MAMMALS

OF COLORADO

MAMMALS
OF COLORADO

James P. Fitzgerald
Carron A. Meaney
David M. Armstrong

Denver Museum of Natural History
and University Press of Colorado

MAMMALS OF COLORADO

Published by the University Press of Colorado, P. O. Box 849, Niwot, Colorado 80544

The University Press of Colorado is a cooperative publishing enterprise supported, in part, by Adams State College, Colorado State University, Fort Lewis College, Mesa State College, Metropolitan State College of Denver, University of Colorado, University of Northern Colorado, University of Southern Colorado, and Western State College of Colorado.

This publication was supported in part by the Colorado Wildlife Commission.

North American maps of mammal distribution are redrafted from *The Mammals of North America*, E. Raymond Hall, © 1981 by John Wiley & Sons, Inc. Reprinted by permission of John Wiley & Sons, Inc.

Composition: Carol Humphrey, University Press of Colorado

Skull drawings: Dave Carlson, Biographics

The Denver Museum of Natural History acknowledges the following individuals:
Design and Production: Ann W. Douden, Cathy Holtz, Kevin Scott
Illustration: Marjorie C. Leggitt, Gail Kohler Opsahl, Barry Syler
Maps: J. Keith Abernathy, Kay Herndon, Lisa McGuire

Library of Congress Cataloging-in-Publication Data

Fitzgerald, James P., 1940–

    Mammals of Colorado / James P. Fitzgerald, Carron A. Meaney, and David M. Armstrong.
      p. cm.
    Includes bibliographical references (p.) and index.
    ISBN 0-87081-333-1 (cloth)
    1. Mammals — Colorado. I. Meaney, Carron A., 1950– . II. Armstrong, David Michael, 1944– . III. Denver Museum of Natural History, IV. Title.
QL719.C6F58 1994
599.09788 — dc20   94-1626
                                                              CIP

10 9 8 7 6 5 4 3 2

Contents

Preface xi

**Chapter 1 — THE LANDSCAPE OF
COLORADO**. 1
Geography. 1
Geology and Landforms. 2
Drainage 6
Climate 6
Soils 8
Humans in the Landscape 8
Ecosystems. 8
    Grasslands. 13
    Semidesert Shrublands 15
    Piñon-Juniper Woodlands. 16
    Montane Shrublands 17
    Montane Forests. 18
    Subalpine Forests 19
    Alpine Tundra 21
    Riparian Systems 22
Patterns of Mammalian Distribution. 23

Chapter 2 — MAMMALS IN GENERAL 27
Mammalian Origins 27
Mammalian Characteristics 27
    Jaw-Ear Complex 28
    Teeth. 28
    Hair 31
    Mammary Glands. 32

Heart. 32
Brain 33
Reproduction 33
Development 34
Skeleton 36
The Diversity of Mammals 41
Orders of Mammals 41
Key to the Orders of Mammals in
Colorado 42

**Chapter 3 — PEOPLE AND WILD
MAMMALS IN COLORADO**. 43
Millenia of Subsistence. 43
The Nineteenth Century: Exploration
and Exploitation 44
The Twentieth Century: Stewardship
for Diverse Values 45
    Recreational and Commercial Values . . 45
    Esthetic Values 50
    Scientific Values 51
    Educational Values. 52
    Urban Wildlife Values 52
Wildlife versus Humans: Nuisance
Aspects of Mammals 53
    Public Health and Wildlife Disease. . . . 53
    Problem Mammals 56
The Futures of Wildlife Management:
The Human Dimension 58
    Conflicting Views 60

Contents

Wildlife Ethics 61
History of Mammalogy in Colorado 63

Chapter 4 — ORDER: MARSUPIALIA —
Marsupials 66
Family Didelphidae — Opossums 67
Didelphis virginiana — Virginia
Opossum 67

Chapter 5 — ORDER: INSECTIVORA —
Insectivores: Moles, Shrews, and Allies 71
Key to the Families of the Order
Insectivora Found in Colorado 71
Family Soricidae — Shrews 71
Key to the Species of the Family
Soricidae Found in Colorado 72
Sorex cinereus — Masked Shrew 74
Sorex hoyi — Pygmy Shrew 75
Sorex merriami — Merriam's Shrew 76
Sorex monticolus — Montane Shrew 78
Sorex nanus — Dwarf Shrew 80
Sorex palustris — Water Shrew 81
Sorex preblei — Preble's Shrew 83
Blarina hylophaga — Elliot's
Short-tailed Shrew 84
Cryptotis parva — Least Shrew 86
Notiosorex crawfordi — Desert Shrew 88
Family Talpidae — Moles 89
Scalopus aquaticus — Eastern Mole 89

Chapter 6 — ORDER: CHIROPTERA —
Bats 92
Key to the Families of the Order
Chiroptera Found in Colorado 95
Family Vespertilionidae —
Vespertilionid Bats 95

Key to the Species of the Family
Vespertilionidae Known or Expected to
Occur in Colorado 95
Myotis californicus — California Myotis . . 97
Myotis ciliolabrum — Western
Small-footed Myotis 99
Myotis evotis — Long-eared Myotis 100
Myotis lucifugus — Little Brown Myotis . 102
Myotis thysanodes — Fringed Myotis 104
Myotis velifer — Cave Myotis* 105
Myotis volans — Long-legged Myotis . . . 106
Myotis yumanensis — Yuma Myotis 108
Lasiurus borealis — Red Bat 109
Lasiurus cinereus — Hoary Bat 111
Lasionycteris noctivagans —
Silver-haired Bat 113
Pipistrellus hesperus — Western
Pipistrelle 114
Pipistrellus subflavus — Eastern
Pipistrelle 116
Eptesicus fuscus — Big Brown Bat 117
Euderma maculatum — Spotted Bat 120
Plecotus townsendii — Townsend's
Big-eared Bat 121
Idionycteris phyllotis — Allen's
Big-eared Bat* 123
Antrozous pallidus — Pallid Bat 124
Family Molossidae — Free-tailed Bats 125
Key to the Species of the Family
Molossidae Found in Colorado 125
Tadarida brasiliensis — Brazilian
Free-tailed Bat 126
Nyctinomops macrotis — Big Free-tailed
Bat 128

Chapter 7 — ORDER: XENARTHRA —
Sloths, Armadillos, Anteaters 130
Family Dasypodidae — Armadillos 130

---

* Species of possible occurence in Colorado.

Dasypus novemcinctus — Nine-banded Armadillo 131

Chapter 8 — ORDER: LAGOMORPHA — Pikas, Hares, Rabbits 134

Key to the Families of the Order Lagomorpha Found in Colorado 135

Family Ochotonidae — Pikas. 135

Ochotona princeps — American Pika. . . . 136

Family Leporidae — Hares and Rabbits . . 138

Key to the Species of the Family Leporidae Found in Colorado. 138

Sylvilagus audubonii — Desert Cottontail 139

Sylvilagus floridanus — Eastern Cottontail 141

Sylvilagus nuttallii — Mountain Cottontail 144

Lepus americanus — Snowshoe Hare . . . 145

Lepus californicus — Black-tailed Jackrabbit 148

Lepus townsendii — White-tailed Jackrabbit 150

Chapter 9 — ORDER: RODENTIA — Rodents 153

Key to the Families of the Order Rodentia Found in Colorado. 154

Family Sciuridae — Squirrels: Chipmunks, Ground Squirrels, Prairie Dogs, Marmots, and Tree Squirrels. 155

Key to the Species of the Family Sciuridae Known or Expected to Occur in Colorado. 155

Tamias dorsalis — Cliff Chipmunk 158

Tamias minimus — Least Chipmunk. . . 159

Tamias quadrivittatus — Colorado Chipmunk. 161

Tamias rufus — Hopi Chipmunk. 163

Tamias umbrinus — Uinta Chipmunk . . 164

Marmota flaviventris — Yellow-bellied Marmot 166

Ammospermophilus leucurus — White-tailed Antelope Squirrel 168

Spermophilus elegans — Wyoming Ground Squirrel. 170

Spermophilus franklinii — Franklin's Ground Squirrel* 172

Spermophilus lateralis — Golden-mantled Ground Squirrel 173

Spermophilus spilosoma — Spotted Ground Squirrel. 175

Spermophilus tridecemlineatus — Thirteen-lined Ground Squirrel 177

Spermophilus variegatus — Rock Squirrel 180

Cynomys gunnisoni — Gunnison's Prairie Dog 183

Cynomys leucurus — White-tailed Prairie Dog 185

Cynomys ludovicianus — Black-tailed Prairie Dog 188

Sciurus aberti — Abert's Squirrel 192

Sciurus niger — Fox Squirrel 194

Tamiasciurus hudsonicus — Pine Squirrel, Chickaree, or "Red Squirrel" 197

Glaucomys sabrinus — Northern Flying Squirrel* 199

Family Geomyidae — Pocket Gophers . . . 200

Key to the Species of the Family Geomyidae Found in Colorado 201

Thomomys bottae — Botta's Pocket Gopher 202

Thomomys talpoides — Northern Pocket Gopher 204

Geomys bursarius — Plains Pocket Gopher 207

---

* Species of possible occurence in Colorado.

Contents

Cratogeomys castanops — Yellow- faced Pocket Gopher 209

Family Heteromyidae — Kangaroo Rats and Pocket Mice 211

Key to the Species of the Family Heteromyidae Known or Expected to Occur in Colorado 211

Perognathus fasciatus — Olive-backed Pocket Mouse 212

Perognathus flavescens — Plains Pocket Mouse 214

Perognathus flavus — Silky Pocket Mouse 216

Perognathus parvus — Great Basin Pocket Mouse 218

Chaetodipus hispidus — Hispid Pocket Mouse 220

Dipodomys ordii — Ord's Kangaroo Rat . 221

Dipodomys spectabilis — Banner- tailed Kangaroo Rat* 224

Family Castoridae — Beavers 225

Castor canadensis — American Beaver . . 225

Family Muridae — Rats, Mice, and Voles . 229

Key to the Subfamilies of the Family Muridae Found in Colorado 230

Subfamily Sigmodontinae — New World Rats and Mice 231

Key to the Species of the Subfamily Sigmodontinae Known or Expected to Occur in Colorado 231

Reithrodontomys megalotis — Western Harvest Mouse 233

Reithrodontomys montanus — Plains Harvest Mouse 235

Peromyscus boylii — Brush Mouse 237

Peromyscus crinitus — Canyon Mouse . . 238

Peromyscus leucopus — White-footed Mouse 240

Peromyscus maniculatus — Deer Mouse . 242

Peromyscus nasutus — Northern Rock Mouse 244

Peromyscus truei — Piñon Mouse 246

Onychomys leucogaster — Northern Grasshopper Mouse 247

Sigmodon hispidus — Hispid Cotton Rat 249

Neotoma albigula — White-throated Woodrat 252

Neotoma cinerea — Bushy-tailed Woodrat 254

Neotoma floridana — Eastern Woodrat . . 256

Neotoma lepida — Desert Woodrat 258

Neotoma mexicana — Mexican Woodrat 260

Neotoma micropus — Southern Plains Woodrat 262

Neotoma stephensi — Stephens' Woodrat* 264

Subfamily Murinae — Old World Rats and Mice 265

Key to the Species of the Subfamily Murinae Known or Expected to Occur in Colorado 265

Mus musculus — House Mouse 265

Rattus norvegicus — Norway Rat 267

Subfamily Arvicolinae — Voles, Meadow Mice, Muskrats 269

Key to the Species of the Subfamily Arvicolinae Known or Expected to Occur in Colorado 269

Clethrionomys gapperi — Southern Red-backed Vole 270

Phenacomys intermedius — Heather Vole 272

Microtus longicaudus — Long-tailed Vole 274

Microtus mexicanus — Mexican Vole . . . 276

Microtus montanus — Montane Vole . . . 278

Microtus ochrogaster — Prairie Vole 280

* Species of possible occurence in Colorado.

viii

Microtus pennsylvanicus — Meadow Vole 283

Lemmiscus curtatus — Sagebrush Vole . . 285

Ondatra zibethicus — Common Muskrat 287

Synaptomys cooperi — Southern Bog Lemming* 289

Family Zapodidae — Jumping Mice 290

Key to the Species of the Family Zapodidae Found in Colorado 290

Zapus hudsonius — Meadow Jumping Mouse 291

Zapus princeps — Western Jumping Mouse 293

Family Erethizontidae — New World Porcupines 295

Erethizon dorsatum — Common Porcupine 295

Chapter 10 — ORDER: CARNIVORA — Carnivores 299

Key to the Families of the Order Carnivora Found in Colorado 300

Family Canidae — Dogs, Foxes, and Allies 301

Key to the Species of the Family Canidae Found in Colorado 301

Canis latrans — Coyote 302

Canis lupus — Gray Wolf 305

Vulpes macrotis — Kit Fox 308

Vulpes velox — Swift Fox 310

Vulpes vulpes — Red Fox 312

Urocyon cinereoargenteus — Gray Fox . . . 315

Family Ursidae — Bears 317

Key to the Species of the Family of Ursidae Found in Colorado 317

Ursus americanus — Black Bear 317

Ursus arctos — Brown or Grizzly Bear . . 321

Family Procyonidae — Raccoons, Ringtails, and Allies 324

Key to the Species of the Family Procyonidae Found in Colorado 324

Bassariscus astutus — Ringtail 325

Procyon lotor — Raccoon 327

Family Mustelidae — Weasels and Allies . . 330

Key to the Species of the Family Mustelidae Known or Expected to Occur in Colorado 330

Martes americana — American Marten . 332

Martes pennanti — Fisher* 335

Mustela erminea — Ermine, or Short-tailed Weasel 336

Mustela frenata — Long-tailed Weasel . . 338

Mustela nigripes — Black-footed Ferret . 341

Mustela nivalis — Least Weasel* 344

Mustela vison — Mink 345

Gulo gulo — Wolverine 348

Taxidea taxus — American Badger 350

Spilogale gracilis — Western Spotted Skunk 352

Spilogale putorius — Eastern Spotted Skunk 354

Mephitis mephitis — Striped Skunk 356

Conepatus mesoleucus — Common Hog-nosed Skunk 359

Lutra canadensis — Northern River Otter 361

Family Felidae — Cats 365

Key to the Species of the Family Felidae Found in Colorado 365

Felis concolor — Mountain Lion 365

Lynx lynx — Lynx 368

Lynx rufus — Bobcat 371

Chapter 11 — ORDER: PERISSODACTYLA — Odd-toed Hoofed Mammals 375

Family Equidae — Horses and Allies 376

* Species of possible occurence in Colorado.

Contents

Equus caballus — Domestic and Feral Horses 376

Chapter 12 — ORDER: ARTIODACTYLA — Artiodactyls, Even-toed Hoofed Mammals 380

Key to the Families of the Order Artiodactyla Found in Colorado 381

Family Cervidae — Deer and Allies 381

Key to the Species of the Family Cervidae Found in Colorado 382

Cervus elaphus — American Elk, or Wapiti 382

Odocoileus hemionus — Mule Deer 386

Odocoileus virginianus — White-tailed Deer 390

Alces alces — Moose 393

Family Antilocapridae — Pronghorn 396

Antilocapra americana — Pronghorn . . . 396

Family Bovidae — Bovids 399

Key to the Species in the Family Bovidae (Including Domestic Livestock) Found in Colorado 400

Bison bison — Bison, or American Buffalo 402

Oreamnos americanus — Mountain Goat 405

Ovis canadensis — Mountain Sheep, or Bighorn Sheep 408

Literature Cited 413

Appendix A — The Metric System 458

Appendix B — Glossary 460

Preface

It has been nearly a quarter century since Robert R. Lechleitner published his *Wild Mammals of Colorado* in 1969. That work provided a modern, general reference on the biology of Coloradan mammals. Although long out of print, the book served well the general audience for whom it was intended. In 1972 David M. Armstrong compiled distributional information on Coloradan mammals and provided technical data on geographic variation. That work also has been out of print for a number of years.

Since those works were published, research in mammalogy has burgeoned and we have learned much more about the species that inhabit Colorado. New state records for several species and changes in known ranges for a number of others have become available. In addition, much improved and extended studies of community and population ecology, behavior, physiology, and management have been performed. Because of Colorado's unique physiography and location, it has a diverse fauna that has attracted investigation by several premier mammalogists from across the country. Indeed, the Literature Cited section of this book reads like a *Who's Who* in mammalogy, including past and present leaders in the field.

This book was begun by the first author in 1983, intended as a revision of Lechleitner (1969). Its purpose is to provide a reasonably detailed, up-to-date account of the mammalian fauna of Colo-

rado. It is intended for college and precollege students of zoology in general and mammals in particular as well as amateur and professional naturalists (in which we include ecologists and resource managers such as wildlife biologists, foresters, range scientists, farmers, and ranchers). Our hope is to provide information useful to understanding, appreciating, managing, and conserving the native mammals with which we share the diverse and magnificent landscapes of Colorado.

Orders, families, and genera are treated in phylogenetic order, generally following Hall (1981). Species are treated alphabetically within genera. This book is not a taxonomic treatise, so we mostly avoid taxonomic controversy, relying instead on recent revisions. Vernacular and formal (scientific) names follow J. K. Jones et al. (1992), except where the common names would be confusing if applied to animals in Colorado or where we have a compelling reason to disagree with nomenclature (as in the case of *Bison*).

Accounts of species are organized under three subheadings. The Description section includes external and cranial measurements in metric units (see Appendix A). More detailed measurements and comparisons (by subspecies) are found in Armstrong (1972). The Natural History section includes information on habitat, population ecology (density, dispersion, home range, for example), predators and parasites, reproduction and development, behavior, food and foraging habits, and general status (including harvest by humans, if relevant). Much of the information in this section is tied by citations to the primary zoological literature. Interested readers are encouraged to pursue these sources for more detailed information. The literature review is not meant to be comprehensive, but we have attempted to cite the major studies of mammals in Colorado, studies of Coloradan species conducted in nearby states, and important general reviews. The Distribution in Colorado section summarizes geographic and ecological distribution and lists subspecies (where recognized); Armstrong (1972) provided greater detail. Taxonomy and nomenclature are addressed in this last section when clarification is important.

Most of the data for the sections on description and distribution are based on museum specimens, summarized by Armstrong (1972), and updated by Meaney (1991). Maps of Coloradan distributions were redrafted after those published by Armstrong (1972). They were supplemented by the database summarized by Meaney (1990a, 1991) and more recent records that have come to our attention from various sources, most notably the Colorado Division of Wildlife. Maps of North American distributions were redrafted after Hall (1981).

We include photographs, line drawings, and maps to assist in recognizing mammals and to encourage readers to make deeper inquiry into geographic ranges and patterns of mammalian distribution in the state. Although the book does not have a separate chapter on Primates, humans (as the sole Coloradan representative of the order) are not neglected, as aspects of human biology and ecology are woven into several chapters, especially Chapter 3, which deals with social and cultural values of mammals and comments on how we hope Colorado will proceed in the future to safeguard its heritage of native mammals.

For most of the states adjoining Colorado there are comprehensive, technical, taxonomic and distributional studies: Wyoming (Long 1965); Nebraska (J. K. Jones 1964); Kansas (Cockrum 1952); New Mexico (Findley et al. 1975); Arizona (Cockrum 1960); Utah (Durrant 1952). In addition, for several of these states and regions there are general accounts of mammals analogous to the present work: Wyoming (T. Clark and Stromberg 1987); Nebraska and the Dakotas (J. K. Jones et al. 1983, 1985); Kansas (Bee et al. 1981); Oklahoma (Caire et al. 1989); New Mexico (Findley 1987); and Arizona (Hoffmeister 1986). We have consulted these references freely in the preparation of this work, and we recommend them to our readers as sources of further information.

This book has been a truly cooperative endeavor. Over a decade ago, the first author organized the project, began to review the vast literature on Coloradan mammals, and started to write drafts of species accounts. He also superintended preparation of the line art.

Meaney joined the project in 1988, updating and augmenting species accounts and preparing drafts of introductory chapters. She also took principal responsibility for updating range maps and locating suitable photographs and played the invaluable role of liaison with the project's sponsors — the Colorado Division of Wildlife and the Wildlife Commission and the Denver Museum of Natural History — and the publisher, University Press of Colorado.

Armstrong began work with the project late in 1991. He expanded the introductory material, revised and augmented species accounts, and served as general technical editor for the project.

Stimulus and encouragement from many persons have allowed us to complete this task. Primary motivation came from R. R. Lechleitner, who provided patient guidance as mentor for Fitzgerald during his doctoral work at Colorado State University. Lechleitner was not only a fine field mammalogist, but a peerless teacher, and he had a major impact on Armstrong during his undergraduate years at CSU.

We all thank Jeanne Remington for her masterful job of copyediting, Bruce A. Wunder for his constructively critical technical review of the manuscript, Jody Berman of the University Press of Colorado, and Betsy Armstrong and Ann Douden of the Denver Museum of Natural History.

We all acknowledge gratefully the efforts of Dave Carlson of BioGraphics for his fine line drawings. Tom McCracken and students in the Biological Illustration Program of Colorado State University also contributed to preliminary development of some of the illustrations.

Barry Syler graciously made available his exquisite drawings for the chapter headings. These were originally prepared for a different project many years ago and were put to good use here. Drawings of additional taxa were prepared by Marge Leggitt of the Denver Museum of Natural History. Lisa McGuire, also of the Museum, drew all the maps with painstaking care. Our thanks to these artists.

Also, our thanks to the many photographers who worked with us to provide the 145 photographs. Our special thanks to Wendy Shattil/Bob Rozinski, Bill Ervin, Jody Fitzgerald, and the Photoarchives of the Denver Museum of Natural History for generously making their photographic collections available to us. Wendy and Bob made extraordinary efforts on our behalf, even going so far as to join a field project to photograph captured mice as they were released. Karen Stephens served as coordinator of photography, tirelessly soliciting and organizing the submissions and selections methodically and meticulously. To her our special thanks.

Individual personnel of the Colorado Division of Wildlife too numerous to mention patiently answered inquiries from each of us. Steven J. Bissell deserves special mention for his friendship and encouragement and for facilitating funding of the project through the Wildlife Commission.

Of course, a tremendous number of individuals — including those named in the Literature Cited, our past and present students, and amateur and professional wildlife biologists scattered throughout Colorado and elsewhere — have provided the hard work and sacrifice that built the database of information presented. We hope that this book will trigger new interests and new efforts in resolving many of the continuing questions presented by the mammals of Colorado.

Like all such projects, this one demanded more of family, friends, and colleagues than was intended, so each of the authors has personal acknowledgments to extend. The first author especially thanks his patient wife, Jody, for all of the years during which she put up with requests for photos of mammals (some of which proudly appear in these pages) or their habitats and with papers scattered about the work space in our house.

Meaney appreciates the support she received from many staff members and volunteers at the Denver Museum of Natural History, including Betsy Webb, Betsy Armstrong, Charles Preston, Andrew Langford, Phyllis Porter, and especially Karen Stephens. Strong support for the project continued at the S. M. Stoller Corporation and is greatly appreciated. And she extends a special kind of gratitude to her parents, who instilled in her the motivation to pursue her scientific interests.

Armstrong singles out for special thanks his partner, Susan Jessup. She patiently tolerated his long hours in front of the computer and for many months negotiated precarious piles of books and papers in the dining room. Further, he celebrates her tenacious stewardship of Sulzer Gulch and Green Ridge, assuring a safe refuge for woodrats and fringed myotis.

JAMES P. FITZGERALD, CARRON A. MEANEY,
DAVID M. ARMSTRONG

MAMMALS
OF COLORADO

Chapter 1

The Landscape of Colorado

This book is about the mammalian fauna of Colorado. Mammals are a familiar and important component of Earth's biodiversity — all the organisms and their genetic and ecological relationships. Biodiversity is an evolutionary and ecological phenomenon in space and time. To understand the diversity of mammals we need to have a perspective of the landscape more generally. Such a perspective is the purpose of this chapter.

Colorado is known for its scenic beauty — from majestic mountain peaks and rushing white rivers tumbling down dark canyons, to red rock deserts and ceaselessly shifting sand dunes, to the expansive sweep of the prairie. Grandeur is wherever we stop to appreciate it, at every scale, from crystalline canyon walls two billion years old, to bold peaks carved by the glaciers of the last Ice Age, to last night's furtive track of a mouse on the snow. We humans appreciate ecological patterns and processes as beautiful or intriguing; to the rest of the mammalian fauna the evolving landscape represents opportunity, and native mammals respond accordingly. Thus, as we seek to understand the distribution and abundance of mammals and the details of their daily lives we must first understand the resource base, the mosaic of Colorado's environments.

GEOGRAPHY

Geography describes broad patterns in the environment. From the standpoint of political geography, Colorado is simple: it is a rectangle, measuring 620 km by 440 km (about 380 by 270 mi) and encompassing 272,800 km^2 (about 103,595 sq mi). Colorado lies between approximately 102° and 109° west longitude and 37° and 41° north latitude and is subdivided into 63 counties (Map 1-1). A few of the counties are nearly natural, ecological units (for example, Jackson, Grand, and Park counties encompass North, Middle, and South parks, respectively), but most are simply administrative artifacts.

From the standpoints of physical and biological geography, Colorado is anything but simple. The marvelous complexity of the scenery is the subject of this chapter, which describes environments of Colorado from several, interrelated points of view. Geologic history and materials underlie environmental patterns. Physiography is the shape of the land, reflecting millions of years of landscape evolution. Patterns of drainage reflect and produce the landforms. Vegetation integrates climate and geological parent material in the development of soils. Biotic communities of plants and animals, fungi and microbes, interact within themselves in systems of symbioses, and they interact with the physical environment in ceaseless cycles of materials powered by a flow of solar energy. We observe — and seek to understand — an ecological whole of extraordinary complexity. But let us begin simply, with a little history.

GEOLOGY AND LANDFORMS

Colorado straddles the "backbone" of North America, the Southern Rocky Mountains. From the mountain front, the Great Plains extend eastward toward the Mississippi Valley. To the west lie canyons and plateaus of the Wyoming Basin and the Colorado Plateau. The juxtaposition of these major physiographic regions affects temperature, precipitation, wind patterns, and water flow.

Colorado is the highest of the United States, with a mean elevation of 2,070 m (6,800 ft) (Map 1-2). The lowest point is 1,020 m (3,350 feet) near Holly, Prowers County, and the highest point is 4,398 m (14,431 feet), the summit of Mount Elbert, Lake County. Because of these varied conditions, species richness is high.

Physiography is the study of landforms. Physiographers divide most of Colorado among three "provinces" (see Fenneman 1931): the Southern Rocky Mountains, the Great Plains, and the Colorado Plateau. Northwestern Colorado is on the periphery of two additional provinces: the Middle Rocky Mountains and the Wyoming Basin.

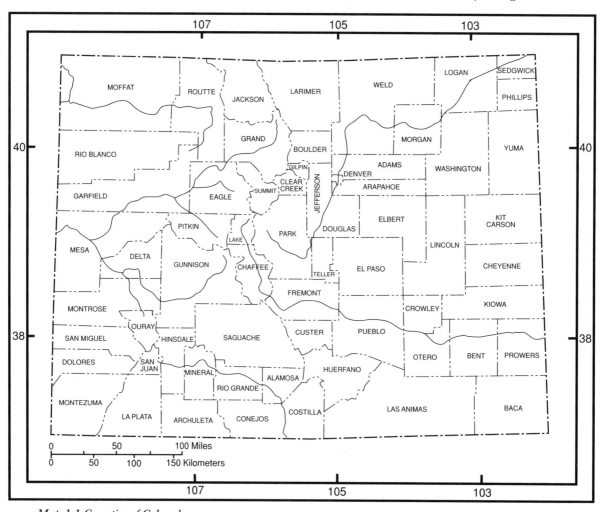

Map 1-1 Counties of Colorado.

The present-day Southern Rocky Mountains arose in a long-term event called the Laramide Orogeny, in Cretaceous to Paleocene times — about the time of the demise of the ruling reptiles, some 70 million years ago. Prior to that time, during the Mesozoic Era, the "Age of Reptiles," Colorado occupied a low-lying area, alternately covered by shallow seas or exposed as deserts and floodplains. With the rise of the Rockies, Mesozoic and older sediments were broken, bent, and tilted on end, resulting in familiar hogback ridges and such features as Boulder's Flatirons. Streams heading in the newly uplifted mountains eroded the rocks, spreading them in a deep "mantle" eastward across the midcontinent.

There is nothing simple about the Southern Rockies of Colorado, but we may think of the basic structure as two great ridges of granitic rocks, arrayed in parallel lines oriented roughly north-south. The eastern series begins north of the Cache la Poudre River as the lower, eastern Laramie Range and the higher, western Medicine Bow Range. The Front Range extends from the Poudre to the Arkansas, ending in the Rampart Range (which includes Pikes Peak). The Wet Mountains are an independent range south of the Arkansas River.

A western chain of granitic mountains begins in southern Wyoming as the Sierra Madre (called the Park Range in Colorado), continues southward as the Gore, Ten Mile, Mosquito, and Sawatch ranges, and then jogs a bit to the east to continue southward into New Mexico in the spectacular ridge of the Sangre de Cristos. Between the granitic ridges are structural basins. North and Middle parks occupy a single basin, which is subdivided by the volcanic Rabbit Ears Mountains. South Park occupies a separate basin. West of the Park Range, the Wyoming Basin is continuous with much of western Wyoming.

The San Luis Valley lies west of the main ranges of the Southern Rockies proper, but it looks like one of the parks, because it is surrounded by mountains, the Sangre de Cristos to the east and the younger, volcanic San Juans to the west. A range of volcanic hills marks the southern border of the San Luis Valley.

The main ranges of the Rockies represent uplifted Precambrian rocks and folded Paleozoic and Mesozoic sediments. Adjacent ranges like the San Juans were produced by Cenozoic volcanic activity. Features like the White River and Uncompahgre plateaus are independent uplifts. Grand and Battlement mesas are built of sedimentary rocks, protected by caps of resistant lava. Chronic and Chronic (1972) provided a readable introduction to the geology of Colorado, and A. Benedict (1991) described the mountains in detail.

The eastern two-fifths of Colorado lies in the Great Plains Province. When the Rockies arose, erosion and sedimentation clothed the area to the east with the pieces. For millions of years, this alluvium covered nearly all of eastern Colorado. During the Pleistocene ice ages, with their high precipitation, however, this so-called "Tertiary mantle" was largely eroded away and carried out of the state. Today it is preserved mostly on the High Plains, a nearly flat landscape interrupted occasionally by sandhills and eroded along stream courses to form canyons, cliffs, and escarpments. Between the High Plains and the mountain front lies the Colorado Piedmont. There the Tertiary mantle has been largely removed, exposing Mesozoic shales, limestones, and sandstones as hogbacks, low rolling hills, and canyons. Remnants of the Tertiary formations along the northern border of eastern Colorado in features like Pawnee Buttes and the escarpment of the Peetz Table suggest just how much material has been removed from the Colorado Piedmont.

The divide between the Platte and the Arkansas rivers is a remnant upland, providing an eastward extension of ecosystems of the foothills. The divide imposes a filter-barrier to north-south movement of organisms between valleys of the master streams of the plains.

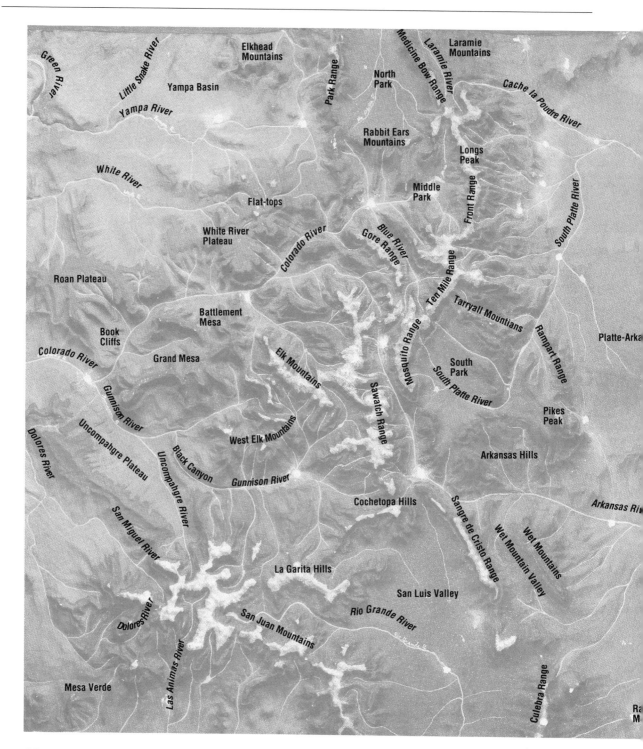

Map 1-2 Physiography of Colorado.

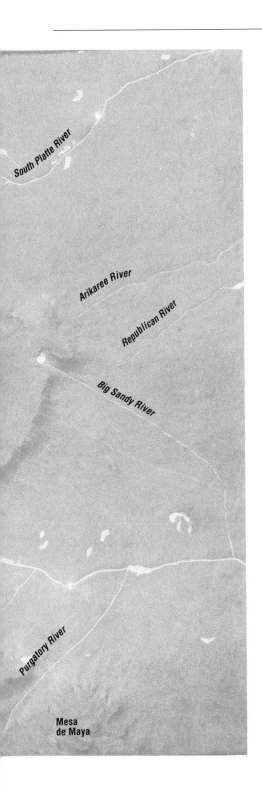

South Platte River

Arikaree River

Republican River

Big Sandy River

Purgatory River

Mesa
de Maya

At the foot of the mountains, the sedimentary units dip steeply eastward, forming a great debris-filled trough, the Denver Basin. The southern rim of the basin is marked by roughlands south of the Arkansas River, which greatly complicate the ecology of southeastern Colorado, providing habitat for a number of species of Mexican affinities. Indeed, the very name of the region, the Raton Section, bespeaks its distinctive mammalian fauna, which includes several species of *ratones* — woodrats, whose dens are conspicuous features of the landscape.

The Colorado Plateau has been called a showplace for the effects of erosion on flat-lying sedimentary rocks. Add to that the complications of a history of volcanism nearby, and the result is a landscape of remarkable ecological diversity. The country is typified by mesas and plateaus dissected by canyons. These include the Book and Roan plateaus, the Piceance Basin, and lava-capped Grand and Battlement mesas. Farther south, the uplifted Uncompahgre Plateau and isolated peaks like Ute Mountain are conspicuous. Mesa Verde is a major highland near the southern boundary of the state.

The boundaries between physiographic provinces are often visible in ecological patterns. The transition from the Great Plains to the Southern Rockies on the Eastern Slope is especially dramatic, with the Front and Rampart ranges rising 2,400 m (nearly 8,000 ft) in less than 30 km. Further, spectacular river canyons often mark gateways from the Rockies to adjacent physiographic provinces: Northgate Canyon on the North Platte, Glenwood Canyon on the Colorado, South Platte Canyon, the Royal Gorge of the Arkansas, the Black Canyon of the Gunnison. These and numerous lesser canyons and gulches provide corridors for movements of the biota, their southfacing slopes providing especially favorable microclimates.

DRAINAGE

Rivers carve landscapes and support moist corridors of opportunity for living things. The influences of rivers are especially striking in the semiarid West. We cannot appreciate natural landscapes of Colorado — or much of human history either — without knowing something of the pattern of drainage, the hydrography of the state.

Colorado lies astride the Continental Divide. Water that falls to the west of the divide ends up in the Sea of Cortez (Gulf of California). Waters of the Eastern Slope are destined for the Gulf of Mexico, via the Missouri-Mississippi system. The San Luis Valley is partly an internal drainage basin, but the Rio Grande flows through on its way to the Gulf of Mexico, having gathered its headwaters in the high San Juans.

The Continental Divide is a fundamental geographic fact in Colorado. The main ridge of the Rockies intercepts moisture coming from the Pacific Ocean. Air is forced up, is cooled, and its water vapor condenses, falling in the mountains as rain or snow. The Eastern Slope is, therefore, in a "rain shadow." The Western Slope has about one-third of the land area of Colorado, but receives over two-thirds of the precipitation. However, because less than 15 percent of the human population lives on the Western Slope, ambitious efforts have been made for over a century to move the water — the lifeblood of agriculture and urban and industrial development — to the Eastern Slope, the center of human population. The actual amount of diversion varies from one year to the next, and the pattern is complex, but typically the amount of Western Slope water diverted annually to the Eastern Slope equals or exceeds the native flow of the South Platte River. Transmountain water diversion has greatly modified environments of Colorado. The South Platte and Arkansas valleys, which nineteenth-century explorer Stephen Long called the Great American Desert, have been transformed into rich agricultural areas, expanding habitat for a number of species of mammals. Also, the tunnels through which diversions flow often provide roosting habitat for bats.

Several of the major rivers of western interior North America originate in the Colorado Rockies. Indeed, the only sizable river that flows into the state is the Green, which heads in the Wind River Mountains of western Wyoming. The master stream of the Western Slope is the Colorado River. The Yampa and White rivers drain northwestern Colorado before they join the Green. The mainstem Colorado — once called the Grand River — drains Middle Park and the western side of Rocky Mountain National Park and then joins the Gunnison at Grand Junction, flowing thence westward into Utah, where it is joined by the Green enroute to the Grand Canyon in Arizona. Southwestern Colorado is drained by several tributaries of the Colorado: the San Miguel (the only river in Colorado that is not dammed), Dolores, and San Juan rivers and their tributaries, all born as mountain snow in the San Juans and destined for a muddy end in the Sea of Cortez.

The North Platte River heads in North Park and drains much of eastern Wyoming before joining the South Platte in Nebraska. The South Platte and its tributaries drain the Front Range and South Park. The Arkansas River heads in the Rampart, Sawatch, and Mosquito ranges. The High Plains of eastern Colorado give rise to the Republican and Arikaree rivers. The Cimarron heads in New Mexico and drains extreme southeastern Colorado.

CLIMATE

Mammals are endotherms; that is, they maintain a high and constant body temperature by elegantly controlled production and retention of metabolic heat. Endothermy partially liberates mammals from the direct influence of climate, but climate still is an important influence on mammals, direct and indirect.

The climate of Colorado is highly variable, from place to place, day to day, and season to season. The Southern Rocky Mountains are the dominant influence on the climate of Colorado. Other important factors are latitude, elevation, exposure, local topography, and location with respect to storm tracks and prevailing winds. Far from the moderating effects of the oceans (roughly 1,600 km and 3,200 km from the West and East coasts, respectively), the state has a so-called "continental climate." Temperate and semiarid overall, relative humidity is low and temperatures vary widely at all elevations. For example, precipitation ranges from over 100 cm in some parts of the San Juan Mountains to less than 25 cm in some of the San Luis Valley, just 80 km away. The frost-free season in the Grand Valley averages 189 days; at Silverton it averages 14 days. The difference in mean annual temperature between Lamar and the summit of Pikes Peak (only 200 km to the west but 3,200 m, or 10,500 ft, higher in elevation) is about 20°C (approximately 35°F).

The Great Plains are typified by low precipitation, high winds, and low humidity. Summer daytime temperatures, although frequently hot, rarely exceed 38°C. Winters have relatively warm periods interrupted by Arctic air masses sweeping down from Canada. Precipitation varies on an east-west gradient from an annual mean of about 45 cm along the Kansas border to 30–35 cm at the foot of the mountains.

Winters near the foothills are milder than on the plains or in the mountains, and the so-called Front Range Corridor, from Fort Collins south to Pueblo, supports over 80 percent of the state's human population. Denver, at an elevation of 1,609 m (5,280 ft) has a mean annual precipitation of 35 cm and a mean annual temperature of 10°C.

In the mountains, temperature decreases with increasing elevation, at roughly 1.7°C per 300 m (985 ft). Above about 2,750 m (9,000 ft), frost is possible any night of the year, particularly in valleys, into which heavier cold air drains. Winter and spring snowfall can be quite heavy in the mountains, but local differences are extreme. More precipitation falls as winter snow than as summer rain in the western mountains. By contrast, winter and summer precipitation are about equivalent on the Eastern Slope. Warm winter winds, or "chinooks," melt or evaporate much of the snow on the Eastern Slope. In spring, rapid snowmelt causes peaks in flow of rivers that head in the mountains. Groundwater from snowmelt contributes to summer stream flow. The enclosed mountain parks and valleys are cooler and drier than the surrounding mountains. They lie in the rain shadow of the mountains and also trap sinking cold-air masses for relatively long periods.

Western Colorado has a diverse climate affected in large part by topography. The high plateaus are similar to the mountains, but the lowlands and river valleys are warmer and drier. Winds generally are less intense than on the Eastern Slope. Stable high-pressure systems often form in winter, resulting in long periods of clear weather with warm days and cool nights. Southern Colorado typically has monsoonal, or summer, rains. This increase in moisture during the warm season contrasts with the pattern for the Western Slope, where the greatest moisture occurs during winter.

There is increasing evidence that climatic patterns are changing at present, due in part to industrial enrichment of Earth's atmosphere with so-called "greenhouse gases," including carbon dioxide released from burning fossil fuels. Colorado, with its high topographic relief and consequent ecological complexity, may expect marked effects from such changes.

There also is evidence of strong, natural climatic change in the recent geological past. Only 15,000 to 20,000 years ago valley glaciers of the Pleistocene Ice Age retreated to their cirques. Some Coloradan mammals are relicts of glacial times, occurring now on the forested "island" of the Southern Rockies, surrounded by an impassable "sea" of grasslands and shrublands. A geologically "mere" 4,000 to 6,500 years ago an interval warmer and drier than the present allowed access to parts of Colorado by a number of species of southwestern affinities, species that are now restricted to particularly warm, dry locations in the foothills, canyons, and other roughlands of the state (Armstrong 1972). Erickson and Smith (1985) summarized a vast amount of information on physical environments of Colorado, including climate. A. Benedict (1991) presented a valuable account of mountain climates.

SOILS

Soils represent the product of interaction over time between the geologic parent material, topography, climate, vegetation, and animal activity. As one would expect, the pattern of soils in Colorado is complex. This complexity is both reflected in and influenced by distributions of biotic communities. The composition, texture, depth, and moisture of soils can influence mammals indirectly through influence on the vegetation of an area. Further, local distribution of fossorial mammals, which depend on specific soil characteristics for their burrowing activities, is affected directly. Kangaroo rats, for example, occur only in sandy soils. In general, soils of Colorado differ from those of more humid regions by being lower in organic matter and higher in total plant nutrients, limes, and soluble salts. Soils of Colorado have been mapped extensively by the Soil Conservation Service in county soil surveys and were summarized broadly by Erickson and Smith (1985).

HUMANS IN THE LANDSCAPE

Human settlement has strongly influenced opportunities for native mammals. Prior to permanent settlement, subsistence populations — first of Native Americans and then of Euroamericans — relied on the native fauna for food and fiber. They influenced local populations of game mammals and furbearers (J. Benedict 1992), but seldom modified environments permanently. The first permanent European settlers came for mineral wealth. The Colorado Mineral Belt extends from Jamestown, Ward, and Gold Hill southwestward to Silverton and Rico. In the second half of the

nineteenth century this region was transformed. Mountains were literally turned inside out, changing the topography and hence the environment for many species, many negatively, a few positively. Roosting habitat for bats, for example, was greatly augmented by mining activities, as were the talus slides favored by pikas and bushy-tailed woodrats (and thus their predators).

Agricultural settlement of the eastern plains and the western valleys came a little later. Wholesale changes in habitats for mammals resulted from irrigated agriculture, impoundment of rivers in reservoirs, transmountain diversion of water, control of floods and prairie fires, and extirpation of the keystone species of the prairie, the bison. Ranching activities often involved predator control (and even eradication, as with the gray wolf and grizzly bear) and overgrazing, expanding opportunities for species like the Wyoming ground squirrel and the black-tailed jackrabbit. Urbanization has had profound effects on the fauna of the state, obliterating habitat for some species, but increasing it for several others, like whitetailed deer, fox squirrels, and raccoons.

ECOSYSTEMS

To this point we have described physical environments of Colorado that provide opportunities for the native fauna. Geology underlies environmental pattern. Physiography describes the broad shape of the land. Climatic patterns describe the distribution and periodicity of precipitation and temperature. Vegetation clothes the landforms, moderates climate, and uses solar energy to integrate air, water, and minerals into the chemical molecules of life. Soils are the dynamic result of the interaction of climate, vegetation, and geologic parent material over time. All of these pieces contribute to the pattern of landscapes that we describe as ecosystems.

For present purposes, Coloradan environments are described in terms of eight ecosystem types. This is not the only way to describe the environment, of course, and it is not the first. Cary

(1911) described environments of Colorado in terms of the classical life-zone concept pioneered by C. Hart Merriam. Pattern in the landscape was described as a series of elevational bands, ranging from the Upper Sonoran Zone grasslands and shrublands, through a Transition Zone typified by ponderosa pine and sagebrush, to a Canadian Zone forest of spruce and fir, through a narrow band of Hudsonian Zone forest at upper treeline, to an Alpine Zone atop the highest mountains. This system describes in broad terms an ecological pattern readily seen in Colorado and elsewhere in the West where environmental change is rapid along steep gradients of elevation. The life-zone map published in Cary's report still is a valuable tool for the ecologist.

Armstrong (1972) tabulated distribution of Coloradan mammals in 14 ecological community types; Gregg (1963) used 31 vegetation types to describe ecological distribution of ants; and Erickson and Smith (1985) mapped 11 vegetation types. Mutel and Emerick (1992) described the Coloradan environment in terms of 15 kinds of ecosystems, A. Benedict (1991) utilized a system of 12 terrestrial ecosystems to describe the landscape, and R. Bailey (1978) mapped 14 types of potential natural vegetation within six ecoregions. For present purposes, we use a simpler array of categories, consistent with the scheme used in the recently renovated Mead Hall at the Denver Museum of Natural History.

This diversity of alternative classification schemes should not be troublesome to the reader who keeps in mind a simple fact: naming and classifying ecosystems is a human activity, done for human purposes. Our particular purpose is to describe the pattern of environmental opportunities for mammals.

An ecosystem is "an ecological unit, a subdivision of the landscape, a geographic area that is relatively homogeneous and reasonably distinct from adjacent areas" (Marr 1967:6). It is a functioning volume of environment, involving interaction of living organisms (the biotic community) and non-living (abiotic) factors in continual cycles of materials powered by a ceaseless flow of solar energy. Ecosystems are arbitrary units, delineated for the convenience of people: naturalists or managers, for example. An ecosystem might be as small as a pond, a field, or even an aquarium. It could be as large as the Great Plains. Indeed, one could argue that Earth has just one ecosystem — a single, integrated, global ecological whole — the ecosphere. Ecologists abstract smaller ecosystems from the whole simply to have something manageable to study and understand.

We describe eight ecosystems for Colorado (Map 1-3). They are defined in large part by the plant communities, the most visible element of the landscape. These eight ecosystems readily lend themselves to subdivision for a further, and often necessary, refinement of the landscape. Estimates of percentage of the state covered by each ecosystem type are rough, determined by tallying townships by ecosystem type from "Major Land Resource Area and Generalized Land Use Map, Colorado" (USDA, Soil Conservation Service, Portland, 1965, approximate scale, 1:2,000,000). In the following descriptions of ecosystems, botanical nomenclature mostly follows Weber (1976).

For each ecosystem type, we provide a brief sketch of the mammalian fauna. More extensive lists of mammalian species in each ecosystem type are presented in Table 1-1. Please note that we highlight mammals only because this is a book about mammals and not about wildlife generally. Sometimes we speak of a "mammalian community." This approach is taxonomically convenient, but ecologically simplistic at best, and at worst actually misleading. A biotic community is the living part of an ecosystem: animals, plants, fungi, and microbes. We might reasonably subdivide the community into *producers* (the green plants and photosynthetic microbes that have the genetic know-how to use solar energy to assemble parts of water and air into chemical bonds of biological molecules) and *consumers* (mammals and other

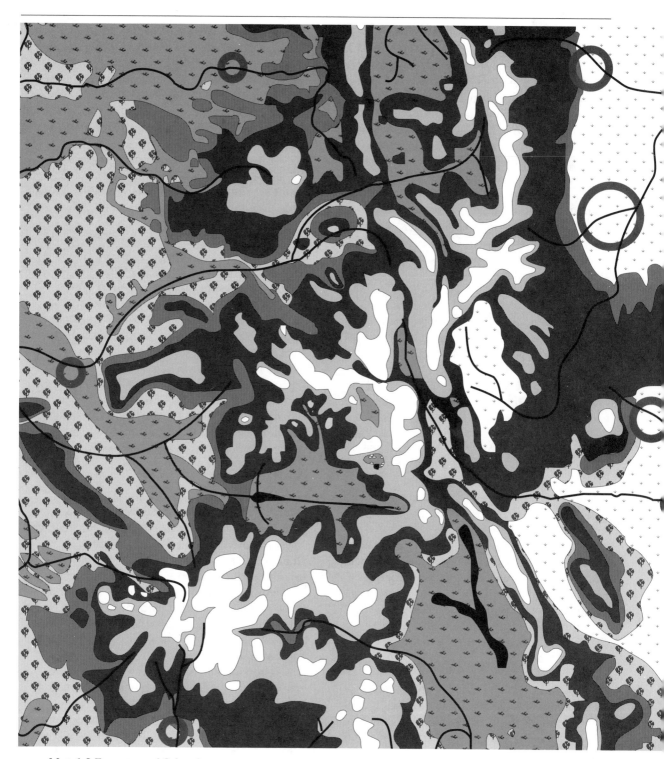

Map 1-3 Ecosystems of Colorado.

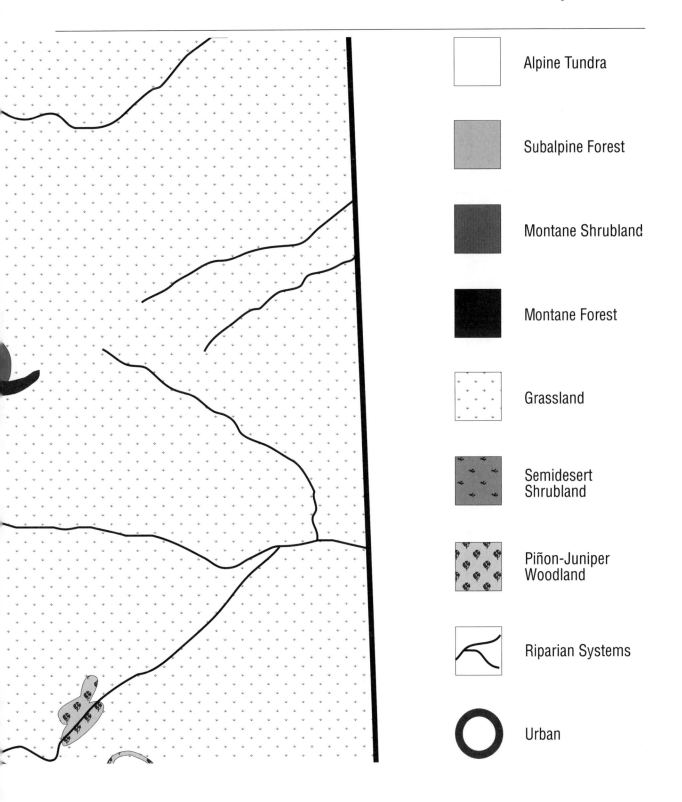

Alpine Tundra

Subalpine Forest

Montane Shrubland

Montane Forest

Grassland

Semidesert
Shrubland

Piñon-Juniper
Woodland

Riparian Systems

Urban

animals as well as fungi and many microbial groups).

Table 1-1. Ecological distribution of native mammals in Colorado. Key: 1 = Grassland; 2 = Semidesert Shrubland; 3 = Piñon-Juniper Woodland; 4 = Montane Shrubland; 5 = Montane Forest; 6 = Subalpine Forest; 7 = Alpine Tundra; 8 = Riparian Systems.

	1	2	3	4	5	6	7	8
MARSUPICARNIVORA — DIDELPHIDAE: OPOSSUMS								
Virginia Opossum — *Didelphis virginiana*								X
INSECTIVORA — SORICIDAE: SHREWS								
Masked Shrew — *Sorex cinereus*					X	X	X	X
Pygmy Shrew — *Sorex hoyi*						X		X
Merriam's Shrew — *Sorex merriami*	X	X		X				
Montane Shrew — *Sorex monticolus*					X	X	X	X
Dwarf Shrew — *Sorex nanus*					X	X	X	X
Water Shrew — *Sorex palustris*								X
Preble's Shrew — *Sorex preblei*				X				
Least Shrew — *Cryptotis parva*	X							X
Elliot's Short-tailed Shrew — *Blarina hylophaga*	X							
Desert Shrew — *Notiosorex crawfordi*		X						
TALPIDAE: MOLES								
Eastern Mole — *Scalopus aquaticus*	X							
CHIROPTERA — VESPERTILIONIDAE: COMMON BATS								
California Myotis — *Myotis californicus*		X	X					
Western Small-footed Myotis — *Myotis ciliolabrum*	X	X	X	X	X			X
Long-eared Myotis — *Myotis evotis*			X	X	X			
Little Brown Bat — *Myotis lucifugus*					X	X		X
Fringed Myotis — *Myotist hysanodes*			X	X	X			
Long-legged Myotis — *Myotis volans*			X	X	X	X		
Yuma Myotis — *Myotis yumanensis*	X	X						X
Red Bat — *Lasiurus borealis*								X
Hoary Bat — *Lasiurus cinereus*				X		X	X	X
Silver-haired Bat — *Lasionycteris noctivagans*				X		X	X	X
Western Pipistrelle — *Pipistrellus hesperus*	X	X						
Big Brown Bat — *Eptesicus fuscus*				X	X	X	X	
Spotted Bat — *Euderma maculatum*				X		X		X
Townsend's Big-eared Bat — *Plecotus townsendii*				X	X	X	X	
Pallid Bat — *Antrozous pallidus*	X	X						
MOLOSSIDAE: FREE-TAILED BATS								
Brazilian Free-tailed Bat — *Tadarida brasiliensis*	X	X						
Big Free-tailed Bat — *Nyctinomops macrotis*		X						
EDENTATA — DASYPODIDAE: ARMADILLOS								
Nine-banded Armadillo — *Dasypus novemcinctus*								X
LAGOMORPHA — OCHOTONIDAE: PIKAS								
Pika — *Ochotona princeps*							X	
LEPORIDAE: RABBITS AND HARES								
Desert Cottontail — *Sylvilagus audubonii*	X	X	X	X				X
Eastern Cottontail — *Sylvilagus floridanus*								X
Nuttall's Cottontail — *Sylvilagus nuttallii*				X	X	X		
Snowshoe Hare — *Lepus americanus*						X		X
White-tailed Jackrabbit — *Lepus townsendii*	X	X	X	X	X		X	
Black-tailed Jackrabbit — *Lepus californicus*	X	X						
RODENTIA — SCIURIDAE: SQUIRRELS								
Cliff Chipmunk — *Tamias dorsalis*		X	X					
Least Chipmunk — *Tamias minimus*		X	X	X	X	X	X	
Colorado Chipmunk — *Tamias quadrivittatus*			X	X	X			
Hopi Chipmunk — *Tamias rufus*		X	X	X				
Uinta Chipmunk — *Tamias umbrinus*						X		
Yellow-bellied Marmot — *Marmota flaviventris*					X	X	X	X
White-tailed Antelope Squirrel — *Ammospermophilus leucurus*		X						
Wyoming Ground Squirrel — *Spermophilus elegans*	X	X		X	X			
Golden-mantled Ground Squirrel — *Spermophilus lateralis*			X	X	X	X	X	X
Spotted Ground Squirrel — *Spermophilus spilosoma*	X	X						
Thirteen-lined Ground Squirrel — *Spermophilus tridecemlineatus*	X	X						
Rock Squirrel — *Spermophilus variegatus*		X	X	X				
Gunnison's Prairie Dog — *Cynomys gunnisoni*	X	X		X				
White-tailed Prairie Dog — *Cynomys leucurus*	X	X		X				
Black-tailed Prairie Dog — *Cynomys ludovicianus*	X	X						
Fox Squirrel — *Sciurus niger*								X
Abert's Squirrel — *Sciurus aberti*				X				
Pine Squirrel, or Chickaree — *Tamiasciurus hudsonicus*						X	X	
GEOMYIDAE: POCKET GOPHERS								
Botta's Pocket Gopher — *Thomomys bottae*	X	X						
Northern Pocket Gopher — *Thomomys talpoides*	X	X		X	X	X	X	
Plains Pocket Gopher — *Geomys bursarius*	X							
Yellow-faced Pocket Gopher — *Cratogeomys castanops*	X	X						
HETEROMYIDAE: POCKET MICE AND ALLIES								
Olive-backed Pocket Mouse — *Perognathus fasciatus*	X	X						
Plains Pocket Mouse — *Perognathus flavescens*	X	X						
Silky Pocket Mouse — *Perognathus flavus*	X	X						
Great Basin Pocket Mouse — *Perognathus parvus*	X	X						
Hispid Pocket Mouse — *Chaetodipus hispidus*	X	X	X					
Ord's Kangaroo Rat — *Dipodomys ordii*	X	X						
CASTORIDAE: BEAVER								
Beaver — *Castor canadensis*								X
MURIDAE: RATS AND MICE								
Western Harvest Mouse — *Reithrodontomys megalotis*	X	X						
Plains Harvest Mouse — *Reithrodontomys montanus*	X							
Brush Mouse — *Peromyscus boylii*			X	X				
Canyon Mouse — *Peromyscus crinitus*		X	X					
White-footed Mouse — *Peromyscus leucopus*								X
Deer Mouse — *Peromyscus maniculatus*	X	X	X	X	X	X	X	X
Northern Rock Mouse — *Peromyscus nasutus*			X	X				
Piñon Mouse — *Peromyscus truei*		X	X	X				
Northern Grasshopper Mouse — *Onychomys leucogaster*	X	X						
White-throated Woodrat — *Neotoma albigula*		X	X					
Bushy-tailed Woodrat — *Neotoma cinerea*				X	X	X	X	X
Eastern Woodrat — *Neotoma floridana*								X
Desert Woodrat — *Neotoma lepida*		X	X					
Mexican Woodrat — *Neotoma mexicana*			X	X	X			
Southern Plains Woodrat — *Neotoma micropus*	X	X						
Hispid Cotton Rat — *Sigmodon hispidus*	X							X
Southern Red-backed Vole — *Clethrionomys gapperi*						X		
Heather Vole — *Phenacomys intermedius*						X		
Long-tailed Vole — *Microtus longicaudus*				X	X	X	X	X

	1	2	3	4	5	6	7	8
Mexican Vole — *Microtus mexicanus*					X			
Montane Vole — *Microtus montanus*				X	X	X	X	X
Prairie Vole — *Microtus ochrogaster*	X							X
Meadow Vole — *Microtus pennsylvanicus*	X							X
Sagebrush Vole — *Lemmiscus curtatus*		X		X				
Muskrat — *Ondatra zibethicus*								X
ZAPODIDAE: JUMPING MICE								
Meadow Jumping Mouse — *Zapus hudsonius*								X
Western Jumping Mouse — *Zapus princeps*								X
ERETHIZONTIDAE: PORCUPINES								
Porcupine — *Erethizon dorsatum*			X		X	X		X
CARNIVORA — CANIDAE: DOGS AND ALLIES								
Coyote — *Canis latrans*	X	X	X	X	X	X	X	X
Gray Wolf — *Canis lupus* *	X	X	X	X	X	X	X	X
Kit Fox — *Vulpes macrotis*	X	X						
Swift Fox — *Vulpes velox*	X							
Red Fox — *Vulpes vulpes*					X	X	X	X	X
Gray Fox — *Urocyon cinereoargenteus*			X	X	X	X		X
URSIDAE: BEARS								
Black Bear — *Ursus americanus*					X	X	X	X
Grizzly Bear — *Ursus arctos* *	X	X	X	X	X	X	X	X
PROCYONIDAE: RACCOONS AND ALLIES								
Raccoon — *Procyon lotor*								X
Ringtail — *Bassariscus astutus*		X	X	X				X
MUSTELIDAE: WEASELS AND ALLIES								
American Marten — *Martes americana*						X	X	
Ermine, or short-tailed Weasel — *Mustela erminea*	X				X	X	X	X
Long-tailed Weasel — *Mustela frenata*	X	X	X	X	X	X	X	X
Black-footed Ferret — *Mustela nigripes*	X	X						
Mink — *Mustela vison*								X
Wolverine — *Gulo gulo*						X		
American Badger — *Taxidea taxus*	X	X	X	X			X	
Western Spotted Skunk — *Spilogale gracilis*		X	X	X	X			
Eastern Spotted Skunk — *Spilogale putorius*								X
Striped Skunk — *Mephitis mephitis*	X	X	X	X	X	X	X	X
Hog-nosed Skunk — *Conepatus mesoleucus*		X	X					
Northern River Otter — *Lutra canadensis* **								X
FELIDAE: CATS								
Mountain Lion — *Felis concolor*			X	X	X	X	X	X
Lynx — *Lynx lynx*						X	X	
Bobcat — *Lynx rufus*			X	X	X	X	X		X
ARTIODACTYLA — CERVIDAE: DEER								
American Elk, or Wapiti — *Cervus elaphus*	X	X	X	X	X	X	X	X
Mule Deer — *Odocoileus hemionus*	X	X	X	X	X	X	X	X
White-tailed Deer — *Odocoileus virginianus*								X
ANTILOCAPRIDAE: PRONGHORN								
Pronghorn — *Antilocapra americana*	X	X						
BOVIDAE: CATTLE AND ALLIES								
Bison, or American buffalo — *Bison bison* *	X	X					X	
Bighorn Sheep, or mountain sheep — *Ovis canadensis*					X	X	X	X

Comments and notes: This list does not include accidentals (for
example, eastern pipistrelle, moose) or adventives, whether inadvertent
"commensals" (for example, Old World rats and mice, feral dogs, cats,
horses) or deliberate introductions (for example, mountain goat).
Used in conjunction with range maps in accounts of individual species,
this list should allow construction of a hypothetical list of the potential
natural mammalian fauna of native ecosystems at any locality in the

state. Nomenclature generally follows J. K. Jones et al. (1992).
Annotations of ecological distribution follow Armstrong (1972) and
Meaney (1991).

* = extirpated within historic time
** = extirpated but restored

The species in a community that exploit similar
resources in similar ways compose an ecological
guild. Visualizing communities of functional
guilds often makes more ecological sense than
visualizing a community organized taxonomically.
One can think of the guilds of primary consumers (grazers, browsers, seedeaters) and secondary
consumers (predators, parasites) regardless of taxonomy. The ecological view focuses attention
where the action is. In semidesert shrublands, for
example, seed-eating kangaroo rats and pocket
mice compete with ants, not with other mammals.
On shortgrass prairie, grazing mammals (like bison and prairie dogs) compete with grazing grasshoppers, not with carnivorous grasshopper mice.

*Photograph 1-1 Grassland, Pawnee National Grassland,
Weld County.*

GRASSLANDS

Dominant Plants

blue grama (*Bouteloua gracilis*), buffalo-grass
(*Buchloë dactyloides*), western wheat-grass (*Agropyron smithii*), silvery wormwood (*Artemisia filifolia*),
yucca (*Yucca glauca*), prickly-pear cactus (*Opuntia*
spp.), needle-and-thread (*Stipa comata*), sand

bluestem (*Andropogon hallii*), sand dropseed (*Sporobolus cryptandrus*)

Elevation: 1,220–3,050 m (4,000–10,000 ft)

Mean Annual Precipitation: 36 cm, range 25–46 cm

Mean Annual Temperature: 11°C

Grasslands occur over the Great Plains and in intermountain parks such as South Park and the Wet Mountain Valley. Prior to permanent settlement and cultivation, grasslands were the single most extensive ecosystem type in Colorado, covering 35 to 40 percent of the state. Roughly half of that area is now under cultivation. Grasslands of the Great Plains and the mountain parks differ in species composition. Generally, grasslands cover a gently rolling topography of fine, deep soils. Winters are dry, and most of the precipitation falls during spring and summer.

Over broad areas this ecosystem is shortgrass prairie of blue grama and buffalo-grass. Western wheat-grass, needle-and-thread, bluestems (*Andropogon* spp.), reed-grass (*Calamogrostis* spp.), and dropseed, interspersed with short grasses, form mixed-grass prairies where soil moisture is greater. Low rolling sand hill areas are typified by sand sagebrush, Indian ricegrass (*Oryzopsis hymenoides*), bluestems, and reed-grass. In southeastern Colorado this ecosystem is characterized by lower precipitation and the presence of the candelabra cactus (*Opuntia imbricata*).

Grasslands evolved with fire and grazing by large and small mammals. Historically, bison, wolves, and black-tailed prairie dogs were a significant component. However, favorable topography and soils have led to such extensive human use of grasslands that there are no known undisturbed tracts in Colorado. Millions of hectares are now devoted to agriculture, with extensive irrigation, dryland grain farming, and grazing. Additional thousands of hectares have been converted to urban landscapes. In many areas, even where never plowed, the prolonged effects of livestock grazing have resulted in alteration of the floristic composition (Costello 1954). Recent efforts to restore grassland and riparian ecosystems have used original land surveys to reconstruct presettlement landscapes (Galatowitsch 1990), and historical photographs are also useful to understand human impacts (McGinnies et al. 1991).

Mammals

Two general "adaptive syndromes" characterize mammals of open grasslands: an ability to move rapidly (to escape predators or inclement weather) or an ability to live underground. The pronghorn and the white-tailed jackrabbit epitomize mammals of open grasslands, where their keen peripheral vision and great speed evolved.

Soil type determines the distribution of many small mammals of grasslands. Plains pocket gophers may become abundant in deep sandy soils, Ord's kangaroo rats excavate sandy banks of ephemeral streams, and plains pocket mice occur in shrubby areas of sand sagebrush and yucca. In contrast to other pocket mice, the hispid pocket mouse is not limited to sandy soils but prefers open areas with a light cover of bunchgrasses. Prairie voles occur adjacent to riparian areas in northeastern Colorado. Northern grasshopper mice are widespread in both grasslands and semidesert shrublands, and they prefer loams because they are obligate dustbathers. Thirteen-lined ground squirrels prefer short bunchgrasses on friable sandy loams where they can dig their burrows. Swift foxes prefer sandy loams or loams where they dig dens for shelter year around. Badgers are wideranging in open habitats with abundant burrowing rodents.

Recently, human disturbance has played a key role on the plains. Black-tailed jackrabbits successfully occupy areas disturbed by human activities, taking cover in and feeding on introduced grasses and weedy forbs; white-tailed jackrabbits do not respond as well to disturbed vegetation and are restricted to more open areas and the mountain parks. Desert cottontails may prefer brushlands and woodland-edge situations, but they occur throughout the open grasslands where they use burrows excavated by other mammals. Black-tailed prairie dogs occur throughout the eastern plains in both short and midlength grasslands, often reaching high densities in unused open space within urbanized areas.

Coloradan grasslands received intensive study during the 1960s when the Grassland Biome component of the International Biological Program (IBP) was headquartered at Colorado State University and Pawnee National Grassland served as a principal research site. In North American grasslands, latitude and moisture gradients underlie broad patterns of community structure, and temporal variability in community composition occurs in all grassland types (Grant and Birney 1979). Flake (1973) compared food habits of four rodents from the IBP Pawnee Site. Lovell et al. (1985) described successional patterns due to development of a dam and canal, agriculture, and irrigation around Barr Lake. Changes in species composition occurred as opportunists (raccoons, least shrews, porcupines) moved in and sensitive species disappeared, while other, more resilient species persisted. A number of studies have focused on the impact of grazing. Moulton et al. (1981a) found small mammals to be adaptable to habitat perturbation and more responsive to vegetational structure than to plant species composition.

SEMIDESERT SHRUBLANDS

Dominant Plants

big sagebrush (*Artemisia tridentata*), mountain sagebrush (*A. tridentata vaseyanum*), greasewood (*Sarcobatus vermiculatus*), shadscale (*Atriplex confertifolia*), four-winged saltbush (*A. canescens*), rabbitbrush (*Chrysothamnus nauseosus*), balsamroot (*Balsamorhiza sagittata*).

Elevation: 1,220–2,440 m (4,000–8,000 ft)

Mean Annual Precipitation: 25 cm, range 15–38 cm

Photograph 1-2 Semidesert shrubland, along the Rio Grande in San Luis Valley, Costilla County.

Mean Annual Temperature: 6°C

Often grayish green in general color, semidesert shrublands cover arid regions at lower elevations in western Colorado and the San Luis Valley, occupying about 15 percent of the state. This is a cold desert ecosystem, occurring at the eastern edge of the Colorado Plateau and the Wyoming Basin. Semidesert shrublands follow the canyon bottomlands of western Colorado, extend up onto mesas and plateaus, and penetrate deep into the mountains along the Yampa, Colorado, and Gunnison rivers. Semidesert shrublands are dominated by shrubs over a sparse understory of grasses and forbs, or even bare ground where poor, alkaline soils and drought prevail. Most of the moisture falls during winter. Early summer drought is common; June is the driest month in western Colorado (whereas it is one of the wettest months in eastern Colorado).

Greasewood is often well developed on alkaline soils and extends over considerable areas in the San Luis Valley, the Grand Valley, and other arid areas of western Colorado. Grass and forb understory is sparse. Rabbitbrush or sagebrush may border greasewood stands, and where soils are less alkaline these species form mixed stands with the greasewood. White-tailed antelope squirrels burrow under rocks and shrubs in such ecosystems in extreme western Colorado.

Saltbush is widespread at lower elevations in western Colorado on soils that are well drained and less alkaline than those dominated by greasewood. Extensive stands are present in western Moffat, Mesa, Garfield, and Rio Blanco counties, and in Delta County between Hotchkiss and the eastern slopes of the West Elk Mountains in Delta County. Typically saltbush plants are widely scattered and often are cushion- or mat-like in appearance. There is little herbaceous understory.

Sagebrush covers thousands of hectares in western Colorado. In North Park and the upper Colorado River drainage (Middle Park, Gunnison Basin, and the Blue River Valley), mountain sagebrush predominates, whereas in the northwestern corner of the state big sagebrush prevails. Grass and forb cover is often well developed. At their lower limits sagebrush stands often merge with either saltbush or greasewood. At the upper limits the transition may be with montane shrubland, montane forest, or subalpine forest. The most significant human use of semidesert shrublands has been for grazing, although portions of the San Luis Valley and the Grand Valley have been converted to irrigated croplands.

Mammals

Foliage of low palatibility and low summer moisture are features of this ecosystem with which herbivores must contend. Desert cottontails feed on sagebrush and rabbitbrush in winter. Black-tailed jackrabbits feed on the forb understory, and turn to shrubs such as winterfat (*Ceratoides lanata*), shadscale, and sagebrush in late fall and winter. Wyoming ground squirrels feed on pasture sagebrush (*Artemisia frigida*), milk vetches (*Astragalus* spp.) and loco-weeds (*Oxytropis* spp.). The Wyoming Basin is home to the white-tailed prairie dog, which favors xeric sites with a mix of shrubs and grasses. Ord's kangaroo rats exploit the rich seed resources of the shrublands. Canyon mice and ringtails favor warm, dry, rocky canyons in semidesert shrublands. Moderately friable sandy loams are favored by northern grasshopper mice. Sagebrush voles feed on the leaves of sagebrush, rabbitbrush, and other aridland shrubs, in areas where they are mixed with grasses. Merriam's shrew and the desert shrew occur locally. The Yuma myotis and pallid bat occur in the canyon country of western and southeastern Colorado. Published studies of mammalian communities of Colorado's semidesert shrublands are few, but studies from adjacent Utah (Armstrong 1979, 1982) are relevant.

Photograph by Carron A. Meaney.

Photograph 1-3 Piñon-juniper woodland, Colorado National Monument.

PIÑON-JUNIPER WOODLANDS

Dominant Plants

piñon pine (*Pinus edulis*), Utah juniper (*Juniperus utahensis*) in western Colorado, red cedar (*J. scopulorum*), blue grama (*Bouteloua gracilis*), June-grass (*Koeleria macrantha*), Indian ricegrass (*Oryzopsis hymenoides*), prickly-pear (*Opuntia* spp.), fescues (*Festuca* spp.), muhly (*Muhlenbergia* spp.), bluegrass (*Poa* spp.)

Elevation: 1,680–2,440 m (5,500–8,000 ft)

Mean Annual Precipitation: 36 cm, range 25–46 cm

Mean Annual Temperature: 10°C

Piñon-juniper woodlands form open stands on warm, well-drained sites, mostly in western and southern Colorado, covering 10 to 15 percent of the state. In southeastern Colorado, they are situated above grasslands and below montane shrublands. Western Colorado presents a more complex pattern. There, piñon-juniper woodlands are bounded below and sometimes also above by semidesert shrublands where the woodlands also interweave with montane shrublands. Piñon-juniper woodlands are found extensively on slopes in western and central Colorado, and along the southeastern edge of the foothills. An isolated grove of about 4,500 ha is located at Owl Canyon, north of Fort Collins. Soils are variable in composition, although generally coarse and shallow. Junipers are more drought tolerant and thus dominate on the lower periphery, whereas piñons are more cold tolerant and hence dominate at the upper extreme. Grasses, cacti, and a variety of annual and perennial composites form much of the sparse ground cover. Many large mammals and birds use this ecosystem seasonally to avoid the rigors of higher elevations. Others are year-round residents. Species diversity in piñon-juniper woodlands is high, in Colorado second only to riparian systems. Native Americans harvested piñon nuts, which are produced by an individual tree only every three to seven years, and they made extensive use of piñon wood and pitch. Early European settlers also used these resources and initiated cattle and sheep grazing, which continues today.

Mammals

During mast years, mammals feed on the rich resource of piñon nuts. Many use the understory grasses and forbs also. Townsend's big-eared bats and fringed myotis pick insects off the trees. The long-eared myotis roosts in tree cavities and under loose bark. Desert cottontails feed on the understory of grasses and forbs. Nuttall's cottontail turns to junipers in winter. Rock squirrels occupy areas of broken rock. Piñon-juniper woodlands are home to four species of *Peromyscus*. The piñon mouse occurs in areas with large rocks where the woodland is well developed. The canyon mouse inhabits the warm, dry canyons of western Colorado. The brush mouse occurs in piñon-juniper woodlands of both the Eastern and Western slopes, especially in the ecotone (area of transition) with oakbrush. The rock mouse occurs only on the Eastern Slope, extending well northward beyond the general range of piñon. Piñon-juniper woodland is the favored habitat of the Mexican woodrat, which reaches its northern limit in Colorado. Ringtails frequent rocky and canyon country, often in association with stream beds. The few records of hog-nosed skunks in Colorado are from piñon-juniper woodlands in the southeastern portion of the state. Gray foxes, mountain lions, and mule deer are common in this ecosystem.

Small mammals of piñon-juniper woodlands often segregate by extent of canopy cover, herbaceous cover, and tree dispersion (Ribble and Samson 1987). Haufler and Nagy (1984) concluded that competition was avoided by selection of different foods. For comparative studies from woodlands in adjacent Utah, see Armstrong (1979, 1982).

MONTANE SHRUBLANDS

Dominant Plants
Gambel oak (*Quercus gambelii*), mountain-mahogany (*Cercocarpus montanus*), serviceberry (*Amelanchier alnifolia*), skunkbrush (*Rhus trilobata*), smooth sumac (*R. glabra*), wax currant (*Ribes cereum*), wild rose (*Rosa woodsii*), needle-and-thread (*Stipa comata*), blue grama (*Bouteloua gracilis*), western wheat-grass (*Agropyron smithii*), side-oats grama (*Bouteloua curtipendula*), mountain muhly (*Muhlenbergia montana*), rabbitbrush (*Chrysothamnus nauseosus*), choke cherry (*Prunus virginiana*)

Elevation: 1,675–2,600 m (5,500–8,500 ft)

Mean Annual Precipitation: 38 cm, range 33–43 cm

Mean Annual Temperature: 7°C

Photograph by David J. Cooper.

Photograph 1-4 Montane shrubland, Black Canyon of the Gunnison.

Montane shrublands generally occur at higher elevations than either grasslands or piñon-juniper woodlands in eastern Colorado, and above semidesert shrublands or piñon-juniper woodlands in western Colorado, and below montane forests. On the Eastern Slope of the Front Range, these shrublands form a distinctive but relatively narrow belt at the mountain front, often in association with sedimentary hogback ridges. West of the mountains, extensive Gambel oak communities often intermingle with piñon-juniper, and mixed stands of serviceberry, snowberry, and rabbitbrush cover extensive areas of northwestern Colorado. All told, such shrublands cover 5 to 10 percent of the state. The topographic setting is rocky, and soils are coarse and well drained. Temperatures are less extreme than in adjacent ecosystems: warmer in winter than ecosystems above and cooler in summer than those lower in elevation. Gambel oak and serviceberry dominate throughout, except for the foothills west of Denver, where Gambel oak reaches its northern limit and is replaced by mountain-mahogany. Montane shrublands are a rich and diverse ecosystem that support plants and animals more typical of adjacent ecosystems, and they serve as a winter refuge for some species. Montane shrublands are often areas of intensive human residential use, and they are quite colorful in fall.

Mammals

Many mammals favor the rocky outcrops and hogbacks common to montane shrublands. Abundant fruits, twigs, and foliage of shrubs provide forage, as does the understory of grasses. Rock squirrels prefer areas that have large rocks and can often be found basking on them or feeding on berries and grass seeds. Brush mice, piñon mice, and rock mice frequent montane shrublands, as do the ubiquitous deer mice. Although four of Colorado's six species of woodrat can be found here, the Mexican woodrat is the most likely. It makes its home in rocky places with shrubs. Ringtails, western spotted skunks, and gray foxes feed on a broad variety of small mammals, reptiles, arthropods, and fruits. The western small-footed myotis frequents rocky areas where they forage and roost in rock crevices and among, or under, rocks on the ground. They winter in tunnels here and in montane forests. Armstrong et al. (1973) described species turnover in communities at different elevations, focused strongly on small mammals of montane shrublands.

MONTANE FORESTS

Dominant Plants

Ponderosa pine (*Pinus ponderosa*), Douglas-fir (*Pseudotsuga menziesii*), quaking aspen (*Populus tremuloides*), white fir (*Abies concolor*), limber pine (*Pinus flexilis*), Colorado blue spruce (*Picea pungens*), lodgepole pine (*Pinus contorta*), wax currant (*Ribes cereum*), Arizona fescue (*Festuca arizonica*), sulphur-flower (*Eriogonum umbellatum*), kinnikinnik (*Arctostaphylos uva-ursi*), mountain maple (*Acer glabrum*)

Elevation: 1,700–2,750 m (5,600–9,000 ft)

Mean Annual Precipitation: 51 cm, range 38–63 cm

Mean Annual Temperature: 7°C

Montane coniferous forests range from open ponderosa pine parklands to dense Douglas-fir forests, and clothe about 10 percent of Colorado.

Photograph 1-5 Montane forest, Boulder.

Bounded below by foothills shrublands, piñon-juniper woodlands, or grasslands, they grade into subalpine forests above. Most precipitation falls as snow in winter and spring, although summer showers are also important. Open ponderosa pine woodlands occur on well-drained sites in the Front Range and eastward on the Platte-Arkansas Divide, in the southern and southwestern mountains to Mesa Verde, and on parts of the Uncompahgre Plateau. Douglas-fir predominates in other mountain regions and generally on moister, steeper slopes at higher elevation, whereas ponderosa pine occupies drier south-facing slopes. In some areas they intergrade along with quaking aspen or lodgepole pine, which will colonize sites after a disturbance such as fire. This ecosystem has been exploited extensively for timber, and also used for mining, grazing, historic and current human settlement, and recreation.

Mammals

Many mammals in both montane and subalpine forests use the dominant conifers for food and shelter. Many feed on the cambium layer and stems and make their nests or roost sites on the trees. Both the long-eared and long-legged myotis roost in tree cavities and under loose bark; the latter forages for moths over openings in the forest. The fringed myotis and the hoary bat also occur in montane forests. Nuttall's cottontails avoid dense forests but can be found at the edge of clearings. Least and Colorado chipmunks feed on fruits, nuts, berries, seeds, leaves, and stems; the Uinta chipmunk also occurs in montane forests, but is restricted to higher areas where it is sympatric with the least chipmunk. Abert's squirrels make nests in ponderosa pine trees and feed on the twigs and seeds, whereas pine squirrels prefer denser Douglas-fir or lodgepole pines. Porcupines feed on the cambium layer, buds, and twigs in coniferous forests. American martens feed on small rodents and are excellent climbers. Numerous studies in Colorado of individual montane species are cited in appropriate accounts. Synecological studies have been remarkably few. Stinson (1978) contrasted communities on north- and south-facing slopes, and many of the observations of Armstrong (1993) pertain to this ecosystem type. Ecology of wildlife diseases in the montane forests of Rocky Mountain National Park was reported by Carey et al. (1980), G. Bowen et al. (1981), and McLean et al. (1981).

SUBALPINE FORESTS

Dominant Plants

Engelmann spruce (*Picea engelmannii*), subalpine fir (*Abies lasiocarpa*), quaking aspen (*Populus tremuloides*), bristlecone pine (*Pinus aristata*), limber pine (*P. flexilis*), lodgepole pine (*P. contorta*), myrtle blueberry (*Vaccinium myrtillus*), broom huckleberry (*Vaccinium scoparium*), heart-leaved arnica (*Arnica cordifolia*), Jacob's ladder (*Polemonium delicatum*)

Elevation: 2,740–3,470 m (9,000–11,400 ft)

Mean Annual Precipitation: 76 cm, range 51–102 cm

Mean Annual Temperature: 2°C

This ecosystem is relatively homogeneous, dense coniferous forest, often occurring on steep slopes. It is the highest elevation forested ecosystem in Colorado and occupies about 15 percent of the land area. Soils are shallow. High winter

Photograph 1-6 Subalpine forest, Rio Grande County.

precipitation, in the form of snow, is augmented by windblown snow from the alpine tundra above. The trees are effective snow fences, and cold temperatures prevent significant melting until late spring. These factors create high snow accumulations. At their upper reaches, subalpine forests become low-growing stands of krummholz. Limber pine and bristlecone pine dominate on windy, exposed sites with rocky soils. Fire or other disturbance may lead to colonization by lodgepole pine or aspen. Spruce and fir seedlings are shade tolerant, allowing them to invade stands of shade-intolerant lodgepole pine and aspen. Regeneration of a spruce-fir forest after disturbance is relatively

slow due to the short growing season. In contrast to lodgepole pine and mature spruce-fir, aspen stands typically have a luxuriant and diverse understory of forbs and grasses. Subalpine forests are used extensively for recreation and provide cover for the watersheds so important to metropolitan areas.

Mammals

A number of mammalian species inhabit subalpine forests. Adaptations to winter include hibernation (yellow-bellied marmots), seasonal color change (long- and short-tailed weasels, snowshoe hares), and use of runways beneath the snow (mice and shrews). Some species, such as the least chipmunks and golden-mantled ground squirrels, prefer forest-edge situations to dense timber. Snowshoe hares select subalpine forests with a well-developed undergrowth of shrubs and forbs where they rest, hidden, during the day. They feed on the leaves and needles, twigs, and bark of the trees and shrubs. Yellow-bellied marmots inhabit rock piles in subalpine clearings, where they bask in the sun and make their hibernacula. Pine squirrels, or chickarees, prefer dense stands of lodgepole pines, spruce, fir, and Douglas-fir, where their chattering calls can often be heard before the squirrels themselves are seen. Southern red-backed voles prefer relatively dense coniferous forests where they nest under logs, roots, and rocks. They are preyed upon by American martens, as are montane and long-tailed voles. Wolverines and lynx, boreal forest predators, are restricted in Colorado to this ecosystem. Lynx feed almost exclusively on snowshoe hares, whereas wolverines are omnivorous. Elk bed down in these forests during the warmer months.

Mammalian communities of the subalpine forest probably have received more attention than those of any other ecosystem type. Armstrong (1977a) reviewed some of the extensive older literature. T. Vaughan (1974) studied differences in feeding strategies of four species of subalpine rodents. The northern pocket gopher (*Thomomys talpoides*) and the montane vole (*Microtus montanus*) were entirely herbivorous but preferred different plants of different sizes and foraged in different microenvironments. Both chipmunks (*Tamias minimus*) and deer mice (*Peromyscus maniculatus*) ate seeds and arthropods but fed at different times. Roppe and Hein (1978) found higher species diversity in a subalpine burn than in adjacent forest. Stinson (1977*a*) described three periods of high mortality among subalpine small mammals: flooding during spring thaw, higher physiological demands and predation during summer, and fall freezes. Merritt and Merritt (1978*b*) emphasized the importance of winter snow to population dynamics of small mammals. In the Upper Williams Fork Basin of Grand County, Armstrong (1977*a*) found that small mammals selected habitat in terms of structural features of the habitat.

© 1993 Wendy Shattil/Bob Rozinski.

Photograph 1-7 Alpine tundra, Rocky Mountain National Park, Larimer County.

ALPINE TUNDRA

Dominant Plants
Kobresia(*Kobresia myosuroides*), alpine avens (*Acomastylis rossii*), Arctic willow (*Salix arctica*), tufted hairgrass (*Deschampsia caespitosa*), sedges (*Carex* spp.), American bistort (*Bistorta bistortoides*), alpine sandwort (*Arenaria obtusiloba*), marsh-marigold (*Caltha leptosepala*), old-man-of-the-mountain (*Rydbergia grandiflora*).

Elevation: Above 3,470 m (11,400 ft)

Mean Annual Precipitation: 76 cm, range about 60–120 cm

Mean Annual Temperature: –3°C

Alpine tundra occurs above subalpine forest. Tundra is arrayed in Colorado as discontinuous islands and occupies less than 5 percent of the state. High winter winds lead to a dry environment characterized by sedges, grasses, low-growing willows, and low-growing perennials that develop as cushion plants. Talus, rock outcrops, and areas of exposed, coarse, poorly weathered rock are common. The density of plant cover varies widely with microclimatic conditions, soil development, and moisture regime. Less precipitation falls on the tundra than on the adjacent forest because storm systems tend to move through mountain passes. Furthermore, the snow that does fall on the high peaks tends to be redistributed by wind, forming large snowbeds interspersed with snowfree areas; some of the snow blows down into subalpine forests. Soils are subject to freeze-thaw action in spring and fall. This action may form polygons of sorted ground as rocks are moved differentially according to their size. Much of this patterned ground effect was formed during glacial episodes of the Pleistocene. Because of its severe climate and inaccessibility, alpine tundra generally has less human activity than most other ecosystems, aside from mining and summer recreationists, including backpackers and off-road vehicle traffic. This ecosystem is fragile and highly susceptible to disturbance. Once disturbed, plants take a very long time to grow back (in some cases up to 500 years) due to the dry, cold climate, short growing season, and slow formation of new soil.

Mammals
Alpine tundra is a relatively inhospitable environment year around, but especially during winter. Adaptations include hibernation (least chipmunks and yellow-bellied marmots), use of runways under the snow (mice, voles, and shrews), migration to lower elevations (elk, mountain sheep), or use of windswept, snowfree ridges (in-

21

troduced mountain goats). In lieu of hibernation, pikas store haypiles of alpine grasses and forbs, which become critical in the event of a late snow-melt. Talus slopes provide cover and protection from predators. Northern pocket gophers feed on roots. Their tunnels aerate the soil, contributing to the slow downward slumping of mountain-sides. Montane and long-tailed voles range into the alpine tundra, where they are prey for coyotes and long-tailed weasels. Elk feed on tundra grasses and forbs on summer nights and move down to the forest edge during the day. Mountain sheep are well known for their preference for remote, rugged areas and are found on the tundra during summer. I. Blake and Blake (1969) reported on alpine mammals of Mount Lincoln. Numerous autecological studies have been conducted on the tundra above Rocky Mountain Biological Laboratory, at Gothic, Gunnison County. The tundra of Niwot Ridge, above the University of Colorado's Mountain Research Station in Boulder County, is the site of ongoing long-term research, including detailed community studies of mammals.

RIPARIAN SYSTEMS

Dominant Plants

Plains cottonwood (*Populus sargentii*), narrowleaf cottonwood (*P. angustifolia*), mountain willow (*Salix monticola*), Geyer willow (*S. geyeriana*), peach-leaved willow (*S. amygdaloides*), sandbar willow (*S. exigua*), broad-leaved cat-tail (*Typha latifolia*), great bulrush (*Scirpus lacustris*), field horsetail (*Equisetum arvense*), salt-grass (*Distichlis spicata*), sand dropseed (*Sporobolus cryptandrus*), alder (*Alnus tenuifolia*), river birch (*Betula fontinalis*), rushes (*Juncus* spp.), water sedge (*Carex aquatilis*), beaked sedge (*C. utriculata*)

Elevation: all elevations, to above 3,350 m (11,000 ft)

Mean Annual Precipitation: variable, comparable to adjacent upland ecosystem

Photograph 1-8 Riparian systems, Conejos County.

Mean Annual Temperature: variable, but generally lower than adjacent upland ecosystem

Riparian ecosystems occur locally throughout the state. They occur as valley-bottom corridors along rivers and streams, well-watered ribbons threading through other ecosystems at all elevations, and occurring as islands of habitat adjacent to ponds, lakes, and marshes. At lower elevations, riparian cottonwoods and willows contrast dramatically with adjacent treeless grasslands and shrublands. Riparian soils are variable. Prior to intensive hydrologic management, many riparian areas, especially at middle to low elevations, were subject to overbank deposition of alluvial material due to seasonal floods during times of intense rainfall or rapid snowmelt.

At higher elevations, willows, alders, and sedges predominate adjacent to streams or other wetlands. This ecosystem is extremely rich in fauna due to the resources it offers: cover, abundant food, travel routes, and water. Riparian systems have the highest species richness of all major ecosystem types in Colorado, but they have the smallest extent, covering only 1 to 2 percent of the land area. As favored sites for human settlement, riparian lands have been extensively altered by introductions and invasions of non-native species such as salt-cedar (*Tamarix gallica*) and Russian-olive (*Eleagnus angustifolia*) and by livestock grazing, which significantly alters streambanks and can lead to substantial problems with erosion. Even greater changes result from dams and water diversion projects. A thorough environmental history of Colorado's riparian ecosystems would be of great interest; rephotography holds great promise for such an effort (G. Williams 1978).

Mammals

Riparian ecosystems of eastern Colorado are home to eastern species (such as eastern cottontails, fox squirrels, and white-tailed deer) that have moved westward along these moist corridors with their abundant food and cover. Statewide, beaver, muskrats, and mink are dependent on riverways for shelter and food. In local areas, meadow voles are excellent swimmers and prefer moist, boggy areas, and jumping mice occupy riparian thickets and lush marshes. In western Colorado, riparian corridors carry some mountain species (montane and long-tailed voles, montane shrews, western jumping mice) to quite low elevations.

Schultz and Leininger (1991) found differences in the mammalian assemblage between riparian areas grazed by livestock and those excluded from grazing along Sheep Creek, at an elevation of 2,500 m, northwest of Fort Collins. Deer mice were more abundant on grazed plots, but western jumping mice were more abundant in exclosures. Moulton et al. (1981*b*) found that grazing affected mammalian assemblages in riparian woodland more than in shortgrass prairie, and small mammals of grazed sand sagebrush were more similar to those in shortgrass prairie than to those of ungrazed sand sagebrush. Moulton (1978) found higher overall species richness in grazed (eight species) than in ungrazed (four species) cottonwood riparian woodlands, although the prairie vole (*Microtus ochrogaster*) was negatively impacted by grazing. By contrast, Samson et al. (1988) found no difference in small mammal communities due to grazing on a floodplain at the South Platte State Wildlife Area near Crook, Logan County. Contrary to the situation found in

birds, mammalian species richness on upland shortgrass prairie is higher than that in nearby riparian communities (Olson and Knopf 1988).

Patterns of Mammalian Distribution

Biogeography is the study of the patterns of distribution of organisms: which species occur where? Why do they occur there? A mammal's occurrence in a particular area is a consequence of history, geology, physiography, climate, and ecological relationships with plants and other animals. Geologic events have shaped the landscape. Physiography influences the occurrence of plant communities, which create historic and present barriers and corridors to movement. Climate can restrict a species at its limit of tolerance. Stochastic, or random, factors may play a role, as in the documented movement of small rodents as stowaways aboard trains or ships. Ecological relationships influence how species assemble into communities, a result of symbiotic interactions (competition, predation, and so forth).

Species diversity is a phenomenon of great interest to biogeographers. Two aspects of diversity are often recognized: *species richness*, the number of species in an area, and *species evenness*, which considers not only numbers of species but their relative abundance. Species richness varies greatly with taxonomic group. Within historic times, Colorado has been home to 130 species of mammals (4 of which have been introduced), 428 species of birds, 50,000 to 100,000 species of insects, and 3,000 species of plants. For comparison, the number of mammals in adjacent states is: Wyoming, 115 (T. Clark and Stromberg 1987); Nebraska, 85 (J. K. Jones et al. 1983); Kansas, 84 (Bee et al. 1981); Oklahoma, 106 (Caire et al. 1989); New Mexico, 149 (Findley 1987); Arizona, 138 (Hoffmeister 1986); Utah, 126 (Armstrong 1977*b*). As a general rule, the more heterogeneous the landscape in a given area, the higher the species richness.

Individual organisms have in the nuclei of their cells genetic information that tells them how to

23

make a living, how to survive, and how to reproduce. No species has genetic information adequate to provide the know-how to operate in all environments. Because they have finite information, species reach distributional limits in the landscape. The limit at a particular time and place may be biotic or physical or some combination of factors. Frequently we do not know why a particular organism occurs in one place but not another, although sometimes we can speculate. The range of tolerance of most species is fairly restricted. Brush mice (*Peromyscus boylii*) in Colorado live almost exclusively under cover of oakbrush, whereas piñon mice (*Peromyscus truei*) are strongly associated with juniper trees. On the Eastern Slope, north of the Palmer Divide (between Colorado Springs and Castle Rock) both oakbrush and juniper trees occur, but neither of these mice is found. Perhaps they cannot (and could not) get to the suitable habitat because of the intervening ponderosa pine woodland on the Palmer Divide. Perhaps the seemingly suitable habitat is not really suitable at all because it is too cold. We simply do not know.

A few species (such as coyotes, striped skunks, and mule deer) are notorious for being broadly tolerant. The deer mouse (*Peromyscus maniculatus*) is another species that occurs just about everywhere. However, it may be scarce or absent where one or more of its larger, more specialized relatives occurs. Further, on closer analysis, it seems that deer mice do particularly well in disturbed areas. The disturbance may be of human origin (a highway margin, a vacant lot, or an overgrazed pasture) or it may be a natural disturbance (a floodplain or an avalanche chute, for example). Any kind of disturbance seems to favor deer mice.

Because all species reach limits, it is possible to map (at least crudely), distributions of species. Biogeographers then analyze distribution maps to reveal regularities. Patterns may indicate the history of the system or they may suggest physical factors controlling the distribution of organisms. Biogeographers frequently describe large-scale patterns of distribution in terms of biotic prov-

inces (Dice 1943). Armstrong (1972) analyzed Colorado's mammals in an analogous way, identifying three major faunal areas (provinces), each subdivisible into smaller units, termed *faunal districts*. Not surprisingly, faunal areas correspond with the physiographic units described earlier in this chapter. The Great Plains Faunal Area is subdivided north-south by the divide between the South Platte and Arkansas rivers, forming faunal districts differentiated by subspecies of a number of mammals. Both the northeastern boundary (Northern High Plains Faunal District) and southeastern Colorado (Raton Faunal District) are distinctive. The latter area is strongly enriched with species of southwestern affinities, species that also extend northward along the foothills of the Eastern Slope. The Rocky Mountains are a coherent faunal unit, although dissected by valleys and canyons of the master streams. Major valleys of the Western Slope are distinctive from the Rockies as well as from each other. The Grand Valley and Dolores–San Juan faunal districts exhibit strong resemblance to areas downstream on the Colorado Drainage — the Four Corners country generally (see Armstrong 1977b). The San Luis Valley, a high, cold desert, is unique in Colorado but has strong faunal affinities with both southwestern and southeastern parts of the state, indirectly through the Rio Grande Valley of New Mexico. The Wyoming Basin shows faunal affinities to the northwest, to adjacent Utah and Wyoming, and beyond. Generally, environmental change is rapid in Colorado, and faunal turnover is more than 80 percent along particularly dramatic boundaries, such as the abrupt transition from the Great Plains to the Rocky Mountains along the Front Range.

Patterns of distribution reflect history. Today, the Southern Rocky Mountains are a forested island surrounded by a "sea" of semidesert shrublands and grasslands. Boreal species like the lynx, pygmy shrews, and snowshoe hare are isolated today from populations to the north. A mere 15,000 to 18,000 years ago, however, there probably was continuous forest (at least along watercourses) from the glaciated Southern Rockies to the Uinta

Mountains of Utah (Findley and Anderson 1956). Species of forest habitats could move freely back and forth, but the forest constituted a barrier to mammals of steppe habitats.

Direct evidence for past distribution of Coloradan mammals is meager. Because of the state's high elevation, most environments have been subject to erosion, not deposition, in the recent geological past. The fossil record of the Pleistocene is therefore poor. An exception in the region is the fauna of Little Box Elder Cave, in Converse County, Wyoming (E. Anderson 1968, Indeck 1987). The site contains a wonderful assemblage of fossils that reflects complex faunal change through the Rocky Mountain Region over the past million years.

In the absence of fossil evidence, careful study of existing distributional patterns can hint at the history of the fauna. Distributional patterns we see today must have been established since the last full glacial period because that interval would have blurred or erased evidence of previous episodes. Armstrong (1972) identified several faunal elements in Colorado based on shapes of overall, continental ranges of species. Most species of Widespread, Cordilleran, and Boreo-Cordilleran elements probably occurred in what is now Colorado even at the height of the last (Pinedale) glacial episode, when coniferous forest and periglacial tundra linked the Southern Rockies with the Middle Rocky Mountains of Utah and Wyoming across what is now the sagebrush steppe of the Wyoming Basin. With glacial recession, more habitats opened for species of adjacent regions. Great Basin and Eastern species moved in from the northwest and east, respectively. A suite of Campestrian (plains) species may have been present on the savannas of eastern Colorado throughout the later Pleistocene, but warming and drying with glacial recession increased opportunities for them. Beginning about 6,500 years ago, there was a period of 20 centuries or more that was warmer and perhaps drier than the present. During that so-called Altithermal Interval, Chihuahuan species moved into Colorado from the south and southwest, along either side of the mountains and into the San Luis Valley. Today several of these species (for example, northern rock mouse, rock squirrel, Mexican woodrat) range northward along the foothills and in the canyons of the Eastern Slope, reaching northern limits at or near the Wyoming boundary (Armstrong 1972).

Organisms have major impacts on one another, and sometimes in improbable ways. Who would have guessed that the introduction of plague from Asia to San Francisco around 1900 would eventually impact ground squirrels in Colorado? Infected Norway rats from arriving ships spread the disease to local rats, which in turn infected local ground squirrels. Plague then spread eastward, eventually reaching Colorado. The first incidence of sylvatic plague in the state showed up in yellow-bellied marmots and rock squirrels in 1941 (Ecke et al. 1952). In the late forties the outbreak extirpated Gunnison's prairie dogs from South Park and adjacent counties. Subsequently, Wyoming ground squirrels, lacking significant physical barriers and relieved of competition from prairie dogs, invaded South Park and are present today.

Much of the change we witness now in mammalian distributions probably results from human influence. For example, the Wyoming ground squirrel (*Spermophilus elegans*) has moved southward over the twentieth century, responding in part to overgrazing (see Hansen 1962), in part to the decimation of Gunnison's prairie dog (*Cynomys gunnisoni*) by plague in areas like South Park. Eastern species like the fox squirrel (*Sciurus niger*) and the raccoon (*Procyon lotor*) have responded positively to urban plantings and stabilization of the riparian corridor by flood control and fire suppression. Of exotic species introduced deliberately, some have prospered (for example, moose, mountain goat) and some (the European hedgehog — *Erinaceus europaeus*, for example, introduced in El Paso County in the belief that it would control rattlesnakes) have not. Further, some inadvertent introductions have prospered (such as the house mouse and the Norway rat) and others (like the Neotropical mouse opossum, *Marmosa*, which probably arrived with shipments of bananas) have not become established.

Species move continually over time. Some movements are rapid and obvious, like the ongoing invasion of fox squirrels into the foothills of the Front Range; others are slower and more subtle. But even if a species expands each generation only the distance that young disperse from their natal burrow, movements of hundreds of miles are possible in only a few hundred generations. The diverse Coloradan landscape, with its array of elevations, vegetation types, moisture regimes, and waterways, presents both significant barriers to and corridors for movement of mammals. The river that is an impassable barrier to a fossorial species like a pocket gopher provides a corridor for an aquatic species like the beaver or a riparian specialist like the raccoon.

Known distributions of some Coloradan mammals have changed over the past couple of decades. Meaney (1990*a*) combined specimen records up through 1988 from a number of institutions (Denver Museum of Natural History; Museum of the High Plains, Hays, Kansas; University of Colorado Museum, Boulder; U.S. Fish and Wildlife Service, Fort Collins; University of Northern Colorado, Greeley) and compared them with distributions mapped in Armstrong (1972). Data were included from annual reports to the Colorado Division of Wildlife from holders of scientific collecting permits for the years 1985 and

1986, as were sight records tabulated for the Mammal Latilong Distribution Study (Meaney 1991). In the past 20 years, 75 species have been newly reported for 254 counties. (Many are simply a matter of new data, and thus represent an expansion in knowledge rather than actual biological activity.) Of 254 new county records, 55 filled in former gaps within supposed geographic ranges of species (shaded areas on maps in Armstrong 1972). Eliminating this group and ignoring deliberate introductions leaves 56 species that showed possible expansion of ranges. These species were sorted by cardinal direction of apparent "expansion." Of the 56 species, 24 expanded northward, 13 moved westward, 12 expanded eastward, and 7 ranges were enlarged southward.

The most common directions of change, northward and westward, may reflect slow post-Pleistocene readjustment. Additionally, a number of species are moving westward along riparian and irrigated corridors. Eastward movement is, at least in part, expansion out from the foothills in response to tree plantings and other human activities by which the demarcation between foothills and plains is being obscured. The southward movement is actually a general southwestern dispersal from the Arkansas and Platte rivers, along irrigated corridors. Such changes are a natural phenomenon, augmented by human activities. Understanding the dynamics of biogeography is critical to management and conservation, and it demands careful observation and reporting, activities in which all knowledgeable naturalists can participate.

Chapter 2

Mammals in General

Mammalian Origins

Long before the origin of dinosaurs, indeed, just barely (in a geologic sense) after the origin of reptiles from amphibians, one branch of the stem reptiles embarked on a course that led eventually to the mammals. Those reptiles were the synapsids, which arose in Carboniferous times, some 300 million years ago. (Among the synapsids were the familiar sail-backed pelycosaurs.) The synapsids produced a side branch, the therapsids — or "mammal-like reptiles" — in the Permian Period, perhaps 270 million years ago. Eventually one of several lines of therapsids gave rise to the earliest mammals, in the Triassic Period, about 230 million years ago.

Two-thirds of mammalian evolution occurred in the Mesozoic Era — the Age of Reptiles. For 180 million years, the early mammals scuttled around in the imposing shadows of the ruling reptiles, or archosaurs. Early mammals were generally small, rat-sized, and rather shrew-like. As archosaurs got larger, diversified, and exploited an increasingly broad spectrum of niches, early mammals stood by, remaining small and rather unspecialized. When the Age of Reptiles had run its course, the descendants of therapsids stood poised on an evolutionary threshold, eventually to assume the dominance that the archosaurs abdicated, ready to stage one of the most dramatic adaptive radiations ever seen on Earth. The mammalian radiation eventually produced a peculiar species that

presumed to name itself *Homo sapiens*, "wise self," and tried to comprehend the cosmos, assuming only that it is comprehensible.

Mammalian Characteristics

Two particularly significant trends stand out in mammalian evolution. One is the evolution of milk-producing glands, the mammae, whence the name Mammalia itself is taken. The mammary glands allow a long-term nutritional and social bond between mother and young. The second is the development of an enlarged brain, especially the neopallium (cerebral cortex), derived from the primitive olfactory lobes. This brain gives mammals an intelligence unparalleled on Earth. Because of longer interaction between mother and offspring and a large brain capacity, mammals can learn much of their adult behavior rather than relying on "hard-wired" or innate behaviors. Complex mental processes and interactions between individuals are then possible. Our own species may represent the zenith of these capacities.

A number of characteristics are unique to mammals, among them hair, sebaceous and sweat glands, mammary glands, a single bone in the lower jaw articulating with a single bone of the skull, three middle ear ossicles, a single left aortic arch, non-nucleated, biconcave red blood cells, a muscular diaphragm separating the thoracic and abdominal cavities, and a highly developed cerebral cortex. These characteristics did not arise from nothing, of course; they have antecedents among the reptilian ancestors of mammals.

Modern mammals differ from modern reptiles in numerous ways. Mammalian traits evolved at different rates over tens of millions of years. Given this mosaic pattern of evolution, to state just when the transition was made from mammal-like reptile to reptile-like mammal is somewhat arbitrary. To avoid undue rancor and speculation, paleontologists generally have agreed on a single character complex — one that fossilizes rather well — as the critical feature defining mammals: the jaw-ear complex.

JAW-EAR COMPLEX

The reptilian jaw consists of three bones (*dentary, prearticulare, articulare*), which articulate with a fourth bone on the skull (the *quadrate*) to form the jaw joint. Among advanced reptiles, this complex jaw arrangement is put to good use. In snakes, for example, the jaw can be essentially disassembled and the animals can swallow prey larger around than themselves. In the middle ear of reptiles is a single bone, the *columella* ("little column").

In mammals, the jaw has been simplified. The lower jaw is a single paired bone, the *dentary*, or *mandible*. The dentary articulates directly with the squamosal bone of the skull. So radical a simplification obviously leaves some bones left over. French Nobel laureate François Jacob characterized evolution as "tinkering." U.S. wildlife biologist and conservationist Aldo Leopold pointed out the First Law of Tinkering: never throw away any pieces. Evolution has tended to follow that rule. Thus, the spare jaw parts were recycled. The prearticulare became the *hammer bone* (malleus) and the quadrate became the *anvil* (incus). The columella remains in place to become the *stirrup bone* (or stapes). The reptilian jaw had three bones, the ear just one; the mammalian ear has three bones, the jaw just one.

The mammalian jaw-ear complex was a net gain for assertive organisms. What was lost in jaw mobility was more than compensated in the strength of the jaw joint and increased effectiveness of the ear. The increased strength of the jaw was important to full exploitation of another mammalian specialty, fancy teeth.

TEETH

Mammalian teeth have three peculiarities, based on trends laid down by their therapsid progenitors: (1) the toothrow is differentiated front to rear (*heterodont*); (2) the teeth are set firmly in sockets (*thecodont*); and (3) the teeth are present in two and only two sets (*diphyodont*), the deciduous (temporary) "*milk teeth*" and the *permanent teeth*. The milk teeth ("baby teeth") are lost as the permanent teeth move into place in the jaws. These conditions contrast with those in primitive vertebrates (including most living reptiles) where teeth are: (1) all the same size and shape (*homodont*), (2) perched atop the jaw bones (*acrodont*), and (3) mostly replaced as needed throughout life (*polyphyodont*).

In primitive mammals, the socketed teeth are of four kinds: (1) *incisors* for nipping, (2) *canines* (or "eye-teeth") for piercing and grasping prey, and (3) *premolars* ("bicuspids" in humans), and (4) *molars* for shearing or grinding the food.

The incisors are usually unicuspid, with a single root. In eutherians (placental mammals) the maximal number of incisors is three per quadrant of the jaw. Canines are generally elongate, conical, unicuspid teeth, attached by a single root. Canines never number more than one per quadrant and they frequently are absent in herbivores. Premolars and molars are distinguished by their embryological development: molars are present only in the permanent dentition. This distinction may not be reflected in adult morphological features. This lack causes difficulty in distinguishing between molars and premolars, so they frequently are referred to collectively as *cheekteeth*. Complex in crown structure, cheekteeth have several roots anchoring them to the jaw. The primitive condition for teeth in placental mammals is three incisors, one canine, four premolars, and three molars. Many mammals have experienced evolutionary loss of teeth, which can lead to the formation of a gap in the tooth row, a *diastema*. Premolars are lost from front to rear. Thus, if there are fewer than four premolars, it is the anterior premolars that have been lost. Molars however, are lost from the back to the front.

Teeth are made of dense, bony material. The *crown* projects above the gum line; the portion of the tooth set in the socket (*alveolus*) in the jaw is the root. Crowns of most teeth are covered by *enamel,* the hardest substance in the vertebrate body. This enamel surface is incomplete in many species, exposing the somewhat less dense *dentine.* Dentine forms the core of the tooth. In many species, normal aging and wear result in loss of enamel and exposure of dentine.

The outer surface of the root of the tooth is covered with a bony material, cementum, which interfaces with the *periodontal membrane,* the fibrous connective tissue that bonds the cementum to the bone of the alveolar wall. In the central core of the dentine a *pulp cavity* contains nerves and a blood supply connected by root canals. In most species, the opening of the root canal constricts and growth ceases when the tooth reaches maturity. Such teeth are termed *rooted.* In other mammals, especially rodents and other herbivores with a fibrous, coarse diet, root canals remain open and the tooth continues to grow throughout life, producing teeth termed *rootless* or evergrowing.

The topography of the *occlusal,* or biting, surface of teeth differs greatly between taxa. Teeth provide clues to diet and evidence of evolutionary relationships. Teeth are readily fossilized; indeed, many extinct mammals are known only from their teeth. Primitive mammals had sharp-cusped, *sectorial* (cutting) cheekteeth. Most insectivores and bats, as well as some primates, retain these primitive cheekteeth. Round-cusped, *bunodont* teeth are found in omnivores (bears, pigs, and hu-

mans, for example); these function in grinding. Herbivores often exhibit expanded grinding surfaces. *Lophodont* teeth (as in horses) have expanded cusps; *selenodont* teeth (as in deer) show elongate, crescent-shaped ridges linking cusps. Often in development the enamel of the crown wears through, exposing the softer dentine. This process establishes an occlusal surface of differential hardness, allowing continual sharpening as the teeth operate on an abrasive diet. Such a surface accompanied by continual growth results in a remarkably effective grinding mechanism. The pattern of alternating dentine and enamel may be important in diagnosis of a taxon.

Teeth with particularly high crowns are termed *hypsodont,* whereas those with low crowns are called *brachydont.* Grazers tend to have higher-crowned teeth than carnivores, as the silicates in grasses cause great wear. The *lingual* side of a tooth is that side closer to the tongue, and the *labial* side is that side closer to the cheeks. Complex evolution necessitates a complex descriptive nomenclature. For a complete discussion of teeth and dental features and structures see DeBlase and Martin (1981), Hershkovitz (1971), or Reig (1977).

The evolutionary plasticity of mammalian teeth has been remarkable as teeth have been greatly modifed within various groups to deal with different specialized diets. The typical deviation from the primitive condition has been to lose teeth. Herbivores, like rodents, rabbits, and the even-toed hoofed mammals have lost the canines and simplified the incisors. Carnivores have sacrificed grinding teeth. Some whales and anteaters have given up on teeth altogether. The toothed whales, by contrast, have re-emphasized teeth; some have over 200 of them. Groups that retain fairly primitive dentition include bats, insectivores, and primates. Tusks of elephants, walruses, the narwhal, and the warthog are teeth turned to tasks other than chewing.

The dental formula of a mammal indicates the number of teeth of each kind for one side of the jaw. The number of upper teeth is indicated above a line (or before a slant line) and the number of lower teeth is indicated below the line (or after a slant line). For example, the primitive placental mammal had a total of 44 teeth expressed in the following dental formula: incisors 3/3, canines 1/1, premolars 4/4, molars 3/3, total = 44. This is conventionally abbreviated to 3/3, 1/1, 4/4, 3/3 = 44. Thus, the dental formula of the deermouse, *Peromyscus maniculatus*, is written: 1/1, 0/0, 0/0, 3/3 = 16. Dental formulae usually do not differ between species within a genus, but they differ greatly above the level of genus. Table 2-1 lists dental formulae for Coloradan mammals. Mammalogists use a variety of shorthand methods to refer to individual teeth. For example, sometimes upper teeth are abbreviated with upper case letters (P4 = fourth upper premolar) and lower teeth are abbreviated with lower case letters (m1 = first lower molar). However, in this book we use a slightly more obvious convention, superscripts for upper teeth (P^4 = fourth upper premolar) and subscripts for lower teeth (M_1 = first lower molar).

Table 2-1. Dental formulae of genera of mammals known or expected to occur in Colorado. I = incisors, C = canines, P = premolars, M = molars.

I	C	P	M	Total	Genus
5/4	1/1	3/3	4/4	50	*Didelphis*
3/3	1/1	4/4	3/3	44	*Sus*
3/3	1/1	4/4	2/3	42	*Canis, Urocyon, Ursus*, Vulpes*
3/3	1/1	4/4	2/2	40	*Bassariscus, Procyon*
3/3	0–1/0–1	3/3	3/3	36–40	*Equus*
2/3	1/1	3/3	3/3	38	*Myotis*
3/3	1/1	4/4	1/2	38	*Gulo, Martes*
2/3	1/1	2/3	3/3	36	*Idionycteris, Lasionycteris, Plecotus*
3/2	1/0	3/3	3/3	36	*Scalopus*
3/3	1/1	4/3	1/2	36	*Lutra*
2/3	1/1	2/2	3/3	34	*Euderma, Pipistrellus*
3/3	1/1	3/3	1/2	34	*Mephitis, Mustela, Spilogale, Taxidea*
0/3	1/1	3/3	3/3	34	*Cervus*
2/2	1/1	2/2	3/3	32	*Homo*
3/3	1/1	2/3	1/2	32	*Conepatus*
2/3	1/1	1/2	3/3	32	*Eptesicus*
3/1	1/1	3/1	3/3	32	*Sorex*
1/3	1/1	2/2	3/3	32	*Lasiurus*
4/2	1/0	2/1	3/3	32	*Blarina*
0/3	0/1	3/3	3/3	32	*Alces, Antilocapra, Bison, Bos, Odocoileus, Oreamnos, Ovis*
1/2–3	1/1	2/2	3/3	30 or 32	*Nyctinomops, Tadarida*
3/3	1/1	3/2	1/1	30	*Felis*
3/2	1/0	2/1	3/3	30	*Cryptotis*
0/0	0/0	7–9/7–9**		28–36	*Dasypus*
3/3	1/1	2/2	1/1	28	*Lynx*
3/2	1/0	1/1	3/3	28	*Notiosorex*
1/2	1/1	1/2	3/3	28	*Antrozous*
2/1	0/0	3/2	3/3	28	*Lepus, Sylvilagus*
2/1	0/0	2/2	3/3	26	*Ochotona*
1/1	0/0	2/1	3/3	22	*Cynomys, Glaucomys, Marmota, Sciurus*, Spermophilus, Tamias, Tamiasciurus*
1/1	0/0	1/1	3/3	20	*Castor, Chaetodipus, Cratogeomys, Dipodomys, Erethizon, Geomys, Thomomys, Perognathus*
1/1	0/0	1/0	3/3	18	*Zapus*
1/1	0/0	0/0	3/3	16	*Clethrionomys, Lemmiscus, Microtus, Mus, Neotoma, Ondatra, Onychomys, Peromyscus, Phenacomys, Rattus, Reithrodontomys, Sigmodon*

*May have one upper premolar missing.
**Premolars and molars combined due to the uncertainty of homologies with teeth of other mammals.

Diverse and highly adapted teeth are one of a number of mammalian features associated with an active lifestyle. Specialization within the toothrow allows thorough and efficient processing of food. In the gut, food comes into contact with digestive chemicals in small bits, with a large ratio of surface to volume. Therefore, digestion can take place rapidly, and the energy-demanding mammalian "engine" can run (or at least "idle") continually, well fueled and ready to spring into action at a moment's notice, regardless of the temperature of the environment.

Teeth and the structure of the ear region provide readily fossilized evidence of the mammalian grade of organization. While these features were changing, major adjustments were occurring in the soft anatomy as well. In particular, there was evolving a whole suite of traits involved with keeping mammals warm and active. Central to those adaptations was hair.

HAIR

We shall see that many of the fundamental features of the mammalian grade of organization are associated with hair. Hairs are specialized structures of the *epidermis* (the outer layers of skin). Hairs develop from roots in a *follicle*, which is an inpocketing of the epidermis into a depression in the *dermis* (the lower part of the skin). Hair is not homologous with feathers or reptilian scales. Rather, hair seems to have evolved independently, as insulation between scales. This pattern actually can be seen today on the nearly naked, scaly tails of some rats and the opossum. Hairs are multicellular and are composed of three layers, the inner *medulla*, the *cortex*, and the outer *cuticle*. The portion of the hair exposed above the skin (the shaft) is composed of dead cells. Hair color results from the presence or absence of pigments, structural arrangements of air spaces, hair texture, hair thickness, or combinations of these features. The medulla is made of shrunken cells that may be pigmented and have air spaces. In the smallest and thinnest hairs the medulla may be absent, whereas in the largest hairs the medulla typically is well developed, with air spaces improving insulating quality, as in the hollow hairs of artiodactyls. The cortex makes up the bulk of the hair; it may or may not be pigmented. The cuticle is not pigmented and consists of a thin outer layer of cells arranged as scales. The scale pattern of the cuticle is fre-

quently diagnostic at the level of genera or even species (Moore et al. 1974).

The principal function of hair clearly is insulation. However, hair has been highly modified to serve other functions. In porcupines, some hairs have become protective quills. Most mammals have facial bristles (*vibrissae*) that serve a tactile function. In many species, hair is colored in a meaningful pattern. In most it provides concealment by cryptic coloration or by countershading, in which the dorsum typically is darker than the venter. Others (like skunks) signal a warning or reminder. Color patterns can serve in communication, such as a white-tailed deer or pronghorn flashing the white rump patch to signal danger. The mane of the male lion increases the apparent size of the head and may be associated with asserting and maintaining social dominance.

Pelage is the collective term for the total hair covering. The pelage is made up of two general types of hair, *guard hairs* and *underhairs*. Guard hairs are the most conspicuous, longest, and coarsest hairs. They protect the underhair and the skin from mechanical injury, screen out dirt and other debris, and shield it from damaging light radiation. Most guard hairs have a *definitive growth* pattern: they reach a certain length, cease growing, are shed, and then are replaced. Some guard hairs — such as the mane of a lion or the mane and tail of a horse — exhibit *angora* growth; the hair continues to grow without replacement. Guard hairs have been modified in some mammals to form stiff, thickened quills. Underhairs usually are dense and soft, and function in insulation. In the fur trade a "sheared" pelt is one on which the guard hairs have been cut to the level of the underhair.

The root of the hair has attached to it a tiny muscle, the *arrector pili* ("hair raiser"). In typical mammals, this muscle can raise the hair to trap an insulating layer of air warmed by the body. In humans, with our minimal body hair, the result is not so much protection from cold, but a frequent sign of cold, so-called "goose bumps."

Associated with skin and hair are glands. Many mammals have *sweat* (sudoriferous) *glands*. Sweat is evaporated from the hair and skin, making the surface cooler. Sweat glands are restricted to the soles of the feet of carnivores, whereas humans and many ungulates have sweat glands over much of the body. Most marine mammals, a number of fossorial types including moles, and rodents lack sweat glands altogether. (Mammals with few sweat glands, such as cats, lick the fur to promote evaporative cooling; or, like the dog, they pant, cooling by evaporation from the tongue.) Perspiration consists of water, salts, and some other compounds, including urea (so the skin is an excretory organ).

Each hair has an associated *sebaceous gland*, which secretes into the follicle an oily substance (*sebum*) that lubricates and weatherproofs the hair. Both sweat and sebaceous glands have been modifed into odor-producing scent glands. Most mammals have at least a few scent glands somewhere on the skin. Tarsal glands occur on the legs of deer; anal glands are found in most carnivores; ventral glands are found on American martens; flank glands on shrews; preorbital glands in deer, elk, and mountain sheep; and cheek glands on pikas and yellow-bellied marmots.

By the way, these scent glands are part of an extensive array of adaptations for olfactory communication. Scent marking is the general name given to behaviors that distribute or place odorous secretions in the environment. In addition to secretions of scent glands, urine and feces are handy and frequently used in scent marking as well. Scent marks may provide information on the identity, status, sex, or reproductive condition of the individual depositing them. Scent marking, not yet well understood by humans, serves functions in reproduction, dispersion and social integration, alarm, and defense.

MAMMARY GLANDS

In the history of mammals, the evolution of the mammary glands surely was the most profoundly significant modification of hair glands. The importance of the milk glands cannot be overstated. The name Mammalia refers to those glands and rightly so: mammary glands are central to the mammalian way of life and its success. Milk from the mammary glands — a highly refined concoction of water, carbohydrates, fats, proteins, and salts, closely tuned to a particular species' developmental needs — provides newborn mammals a nutritional headstart. Further, nursing makes of young mammals a captive audience and offers a period of interaction with the mother (and often with siblings) that allows training and socialization.

HEART

Like birds, mammals have an efficient, four-chambered (double pump) heart, with separate circuits for oxygen-poor and oxygen-rich blood. This circulatory system allows the efficient delivery of oxygen (and removal of carbon dioxide) that high activity demands. Evidence from comparative anatomy and embryology indicates that the four-chambered hearts of mammals and birds evolved independently. The common ancestor of birds and mammals was an ancient stem reptile that probably had a three-chambered heart.

The efficient circulatory system of mammals, along with insulating hair, allows mammals to be *endothermic* (warm-blooded), maintaining a relatively constant body temperature despite changes in the external environment. The constant body temperature of both birds and mammals is fairly high, far closer to the upper limit of environmental conditions than to the lower limit. One explanation for this is that heating is less costly — in terms of water — than cooling. Animal cooling systems mostly are based on evaporation (perspiration, panting, mudbathing, and so forth). Water loss is expensive (or even destructive) to animals on dry land (animals that already are struggling hard to maintain the homeostasis of those little bags of sea water called cells).

Mature red blood cells of mammals lack a nucleus, an adaptation that maximizes their oxygen-carrying capacity, and they are biconcave in shape, maximizing the exchange surface. The body cavity of mammals is subdivided into thoracic and abdominal cavities by the *diaphragm*, a complex muscle that functions in ventilation.

BRAIN

Another element in the success of early mammals was their behavior. Early mammals were small, probably nocturnal, and surely secretive (as most groups still are). The land and the shallow waters of the Mesozoic Earth were dominated by a great variety of reptiles. The sophisticated brains of early mammals must have been critical to their survival alongside their extravagantly large and successful contemporaries.

The mammalian brain shows several advances over the brain of reptiles. The *neopallium* of the forebrain is substantially enlarged, and development of the corpora quadrigemina of the midbrain allows them to serve as auditory and visual reflex centers. With this expansion of brain capacity, mammals have achieved much greater development of learning and cognitive processes than other vertebrates.

The most dim-witted of mammals is wittier than the brightest bird, reptile, or fish. Please do not misunderstand this assertion. Bird brains are perfectly adequate for birds and birds' behavior, and bird behavior can be wonderfully complicated. (Have you tried to fly home in the dark recently, to Tierra del Fuego?) But generally bird behavior is not what one would term creative (the fabulous vocal mimicry of some species notwithstanding). The same can be said of most reptiles, amphibians, and fish. Their behavior is not as individually variable or flexible as that of mammals and not as responsive to novel environmental opportunity. Mammals are more highly dependent on learned behavior than are any other animals. Lacking built-in solutions to many of the problems they face, mammals must piece together effective solutions based on individual experience. That takes a brain built for such work. The mammalian brain differs from that of reptiles in degree, not in kind. The basic pieces of the mammalian brain are present in reptiles and even fish. What mammals have done is to elaborate parts of the brain, especially those parts involved with learned behavior.

REPRODUCTION

The reproductive tract of female eutherians (placental mammals) includes paired *ovaries* and *oviducts*, and a *uterus*, *cervix*, and *vagina* of variable structure. In the *duplex* system, typical of lagomorphs and most rodents, there are two uteri, two cervices, and a single vagina. In a *bipartite* tract there are two uteri with a single vagina and cervix. Most carnivores and the pigs show this type. In insectivores, most ungulates, bats, and some primates the reproductive system is *bicornuate*, with the lower half of the uteri fused and the upper portion of the uteri remaining separate as horns, or cornua. A *simplex* uterus found in higher primates and the xenarthrans (armadillos and sloths) involves a single uterus, cervix, and vagina. The external genitalia of female mammals are termed the *vulva*. In many species, swelling of the vulva indicates the period of sexual receptivity. The female reproductive tract of marsupials lacks a true vagina. Paired oviducts lead to paired uteri, which in turn connect to two lateral vaginal canals (pseudovaginae) that receive the forked penis of the male.

Environments often exhibit seasonal variation in the availability of resources. Reproduction is an expensive process, so it usually is cued to seasonal rhythms of the environment so that young are produced at optimal times. In most female mammals there is a fixed period of time, termed *estrus*, or "heat," during which she will receive the male. This period of receptivity is part of a generalized *estrous cycle*. Mammals in which the female has a single reproductive cycle during the breeding season are termed *monestrous*. Those that exhibit recurrent cycles of estrus are termed *polyestrous*. The timing and frequency of reproduction is dictated by environmental conditions such as availability of food, stability of the environment, and weather. The white-footed mouse, deer mouse, and hispid cotton rat have restricted breeding seasons in northern parts of their ranges but breed throughout the year in more equable climes. Ovulation (the release of eggs from the ovary) may occur spontaneously, usually toward the end of estrus (*spontaneous ovulation*) or it may result from the stimulus of copulation (*induced ovulation*).

Humans exhibit a distinctive reproductive cycle — the *menstrual cycle*. Some features typical of the menstrual cycle (such as menstrual bleeding, which is sloughing of the uterine lining) are found in other Old World primates, but the situation in human females — involving more or less continual sexual receptivity, no obvious point of estrus, cryptic ovulation, and menstruation approximately on a lunar-monthly cycle — is a human specialty, an evolutionary descendent of the typical mammalian estrous cycle.

In males of most mammals paired *testes* are contained in an external pouch, the *scrotum*, at least during the breeding season. High temperatures are deleterious to sperm cell production. The scrotum maintains the testes at cooler temperatures. In some groups, including primates, artiodactyls (even-toed ungulates), and most perissodactyls (odd-toed ungulates), the testes of adults are scrotal at all times. In other mammals (including many carnivores and most rodents) the testes remain in the abdominal cavity until the actual breeding season, at which time they migrate to the scrotum and begin to function. Whales, insectivores, and bats lack a scrotum and the testes remain in the body cavity permanently. Ducts carry sperm from the testes and seminal products from the accessory sex glands to the *penis*, the intromittant organ.

Males of many species of carnivores, bats, and most rodents have a supportive bone, the *os penis* or *baculum*, in the penis. The shape of the baculum frequently differs between closely related species and thus has value as a taxonomic character. The *os clitoridis*, or *baubellum*, is the homologous bone in females. Primates and bats have a pendulous penis; the phallus of most mammals is not pendulous, however, but rather is withdrawn into a penile sheath when not in use.

The reproductive cycle in both sexes is closely controlled by hormones of the pituitary gland and the gonads. Estrogenic hormones of the ovaries and androgenic hormones of the testes regulate development of secondary sexual characters of females and males, respectively.

DEVELOPMENT

Except for the peculiar, reptile-like monotremes (platypus, echidnas) of Australia and New Guinea, mammals do not lay eggs. Rather, the embryo develops to some degree within the mother and then is given birth, rather than hatched. In mammals other than marsupials (the pouched mammals of the Americas and Australia), some sort of intimate relationship develops between the mother and the embryos. The mediator of this relationship is the *placenta*, a remarkable, cooperative structure built of maternal and embryonic tissues.

The embryonic contribution to the placenta is built from membranes first seen in the reptilian *land egg* (also called the cleidoic egg, a shelled egg that can be laid on dry land). The *amnion* retains its ancestral function as a fluid-filled, shock-absorbing bag. The *chorion*, too, remains as a tough, protective sack that provides the surface for gaseous exchange. However, the reptilian *allantois* and *yolk sac* no longer are needed. In the reptile, the yolk sac stores food; embryonic eutherian mammals derive their nutrients from the mother's bloodstream. The reptilian allantois is a receptacle for embryonic wastes; embryonic mammals pass their wastes to the maternal circulation.

A handy fact about the yolk sac and the allantois is that they have blood vessels leading to and from (respectively) the embryo. In placental mammals the ancestral reptilian structures have been recycled, the blood vessels commandeered to participate in the *umbilicus*, which connects the embryo to the placenta. The ancestral membranes of the yolk sac and the allantois lend strength to the umbilicus.

The maternal contribution to the placenta is the uterine lining, or *endometrium*. Across the placenta the embryo receives oxygen, food molecules — carbohydrates and fats for energy and amino acids for building materials — and also antibodies to fight infection. From the embryo, wastes — urea and carbon dioxide — diffuse back to the mother. Increased maternal mobility coupled with optimal parental care and the advanced stage of development at birth have contributed to the success and diversity of placental mammals. An almost solid mass of blood vessels, the placenta creates a very large surface area between the two circulatory systems to promote efficient diffusion.

Villi — finger-like projections of the chorion into the uterus — further increase the area of contact and exchange, enhancing this function. In contrast to placentals, marsupials produce embryos covered by a shell membrane. When the membrane dissolves, only a weak placental attachment develops, and it has no villi.

In most mammals the placenta is deciduous, tearing away from the uterine wall at birth. The result is *uterine scars*, which may be used to estimate the number of young a particular female has produced. A nulliparous (literally, "never-birthed") female shows no evidence of scarring and has not produced young. A parous female is one that is pregnant or shows placental scars. A multiparous female could show several series of different-aged placental scars.

The placenta is remarkable enough when we appreciate its structure and its function. But there is more to the story than just remodeling a reptilian egg. Obviously, keeping embryos inside the mother is an adaptive thing to do. They are pro-

tected, nourished, and — stored as they are within a warm body — incubated. But before this "big idea" would work there was a serious problem to solve: the mother's immune system.

At the level of molecules, animal cells are able to recognize "self" and "not-self." There are mechanisms at various levels to destroy all that is not-self: foreign organisms, toxins, foreign proteins. From the mother's standpoint, the embryo is, of course, one-half not-self, because half of its genetic information (and hence something like half of its proteins) came from the father. Before the embryo can implant in the uterine wall and establish the placenta, it must, therefore, overcome the maternal immune system. Just how this works still is poorly understood. However, solving the problem of immunologic incompatibility between the mammalian mother and her half-alien embryos allowed the perfection of internal development.

Timing of reproduction and development frequently is tied to particularly favorable seasons. In some species, especially bats that hibernate in the temperate zone, *delayed fertilization* occurs. The animals mate in late summer or early fall while gathering at the hibernation site. Sperm are stored for the winter in the uterus or vagina. Actual fertilization occurs in late winter or spring. A somewhat similar condition, *delayed implantation*, occurs in many of the mustelids, bears, armadillos, seals, and some deer. Fertilization occurs at the time of mating but the resulting zygote does not implant in the uterine lining for up to several months, remaining instead in a state of suspended animation in the upper regions of the uterine cavity. Both phenomena appear to have evolved as mechanisms to allow mating during peaks of activity in late summer or fall, but delaying development and parturition to coincide with favorable environmental conditions.

The *gestation period* is the length of time from fertilization until birth (*parturition*) of the young. Gestation lasts only 16 to 17 days in some rodents and up to 22 months in the African elephant.

Length of gestation generally increases with increasing body size, but there are exceptions. For instance, the porcupine has a much longer gestation period (nearly 7 months) than one would predict from body size, giving birth to well-developed young.

Litter size is the number of young born at any one time, ranging from one to a dozen or more. Smaller mammals tend to have larger litters than do larger mammals. Bats are a major exception to the rule, many species being among the smallest of mammals, but most having only one young per year. *Altricial* young are those born at an early stage of development. In most mammals, neonates have the eyes unopened, have little hair and poorly developed limbs, capable of little more than crawling. Altricial young usually are reared in a nest. *Precocial* young are born furred, with eyes open, and are capable of walking shortly after birth.

SKELETON

The mammalian skeleton is frequently subdivided into *cranial* (head) and *postcranial* anatomy. Mammalogists tend to emphasize cranial features because they are so useful in identification. Cranial adaptations often are concerned with dietary habits and with sensing the environment; the postcranial skeleton is adapted to locomotion.

Another frequent subdivision of the skeleton is *axial* versus *appendicular.* The axial skeleton is the skull and the vertebral column; it protects the central nervous system. The appendicular skeleton is the limbs and their points of attachment, the *pectoral* (or shoulder) and *pelvic* (or hip) *limb girdles.* These subdivisions are simply for descriptive and interpretive convenience, of course: organisms function as integrated wholes.

SKULL — Mammals are the epitome and the apogee of a general evolutionary trend that commenced with the flatworms: *cephalization,* the tendency to concentrate structures and functions in a *head,* that end of the organism that meets the environment. Heads are organized and adapted to deal with environmental resources and perils. In the head are the major organs of sensation: transducers for light, sound, and chemical (olfaction, gustation) inputs; the skull houses the brain, the centerpiece of the central nervous system; it incorporates the front ends of the digestive and ventilatory (respiratory) systems. The head is the business end of a mammal; the skull is its bony infrastructure.

Although the mammalian skull is a rather complicated affair, it is much simpler than its reptilian precursor. Many reptilian bones have been lost or rearranged. Adapted to a vast array of lifestyles, mammalian skulls are very diverse. The skull can therefore be used effectively to classify and identify orders, families, genera, and sometimes individual species. Taxonomic keys rely heavily on knowledge of cranial and dental characters. The skull, or *cranium,* is commonly divided into two major regions: the *braincase* and the *rostrum.* The braincase is the portion of the cranium containing the brain. Compared to other vertebrates, it is particularly well developed in mammals. The rostrum is the bony part of the snout or muzzle. The *mandible* is simply the lower jaw. Figures 2-1 and 2-2 illustrate major bones and regions of the skull of a coyote, including *foramina* (openings), *processes* (projections), *fossae* (depressions), and *condyles* (prominences that provide articular surfaces with another bone). The figures can be used to identify bones of the skull of most other mammals.

The rostrum extends forward from the anterior margin of the *orbits,* or eye sockets. At its anterior end are two large *external nares,* the openings of the nasal chambers. The nasal septum that separates the chambers is made of cartilage anteriorly and merges posteriorly into a bone, the *vomer.*

The braincase surrounds the brain and serves as the attachment point for jaw muscles and the bony *auditory bullae,* in which the middle and inner ear are housed. At the back of the braincase, two prominent *occipital condyles* surround the base

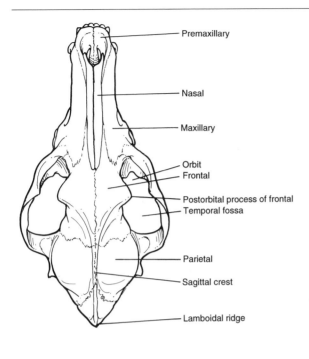

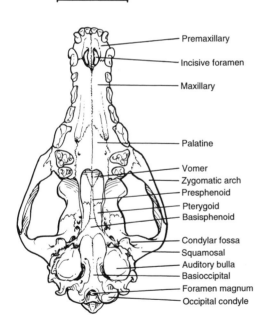

Figure 2-1 Dorsal and ventral views of the skull of the coyote (Canis latrans). Scale = 5 cm.

of the *foramen magnum*, the large opening allowing for passage of the spinal cord. These condyles serve as articulation surfaces with the first cervical vertebra, the *atlas*. The posterior wall of the braincase is the *occipital bone*, which bounds the foramen magnum and is composed of four fused elements: a dorsal *supraoccipital*, two lateral *exoccipitals*, and a ventral *basioccipital*. In most adult mammals sutures between these bones are fused, making them difficult to distinguish. In many species, a small *interparietal* bone lies between the posterior border of the *parietals* and the *supraoccipital* (see Figure 8.2).

The *zygomatic arches*, or cheekbones, are formed by a posterior extension of the *maxillary* bone, a *jugal* (malar) bone, and the forward-projecting zygomatic process of the *squamosal* bone. The orbits, which house the eyes and the external eye muscles, are bounded posteriorly by *postorbital processes* of the frontal and jugal bones. In some mammals, like deer, these processes fuse to form a *postorbital bar* separating the orbits from the *temporal fossa*. In primates, there is a solid *postorbital plate* in this position. The temporal muscles, used in mastication, fill the temporal fossae.

Elevated ridges on the skull form points of attachment for muscles of the head and neck. Generally these increase in size with age, attesting to the fact that bone is a dynamic tissue, continually remodeling itself in response to the stresses of living. A prominent *sagittal crest* arises on the frontals near the postorbital processes and extends posteriorly along the medial sutures of the skull. A *lambdoidal ridge*, formed along the posterior border of the cranium from the dorsal surface of one auditory bulla to the other, may intersect the posterior edge of the sagittal crest.

The paired *premaxillary bones* bear the incisors, form the anterior portion of the hard *palate* (the bony shelf separating the oral cavity from the nasal chambers), and send wings dorsally along the nasal bones. The paired *maxillary bones* form the sides of the rostrum and most of the hard palate, and bear the canines, premolars, and molars. The

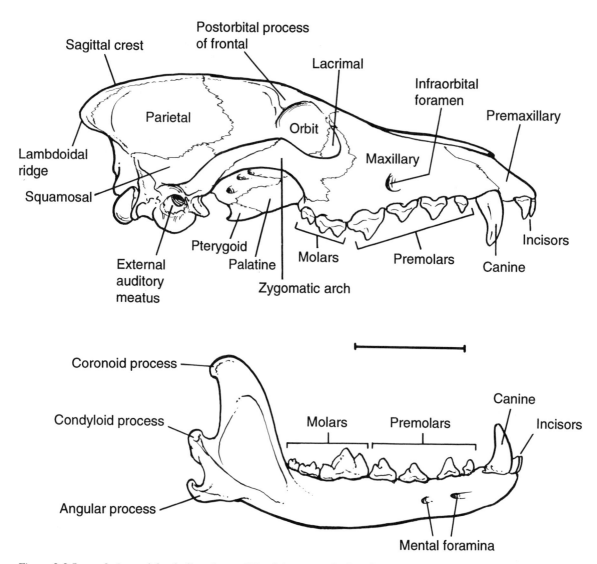

Figure 2-2 Lateral views of the skull and mandible of the coyote. Scale = 5 cm.

smaller, paired *palatine bones* form the posterior margins of the palate. This extensive palate is another feature associated with the active mammalian lifestyle. The palate separates the air passage from the food passage, and thus allows breathing and chewing at the same time. Animals without such a palate have to bolt their food whole or suffocate. If they do bolt the food, the meal arrives at the stomach intact, poorly prepared for effi-

cient chemical dismantling by the digestive organs. The palate also allows the young to suckle and breathe at the same time.

The *mandible* (Figure 2-2) consists of a single bone on either side, the *dentary*. The dentaries are fused at the *mandibular symphysis*, on the anterior midline. In rodents and most artiodactyls the symphysis is flexible and allows for considerable disarticulation, whereas in most other mammals the symphysis is fused and immobile. (Artiodactyl mandibles in museum collections are frequently disarticulated.) The *ramus* is the tooth-bearing horizontal portion of the dentary. The *coronoid process* extends up into the temporal fossa when the jaws are shut. The *mandibular condyle* (condylar process) articulates with the mandibular fossa of the cranium. In many mammals, including most rodents and lagomorphs, the mandibular condyle and fossa are rounded, allowing for lateral movement, rather than elongated transversely as they are in the coyote. The numerous foramina that penetrate the skull provide passage for blood vessels and nerves.

POSTCRANIAL SKELETON — Mammal-like reptiles from the later Permian and Triassic not only exhibited mammalian cranial features but also advances in postcranial structure. They stood more erect than typical reptiles, the elbows pointed backward, the knees forward.

The shoulder or *pectoral girdle* of most mammals is composed of two elements, the *scapula* and the *clavicle* (collar bone). Mammals that run on hard ground often have a reduced clavicle or none at all, lacking a bony connection between pectoral and axial parts of their skeletons. The shock of the running body striking the ground is absorbed by the soft tissues around the scapula.

The pectoral limb itself consists of three major parts, a proximal *humerus*, and distal *ulna* and *radius*. The ulna and radius usually can rotate around each other, enhancing mobility of the forefoot. The hand (*manus*) includes three different sets of bones. The first, proximal group form the *carpus*, or wrist; individual elements are *carpals*. They are followed by the *metacarpals*, one for each *digit* (finger). The most distal series of bones is the *phalanges* (singular, *phalanx*). In the primitive pattern, the first digit of the forelimb, or *pollex*, has two phalanges; other digits have three. Hence, the primitive *phalangeal formula* is 2-3-3-3-3, a simplification of the general reptilian formula (as seen in modern lizards): 2-3-4-5-3.

The hip or *pelvic girdle* is composed of two symmetrical halves, the *innominate bones*, which form a ring through which the reproductive, urinary, and digestive tracts leave the body. The pelvic limb is similar to the front limb. The proximal bone (corresponding humerus) is the *femur*. The middle segment of the hindlimb includes the larger *tibia* and narrower *fibula*. These two bones are often partly fused. Many mammals have a *patella*, or knee-cap. This bone is formed independently from the other leg bones and is unique to the Mammalia; it protects the knee joint. The hindfoot, or *pes*, consists of three series of bones. The most proximal are the *tarsals*, followed by *metatarsals* and, as in the manus, distal *phalanges*. The number of phalanges is the same as in corresponding digits of the forefoot. The first digit (the "big toe") is the *hallux*. Carpals and tarsals are often referred to collectively as *podials*; metacarpals and metatarsals together are called *metapodials*.

The basic mammalian stock was four-footed (*quadrupedal*) and each of those feet had five toes (*pentadactyl*). (Humans retain this primitive arrangement, modifed in detail, of course, to allow a peculiar bipedal gait). This is the same arrangement of toes found in a primitive quadruped, such as the salamander. Mammals have pushed the basic plan in myriad ways, showing diverse adaptations in both *stance* and *locomotion*.

Stance describes the way an animal stands; locomotion describes how an animal moves. Some species change their stance as they change their mode of locomotion. For example, a human runner stands and walks on the soles of her feet (a *plantigrade* stance). Leaving the starting blocks, she runs on her toes — that is, she becomes *digitigrade*. Loping along in full stride, she may again become plantigrade. Stance and locomotion (gait) are easy to confuse but they are different phenomena. (Whales move but they do not stand.)

Some prey animals elaborated this principle further, rising to stand only on the longest, medial digits. The side toes were reduced, the remaining digits strengthened and elongated. Claws increased in size to support the toes and eventually surrounded the entire structure. These *hooves* became the only parts of the feet in contact with the ground. Members of two living orders show this *unguligrade* stance — most artiodactyls and the family Equidae, order Perissodactyla. Most artiodactyls have two principal digits of equal size on each foot, the *paraxonic* condition, the toes being beside (para-) the axis of symmetry. Metacarpals and metatarsals are often fused to form a single so-called cannon bone, increasing the legs' stability. Horses have only the median digit in each foot, a *mesaxonic* foot, its axis of symmetry passing through the middle (meso-). In many artiodactyls and the horses ulna and radius and fibula and tibia are fused, resulting in a single bone in the middle segment of the limbs. The trend toward longer, simpler limbs specialized for high speed is generally accompanied by reduced lateral mobility.

In *saltatory* locomotion, as in rabbits, the stronger and longer hindlegs leave the ground last, and the front legs touch down first when the animal lands. Hindlimbs provide the major part of the thrust. In contrast, kangaroo rats, like kangaroos proper, are bipedal; the front feet are not used for locomotion. The hindfeet are elongate and the strong, long tail provides support and counterbalance in such *ricochetal* locomotion.

Some heavy terrestrial mammals like elephants have *graviportal* limbs. The leg bones are arranged in a straight, vertical line, and the feet are large and broad, distributing the weight of the animal over a great area.

Many mammals are capable of digging, and most smaller mammals do so at least sporadically, often to nest. Prairie dogs, marmots, and other *semifossorial* species — which often have small external ears (pinnae) and especially strong limbs and claws — dig elaborate burrows and use them as permanent homes, but they gather food outside their retreats. Semifossorial prey species tend to retain keen senses of sight and hearing and swift mobility.

The seemingly small step to a truly *fossorial* habit is accompanied by major anatomical specialization. Fossorial mammals usually have sturdy, compact bodies, short necks and tails, improved tactile and olfactory senses, reduced pinnae, small and sometimes completely nonfunctional eyes, and fur with no direction of lay. Both true moles (Insectivora) and the marsupial mole (*Notoryctes*) have front limbs with large, shovel-like hands, strong claws, and powerful shoulder muscles. Fossorial rodents (pocket gophers, mole rats) use strong, procumbent incisors for digging.

Mammals without obvious adaptations for climbing are often seen to take to the trees, to reach food or safe, elevated places to rest. Many smaller rodents and insectivores with unspecialized limbs are excellent climbers and forage in trees and shrubs. Not only cats, martens, raccoons, and bears, but even foxes and goats spend time in trees. Tree squirrels have a basically terrestrial structure. Specializations are limited to sharp, curved claws and bushy tails that aid in balance. They tend to nest in trees, but in part they forage on the ground. Tree squirrels exhibit *scansorial* ("scampering") locomotion. Mammals like monkeys are specialized for more exclusive *arboreal* locomotion, with opposable digits or prehensile tails, or both. The so-called "flying" squirrels have flaps of skin that extend between hind and front legs to greatly increase the surface area of the body, giving the animal the properties of a glider. Such *glissant* animals can travel great distances in one leap and often can maneuver well. However, no glissant mammal really flies; that is, none can gain altitude by its own power. Bats are the only mammals exhibiting true flight. These *volant* mammals are enormously successful and represent the second largest mammalian order after the Rodentia.

When pressed, virtually any mammal can swim, but some kinds are specialized for swimming (*natatorial* locomotion). Amphibious mammals like the watershrew, muskrat, and beaver have webbed feet or strong hairs growing at the edges of their toes. The tail may be flattened as a rudder or propeller. The whole body is more streamlined than that of terrestrial relatives. However, amphibious mammals are well equipped to travel the land. A few mammalian groups, including some carnivores (seals, sea lions, walruses), the dugongs and manatees, and the whales, are so strongly specialized for life in the water that they have little or no capacity for movement on land.

THE DIVERSITY OF MAMMALS

The several distinctive traits of mammals evolved through the long millenia of the Age of Reptiles. With the demise of the ruling reptiles in the Cretaceous, mammals were "ready and waiting" to undergo a profound adaptive radiation in the Cenozoic, the most recent 70 million years. It is with good reason that the Cenozoic is called the Age of Mammals.

Most living mammals are placentals (the Eutheria, which build a placenta and carry the embryos inside) or marsupials (Metatheria, which carry "embryos" in an external pouch). The common ancestor of both placentals and marsupials was a rat- to opossum-sized mammal, quadrupedal, omnivorous, and basically terrestrial. The primitive marsupial looked very much like the living opossum. From those arose the insectivores (the order that includes modern shrews and moles), the basal placental stock. From those beginnings there quickly evolved forms as diverse as bats, whales, hoofed herbivores, and specialized carnivores. Most existing orders of mammals had appeared by the Eocene, 60 million years ago.

Although not the most numerous of vertebrates (there are 4,200 living mammalian species compared to 8,600 birds, 5,000 reptiles, 2,000 amphibians, and 25,000 bony fishes), mammals are by far the most diverse in body form and general

lifestyle. Earlier in the Age of Mammals, some 20 to 30 million years ago, our class was even more diverse than it is today.

The variety of mammals is truly remarkable. Existing mammals differ in mass (for practical purposes a synonym of weight) by a factor of 10 million, from 3-gram shrews (the weight of a U. S. penny) and tiny bats and mice to 190-tonne whales (the mass of three full railway freight cars). They differ in length by a factor of 10,000, from bats shorter than your little finger (50 mm) to whales the length of a gymnasium (35 m).

Of the numerous fine references on mammals in general, we mention a brief selection. The standard textbook of mammalogy is T. Vaughan (1986); Eisenberg (1981) provided an advanced analysis of the diversity of mammals. DeBlase and Martin (1981) provided a laboratory manual that also includes keys to families of mammals of the world, a vast amount of descriptive information, and a summary of field techniques. Savage and Long (1986) provided an accessible evolutionary account of mammals, emphasizing extinct forms, and Kurtén (1971) published the classic, semitechnical synopsis of the Age of Mammals. Honacki et al. (1982) and D. Wilson and Reeder (1993) outlined mammalian species of the world, Nowak (1991) provided brief accounts of all Recent genera, and S. Anderson and Jones (1984) detailed orders and families. Relationships among mammalian orders based on traditional morphological and paleontological information were reviewed by Novacek (1990), and Czelusniak et al. (1990) assessed relationships using comparative molecular data. For a thorough review of higher classification, see Stucky and McKenna (1993).

ORDERS OF MAMMALS

Mammals are classified in 30 to 40 orders (depending upon how finely one chooses to subdivide such groups as marsupials, whales, and insectivores), of which 20 to 25 are alive today. Extinct orders mostly were large, hoofed beasts, or the archaic forerunners of existing orders (the creodont ancestors of carnivores and the condylarth ancestors of ungulates, for example). Native Coloradan mammals represent nine orders. The approximate percentage of worldwide mammalian diversity (by order) indigenous to Colorado is: Marsupialia, 0.4; Insectivora, 2.7; Chiroptera, 1.9; Primates, 0.6; Xenarthra, 3.4; Lagomorpha, 10.8; Rodentia, 3.3; Carnivora, 8.9; Artiodactyla, 3.3. In total, Colorado is the natural home of 126 of some 4,175 mammalian species, or about 3 percent of extant mammalian diversity.

Key to the Orders of Mammals in Colorado

1. First toe on hindfoot thumblike, apposable; marsupium present in females; incisors 5/4 . . . . Marsupialia, p. 66

1' First toe on hindfoot not thumblike or apposable; marsupium absent; incisors never more than 3/3 2

2. Forelimbs modified for flight; canines prominent; greatest length of skull less than 35 mm . . . . Chiroptera, p. 92

2' Forelimbs not modified for flight; if canines prominent, then greatest length of skull greater than 35 mm 3

3. Stance bipedal, plantigrade; body thinly haired, without bony plates; thumb completely apposable; digits with nails . . . . Primates

3' Stance quadrupedal; body well furred, or if thinly haired then dorsum covered with bony plates; thumb (if present) not apposable or incompletely so; digits with claws or hooves 4

4. Cheekteeth peglike, lacking enamel; dorsum covered with bony plates . . . . . . Xenarthra, p. 130

4' Cheekteeth not peglike, bearing enamel; dorsum covered with fur 5

5. Feet with hooves; upper incisors absent, or if present, then toothrow either not continuous or teeth bunodont 6

5' Feet with claws; upper incisors present 7

6. Hooves even-toed; upper incisors absent, or if present, then cheekteeth bunodont (e.g., Suidae) . . . . Artiodactyla, p. 380

6' Hoof single; upper incisors present . . . . Perissodactyla, p. 375

7. Toothrow continuous (without conspicuous diastema); canines present 8

7' Toothrow with conspicuous diastema between incisors and cheekteeth; canines absent 9

8. Canines approximately equal in height to adjacent teeth; total length less than 200 mm . . . . Insectivora, p. 71

8' Canines conspicuously longer than adjacent teeth; total length greater than 200 mm . . . . Carnivora, p. 299

9. Ears approximately same length or longer than tail; incisors 2/1 . . . . Lagomorpha, p. 134

9' Ears much shorter than tail; incisors 1/1 . . . . Rodentia, p. 153

Chapter 3

People and Wild Mammals in Colorado

Colorado has a diverse and abundant mammalian fauna that is valued and enjoyed in numerous ways by residents and visitors alike. People are fascinated by wild mammals and find in them a range of recreational opportunities. The U.S. Fish and Wildlife Service estimated that $24.4 billion was spent nationwide on wildlife-related recreational interest in 1985 alone, nearly $1,000 per person (Decker 1989). During that same year almost three-quarters of all Americans aged 16 and older participated in wildlife-related activities. Between 1980 and 1985, the number of adults in the U.S. who participated in nonconsumptive wildlife activities increased from 93.2 to 134.7 million (Decker 1989). This upward trend is predicted to continue because of the increased interest in wildlife seen in children and because of a steadily growing retired population, people with the leisure time to pursue their interests.

Wild mammals enrich our lives in numerous ways, and their value for many of us grows as Earth is increasingly dominated by people. With technical developments like satellite mapping, radiotelemetry, and computer-based habitat models, the sophistication of our insights into the lives of wild mammals has increased dramatically, yet many of us still feel the same wonder and excitement at the marvelous grace of a deer, the strength of a mountain lion, the astonishing agility of a bat harvesting insects from the night air, or the stubborn industry of a pocket gopher or beaver.

Humans have interacted with the rest of the native Coloradan mammalian fauna from time immemorial. Over the past 10,000 years or more, these interactions have changed significantly. Indeed, we may consider the interactions in three broad historical phases: several thousand years of subsistence use, a century of largely unregulated exploitation, and several decades of increasingly sensitive and scientific stewardship of wildlife. Let us look at each of these phases in turn, with special focus on changing views of wildlife in the last quarter of the twentieth century.

Millenia of Subsistence

Just when humans first came to what is now Colorado is a matter for debate. It was at least 11,500 years ago, and it may have been much earlier (Cassells 1983). Whenever it was, this much we know: prehistoric peoples in Colorado depended on native mammals for subsistence and therefore they knew the fauna well. Paleoindians left numerous clues to the fundamental importance of mammals in their lives. Clovis people used stone tools to hunt and butcher mammoths. Opportunistic omnivores, these Paleoindians also hunted and scavenged camels, native horses, and numerous smaller mammals. The most significant game species was the bison, which continued in a central role for later Native Americans and then for early European settlers. Bison meat, fat, and bone marrow were eaten. Bison skin provided clothing, sleeping mats, and, eventually, tepees. Containers were made from horns and the stomach, and tools were fashioned from bone. Even the brain was used — to tan the hide.

Paleoindians developed techniques for driving herds of large mammals into natural traps (J. Benedict 1992). Major bison kill sites have been described from the plains in Yuma (Stanford 1974, 1975) and Kit Carson (Wheat 1967) counties. In the Front Range, rock walls were built to funnel game into traps. A game-drive system for mountain sheep and elk on Arapahoe Pass is 1.2 km long, with the most recent construction phase dated at 800 years ago (J. Benedict 1985). A nearby site on Mount Albion was used by communal hunters for 5,800 years to drive mountain sheep (J. Benedict and Olson 1978).

The Pleistocene fauna of Colorado included many mammals that no longer occur here: archaic camels and llamas, native horses, the short-faced bear, and even an American subspecies (*Felis leo atrox*) of what is today the African lion. There is considerable evidence that early human populations in the Americas hunted much of the Ice Age megafauna to extinction, or at least helped to push over the brink a fauna already stressed by global climatic change (P. Martin and Klein 1984).

Later Native Americans in Colorado were entirely dependent on local ecosystems for food, clothing, and shelter. Not only were bison used for food; deer, elk, and mountain sheep were taken, as was smaller game, including rodents. Carnivores provided decorative skins for headdresses and ritual objects. Mammals also figured prominently in ceremony and religion, as symbols, totems, and figures in tribal stories. There clearly were situations in which subsistence hunters slaughtered animals that were not fully used, but theirs seemingly was a sustainable, long-term relationship with the plants and animals upon which they depended. Hunting traditions of Native Americans reflect a deep knowledge of the ecology and behavior of mammals. Some would attribute the apparent equilibrium between human predators and their prey to the hunters' respect for — or even spiritual connection with — the hunted. This may, in part, make a virtue of necessity, however. Both predator and prey were migratory, following shifting resources and leaving disturbed areas behind with time to recover. Habitat alteration sometimes occurred on a massive scale, as when game was driven by prairie or forest fires, although on the longer timescales that ecologists must use, these are lesser disturbances than building cities, airports, or diverting western rivers into concrete-lined irrigation canals on the Eastern Slope.

The Nineteenth Century: Exploration and Exploitation

European exploration opened a new era of interaction between wildlife and people. In the early nineteenth century, explorers from the newly established United States began to explore the West. Colorado lay north of the Santa Fe Trail and south of the route of Lewis and Clark, and it was left to Zebulon K. Pike — under orders from President Thomas Jefferson — to begin formal exploration of our corner of "Louisiana." Pike returned to the East with reports of an inhospitable landscape, largely unsuited to civilization. That description in itself may have been enough to lure the first wave of commercial exploiters, the storied Mountain Men. The young nation was at war in 1812 when Ezekiel Williams led the first band of trappers from the Big Horn Mountains of Wyoming to Colorado's mountain parks. The real frenzy began after William Ashley's Rocky Mountain Fur Company encouraged trappers to go to northern Colorado in 1822. Their quarry was beaver, whose fur was made into hatters' felt. At the peak of the boom, 100,000 beaver pelts a year flowed eastward, many from Colorado, gathered by near-legendary characters with names like Jim Bridger, Jedidiah Smith, Kit Carson, and Lucien Maxwell, and traded at Fort Davy Crockett in Brown's Hole, Antoine Robidoux's Fort Uncompahgre, Fort St. Vrain, Bent's Fort, and other wilderness outposts. A shift of tophat fashion from beaver felt to silk may have saved the beaver from extermination; it led to the extinction of the Mountain Men by 1840.

Colorado and its wildlife largely avoided the migration of the 1840s to Oregon and the rush of the 1850s to the goldfields of California, for topographic explorations by John C. Frémont and by John W. Gunnison found Colorado impassable for the trails and rails to Manifest Destiny. But then, in 1858, gold was discovered in what is now downtown Denver, and Colorado had a landrush of its own. With the influx of settlers, the focus of exploitation was no longer on furbearers but on game mammals, and what began as subsistence hunting soon shifted to commercial exploitation. Hunters supplied the mining camps and the settlements along the mountain front. The great herds of bison, elk, deer, and pronghorn that had defined and dominated the ecosystems of the mountain parks and the Great Plains were slaughtered in a few years. At first they supplied the local market, but then — when General William J. Palmer's Denver Pacific Railroad linked Denver to the outside world, as represented by the Union Pacific at Cheyenne — markets expanded to the Midwest and even the East Coast. Native wildlife was no match for a settled human population with modern firearms and transportation. Elk were becoming rare in South Park in the early 1870s and were nearly extirpated by 1910, reduced to a herd of 500 to 1,000 animals on the Upper White River. Cary (1911) reported neither seeing nor hearing reports of mule deer in Boulder and Larimer counties in 1906. Bison had been removed from the Denver Basin by about 1875, and the last native bison in eastern Colorado was killed at Springfield in 1889. The end of the bison in northwestern Colorado came in 1884, and the last wild bison in the state were slaughtered in South Park in 1897. Pronghorn were so heavily impacted that all seasons were closed as early as 1893 and not reopened until 1945. Mountain sheep retreated to the higher mountains from the foothills where they had been abundant. To allow recovery from their decimation by market hunting, the sheep season remained closed from 1885 to 1953 (Barrows and

Holmes 1990). Furthermore, as domestic livestock replaced native species on Coloradan rangelands, competitors, alleged and real, from grizzly bears and wolves to jackrabbits, prairie dogs, and pocket gophers, were shot, poisoned, or simply rounded up and clubbed to death. The nineteenth century was an age of unregulated exploitation and extermination that forced the development of new concepts of both wildlife management and wildlife ethics.

The Twentieth Century: Stewardship for Diverse Values

The twentieth century has been a time of deepened knowledge of wildlife and its environments, a diversification of the values that wildlife has to people, and fundamental shifts in attitudes (Kellert 1988). We have looked at a historical shift from subsistence use of wildlife to commercial exploitation. Over the past several decades — especially in the past 20 years, after the elimination of indiscriminant poisoning on public lands — the trend has been toward stewardship in an increasingly complex cultural and political environment. The complexity stems from the fact that some values of wildlife and attitudes about wildlife are in potential or actual conflict. Let us examine the diversity of wildlife values and attitudes and explore some avenues for wildlife and its management in the rapidly changing human culture of Colorado.

RECREATIONAL AND COMMERCIAL VALUES

Probably the most obvious value to humans of wildlife in Colorado is recreational. Mammals have both measurable and immeasurable recreational value. Many of us delight in simply seeing native mammals. We may chuckle at their antics or be inspired and excited by their strength or their ability to make a living off the land. To increase these opportunities, we create national parks, wilderness areas, open spaces, and corridors for wildlife and recreation. Rocky Mountain National Park and the Denver Museum of Natural History are the two largest tourist attractions in Colorado. The recently authorized Rocky

Mountain Arsenal Wildlife Refuge doubtless will become a major attraction as well. In recent years, roughly one-quarter of the state's tourist income, an estimated $2 billion, is attracted by wildlife, of which $30 to 50 million comes directly from license fees.

Wildlife recreational values are often categorized as consumptive and nonconsumptive. Consumptive use of resources refers to activities that actually consume organisms, removing individuals from the ecosystem: hunting, trapping, catch-and-keep fishing, and berry picking all are consumptive uses. Nonconsumptive uses do not directly destroy organisms. Birdwatching, hiking, rafting, and wildlife photography are examples. Many people enjoy a variety of different recreational values from mammals, both consumptive and nonconsumptive. The distinction between consumptive and nonconsumptive is hardly absolute. However, it raises questions of values to which we return below. Some nonconsumptive users think that consumptive use is inappropriate or even immoral. Some people even argue that any deliberate use of wildlife — consumptive or not — is unethical (for general review, see Mighetto 1991).

Trapping and hunting were important activities in Colorado's recent history, encouraging exploration and supporting permanent settlement. The obvious excesses of the nineteenth century began to be curbed when the State Fish Commissioner became the State Game and Fish Warden in 1891. The Colorado Department of Game and Fish was established in 1899. Laws were passed to help preserve the rich wildlife resource. However, enforcement was difficult at first because of chronic understaffing and widespread ignorance of the law. The first hunting licenses were approved in 1903 and cost $1.00 for residents. Deer were the only game mammals that could be hunted legally in 1907. Increasingly, Colorado developed a scientific management strategy to protect and enhance the state's wildlife resources (Barrows and Holmes 1990).

The Colorado Wildlife Commission, a six-member board appointed by the governor, was established by the Legislature in 1937. The commission took on the tasks of issuing hunting regulations and setting seasons, acquiring land, appointing the director of the Colorado Department of Game and Fish, and establishing overall organization. By the late 1930s game had again become abundant as a result of long-closed hunting seasons (the elk season was closed for 26 years), strict bag limits, stiffer fines, and better law enforcement. During the 1940s hunting seasons expanded. Since that time, there has been a steady increase in large game populations and harvest figures, especially for deer and elk.

In 1973, the Department of Game and Fish was renamed the Colorado Division of Wildlife and its mission was broadened greatly, to focus on wildlife species as components of ecosystems and to take responsibility for management of the vast majority of native species that were not game animals. The same year, the Nongame Wildlife Program was started. Now native mammals are categorized as big game, small game, furbearers, livestock, or nongame (Table 3-1). A majority of Coloradan mammals are nongame species. The Nongame Wildlife Cash Fund receives proceeds from voluntary contributions, much of which comes from a check-off from individual state income tax refunds. Check-off proceeds average about $500,000 annually. The restoration of the river otter to Colorado is one of the more visible success stories of the division's Nongame Program, but there are many others.

Table 3-1. Management status of mammals in Colorado, as established by Colorado statute. See text for explanation of categories.

MARSUPIALS	
Virginia Opossum (*Didelphis virginiana*)	Furbearer

INSECTIVORES	
Masked Shrew (*Sorex cinereus*)	Nongame
Pygmy Shrew (*Sorex hoyi*)	Nongame
Merriam's Shrew (*Sorex merriami*)	Nongame

Table 3-1 (continued).

Dusky or Montane Shrew (*Sorex monticolus*)	Nongame
Dwarf Shrew (*Sorex nanus*)	Nongame
Water Shrew (*Sorex palustris*)	Nongame
Elliot's Short-tailed Shrew (*Blarina hylophaga*)	Nongame
Least Shrew (*Cryptotis parva*)	Nongame
Desert Shrew (*Notiosorex crawfordi*)	Nongame
Eastern Mole (*Scalopus aquaticus*)	Nongame

BATS

California Myotis (*Myotis californicus*)	Nongame
Long-eared Myotis (*Myotis evotis*)	Nongame
Western Small-footed Myotis (*Myotis ciliolabrum*)	Nongame
Little Brown Myotis (*Myotis lucifugus*)	Nongame
Fringed Myotis (*Myotis thysanodes*)	Nongame
Long-legged Myotis (*Myotis volans*)	Nongame
Yuma Myotis (*Myotis yumanensis*)	Nongame
Red Bat (*Lasiurus borealis*)	Nongame
Hoary Bat (*Lasiurus cinereus*)	Nongame
Silver-haired Bat (*Lasionycteris noctivagans*)	Nongame
Western Pipistrelle (*Pipistrellus hesperus*)	Nongame
Eastern Pipistrelle (*Pipistrellus subflavus*)	Not listed
Big Brown Bat (*Eptesicus fuscus*)	Nongame
Spotted Bat (*Euderma maculatum*)	Nongame
Townsend's Big-eared Bat (*Plecotus townsendii*)	Nongame
Pallid Bat (*Antrozus pallidus*)	Nongame
Brazilian Free-tailed Bat (*Tadarida brasiliensis*)	Nongame
Big Free-tailed Bat (*Nyctinomops macrotis*)	Nongame

XENARTHRANS

Nine-banded Armadillo (*Dasypus novemcinctus*)	Nongame

LAGOMORPHS

Pika (*Ochotona princeps*)	Nongame
Desert Cottontail (*Sylvilagus audubonii*)	Small Game
Eastern Cottontail (*Sylvilagus floridanus*)	Small Game
Nuttall's or Mountain Cottontail (*Sylvilagus nuttallii*)	Small Game
Snowshoe Hare (*Lepus americanus*)	Small Game
Black-tailed Jackrabbit (*Lepus californicus*)	Small Game
White-tailed Jackrabbit (*Lepus townsendii*)	Small Game

RODENTS

Cliff Chipmunk (*Tamias dorsalis*)	Nongame
Least Chipmunk (*Tamias minimus*)	Nongame
Colorado Chipmunk (*Tamias quadrivittatus*)	Nongame
Uinta Chipmunk (*Tamias umbrinus*)	Nongame
Yellow-bellied Marmot (*Marmota flaviventris*)	Small Game
White-tailed Antelope Squirrel (*Ammospermophilus leucurus*)	Nongame
Wyoming Ground Squirrel (*Spermophilus elegans*)	Small Game
Golden-mantled Ground Squirrel (*Spermophilus lateralis*)	Nongame
Spotted Ground Squirrel (*Spermophilus spilosoma*)	Nongame
Thirteen-lined Ground Squirrel (*Spermophilus tridecemlineatus*)	Small Game
Rock Squirrel (*Spermophilus variegatus*)	Small Game
Gunnison's Prairie Dog (*Cynomys gunnisoni*)	Small Game
White-tailed Prairie Dog (*Cynomys leucurus*)	Small Game
Black-tailed Prairie Dog (*Cynomys ludovicianus*)	Small Game
Abert's Squirrel (*Sciurus aberti*)	Small Game
Fox Squirrel (*Sciurus niger*)	Small Game
Red Squirrel (Pine Squirrel, Chickaree) (*Tamiasciurus hudsonicus*)	Small Game
Botta's Pocket Gopher (*Thomomys bottae*)	Small Game
Northern Pocket Gopher (*Thomomys talpoides*)	Small Game
Plains Pocket Gopher (*Geomys bursarius*)	Small Game
Yellow-faced Pocket Gopher (*Cratogeomys castanops*)	Small Game
Olive-backed Pocket Mouse (*Perognathus fasciatus*)	Nongame
Plains Pocket Mouse (*Perognathus flavescens*)	Nongame
Silky Pocket Mouse (*Perognathus flavus*)	Nongame
Hispid Pocket Mouse (*Chaetodipus hispidus*)	Nongame
Great Basin Pocket Mouse (*Perognathus parvus*)	Nongame
Ord's Kangaroo Rat (*Dipodomys ordii*)	Nongame
Beaver (*Castor canadensis*)	Furbearer
Western Harvest Mouse (*Reithrodontomys megalotis*)	Nongame
Plains Harvest Mouse (*Reithrodontomys montanus*)	Nongame
Brush Mouse (*Peromyscus boylii*)	Nongame
Canyon Mouse (*Peromyscus crinitus*)	Nongame
White-footed Mouse (*Peromyscus leucopus*)	Nongame
Deer Mouse (*Peromyscus maniculatus*)	Nongame
Northern Rock Mouse (*Peromyscus nasutus*)	Nongame
Piñon Mouse (*Peromyscus truei*)	Nongame
Northern Grasshopper Mouse (*Onychomys leucogaster*)	Nongame
Hispid Cotton Rat (*Sigmodon hispidus*)	Nongame
White-throated Woodrat (*Neotoma albigula*)	Nongame
Bushy-tailed Woodrat (*Neotoma cinerea*)	Nongame
Eastern Woodrat (*Neotoma floridana*)	Nongame
Desert Woodrat (*Neotoma lepida*)	Nongame
Mexican Woodrat (*Neotoma mexicana*)	Nongame
Southern Plains Woodrat (*Neotoma micropus*)	Nongame
Southern Red-backed Vole (*Clethrionomys gapperi*)	Nongame
Heather Vole (*Phenacomys intermedius*)	Nongame
Long-tailed Vole (*Microtus longicaudus*)	Nongame
Mexican Vole (*Microtus mexicanus*)	Nongame
Montane Vole (*Microtus montanus*)	Nongame
Prairie Vole (*Microtus ochrogaster*)	Nongame

47

Table 3-1 (continued).

Meadow Vole (*Microtus pennsylvanicus*)	Nongame
Sagebrush Vole (*Lemmiscus curtatus*)	Nongame
Muskrat (*Ondatra zibethicus*)	Furbearer
Norway Rat (*Rattus norvegicus*)	Non-native, not listed
House Mouse (*Mus musculus*)	Non-native, not listed
Meadow Jumping Mouse (*Zapus hudsonius*)	Nongame
Western Jumping Mouse (*Zapus princeps*)	Nongame
Porcupine (*Erethizon dorsatum*)	Small Game

CARNIVORES

Coyote (*Canis latrans*)	Furbearer
Gray Wolf (*Canis lupus*)	Endangered*
Kit Fox (*Vulpes macrotis*)	Furbearer
Swift Fox (*Vulpes velox*)	Furbearer
Red Fox (*Vulpes vulpes*)	Furbearer
Gray Fox (*Urocyon cinereoargenteus*)	Furbearer
Black Bear (*Ursus americanus*)	Big Game
Grizzly or Brown Bear (*Ursus arctos*)	Endangered**
Ringtail (*Bassariscus astutus*)	Furbearer
Raccoon (*Procyon lotor*)	Furbearer
Marten (*Martes americana*)	Furbearer
Ermine (*Mustela erminea*)	Furbearer
Long-tailed Weasel (*Mustela frenata*)	Furbearer
Black-footed Ferret (*Mustela nigripes*)	Endangered*
Mink (*Mustela vison*)	Furbearer
Wolverine (*Gulo gulo*)	Endangered
Badger (*Taxidea taxus*)	Furbearer
Western Spotted Skunk (*Spilogale gracilis*)	Furbearer
Eastern Spotted Skunk (*Spilogale putorius*)	Furbearer
Striped Skunk (*Mephitis mephitis*)	Furbearer
Hog-nosed Skunk (*Conepatus mesoleucus*)	Furbearer
River Otter (*Lutra canadensis*)	Endangered
Mountain Lion (*Felis concolor*)	Big Game
Lynx (*Lynx lynx*)	Endangered
Bobcat (*Lynx rufus*)	Furbearer

ARTIODACTYLS

Elk or Wapiti (*Cervus elaphus*)	Big Game
Mule Deer (*Odocoileus hemionus*)	Big Game
White-tailed Deer (*Odocoileus virginianus*)	Big Game
Moose (*Alces alces*)	Big Game
Pronghorn (*Antilocapra americana*)	Big Game
Bison (*Bison bison*)	Livestock
Mountain Goat (*Oreamnos americanus*)	Big Game
Mountain Sheep (*Ovis canadensis*)	Big Game

* Appears on 1993 Federal Endangered Species List as Endangered.
** Appears on 1993 Federal Endangered Species List as Threatened.

HUNTING AND TRAPPING — Mammals provide recreational and cultural value to hunters. A number of different elements such as enjoyment of nature, getting away from home, developing tracking and shooting skills, and companionship add to the recreational pleasure that this activity offers (Beattie and Pierson 1977). For many people this yearly experience is an unparalleled thrill. Hunting involves both an experiential value and a measurable monetary value to local economies.

Sport hunting in Colorado attracts a large number of both residents and nonresidents. In 1990, some 1.47 million mammals of over 40 species were harvested by about 530,000 hunters and trappers, for a total net license income of $33.5 million (Table 3-2). Interestingly, the outcome of the hunt is not the only criterion of the success of the hunting experience (Hammitt et al. 1990, Langenau et al. 1981). Being outdoors in an uncrowded environment and the hunting success of partners may be more important than individual harvest success in determining hunter satisfaction.

Between 1960 and 1990, the number of resident hunting licenses increased from 320,000 to 456,000. However, there was a decline in the percentage of the population that actually hunted. The number of licenses sold per 100 people over age 12 in Colorado has declined by one-third, from 25 to 17 percent, during the same period (Colorado Division of Wildlife 1990). And nationally, there were fewer hunters in 1985 than in 1980 (Heberlein 1987). Factors contributing to the relative decrease in hunting in Colorado and nationally include urbanization, an increase in single-parent households, competition with myriad other recreational activities, an increased environmental awareness, and the development of organized antihunting movements. The overall increase in hunting in Colorado is attributable largely to nonresident elk licenses and other special licenses that contribute 75 to 80 percent of the game management budget for the state. On balance, herds of game mammals have been managed well since the turn of the century, and Colo-

Table 3–2. Harvest of small game mammals, big game mammals, and furbearers, and estimated numbers of hunters or trappers, 1975, 1980, 1985, and 1990. Total license revenues are shown by year.

Species/Genus	1975 Harvest	1975 Hunters	1980 Harvest	1980 Hunters	1985 Harvest	1985 Hunters	1990 Harvest	1990 Hunters
*Opossum	29	36	99	58	20	14	320	73
Cottontail	184111	36284	230583	43546	107957	29779	188726	26770
Snowshoe Hare	10383	5811	13401	5762	7248	3842	14610	4602
Jackrabbit	44793	11901	121765	14857	70420	9779	50907	7223
Marmot	10218	1827	9720	1543	12111	1287	30285	1253
Prairie Dog	279269	8691	186050	6282	187263	6960	935299	12345
Abert Squirrel			198	61			4376	780
Fox Squirrel	5762	1459	2812	1267	3726	1135	7246	1496
Pine Squirrel	8021	1846	13266	1894	11461	2575	13963	2531
*Beaver	5914	406	8940	843	8448	374	3888	258
*Muskrat	36628	564	94005	1565	16302	427	4877	181
Porcupine	5534	2217	4525	1152	1621	711	2209	1330
*Coyote	34415	14409	29080	13636	43065	12753	38164	10090
*Swift Fox	1070	319	3486	417	1466	303	376	139
*Red Fox	2304	1087	2881	935	4119	1359	2024	545
*Gray Fox	733	423	905	405	2238	422	576	239
Black Bear	895	13899	651	8454	619	4875	412	3514
*Ringtail	148	19	120	65	337	84	40	21
*Raccoon	6347	1591	5655	1776	6854	1621	8848	2722
*Marten	143	38	738	120	1717	131	1098	110
*Short-tailed Weasel	3	3	37	27	26	218	13	9
*Long-tailed Weasel	76	38	299	88	14	56	129	30
*Mink	113	41	399	136	859	62	255	43
*Spotted Skunk	198	46	354	193	292	68	88	30
*Striped Skunk	2139	227	4103	541	3446	265	12735	2167
*Badger	1204	818	3536	1434	1646	980	820	615
Mountain Lion	90	143	82	200	155	363	240	576
*Bobcat	2544	1453	3051	1390	5485	1403	309	101
Elk	22632	143319	27623	180797	23349	139033	51595	192907
Deer	40449	156191	54546	175600	58399	169439	90490	246797
Moose					3	5	5	5
Pronghorn	3519	4398	6873	9091	7475	12380	8621	11851
Mountain Goat	35	40	54	79	45	83	102	113
Bighorn Sheep	28	127	79	305	112	412	134	368

Revenues

	1975	1980	1985	1990
Big Game Licenses	$7,410,236	$15,801,060	$21,728,270	$34,512,960
Furbearer/Small Game Licenses	$608,235	$915,405	$1,306,472	$1,339,110
Total CDOW License Revenue	$11,890,868	$22,191,270	$31,273,738	$46,955,870

Source: Colorado Division of Wildlife; Lipscomb et al. 1983.
*Species classified as furbearers.

rado usually offers excellent hunting opportunities. In fact, deer and elk populations are at all-time highs, elk harvest figures for 1991 are the highest for any state in any year, and hunting is presently an effective and essential management tool.

In addition to the big game already discussed, game species, as defined by the Wildlife Commission, also include small game and furbearers. Small game species are the smaller mammals (lagomorphs and rodents) that may be hunted. Furbearers are species whose pelts have commercial value and provide sport harvest opportunities. Unlike big game, other game mammals are not managed intensively, with a few exceptions. Many young hunters develop their skills on rabbits and squirrels and turn to other game as their skills and interest change. Hunters are not a homogeneous group, and those who hunt small game are the most difficult to characterize. Small game licenses provide more recreation days, more animals harvested, and a wider variety of species than do big game licenses (Table 3-2). Considered a bargain by many, small game licenses offer year-round hunting or shooting opportunities.

Fur trapping is the only legal consumptive use of Coloradan wildlife where the catch can be sold commercially. The annual harvest is highly variable (Table 3-2) in terms of numbers of individuals of particular species taken and dollar value. Historically, beaver have been significant furbearers. They lured trappers to Colorado originally, have served as a valuable fur resource, profoundly alter the riparian environment, and can become a nuisance. Mandated by unpredictable fashions, demand has been variable. The market for beaver skins was strong in the early 1800s, the 1920s, and the 1940s. In the 1970s, demand for long-haired furs rose again and sales of coyote pelts outnumbered beaver (Barrows and Holmes 1990). When demand for beaver fur (hence trapping effort) is low, populations have tended to increase, allowing the animals to become nuisances locally, plugging canals and cul-

verts, thus flooding fields and roads. Both public and private funds have been spent on attempts to control them. Ironically, in the 1930s ranchers bought live beavers and restored them on their lands to help contain scarce water resources, after having spent much effort in their control in previous years (Barrows and Holmes 1990).

The past few decades have seen major changes in uses of mammals by humans. Historically the focus (and funding source) for the Colorado Division of Wildlife has been hunting and fishing. There is now a measurable move toward nonconsumptive uses. This change is related to demographic and cultural changes in Colorado's human population, which is becoming more urbanized, less agrarian, more "white collar," older, more broadly multicultural, and less male dominated. An increasingly vocal constituency of wildlife enthusiasts is evolving who are nonhunters or even antihunters. In some cases this evolution has led to conflict, as indicated by a recent debate over spring bear hunting, resulting in a referendum in the General Election ballot in 1992 that banned the activity.

ESTHETIC VALUES

"When the Grizzly is gone we shall have lost the most sublime specimen of wild life that exalts the western wilderness." These words by John A. McGuire, founder of *Outdoor Life* magazine, are inscribed on the famous statue of the grizzly bear that graces the west entrance of the Denver Museum of Natural History. They express a sentiment that assigns esthetic value to a species' mere presence. Something invaluable is lost with the extirpation of a species. There are many people who hold no hope that they will ever actually see a black-footed ferret, but who nevertheless are deeply enriched by the simple knowledge that black-footed ferrets still exist, that the system retains its integrity.

Other people find esthetic value in actively seeking and seeing wildlife, perhaps in wilderness areas or state and national parks. Seeing a large carnivore in the wild is an exciting experience, as is the sight of a herd of elk or a band of mountain sheep. Sometimes a high point is reached by a more uncommon sighting of a common species, such as a long-tailed weasel, a marten, or even a meadow vole. Nature's beauty is an intangible but important resource for those who find comfort in the fact that Earth has wild animals in wild places, often even when the animal is as common as a muskrat or big brown bat, as close to home as a pond in the park or twilight in the backyard. Difficult to articulate and impossible to measure, this value reaches to the core in many of us.

The Colorado Division of Wildlife has recognized people's desire to view wild animals. The Watchable Wildlife Program was established in 1988. At that time a marketing survey indicated that 60 percent of Colorado's population actively watched wildlife. The purpose of this program is to enhance people's enjoyment of wildlife by providing tools and opportunities for them to observe, photograph, and learn. The tools include interpretive signage and brochures, books (including Rennicke 1990 and Shattil and Rozinski 1990), and volunteer programs. The opportunities include developed viewing sites, such as the mountain sheep viewing station near Georgetown, elk viewing sites near Leadville and west of Vail, and a site on the Arkansas River between Salida and Canon City. Watchable Wildlife is a broadly cooperative effort, involving the schools, cities, counties, federal agencies, nongovernmental organizations, and private landowners.

SCIENTIFIC VALUES

Wildlife has immense scientific value. This value is complex and obviously is interrelated with other values, including esthetic, recreational, and educational values, for example. Scientists study the natural world for two broad reasons. Simply put, basic science asks "how do things work?" Many human cultures give scientific knowledge an implicit value, for its own sake. Other science is meant to be applied, asking not "how does the system work?" but "how can we make the system

work for our benefit?" Of course, basic and applied science are related and they merge into each other. For example, ecologists study populations and communities of species to unravel the complex interrelationships in natural systems. This knowledge serves as a basis for management of species and their habitats.

A number of features of Coloradan mammals are of scientific interest. Biodiversity is not merely an issue in the tropical rainforest. It is an issue in Colorado as well. The importance of biodiversity — the number of species in a biotic community and their relative abundances — to the stability and healthy functioning of ecosystems has become apparent in recent years. Yet there are threats to Coloradan biodiversity, chronic and acute. For example, water is a critical resource in the West, and numerous plans to divert, pump, dam, or otherwise relocate water in Colorado may have tremendous impacts on mammalian populations. Wildlife concentrates at sources of water, and research on mammalian communities in riparian ecosystems and wetlands is critical to their survival.

Some scientific studies of wild mammals have practical value. Humans are mammals, so comparative study of nonhuman mammals is critical to biomedical progress. Laboratory studies of native mammals have contributed to our understanding of genetics, physiology, behavior, and disease. Studies on circadian rhythms in wild mammals have been applied to problems in human productivity and jetlag. Knowledge of hibernation in black bears and ground squirrels may be applied to research on reduced metabolic activity in humans. From mammalian models we have learned the importance of control and predictability in our ability to cope with stress. Mammalian models have also revealed the significance of the social environment on reproductive and immune system functioning. For example, the development of sonar — which has both military and medical applications — was facilitated by studying echolocation in bats.

Coloradan mammals and wildlife biologists have contributed much to the knowledge base of wildlife management. Specifically, much of the published research on game species such as mule deer, elk, and bighorn sheep has been conducted in Colorado.

Mammalian species may also be indicators of habitat quality. The meadow jumping mouse may indicate intact stands of relict tallgrass prairie on the Colorado Piedmont. The presence of house mice is a sure sign of human disturbance. Sagebrush voles occur mostly on well-managed sagebrush rangelands. Martens and southern red-backed voles are mammalian indicators of old-growth conditions in some subalpine forest types. The Colorado Division of Wildlife and the U. S. Forest Service have cooperated on efforts to improve forest management by considering many of these indicator species and their habitat needs (Hoover and Wills 1987).

Other scientific values are less practical and more philosophical. As natural scientists study nonhuman mammals, the animals teach us more about ourselves, perhaps helping us to move beyond mere anthropocentrism. They provide a sense of perspective. To learn about the remarkable adaptations of mammals to environments underscores human physiological, ecological, and social adaptations.

EDUCATIONAL VALUES

Wild mammals offer educational benefits. Perhaps the greatest educational values of mammals are informal, in the simple observations of them in their element: to see a beaver slap the water in warning with its flat, paddle-shaped tail at twilight; to watch two mule deer bucks test each other as they spar on a bed of fresh snow; to sit atop a mountain and count the trips a pika makes to collect its haypile; to walk alone in the foothills and glimpse a gray fox foraging for fruit in a tree; or to be surprised by a mock attack from a badger who has young in her den. These are examples of

mammalian form and function in their natural contexts.

We also educate students and ourselves by observing and unpacking the connections in the natural world. Project Wild, sponsored by the Colorado Division of Wildlife, reaches 12,000 teachers annually, who work with some 300,000 to 400,000 students in Colorado's schools, helping to put people and wildlife in context. Observing wild mammals to let them teach us, as we develop an understanding of their world, enriches all who have the humility and patience to try, watch, and wonder.

URBAN WILDLIFE VALUES

In the nineteenth century, direct exploitation of particular species had the greatest human impact on wild mammals. In the twentieth century, indirect human effects on wildlife — especially habitat change — are surely much more important. The urban landscape is the most rapidly expanding habitat in Colorado, as elsewhere in the United States.

As Colorado's habitats and human population become increasingly urban, the ways that people interact with wildlife are changing. By the year 2000, almost half of the six billion humans on Earth will live in urban areas. In Colorado, over 80 percent of Colorado's human population lives along the Front Range corridor between Pueblo and Fort Collins (Webb 1990). Fortunately, there are rich opportunities to see free-roaming mammals close to home (Webb and Foster 1991). A number of Front Range cities, including Fort Collins, Boulder, and Denver, have considered wildlife in planning for parks and open space.

How do nonhuman mammals respond to this? Certain species respond positively to habitat alterations associated with human activities, including noxious invaders like the Norway rat and the house mouse, both of which were introduced to this continent from Eurasia. But other, more benign, native species, such as the red fox, raccoon, fox squirrel, and striped skunk, also have become more widespread and abundant as a result of human activities.

Fox squirrels entered Colorado within historic times, along the riparian corridors of the South Platte and Republican rivers. Human activities, including deliberate introductions, the planting of deciduous trees, irrigation, and control of flooding and prairie fires, have encouraged these animals to the point that they are now abundant in areas where they did not even occur a century ago.

Similarly, striped skunks and raccoons have become more common. Both are species of riparian woodland on the eastern plains, and they have responded positively to human intervention in the landscape. With the development of suburbs in the foothills of the Front Range, raccoons have expanded their elevational range, taking advantage of new food resources such as tree fruits, garden crops, and garbage. Red foxes also respond to expanded deciduous woodland and irrigated cropland and they are quite tolerant of human proximity, so many people have had the opportunity to observe them in urban environments.

Muskrats and beavers are also tolerant and may become nuisances. Sometimes chainlink or sheet-metal guards must be installed to protect trees from beavers. Black-tailed jackrabbits are problematic at Denver's Stapleton Airport. Mule deer have become pests to many a gardener in Boulder, and mountain lions, habituated to people, have settled in to feed on the deer and an occasional pet dog or cat.

The species that succeed in the urban environment are often habitat generalists, whose diet is somewhat opportunistic. In Colorado, they frequently are eastern species of riparian ecosystems: fox squirrel, raccoon, opossum. They have expanded because human settlement has brought irrigation (both on croplands and in urban landscaping) and deciduous trees. Thus the urban wildlife community usually has a different species composition than the native ecosystems the city replaced.

WILDLIFE VERSUS HUMANS: Nuisance Aspects of Mammals

As part of a larger ecological whole, human interactions with other mammals form a complex web. Some interactions are positive, many are relatively neutral, and some are negative. The negative impacts include diseases and problems created by certain species.

PUBLIC HEALTH AND WILDLIFE DISEASE

Wild mammals of Colorado can be infested with a variety of endo- or ectoparasites or infected with pathogenic organisms capable of infecting humans or their pets and livestock. Thorne et al. (1982) provided a good survey of over 50 important diseases of mammals in Wyoming, and their insights are relevant in Colorado as well. Endoparasites include a variety of roundworms, flatworms, and protozoans, many of which have complicated life cycles that involve more than one host species. Accidental infection of humans or domestic mammals can occur from eating uncooked or improperly cooked meat, handling and cleaning wild game, feeding on contaminated vegetation, or drinking from contaminated waters, leading to infection with tapeworm or hookworm, lungworm, or giardia. Many of these organisms, depending on the severity of infection, can affect the general health and condition of the host and in severe instances can cause death. Ectoparasites include fleas, ticks, lice, mites, and true bugs (Hemiptera). Such species can cause skin irritation and general discomfort or may transmit microbial diseases such as plague, tularemia, tick fever, and spotted fever.

The more important wildlife diseases are summarized in Table 3-3. Zoonotic diseases are wildlife diseases transmissible to humans. Because many people engage in outdoor activities in Colorado that place them close to wild animals and their diseases, a number of zoonoses are of importance

53

Table 3–3. Important microbial diseases of wild mammals in Colorado.

Disease	Typical hosts	Transmission	Host Mortality
Viral Diseases			
Contagious ecthyma	bighorn sheep, mountain goat	direct contact	low
Blue tongue	elk, deer, pronghorn, bighorn sheep	gnats	may be high
Canine distemper	canids, mustelids, raccoon	direct contact	may be high
Parvoviruses	most canids, felids		low
Rabies*	all mammals, especially carnivores, bats	bites, rarely aerosol	high
Bacterial Diseases			
Brucellosis	elk, moose, bison, cattle	ingest contaminated vegetation	low
Tularemia*	lagomorphs and rodents	ticks, blood-blood contact, eating infected meat	high
Plague*	rodents	fleas	high
Pasteurellosis	most ruminants, especially bighorn sheep, pronghorn	droplet infection, ingestion	high

*Zoonotic disease; transmissible from wild mammals to humans.
Source: After E.T. Thorne, N. Kingston, W. R. Jolley, and R. C. Bergstrom, eds. 1982. *Diseases of Wildlife in Wyoming*, second ed. Wyoming Game and Fish Dept., Cheyenne.

to human health. Rabies and plague are of particular importance because they are life threatening.

Rabies is a virus, associated mostly with bats and carnivores, that is transmitted through the saliva of infected mammals. Infection typically occurs as saliva passes into a bite wound. Although human exposure usually is caused by the bite of a carnivore or bat, rabies can infect and kill any mammalian species, and animals ranging from squirrels to elephants are known to have passed the disease. Any person whose skin is broken by the bite of a wild or domestic mammal whose history is unknown should consult a physician as soon as possible. Individuals who routinely work with wild mammals should consider preventative vaccination.

The incubation period for rabies is highly variable, but symptoms usually show within two to eight weeks in most species. (Dogs that bite people usually are quarantined for 10 days.) Once symptoms manifest themselves the disease is untreatable and death invariably results. The only way to determine the presence of infection is to kill the animal and inspect brain tissue for the virus.

Biologists have identified a number of strains of the rabies virus that are host-specific (and especially virulent) for particular terrestrial mammals such as skunks, raccoons, and foxes (MacInnes 1987). Other strains are found in bats. Most regular and recurring epizootics (an outbreak in a population of wild animals) of rabies in terrestrial carnivores occur east of the 105th meridian (roughly the alignment of Interstate Highway 25); hence, a major part of Colorado lies just west of such outbreaks and rabies in wild carnivores in the state is episodic and rare. In the West, bats are the main source of rabies (MacInnes 1987). Thorne et al. (1982) summarized rabies incidence in Colorado and Wyoming from 1938 to 1979. In Colorado, 43 percent of cases were from bats, 31 percent from dogs, and 17 percent from skunks. (Interestingly, in Wyoming 61 percent of cases were from skunks and only 17 percent from bats.)

Over the past decade or so, the number of humans who have died from bat-transmitted rabies in the United States is very low. Although the risk is low, however, it is higher than for dog- or cat-transmitted rabies because of the active vaccination programs for domestic pets (John Pape, Colorado Department of Health, pers. comm.).

It is very difficult to determine the incidence of infection of rabies (and most other wildlife diseases) in wild populations because diseases can spread rapidly, infected individuals may be difficult to observe, and it is costly to maintain monitoring systems. Therefore, data on infection rates should be viewed with caution unless they are specific to a given area and have been obtained over long periods. However, it has been estimated that infection rates in wild bat populations are less than 0.1 percent, and fewer than 1 percent of these infected bats ever attack another animal. Most simply become paralyzed and die. Sick or injured bats are often obvious in their behavior and frequently are taken to the Colorado Health Department for testing. A relatively high number of these test positive for rabies. Of course, this is a highly biased sample of the whole population. Nonetheless, although rabies is uncommon, care should always be taken with a bat or other wild mammal that acts unhealthy or abnormal. By the way, canine distemper, a disease that does not infect humans, is not uncommon in raccoons and wild canids and mustelids in Colorado. Symptoms are almost identical to those of rabies, including apparent disorientation, lack of fear, and extreme aggressiveness.

Plague, known as the Black Death in the Middle Ages, is caused by a bacterium (*Yersinia pestis*). The bacterium lives in the gut of a flea (the intermediate host), where it reproduces. The pathogen is then regurgitated into the saliva and enters the definitive host — a mammal — when the flea takes a blood meal. This leads to infection of the mammal. The disease can also be transmitted by eating or handling infected carcasses if cuts or abrasions allow entry to the bloodstream. Because of the potential for human cases to become pneumonic (transmissible by aerosol), the disease is monitored closely by the U. S. Public Health Service and is quarantinable. If misdiagnosed (initial

symptoms are much like those of flu) and left untreated, the disease typically is fatal. From 1925 to 1964 plague cases in the western United States averaged two per year, most in California. Since then the annual number of cases in humans has increased steadily (average 16 per year since 1975) with most of them reported from New Mexico (Barnes, in press). Less frequently plague may produce infections in cottontails or even carnivores; human infection occurs as hunters or trappers skin infected animals. Not infrequently, dogs or cats are implicated in human cases of the disease, especially in the Southwest.

Plague has been known in North America since 1900, probably introduced to port cities on commensal rodents but then spreading rapidly over the western United States. Plague was first documented in Colorado in 1941 (Ecke and Johnson 1952). By contrast with rabies, plague is a western disease, not maintained in the wild much east of the 101st meridian (Barnes, in press). In Colorado, plague is most often associated by the general public with prairie dogs, because nearly every summer the news media report dramatic die-offs (often mortality is close to 100 percent) of these rodents from the disease. Only about 3 percent of human plague cases are attributable to contact with prairie dogs, however (Barnes, in press). Practically any rodent in the state, from grasshopper mice and voles to woodrats, chipmunks, and ground squirrels, can harbor infected fleas, although such populations usually do not exhibit major die-offs. The mammal most often implicated in our area with transmission of sylvatic plague to humans is the rock squirrel, which often occurs close to homes and whose fleas readily bite humans or their pets. Use of insecticidal powder at burrows or bait stations is an effective control.

Tularemia is caused by a bacterium (*Francisella tularensis*) that produces chills or fever in infected humans. The disease is usually contracted as people skin infected rabbits or beaver. It can also be contracted by eating undercooked rabbit meat, drinking contaminated water, or inhaling contaminated dust. Flies and ticks also carry and transmit the disease. Broad-spectrum antibiotic treatment is effective. In the wild, the pathogen is associated with a wide range of mammals, from muskrat and beaver to ground squirrels, mice, and lagomorphs, especially cottontails. Two major strains exist, with Type A, associated with terrestrial rodents and rabbits, causing most human infection. Type B is associated with wetlands and aquatic environments and is passed by water or aquatic rodents. Addison et al. (1987) and Thorne et al. (1982) provided useful summaries.

During spring and summer, people active outdoors may be exposed to three different tickborne diseases in addition to tularemia: Colorado tick fever (caused by a virus), Rocky Mountain spotted fever (caused by a rickettsia), and Lyme disease (caused by a spirochaete bacterium). All three diseases are transmitted by tick bites, and the respective species of ticks require small to medium-sized mammals to complete their life cycles. The diseases appear similar in humans, including cold or flu-like symptoms, chills, fever, and headache. Although recovery may take time, these diseases usually are not fatal. Although first described from our region, Rocky Mountain spotted fever actually is much more prevalent in the Southeast. Lyme disease tends to be more common in the Northeast. Very few cases have occurred in Colorado; two were reported in 1988, one in 1989, none in 1990, and one in 1991 (J. Pape, Colorado Department of Health, pers. commun.).

Hantavirus is a newly discovered disease in the United States that has recently received attention in western North America. This virus is related to the Asian Hantaan virus, which has been known for many years. Cases of hantavirus infection have now been documented in Texas, New Mexico, California, Colorado, Arizona, Oregon, Nevada, Utah, and Louisiana. However, the majority of these cases have occurred in the Four Corners area. Of those, Colorado has reported five cases with four fatalities as of September 1993. It is very

likely that previous deaths from hantavirus have gone unrecognized.

Early symptoms of the disease include fever and chills, muscle pain, headache, fatigue, and cough. Within one to five days severe breathing difficulties and respiratory complications will develop. The disease can progress extremely rapidly, and the mortality rate is high.

Hantavirus is transmitted via the inhalation of aerosols of urine and feces of infected rodents. Contact with saliva via bites is also a potential mode of transmission. Most cases are associated with concentrations of urine and feces in enclosed environments, such as in a cabin or trailer where deer mice, *Peromyscus maniculatus*, have set up home. Deer mice appear to be the predominant reservoir of infection of hantavirus, although it has been documented in other rodents such as piñon mice (*P. truei*), brush mice (*P. boylii*), and chipmunks (*Tamias* spp.). It is suspected that hantavirus occurs throughout wild mouse and rat populations in the United States.

The causes of outbreaks in humans, other than factors associated with the mode of transmission, are not well understood at this time. Centers for Disease Control (1993) published recommendations for mammalogists and others working in the field with rodents. These measures include the use of rubber or plastic gloves and respirators, and disinfecting traps. The virus is susceptible to most common household disinfectants. At the present time we do not know very much about this disease, and the risks can be very difficult to assess. Much more information will surely be gathered in the near future to clarify the risks to field workers and the precautions that should be taken.

PROBLEM MAMMALS

Mammals have impacts on people's livelihood and property in a number of different ways. Skunks, raccoons, and beaver create nuisance problems in urban neighborhoods, rodents and ungulates feed on crops and forage grasses, and predators feed on livestock. Nearly $17 million of damage by prairie dogs, pocket gophers, and ground squirrels was reported for 1989 in Colorado (Colorado Department of Agriculture 1990). During the decade 1982 to 1992, claims for damage by deer, elk, pronghorn, bear, and mountain lion paid by the Colorado Division of Wildlife ranged from a low of $137,600 in 1987 to a high of $879,600 in 1984, a particularly severe winter. In 8 of the 10 years, claims were less than $200,000 (Tully 1990). Although much of the human population resides along the Front Range and is unaware of these problems on a daily basis, ranchers and farmers feel the financial impact and have legitimate concerns.

Prairie dogs, pocket gophers, ground squirrels, and beavers are frequent subjects of damage complaints. On Colorado rangelands, ranchers feel the greatest impact from prairie dogs. Their concerns are that prairie dogs compete with cattle for forage and alter the plant species composition, generally causing "destruction of rangeland," which translates to more acres needed per head of livestock. Horses and cattle can be injured by stepping into prairie dog burrows. Burrows can divert valuable water from irrigation ditches. Some people are concerned about plague in prairie dog populations. At airports, prairie dogs even violate Federal Aviation Administration regulations, which disallow holes greater than two inches in diameter near runways! An estimated two million acres of private land are inhabited by prairie dogs in Colorado. Landowners may feel that they are carrying the public burden of hosting prairie dogs and are frustrated at the expense of control. Reduced funds for rodent control from the Colorado Department of Agriculture and increasing emphasis on education have reduced control efforts in recent years.

Pocket gophers cause cropland destruction as plants are killed in the vicinity of tunnels and species composition is altered as new seedbeds are formed by their diggings. They may disturb or destroy stands of alfalfa and other crops. Gopher mounds can even damage farm machinery, dull-

ing or breaking sickleblades, for example. Pocket gophers also chew on underground cables and irrigation pipes, and irrigation water is lost through their burrow systems. In various parts of the state, thirteen-lined and Wyoming ground squirrels, rock squirrels, and marmots compete with livestock for forage, destroy food crops, invade hay pastures, dig up newly planted seeds and eat sprouting seedlings, and excavate burrows and build mounds that are destructive to machinery. Current control methods for all these rodents include burrow fumigants and zinc phosphide.

The establishment of commercial cattle and sheep operations in the western United States in the nineteenth century created today's predator and rodent control problems. Livestock provided an easy food source for predators. Bounties were first set on wolves and coyotes in 1876 (Barrows and Holmes 1990). Subsequently, coyotes expanded their distribution and wolves were extirpated from most states. Coyotes cause the heaviest damage losses to sheep and, to a lesser extent, to calves. A number of nonlethal methods for coyote control are being developed and implemented to varying degrees. Black bears occasionally prey on livestock but probably do more damage by raiding apiaries and orchards. Each situation is unique and may require experimenting with different combinations of techniques for relief from predation (Andelt 1987).

Beavers can be a nuisance in both rural and urban environments by felling trees, building dams in irrigation ditches, burrowing in banks, and flooding hay meadows. Urban examples include Confluence Park along the South Platte River in Denver, where trees have metal guards to protect them from beavers. An unusual problem occurred in the 1930s when beavers dammed up tunnels two miles underground at the Bonanza gold and silver mine (Barrows and Holmes 1990).

Raccoons and striped skunks can be a nuisance around homes and sometimes prey on poultry. Skunks get under houses and foundations, causing concern to homeowners. Raccoons climb into chimneys, enter houses and yards, and topple garbage cans in search of food. An especially bold raccoon may even remove used charcoal from a patio barbecue grill and rinse it in a nearby wading pool. During outbreaks of distemper, raccoons may be especially visible and approachable, although they may also exhibit rabies-like symptoms of aggressiveness.

Deer and elk feed on irrigated hay meadows and alfalfa, especially in spring. In severe winters, they get into haystacks that are not protected by fencing. In particularly severe winters, public sentiment motivated the Division of Wildlife to supply alfalfa and deer pellets to avoid massive winter kill. This winter feeding activity is of disputed benefit as it is a short-term solution that, in fact, aggravates the problem. These die-offs are a function of insufficient winter range, and supplemental feeding only exacerbates the problem (Gill and Carpenter 1985). The present policy of the Wildlife Commission and the Colorado Division of Wildlife is not to feed ungulates.

A few other species deserve mention for the problems they cause. Kangaroo rats have become a concern recently as large tracts of sandy soils (their preferred habitat) have been developed for sprinkler-irrigated corn and alfalfa production. They feed on newly planted seeds and emerging seedlings. Hispid cotton rats feed on crops, especially melons and sugar beets. Exotic house mice and Norway rats contaminate food and carry disease. Although house mice may not consume large quantities of food, they do chew through packaging and foul the contents with their feces and urine. Rats can substantially impact stores of livestock feed and are common residents of feedlots. Both species can also cause structural damage. Voles and porcupines damage orchards, landscape plantings, and forests by girdling seedlings, branches, and ornamentals, especially in fall and winter.

A cooperative approach has been taken by various agencies to handle these problems. Generally, the State Department of Agriculture advises on rodent problems and oversees the cooperative agreement with the Animal Damage Control unit (under the Animal and Plant Health Inspection Services — APHIS) of the U.S. Department of Agriculture, which controls predators. The Colorado Division of Wildlife responds to big game problems and damage claims. The Cooperative Extension Service, headquartered at Colorado State University in Fort Collins, has county agents statewide who provide information to the public on nuisance mammals and develop outreach programs, educational materials, and programs for landowners.

Colorado is fortunate to be the location of several federal wildlife research agencies. The National Ecology Research Center in Fort Collins is a unit of the U.S. Fish and Wildlife Service, Bird and Mammal Laboratories, and is involved in studies at the level of ecosystems and regional landscapes. The Denver Wildlife Research Center, under the U.S. Department of Agriculture, is actively involved in research on new and progressive ways to handle animal damage problems. Currently, they are developing technology for immunocontraception as a population control measure for deer. Other nonlethal methods developed at the center include devices designed to frighten coyotes and discourage them from preying on sheep. Certain breeds of dogs (Komondors, Akbosh, and Great Pyrenees, among others) and also llamas have been used to guard sheep from coyotes and other predators and are effective in many situations. Among the diversity of developing projects are protective collars for livestock, which impact only offending coyotes, and assessment research on diameter and hardness of utility cables that resist rodent chewing. These efforts are important. Solutions to nuisance and damage problems enhance the positive values of wildlife.

THE FUTURES OF WILDLIFE MANAGEMENT: The Human Dimension

The management of wildlife resources has changed over the years. The nineteenth century, an era of exploitation with decades of active and uncontrolled harvest, was followed by intense and careful management of selected game species with successful results. Biological (and sometimes political) factors drove these management schemes, and results could be measured with basic economics. Dollars spent directly or indirectly by hunters were the measure of the value of the resource. The passage of time, increased knowledge, and cultural changes have made this an oversimplification, however. Mammals have immense value that is measured indirectly by such indices as the flow of tourist dollars, but no fee is levied for this use and it is difficult to compile data documenting income per head of golden-mantled ground squirrel seen and appreciated.

The urbanization (and perhaps the relative feminization) of our society has had a major impact on the way wildlife is viewed and valued by the public and is beginning to influence approaches to resource management. Most Americans value wildlife for one reason or another. However, 9 out of 10 hunters are men; only 2 percent of American women hunt (Heberlein 1987). Thus, perhaps half the population values wildlife in a nonhunting context and its voice in the political arena is being heard increasingly. Urbanites, who often have grown up with little contact with wild animals, hold different views and values of wildlife and hunting than do people from rural backgrounds. Furthermore, interest in wildlife has broadened in recent years. Between 1982 and 1987, memberships in wildlife organizations increased by 47 percent (Decker 1989). This high level of public interest comes from many different sectors. We no longer have a homogeneous view of the nonhuman animals among whom we live; our views are varied and often in conflict.

Over the past 20 years, a growing body of knowledge has developed on the human dimensions of wildlife management. A number of universities have developed the theory; applications research generally has been carried out by wildlife agencies, which increasingly recognize the importance of the "people factor" in management decisions.

This approach links wildlife management with the social sciences to meet societal needs (Decker 1989). Examples of efforts that address the human dimension are hunter and nonhunter attitudes toward a program, public preferences for game and nongame management, and farmers' attitudes toward crop damage by deer. How we manage wildlife is largely a function of how, and to what extent, we value it.

The value that we place on mammals is a function of our attitudes, perceptions, and knowledge about them. Once the managers' view of the public was simple: there were hunters and nonhunters. Over the past 15 years, a body of knowledge has developed on the values people place on wildlife and the relationship of human behavior to these values (Decker and Goff 1987). In a first step, Kellert (1977, 1980) outlined a number of basic human attitudes toward animals. People exhibiting a *naturalistic* attitude have an interest in and affection for wildlife and the outdoors. The *ecologistic* attitude has primary concern for the environment as a system, for interrelationships between wildlife species and their natural habitats. A *humanistic* attitude expresses a primary interest in and strong affection for individual animals, especially pets. People with a *moralistic* attitude show primary concern for right and wrong treatment of animals, and strong opposition to exploitation of and cruelty toward animals. The *scientistic* attitude has its primary interest in understanding the physical attributes and biological functioning of animals. People with a predominantly *esthetic* attitude place their primary interest in the artistic and symbolic characteristics of animals. Those with a *utilitarian* attitude focus concern on the practical and material value of animals. A *dominionistic* attitude derives primary satisfaction from mastery and control over animals, typically in sporting situations. People with *negativistic* attitudes toward wildlife actively avoid animals because of dislike or even fear. Finally, those with a *neutralistic* attitude exhibit passive avoidance of animals, indifference, a general lack of interest. Obviously, there is a possibility for conflict between people with these different attitudes, some of them diametrically opposed. Although few people would hold one or another of these attitudes exclusively, a focus on primary attitudes reveals interesting and important trends.

Through personal interviews with 3,107 randomly selected persons, Kellert (1980) found that the most common attitudes toward animals in the United States were humanistic, moralistic, utilitarian, and negativistic. The humanistic attitude would characterize some members of animal welfare organizations, which often work against activities that cause animals to suffer or die. The moralistic attitude is consistent with the beliefs of some animal rights advocates, who sometimes oppose any and all exploitative uses of animals. The utilitarian attitude, by contrast, embraces hunting as a valuable and positive (or even necessary) use of animals. The clash between these three attitudes is a cause of much controversy. Overall, gender emerges as the most significant factor affecting attitudes toward animals (Kellert and Berry 1987). Addressing the many different views can provide directions for future educational thrusts in our attempt to ensure that wild mammals remain an integral part of the landscape.

Carrying capacity is an estimate of the population of a species that can be supported indefinitely on a particular area of habitat. Although it is far too simple for actual prediction, the concept of carrying capacity traditionally has been an important tool for understanding the biological relationship between wildlife populations and habitats in ecological and management contexts. To expand beyond this, Decker and Purdy (1988) developed a new capacity concept to account for the relationship between human beliefs and preferences and decisions of wildlife management. The *wildlife acceptance capacity* (WAC) recognizes the importance of public opinion and, for a given area, projects the optimal wildlife population that is acceptable to people. This measure incorporates numerous negative elements such as tolerable amounts of damage and nuisance, competition with other species, and disease transmission, and weighs them against the esthetic, educational, eco-logical, and scientific value of the species in question.

The WAC is a dynamic factor. It varies by region, culture, level of education, degree of urbanization, point in time, and numerous other factors. Different constituencies, with different fundamental attitudes toward wildlife, have different WACs. Educational programs and good communication with these constituencies can go far toward maintaining wildlife populations that integrate the values of various constituencies. For example, important elements of allaying ranchers' concerns about the gray wolves that are repopulating Montana are listening to stockgrowers, informing them about wolf biology, and providing an effective damage claim program.

CONFLICTING VIEWS

Because humans have strong feelings about animals, both negative and positive, it is inevitable that conflict will arise, and it does. For example, "it will seem ridiculous to a sportsman to say that snail darters and louseworts have more recreational value than the reservoir behind a dam, full of fish; while a naturalist will find extermination of a rare life form in trade for yet another place to water-ski an obscenity" (Rolston 1986:79). Conflicts also arise in determining how best to handle problem species. What means of control are effective and acceptable? How much damage is tolerable?

Mule deer and mountain lion populations along the Front Range are subjects of controversy. Due to a combination of factors including successful management programs, city or county ordinances banning harvest or control in populated areas, the palatibility of ornamental plantings, and the lack of wildlife management tools to regulate populations without killing, deer are at very high population levels. Mountain lions apparently have become both abundant and habituated to people. On a given street, one person's family may enjoy seeing deer in their neighborhood, while a neighbor may resent their intrusion on carefully tended plantings. One person may feel that mountain lions are a welcome attraction and people are the intruders, but another person may be fearful of harm to family or pets. Where management calls for population reduction, the difficulty of culling operations in suburban neighborhoods is apparent. Nonlethal approaches, such as immunocontraception for the deer, may offer solutions to overabundance where traditional population control methods (such as natural predation and hunting) are inappropriate.

Consumptive and nonconsumptive uses sometimes come into conflict. This conflict happens most frequently in areas of high use, such as on Mount Evans where people expecting to enjoy nonconsumptive wildlife recreation have observed bighorn sheep and mountain goat hunters stalking and killing animals. It may be painful to nonhunters to see hunters in action, especially if illegal behavior is involved, such as poaching or shooting from the road. Surveys have shown that 18 percent of the population of Colorado disapproves of hunting, whereas 72 percent of Coloradans strongly disapprove of the use of steel-jaw traps for taking wild mammals (Gill 1991).

Heated wildlife issues are legion: poisoning or shooting nuisance species like prairie dogs, the use of leg-hold traps, the spring bear hunt, hunting with bait and dogs, and the use of furs for coats. These conflicts cannot be eliminated. They are rooted in deeply held beliefs, values, and attitudes. We humans can, however, recognize different points of view, educate ourselves and others about biology and the decision-making process, develop new techniques, and — when needed — make the hard decisions on what can or cannot be done both for managing wildlife and facilitating public involvement.

WILDLIFE ETHICS

Holmes Rolston, Distinguished Professor of Philosophy at Colorado State University, wrote (1986:74): "to ask about values in nature is . . . to form a misleading question, for values are only in people, created by their decisions." We readily discuss how we *do* value nature, and the spectrum of different and sometimes conflicting views, and some thinkers have begun to ask how we *should* value nature. We can readily value things as we ascribe some extrinsic, or monetary, value to them. If we ascribe value simply for the sake of its being there, untrammeled, have we perhaps reached a higher level of understanding? Is nature a resource to be used simply for our benefit, or a greater entity to be treated with respect for its own sake and allowed to flourish?

There are two levels of environmental ethics. The first is anthropocentric: preserve nature because it benefits humans, actually or potentially. This is often the most effective argument to justify preservation of natural resources. We are told to preserve tropical rainforests because yet undiscovered medicines and food plants abound that eventually will benefit us. The second level of environmental ethic can be termed naturalistic (Rolston 1986). This view is held by a growing number of people, based on a belief in the unity of the earth with all its inhabitants and respect for its integrity. A naturalistic ethic values and preserves both resources and nonresources (Ehrenfeld 1974). Leopold (1949) foresaw such thinking when he observed that "a system of conservation based solely on economic self-interest is hopelessly lopsided."

Currently, there is a thrust to encourage a stewardship approach toward natural systems. Dasmann (1966) wrote on the "old conservation," which emphasized the quantity of resources; in Colorado, that has meant mule deer, elk, and trophy bighorn rams. The "new conservation," by contrast, sees things whole. It is about quality, not just quantity — the quality of ecosystems and hence of human life. In wildlife management, such ideas are traceable in part to Aldo Leopold, whose ideas were epitomized in an essay titled "The Land Ethic." Leopold urged (1949:224–225) that we "quit thinking about decent land-use as solely an economic problem. Examine each

61

question in terms of what is ethically and esthetically right, as well as what is economically expedient. A thing is right when it tends to preserve the integrity, stability, and beauty of the biotic community. It is wrong when it tends otherwise." Responsible decisions are beneficial to the resource and also to people. The notion of stewardship does, of course, make a subtle separation between humans and nature, implying that we humans know better and must be the responsible guardians of a landscape that needs our care. From a management standpoint this view probably is necessary, although some would urge that we approach the landscape as students rather than stewards (Kellert 1987), becoming a part of the system that we manage.

Human interactions with other Coloradan native mammals have passed through two broad evolutionary phases: a long-term phase of subsistence and a short-term phase of exploitation. We are now in the midst of a third phase, typified by new forms of stewardship and a diversity of values and attitudes, in a state where wildlife economics and politics are connected in complex ways. Where present trends will lead and how our descendants seven generations hence will characterize and evaluate our times we cannot know.

Given the changes in society and science that can lead to a new relationship between humans and the other native mammals of Colorado, what are some outstanding questions that deserve discussion? We suggest the following merely as a starting point; a recent workshop (Winternitz and Crumpacker 1985) suggested many others.

- How do we maintain the integrity of managed ecosystems with their mammalian fauna, especially riparian systems (not only on the eastern plains but on the Western Slope) and grasslands with their native fauna — white-tailed jackrabbits, prairie dogs, swift fox, grasshopper mice?

- In an age of enlightened wildlife management, is it not time to consider the fact that 20 mammalian species (about 16 percent of native species) are not provided any protection on public lands in Colorado? Should there be year-round open season on public lands for species whose status and distribution are essentially unknown — such as eastern spotted skunks and hog-nosed skunks?

- Should we continue to allow "recreational" trapping of species whose populations apparently are low and whose pelage has minimal commercial value, such as ringtails, ermine, swift fox?

- When should the state begin to insist that all consumptive users of wildlife use the most humane methods possible? Canadian regulations on trapping are far more humane than those in force in Colorado (Novak et al. 1987).

- How should decisions about introduction of exotic species be weighed against the integrity of a native ecosystem? Moose and mountain goats are prospering in Colorado today thanks to human intervention, although neither species managed to get to Colorado on its own, despite the dramatic ecological changes that characterized the Pleistocene. What is the ecological and esthetic cost of these introductions, to balance with the benefits?

- That the State of Colorado can manage wildlife resources is beyond question. But what is Colorado's appropriate relationship with the "nonresources" represented by nongame mammals? Public interest is amply demonstrated by people's responses to the Colorado Bat Society's annual Bat Trend Survey and the Bats/Abandoned Mines Project of the Colorado Division of Wildlife and the Office of Mined Land Reclamation. Should we be establishing preserves for species like meadow jumping mice and olive-backed pocket mice — species whose habitats are being overrun by urbanization of the Front Range Corridor?

We suppose that the future will bring new challenges to Colorado and its wild mammals: human population growth, continued and expanded human impact on native ecosystems, losses of biodiversity, development of oil shale, local effects of global climatic change, and myriad others, unforeseen. We can speculate but we cannot predict. Still, we do know a few things. Writer-conservationist John Muir was right: everything *is* hitched to everything else. Biologist Sir Julian Huxley was also right: we humans are "no longer insignificant in relation to the cosmos," for we find ourselves "in the unexpected position of business manager for the cosmic process of evolution" (1953:132). And ecologist Garrett Hardin was right: we can't do nothing. Not to choose is a strong choice.

HISTORY OF MAMMALOGY IN COLORADO

Just as we can visualize human exploitation of the Coloradan fauna as a history of changing values and attitudes, we can imagine the development of Coloradan mammalogy as a series of broadly overlapping phases. Initial study of the native fauna by humans doubtless began as the first waves of immigrants from Asia expanded down the Americas during the last Ice Age, relying on some mammalian species for food and avoiding becoming prey for some other species. Though unrecorded, there is ample archaeological evidence to suggest that from the beginning humans distinguished the more obvious and important kinds of mammals and knew their ecology and habits. From that day forward, often the most accurate and insightful knowledge of the fauna of a particular area is not to be found in books but in the minds and stories of ranchers, farmers, hunters, trappers, and other natural resource managers, who frequently get beyond merely exploiting the fauna, to enjoy and admire it as well. D. Wilson and Eisenberg (1990) provided a broad outline of the history of North American mammalogy.

European encounters with the Coloradan fauna began with the explorations of Fray Silvestre Vélez de Escalante and Fray Francisco Atansio Dominguez and continued with the expedition of Zebulon K. Pike, who made a few informal notes on his observations of the fauna in 1806–1807. We may date scientific study of mammals of Colorado from 1820, when Thomas Say, the first trained naturalist to work in Colorado, entered the area with the Stephen H. Long's expedition, sent to explore the southern parts of "Louisiana," an area ignored by the earlier expedition of Meriwether Lewis and William Clark. Long returned home with reports of "the Great American Desert," reports that only military necessity and the lure of gold would overcome.

From 1820 until about 1870, most mammalogical exploration was conducted incidental to military exploration. Specimens obtained by such people as John Charles Frémont and J. W. Abert were sent east for description by naturalists like John James Audubon and John Bachman. The most productive of these expeditions was that of Captain John Gunnison, whose surveys for a possible route for a transcontinental railway along the 38th parallel led him across southern Colorado. He obtained several mammals of significance, despite the fact that the expedition came to an untimely end in Utah. Much of the material obtained by the military expeditions was returned to the fledgling Smithsonian Institution and published by Baird (1855) and summarized in his monumental *Mammals of North America* (1858). Specimens from later geological and topographic expeditions were reported by Coues and Yarrow (1875) and Coues and Allen (1877).

During the 1870s, private expeditions to Colorado provided new insights, including work by Brewer (1871), Trippe (1874), and J. A. Allen (1874). The first local naturalist of note was Martha Maxwell, a hunter and taxidermist who settled in Boulder in 1868. Her magnificent collection was exhibited in Philadelphia at the Centennial Exposition of 1876, and then in Washington, and was reported by Coues (in Dartt, 1879). Edwin Carter (1812–1900) also developed renown for his taxidermy, which in 1900 (shortly after his death) provided the founding collections of the Denver Museum of Natural History. Although never published, Carter's extensive records of observations on small slips of paper were strung up around his cabin in Breckenridge. The cabin is being restored and will eventually be opened to the public.

The 1890s saw a new impetus for vertebrate natural history, under the leadership of C. Hart Merriam. Merriam promoted the idea that one could judge appropriate land use from an understanding of the natural distribution of organisms, a useful lesson that still is not well understood in some circles. Merriam developed the notion of life zones (which he also called "crop zones"). He organized the Bureau of Biological Survey in the Department of Agriculture to conduct field research, especially in the West, to extend his ideas. In Colorado, this effort was conducted intensively from 1905 to 1909, led by Merritt Cary, culminating in fine collections in the National Museum of Natural History (Smithsonian Institution) and *A Biological Survey of Colorado* (Cary 1911), a work that is still of value to the field naturalist. The Bureau of Biological Survey eventually evolved into the U.S. Fish and Wildlife Service, which continues active mammalogical research in Colorado from offices in Fort Collins.

In the 1890s, "homegrown" natural history began to mature. E. R. Warren (1865–1942) was a mining engineer who was introduced to the wildlife of Colorado around the mining camps in northern Gunnison County: Crested Butte, Ruby, Gothic, Irwin. Retiring to Colorado Springs he met W. L. Sclater, son of an officer of the London Zoological Society and son-in-law of W. J. Palmer. The younger Sclater had intended to prepare a book on Coloradan mammals but found that he had challenges enough with the birds, so Warren took over the mammals, becoming the most prolific of Coloradan mammalogists, publishing 3 books and some 40 papers on mammals and nearly that many on birds. Warren's history of Coloradan mammalogy (1911) provided details on earlier workers. The revised (1942) version of his

Mammals of Colorado (1910) appeared posthumously. Warren died shortly after reviewing the first proofs, and his wife, Maude Baird Warren, saw the book through to completion. Armstrong (1986) published an appreciation of Warren's work, concluding that although he made no lasting contribution to systematics or biological theory, his collections (now in the University of Colorado Museum) and accompanying fieldnotes and photographs are an invaluable research resource and a rich legacy from a peerless field naturalist.

World-famous naturalists were attracted to the Coloradan fauna around the turn of the century. Theodore Roosevelt wrote popular articles on his mountain lion and bear hunts, and Ernest Thompson Seton published articles on large mammals in *Scribner's Magazine* in 1906 and 1907. Local naturalists like Enos Mills — "Father of Rocky Mountain National Park" — achieved national prominence with their writing on Coloradan wildlife.

Since the days of Cary and Warren, much of the mammalogical work in Colorado has been conducted through universities and colleges. Polymath T.D.A. Cockerell, of the University of Colorado, was mostly an entomologist, but he did study mammals of Boulder County and wrote on zoology in Colorado. W. L. Burnett, State Entomologist at Colorado A&M College (now Colorado State University), was involved in mammalian pest control. He published numerous papers on rodents, the eastern mole, and jackrabbits from 1913 to 1926. During the 1960s, when basic distributional and taxonomic work was well underway, academic research shifted toward studies of behavior and ecology. R. M. Hansen and T. A. Vaughan were both active in the state during that decade, concentrating on pocket gophers, other rodents, and jackrabbits. Their work is cited in accounts of several species in this book. R. R. Lechleitner, also of Colorado State University, focused his field efforts on the ecology of prairie dogs. His *Wild Mammals of Colorado* (1969) was a thorough and up-to-date treatment of abundance, distribution, and habits. Lechleitner died shortly after its publication. Armstrong (1972), influenced as an undergraduate by Lechleitner, prepared a zoogeographic account of Coloradan mammals, based on museum and field work on geographic variation and distribution. In addition, the Denver Museum of Natural History made early and continuing contributions, commencing with the work of F. W. Miller, J. D. Figgins, R. J. Niedrach, and their colleagues.

Not only Coloradan institutions have been involved in research in the state. Significant contributions over several decades have been made by faculty and students from the University of Kansas Museum of Natural History, the University of Utah, the Museum of Southwestern Biology at the University of New Mexico, and Fort Hays State University, Kansas. Additional major collections of Coloradan mammals are in the American Museum of Natural History in New York and the Carnegie Museum in Pittsburgh.

The Colorado Division of Wildlife (DOW) has made important contributions to mammalogy. Much of the earlier research was on harvested species: big game, small game, and commercial fur-bearers (Barrows and Holmes, 1990). However, since about 1970, there has been increasing emphasis on nongame species, stemming from statutory recognition that wildlife has value even when it is not exploited for human pleasure or profit. The diverse values of Coloradan mammals are the subject of this chapter.

The pattern of discovery and reporting of the fauna summarizes the history of mammalogy in Colorado. Of 124 species of native mammals, some 90 percent were accounted for by 1925 and 95 percent by 1955. In the past 40 years only a half-dozen species have been added to the list. Beginning with the 1820s, when about 11 percent of the fauna had been reported, the decades of greatest increase in knowledge of mammalian biodiversity were the 1870s (a decade of local faunal lists, with an increase of 28 percent), the 1890s (initiation of formal biological survey, adding 14 percent), and the 1900s (research by Cary and by Warren, adding 25 percent). Of course, some species are more difficult to document than others. On average, artiodactyl species were reported by 1835, lagomorphs by 1873, and carnivores by 1875. By contrast, average date of reporting of rodents was 1883, bats, 1897, and insectivores, 1925.

Chapter 4

Order: Marsupialia

Marsupials

Zoologists traditionally have considered the infraclass Metatheria to contain a single living order, the Marsupialia, a group including mammals as diverse as opossums, wombats, marsupial "moles," koalas, and kangaroos (G. Simpson 1945). Recent workers (Kirsch 1977; Kirsch and Calaby 1977; Ride 1964, 1970; Stucky and McKenna, in press) have recognized three or more orders within this diverse group. Depending on the author, there are 8 (G. Simpson 1945), 11 (Stucky and McKenna, 1993), or 16 (Kirsch 1977) families of marsupials, containing about 70 genera and 242 species. Two families, Didelphidae and Microbiotheriidae, with 12 genera and 71 species, live in the Americas, but only one species, *Didelphis virginiana*, occurs in the United States.

Debate about their classification aside, marsupials have a suite of common characteristics. Females give birth to young at a very immature stage of development and nourish them with milk for a relatively long period. The mammary glands usually are contained within an abdominal skin fold or pouch, the marsupium. The basic metatherian dental formula is 5/4, 1/1, 3/3, 4/4 = 50 (thus differing from placentals in having a greater total number of teeth, more incisors, with numbers of incisors different in the lower and upper jaw, and more molars than premolars). The palate is poorly ossified with many openings (fenestrae or vacuities). Auditory bullae are incompletely developed or lacking. The jugal bone is large and joins with the squamosal to form the glenoid fossa for articulation of the lower jaw. The horizontal ramus of the mandible is turned inward (inflected) at the angle of the dentary, a very distinctive feature. Two small epipubic bones project forward from the anterior rim of the pelvic girdle. Females have a double reproductive tract with two ovaries, two oviducts, two uteri, and two lateral vaginae. In males the penis typically is forked at the tip and the testes are located in a scrotum anterior to the penis. The brain is small, with poorly convoluted cerebral hemispheres, no corpus callosum, and large olfactory lobes.

There is a widespread, but mistaken, tendency to dismiss marsupials as merely primitive mammals, somehow inferior to placentals. It is true that when faced with competition from ecologically equivalent placentals — such as occurred with successive invasions of South America from North America through the Cenozoic and with introduction of non-native placentals to Australia — marsupials have tended not to fare very well. Mostly, however, it probably is more accurate to view them as different rather than inferior. Marsupials are a highly successful and diverse group, and the range of their adaptations is nearly as broad as that of placentals. Only placental bats and whales lack some analogous group among the marsupials, and that fact probably is explainable by the nature of marsupial reproduction. (Both aerial and marine habitats would be awkward or impossible for pouch-young.)

Placental mammals have emphasized internal development, investing in an efficient mechanism for resource exchange, the placenta. In marsupials, however, internal development is limited. A rudimentary yolk sac placenta forms in most groups, but it is transitory. The emphasis of maternal care is on lactation. In mammals the total duration of maternal care (gestation plus lactation) tends to be proportional to body size. Interestingly, the period of care in marsupials and placentals is essentially the same. The difference between the groups is not the duration of care but the timing of birth during the period of maternal care. Marsupials are born early, placentals late. Maternal care in marsupials mostly is invested after parturition.

FAMILY DIDELPHIDAE — Opossums

Didelphids are confined to the Americas, with the greatest diversity being in South America. In many ways they resemble ancestral marsupials from the Cretaceous Period, and they have been called "living fossils." The teeth are rooted and heterodont, and all species have the primitive metatherian dental formula, 5/4, 1/1, 3/3, 4/4 = 50. The snout is pointed and the tail is more or less prehensile and partly naked. The hallux, or big toe, is clawless and apposable to the other toes. The marsupium is well developed in *Didelphis* but completely lacking in some other genera. There are 11 genera and 75 species in the family. The genus *Didelphis* includes three species, of which one, the Virginia opossum (*D. virginiana*), occurs in Colorado. Some older references, including Lechleitner (1969), used the name *Didelphis marsupialis* for this species.

Didelphis virginiana
VIRGINIA OPOSSUM

DESCRIPTION — About the size of a house cat, opossums have pointed snouts; naked, rounded ears; and long, scantily haired, prehensile tails. The fur is long, with coarse guard hairs and dark-tipped underfur. The color usually is gray

Photograph 4-1 Virginia opossum (Didelphis virginiana). *Photograph by Joseph Van Wormer.*

with a paler facial area, but varies considerably between individuals, from nearly black to quite pale. The nose pad is pink, the eyes dark, and the tail dark at the base, but becoming paler toward the tip. Measurements are: total length 650–1,020 mm; length of tail 250–400 mm; length of hindfoot 50–80 mm; length of ear 50–53 mm; weight 2–7 kg. The sexes are similar in appearance, although males usually are heavier than females. The feet are plantigrade with naked soles. The nasal bones are expanded at their posterior ends. The palate has several large vacuities. Skulls of older animals have prominent sagittal crests and lambdoidal (occipital) ridges. The cranium is small and the skull is constricted posterior to the postorbital process. The auditory bullae are incomplete.

NATURAL HISTORY — Opossums generally are secretive and nocturnal, and their presence may go undetected even in areas where they are fairly abundant. They use a variety of temporary shelters, including rocks, brush, hollow trees, woodpiles, and burrows of other animals. Radio-tracking and live-trapping studies indicate that opossums are highly transient. Except for females with litters of young, they rarely spend

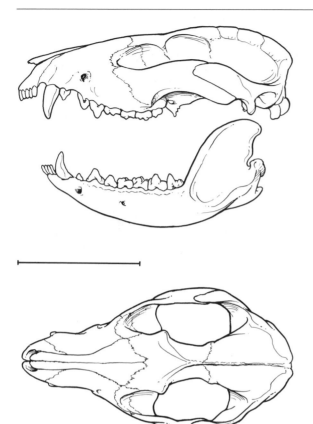

Figure 4-1 Dorsal and lateral views of the skull of the opossum (Didelphis virginiana). *Note the constricted cranium and the flared posterior ends of the nasal bones. Scale = 5 cm.*

more than a few days in one particular den (Fitch and Sandidge 1953, Fitch and Shirer 1970). Opossums may construct a nest of grass. Nesting materials are carried wrapped in the prehensile tail (L. Smith 1941).

Omnivorous and opportunistic, opossums eat almost any organic matter available. Insects, other invertebrates, and carrion appear to provide most of the animal protein in the diet (Lay 1942, Sandidge 1953). Amphibians, reptiles, birds, and small mammals are eaten, but some of these are taken as carrion. Opossums are resistant to the venom of crotalid snakes (rattlesnakes, copperheads, and water moccasins) and can feed on them with impunity (Werner and Vick 1977). Ber-

ries, apples, cherries, grapes, and corn and other grains may be eaten in considerable quantities when available.

Opossums are active at all times of the year, but in the northern portions of the range (including Colorado) activity is reduced during colder periods and they may not emerge from the den for several days at a time. In cold weather some foraging occurs during the day. Due to transiency, home ranges are highly variable and have been estimated from 5 to about 260 ha, depending on sex, age, locality of study, and method of calculation (Gillette 1980, Holmes and Sanderson 1965). Nightly foraging activities rarely exceed 500–700 m from the den site (Fitch and Shirer 1970, Gardner 1982).

Opossums are generally solitary except during the breeding season or when females are rearing young. Most encounters between adults are agonistic, marked by hisses, growls, or screeches, and fierce fighting. During the breeding season the female normally remains aggressive toward the male except for the brief periods when she is in estrus (McManus 1970, H. C. Reynolds 1952). Response of an opossum to being cornered varies from docility to bared teeth and profuse salivation. Opossums will bite if provoked and their large canines can be very effective. When pressed, the animals will often "play 'possum," rolling over on the side, with tongue protruding and eyes closed. The profound physiological changes of this catatonic period may last from less than a minute up to six hours (Wiedorn 1954). An effective defense against some predators, this behavior is maladaptive when the danger is a speeding vehicle, so opossums are traffic casualties in disproportionate numbers.

Opossums breed in late winter, spring, and summer in temperate areas. Two general peaks of breeding occur, one early in the season, and later, a longer period (Gardner 1982). Females are polyestrous, and five or six cycles can occur during the breeding season. The estrous cycle averages 29 days, with estrus limited to about 36 hr

Map 4-1 Distribution of the Virginia opossum (Didelphis virginianus) *in North America.*

Seidensticker et al. 1987) indicate that very few animals live beyond one year of age, and a population turnover period of less than three years is to be expected. The opossum is listed as a furbearer in Colorado. Hunters and trappers take opossums for both food and fur, although the pelt is of low value and very few are harvested in Colorado. Opossums are not seriously detrimental to humans despite an occasional raid on poultry pens and consumption of some cultivated crops and fruits. The animals support high parasite loads and may carry a number of infectious diseases including rabies and tularemia. McManus (1974), Gardner (1982), and Seidensticker et al. (1987) provided thorough reviews of natural history.

DISTRIBUTION IN COLORADO — In Colorado, opossums are most abundant in riparian situations bordering agricultural lands (Armstrong 1972, Beidleman 1952, Gruchy 1950, Lechleitner 1969). However, the species is extremely adaptable and can survive in marshes, forests, grasslands, agricultural and urban areas, and wooded or brushy canyon country. The subspecies in Colorado is *Didelphis virginiana virginiana.*

(Reynolds 1952). Females breed the first season following their birth and produce two litters a year in warmer parts of their range. The young, numbering up to 25 (average 6 to 9), are born after a gestation period of 12 to 13 days (Reynolds 1952). At birth, young average less than 1 g in weight and 20 mm in length. The relatively well-developed forelimbs drag the otherwise fetal newborn to the pouch. There it attaches itself to a teat where it remains for the next 50 to 65 days. The number of teats averages 13, so many of the offspring perish from lack of nourishment. By 80 days after birth the young can leave the pouch and cling to the mother's fur while she forages. By about 100 days they become independent of her and disperse. Seidensticker et al. (1987) summarized development.

A variety of animals (including coyotes, dogs, bobcats, and great horned owls) can capture opossums, but the species is not commonly reported in their diets. Population studies (summarized by

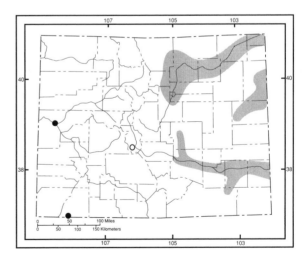

Map 4-2 Distribution of the Virginia opossum (Didelphis virginianus) *in Colorado. Solid circles represent introductions. Open circle represents isolated sighting.*

The opossum is a Neotropical mammal, but since Pleistocene times it has become firmly established in the United States (Ride 1964). In recent years it has extended its range to the north and west. Although museum specimens are few for the state, viable populations exist along the South Platte, Republican, and Arikaree rivers. Opossums have been observed near Orchard in Morgan County, and raccoon hunters in Weld County occasionally take them while hunting with dogs. Opossums are not uncommon in Denver. The status of the animal in the Arkansas drainage is poorly known, with a record from Bent County (Cary 1911) still the only one from that area. The population in the Grand Junction area is the result of introductions made in 1920, 1930, and 1940 (Armstrong 1972). This population does not appear to be significantly expanding its range. Reports of opossum sightings, road kills, and captures by trappers have increased in recent years, even in several mountainous areas of the state.

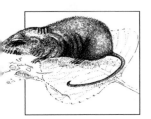

Chapter 5

Order: Insectivora

Insectivores — Moles, Shrews, and Allies

Insectivores are the ancestral group from which eutherian mammals evolved — "the trunk of the phylogenetic tree" — although many modern representatives are highly specialized, including shrews, moles, and hedgehogs. The predilection of several groups for feeding on insects gave rise to the ordinal name. There is no firm agreement on the classification of insectivores. Elephant shrews and tree shrews are both sometimes placed in their own separate orders (Findley 1967), and the latter sometimes are considered to be primates. Further, some authors (McKenna 1975; Stucky and McKenna, 1993) have elevated Insectivora to the level of grandorder, recognizing orders Erinaceomorpha and Soricomorpha, thus separating shrews and hedgehogs at the ordinal level.

Most insectivores are small, ranging from the pygmy and dwarf shrews (*Sorex hoyi* and *S. nanus*), which measure 80–90 mm in length and weigh 2 to 3 g, to about 600 mm in length for the tenrecs and African water shrews. Some hedgehogs may weigh up to 1.4 kg.

Characteristics common to North American insectivores include a small brain; specialized dentition; reduced eyes, a long, pointed snout; poorly developed auditory bullae; and the jugal reduced or absent, resulting in a weak or incomplete zygomatic arch. The pelage is composed of hairs all of the same type, each foot has five clawed digits, and the feet are plantigrade. The testes are usu-

ally abdominal or inguinal and a baculum has been reported in only a few taxa. The uterus is usually bicornuate with a single cervix and vagina. Insectivores have large olfactory bulbs and a well-developed sense of smell. A vomeronasal organ is present, as are a variety of scent-producing glands. Glandular secretions vary seasonally and may serve as signposts and as a means to facilitate encounters between solitary individuals (Holst 1985).

The order Insectivora includes about 60 genera and 379 species in 8 different families. Insectivores are present in Eurasia, Africa, Madagascar, North America, Central America, northern South America, and the West Indies. In Colorado, 2 families, 5 genera, and 10 species occur.

Key to the Families of the Order Insectivora Found in Colorado

1. Forefeet not spade-like; zygomatic arch absent; total teeth fewer than 36; teeth with brown tips . . . . Family Soricidae, p. 72

1' Forefeet spade-like; zygomatic arch present; total teeth 36; teeth without brown tips . . . . Family Talpidae, p. 89

FAMILY SORICIDAE — Shrews

Most shrews are very small mammals. None of the species in Colorado exceeds 175 mm in total length or 30 g in weight. Shrews are somewhat mouse-like in appearance but their snouts are longer and more pointed. Their eyes are small and their vision is poor. The olfactory sense is strong and hearing is acute, especially for high-frequency sounds. Shrews produce high-pitched twittering vocalizations, and some may echolocate. The tactile sense probably is well developed. The fur is short and dense with all the hairs of one kind. Colors vary from gray through brown to almost black, and there is little difference between the dorsal and ventral color on most species. The feet have five clawed digits. The tail is always haired; length varies with species. Skulls are relatively long and narrow without a zygomatic arch or auditory bullae. The teeth are tubercular and sectorial, well suited to a diet of small invertebrates. Homologies of teeth with those of other placentals are poorly understood. The first tooth on each side of the upper jaw is bicuspid, with a variable number of unicuspid teeth immediately behind. Unicuspid teeth are followed in turn by a variable number of teeth with three or more cusps. Teeth are rooted, and the bicuspids and unicuspids have brown tips.

Flank glands, located anterior to the hindlimbs, have been found in all species investigated (Holst 1985). These glands create a darker, moist-looking oval on the flanks. They are present in both sexes, and glandular activity correlates with reproduction, although patterns are not always clear.

Coloradan shrews are terrestrial. They typically live in shallow tunnels or form runways in the litter of the surface of the soil. Some species use the tunnels of other mammals such as moles or voles. Shrews seldom live much more than one year.

Shrews are active animals with high metabolic rates, so the animals must forage almost constantly, consuming one to two times their body weight in food every 24 hours. Their prodigious appetites cause them to take practically any available animal matter including small mammals, but mostly they rely on insects and other small invertebrates. Apparently, they are limited by the ability

and speed of their digestive tract to assimilate food. Foraging periods are brief, averaging 55 minutes in the European common shrew *Sorex araneus*, and are followed by periods of sleep that average 64 minutes. Foraging bouts are interrupted by rest periods of 5 to 10 minutes, which occur when the gut is full. During these brief rest periods, the shrew stands, moving its muzzle from side to side (Saariko and Hanski 1990).

There are about 20 genera and 265 species of shrews distributed on all continents except Australia. There are 4 genera and 10 species in Colorado. In some parts of the mountains as many as 5 species of shrews occur at a single locality. Identification of long-tailed shrews (genus *Sorex*) is difficult at best. An annotated key developed by Junge and Hoffmann (1981) may be of help. The evolution, systematics, and biogeography of the genus *Sorex* (George 1986*a*, 1988) and the genus *Blarina* (George et al. 1982) have been addressed recently.

Key to the Species of the Family Soricidae Found in Colorado

1. Total teeth 28 with three unicuspid teeth in each side of the upper jaw . . . . Desert Shrew — *Notiosorex crawfordi*, p. 88

1′ Total teeth more than 28 with more than three unicuspid teeth in each side of the upper jaw . . . 2

2. Total teeth 30 with four unicuspid teeth in each side of the upper jaw (the last upper unicuspid is tiny, not visible from the side but visible ventrally) . . . . Least Shrew — *Cryptotis parva*, p. 86

2′ Total teeth 32 with five unicuspid teeth in each side of the upper jaw (one or more of the unicuspid teeth may be tiny and difficult to see without use of hand lens or microscope) 3

3. Tail less than one third of body length, body stout . . . . Elliot's Short-tailed Shrew — *Blarina hylophaga*, p. 84

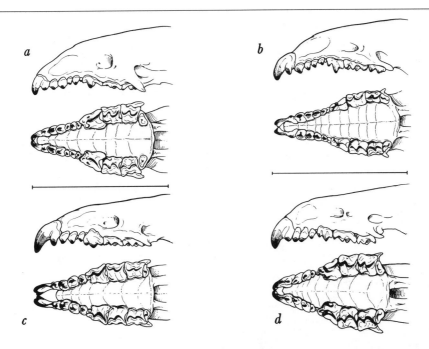

Figure 5-1 Ventral and lateral views of the upper jaws of shrews showing relative size and position of unicuspid teeth. A. montane shrew (Sorex monticolus); *B. masked shrew* (Sorex cinereus); *C. pygmy shrew* (Sorex hoyi); *D. least shrew* (Cryptotis parva). *Scale = 1 cm.*

3′ Tail greater than one third of body length; body rather slender . . . . Sorex 4

4. Third and fifth unicuspid teeth tiny and barely or not at all visible from side . . . .
. . . . Pygmy Shrew — *Sorex hoyi*, p. 75

4′ Third unicuspid tooth not especially tiny so four unicuspid teeth are visible from side 5

5. Size large for a shrew; total length over 130 mm; upperparts blackish gray; underparts pale to dark gray; hindfoot with conspicuous fringe of stiff hairs. . . . Water Shrew — *Sorex palustris*, p. 81

5′ Size small; total length less than 130 mm; upperparts brownish, never blackish gray; underparts brownish; hindfoot without fringe of stiff hairs 6

6. Third unicuspid conspicuously smaller than fourth (Fig. 5-1) 7

6′ Third unicuspid not conspicuously smaller than the fourth (Fig. 5-1) 8

7. Braincase with convex profile; foramen magnum relatively ventral, extending more into basioccipital than supraoccipital; occiput with rounded appearance when viewed from behind; hindfoot generally more than 11 mm; greatest length of skull generally more than 15 mm; total body length usually more than 100 mm . . . .
. . . . Montane Shrew — *Sorex monticolus*, p. 78

7′ Braincase with flattened profile; foramen magnum not relatively ventral, extending more dorsally into supraoccipital; occiput with shield-shaped profile when viewed from behind; hindfoot less than 11 mm; greatest length of skull usually less than 15 mm; total length generally less than 100 mm . . . .
. . . . Dwarf Shrew — *Sorex nanus*, p. 80

8. Feet and underparts whitish; skull with short, broad rostrum abruptly truncated anteriorly; maxillary breadth usually greater than 4.8 mm; teeth stout, molars as broad as long . . . .
. . . . Merriam's Shrew — *Sorex merriami*, p. 77

8′ Feet and underparts not whitish, only slightly paler than dorsum; skull with long, narrow rostrum not abruptly truncated anteriorly; maxillary breadth usually less than 4.6 mm; teeth no noticeably stout, molars longer than broad . . .
. . . . Masked Shrew — *Sorex cinereus*, p. 74**

Map 5-1 Distribution of the masked shrew (Sorex cinereus) *in North America.*

Photograph 5-1 Masked shrew (Sorex cinereus).

Sorex cinereus
MASKED SHREW

DESCRIPTION — The masked shrew is medium grayish to brownish, slightly paler on the ventral surface. The tail is indistinctly bicolored. Pelage is slightly paler in winter than in summer. Measurements are: total length 80–109 mm; length of tail 35–46 mm; length of hindfoot 11–12 mm; weight 3–6 g. Greatest length of skull is 14–16 mm. The third unicuspid is as large as or larger than the

fourth. This shrew is difficult to distinguish from the montane shrew without examining the teeth carefully.

NATURAL HISTORY — The most common shrew of Colorado's central mountains, the masked shrew occurs in moist habitats within the montane and subalpine forests of the state, especially in willow thickets and moist meadows. It extends eastward onto the plains in situations with lush vegetation and suitable moisture such as cat-tail marshes and cottonwood river bottoms. In general, the ecology of this species over much of its range is similar to that of the montane shrew (T. Clark 1973, A. Spencer and Pettus 1966) and they are frequently taken in the same habitat, although the montane shrew has a more restricted range than the masked shrew. Generally, masked shrews seem to be more abundant on the Eastern Slope

_____

**Sorex preblei*, reported recently from Colorado, is smaller but otherwise very similar; for comments on identification, see the account of Preble's shrew.

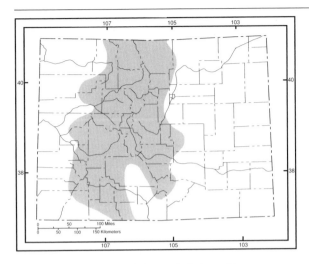

Map 5-2 Distribution of the masked shrew (Sorex cinereus) *in Colorado.*

and montane shrews are more abundant on the Western Slope (Armstrong 1972). The masked shrew is active at any time of day and at all times of year, but it leaves little sign of its presence. Masked shrews hunt above ground, among leaf litter, in burrows of their own making, or in those dug by other animals. Plant cover greater than 75 percent is preferred, and they are rarely found away from standing water (T. Clark 1973).

Food is mostly small invertebrates, especially insects. A captive individual readily ate grubs, mealworms, grasshoppers, and earthworms (Pokropus and Banta 1966). The masked shrew apparently reproduces throughout the warmer months of the year. Females may have several litters during the summer with 4 to 10 young per litter. The young become self-sufficient at about four weeks of age (Forsyth 1976). In Wyoming, litter size averaged 4.6 (range 3–7) (T. Clark 1973).

DISTRIBUTION IN COLORADO — The masked shrew occurs over much of the mountainous central portion of the state, and eastward onto the piedmont (Beidleman 1950). The elevational range is 1,500-3,350 m (5,000–11,000 ft). A single subspecies, *Sorex cinereus cinereus*, occurs in Colorado. The masked shrew was reported recently from Tama-

rack Ranch in Logan County (Samson et al. 1988). Specimens of long-tailed shrews from that area should be examined with great care and with the benefit of comparative material, as they may represent the closely related Hayden's shrew (*Sorex haydeni*), sometimes treated as a subspecies of *S. cinereus*. J. K. Jones (1964) reported *S. c. haydeni* from along the North Platte River in Nebraska; in Wyoming, Hayden's shrew apparently is restricted to the Black Hills (T. Clark and Stromberg 1987). Junge and Hoffmann (1981) provided illustrated keys to distinguish the species.

Sorex hoyi
PYGMY SHREW

DESCRIPTION — Well named, the pygmy shrew is very small. The pelage in Colorado specimens is dark brown shading to slightly paler on the venter. In other populations, color varies from reddish brown to gray-brown. The tail is indistinctly bicolored and relatively short. Measurements of Colorado and Wyoming specimens (L. N. Brown 1966, Armstrong 1972) are: total length 70–90 mm; length of tail 25–31 mm; length of hindfoot 9–11 mm; weight 2–5 g. Greatest length of skull is under 16 mm for these Rocky Mountain specimens. The skull is narrow and flattened, similar to other small species of *Sorex*. The third unicuspid tooth has a flattened disc-like shape, and the fifth unicuspid is minute; both are barely or not at all visible from the side, but may be seen in a ventral view. The dentition of *S. hoyi*, its small size, shorter tail, and normally darker color help to distinguish it from the montane shrew. Some authors (Long 1974) placed this species in the genus *Microsorex*; however, Diersing (1980) placed it in the genus *Sorex*, as originally described by S. F. Baird in 1858.

NATURAL HISTORY —The pygmy shrew apparently is able to survive under a variety of ecological conditions. It has been captured in subalpine forests (spruce, fir, and lodgepole pine), clear-cut and selectively logged forests, forest-meadow edges, boggy meadows, willow thickets, aspen-fir forests, and subalpine parklands (DeMott and Lindsey

Map 5-3 Distribution of the pygmy shrew (Sorex hoyi) in North America.

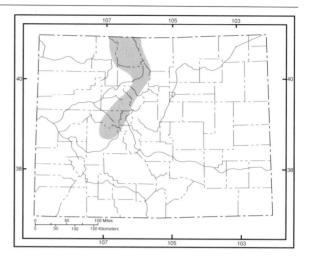

Map 5-4 Distribution of the pygmy shrew (Sorex hoyi) in Colorado.

1975, Pettus and Lechleitner 1963, A. Spencer and Pettus 1966, T. Vaughan 1969). In more northern parts of its range this shrew has been reported from sandy areas and even cultivated fields. In Wisconsin, pygmy shrews move from wet marshy areas to peripheral, drier areas as populations build up in late summer (Long 1972).

Behavior of the pygmy shrew is poorly known. It builds runways under stumps, fallen logs, and litter and has been observed to build nests in captivity. The animals are active both day and night, and, like other shrews, prey on a variety of small invertebrates and carrion of vertebrates including mice and other shrews. One captive shrew ate 11 g of food over a two-day period. As other members of the genus, the pygmy shrew probably eats one to two times its weight daily, with alternating periods of foraging and sleeping.

Pygmy shrews breed in the warmer months, with up to eight young reported from a Colorado specimen (DeMott and Lindsey 1975). There are no re-

ports of more than one litter per year in this species. The low reproductive rate combined with the difficulty of capturing these animals may explain the lack of data on the species (Long 1974).

Data on populations are scarce. Manville (1949) estimated 0.52 animals per hectare in Michigan. A. Spencer and Pettus (1966) took over 40 specimens from their 25-ha study area in Colorado over a 4-year period.

DISTRIBUTION IN COLORADO — Until 1961 this shrew was not known in the Rocky Mountains south of Montana. In that year the first specimens from Colorado were taken around the edge of a small sphagnum bog in coniferous forest at 2,950 m (9,700 ft), west of Fort Collins (Pettus and Lechleitner 1963). The pygmy shrew has since been captured on Rabbit Ears Pass in western Grand County (T. Vaughan 1969) and near Gothic in Gunnison County (DeMott and Lindsey 1975). The latter record extended the known range of the species 145 km south. It is possible that the pygmy shrew occupies suitable habitat throughout the mountains of central Colorado; however, populations may be discontinuous relicts remaining from glacial times. All captures have been at elevations above 2,900 m (9,600 ft).

One subspecies, *Sorex hoyi montanus*, occurs in Colorado.

Photograph by Claude Steelman/Wildshots.

Photograph 5-2 Merriam's shrew (Sorex merriami).

Sorex merriami
MERRIAM'S SHREW

DESCRIPTION — Merriam's shrew is medium-sized and grayish with whitish feet and underparts. The tail is conspicuously bicolored and sparsely haired. Measurements are: total length 88–107 mm; length of tail 33–42 mm; length of hindfoot 11–13 mm; weight 4–7 g. Greatest length of skull is 16–18 mm. The skull has a short, broad rostrum, abruptly truncated anteriorly, with the braincase flattened and not much higher than the rostrum. The dentition is stout; the second unicuspid is the largest and the third unicuspid larger than the fourth.

NATURAL HISTORY — Little is known of the habits of this shrew anywhere in its range and virtually nothing is known of them in Colorado. *Sorex merriami* occupies drier habitats than other shrews in the state, particularly sagebrush of semidesert shrublands. The species has also been captured in montane shrublands, piñon-juniper woodlands, mixed montane and subalpine forests, and grasslands. The largest numbers of this species in Colorado have been captured in montane shrublands in the Arkansas River drainage of Fremont and Custer counties (Armstrong et al. 1973).

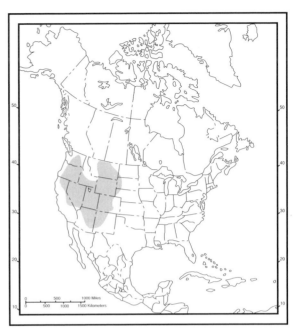

Map 5-5 Distribution of Merriam's shrew (Sorex merriami) in North America.

Merriam's shrews frequently use burrows and runways of other mammals, especially sagebrush voles (*Lemmiscus*) and other arvicolines (Armstrong and Jones 1971). Diet includes spiders, bee-

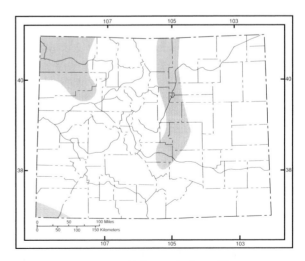

Map 5-6 Distribution of Merriam's shrew (Sorex merriami) in Colorado.

tles, caterpillars, and other small invertebrates. Flank glands are prominent on the males during the breeding season and are thought to be associated with mate attraction. Breeding occurs during the spring and early summer, and females have five to seven young. It is not known whether the species has one or two litters a year (M. L. Johnson and Clanton 1954).

DISTRIBUTION IN COLORADO — Specimens of Merriam's shrew in Colorado have generally come from elevations between 1,370 and 2,920 m (4,500–9,600 ft) and are summarized by Armstrong (1972). Subsequent specimens have been reported for El Paso, Gunnison, Rio Blanco, and Garfield counties (Diersing and Hoffmeister 1977, Finley et al. 1976, A. Spencer 1975). These data suggest a broad distribution over much of the lower foothills and mountains of the state. As with several other shrew species, Merriam's shrew is probably more common and widespread in Colorado than once thought. One subspecies, *Sorex merriami leucogenys*, occurs in the state. The species was named for C. Hart Merriam, who served as first Chief of the U.S. Biological Survey (now the U.S. Fish and Wildlife Service) and first president of the American Society of Mammalogists, and was instrumental in the establishment of the Wildlife Society.

Sorex monticolus
MONTANE SHREW

DESCRIPTION — The montane shrew is stout-bodied and brown with a relatively long tail. It is the largest of the brown shrews (*S. monticolus, S. cinereus, S. nanus, S. hoyi*) of the mountainous areas of the state, although only slightly larger than the masked shrew (*S. cinereus*). Dorsal color is medium to dark brown, becoming slightly paler on the venter. The tail is bicolored but not conspicuously so. Measurements are: total length 90–125 mm; length of tail 35–50 mm; length of hindfoot 10–14 mm; weight 4–7 g. The skull varies in total length from 15 to 17 mm. The braincase is rounded or convex in profile, and the foramen magnum extends farther into the basioccipital

Photograph 5-3 Montane Shrew (Sorex monticolus).

than into the supraoccipital. The third unicuspid is smaller than the fourth, as in the smaller, slimmer, dwarf shrew (*S. nanus*). The teeth are more robust than in the latter species. In Colorado this shrew can also be confused with the masked shrew, which it greatly resembles in color and general size. However, the teeth of the masked shrew are characterized by a third unicuspid as large as the fourth. Flank glands are apparent, especially in males, from January through the breeding season. Darker winter pelage and paler summer pelage result from spring and fall molts (Clothier 1955).

NATURAL HISTORY — The montane shrew is most frequently associated with the mesic habitats of aspen stands, willow thickets, moist openings in subalpine forests, and riparian communities. Marshy and clear cut areas in the subalpine forest are also used, as is the case for the ecologically similar and sympatric masked shrew (A. Spencer and Pettus 1966). In South Park, this species and *S. cinereus* are commonly taken around beaver ponds and similarly flooded lowlands and boggy areas at the margin of ponderosa-bristlecone pine forest. The montane shrew has also been collected in relatively dry subalpine meadow and coniferous forest edge (T. Vaughan 1969), in streamside communities (O. Williams 1955*a*), and in alpine rockslide areas and alpine bogs (L. N. Brown 1967*b*). In moist forested areas the animal lives in humus or under downed and rotting

Map 5-7 Distribution of the montane shrew (Sorex monticolus) *in North America.*

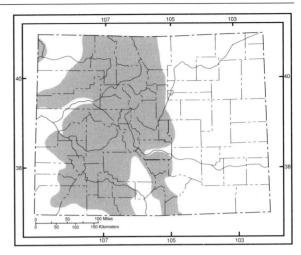

Map 5-8 Distribution of the montane shrew (Sorex monticolus) *in Colorado.*

timber. Montane shrews are greatly affected by temporal variation in ground cover. Dense herbaceous ground cover or woody ground cover such as logs and shrubs are preferred (Belk et al. 1990). When herbaceous growth declines at the end of summer, these animals move to more mesic, adjacent aspen stands where dense cover persists. In mesic habitats along streams the species has been taken at elevations as low as 2,075 m (6,800 ft) in the Arkansas River drainage (Armstrong et al. 1973). Armstrong (1977) presented information on habitat preferences of the largely sympatric masked shrew (*S. cinereus*) in Colorado.

Montane shrews are active all year. During the winter months they forage under snow cover. Stomach contents consist primarily of insects (both adult and larvae), earthworms, other invertebrates, and some plant material (Clothier 1955). As in other shrews, alternating hour-long bouts of foraging and sleeping probably occur. Shorter rest periods may be interspersed with activity and apparently serve to allow passage of

food in a full digestive tract (Saariko and Hanski 1990). The montane shrew does not construct elaborate tunnels or burrows but utilizes runs of other small mammals. It constructs a nest of grasses and leaves. In captivity the animals are solitary and tend to avoid one another. Intruders elicit agonistic behavior and nest defense (Eisenberg 1964). The species has a high level of activity both day and night (Ingles 1960) but seems to fare well in captivity.

Montane shrews breed from April through August in the Rocky Mountains; more than one litter per year has been reported in Montana. In Wyoming, pregnant females were first seen in mid-June (T. Clark 1973). Gestation lasts 20 to 22 days and the young are born blind and naked. An average of six young are produced per litter, with a range of two to nine. A nest in Montana consisted of a ball of dried grass about 10 cm in diameter with no definite nest cavity (Clothier 1955). Although the young develop rapidly, females apparently do not breed until the summer after their birth.

In a given area the montane shrew may be abundant one year but scarce in a subsequent year. A. Spencer and Pettus (1966) indicated that populations of montane and masked shrews varied synchronously in an area west of Fort Collins, suggesting that the two species were being affected either by similar environmental conditions or by each other. In California, home ranges were 260 to 6,758 m^2 , with the longest axis 14 to 59 m (Ingles 1961). The size, shape, and part of the home range used seems to vary with season and age; mature animals have larger home ranges than do immatures.

DISTRIBUTION IN COLORADO — The montane shrew is found over much of western North America in coniferous forests and mountainous areas (Hawes 1977). In Colorado the species has been taken from a variety of habitats throughout the foothills and mountains, at elevations from 1,620 to 3,500 m (5,300–11,500 ft). One subspecies, *Sorex monticolus obscurus*, occurs in Colorado. There has been considerable confusion regarding the taxonomy of this species. Because of great similarities between *Sorex vagrans* and *Sorex obscurus*, Findley (1955) lumped them as *Sorex vagrans*. However, Hennings and Hoffmann (1977) showed that these shrews are specifically distinct and that *obscurus* is a subspecies of *S. monticolus*. Coloradan montane shrews, *S. monticolus obscurus*, may be referred to in earlier literature as *S. obscurus* or *S. vagrans*, under the common names wandering or vagrant shrew.

Sorex nanus
DWARF SHREW

DESCRIPTION — Colorado's smallest-bodied mammal, the dwarf shrew is a delicate animal with a relatively long tail. Although total length of the pygmy shrew is less, its body length is greater. The color is generally medium brown dorsally merging to a grayer color ventrally. The tail is indistinctly bicolored. Winter pelage is paler and grayer. Measurements are: total length 82–105 mm; length of tail 27–45 mm; length of hindfoot 10–11 mm; weight 1.8–3.2 g. The skull is slim and delicate, with a braincase that appears flattened when viewed from the side. The foramen magnum is dorsally placed, extending farther into the

Photograph by Donald L. Pattie

Photograph 5-4 Dwarf shrew (Sorex nanus).

supraoccipital than into the basioccipital. The condylobasal length is less than 15 mm. The third unicuspid is smaller than the fourth but is visible from the side. The fifth unicuspid is also small. A diagnostic dental measurement for the dwarf shrew is that the distance from the posterior border of the alveolus of the fifth unicuspid to the anterior margin of the alveolus of the incisor ranges between 1.8 and 2.4 mm (A. Spencer 1966). This measurement can be taken on fluid-preserved specimens by slitting the cheek and displacing the proboscis. This measurement and the size of the third unicuspid allow distinction of the dwarf shrew from similar species.

NATURAL HISTORY — Although the type specimen of the dwarf shrew is from Estes Park, Larimer County, we know very little about the ecology, behavior, or reproductive cycles of this species in Colorado. The animal has been taken from a variety of habitats in the Southern Rocky Mountains, ranging from the edges of alpine and subalpine rockslides to spruce-fir bogs; coniferous forest; sedge marsh; dry, brushy hillsides; and open woodland. In Colorado the species has not been captured at low elevations on either side of the mountains, but in South Dakota it has been found in grasslands (Cinq-Mars et al. 1979). The dwarf shrew apparently can tolerate arid to semiarid conditions as captures have been made

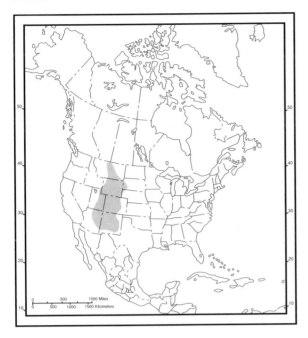

Map 5-9 Distribution of the dwarf shrew (Sorex nanus) *in North America.*

up to 0.8 km (0.5 mile) from water sources. The wide diversity of habitats occupied suggests that the animal is probably more widely distributed than records indicate.

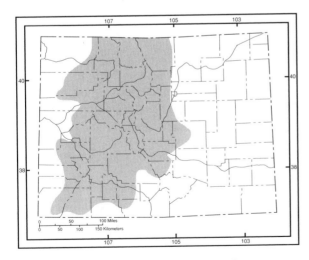

Map 5-10 Distribution of the dwarf shrew (Sorex nanus) *in Colorado.*

In Montana, breeding occurs in June and July in alpine and subalpine areas (R. Hoffmann and Owen 1980) and probably earlier at lower elevations. A number of pregnant, lactating females have been taken, indicating that second litters are common, at least in some areas. The average number of embryos varies from four to eight. Juvenile males may reach breeding condition the summer of their birth, but there is no evidence for such early sexual maturity in females. A. Spencer and Pettus (1966) observed captive dwarf shrews feeding on carrion of vertebrates as well as insects and spiders.

DISTRIBUTION IN COLORADO — The dwarf shrew is known from the Southern Rocky Mountains at elevations above 1,680 m (5,500 ft). Two collections from Colorado represent some of the greatest numbers of these animals ever captured. Armstrong et al. (1973) reported a total of 81 dwarf shrews collected at elevations of 1,600 to 3,050 m (5,300–10,000 ft) in the Arkansas River drainage. A. Spencer and Pettus (1966) captured over two dozen specimens at their Larimer County study area. In south-central Wyoming, L. N. Brown (1967) captured 25 of the animals in subalpine and alpine areas of the Medicine Bow Mountains. These reports indicate that in suitable locations this tiny mammal may be quite common. Hoffmeister (1967) and Spencer (1975) have captured the dwarf shrew at Mesa Verde and Durango. The dwarf shrew is monotypic; subspecies are not recognized.

Sorex palustris
WATER SHREW

DESCRIPTION — The water shrew is a beautiful, distinctive mammal, a large dark shrew with a long tail. The color is blackish gray above and silvery gray below. The tail is distinctly bicolored and about the same length as the body. There is a conspicuous fringe of stiff hairs along the toes and margin of the relatively large hindfeet. The sexes are similar in size and coloration although mature males generally weigh more than females. There are two molts per year, but little difference

Photograph by J. Perley Fitzgerald.

Photograph 5-5 Water shrew (Sorex palustris).

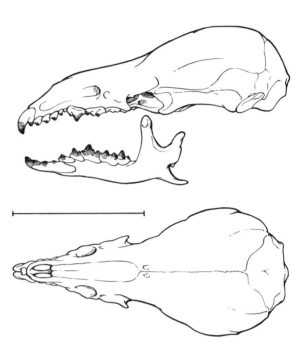

Figure 5-2 Dorsal and lateral views of the skull of the water shrew (Sorex palustris). *Scale = 1 cm.*

in color or texture between them. Measurements are: total length 140–175 mm; length of tail 63–80 mm; length of hindfoot 18–21 mm; weight 13–19 g, four times the size of the diminutive pygmy shrew. The skull is stout and long for a shrew of the genus *Sorex*, with greatest length up to 22 mm. There are five unicuspid teeth in each side of the upper jaw, with the fifth much smaller than the others but still visible in a lateral view. The third unicuspid is smaller than the fourth, a trait shared with *S. monticolus* and *S. nanus*.

NATURAL HISTORY — Restricted to riparian ecosystems, this is one of the better studied soricids (Beneski and Stinson). The study by Conaway (1952) in Montana remains the most detailed field investigation of the species to date. The water shrew has several morphological adaptations to semiaquatic life and it is seldom seen or captured far from water. The animal is not uncommon along the banks of rivers and streams (especially in the tangle of roots under cutbanks), beside ponds and lakes, or in marshes in forested areas. It swims well both on top of and under the water. While under water, tiny air bubbles become trapped in the short, velvety fur, giving it a silvery appearance while keeping the animal dry. Reports by anglers of a mouse-like animal swimming under the water are undoubtedly sightings of this shrew. The stiff hairs on the hindfeet allow

the animal to race across the surface of water for short distances without breaking the surface.

The water shrew feeds mainly on aquatic insects, but other insects, small fish, and other animal matter may be eaten. Green plant material is also consumed (T. Clark 1973). Apparently this animal is capable of capturing smaller fish although they are not an important part of the diet. The water shrew remains active all winter and forages along stream banks under the protective cover of ice and snow (Conaway 1952).

Water shrews have two periods of intense activity, one between sunset and 2300 hours (11 P.M.) and another shortly before sunrise. Captive animals dig short tunnels and make nests from available materials. Nests average 8 cm in diameter. Excess food is cached under logs. Individual water

The animals reproduce from January through August in Montana, and females have several litters per year (Conaway 1952). The number of young varies from about five to seven. Ovulation is thought to be induced by copulation. The gestation period is about three weeks. Males apparently are not sexually active during the season of their birth, but a few females may breed in their first summer.

DISTRIBUTION IN COLORADO — In Colorado the water shrew is found in mountainous areas in the western two-thirds of the state from 1,800 to 3,050 m (6,000–10,000 ft) in elevation (Armstrong 1972). *Sorex palustris navigator* is the sole subspecies in Colorado.

Sorex preblei
PREBLE'S SHREW

DESCRIPTION — This tiny shrew is generally similar to the masked shrew, but smaller. Measurements of the only Coloradan specimen are: total length 81 mm; length of tail 30 mm; length of hindfoot 10 mm; condylobasal length 14.6 mm, maxillary breadth 3.8 mm (Long and Hoffmann 1992); average weight of three individuals from Montana was 2.8 g (R. Hoffmann et al. 1969).

NATURAL HISTORY — Virtually nothing is known of the natural history of this species anywhere in its range. The animals are known from the Columbia Plateau and northern Great Basin, extending eastward to Montana and Wyoming. The recent report from Colorado extended the known range by over 500 km, from western Utah. Habitats of capture generally are semiarid shrublands, including sagebrush, grasslands, alpine tundra, and sagebrush openings in subalpine forest (R. Hoffmann and Fisher 1978). The meager literature on this species was reviewed by Cornely et al. (1992).

DISTRIBUTION IN COLORADO — Preble's shrew was reported in Colorado on the basis of a single specimen captured in oakbrush on the South Rim of the Black Canyon of the Gunnison, Montrose County, in 1966 (Long and Hoffmann

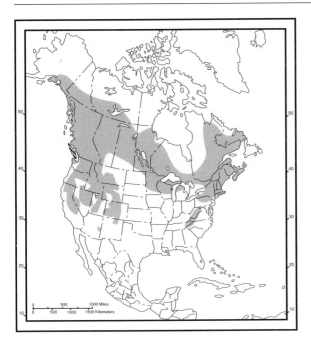

Map 5-11 Distribution of the water shrew (Sorex palustris) *in North America.*

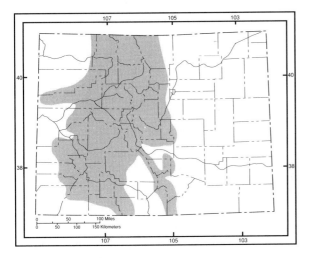

Map 5-12 Distribution of the water shrew (Sorex palustris) *in Colorado.*

shrews are solitary and aggressive toward others of the species in captive colonies (Sorenson 1962).

Map 5-13 *Distribution of Preble's shrew* (Sorex preblei) *in North America.*

Photograph by R. B. Forbes.

Photograph 5-6 Elliot's short-tailed shrew (Blarina hylophaga).

1992). In the absence of information on morphological variation of the species in this part of its range, we have not included Preble's shrew in the key to Coloradan shrews, referring the reader instead to illustrated keys provided by Junge and Hoffmann (1981). Any tiny, long-tailed shrew from Colorado with the third unicuspid tooth obviously larger than the fourth should be submitted to a specialist for identification.

Blarina hylophaga
ELLIOT'S SHORT-TAILED SHREW

DESCRIPTION — This stout-bodied shrew has a tail less than one-third the length of the body. The color varies from silvery gray through brown to almost black and lacks significant countershading. Ear openings are large but hidden by fur. The tiny eyes are apparently of little use. The vibrissae on the snout are well developed. The paired flank glands are well concealed by fur, unlike the con-

spicuous scent glands of the desert shrew. In addition to flank glands, *Blarina* has large ventral glands on the midline of the abdomen (O. Pearson 1946). Males are heavier than females and have better developed scent glands. The animal's range in Colorado overlaps that of the least shrew, but *Blarina* is readily distinguished from *Cryptotis* by its heavy build, larger size, and lack of significant countershading. Measurements are: total length 95–135 mm; length of tail 17–30 mm; length of hindfoot 11–17 mm; weight 15–30 g. The skull is quite stout and angular for a shrew and varies from 18 to 25 mm in length. The teeth are robust with dark brown tips, but as the animal ages the brown tips may be worn away. There are five unicuspid teeth in each side of the upper jaw. The fifth is smaller than the others but readily visible from the side.

NATURAL HISTORY — Considerable information exists on the life history of the closely related *B. brevicauda* of the Midwest (George 1986*b*; I. Martin 1980, 1981, 1983; O. Pearson 1944; Pruitt 1953; Randolph 1973; Tomasi 1978, 1979). Due to a dearth of information on the newly recognized *B. hylophaga*, we draw on this body of literature, although the extent to which these studies characterize Elliot's short-tailed shrew is not known.

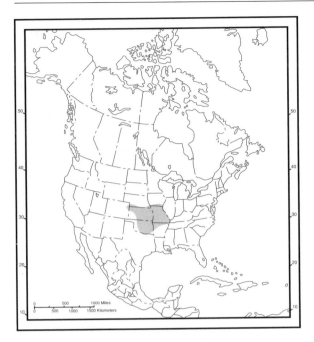

Map 5-14 Distribution of Elliot's short-tailed shrew (Blarina hylophaga) *in North America. After George et al. (1982).*

Blarina is most common in forests (the specific name *hylophaga* translates to "feeding in the woods") and moist brushy areas, and less common in fields, meadows, and marshes. In the eastern portion of its range it may be found in both coniferous and deciduous forests, but on the Great Plains it is most common in riparian situations with cottonwoods or in rank grasses and weeds along roadsides and irrigation ditches. *B. hylophaga* may be more dependent on mesic environments with mulch for burrowing than the least shrew (*Cryptotis parva*), which tolerates more arid environments and shallower soils (Choate and Fleharty 1973). Scarcity of short-tailed shrews in Colorado may be linked to aridity and lack of herbaceous cover in bottomlands of the South Platte and Republican river systems because of overgrazing by livestock.

The diet consists mostly of insects, snails, earthworms and other small invertebrates but is known to include vertebrates (salamanders, snakes, birds, and small rodents). Short-tailed shrews are aided in killing such large prey by a toxic secretion from the submaxillary glands that enters the wounds made by its initial bites (Tomasi 1978). Humans who have been bitten have reported intense pain and swelling at the site of the bite (O. Pearson 1942). The venom closely resembles those of elapid snakes (cobras and coral snakes).

Blarina digs its own tunnels under surface litter or in loose soil, or utilizes burrows of other mammals. Runways may be as much as 50 cm below the ground surface. The animal makes a nest from shredded grasses, leaves, other plant material, or even the fur of voles. The nest has several openings. Nests are most often under decaying logs, old hay bales, or similar surface structures or in deeper burrow systems. Captive behavior studies of *B. brevicauda* indicate that they are solitary and highly territorial (I. Martin 1981). Territories range in size from 300 to over 4,000 m², depending on habitat. Total daily activity is highly correlated with mean ambient temperature (I. Martin 1983). Daily activity out of the nest is 7 to 31 percent. Shaking or shivering occurs upon awakening, probably helping to raise body temperature. Temperature extremes of summer days and winter nights are avoided.

The breeding season is from late February to October. Adult females have one or two litters of 3 to 10 young (average 5 to 7). The gestation period is about 22 days (W. Hamilton 1929, O. Pearson 1944). The young are able to leave the nest by about 30 days of age. Maturity is reached in three months. In Nebraska, *B. brevicauda* breeds once in the spring and once in the fall (J. K. Jones 1964).

Although other shrews have been reported to eat their weight in food daily, *Blarina* normally eats about one-half of that amount. Periods of activity are interspersed with periods of lower metabolic output, possibly allowing these animals to survive in cold climates without meeting the energy demands faced by other shrews (Martinsen 1969,

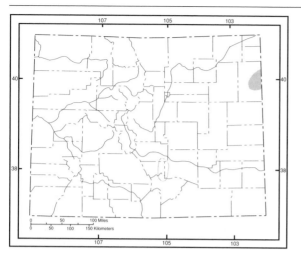

Map 5-15 Distribution of Elliot's short-tailed shrew (Blarina hylophaga) *in Colorado.*

Photograph 5-7 Least shrew (Cryptotis parva).

Randolph 1973). Known predators include owls, hawks, house cats, foxes, reptiles, and fish.

DISTRIBUTION IN COLORADO — Elliot's short-tailed shrew occurs on the southern Great Plains from southern Nebraska and southern Iowa, through Oklahoma and Kansas, and into Missouri and northwestern Arkansas. The species is known in Colorado only from specimens taken by J. K. Jones and Loomis (1954) along the Republican River one mile east of Laird in Yuma County. *Blarina hylophaga* is monotypic. Recent systematic studies of the genus *Blarina* have assigned Colorado's representative to the species *B. hylophaga.* Prior to this, *B. brevicauda* was thought to range westward to North Dakota, South Dakota, Nebraska, Colorado, Oklahoma, and Texas. Now three species are recognized, *B. hylophaga* at mid-latitudes in the west, *B. brevicauda* at northern latitudes, and *B. carolinensis* at southern latitudes (George 1986b; George et al. 1981, 1982).

Cryptotis parva
LEAST SHREW

DESCRIPTION — The least shrew is small, with a long pointed snout and a short tail. The color varies from brown to grayish brown, often slightly darker on the back than on the belly. The ear openings are large but hidden by fur. The limbs and feet are small. Measurements are: total length 70–100 mm; length of tail 12–22 mm; length of hindfoot 9–13 mm; weight 3–5 g. The skull is delicate, but higher and broader than in *Sorex.* Greatest length of skull ranges from 14 to 16 mm. The teeth are brown tipped. There are four unicuspid teeth in each side of the upper jaw, each of them slightly smaller than the one in front. The last unicuspid is minute and rarely visible from the side. Students often mistake the skull of this shrew with that of *Notiosorex crawfordi,* failing to notice the last small unicuspid tooth. Externally the two species may also be confused unless one looks for the conspicuous ears, heavier tail, and grayish color of the desert shrew.

NATURAL HISTORY — The least shrew inhabits a variety of habitats, but it seems to occur most often in grassy, weedy, or brushy areas that sometimes are quite dry. In Colorado, the species has been taken in the following habitats: shortgrass prairie (Marti 1972), old field communities (O. Williams and McArthur 1972), marshy areas (Beidleman and Remington 1955, Lechleitner 1964, O. Williams and McArthur 1972), and riparian woodland (Choate and Reed 1988; Fitzgerald, unpublished). Occasionally they are taken from beehives, window wells, basements, and garages

Map 5-16 *Distribution of the least shrew* (Cryptotis parva) *in North America.*

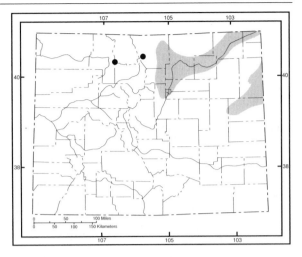

Map 5-17 *Distribution of the least shrew* (Cryptotis parva) *in Colorado.*

in suburban areas. The animals may construct burrows and runways in leaf litter or along the soil surface or may utilize runways of other animals. When digging, least shrews root with the nose while using the front and hindfeet to remove dirt. Nests are made of loosely piled grass or leaves and are 8 to 15 cm around. Latrines are frequently located near nests. Least shrews are relatively gregarious with up to 31 individuals reported in communal nests (McCarley 1959). Such behavior conserves heat. The least shrew is most active at night but may forage at all hours. When fed they may sleep for considerable periods of time.

Females have an aural gland, located in front of and below the ear, which seems to inform males of their reproductive condition (Kivett and Mock 1980). Least shrews appear to be induced ovulators. Mating pairs form a "lock" or "tie" and copulation may last up to 40 min (Kivett and Mock 1980). Least shrews probably breed from March to November in the northern parts of their range and year around farther south.

Choate (1970) suggested that most breeding was in spring and summer. More than one litter may be born per year, with litter size ranging from three to seven. Gestation takes 21 to 23 days. Young are born blind and hairless. By day 14 the eyes open; young are close to adult size by 30 days of age. Weaning apparently occurs about 21 to 23 days postpartum (Conaway 1958).

Food habits are similar to those of other shrews and include insects, other arthropods, and earthworms. In captivity the animals have been reported to kill and eat leopard frogs. Food hoarding behavior, especially by females, is well documented (Formanowicz et al. 1989). Owls, skunks, foxes, and snakes of several species prey on least shrews. Remains of least shrews found in long-eared and barn owl pellets were instrumental in documenting the first record for Weld County (Marti 1972). Few detailed studies have been made on this species, and its biology is poorly understood in Colorado. Whitaker (1974) summarized the general literature on the least shrew.

DISTRIBUTION IN COLORADO — Colorado marks the western edge of the distribution of the least shrew. The species occurs along the South Platte and Republican drainages in northeastern Colorado and is not rare on the Colorado Piedmont along the northern Front Range. It has been reported recently from southeastern Colorado, taken in riparian habitat in Baca County (Choate and Reed 1988). A single subspecies, *Cryptotis parva parva* (Say), occurs in Colorado.

Photograph 5-8 Desert shrew (Notiosorex crawfordi).

Notiosorex crawfordi
DESERT SHREW

DESCRIPTION — This species is a small, slender shrew with a tail less than one-third the total length. The pinnae are quite conspicuous in contrast to those of many other soricids. Color varies from silvery gray to a darker brownish gray, with the undersides slightly paler. Juveniles are often paler than adults. Measurements are: total length 77–93 mm; length of tail 24–32 mm; length of hindfoot 9–11 mm; length of ear 7–8 mm; weight 4–6 g. The skull is relatively long and narrow, with the greatest length generally exceeding 16 mm. The cranium is flattened; the braincase is only slightly elevated from the rostrum. Flank glands are conspicuous, especially in mature males. The glands are usually marked by a halo-like ring of hair or thinned pelage.

NATURAL HISTORY — The desert shrew occupies various habitats in arid and semiarid regions of southwestern North America. Most often it occurs in semidesert shrublands but it has also been reported from riparian woodland, grasslands, piñon-juniper woodlands, piñon–ponderosa pine stands, and dry, rocky areas.

The desert shrew constructs a nest of leaves, bark, or grass under surface debris such as plant litter, building materials, trash, and car bodies. Nests are variable in size, ranging from 50 to over 150 mm in diameter. The species is often reported to occupy woodrat dens, including those of *Neotoma micropus* and *N. albigula* (Brach 1969, Hoffmeister and Goodpaster 1962, Preston and Martin 1963).

There are conflicting data on the degree of burrowing activity shown by this species. In certain situations it may use fissures and cracks in the ground for cover and passageways. Armstrong (1972) noted that behavioral observations reported by Pokropus and Banta (1966) for *Cryptotis parva* actually apply to the desert shrew. Movements appear erratic and nervous, and while foraging the shrew may utilize runways of other small animals. Desert shrews apparently are not as agonistic toward conspecifics as are some other soricids, and if food is abundant they can be maintained together in captivity without much conflict.

Reproduction occurs as early as April in Arizona (Turkowski and Brown 1969) and as late as mid-November in Oklahoma (R. Baker and Spencer 1965), and varies with locality. The gestation period and number of litters per year are unknown. Litter size ranges from three to five. Young are naked and blind at birth. By 3 days they have a fine covering of hair and by 11 days are completely furred. The animals are adult size in less than 90 days (Hoffmeister and Goodpaster 1962).

Foods eaten include juvenile and adult insects of various kinds, such as moths, beetles, crickets, grasshoppers, and cockroaches; and carrion or fresh-killed mammals, birds, and reptiles; but not live rodents, scorpions, or earthworms (Hoffmeister and Goodpaster 1962). The animals apparently can survive without free water but will drink when water is available. Fecal material is fre-

Map 5-18 Distribution of the desert shrew (Notiosorex crawfordi) *in North America.*

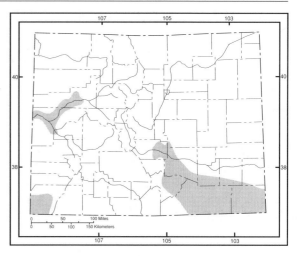

Map 5-19 Distribution of the desert shrew (Notiosorex crawfordi) *in Colorado.*

quently deposited at regularly used defecation stations, often on objects elevated from their surroundings. The significance of marking behavior is not known.

No data exist on the population dynamics of the species; however, it is unlikely that animals live much more than one year. Barn owls and great horned owls prey on desert shrews. Armstrong and Jones (1972) reviewed the literature on the species.

DISTRIBUTION IN COLORADO — The desert shrew has been documented from southeastern, southwestern, and west-central parts of the state. The northernmost record of the species is of an animal captured in a pitfall in a juniper woodland near Rifle (Caire and Finley 1977). A single specimen has been reported from Mesa Verde National Park, Montezuma County (C. L. Douglas 1967). In southeastern Colorado the species has been collected from Otero (Finley 1954), Fremont (Armstrong et al. 1973), and Baca and Huerfano counties (Armstrong 1972). Elevations

of capture range from 1,280 m (4,200 ft) in Otero County to 2,075 m (6,800 ft) in Fremont County. The species is apparently not as rare as once suspected, and populations probably exist at moderate elevations on either side of the mountains from the Grand Valley in western Colorado to at least as far north as Monument Divide along the Eastern Slope. One subspecies, *Notiosorex crawfordi crawfordi*, occurs in Colorado.

FAMILY TALPIDAE — Moles

Moles are stocky animals with structural modifications for digging and a fossorial existence. There are about 27 species of moles in the world in 12 genera, of which 8 are monotypic. The family is distributed widely in Eurasia and in North America from southern Canada to northern Mexico. In North America there are 5 genera and 7 species. Only the eastern mole, *Scalopus aquaticus*, is found in Colorado.

Scalopus aquaticus
EASTERN MOLE

DESCRIPTION — The eastern mole has a stocky body and large, muscular feet. The front feet are

89

Photograph by Roger W. Barbour.

Photograph 5-9 Eastern mole (Scalopus aquaticus).

spade-like, the palms wider than long. The toes on all four limbs are webbed. The snout is pointed with a naked tip. The eyes are vestigial and are not detectable externally. Pinnae are lacking and the ear openings are tiny holes. The fur is dense, short, and soft; colors range from pale gray or silver to nearly black. The tail is scantily haired and short, and its length is less than one-fourth of the total length of the animal. Measurements are: total length 133–190 mm; length of tail 19–36 mm; length of hindfoot 17–24 mm; weight 65–100 g. The forelimbs and pectoral girdle are highly modified, with a greatly shortened and flattened humerus and a keeled sternum. These modifications allow for attachment points and maximum development of the forelimb muscles for digging. Males are only sightly larger than females.

NATURAL HISTORY — The eastern mole is a fossorial mammal, spending an estimated 99 percent of its life below ground. Despite being abundant over much of the eastern United States, little ecological research has been conducted on the species. Moles are active all year. They construct both deep and shallow burrow systems. The shallow tunnels consist of runs several centimeters below the ground surface resulting in the characteristic surface ridges that can annoy lawn owners in the eastern states (Silver and Moore 1941). These tunnels are used primarily for forag-

ing. Deeper tunnels, 10–50 cm below the surface, are used for nesting and for access to shallower runs. Although new runs may be constructed at any time of the year, most activity seems to occur in the spring or following precipitation when soils are softer and not frozen (Harvey 1976). Shallow tunnels of moles can be confused with those of pocket gophers but moles do not typically leave the large accumulated mounds of soil so characteristic of pocket gopher activity. Moles are most numerous in loose, loamy, or sandy soils that are sufficiently moist to allow for tunneling. The animals are not found in heavy clay, stony, or gravel soils (Jackson 1915).

Moles feed mostly on invertebrates, especially earthworms and insects. In captivity the animals have also eaten dead mice and small birds. Some vegetable matter is consumed. Several researchers have reported that moles consume food equal to 25 to 100 percent of their body weight daily (Arlton 1936, W. B. Davis 1942).

Map 5-20 Distribution of the eastern mole (Scalopus aquaticus) *in North America.*

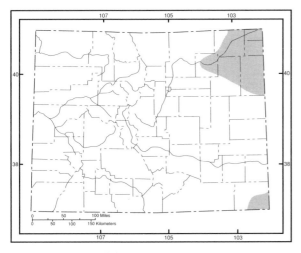

Map 5-21 Distribution of the eastern mole (Scalopus aquaticus) *in Colorado.*

Moles construct nests of dried grass or leaves in the deeper runways of their tunnel system and appear to utilize only one nest at a time, although they may move to new nests and abandon old ones. Moles tracked with radioisotopes (Harvey 1976) did not move more than 280 m from their nests during a foraging period. About 35 to 40 percent of a mole's time is spent in the nest, sometimes for periods of over six hours at a time. Activity peaks for moles occur bimodally between 0800 and 1600 hours (8 A.M. and 4 P.M.) and from 2300 and 0400 hours (11 P.M. to 4 A.M.). The home range of males averaged 1.9 ha, that of females 0.28 ha. The size of home ranges of males exceeds that reported for a number of fossorial rodents including the plains pocket gopher (*Geomys bursarius*) and the valley pocket gopher (*Thomomys bottae*), animals considerably larger than the eastern mole. This difference in home range size may relate to the insectivorous diet of the mole compared to herbivory in the gophers (Harvey 1976).

Little is known about reproduction in the eastern mole. The species is reported to have only one litter per year with two to five young (Jackson 1915). The gestation period is estimated to be 28 to 45 days (Arlton 1936, Conaway 1959). Most breeding apparently occurs in March or April in northern portions of its range including Colorado. The young are naked and blind at birth but develop a covering of grayish fur in about 10 days (Jackson 1915). They become independent of the mother in about one month.

Moles may live over three years in the wild (Harvey 1976) although there are no data on population dynamics and turnover rates. Moles appear to have few natural enemies other than humans. Skunks, cats, dogs, and other predators capture them on occasion, as do snakes. In their rare appearances above ground, they may be taken by owls. Floods may be the most important natural control on populations. Although moles may create unsightly mounds on lawns, their activities mostly are beneficial because they eat insect larvae and aerate the soil. Yates and Schmidly (1978) and Yates and Pedersen (1982) reviewed the literature on eastern moles.

DISTRIBUTION IN COLORADO — The eastern mole reaches its western distributional limit in Colorado and Wyoming. The species appears to be limited to well-developed, well-drained soils of floodplains and sandhills in northeastern and extreme southeastern Colorado. Although seemingly suitable habitat exists along much of the South Platte River and other drainages on the plains, the species does not appear to be expanding its range in the state. The subspecies *Scalopus aquaticus caryi* occurs in Morgan, Logan, Sedgwick, Phillips, Yuma, and Washington counties; *S. a. intermedius* is known from a single record in Baca County (T. Vaughan 1961*a*).

Chapter 6

Order:
Chiroptera

Bats

Bats are the only mammals capable of true flight. They are excellent fliers with numerous remarkable anatomical and physiological specializations. Delicately built, their long bones are slender and filled with large amounts of marrow. The forelimbs and elongated digits support a flexible, often leathery, membrane (the patagium) extending from the shoulders to the hindlimbs. Another membrane (the uropatagium or interfemoral membrane) connects the hindlimbs and part or all of the tail. The humerus is short, the radius long, and the ulna rudimentary. The wrist has six carpals, and the hand has five metacarpals and five digits. The thumb is free from the flight membrane, very short, and usually clawed. In one of the two suborders of bats, the Megachiroptera, the second digit ("index finger") is also clawed and free. The pectoral girdle of bats includes a stout scapula and a well-developed clavicle. The sternum is usually keeled, increasing the surface area for attachment of flight muscles. In contrast to the shoulder, the pelvic girdle is relatively weak and the hindlimbs are rotated so that the knee is directed outward and backward. The femur is long and the tibia stout. The fibula may be rudimentary. There are five clawed digits on each hindfoot. For excellent discussions of the origin, mechanics, physiology, and anatomy of flight, and adaptations in wing shape, see Fenton et al. (1987).

Bats date back to the Eocene Epoch, 50 to 60 million years ago. The Chiroptera evolved from arboreal insectivores. The order is divided into two suborders, the Megachiroptera and the Microchiroptera. The Megachiroptera are the large Old World fruit bats, or "flying foxes"; the Microchiroptera are the small echolocating bats. The organization of the optic structure in the Megachiroptera is similar to that in primates, suggesting to some that they are more closely related to primates than to microchiropterans (Pettigrew 1986). That is, bats might be an unnatural group, with a diphyletic origin (and therefore bat wings must have evolved twice). Although this theory is intriguing, other morphological and molecular evidence indicates that it is more likely that the similarity between megachiropterans and primates is the result of convergent evolution and that bat wings evolved only once (R. Martin 1986).

The use of sound for orientation in bats was first studied and reported in the 1700s, but not again until 1912, and then reconfirmed in 1922. However, it was not until the 1930s that we came to understand bats' use of echolocation. Echolocation, a form of sonar, is used by most microchiropterans. They investigate their surroundings and navigate by emitting a series of ultrasonic sounds through the nose or mouth and then detecting the echoes that return (Fenton 1985). Many species have recognizably distinctive echolocatory calls (Fenton and Bell 1981). Not all are ultrasonic. For example, spotted bats, pallid bats, and big free-tailed bats have calls that are audible to humans.

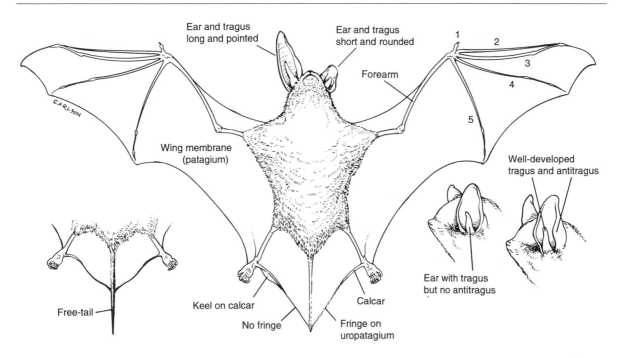

Figure 6-1 A composite, generalized bat showing various features of diagnostic importance.

"Blind as a bat" is not quite blind. Microchiropterans have small but well-developed eyes, at least capable of distinguishing light and dark. The ears of many species are large and conspicuous and they often have a projecting central lobe, the tragus. A flap-like lobe, the antitragus, may be present on the lower edge of the outer margin of the pinnae. The degree of development of these structures is of value in identification. Many microchiropterans have well-developed facial protuberances, flaps, or folds that give their faces a grotesque appearance. These structures, along with the well-developed pinnae, are thought to function as deflectors or funnels for echolocatory pulses, allowing them to locate targets at angles above the horizontal. Facial vibrissae are present in many species and sensory hairs are also located on the flight membranes and on the feet.

The dentition of most insectivorous bats is simple and features a reduced number of incisors and premolars. The front teeth are sectorial, having blade-like cutting edges that shear against another tooth. Molars and premolars have sharp cutting edges as well, allowing rapid dissection of prey. The brain has a small cerebrum with few convolutions. Male and female bats generally are of similar size (monomorphic), but males have a readily visible, pendant penis. A baculum is present. The testes may be abdominal or descend into a scrotum during the breeding season. The uterus is bicornuate and often only the right ovary is functional. The placenta is usually discoidal and hemochorial. The young are usually delivered rump first, the so-called breech position. The two mammae are thoracic.

A major adaptive radiation of bats has occurred in diets. Ancestral bats doubtless were insectivorous, and about 70 percent of living species still feed on insects, but others are specialized to prey on fish, frogs, lizards, birds, and small mammals, including other bats. Vampire bats feed on the blood of mammals or birds, and other bats have become specialized to feed on fruits, pollen, and nectar. This dietary divergence has allowed for tremendous evolutionary success. Almost one-fourth of mammalian species worldwide are bats, although only about one-seventh of Coloradan mammals are bats, as bats are more diverse in tropical areas.

The behavior and ecology of bats still are poorly known, although in recent years tremendous research efforts have been made. Bats are mostly nocturnal, although some are crepuscular, and a few may even fly on cloudy days. Coloradan bats tend to be active during the first four hours after sunset (Freeman 1984). This preference may be due to cooling during the night (which increases the energetic expense of flight) and to reduced insect activity. Some species are seasonally migratory, but others hibernate in Colorado. These different winter ecologies and the general difficulty of working with flying animals at night have influenced our level of knowledge and led to much speculation, superstition, and folklore. General texts on bat biology correct many misconceptions (Fenton 1983, Tuttle 1988).

Natural history traits and gregariousness differ widely among species. Some species form colonies that number in the thousands or millions of individuals. Other species are solitary, roosting in trees, under bark, in cracks and crevices of rock faces, or other similar sites. Some species use caves, mines, tunnels, or buildings (abandoned or occupied) for roosts.

Habitat of bats in Colorado is diverse. The big brown bat and the little brown bat can be found in almost all ecosystems, including urban environments, but other species are more particular. For example, the red bat is restricted to deciduous riparian woodlands. The two community types most commonly used by bats are piñon-juniper and sagebrush (R. Adams 1990). Although only an estimated 10 to 15 percent of Colorado is covered in piñon-juniper woodland, 86 percent of bat species use this habitat, which contains the highest bat diversity. This concentration is likely a consequence of several factors: the high insect diversity in the woodlands, the frequent association with Gambel oak brushlands (which also support high insect diversity); the open structure of the woodland; rocky, broken substrate; and mild temperatures compared to ecosystems at both lower and higher elevations.

Recently there has been widespread concern about the status of bat populations. A number of characteristics contribute to the vulnerability of bats. They have a low reproductive rate; most produce only one young per year. They are susceptible to pesticides, especially DDT (which is still used in many countries). Some bats are unable to tolerate the energetic stress of disturbance during hibernation. Unfortunately, large numbers of bats may be impacted when people explore old mines or caves and unintentionally disturb the animals to the point that they abandon their roosts. Most caves and many old tunnels, mines, and abandoned buildings in Colorado have been visited so frequently by people that they no longer offer safe, secure habitat for bats. Mines in the western United States, including Colorado, are being closed as a safety measure; summer roosts are lost as old buildings are torn down. Add to this the fact that the biology of most bat species is poorly known, and their public image is often negative (simply because they are so different from other mammals). Education and conservation efforts should be encouraged in an effort to improve this situation. All Coloradan bats are protected as nongame mammals (see Table 3-1).

Like most mammals, bats can harbor rabies, although less than one-half of 1 percent of bats in the field are thought to be rabid. Most bats attempt to bite if handled. People who come in contact with bats on the ground, roosting in exposed areas, or captured by the pet cat should be cautious. Such animals may be unable to act normally because of rabies. Children should always be cautioned not to handle wild mammals, and bats are no exception. The first author was bitten by a rabid big brown bat while removing it from a Greeley hardware store. That particular animal was not acting normally and died four days later. Despite concerns of disease, rabies in bats is an extremely rare event and the animals should not be persecuted. Moreover, bats are quite beneficial to the interests of humans because of their consumption of immense numbers of insects, although on occasion they invade attics and older buildings where they may cause noise and odor problems.

There are 42 genera and about 170 species in the Pteropodidae, the sole family in the suborder Megachiroptera, and about 133 genera and 770 species in 18 families in the Microchiroptera. Bats are widespread in tropical and temperate regions throughout the world but do not extend into the Arctic or Antarctica. Most of the species occur in the tropics. About 9 families, 70 genera, and 190 species of bats live in North America, with 2 families, 10 genera, and 18 species reported in Colorado. Most of these reach distributional limits in Colorado (Armstrong 1972, Freeman 1984). As efforts to learn about these animals continue we may find that several more species of bats occasionally enter the state. All bats in Colorado eat insects, rest during the day in a variety of situations such as trees, buildings, caves, and crevices, and fly in the evening or at night.

Key to the Families of the Order Chiroptera Found in Colorado

1. Tail contained within interfemoral membrane; fibula slender or rudimentary . . . .
. . . . Family Vespertilionidae, p. 95

1' Tail free from interfemoral membrane for approximately 1/3 its length; fibula well developed, about diameter of tibia . . . .
. . . . Family Molossidae, p. 125

FAMILY VESPERTILIONIDAE —
Vespertilionid Bats

This is a family of small to medium-sized bats. The muzzle and lips are simple. The ears are usually separate from each other at their bases and exhibit well-developed tragi. Both the ulna and

fibula are vestigial (T. Vaughan 1959). The second digit consists of a metacarpal and a single, small phalanx. The interfemoral membrane is well developed and includes the tail. This is the largest family of bats, and nearly all species are insect feeders. In most species, females are slightly larger than males (D. Williams and Findley 1979). Ranges of many species extend well into the North Temperate Zone. The family includes 37 genera and 324 species, of which 10 genera and 27 species occur in the United States, and 8 genera and 16 species are known in Colorado.

The vespertilionid bats of the western United States constitute a guild of aerial insectivores (Black 1974, Ellinwood 1978, Freeman 1984, C. Jones 1965, M. O'Farrell and Bradley 1970, M. O'Farrell et al. 1967, Ruffner et al. 1979). Within that guild, certain aspects of morphology are predictive of habitat utilization and different foraging modes such as gleaning, aerial capture with the interfemoral membrane, filter-feeding, and terrestrial foraging (Freeman 1984). Interestingly, there seems to be little or no competition in present-day communities, and food resources do not seem to be limiting.

Key to the Species of the Family Vespertilionidae Known or Expected to Occur in Colorado

1. Ears long, greater than 26 mm; teeth fewer than 38 2

1' Ears shorter, generally less than 25 mm; if ears approach 25 mm then dentition totals 38 teeth 5

2. Dorsal color black with three large white spots; total teeth 34, cheekteeth 5/5 . . . .
. . . . Spotted Bat — *Euderma maculatum*, p. 120

2' Dorsal color brownish, or if black then lacking white spots; total teeth 36 or 28; cheekteeth 5/6 or 4/6 3

3. Ears usually less than half length of forearm, not joined at bases; color pale yellowish, almost

white in some individuals; total teeth 28, cheek-teeth . . . . . . Pallid Bat — *Antrozous pallidus*, p. 124

3′ Ears longer, usually more than half length of forearm, joined at bases; color usually brown; total teeth 36, cheekteeth 5/6 4

4. Accessory basal lobe of ears forming two prominent leaf-like lappets projecting over forehead; calcar keeled; breadth of braincase more than half greatest length of skull . . . . Allen's Big-eared Bat — *Idionycteris phyllotis**, p. 123

4′ Leaf-like structures not obvious over forehead; calcar not keeled; breadth of braincase less than half greatest length of skull . . . . Townsend's Big-eared Bat — *Plecotus townsendii*, p. 121

5. Dorsal surface of interfemoral membrane densely furred to trailing edge; incisors 1/3 6

5′ Dorsal surface of interfemoral membrane not densely furred to trailing edge; incisors 2/3 or 1/2 7

6. Dorsal color brown with many hairs white tipped, giving a frosted appearance; ears with black rim; greatest length of skull more than 16 mm . . . . Hoary Bat — *Lasiurus cinereus*, p. 111

6′ Dorsal color brick red to yellowish red with only a few white-tipped hairs; ears without black rim; greatest length of skull less than 15 mm . . . . Red Bat — *Lasiurus borealis*, p. 109

7. Dorsal color blackish, some hairs white tipped; interfemoral membrane densely furred on proximal half of dorsal surface . . . . Silver-haired Bat — *Lasionycteris noctivagans*, p. 113

7′ Dorsal color not blackish; hairs not white tipped; interfemoral membrane almost naked . . . 8

8. Total teeth 34 or 32; cheekteeth not 6/6 9

8′ Total teeth 38; cheekteeth 6/6 . . . . *Myotis* 11

9. Total teeth 32; size large, forearm longer than 40 mm; color not yellowish gray, generally brown . . . . Big Brown Bat — *Eptesicus fuscus*, p. 117

9′ Total teeth 34; size small, forearm shorter than 36 mm; color yellowish gray . . . . *Pipistrellus* 10

10. Dorsal hairs distinctly tricolored, dark at tips and base and paler in middle . . . . Eastern Pipistrelle — *Pipistrellus subflavus*, p. 116

10′ Dorsal hairs not distinctly tricolored . . . . Western Pipistrelle — *Pipistrellus hesperus*, p. 114

11. Calcar with well-developed keel 12

11′ Calcar without noticeable keel 14

12. Underside of wing furred to level of elbow or beyond; foot usually longer than 8.5 mm; forearm usually longer than 35 mm; rostrum noticeably short . . . Long-legged Myotis — *Myotis volans*, p. 106

12′ Underside of wing not furred to level of elbow; foot shorter than 8.5 mm; forearm usually shorter than 35 mm; rostrum not noticeably short 13

13. Braincase rising abruptly from rostrum, skull with steep profile when viewed from side; third metacarpal as long or longer than forearm; hair on back dull, lacking burnished tips . . . . California Myotis — *Myotis californicus*, p. 97

13′ Braincase sloping gently from rostrum, skull with flattened appearance when viewed from side; third metacarpal not as long as forearm; hair on back shiny, with burnished tips . . . .

---

* Species of possible occurrence in Colorado.

Western Small-footed Myotis — *Myotis ciliolabrum,*
. . . . p. 97

14. Conspicuous fringe of stiff, short hairs along
trailing edge of uropatagium . . . .
. . . . . . Fringed Myotis — *Myotis thysanodes,* p. 104

14′ No conspicuous fringe of stiff, short hairs
along trailing edge of uropatagium 15

15. Ears longer, usually 21–24 mm, extending
well beyond nose when laid forward . . . .
. . . . Long-eared Myotis — *Myotis evotis,* p. 100

15′ Ears shorter, usually less than 16 mm, not
extending beyond nose when laid forward 16

16. Hairs short, somewhat coarse; condylobasal
length greater than 16 mm; sagittal crest well
developed in adult; forearm usually greater than
44 mm. . . . . . Cave Myotis — *Myotis velifer*[*], p. 105

16′ Hair not especially short and coarse;
condylobasal length less than 16 mm; sagittal
crest not well developed; forearm usually less
than 44 mm 17

17. Dorsal hairs glossy, with burnished tips;
greatest length of skull usually greater than 14.2
mm; mastoid breadth 7.5 mm or more. . . . .
. . . . Little Brown Myotis — *Myotis lucifugus,* p. 102

17′ Dorsal hairs not glossy, without burnished
tips; greatest length of skull less than 14.2 mm;
mastoid breadth 7.4 mm or less . . . .
. . . . Yuma Myotis — *Myotis yumanensis,* p. 108

Myotis californicus
CALIFORNIA MYOTIS

DESCRIPTION — The California myotis is a small,
generally yellowish brown bat, although individu-

Photograph 6-1 California myotis (Myotis
californicus).

als may range from pale tan to nearly black. The
pelage is typically dull and the hairs lack burnished tips. The calcar is distinctly keeled. Hair
on the ventral side of the patagium does not extend to the level of the elbow. Measurements are:
total length 70–84 mm; length of tail 30–40 mm;
length of hindfoot 5.5–8.2 mm; length of ear 11–
15 mm; length of forearm 29–36 mm; weight 3–5
g. This species needs careful comparison with *M.
ciliolabrum.* The length of the small, fragile skull is
less than 13.5 mm in most specimens (Findley et
al. 1975). The braincase has an abruptly rising
profile whose height is equal to or greater than
32 percent of the greatest length of the skull in
three-fourths of specimens examined (Findley et
al. 1975). Height of the skull in *M. ciliolabrum* is
typically less than 32 percent of the greatest
length. Rostral breadth does not exceed 5.0 mm
in *M. californicus,* and in *M. ciliolabrum* it exceeds
5.2 mm (Bogan 1974). The ears of the California
myotis are long, extending beyond the nose when
laid forward. Even in hand, these two species can
be confused.

NATURAL HISTORY — The biology of the California myotis is poorly known, and the species does

* Species of possible occurrence in Colorado.

Map 6-1 Distribution of the California myotis (Myotis californicus) *in North America.*

not appear to be common in Colorado. During a three-year study in Moffat County, Freeman (1984) captured only 44 individuals. The California myotis uses abandoned structures, mines, caves, and cracks and crevices in cliff faces for night roosts. Day roosts are similar and include hollow trees and spaces under bark. These bats occur in piñon-juniper woodlands and semidesert shrublands at lower elevations in the canyons and valleys of western Colorado, a habitat similar to that of the western pipistrelle in northwestern Colorado (Finley et al. 1976).

The California myotis starts to forage early in the evening, shortly after western pipistrelles emerge. They usually fly 2 to 3 m above the ground in search of spiders, moths, and flies. Foraging occurs over stock tanks, riparian canyons, arroyos, open areas, and along cliff faces (Freeman 1984). The animals may be somewhat transient, not spending much time at any particular roost, although frequenting the same general roosting area. Breeding occurs in the fall. In Colorado,

young are probably born in May and June, although pregnant females have been captured in June and July, and lactating females in August (R. Adams 1988), so at least some females give birth later. Although the gestation period is not known, it likely is 50 to 60 days. Females give birth to a single young.

The winter range of the California myotis is not known, and information on migration is not available. They may migrate out of Colorado to winter, although hibernation records are common in many of the western states where the animals have been found in mines, caves, and stone buildings. M. Simpson (1993) reviewed the literature on the California myotis.

DISTRIBUTION IN COLORADO — The California myotis occurs in dry canyon and mesa country of the western United States. It is most common in semidesert shrublands and piñon-juniper woodlands up to elevations of about 2,290 m (7,500 ft). The species has been captured all along Colorado's western boundary except in San Miguel and Dolores counties, where it will likely be found eventually. One subspecies, *Myotis californicus stephensi*, occurs in Colorado.

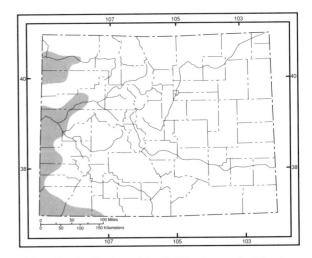

Map 6-2 Distribution of the California myotis (Myotis californicus) *in Colorado.*

Photograph by William E. Ervin.

Photograph 6-2 Western small-footed myotis (Myotis ciliolabrum).

Myotis ciliolabrum
WESTERN SMALL-FOOTED MYOTIS

DESCRIPTION — This is one of the three species of Colorado *Myotis* with a keeled calcar (the other two being *M. californicus* and *M. volans*). *M. ciliolabrum* is smaller than *M. volans*, and slightly larger than *M. californicus*. Coloration of *M. ciliolabrum* varies geographically in Colorado. Specimens from eastern Colorado (*M. c. ciliolabrum*) are paler than the rich reddish brown of the west-

ern subspecies (*M. c. melanorhinus*), although the latter shows clinal variation in color and is paler in northwestern Colorado (Armstrong 1972). The pelage often has a pronounced sheen due to the burnished tips of the hairs. A dark facial mask is present on some individuals. Measurements are: total length 75–88 mm; length of tail 33–42 mm; length of hindfoot 5–8 mm; length of ear 12–16 mm; length of forearm 30–35 mm; weight 3.5–5.5 g. The skull of *M. ciliolabrum* is relatively flattened in lateral view. When laid forward the ears barely extend beyond the muzzle. For differences from the very similar *M. californicus*, see the account of that species.

NATURAL HISTORY — The western small-footed myotis is widely distributed in many habitats throughout the western United States. In summer it has been found roosting in rock crevices, caves, dwellings, burrows, among rocks, under bark, and even beneath rocks scattered on the ground. Along the Rockies and adjacent plains, the bat is generally found in the broken terrain of canyons and foothills, commonly in places with cover of trees or shrubs.

The western small-footed myotis forages only a meter or so above the ground and flies with an erratic, butterfly-like pattern. Half of the foraging time is spent near rocks and cliffs (Freeman 1984). The rest of the time is spent foraging over open areas, arroyos, and forest canopy. Like other small bats of Colorado (western pipistrelle, California myotis), the western small-footed myotis tends to fly early in the evening. Early evening flight behavior may help reduce predation by larger species such as the hoary bat. In northern Weld County the species is not uncommon along the High Plains escarpment, but is difficult to capture at cattle tanks (the principal water supply) because of its ability to detect and avoid mistnets. The western small-footed myotis was relatively abundant at a study site in Moffat County (Freeman 1984).

The diet of the small-footed myotis has not been studied in detail. Highly maneuverable in flight,

Map 6-3 Distribution of the western small-footed myotis (Myotis ciliolabrum) *in North America.*

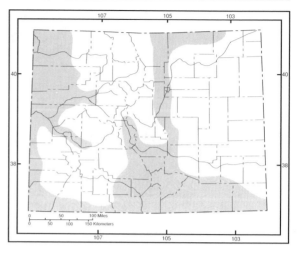

Map 6-4 Distribution of the western small-footed myotis (Myotis ciliolabrum) *in Colorado.*

this species forages among rocks, shrubs, and trees for small beetles, flies, and ants.

The reproductive cycle is poorly known. Apparently most females give birth to one young, although twins have been reported. Parturition probably occurs in June, July, and August in Colorado. Aside from forming small nursery colonies of 10 to 20 individuals, these bats generally are thought to be solitary.

The animals overwinter in caves and rock crevices in the state (Armstrong 1972, Warren 1942), often in locations with temperatures near freezing, low humidity, and significant air circulation. Such hibernacula are atypical for bats, as most species select more protected, humid sites with somewhat higher temperatures.

DISTRIBUTION IN COLORADO — In Colorado the species is not uncommon at elevations below 2,591 m (8,500 ft) where suitable roosting and foraging habitat is available. It is probably absent

from most of the eastern plains where suitable roosting cover is scarce; records are restricted to the rocky, eroded terrain along the southern and northern margins. Nomenclature of this species has long been problematic (Armstrong 1972, Hall 1981). Van Zyll de Jong (1984) revised the small-footed myotis, recognizing two distinct species; *Myotis leibii* (the eastern small-footed myotis) and *M. ciliolabrum* (the western small-footed myotis). Previously the forms were treated together as *M. leibii*; in older literature this bat was called *Myotis subulatus*. Coloradan subspecies are *M. c. melanorhinus* in western Colorado and the San Luis Valley, and *M. c. ciliolabrum* in the eastern part of the state.

Myotis evotis
LONG-EARED MYOTIS

DESCRIPTION — The long-eared myotis is a medium brown bat with notably long ears. The black ears and membranes contrast markedly with the paler pelage. There is a pale, inconspicuous fringe of hairs on the posterior margin of the interfemoral membrane. The underside is paler than the dorsum. Measurements are: total length 88–92 mm; length of tail 41–46 mm; length of hindfoot 8–10 mm; length of ear 18–23 mm;

Photograph 6-3 Long-eared myotis (Myotis evotis).

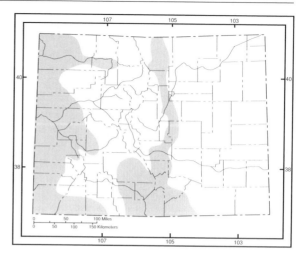

Map 6-6 Distribution of the long-eared myotis (Myotis evotis) *in Colorado.*

length of forearm 35–41 mm; weight 5–7 g. Greatest length of skull is 16–16.8 mm, similar to that of *M. thysanodes* but lacking the well-developed sagittal crest. The braincase rises gradually from the rostrum. The long ears of this bat, coupled with relatively small size and lack of a conspicuous fringe of hair on the trailing edge of the uropatagium, distinguish it from other Colorado bats.

NATURAL HISTORY — The species occurs in coniferous forests at moderate elevations. It is most common in ponderosa pine woodlands and is also found in piñon-juniper woodlands and subalpine forests. The animals use day roosts in tree cavities, under loose bark, and in buildings. These sites as well as caves and mines are used for night roosts.

The long-eared myotis feeds over water and along the margins of vegetation. A gleaner, it picks individual insects from leaves (Freeman 1984). The long ears probably facilitate auditory sensitivity to allow this behavior. They have been reported to specialize in feeding on beetles (Black 1974), but also feed on moths and other insects, including caddisflies (Freeman 1984). The long-eared myotis tends to emerge late in the evening.

Maternity colonies contain up to 20 individuals. G. Miller and Allen (1928) reported a small nursery colony in an abandoned ranch building near Dolores, Montezuma County. Birth of a single

Map 6-5 Distribution of the long-eared myotis (Myotis evotis) *in North America.*

young probably occurs in June and July. In Colorado, lactating females have been taken in June, July, and August, with greatest numbers from August (R. Adams 1988, R. Finley et al. 1983, Freeman 1984). Males are scrotal in July, August, and September, and mating probably occurs in fall, with fertilization delayed until spring. Manning and Jones (1989) reviewed the literature on the species.

DISTRIBUTION IN COLORADO — An inhabitant of ponderosa pine forests in Colorado, the long-eared myotis has been taken from scattered areas in the western two-thirds of the state at elevations between 1,830 and 2,750 m (6,000–9,000 ft). One subspecies, *Myotis evotis evotis*, occurs in Colorado.

Photograph 6-4 Little brown myotis (Myotis lucifugus).

Myotis lucifugus
LITTLE BROWN MYOTIS

DESCRIPTION — The little brown myotis is pale brown to dark brown above with somewhat paler undersides. The hairs are relatively long; burnished tips lend a definite sheen to the pelage. There usually are long hairs on the toes that extend beyond the tips of the claws. Measurements are: total length 90–100 mm; length of tail 36–47 mm; length of hindfoot 8–10 mm; length of ear 11–15 mm; length of forearm 33–41 mm (usually

in the 39–41 range); weight 4.5–5.5 g. Females are slightly larger than males. The ears of *M. lucifugus* barely reach the tip of the nose when laid forward. The greatest length of the skull is 14.0–15.9 mm. The little brown bat can be confused with most other myotis species. Probably the most productive approach for identification is to search for the characters that distinguish other, more distinctive species known to occur in the area. The most similar Coloradan species is the Yuma myotis, from which the little brown bat differs in having a greater mastoid breadth (greater than 7.5 mm versus less than 7.4) and glossy, darker pelage (Findley et al. 1975).

NATURAL HISTORY — The little brown myotis is the "deer mouse" of the vespertilionid bats; there are more publications on this species than any other North American bat (Fenton and Barclay 1980, Fenton et al. 1987, Humphrey and Cope 1976). It inhabits most of North America, roosting by day under bark, in trees, under rocks, in wood piles, buildings and other structures, and less frequently in caves and mines. Similar areas are used for night roosts. If the same site is used for both day and night roosts, different locations are utilized within the roost. Due to a lack of food resources, in winter little brown bats must hibernate. Caves, mines, and buildings are typical hibernacula, but little is known about wintering habits of the little brown bat in Colorado or elsewhere in the western United States.

Nursery colonies form in summer, numbering up to 800 individuals in the East. In Colorado, nursery colonies typically contain fewer than 100 adult females and have invariably been found in buildings, usually in warm attics. Females and young are tolerant of extremely high temperatures (Studier and O'Farrell 1972). A nursery colony in Stonewall, Las Animas County, was located behind ponderosa pine slabs 15–25 cm wide, which were nailed to the side of a rustic lodge (Ellinwood 1978). In early August it contained an estimated 180 to 200 bats, most of which were little brown bats. Of 89 little brown myotis captured, most (73) were juveniles that had only recently be-

Map 6-7 Distribution of the little brown myotis (Myotis lucifugus) *in North America.*

gun to fly. A site in an attic at Red Feather Lakes, Larimer County, contained an estimated 250 bats on July 20. The young, probably about two weeks old, were only one-half the size of the females and not yet volant (Ellinwood and Fitzgerald, unpublished). Unfortunately, the colony was exterminated before the young reached maturity. Another nursery colony, on the Colorado State University campus, shared its roost for part of the year with big brown bats (L. Wunder 1987; L. Wunder and Nash 1980, 1981). M. O'Farrell and Studier (1973) discussed maternity roosts of *M. lucifugus* and *M. thysanodes* in northeastern New Mexico.

Little brown bats mate in late fall and winter while the animals are in the vicinity of their hibernacula. Copulation may occur with both sexes alert, or the male may copulate with torpid females (D. Thomas et al. 1979). Mating is promiscuous and both sexes mate more than once. Ovulation occurs one or two days after arousal from hibernation (Buchanan 1987). Sperm are

stored and fertilization occurs when females leave the hibernaculum. The gestation period is 50 to 60 days. Little brown bats give birth in late May or early June (early for Coloradan bats), and lactation is terminated by the end of June (R. Adams 1988). Delivery is remarkable because the female reverses her normal head-down roosting posture and hangs from her thumb claws, capturing the newborn bat in her interfemoral membrane as it is expelled. Other species of bats often give birth in the head-down position. Young are born with fine, silky hair, and their eyes and ears open two to three days after birth. Occasionally, the young are carried attached to the female's nipples while she forages, but usually they are left in the roost. They develop rapidly, fly by about three weeks of age, and reach adult weight in about one month.

Little brown myotis emerges at dusk to drink and feed and generally forages over water or in clearings, in a zigzag flight. It forages at 3 to 6 m above ground, zigzagging over the area. Insect prey are knocked into the uropatagium with the wing tip and then lifted to the mouth and consumed in flight. During this procedure, the bats appear to tumble briefly. Known as moth specialists, they also take many other prey items, including mosquitoes. In fact, one individual can capture up to

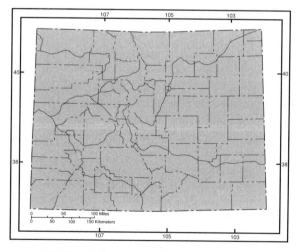

Map 6-8 Distribution of the little brown myotis (Myotis lucifugus) *in Colorado.*

600 mosquitoes per hour (Tuttle 1988). A bat colony can thus have a substantial impact on insect populations. These bats feed periodically through the night, rapidly fill their stomachs, then rest and eliminate undigested food for an hour or so, and then resume foraging activities. Females at maternity colonies show seasonal selectivity in foraging and diet (Aldridge 1976).

As with many bats, the species has remarkable longevity for a small mammal. The oldest reported age is 31 years and many survive over 10 years. Mortality is highest in the first year, occurring mostly in hibernation or as the young learn to fly. Foraging skills must develop, and the young are not as adept as adults. A variety of predators feed on this species, including snakes, passerine birds, birds of prey, domestic pets, and other small carnivores. Rabies is rare.

DISTRIBUTION IN COLORADO — In Colorado, the little brown bat is common in wooded areas of the western two-thirds of the state at elevations of 1,530 to 3,360 m (5,000-11,000 ft). Frequently associated with ponderosa pine forests, it is also found in piñon-juniper woodlands, montane shrublands, and riparian woodlands (Armstrong 1972, Ellinwood 1978, Freeman 1984). *Myotis lucifugus carissima* is distributed over the state in suitable habitat.

Myotis thysanodes
FRINGED MYOTIS

DESCRIPTION — The fringed myotis is yellowish brown to reddish brown, with the ventral color similar to the dorsum. The ears are quite large, extending 3 to 5 mm beyond the nose when laid forward. The free edge of the interfemoral membrane has an obvious fringe of stiff hairs, hence the common name. This feature most readily distinguishes this bat from others in Colorado. Measurements are: total length 77–100 mm; length of tail 34–45 mm; length of hindfoot 9–11 mm; length of ear 16–21 mm; length of forearm 39–46 mm; weight 6–7 g. The skull is relatively large, slender, and fragile; greatest length of skull

Photograph by Roger W. Barbour.

Photograph 6-5 Fringed myotis (Myotis thysanodes).

is 16–17.2 mm. A well-developed sagittal crest is present.

NATURAL HISTORY — The fringed myotis apparently is not common in Colorado. It is found in ponderosa pine woodlands, greasewood, oak-brush, and saltbush shrublands.

These bats may begin to forage shortly after sunset, although most of their activity occurs a couple of hours after dark. As with some other bat species, precipitation does not necessarily affect activity. Gleaners, they forage close to the plant

Map 6-9 Distribution of the fringed myotis (Myotis thysanodes) in North America.

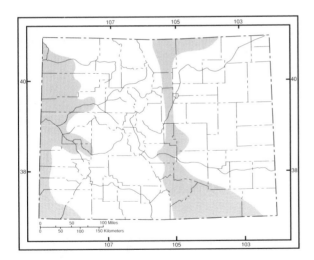

Map 6-10 Distribution of the fringed myotis (Myotis thysanodes) in Colorado.

canopy where they pick prey off the vegetation during a slow, maneuverable flight. The fringed myotis has a relatively broad diet, feeding on moths, beetles, caddis flies, Hymenoptera (ants, bees, and wasps), and other insects (Freeman 1984).

Females mate in the fall; ovulation and fertilization occur in late April and May. The gestation period is 50 to 60 days with one young per year. Barbour and Davis (1969) captured pregnant fringed myotis near Colorado Springs in mid-June. The young are capable of flight by two and one-half weeks of age and are indistinguishable from adults in size by three weeks. Nursery colonies of several hundred fringed myotis have been reported in other areas but records on distribution, behavior, and ecology of this species in Colorado are scarce.

Caves, mines, and buildings are used as both day and night roosts. Localized migrations are thought to occur, but firm data are lacking. Hibernation sites include caves and buildings. The literature on the species was reviewed by M. O'Farrell and Studier (1980).

DISTRIBUTION IN COLORADO — The fringed myotis is a species of coniferous woodlands and shrublands at elevations to 2,290 m (7,500 ft). The few Coloradan records are widely scattered both east and west of the Continental Divide (J. Fitzgerald et al. 1989). One subspecies, *Myotis thysanodes thysanodes*, occurs in Colorado.

Myotis velifer
CAVE MYOTIS

DESCRIPTION — The cave myotis, a species of possible occurrence in Colorado, is large for the genus, with a pale brown dorsal pelage and a somewhat paler venter. The hair is of moderate length, coarse, has no sheen, and is described as "woolly." This species may be confused with *M. lucifugus* or *M. yumanensis* and is best distinguished by having a forearm longer than 41 mm, condylobasal length greater than 16 mm, and a well-developed sagittal crest.

NATURAL HISTORY — The cave myotis is mostly a cave-roosting species that forms large colonies in

Map 6-11 Distribution of the cave myotis (Myotis velifer) *in North America.*

Photograph by Roger W. Barbour.

Photograph 6-6 Long-legged myotis (Myotis volans).

caves, mines, and sometimes buildings. They leave the roost a few minutes after sunset and generally forage 4 to 6 m over open water. Their flight is strong and not as erratic as other *Myotis*.

DISTRIBUTION IN COLORADO — The cave myotis is not yet documented in Colorado. It occurs at lower elevations in the Southwest (to south-central Kansas) and Mexico. Individuals of the High Plains subspecies, *Myotis velifer incautus*, may occasionally enter extreme southeastern Colorado; the westernmost record from Kansas (J. K. Jones et al. 1967) is only 140 km from the Colorado border, and Caire et al. (1989) reported captures in the Oklahoma Panhandle. The closest record of this subspecies from New Mexico is 320 km from the Colorado border (Findley et al. 1975). The southwestern subspecies, *M. v. velifer*, is known from New Mexico no closer than 400 km from Colorado (Findley et al. 1975).

Myotis volans
LONG-LEGGED MYOTIS

DESCRIPTION — The long-legged myotis is a large representative of the genus. The color is reddish or orangish brown to dark brown, with paler undersides. The pelage is relatively long and soft. The underside of the patagium is furred to the level of the elbow or beyond. The ears are short, barely reaching the nose when laid forward. The calcar is long and conspicuously keeled. Measurements are: total length 95–108 mm; length of tail

Map 6-12 Distribution of the long-legged myotis (Myotis volans) in North America.

40–43 mm; length of hindfoot 8–9 mm; length of ear 11–14 mm; length of forearm 35–41 mm; weight 8–10 g. Greatest length of the small, fragile skull is 12–15 mm. The rostrum is short and the braincase rises abruptly. This animal can be confused with *M. lucifugus*, frequently found in the same area. The latter species lacks a keel on the calcar and has a glossier pelage.

NATURAL HISTORY — A western species, the long-legged myotis is relatively common in ponderosa pine forests and piñon-juniper woodlands. This bat roosts in a variety of sites including trees, buildings, crevices in rock faces, and even fissures in the ground in severely eroded areas. Caves and mines do not appear to be important as day roosts, but are used as night roosts if available. Animals roost in small groups or alone. Hibernacula have not yet been found in Colorado, but the animals probably hibernate locally or make only short migrations (Schowalter 1980). Probably, they hibernate singly in mines and caves.

The long-legged myotis emerges at early dusk and forages over openings in forested areas or over water, usually at a height of 3 to 5 m. Rapid, direct fliers, they are capable of long-distance pursuit of prey (Fenton and Bell 1979, Fenton et al. 1980). They forage singly and feed on large numbers of moths (Freeman 1984). Typical of vespertilionids, as they approach their flying prey, the rate of echolocatory clicks increases to a "feeding buzz."

The reproductive biology of the long-legged myotis is poorly known. The species breeds in late June, July, and August in our area. In Colorado, pregnant females have been captured from June to August, and lactating females have been captured in August (R. Adams 1988, W. H. Davis and Barbour 1970). A single young is produced annually. Large nursery colonies are formed. Forty-five females were banded in the Conejos County Courthouse in the San Luis Valley (W. H. Davis and Barbour 1970). Both little brown myotis and long-legged myotis were captured at a nursery colony behind pine siding on a building in Las Animas County (Ellinwood 1978). Males may become reproductively active their first year (Schowalter 1980). These bats are believed to mi-

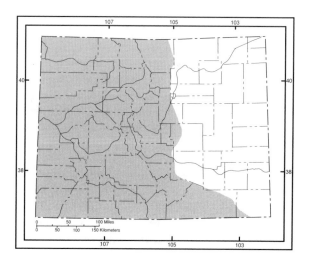

Map 6-13 Distribution of the long-legged myotis (Myotis volans) in Colorado.

grate but little is known of their movements or wintering areas. Literature on the long-legged myotis has been reviewed by Warner and Czaplewski (1984).

DISTRIBUTION IN COLORADO — The long-legged myotis occupies montane forests, piñon-juniper woodlands, montane shrublands, and subalpine forests up to 3,700 m (12,369 ft). One of Colorado's higher elevation bats, it has been taken at numerous locations in the western two-thirds of the state. Although there are no records, it would not be surprising to find them in the chalk bluffs escarpment in northern Weld and Larimer counties, the Black Forest in Elbert and El Paso counties, or the roughlands of Baca County. One subspecies, *Myotis volans interior*, occurs in Colorado.

Myotis yumanensis
YUMA MYOTIS

DESCRIPTION — The Yuma myotis is a pale, tawny to buff-colored bat with undersides somewhat paler than the dorsum. The animal is similar in size to the little brown myotis. Measurements are: total length 78–90 mm; length of tail 32–37 mm; length of hindfoot 7–9 mm; length of ear 12.5–14 mm; length of forearm 32–38 mm; weight 3.5–5 g. The braincase rises steeply from the rostrum, and there is no sagittal crest. The calcar is not keeled. The animal can be confused with the little brown myotis, from which it differs by having a duller, paler pelage, paler ears, a steeply sloping forehead, and a mastoid breadth of 7.4 mm or less (Harris 1974).

NATURAL HISTORY — The Yuma myotis is associated with riparian lands of the western United States, although some of these areas may be relatively dry and shrubby. These bats roost by day in rock crevices, buildings, caves and mines, and in swallows' nests. Night roosts typically are in buildings, under ledges, or similar shelters. Nursery colonies are usually in buildings or caves and may contain a large number of individuals.

Photograph by Roger W. Barbour.

Photograph 6-7 Yuma myotis (Myotis yumanensis).

These bats forage early, not infrequently before dark in shadowy canyons. A shorter feeding period may occur in the morning (Ellinwood 1978). Foraging typically occurs rather low over water, often just a few centimeters above the surface. The diet is not well studied, but probably aquatic insects make up much of it. Moths, flies, and beetles are taken, as are a number of other insects including grasshoppers.

Reproduction in this species also is not well known. The animals have a single young, generally born from late May to July. Lactating females

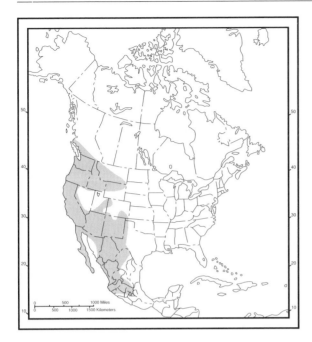

Map 6-14 Distribution of the Yuma myotis (Myotis yumanensis) in North America.

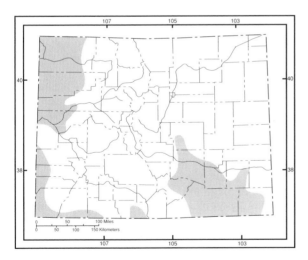

Map 6-15 Distribution of the Yuma myotis (Myotis yumanensis) in Colorado.

have been captured in early and mid-July in Colorado (W. H. Davis and Barbour 1970, Ellinwood 1978), which suggests that the young were born in June and early July. Wintering habits of the spe-cies are poorly documented, but the animals may hibernate near their summer range. Dalquest (1947) made a thorough study of this species in California.

DISTRIBUTION IN COLORADO — The Yuma myotis is frequently associated with semiarid canyon-lands and mesas at lower elevations in southern and western Colorado, but it also ranges into mixed coniferous forests in the Pacific Northwest. The species is not uncommon in suitable canyon country in the western third of the state and in southeastern Colorado, and is represented in both areas by one subspecies, *Myotis yumanensis yumanensis*.

Lasiurus borealis
RED BAT

DESCRIPTION — This is a medium-sized reddish to yellowish red bat with some of the dorsal hairs tipped white. Males are generally brighter and redder in color than females. The shoulders may have paler buffy spots, and the ventral surface is paler than the dorsum. The white-tipped hairs have a reddish band below the white, then a brown band, and then a black basal band. The ears are short, rounded, and lack a black rim. The interfemoral membrane is densely furred above and sparsely furred below. Measurements are: total length 107–128 mm; length of tail 40–60 mm; length of hindfoot 11 mm; length of ear 8–13 mm; length of forearm 35–46 mm; weight 7–16 g; wingspan 232–290 mm. The skull is short and robust but smaller than that of the hoary bat. The rostrum is nearly as broad as the braincase. Greatest length of skull usually is less than 15 mm. As with the hoary bat, a tiny peg-like first pre-molar is present.

NATURAL HISTORY — The red bat is a solitary, tree-roosting species, similar to the hoary bat. On occasion red bats have been taken in or on the sides of buildings. Although rare in Colorado, red bats are common in the Midwest and east-central states where they roost in deciduous trees (Constantine 1966). Suspended from leaf petioles or

Most foraging occurs within the first few hours after dark, although some foraging occurs throughout the night (Mumford 1973).

The animals feed from treetop level to within a meter of the ground. The foraging flight pattern is swift and straight, a series of broad, sweeping arcs. Red bats appear to be relatively sedentary, foraging over the same areas night after night and frequently close to the day roost. The varied diet consists of moths, flies, beetles, and crickets. The bats are often attracted to insects congregating around lights and will forage at such sites with little apparent fear. They also land on the ground and forage for crickets, beetles, and other insects.

Red bats probably mate in August and September over most of their range, and store sperm over winter in the oviducts. Glass (1966) reported that copulation was initiated in flight. Gestation is 80 to 90 days with two to five young (average two to three) born from late May to early July (R. Hamil-

Photograph by Roger W. Barbour.

Photograph 6-8 Red bat (Lasiurus borealis).

small twigs and branches, they may look like dead leaves from a distance. Like the hoary bat they appear to favor trees located on the edge of clearings or along fencerows, generally roosting on the south and east side of such trees. The roost area is protected from the sides and from above, with a clear flight path below. Roost height ranges from 1.5 to 4 m above ground.

The red bat emerges relatively early in the evening, but typically after other bats have begun to fly. Some of the early flight behavior is erratic and is carried on at altitudes well above the treetops.

Map 6-16 Distribution of the red bat (Lasiurus borealis) *in North America.*

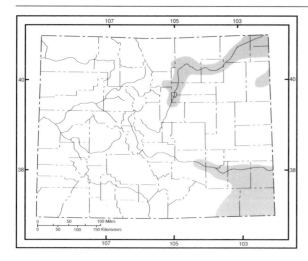

Map 6-17 Distribution of the red bat (Lasiurus borealis) *in Colorado.*

ton and Stalling 1972). This is an unusually high number of young for a bat. The young are usually left at the roost while the female forages. The young bats reach flight age by about four weeks and are weaned at about five weeks of age.

Red bats are thought to undertake long-distance migrations, at least in their northern ranges. Spring migrations occur in May and early June, and fall movements in September, October, and November (LaVal and LaVal 1979). Perhaps Coloradan individuals migrate eastward and southward but data are lacking. Shump and Shump (1982*b*) reviewed the literature.

DISTRIBUTION IN COLORADO — Only a handful of specimens were known in Colorado prior to the 1980s, collected in riparian woodlands on the eastern plains in Weld, Arapahoe, Yuma, Otero, and Baca counties (Armstrong 1972, Ellinwood 1978). In 1985 an animal was found in Boulder, and in 1990 one was found dead on a barbed wire fence in Las Animas County. Four records from Greeley, dating back to 1898, suggest that the species was not uncommon in the early days of that city. Colorado now has more extensive deciduous woodland habitat (both along streams and in towns) on the eastern plains than existed 80 to

100 years ago. These changes are directly related to irrigation and would seem to have increased the available habitat for the red bat. With more collecting we may find that the red bat is not unusual at certain times of year in Colorado. One subspecies, *Lasiurus borealis borealis,* occurs in Colorado.

Lasiurus cinereus
HOARY BAT

DESCRIPTION — The hoary bat is Colorado's largest vespertilionid. Quite handsome, its white-tipped dorsal hairs lend a hoary (frosted) appearance. The ventral surface is yellowish in the neck area, brown on the chest, and almost white on the belly. The dorsal hairs are black at the base, followed by a yellow band, a brown band, and a white tip. The ears are short and rounded, with conspicuous black rims. The wings are long and pointed with a span of 380 to 410 mm. The interfemoral membrane is heavily furred on its dorsal surface. Measurements are: total length 120–145 mm; length of tail 49–60 mm; length of hindfoot 9–11.8 mm; length of ear 12.5–18 mm; length of forearm 46–56 mm; weight 18–32 g. The skull is large (greatest length, 17–18.5 mm) and robust, with the upper first premolar very small and peg-like.

NATURAL HISTORY —The hoary bat is a solitary, wide-ranging species (the only land mammal native to Hawaii). It uses a variety of trees as roost sites. It appears to favor deciduous trees for roosts in the eastern United States, but in Colorado the species is frequently taken in ponderosa pine forests where large deciduous trees are lacking (Armstrong 1972, Ellinwood 1978). Roosts are located 4 to 5 m above ground, protected from above with good leaf cover and branches, but allowing a clear flight path below. Such trees are frequently associated with the margins of clearings or with windbreaks of the narrow fringe of deciduous trees along irrigation canals on the plains. The species never seems to be abundant in any area and most collections are of single individuals unless small groups are encountered in migration.

Photograph 6-9 Hoary bat (Lasiurus cinereus).

Males and females are segregated in summer, males tending to stay in Colorado while females continue north to bear and rear the young.

Hoary bats emerge well after dark, although migrants are known to emerge shortly after nightfall. Flight is straight and rapid. These bats make a distinctly audible chatter during flight, enabling researchers to detect their presence with relative ease. The diet is mostly moths, although other insects — including beetles and wasps — may also be taken (Black 1974, Freeman 1984), as are smaller bats such as pipistrelles (Orr 1950).

The reproductive biology is poorly known. Mating is thought to occur on the winter range, although males with scrotal testes have been captured in Colorado in July and August. Pregnant females have been collected in June, July, and August (Adams 1988). Unusual for a microchiropteran, two young are typical, and single births are rare (Bogan 1972). The young are capable of flight by 34 days of age. Most young are born in the northern and eastern parts of North America (Findley and Jones 1964).

The species apparently migrates north and south in distinct waves, with northward movement occurring mostly in May and June, and southward movement in late August or early September. Females migrate north earlier than males. Winter range is unknown. Shump and Shump (1982a) reviewed the literature on the hoary bat.

DISTRIBUTION IN COLORADO — The hoary bat probably occurs throughout Colorado in suitable

Map 6-18 Distribution of the hoary bat (Lasiurus cinereus) *in North America.*

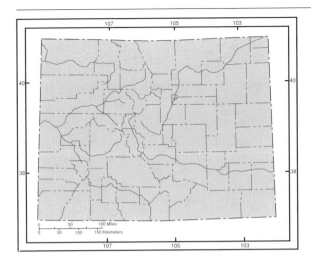

Map 6-19 Distribution of the hoary bat (Lasiurus cinereus) in Colorado.

habitat from the eastern plains to elevations of 3,050 m (10,000 ft) in the mountains. Armstrong (1972) suggested that only migrants were to be expected on the plains of Colorado, but specimens (a female and young) were taken in early summer in Greeley; they are now in the collection at the University of Northern Colorado (Fitzgerald, unpublished). This record suggests that females may give birth on the eastern plains in suitable habitat. One subspecies, *Lasiurus cinereus cinereus*, is recognized throughout North America.

Lasionycteris noctivagans
SILVER-HAIRED BAT

DESCRIPTION — The silver-haired bat is medium-sized and blackish brown with a variable wash of white-tipped dorsal hairs. The ears are relatively short, naked, and rounded. The interfemoral membrane has fur on its dorsal surface. Measurements are: total length 90–112 mm; length of tail 35–48 mm; length of hindfoot 8–11 mm; length of ear 13–16 mm; length of forearm 37–44 mm; weight 7–15 g. The skull is somewhat flattened and the rostrum is broad. This is the only short-eared bat in Colorado with a total of 36 teeth. This, coupled with the presence of white-tipped

Photograph 6-10 Silver-haired bat (Lasionycteris noctivagans).

hairs on the dorsum, separates this species from any of the darker species of *Myotis*.

NATURAL HISTORY — Despite its solitary habits this is one of the more common bats of North America. The silver-haired bat is thought to use tree cavities or crevices under loose bark for summer roosts but has been found in buildings, caves, and woodpiles during migration or hibernation. The animals seem to prefer forest edges and are most frequently seen foraging over open areas or over streams and ponds.

The silver-haired bat has been reported as a late flyer (Kunz 1973) and as an early flyer (Whitaker et al. 1977). When foraging, its flight is slow and methodical, often close to the ground, but on occasion up to 6 m high. At times the animals feed on the ground. They may form small foraging groups of three or four animals. Silver-haired bats feed on a variety of insects including moths, beetles, flies, wasps, mayflies, and termites, but moths probably are the most important food (Black 1974, Freeman 1981).

This species migrates in spring and fall. In summer, males tend to stay at higher elevations in the Rocky Mountains while females move farther north to rear their young. The animals have been captured in Colorado from March through early October (Armstrong 1972).

Two young are born from June to mid-July (Druecker 1972). Males examined in Colorado were scrotal in July, August, and September

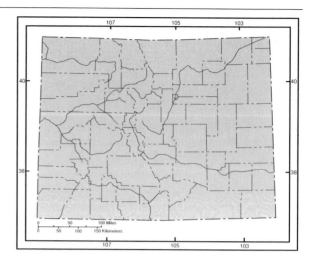

Map 6-21 *Distribution of the silver-haired bat* (Lasionycteris noctivagans) *in Colorado.*

(Adams 1988). Mating occurs in the late summer and fall, and sperm overwinter in the female reproductive tract. Kunz (1982) reviewed the literature.

DISTRIBUTION IN COLORADO — The silver-haired bat probably occurs statewide at elevations of 1,370 to 2,900 m (4,500–9,500 ft), at least during migration. Most records are from along the mountains on either side of the Continental Divide at elevations of 2,100 to 2,700 m (7,000–8,900 ft). Nowhere in Colorado does it appear to be abundant, but neither is it an unusual species, especially during spring and fall. *Lasionycteris noctivagans* is monotypic; subspecies have not been recognized.

Pipistrellus hesperus
WESTERN PIPISTRELLE

DESCRIPTION — Colorado's smallest bat, the western pipistrelle is pale yellowish gray. The pale color of the body contrasts with the dark, sparsely haired membranes of the ears, muzzle, patagium, and uropatagium. Wing venation is conspicuous, forming a delicate pattern. The tragus is blunt and club shaped, and the calcar is keeled. Measurements are: total length 60–86 mm; length of

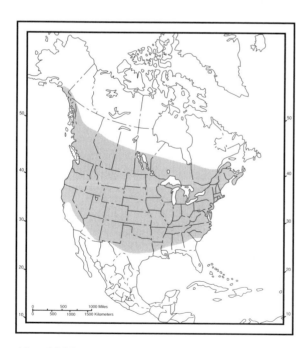

Map 6-20 *Distribution of the silver-haired bat* (Lasionycteris noctivagans) *in North America.*

Photograph 6-11 Western pipistrelle (Pipistrellus hesperus).

tail 25–36 mm; length of hindfoot 5.5–7.1 mm; length of ear 12–14 mm; length of forearm 27–33 mm; weight 4–6 g. The skull is delicate and flattened, with virtually no rise between the rostrum and cranium. The first upper premolar is tiny and peg-like, and the inner upper incisor is unicuspidate.

NATURAL HISTORY — The western pipistrelle is one of the more common bats in canyon and desert country of the southwestern United States (Barbour and Davis 1969). The animals roost under loose rocks, in crevices or caves, and occasionally in buildings. It will also use the burrows of animals in open desert scrub communities.

These bats fly very early in the evening or even in late afternoon, when canyon walls shade them from the setting sun. The flight pattern is weak and erratic, somewhat butterfly-like. Fluttering flight and small size generally restrict activity to calm weather. On windy evenings they remain in their roosts. In Colorado, as elsewhere, two peaks of feeding activity occur, one early in the evening and a second, lesser peak, at dawn (Ellinwood 1978). Their early foraging may result in some competition with swallows or other diurnal insectivorous birds, but insects are an abundant resource and neither competition nor competitive exclusion has been documented.

The western pipistrelle appears to be a rather sedentary bat that roosts and hibernates close to its summer range. In some areas, including Nevada (M. O'Farrell et al. 1967) and Utah (Ruffner et al. 1979), the animals are active even in the colder months at temperatures close to 1 to 2°C (34–36°F). In Colorado National Monument they are active in all months except December, January, and February (P. Miller 1964). Small populations probably occur in suitable habitat along the entire western margin of Colorado and in extreme southeastern parts of the state. The animals may be observed flying about mistnets, but very few individuals are captured because they can avoid the nets with their slow, deliberate flight (Barbour and Davis 1969). Future studies may find them more widespread than current records indicate.

One or two young are born in June or July (Krutzsch 1975). Small nursery colonies have

Map 6-22 Distribution of the western pipistrelle (Pipistrellus hesperus) *in North America.*

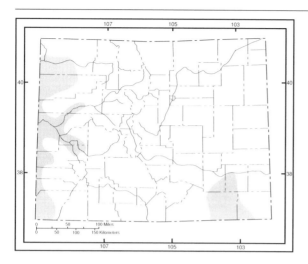

Map 6-23 Distribution of the western pipistrelle (Pipistrellus hesperus) in Colorado.

been reported, as have solitary females with young (Ellinwood 1978).

DISTRIBUTION IN COLORADO — *Pipistrellus hesperus hesperus* occurs in the western quarter of the state, and *P. h. maximus* is known from a few specimens from southeastern Colorado (Armstrong 1972, Ellinwood 1978, Freeman 1981).

Pipistrellus subflavus
EASTERN PIPISTRELLE

DESCRIPTION — This is one of the smallest bats found in the United States, only slightly larger than the western pipistrelle. It has distinctly tricolored dorsal hairs, the dark bases and tips being separated by a relatively broad band of paler yellow. The general color of the fur varies from brownish to yellowish gray on the dorsum with the venter slightly paler. The wing venation is not as pronounced as in the western pipistrelle. The ears are rounded at their tips and of moderate length, barely reaching beyond the tip of the nose if pushed forward. The tragus is straight and tapered. Measurements are: total length 70–90 mm; length of tail 32–42 mm; length of hindfoot 8–11 mm; length of ear 12–14 mm; length of fore-

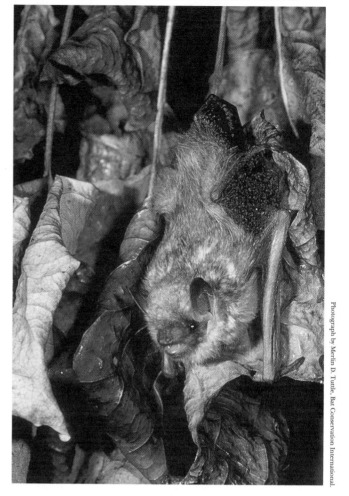

Photograph by Merlin D. Tuttle, Bat Conservation International.

Photograph 6-12 Eastern pipistrelle (Pipistrellus subflavus).

arm 30–35 mm; weight 4.5–8 g. The inner upper incisor is bicuspidate. The calcar is not keeled.

NATURAL HISTORY — Although a common bat over much of the eastern United States, the species' ecology is not well known. It is thought to be mostly a bat of open woodlands, typically foraging along the edge of openings or over water. An early flier, its movements are erratic, similar to those of the western pipistrelle. In summer the bat is thought to roost in trees, using foliage for diurnal cover, as does the red bat. The animals seem more tolerant of exposure to light than are most other vespertilionids, and they may roost in full daylight under porch roofs and similar overhangs. Except for small maternity colonies, the species is not often found in buildings (Barbour and Davis 1969). Mines, rock crevices, and caves are typical hibernation sites and are often used as summer night roosts as well. Hibernation sites are often in locations warmer than those chosen by other species (Raesly and Gates 1987). The bats generally are solitary during summer but considerable numbers may congregate at hibernacula. Swarming around caves in suitable wintering areas may occur in late summer (Barbour and Davis 1969). Moths are a principal food for the species.

Although reproductive biology is poorly known, adults can be found in breeding condition from November to April in the southeastern United States. Young are born in late June or early July in the eastern United States, with a typical litter size of two. Mortality is highest in the first several

years of life. Females may live to 10 years and some males to 15 years. Eastern pipistrelles are not highly migratory; studies to date indicate that they generally stay within 60 to 100 km of winter hibernacula. Fujita and Kunz (1984) reviewed the literature on the species.

DISTRIBUTION IN COLORADO — The eastern pipistrelle was only recently reported for Colorado. A single adult female was collected on the side of a dwelling in Greeley in early September 1987 (J. Fitzgerald et al. 1989). This site is approximately 480 km northwest of its previously known range in central Kansas. The animal appeared to be in good condition with considerable body fat and no evidence of disease. The Coloradan specimen (housed in the Denver Museum of Natural History) was assigned on geographic grounds to *Pipistrellus subflavus subflavus*, the subspecies of the northern Great Plains.

Eptesicus fuscus
BIG BROWN BAT

DESCRIPTION — The big brown bat is large and its dorsal color ranges from pale to dark brown. The venter is somewhat paler than the dorsum. Ears, muzzle, and flight membranes are dark. The ears are relatively small, and the tragus is broad and rounded. The interfemoral membrane may be sparsely haired. Measurements are: total length 90–138 mm; length of tail 34–56 mm; length of hindfoot 11–13 mm; length of ear 14–18 mm; length of forearm 39–54 mm; weight 12–20 g. The wingspan, 335–350 mm, is large for a Coloradan bat. The calcar is keeled. The skull is rather large and robust (greatest length, 15–23 mm). To the novice, young individuals of *Eptesicus fuscus* could be confused with some of the *Myotis* species, but the dental formula is different (*Eptesicus* has 32 teeth and *Myotis* has 38 teeth). Only *M. volans*, *M. californicus*, and *M. ciliolabrum* have keeled calcars, but the small size and generally paler color of the latter two species differentiate them from the big brown bat.

Map 6-24 Distribution of the eastern pipistrelle (Pipistrellus subflavus) *in North America.*

Photograph 6-13 Big brown bat (Eptesicus fuscus).

aging habitat is frequently a considerable distance away from the roost. Individuals tend to patrol the same feeding areas night after night (Goehring 1972). The diet consists mostly of beetles (G. Phillips 1966); moths are not as important to this species as they are to many other bats (Black 1974, Freeman 1981). Big brown bats are efficient foragers and may fill their stomachs in an hour or less. They use feeding stations or perches where they rest between foraging bouts or they return to the day roost. Guano and food

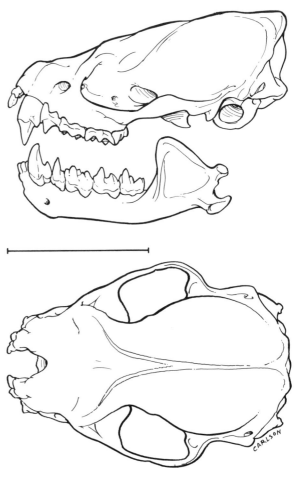

NATURAL HISTORY — This bat is found in almost every habitat in the United States. Unlike many bats, it is common in urban areas (Tuttle 1988) and frequents buildings as roost sites. Despite its wide distribution, few detailed studies exist. The animals roost in dwellings and other structures, in hollow trees, rock crevices, caves, under bridges, and in practically any other location that offers concealment and cover from the elements.

They generally emerge from their day roost at dusk and fly with a steady, straight flight. Foraging generally occurs at altitudes of 7 to 10 m. For-

Figure 6-2 Lateral and dorsal views of the skull of the big brown bat (Eptesicus fuscus). *Scale = 1 cm.*

Map 6-25 Distribution of the big brown bat (Eptesicus fuscus) in North America.

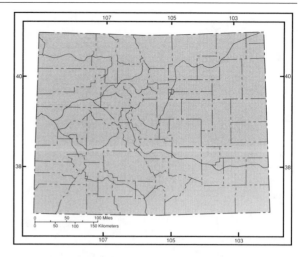

Map 6-26 Distribution of the big brown bat (Eptesicus fuscus) in Colorado.

debris on the doorstep of a house is a sign of such a resting station.

The big brown bat is thought to be rather sedentary, staying in the same general area both winter and summer. However, little is known about the location of hibernacula in Colorado. Big brown bats have been reported wintering in mines and tunnels in the state (Armstrong 1972) and occasionally a few are discovered in an attic or building being remodeled. The numbers thus encountered in no way compare with the densities of the animals observed in summer, however, when nursery colonies may exceed 300 bats. Gillis (1968) studied aspects of their biology in Fort Collins.

Mating occurs in fall and winter; spermatozoa are stored in the female's reproductive tract until spring. Testes are scrotal in August and yearlings do not reproduce. Parturition occurs 60 days after fertilization. Lactating females have been collected from June to September, but highest

numbers are found in July (Adams 1988). Young are born naked and helpless, but reach flight age in about one month (Kunz 1974). The usual litter size is two in the eastern United States, but a single young is produced in the west (Christian 1956, Cockrum 1955). As in many other bats, the big brown bat forms nursery colonies during the summer months and males are segregated from females and young. Nursery colonies may be as large as a couple of hundred individuals, but average 12 to 24. In Maryland, young were apparently born in maternity colonies in hollow trees, weighing 2.5 g (Christian 1956). In late June or July, the colony moved to cover behind window shutters where they remained until October. Considerable shifting occurs, and the sexes mix in July. Females first give birth at one year of age.

DISTRIBUTION IN COLORADO — The big brown bat is one of the commonest bats in North America and the one most frequently observed by residents of urban areas. These bats probably exist throughout Colorado in all habitats to elevations of about 3,050 m (10,000 ft). Roosting areas on the eastern plains are now available because of human settlement, which provides abandoned buildings and similar cover. A single subspecies, *Eptesicus fuscus pallidus*, occurs in Colorado.

Photograph by Roger W. Barbour.

Photograph 6-14 Spotted bat (Euderma maculatum).

Euderma maculatum
SPOTTED BAT

DESCRIPTION — The spotted bat is a beautiful and unmistakable animal. It is medium-sized, with enormous ears and a conspicuous black dorsum with three large white spots. The venter has a frosted appearance due to the hairs having black bases and white tips. White hairs are usually present at the posterior base of each ear. The ears are pink to gray-brown in color. Measurements are: total length 107–119 mm; length of hindfoot 10–12 mm; length of ear 37–47 mm; length of

forearm 48–52 mm; weight 13–14 g. The large skull measures 18–19 mm in greatest length. The braincase is elongate and the zygomatic arches are stout and expanded near their midpoints. The auditory bullae are elliptical and enlarged. The lower canine is somewhat reduced in size.

NATURAL HISTORY — The ecology and distribution of the spotted bat are poorly understood. The most significant studies are from Utah (Poché and Bailey 1974) and Texas (Easterla 1973, Easterla and Whitaker 1972). The animal has been captured in ponderosa pine of montane forests, piñon-juniper woodlands, and open semidesert shrublands. Rocky cliffs are necessary to provide suitable cracks and crevices for roosting, as is access to water. The animals show apparent seasonal change in habitat, occupying ponderosa pine woodlands in the reproductive season and lower elevations at other times of the year.

Map 6-27 Distribution of the spotted bat (Euderma maculatum) *in North America.*

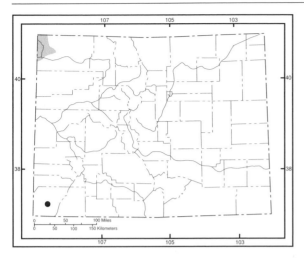

Map 6-28 *Distribution of the spotted bat* (Euderma maculatum) *in Colorado.*

Spotted bats forage alone in open habitat, flying 5 to 10 m above ground. Foraging usually occurs after midnight. The diet appears to consist of moths, with only the abdomens eaten, but grasshoppers, beetles, katydids, and perhaps smaller insects may also be taken. Their calls (which are audible to humans, thus facilitating their detection) apparently help individuals space themselves in suitable habitat (Leonard and Fenton 1984).

Little is known of reproduction in spotted bats although lactating females have been captured from June until mid-August in various areas of the range. Litter size is thought to be one. Watkins (1977) reviewed the literature on the species.

DISTRIBUTION IN COLORADO — Finley and Creasy (1982) reported the first record of the spotted bat from Colorado, an individual from Brown's Park, Moffat County. The species likely will be captured elsewhere in the suitable habitat in western and south-central Colorado. The species ranges in elevation from below sea level in California to 3,230 m (10,600 ft) in New Mexico. *Euderma maculatum* is monotypic; subspecies are not recognized.

Photograph 6-15 *Townsend's big-eared bat* (Plecotus townsendii).

Plecotus townsendii
TOWNSEND'S BIG-EARED BAT

DESCRIPTION — Townsend's big-eared bat is medium-sized. The color is brown to grayish brown, and the ventral surface is slightly lighter in color than the dorsal surface. There are a pair of protruding glandular masses between the eyes and the nostrils. The hairs are usually brown at the tips and grayish at their bases. The markedly long ears have conspicuous transverse ridges. The tragus is well developed. Measurements are: total length 90–112 mm; length of tail 35–54 mm;

121

Map 6-29 Distribution of Townsend's big-eared bat (Plecotus townsendii) *in North America.*

length of hindfoot 9–12 mm; length of ear 30–38 mm; length of forearm 39–48 mm; weight 9–14 g. The skull is slender, the rostrum is rather short, and the auditory bullae are large. The greatest length of the skull is 15–17 mm. The calcar is not keeled as it is in *Idionycteris phyllotis*, which it greatly resembles. *Plecotus townsendii* also lacks the well-developed lappets that project over the forehead of Allen's big-eared bat.

NATURAL HISTORY — Townsend's big-eared bat is a western species occupying semidesert shrublands, piñon-juniper woodlands, and open montane forests. Where the species does occur on the Great Plains, it is restricted to deciduous woodland near suitable caves and rocky outcrops. It is frequently associated with caves and abandoned mines for day roosts and hibernacula but will also use abandoned buildings and crevices on rock cliffs for refuge. Several animals were captured in an abandoned mansion near Larkspur, Douglas County, in September (J. Fitzgerald et al. 1989). Recently, a hibernaculum was found in an

active gold mine in the La Plata Mountains near Mancos (Armstrong, unpublished). Armstrong (1972) reported use of water diversion tunnels by this and associated species (*M. ciliolabrum* and *E. fuscus*) of hibernating bats in Larimer County. During the summer single individuals may be encountered hanging in cracks of cliffs. Townsend's big-eared bats are relatively sedentary. They do not move long distances from hibernacula to summer roosts nor do they move or forage far from their day roosts.

Townsend's big-eared bats breed in late fall and winter while in their hibernacula. Females store sperm until spring. Gestation lasts 50 to 60 days and a single young is born in May or June. Females assemble into nursery colonies of a few to several hundred individuals, forming dense clusters to take advantage of shared metabolic heat. Warm nursery sites are essential for reproductive success (Humphrey and Kunz 1976). Females leave the young in the roost when they forage. The young develop rapidly, achieving volancy at about three to four weeks. Adult males at this time are segregated from females, either in the same cave or in separate roost sites. Males are usually found as solitary individuals or in small groups. At summer roosts individuals do not hide in cracks or crevices, but rather hang exposed from the roof or walls of the chamber, taking flight if disturbed.

These bats are late flyers, generally emerging from the roost well after dark. Caddisflies appear to be a staple of the diet (Freeman 1984), which also includes moths, flies, and other insects. These bats are gleaners, picking insects from leaves. Much of the foraging occurs over water, along the margins of vegetation, and over sagebrush. Their late flight, seclusive habits, and their capable avoidance of mistnets may allow this species to go undetected in an area unless roost sites are found.

During hibernation Townsend's big-eared bats coil their long ears back and fluff the fur to conserve heat. They are very sensitive to fluctuations

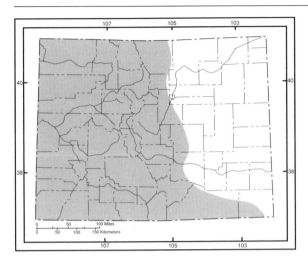

Map 6-30 Distribution of Townsend's big-eared bat (Plecotus townsendii) *in Colorado.*

in temperature and humidity and move in response to them. Hibernacula with the appropriate stable temperature and humidity appear to be a limiting resource for this bat. Both males and females lose half their body weight before spring, leading to the suggestion that winter mortality may be a prevailing factor limiting populations (Humphrey and Kunz 1976). Furthermore, they are easily disturbed and leave caves or mines where human harassment occurs even though such disturbance may be unintentional. This sensitivity suggests that caves and mines should be closed or access strictly limited to protect the species. The ecology and habits of this species were summarized by Barbour and Davis (1969) and Kunz and Martin (1982).

DISTRIBUTION IN COLORADO — One subspecies, *Plecotus townsendii pallescens*, occurs over most of the western two-thirds of the state and extreme southeastern Colorado to elevations of about 2,900 m (9,500 ft).

Idionycteris phyllotis
ALLEN'S BIG-EARED BAT

DESCRIPTION — Allen's big-eared bat is medium-sized, tan to olive-brown to nearly black on the

dorsum, with the venter slightly paler. The bases of all hairs are black or brown. A blackish shoulder patch is usually present, as is a patch of white hair at the base of each ear. Measurements are: total length 103–121 mm; length of tail 46–55 mm; length of hindfoot 9–12 mm; length of ear 38–43 mm; length of forearm 43–49 mm; weight 10–12 g. Greatest length of the skull is 17.5 mm, and the breadth of the braincase is more than half that. This bat has conspicuous accessory facial lappets, two leaf-like structures that project over the forehead from the bases of the ears. These lappets distinguish this animal from any other bat in Colorado. The calcar is keeled.

NATURAL HISTORY — Allen's big-eared bat seems to be most typically associated with montane forests, piñon-juniper woodland, and shrublands. It has also been captured in riparian cottonwood stands in the Southwest. Similar to Townsend's big-eared bat, this species prefers caves, mines, and similar shelters for the day roost, and also utilizes cracks and spaces between boulders and

Map 6-31 Distribution of Allen's big-eared bat (Idionycteris phyllotis) *in North America.*

123

fallen rock. Roosts may be shared with other species such as the fringed myotis and Townsend's big-eared bat.

This bat seems to fly relatively late, at least several hours after dark. Its major foods include moths and beetles that are probably gleaned from the ground or vegetation. They reportedly emit low cheeping sounds in flight. Reproductive biology is poorly known, but one young per year is reported. The literature was reviewed by Czaplewski (1983).

DISTRIBUTION IN COLORADO — Allen's big-eared bat is a species of probable occurrence in Colorado. It has been reported in southeastern Utah from piñon-juniper woodlands close to the Colorado border (Armstrong 1974, Black 1970). The animal can be expected in similar habitat in extreme southwestern Colorado. Known elevational range is from about 1,100 to 3,225 m (3,500–9,800 ft). This bat sometimes is referred to as *Plecotus phyllotis* and given the vernacular name Mexican big-eared bat. The genus *Idionycteris* contains a single species; on geographic grounds, the subspecies to be expected in Colorado is *I. phyllotis hualapaiensis,* named recently by Tumlison (1993).

Antrozous pallidus
PALLID BAT

DESCRIPTION — The pallid bat is large and pale yellowish gray with big ears. The eyes are large, and the face has numerous sebaceous glands that resemble warts. Measurements are: total length 90–113 mm; length of tail 40–47 mm; length of hindfoot 10–12 mm; length of ear 23–37 mm; length of forearm 48–60 mm; weight 14–17 g. The skull has a large braincase, large auditory bullae, and a relatively long rostrum. Large size, pale color, and dental formula distinguish this from other bats in Colorado.

NATURAL HISTORY — The pallid bat is found mostly in semidesert and montane shrublands, piñon-juniper woodlands, and riparian woodland

Photograph by Claude Steelman/Wildshots

Photograph 6-16 Pallid bat (Antrozous pallidus).

in the foothills and canyon country. Cliff faces with crevices and fissures, shallow caves and grottos, or dwellings, are needed for day roosts (T. Vaughan and O'Shea 1976; O'Shea and Vaughan 1977). Males and females may segregate from one another at roosts or seasonally. Pallid bats are not thought to be highly migratory, and it is likely that they hibernate in Colorado.

The pallid bat generally begins to forage an hour or so after dark, later than most species of *Myotis,* western pipistrelles, or the big brown bat, all of which may forage in the same areas. However, Ellinwood (1978) reported observing pallid bats leaving roosts before dark in southeastern Colorado and also reported bimodal peaks of feeding in the species, at about 2 and 8 hours after dark. A ground forager (Freeman 1984), the pallid bat feeds mostly on beetles, and also on crickets, moths, scorpions, and small vertebrates including lizards, other bats, and small mice. Taking much of their prey on the ground, they typically fly within 3 m of the surface. While foraging, pallid bats emit clicks audible to the human ear.

Reproductive biology is poorly understood. Copulation probably occurs in fall and winter. Gestation is thought to take about 9 weeks. Females hang upright when giving birth and catch the young in the uropatagium. Two young, naked

Map 6-32 Distribution of the pallid bat (Antrozous pallidus) *in North America.*

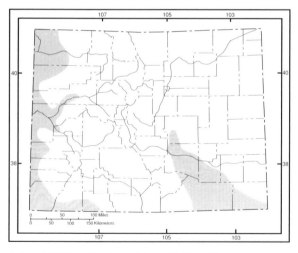

Map 6-33 Distribution of the pallid bat (Antrozous pallidus) *in Colorado.*

and blind at birth, are the mode. Eyes open by day 9, and young are furred by day 24. Young pallid bats can fly by 6 weeks of age. Births in Colorado probably occur in June. Natural history and

literature are reviewed by Hermanson and O'Shea (1983) and Orr (1954).

DISTRIBUTION IN COLORADO — One subspecies, *Antrozous pallidus pallidus*, is found over much of the semiarid canyon country of western Colorado, and similar rocky habitat in the southeastern corner of the state. Stromberg (1982) reported the species from near Torrington, Wyoming, signaling its possible occurrence in northeastern Colorado.

FAMILY MOLOSSIDAE — Free-tailed Bats

Molossid bats are freetailed, insectivorous, and most are highly colonial. The ears vary in size and often are joined at their bases. The tragus is small, and the antitragus is large. The well-developed fibula is bowed outward from the tibia. The second digit has only one rudimentary phalanx. The wings are narrow with thick, leathery membranes. The interfemoral membrane is narrow, allowing the tail to project about two-thirds of its length beyond the trailing edge of the membrane. This characteristic has given the group the common name— free-tailed bats. There are 11 genera and 33 species of molossids (also called mastiff bats), most of them in the warmer temperate and tropical areas of the world. Two genera and two species occur in Colorado.

Key to the Species of the Family Molossidae Found in Colorado

1. Greatest length of skull less than 22 mm; length of forearm less than 54 mm; ears not united at bases; ears short, not extending much beyond nose when laid forward; second phalanx of fourth digit more than 5 mm; anterior rostral breadth much greater than interorbital breadth. . . . . Brazilian Free-tailed Bat —*Tadarida brasiliensis*, p. 126

1′ Greatest length of skull greater than 22 mm; length of forearm greater than 54 mm; ears united at bases; ears relatively long, extending well beyond the nose when laid forward; second

phalanx of fourth digit less than 5 mm; anterior rostral breadth only slightly greater than interorbital breadth . . . .
. . . Big Free-tailed Bat — *Nyctinomops macrotis,* p. 128

Photograph 6-17 Brazilian free-tailed bat (Tadarida brasiliensis).

Tadarida brasiliensis
BRAZILIAN FREE-TAILED BAT

DESCRIPTION — The Brazilian free-tailed bat is chunky and dark-colored. The dorsum is grayish brown and the venter is slightly paler. The ears and the flight membranes are thick, leathery, and dull black. There usually are several thickened papillae on the anterior rim of the ears. The rounded ears are not united at their bases. Prominent vertical wrinkles or grooves are present on the upper lip. The calcar is not keeled. The tail projects beyond the margin of the interfemoral membrane for more than one-third its length. Measurements are: total length 90-105 mm; length of tail 32–40 mm; length of hindfoot 10–11 mm; length of ear 11–14 mm; length of forearm 36–46 mm; weight 8–12 g. The species is sometimes called the Mexican free-tailed bat.

NATURAL HISTORY — In the southwestern United States, the Brazilian free-tailed bat occurs at lower elevations, in piñon-juniper woodlands, arid grasslands, and semidesert shrublands. The animals typically roost in caves, mines, rock fissures, or buildings. Instances of roosting under bridges have also been reported. In the southeastern United States the Brazilian free-tailed bat lives primarily in buildings.

The species is gregarious, capable of forming colonies of as many as 5 to 10 million individuals. This is the bat responsible for the spectacular summer exit flights from Carlsbad Caverns, in New Mexico. One of the largest known summer concentrations of male Brazilian free-tailed bats is located at the Orient Mine in Saguache County, Colorado, where over 100,000 individuals have been estimated (Freeman and Wunder 1988, Svoboda and Choate 1987). That colony, first reported by Meacham (1971, 1974), has shown considerable expansion. The distribution of populations of Brazilian free-tailed bats is limited and patchy because of their need for secure, properly ventilated roosts. At roosts, the bats literally cover the walls and ceiling and make constant noise late at night and early in the morning. The animals are quiescent in early afternoon and arouse shortly before sunset.

Evening foraging starts shortly after sunset, and they may forage up to 40 or 50 km from the roost. Flight speed can exceed 40 km per hour. The animals forage almost exclusively on small moths taken on the wing. They forage 6 to 15 m above the ground and may reach altitudes of 3,000 m (9,840 ft) when traveling from the roost to distant foraging areas. Brazilian free-tailed bats do not appear to use night roosts, and simply return to the day roost when foraging is completed. Average foraging time is about 4 hours. At the Orient Mine, there are three separate outflights of bats, each lasting 20 minutes and separated by about 30 minutes. The bats return individually throughout the night, and a few stragglers return only as the sun rises.

The sexes are together during the winter but typically segregate in the warmer months when females are rearing young. Breeding occurs from February to April with no delayed fertilization.

126

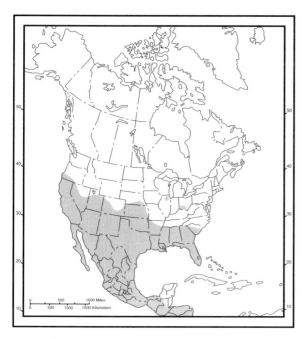

Map 6-34 Distribution of the Brazilian free-tailed bat (Tadarida brasiliensis) *in North America.*

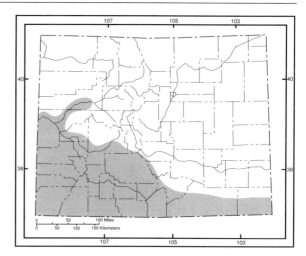

Map 6-35 Distribution of the Brazilian free-tailed bat (Tadarida brasiliensis) *in Colorado.*

Gestation takes 77 to 100 days and usually a single young is born, in June or early July, although up to three young have been reported. Pups may reach densities of 5,000 individuals per square meter (Loughry and McCracken 1991). Yearling females can produce young, unlike many vespertilionid bats, which do not even mate until they are yearlings. While giving birth the female remains suspended head down. The young are left in large nursery groups while the females fly off to forage. Although hundreds or thousands of young are present in some roosts, females identify and nurse their own offspring (Gustin and McCracken 1987, McCracken 1984). This ability is facilitated by olfaction, but the source of the odor is not known. In addition, females can discriminate, and show preference for, the calls of their own pups (Balcombe 1990). Young can fly at about five weeks of age. Although the Orient Mine population in Colorado is mostly composed of males, a few females and young have been captured in July, August, and September, indicating that the animals do reproduce in Colorado.

Seasonal migrations typically occur from summer to winter range, with only a few reports of animals overwintering in the West. Populations in the Southeast appear to be more sedentary. Migrations of 1,200 to 1,700 km are common in bats from Oklahoma and New Mexico that winter in Mexico. Such migrations take about two months to complete. In Colorado, bats begin to appear at the Orient Mine in mid-June and reach highest numbers between July and early September. By late September numbers are reduced to a few hundred individuals (Freeman and Wunder 1988).

Longevity is about 7 to 8 years in the wild, with some individuals living up to 15 years. This is one of several bat species seriously impacted by widespread use of insecticides in this country and in Mexico. For example, the large population at Carlsbad Caverns has dropped from an estimated 8 to 9 million to about 250,000–350,000 individuals. The Orient Mine population in Colorado has low levels of pesticide contamination (Freeman and Wunder 1988). The species is preyed on by a variety of raptors and by cave-dwelling mammals and reptiles, including raccoons, skunks, opossums, and several species of snakes. Rabies occurs in Brazilian free-tailed bats, although not in any higher concentrations than in less colonial species. Histoplasmosis is commonly associated with cavernicolous populations in the Southwest. Wilkins (1989) reviewed the literature on this species.

DISTRIBUTION IN COLORADO —The Brazilian free-tailed bat has been recorded from Garfield, Mesa, Gunnison, Montezuma, Rio Grande, Saguache, Las Animas, and Baca counties. The lack of specimens from southeastern Colorado is somewhat surprising as the species is not uncommon in Oklahoma, Kansas, and northeastern New Mexico. One subspecies, *Tadarida brasiliensis mexicana*, occurs in Colorado.

Photograph by J. Scott Altenbach.

Photograph 6-18 Big free-tailed bat (Nyctinomops macrotis).

Nyctinomops macrotis
BIG FREE-TAILED BAT

DESCRIPTION —The big free-tailed bat is the largest bat in Colorado. The dorsal surface is pale reddish to dark brown; the ventral surface is slightly paler. The hair is bicolored with the bases nearly white. The tail extends about one-fourth its length beyond the interfemoral membrane. The tail membrane has a well-developed pocket at the angle of the tibia and the femur. The ears are united at their bases and when laid forward extend well beyond the nose. Measurements are: to-

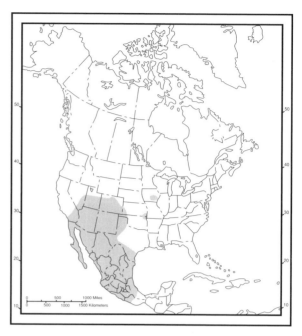

Map 6-36 Distribution of the big free-tailed bat (Nyctinomops macrotis) *in North America.*

tal length 125–140 mm; length of tail 48–54 mm; length of hindfoot 14–16 mm; length of ear 9–11 mm; length of forearm 58–64 mm; weight 12–18 g. The wingspan is 417–436 mm compared to 380–410 mm for the hoary bat, Colorado's largest vespertilionid bat.

NATURAL HISTORY —The big free-tailed bat occupies habitat similar to the Brazilian free-tailed bat but does not reach the densities of the latter species. The animals roost in crevices on cliff faces or in buildings, but little is known of their natural history. Big free-tailed bats generally leave the roost after dark and forage mostly on large moths. When foraging, both *N. macrotis* and *T. brasiliensis* make loud piercing calls that can be discriminated by observers familiar with the two species.

Females congregate into small nursery colonies during the summer months and give birth to single young in late June or July (Hasenyager 1980). Lactating females have been reported in August

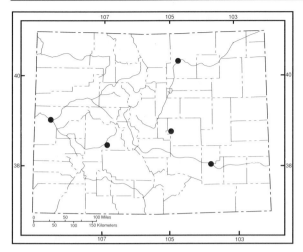

Map 6-37 Distribution of the big free-tailed bat (Nyctinomops macrotis) *in Colorado. Solid circles represent records of occurrence.*

and mid-September in New Mexico (Findley et al. 1975). No breeding records exist for Colorado. The literature was reviewed by Milner et al. (1990), and Hasenyager (1980) presented information on the animals in Utah that may be particularly useful to Coloradan workers.

DISTRIBUTION IN COLORADO —Only five scattered records exist from Mesa, Otero, El Paso, Gunnison, and Weld counties, with the northernmost from Greeley (Armstrong 1972, J. Fitzgerald et al. 1989). Individual wanderers may be expected over most of the state, but probably no breeding population exists within Colorado. *Nyctinomops macrotis* is monotypic.

Chapter 7

Order:
Xenarthra

Xenarthrans — Sloths, Armadillos, Anteaters

The order Xenarthra (formerly called Edentata) contains three infraorders of superficially very different mammals, the armadillos, sloths, and anteaters (or vermilinguas). Despite their diversity, however, these animals do share a number of morphological similarities: usually the forefoot has two or three of the digits enlarged and equipped with long, curved claws. (The hindfoot typically has five toes.) All of the living forms have a double posterior vena cava (the vessel that returns systemic blood to the heart). The clavicle is usually well developed. The dentition is generally reduced, and in anteaters it is absent entirely. Incisors and canines are absent, the cheekteeth are usually homodont, and often lack an enamel covering. All xenarthrans have extra articulations (points of contact), the so-called xenarthrous processes, between the lumbar vertebrae. In females, the urinary and genital tract is shared. In males, testes are abdominal. Differences are seen among species in diets, dentition, and preferred habitats. The only Coloradan xenarthran, the nine-banded armadillo, is a semifossorial omnivore.

Except for tantalizing fossils from Germany (Storch and Richter 1988), xenarthrans are strictly a New World group, with a fossil record dating to the Paleocene Epoch, 60 million years ago. The earliest adaptive radiation occurred in South America, but some species eventually entered Central and North America, including the giant ground sloths of the Pleistocene, some of

which were 3 m in length. There are 4 living families with 24 species in 13 genera.

FAMILY DASYPODIDAE — Armadillos

Armadillos are small to medium-sized mammals, ranging in weight from less than 1 kg up to 60 kg. The body is covered with bony plates that have a dermal covering of horny, cornified epidermis. At the junctions of the plates are areas of thinner skin that allow for considerable flexibility and movement. The word *armadillo* is Spanish, referring to this armor-like coat. The limbs are protected by smaller cornified plates and can be partly withdrawn into spaces shielded by the dorsal and lateral body plates. The head and tail are also covered with ossified plates or rings. The belly and medial margins of the legs have haired skin and are not protected by these plates. The forefeet have three to five clawed digits. The tibia-fibula and radius-ulna are fused at their ends.

The ears are of modest size, either rounded or pointed at their tips. Armadillos appear to have good visual, auditory, and olfactory senses. The muzzle is elongated and the tongue is long and extensile. Incisors and canines are absent and the numerous cheekteeth are peg-like, ever growing, and may number 40 or more.

Females usually have a pair of pectoral mammae and some genera have inguinal mammae as well. The uterus is simplex with a combined urogenital tract that transports urine and serves as the birth canal. Females give birth to genetically identical young produced from a single fertilized egg. Delayed implantation is common. Litter size ranges from one to 12. Males lack a scrotum, and no baculum is present. Armadillos are terrestrial mammals. They are excellent burrowers and usually seek security underground during periods of inactivity. Various species may be diurnal, nocturnal, or crepuscular. Generally solitary, most live in relatively open habitats such as grasslands, brushlands, and open woodland. Their broad dietary habits range from insectivory and carrion feeding to omnivory. There are 8 genera and 20 species in the family, with one species present in Colorado.

Photograph 7-1 Nine-banded armadillo (Dasypus novemcinctus).

Dasypus novemcinctus
NINE-BANDED ARMADILLO

DESCRIPTION — With their bony carapace, nine-banded armadillos are unique among Coloradan mammals. They are about the size of a large house cat, and males are larger than females. The body is well protected by the carapace of bone and cornified skin, with scutes extending onto the head, tail, and lateral margins of the legs. "Nine-banded" is a reference to the 8 to 11 rows of scutes lying between the much larger scapular

and pelvic shields. Sparse, stiff hairs may be present at junctions between scutes and on the face. The belly and inner legs are covered with long, coarse hair. The dorsal color is mottled dark to grayish ivory. The sides are typically paler in color. The belly is whitish to yellow. The ears are relatively long and conspicuous. Measurements are: total length 600–800 mm; length of tail 240–370 mm; length of hindfoot 75–110 mm; length of ear 40 mm; weight 3–7 kg. The skull is dorsoventrally flattened with an elongate, narrow rostrum. The zygomatic arch is complete. Auditory bullae, incisors, and canines are lacking. Cheek-teeth are peg-like, ever growing, and not covered with enamel in adults. The tooth count varies from 28 to 32, the latter being the mode. The limbs are short with five toes on the hindfeet and four toes on the forefeet. The digits are equipped with long, stout claws. Both sexes have well-developed anal scent glands that produce a strong musky odor.

NATURAL HISTORY — Nine-banded armadillos are highly adaptable, capable of existing in a variety

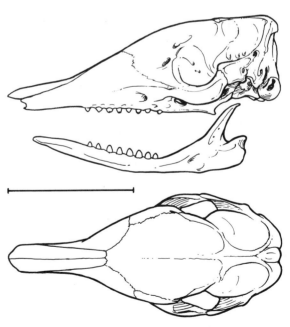

Figure 7-1 Lateral and dorsal views of the skull of the nine-banded armadillo (Dasypus novemcinctus). *Scale = 5 cm.*

Map 7-1 Distribution of the nine-banded armadillo (Dasypus novemcinctus) *in North America.*

of habitats as suggested by their broad distributional range. They are intolerant of arid conditions and seem to reach highest populations in areas with good ground cover and high humidity. In the plains states they are most commonly associated with wooded river bottoms, rather than upland prairie. Humphrey (1974) considered 38 cm of precipitation to be minimal to support viable populations in the United States. Extreme eastern and southeastern Colorado barely meet this requisite, and our cold winters probably impose limitations on long-term survival of sufficient animals to form reproductive populations. Other authors have attributed range limitations to lack of deep moist soils and lack of rotting litter, with its frequently rich concentration of arthropods for prey (Galbreath 1982).

The diet of the armadillo in the southeastern United States emphasizes insects, especially scarabaeid beetles and a variety of Hymenoptera (bees and wasps), Lepidoptera (butterflies and moths), and Orthoptera (grasshoppers, crickets). Animal

matter constitutes about 93 percent of the diet, of which 77 percent is insects (Kalmbach 1943). Other invertebrate prey includes earthworms, centipedes, and snails. Vertebrate prey and carrion are also eaten, including cottontails, birds, bird eggs, lizards, snakes, frogs, and salamanders. Plant matter in the diet includes berries, fruits, and seeds. Free water is necessary for survival.

Armadillos are generally reclusive, solitary animals, except when females are caring for young or during the breeding season, when transitory pair bonding may occur. Most activity is either nocturnal or crepuscular although some authors believe temperature is more critical to activity than is light. When foraging, armadillos "follow their noses" in seemingly erratic movements. The animals are not territorial and several individuals may use the same general foraging area. Armadillos seek shelter in nests constructed below ground or in rocky outcrops. Burrows may be more than a meter deep and up to 4 or 5 m in length. They may have multiple entrances, and one chamber typically is modified as a nest. Armadillos bring leaves, twigs, and grasses to the nest tucked against the belly with the forelegs, and then they back into the burrow (W. K. Clark 1951). When alarmed above ground, armadillos attempt to reach the security of a burrow where they anchor the feet against the burrow wall with the carapace protecting the entrance. In this defensive position they are almost impossible to extract.

Data on home ranges and population densities are scanty. Home ranges have been estimated between 1.6 and 13.8 ha (Layne and Glover 1977) and up to 20 ha (Fitch et al. 1952). Densities vary from 0.05 animals/ha to over 3 animals/ha (Kalmbach 1943, Taylor 1946). Although not territorial, the animals compete for preferred open areas (Galbreath 1982).

Armadillos exhibit delayed implantation and are capable of breeding at two years of age (Galbreath 1982). Ovulation occurs during July and August (Asdell 1964). Five to seven days following

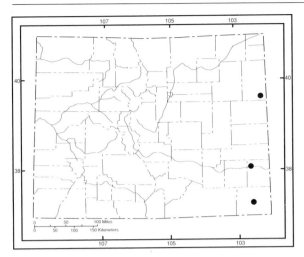

Map 7-2 Distribution of the nine-banded armadillo
(Dasypus novemcinctus) *in Colorado. Solid circles*
represent records of occurrence.

ovulation and fertilization, development of the blastocyst ceases and the developing egg is retained in the uterine cavity until late October, November, or early December, when implantation occurs. In Texas, young are born in March and April, suggesting a postimplantation gestation period of about 120 days, long for a mammal of this size (A. Enders 1966). Polyembryony is the rule, with four genetically identical offspring developing from one fertilized egg. A few authors have reported triplets, twins, and sextuplets (McBee and Baker 1982). The precocial young are born with eyes open and the carapace fully developed although not hardened. At birth the animals weigh about 85 g. They are weaned by about three months of age.

Armadillos are reported to have few natural predators. Untold thousands of them are killed annually on highways in the South, however, and some people hunt them for food. Longevity may exceed eight years although wild animals probably do not survive that long (Galbreath 1982). The species has been a subject of research interest because of its embryology and morphology, and also because it provides a useful model for studies of leprosy, a bacterial infection not known to afflict animals other than armadillos and humans.

DISTRIBUTION IN COLORADO — The nine-banded armadillo has the broadest range of any xenarthran. It was introduced to Florida and expansion of that population as well as natural population expansion in the central Gulf states has firmly entrenched the species in the United States. For reviews of the history of this range expansion see McBee and Baker (1982) and Humphrey (1974). The status of armadillos in Colorado is uncertain. There are no early records, but a few specimens have been reported in recent years (Choate and Pinkham 1988, Hahn 1966, Meaney et al. 1987). Colorado mostly provides marginal habitat for the species, and no actual breeding populations have been reported. However, more reports undoubtedly will come from the southeastern and eastern parts of the state, because armadillos are known from Nebraska (R. Hoffmann and Jones 1970) and Kansas (J. Smith and Lawlor 1964). The armadillo is a nongame mammal in Colorado (see Table 3-1) and thus protected by statute. *Dasypus novemcinctus mexicanus* is the only subspecies recognized in the United States.

Chapter 8

Order: Lagomorpha

Pikas, Hares, Rabbits

The order Lagomorpha contains small to medium-sized mammals that superficially resemble rodents. The order is old, dating from the late Paleocene in Asia, approximately 60 million years ago. Our understanding of the phylogeny of the lagomorphs is in a state of flux and has undergone numerous revisions. Some degree of affinity between lagomorphs and rodents has long been suspected and has been emphasized recently by several mammalogists and paleontologists (Eisenberg 1981; Li and Ting 1985; Novacek 1985, 1990). The likelihood of a common ancestor in the Paleocene has led to placement of lagomorphs and rodents together in a grandorder Anagalida, along with the order Macroscelidea, the elephant shrews (Stucky and McKenna, 1993).

Lagomorphs are herbivorous mammals with a short or vestigial tail. The skull tends to be light, often with numerous intricate perforations (fenestrae). The palate is short, with large incisive foramina. Chewing movements are mostly lateral, facilitated by a small amount of surface contact at the articulation of the mandibular fossa and the condyloid process. There are four incisors above and two below; the second upper incisors are small, peg-like teeth located directly behind the larger front incisors. A longitudinal groove marks the face of the upper incisors. A transitory pair of third upper incisors is lost soon after birth. The cheekteeth are hypsodont, and both incisors and cheekteeth are rootless and ever growing. Several teeth have been lost and a long diastema is present in both upper and lower jaws. The radius and ulna are distinct but the elbow prevents rotation of the forearm. The tibia and fibula are fused distally, and the latter bone articulates with the calcaneus. The forefeet are digitigrade and the hindfeet are plantigrade during walking and digitigrade during running.

The caecum is very large and contains a spiral valve. Coprophagy (the process of reingesting a specialized fecal material) is common in this group (Lechleitner 1957). Bacteria in the caecum break down cellulose, rendering it a nutrient-rich food source. The uterus is duplex. A baculum is lacking in the males, and the testes are abdominal except during the breeding season. The scrotum, when it develops, is anterior to the penis. The position of the genitalia and the lack of a scrotum in nonbreeding males make it difficult to sex these animals externally.

There are 2 families, 9 genera, and about 63 species of lagomorphs. The natural distribution of the order was worldwide except for southern South America, west-central Africa, Australia, and New Zealand. Several species, particularly the European rabbit (*Oryctolagus cuniculus*), have been introduced widely, even onto remote islands, and they have become pests in many areas. In Colorado, 2 families, 3 genera, and 7 species occur.

134

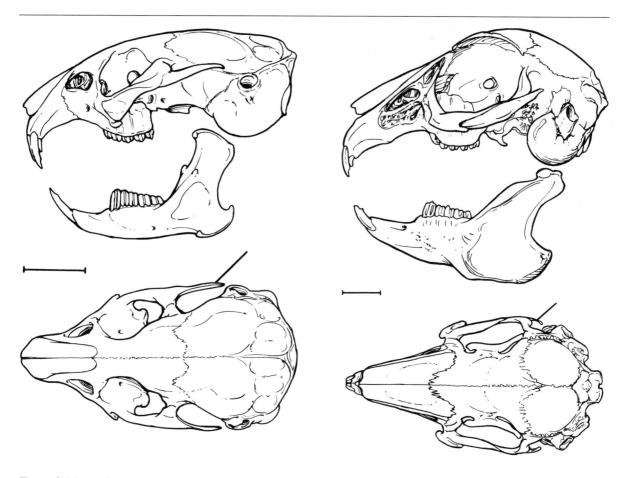

Figure 8-1 Lateral and dorsal views of the skull of the pika (Ochotona princeps — *left*) *and the desert cottontail* (Sylvilagus audubonii — *right*) *to show comparative length of the jugal bones. Scale = 1 cm.*

Key to the Families of the Order Lagomorpha Found in Colorado

1. Ears about as wide as long; tail not visible externally; five cheekteeth on one side of upper jaw; no supraorbital shield; jugal bone elongated and projecting far posterior of zygomatic process of squamosal . . . . Ochotonidae, p. 135

1′ Ears longer than wide; tail short, visible externally; six cheekteeth on one side of upper jaw; supraorbital shield present; jugal not extending far posterior of zygomatic process of squamosal. . . . . Leporidae, p. 138

FAMILY OCHOTONIDAE — Pikas

Pikas are small and short eared. The hindlimbs are only slightly longer than the forelimbs. There are five digits on each foot, and the soles of the feet are well haired. The tail is not visible externally. There is only one genus, *Ochotona*, and 14 species. In Eurasia, including Japan, 12 species occur. In North America, 2 species occur: *O. princeps* in mountain ranges of the western United States and southwestern Canada and *O. collaris* in Alaska and northwestern Canada. The collared pika is disjunct from the southern species by about 800 km.

Photograph 8-1 American pika (Ochotona princeps).

Ochotona princeps
AMERICAN PIKA

DESCRIPTION — The pika, sometimes called cony (a term also used in the Bible for the hyrax), chief hare, or rock rabbit, is small and grayish brown, with short, rounded ears and no visible tail. The pelage is fairly long, soft, and fine textured. The ventral surface is paler than the dorsum and is usually washed with buff. The hindlimbs are not elongated and are only slightly longer than the forelimbs. Pikas are sexually monomorphic, and the gender of a captured animal can be determined only by extrusion of the genitalia (Duke 1951). Measurements are: total length 162–216 mm; length of hindfoot 25–35 mm; length of ear 19–25 mm; weight 120–250 g. The skull is dorsoventrally flattened, lacks a supraorbital ridge, and has a long jugal bone forming a prominent projection from the posterior zygomatic arch. The maxillae have a single large fenestration rather than the numerous small fenestrae of the Leporidae.

NATURAL HISTORY — Pikas inhabit talus slopes in the mountains of Colorado. They are restricted to alpine tundra and subalpine forests in areas adjacent to alpine grasses, forbs, and sedges, which serve as their food. Occasionally, pikas use burrows or woodpiles for cover (Pruitt 1954).

Leaves and stems of forbs and shrubs constitute 78–87 percent of the diet, with alpine avens, clovers, and sedges as important components (D. R. Johnson 1967). Needles of conifers and bark of several woody species are also eaten. Starting in mid-July pikas collect vegetation and store it in haypiles located under overhanging rocks and underground among the rocks. It is more correctly referred to as a haypile complex, as these stashes may easily cover an area of a hundred square meters. Haypiles are not the exclusive winter food source for this nonhibernating mammal; rather, they serve as insurance against an unusually harsh or prolonged winter (Conner 1983). The volume of a haypile is perhaps that of a bathtub, and 30 species of plants may easily be found in one haypile (Beidleman and Weber 1958).

Map 8-1 Distribution of the American pika (Ochotona princeps) *in North America.*

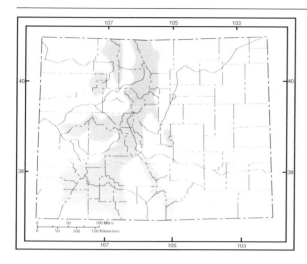

Map 8-2 Distribution of the American pika (Ochotona princeps) *in Colorado.*

Pikas are diurnal and have peaks of activity in the morning and in the late afternoon to early evening, although their calls can also be heard at night. In late fall and winter, activity decreases and the animals spend large portions of time in their dens. When snow covers the talus, they dig snow tunnels up to the surface where they forage.

Pikas are individually territorial. Territory sizes vary from 680 m^2 in June to 300 m^2 in September (Svendsen 1979, Meaney 1990b). Some overlap occurs at territorial boundaries. Home ranges vary from 860 to 2,100 m^2 (A. Smith and Ivins 1984) and considerable overlap occurs between males and females. It has been suggested that adjacent home ranges are occupied by members of the opposite sex (A. Smith and Weston 1990), although the data do not always support this claim (R. Brown et al. 1989). Pikas are philopatric, tending to stay near their site of birth (A. Smith and Ivins 1983, 1984). Females are more likely to disperse as a result of unsuccessful competition with male siblings (Whitworth and Southwick 1984). Pikas have notably low levels of genetic heterozygosity for a mammal of broad distribution (Tolliver et al. 1985), perhaps a consequence of insular populations and philopatry.

Dominance is influenced by age, sex, and resident status and is a key factor in the defense of territorial boundaries. Chases and short fights are frequent between animals involved in territorial disputes. Territorial behavior in late summer and fall centers around protection of haypiles (Kawamichi 1976).

Vocalizations and scent marking are well developed in this species and are significant in maintenance of territorial boundaries (Conner 1984, Meaney 1990b). There are a number of different vocalizations (Conner 1985a) as well as geographic differences in dialects (Somers 1973, Conner 1982). Urine, feces, and cheek marks are all used in scent marking. The cheek gland is located at the angle of the jaw and perfunctorily rubbed against rocks. Pikas can discriminate individual differences in calls and cheek-gland secretions (Conner 1985b, Meaney 1987). Cheek marking also serves to facilitate breeding, in that females are more likely to breed with males whose odors are familiar (Meaney 1986). Urine and feces are strategically placed by haypiles.

Pikas breed in April, May, and June. Females have a postpartum estrus and initiate two litters per season, although only one litter is produced. The gestation period is 30 day; an average litter size is three. Young are altricial at birth, and growth is relatively rapid (Whitworth and Southwick 1980).

Population densities vary from 3.4 to 9.8 pikas per ha in Colorado (Southwick et al. 1986). They are surprisingly stable, perhaps as a consequence of their highly developed territoriality (Southwick et al. 1986). Pikas are relatively long lived for a mammal of their size. A number of predators feed on pikas including golden eagles, weasels, coyotes, and martens. A. Smith and Weston (1990) reviewed the literature.

DISTRIBUTION IN COLORADO — Pikas are distributed throughout the higher mountains on talus slopes above 3,000 m (10,000 ft). *Ochotona princeps figginsi* occurs in the West Elk and Elk mountains and the Park range; *O. p. incana* occurs in the San-

gre de Cristo and Culebra ranges, and the Spanish Peaks; and *O. p. saxitilis* occurs in the Front
Range, Sawatch and nearby ranges, and the San
Juan Mountains. The pika is a protected nongame mammal in Colorado (see Table 3-1).

FAMILY LEPORIDAE — Hares and Rabbits

Leporids are medium-sized mammals with elongated hindlegs and hindfeet, and ears longer
than wide. The tail is short but visible. The skull is
strongly arched and has well-developed supraorbital processes. The jugal bones are long but do not
project significantly beyond the zygomatic process of the squamosals. There are 8 genera and 49
species of hares and rabbits in the world. Colorado has 2 genera and 6 species.

Colorado's hares, species of the genus *Lepus*, are
larger than rabbits, have longer ears and legs,
give birth to precocial young fully furred with
their eyes open at birth, and do not dig or live in
burrows. Colorado's rabbits, species in the genus
Sylvilagus, are smaller than hares, have shorter
ears and legs, give birth to altricial young that are
naked, blind, and helpless, and often dig or use
burrows for shelter. When leporids were given
common names by early explorers little heed was
paid to the distinction between hares and rabbits,
thus leading to much confusion. Cottontails are
rabbits, but the snowshoe "rabbit" and jackrabbits are hares. Many members of this family are
important locally as food species or species with
sport hunting value. The fur is sometimes used by
the clothing industry but the skin is thin, easily
torn, and does not wear well. Many members of
the group are looked on as agricultural pests competing with livestock for forage, or raiding cultivated crops. In Colorado, all leporids are
recognized by statute as small game mammals
(see Table 3-1).

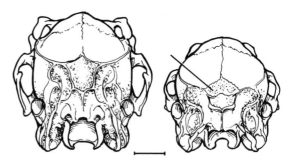

*Figure 8-2 Dorsal view of the skull of a hare (*Lepus* —
left) and a cottontail (*Sylvilagus* — right) to show the
distinct interparietal bone in the latter. Scale = 1 cm.*

**Key to the Species of the Family Leporidae
Found in Colorado**

1. Hindfoot more than 105 mm in adults;
interparietal not distinct, fused to parietals . . . . . .
. . . . *Lepus* 2

1' Hindfoot 105 mm or less in adults;
interparietal distinct, not fused to parietals . . . . . .
. . . . *Sylvilagus* 4

2. Ear of adults less than 80 mm long; little or no
development of anterior projection on
supraorbital process . . . .
. . . . . . Snowshoe Hare — *Lepus americanus*, p. 145

2' Ear of adults 80 mm or longer; well-developed
anterior projection on supraorbital process 3

3. Dorsal surface of tail with prominent medial
black stripe extending onto rump; skull relatively
low and flattened; rostrum relatively long and
shallow . . . .
. . Black-tailed Jackrabbit — *Lepus californicus*, p. 148

3' Dorsal surface of tail white, sometimes with
gray medial stripe, but not extending onto rump;
skull relatively arched; rostrum relatively short
and deep . . . .
. . White-tailed Jackrabbit — *Lepus townsendii*, p. 150

4. Predominant dorsal color pale grayish; patch on throat and chest often orangish; auditory bullae large, nearly as long as basioccipital (as measured from anterior end of basioccipital to posterior plane of occipital condyles) . . . .
. . . Desert Cottontail — *Sylvilagus audubonii*, p. 139

4′ Predominant dorsal color grayish but with many dark (reddish to blackish) hairs; patch on throat and chest rusty brown; auditory bullae smaller, usually shorter than basioccipital 5

5. Inside of ears densely furred; neck and chest patch dark rusty brownish; diameter of external auditory meatus greater than crown length of upper molars . . . .
. . . Mountain Cottontail — *Sylvilagus nuttallii,* p. 144

5′ Inside of ears not densely furred; neck and chest patch bright rusty brown; diameter of external auditory meatus less than crown length of upper molars . . . .
. . . Eastern Cottontail — *Sylvilagus floridanus,* p. 141

Sylvilagus audubonii
DESERT COTTONTAIL

DESCRIPTION — A small rabbit, the desert cottontail has long hindlegs and long, sparsely furred ears. The dorsum is pale grayish brown with a few blackish hairs on the mid-dorsum. The sides are paler than the back. The underparts are white, except for an orangish brown spot on the throat extending to the chest between the front legs. Measurements are: total length 360–420 mm; length of tail 30–60 mm; length of hindfoot 70–90 mm; length of ear 60–90 mm; weight 700–1200 g. The auditory bullae are greatly enlarged but are only roughly rounded, with a rugose surface. The external auditory meatus is also very large. The supraorbital process is generally prominent, with an upward flare to the margin. Both the mandibular and maxillary toothrows are reportedly shorter than in the other two species (J. K. Jones et al. 1983, Hoffmeister 1986). Differences between cottontails in Colorado are subtle (Scrib-

Photograph by Andrew Langford.

Photograph 8-2 Desert cottontail (Sylvilagus audubonii).

ner and Warren 1986), and it can be difficult to separate the three species by external characters alone. Hoffmeister and Lee (1963) revised the subspecies in the Southwest, including southwestern Colorado.

NATURAL HISTORY — Although desert cottontails are widely distributed, their biology has not been studied thoroughly. They occur on grasslands on the eastern plains, especially in prairie dog colonies where burrows provide excellent cover. The species inhabits a variety of other situations including montane shrublands, riparian lands, semidesert shrublands, piñon-juniper woodlands, and various woodland-edge habitats in Colorado. It can exist in areas with minimal vegetation provided that adequate cover is present in the form of burrows, scattered trees and shrubs, or crevices and spaces under rocks. Studies in southern New Mexico indicated that chaining of piñon-juniper is detrimental to cottontails unless at least 70 living shrubs or downed trees are left per acre. (Widely in the West, woodland is cleared by "chaining" — dragging an anchor chain between two bulldozers.) High density of trees reduces the density of desert cottontails by discouraging growth of shrubs (Kundaeli and Reynolds 1972).

Desert cottontails forage mostly on forbs and grasses, which constitute 80 percent of the diet.

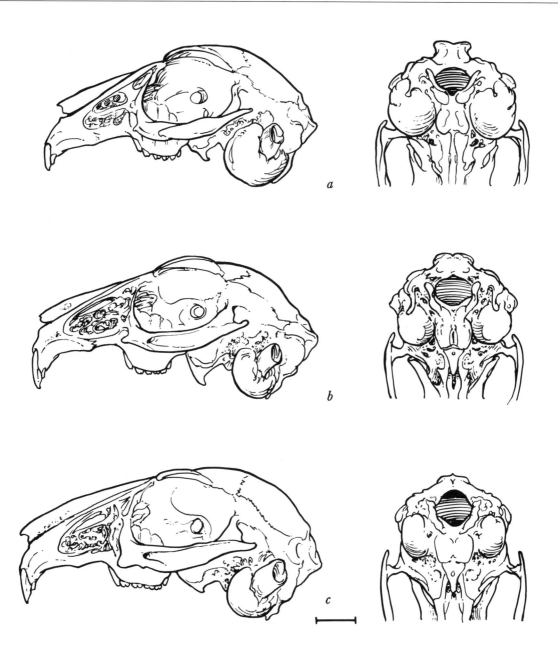

Figure 8-3 Lateral and posterior views of the skulls of the three species of cottontail found in Colorado. A. desert cottontail (Sylvilagus audubonii); *B. mountain cottontail* (Sylvilagus nuttallii); *C. eastern cottontail* (Sylvilagus floridanus). *Note relative size of the diameter of the external auditory meatus and of the auditory bullae. Scale = 1 cm.*

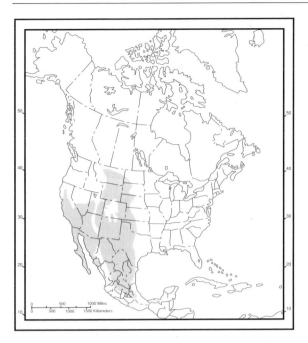

Map 8-3 Distribution of the desert cottontail (Sylvilagus audubonii) *in North America.*

Shrubs are of relatively little importance except as cover (DeCalesta 1971, Turkowski 1975). Desert cottontails are mostly nocturnal or crepuscular, and, like other leporids, are active throughout the year. They are able to swim and will also clamber into trees and brush piles.

Ovulation is induced by copulation. The gestation period is about 28 days, followed by postpartum estrus. Young of early litters are able to breed in the first year. In northcentral Colorado, three to five litters are produced per season with an average litter size of four (Wainwright 1968). The young are reared in sheltered nests lined with fur, grass, and weeds. Typical of lagomorphs, females are "absentee mothers" and up to 30 hours may elapse between nursing bouts.

Desert cottontails are not territorial. Home ranges are from about 0.5 ha to 6 ha. Densities of two to seven cottontails per ha are typical, with highest densities (16 per ha) reported in northeastern Colorado (Flinders and Hansen 1973).

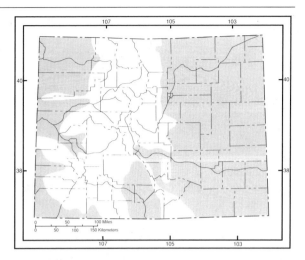

Map 8-4 Distribution of the desert cottontail (Sylvilagus audubonii) *in Colorado.*

Moderate cattle grazing tends to promote increased cottontail densities by favoring broad-leaved herbs and shrub cover (Flinders and Hansen 1975). A wide variety of predators including coyotes, foxes, badgers, weasels, eagles, hawks, owls, snakes, and humans prey on the desert cottontail. Tularemia and plague are not uncommon, and large fluctuations in population numbers occur periodically. The literature was reviewed by Chapman and Willner (1978) and Chapman et al. (1982).

DISTRIBUTION IN COLORADO — Desert cottontails occur throughout eastern Colorado, up into the lower foothills of the Front Range. In western Colorado they are common in semidesert and montane shrublands, below about 2,135 m (7,000 ft). The subspecies *Sylvilagus audubonii baileyi* occurs on the eastern plains and in northwestern Colorado, and *S. a. warreni* occurs in the San Luis Valley and in western Colorado.

Sylvilagus floridanus
EASTERN COTTONTAIL

DESCRIPTION — The eastern cottontail is generally larger and darker than the other two cottontails in Colorado, and its ears are shorter relative

141

Photograph by Bill Bevington.

Photograph 8-3 Eastern cottontail (Sylvilagus floridanus).

to body size. Measurements are: total length 380–490 mm; length of tail 40–70 mm; length of hindfoot 75–111 mm; length of ear length 45–70 mm; weight 500–1,500 g.

NATURAL HISTORY — The eastern cottontail has been studied in eastern North America probably more than any other small game species. However, information about the ecology and biology of the species in the western portions of the range is scant. This cottontail occupies a wide variety of habitats and is common in brush, rank weeds, and grassy areas. In Colorado it inhabits

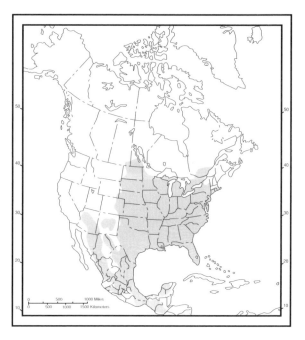

Map 8-5 Distribution of the eastern cottontail (Sylvilagus floridanus) *in North America.*

lowland riparian situations on the eastern plains and lower foothills and is the typical cottontail of cultivated areas of the Colorado Piedmont. It is mostly nocturnal but can also be seen in early morning or late evening. The species is mostly solitary except for the brief estrous period and when the female is rearing her young.

Eastern cottontails eat a variety of grasses and forbs. In winter the diet shifts to woody plants and buds, bark, twigs, and shoots from shrubs and smaller trees. They are coprophagous, re-ingesting their soft feces in order to extract a maximal amount of nutrients.

Eastern cottontails breed during the warmer months; in the southern part of their range they may breed year around. Females of reproductive age achieve almost 100 percent pregnancy rates (Trethewey and Verts 1971, Chapman et al. 1977). In Colorado the breeding season is probably similar to that of the desert and mountain

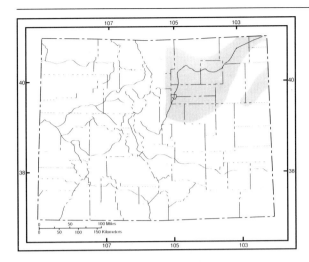

Map 8-6 Distribution of the eastern cottontail (Sylvilagus floridanus) *in Colorado.*

cottontails, with initiation in February or March and termination in August, but firm data are lacking. Eastern cottontails are induced ovulators. The gestation period is 28 to 32 days with a post-partum estrus. The number of litters ranges from three to eight per year depending on latitude. Litter size varies from two to seven with an average of three or four. Sex ratios of young approximate 1:1; sex ratios of adults may slightly favor females (Chapman et al. 1982).

Young are blind, naked, and helpless at birth and are kept in a nest lined with fine grass and hair from the female's underside. The nest is usually in a thicket or dense stand of grass. The young grow rapidly and by the end of two to four weeks are ready to leave the nest and forage on their own. Juveniles from early litters may become reproductively active by late summer.

Social behavior of the eastern cottontail is characterized by a dominance hierarchy established by postures, displacements, scent marking, and occasional direct aggression. Dominant males paw-rake with the forepaws and copulate with the majority of females. Eastern cottontails scent mark by chinning (rubbing objects in their environment with a gland on the underside of the

chin), and marking vegetation with the corner of the eye (Marsden and Holler 1964). During courtship, the male approaches the female, who adopts a threat posture. They face off, the male then makes a running dash by the female, she boxes him or jumps, and they face off again. This sequence is repeated and eventually the female becomes receptive to the male (Marsden and Holler 1964). As with other leporids, vocalizations include a shrill scream given when attacked. Cottontails communicate danger or threat by thumping their hindfeet and emit squeals during copulation; females use soft vocalizations with the young.

Densities in favorable habitat range from about 3 to 15 per ha (Chapman et al. 1980, 1982; R. Baker et al. 1983). Home ranges have been estimated to be about 2 ha (Janes 1959), but seasonal, age, and sex differences introduce much variation. The species is not considered to be territorial (Trent and Rongstad 1974). Adult females show little range overlap during the breeding season but other age and sex classes may show considerable sharing of ranges. The turnover of eastern cottontail populations is high. Rose (1977) estimated that mortality averaged 79 to 81 percent in Illinois, and although individuals can live up to 10 years in captivity, few survive past their second year in the wild.

Eastern cottontails are preyed on by numerous medium- to large-sized avian and mammalian carnivores, including bobcats, coyotes, ringtails, foxes, owls, hawks, eagles, and humans. Predation may be the major cause of death in cottontails. Cottontails are host to numerous internal and external parasites, and they are also susceptible to enzootic tularemia, which can decimate populations. Chapman et al. (1980, 1982) reviewed the abundant literature.

DISTRIBUTION IN COLORADO — As the name suggests, the eastern cottontail is a mammal of eastern North America. In Colorado it occurs only below about 1,980 m (6,500 ft). *Sylvilagus floridanus similis* is restricted to the eastern plains and foothills of the northeastern quarter of Colorado; *S. f. llanensis* is known only from extreme southeastern Colorado (Armstrong 1972).

Photograph by Andrew Langford.

Photograph 8-4 Mountain or Nuttall's cottontail (Sylvilagus nuttallii).

Sylvilagus nuttallii
MOUNTAIN COTTONTAIL

DESCRIPTION — The mountain cottontail (also called Nuttall's cottontail) is similar in general appearance to both desert and eastern cottontails. It differs from the former in being darker, with more blackish hairs dorsally, and by having smaller ears and hindlegs. The auditory bullae are much smaller than in the desert cottontail. It is distinguished from the eastern cottontail by having a paler dorsal color, a duller brownish throat patch, and more densely furred ears. The supraoccipital process is pointed posteriorly, the posterior extension of the supraorbital ridge is typically free from the braincase, and the external auditory meatus is slightly larger than in the eastern cottontail. Measurements are: total length 340–415 mm; length of tail 30–55 mm; length of hindfoot 90–110 mm; length of ear 56–65 mm; weight 900–1,100 g. In some parts of Colorado, this cottontail is sympatric with the other two species of cottontail, and identification can be difficult.

NATURAL HISTORY — The mountain cottontail is a species of the intermountain west. In Colorado, it is most frequently found in montane shrublands and semidesert shrublands and on the edges of piñon-juniper woodlands and montane and subalpine forests. It also inhabits open parklands with sufficient shrub, rock, or tree cover. It does not construct its own burrow but uses burrows of other species. This cottontail tends to avoid dense riparian vegetation and heavy coniferous forest.

During warmer months, grasses and forbs are the mainstay of the diet. In southern Idaho several grasses, globemallow, vetches, sage, winterfat, and prickly-pear were favored (M. K. Johnson and Hansen 1979). Sagebrush, rabbitbrush, and junipers are important in winter. Mountain cottontails are somewhat more crepuscular than other cottontails, often feeding early in the afternoon or from dawn to midmorning if undisturbed. They are active year round, but temperature, precipitation, and wind may alter behavioral pat-

Map 8-7 Distribution of mountain or Nuttall's cottontail (Sylvilagus nuttallii) *in North America.*

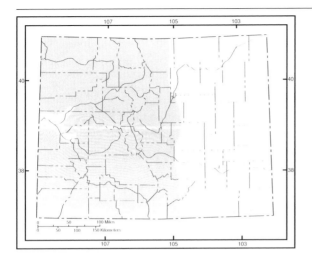

Map 8-8 Distribution of mountain or Nuttall's cottontail (Sylvilagus nuttallii) in Colorado.

terns. They retreat to cover during the middle of the day. When frightened they typically dash a short distance, stop, crouch, and face away from danger. If approached they repeat the process, or retreat to heavy cover, a burrow, or similar shelter (Chapman 1975).

Data on reproduction in Colorado are lacking. In Oregon, mountain cottontails breed from late February to early July (Powers and Verts 1971). Juvenile females can breed but few apparently do. Juvenile males are nonbreeding. Adult females have four litters a year with an average embryo count of 4.3. A few females were reported to have five litters. Gestation is 28 to 30 days, followed by a postpartum estrus. Drought-induced curtailment of plant production appears to trigger cessation of reproduction. Sex ratios approximate 1:1. The young are reared in a nest of dried grass lined with fur. Nests are typically covered with sticks, grass, or fur. The young are mobile when they weigh as little as 40 to 75 g (Orr 1940).

Population densities in juniper scrubland in Oregon ranged from about 2.5 per ha in August to as low as 0.06 per ha in November, December, and January (McKay and Verts 1978). Peaks in population coincided with production of the third litter.

Most mortality occurred in fall and early winter; drought and cold temperatures contributed to juvenile mortality. Dispersal and mortality are key elements in population control. Predators include bobcats, coyotes, badgers, eagles, great horned owls, and humans.

The three species of cottontails are sympatric in Rist Canyon west of Bellvue, Larimer County (Armstrong 1972), and doubtless elsewhere along the Front Range. As with other cottontails, this species is in need of more detailed ecological investigation in Colorado. Chapman (1975) and Chapman et al. (1982) provided review of the literature.

DISTRIBUTION IN COLORADO — Mountain cottontails inhabit the mountainous western three-fifths of the state between 1,830 and 3,500 m (6,000–11,500 ft). *Sylvilagus nuttallii grangeri* occurs in Moffat and northern Rio Blanco counties in the White and Yampa river basins; *S. n. pinetis* occurs over the remainder of this species' distribution in the state.

Lepus americanus
SNOWSHOE HARE

DESCRIPTION — The snowshoe hare, also termed snowshoe rabbit (a misnomer, as it is not a rabbit), or varying hare, is medium sized with disproportionately large hindfeet and only moderately large ears. The summer pelage is rusty brownish to gray-brown above and white below. The tips of the ears are blackish, and frequently the animal shows striking, whitish gray stockings. During the fall the animals molt to a white winter pelage with only the tips of the ears remaining black. This pelage is shed in the spring. For a short time in spring and fall the animals are mottled brown and white. Measurements are: total length 365–525 mm; length of tail 25–55; length of hindfoot 110–150 mm; length of ear 60–80 mm; weight 1–1.5 kg. The interparietal bone is indistinct, entirely fused with the parietals. The supraorbital process is present but lacks the conspicuous anterior projection of jackrabbits. In winter pelage,

Photograph by J. Perley Fitzgerald.

Photograph 8-5 Snowshoe hare (Lepus americanus).

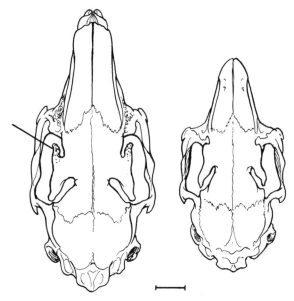

Figure 8-4 Comparison of the development of the anterior projections of the supraorbital shield in the black-tailed jackrabbit (Lepus californicus — *left*) *and snowshoe hare* (Lepus americanus — *right*). *Scale = 1 cm.*

the species can be mistaken for the white-tailed jackrabbit, which also changes color, but the snowshoe hare has much shorter, black-tipped ears, and relatively larger, more densely furred feet.

NATURAL HISTORY — Ecological information on snowshoe hares in the Southern Rocky Mountains is scant. In Colorado the species is restricted to the mountains, most commonly in or near dense stands of montane or subalpine forest and alpine tundra near treeline. The species is most abundant in willow thickets where forbs and shrubs are dense. Forests subjected to forest fires, windfall, or logging provide excellent habitat, once sufficient succession has occurred.

The diet consists of foliage, twigs, and bark of deciduous and evergreen trees and shrubs, as well as a variety of grasses and forbs when available (Hansen and Flinders 1969). Snowshoe hares need to ingest 91 to 122 kcal/kg of body weight to meet energy demands of minimal activity (Holter et al. 1974). On *ad libitum* diets the animals ate about 6.4 percent of their body weight per day. Free water and snow are both consumed. Green succulents, including clovers, sedges, and grasses, are important in late spring and summer. During winter the diet consists mostly of needles, browse, and bark of coniferous trees, especially Douglas-fir, subalpine fir, and spruce. Aspen, willow,

birch, and even oakbrush are also acceptable winter foods. When the animals turn to a dry, high-fiber diet of browse they typically show an enlargement of the cecum (R. L. Smith et al. 1980). Locally the species may cause some damage to tree plantings and seedlings from browsing. Favored browse generally has a diameter of 4 mm or less. Browsing effects of snowshoe hares may reach heights of 2 m in deep snow conditions. In Canada, Ferguson and Merriam (1978) reported considerable consumption by snowshoe hares of twigs cut and dropped by porcupines.

Snowshoe hares do not appear to venture more than 60 to 120 m into clearings, so large openings created by burning may not be used effectively (Roppe and Hein 1978). The hares are mostly nocturnal and spend the day in scrapes or "forms" in concealed, protected areas such as a dense tangle of shrubs or young conifers. Unless flushed, snowshoe hares remain quiescent during the day. At night they leave the resting place and forage, usually traveling on well-used runways.

Map 8-9 Distribution of the snowshoe hare (Lepus americanus) *in North America.*

40 days, and females have a postpartum estrus (W. R. Clark 1973). Pregnancy rates for females are 94 to 100 percent for the first two litters and about 38 percent for third litters (Dolbeer and Clark 1975). Females rarely breed as juveniles. The young are precocial and huddle in the form for their first few days. They are weaned at about one month and reach adult size by five months of age.

In the northern portions of their range snowshoe hares are noted for dramatic 10-year population cycles, which in turn affect predator populations. A number of hypotheses have been presented to account for the cycles, including behavioral interactions, endocrine responses, food shortages, and interactions of food and predators (L. Keith 1974, Keith and Windberg 1978, M. Vaughn and Keith 1981, Graf 1985, Boutin et al. 1985). In Colorado little is known of their population dynamics. The discontinuous nature of suitable habitat, the tendency to force juveniles to suboptimal open habitats, and sustained pressure by facultative predators may act to dampen population fluctuations (L. Keith 1990).

Adult survival averages 45 percent, with an estimated 15 percent survival in juveniles. Juveniles living in more open, less favorable habitat have the highest mortality. An estimated 16 percent of juveniles need to survive to maintain stability of the populations in Colorado (Dolbeer and Clark 1975). A variety of predators including coyotes, bobcats, lynx, weasels, marten, golden eagles, hawks, great horned owls, and humans feed on this species (T. Williams 1957). In appropriate habitat, snowshoe hares provide a significant component of the predator food base. This species is subject to internal and external parasites. Epizootics of tularemia seem to have little impact. The literature was reviewed by Bittner and Rongstad (1982).

DISTRIBUTION IN COLORADO — Snowshoe hares are common in coniferous forests over most of mountainous Colorado. Elevational distribution ranges from 2,438 to 3,505 m (8,000–11,500 ft).

Snowshoe hares are solitary and have intersexual overlapping home ranges (Boutin 1979). In addition to territorial aggression, these hares show dominance interactions. Males are generally dominant in winter and females are dominant during the breeding season (Graf 1985). Home ranges were estimated to be about 8 ha in subalpine forests in Colorado; juveniles were forced to utilize marginal areas (Dolbeer and Clark 1975). In prime habitat, densities of adults reach 46 to 73 per km^2 (Dolbeer and Clark 1975).

During the breeding season males fight frequently; unless in estrus, females repel male advances. Breeding starts in mid- to late April in Colorado and typically is over by late August or early September. Females have two or three litters of one to seven young (average three or four). The abundance of winter food supply influences the timing of reproduction and the numbers of young produced a year. Average natality per female per year was estimated at 8 to 11 young in Colorado and Utah. The gestation period is 37 to

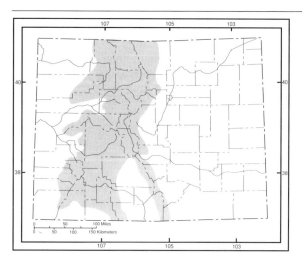

Map 8-10 Distribution of the snowshoe hare (Lepus americanus) *in Colorado.*

Photograph 8-6 Black-tailed jackrabbit (Lepus californicus).

The lowest elevational record is 1,980 m (6,500 ft) from Gunnison County (Warren 1942). The westernmost specimen is from Anvil Points, near Rifle, Garfield County (Finley et al. 1976). The Colorado Division of Wildlife considers the snowshoe hare common in Colorado and has a liberal hunting season during fall and winter. Unfortunately, nothing is known of population fluctuations in Colorado and how hunting impacts them. One subspecies, *Lepus americanus bairdii*, occurs in the state.

Lepus californicus
BLACK-TAILED JACKRABBIT

DESCRIPTION — The black-tailed jackrabbit is medium sized to large with a grayish black dorsum and white venter. A black dorsal stripe extends from the tail onto the rump. The ears are dark on the outer tips. The young have a pronounced white spot on the forehead. Winter pelage is paler than summer pelage but never approaches white. Measurements are: total length 470–630 mm; length of tail 50–112 mm; length of hindfoot 110–145 mm; length of ear 100–130 mm; weight 1.3–3.2 kg, slightly less than the white-tailed jackrabbit. The supraorbital process may be somewhat concave in profile, with the projections

never denticulate. The interparietal is indistinct. The skulls of some individuals of the two species of jackrabbit are virtually impossible to differentiate.

NATURAL HISTORY — The black-tailed jackrabbit is a common resident of grasslands and semidesert shrublands of the western United States. The species has been studied in a variety of situations, in part because of their foraging on crops and supposed competition with livestock (Tiemeier 1965, Currie and Goodwin 1966, R. M. Hansen 1972, Westoby and Wagner 1973, Fagerstone et al. 1980) and partly because they may constitute the primary food base for a number of predators, especially coyotes (T. Clark 1972, Wagner and Stoddart 1972, Stoddart 1985). Because of a tendency of large populations to degrade poorly managed rangeland, black-tailed jackrabbits sometimes have become serious pests in parts of eastern Colorado. From 1893 to 1895, 32,000 jackrabbits were killed in Las Animas and Prowers counties in organized hunts (Warren 1942).

The diet consists of a variety of grasses, sedges, forbs, and shrubs. Diet is closely linked with seasonal changes in palatability and availability of forage, and may vary from year to year depending on local conditions. In northeastern Colorado, 65 percent of the diet consisted of western wheat-

Photograph by William E. Ervin.

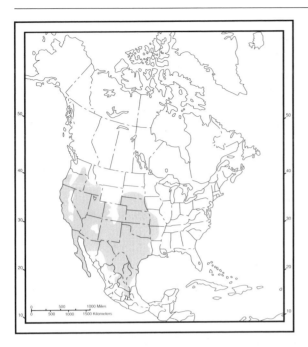

Map 8-11 Distribution of the black-tailed jackrabbit (Lepus californicus) *in North America.*

grass, alfalfa, burning-bush (summer-cypress), winter wheat, crested wheat-grass, rabbitbrush, and sedge (Flinders and Hansen 1972). In eastern Colorado, grasses were eaten in early spring and summer, forbs were mostly consumed during summer and fall, and shrubs were eaten in fall and winter (Sparks 1968). Studies in Arizona and Utah also indicated preference for grasses and forbs, with shrubs important in the winter months. In Utah, sagebrush, greasewood, and salt-bush were important browse species (Wagner and Stoddart 1972). Studies in Arizona and Utah suggested that forage consumption of 5.8 to 30 jackrabbits equals that of one domestic sheep, and 74 jackrabbits equal one cow. During certain seasons and on certain ranges competition between sheep and jackrabbits occurs. Hansen (1972) estimated that jackrabbits cost ranchers about $9.35 per hectare in the sandhills country of northeastern Colorado because of consumption of forage. C. Cook (1972) estimated that adult jackrabbits consumed an average of 0.54 pounds of food per day. He also reported them to be 1.82

times as efficient as domestic cattle and sheep at converting forage to animal biomass.

Black-tailed jackrabbits, as other lagomorphs, practice coprophagy, the reingestion of specialized feces. This activity enables them to assimilate the nutrients made by the bacteria in the cecum (Lechleitner 1957).

Black-tailed jackrabbits breed from January to July in southwestern North America, and later in this state. In southeastern Colorado breeding may start as early as February in some years (Esch et al. 1959). The reproductive cycle, from conception through gestation and postpartum estrus, to the next conception takes 40 days. Up to 5 litters are produced, with ranges in mean litter size from 1.9 for late litters to 6.4 for litters in the middle of the breeding season. The young are precocial and are raised in fur-lined nests under dense vegetation. An estimated 27 percent of juvenile females are born early enough in the year to breed that year (Gross et al. 1974). In California, young jackrabbits were capable of breeding at 8 months of age (Lechleitner 1959). The natal sex ratio approximates 1:1. Black-tailed jackrabbits are mostly nocturnal or crepuscular. They may forage in open areas at night but typically move to denser vegetation during the day. They are most active on well-lit nights and least active during high winds (G. Smith 1990). They usually spend the day in forms, shallow depressions under shrubs, and will occasionally use abandoned badger dens for cover and protection from predation. In winter they become more social, and may congregate in groups of 30 or so animals.

Density estimates range from 0.1 to 34.6 jackrabbits per ha, with home ranges of 16 to 20 ha (Lechleitner 1958, Tiemeier 1965). Home ranges overlap.

In semidesert shrublands in northern Utah, populations fluctuated by a factor of nine. Average mortality ranged from 45 to 62 percent depending on year. Juvenile mortality ranged between 55 and 70 percent (Gross et al. 1974). In California,

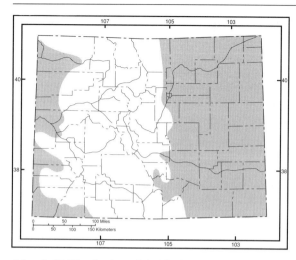

Map 8-12 Distribution of the black-tailed jackrabbit (Lepus californicus) *in Colorado.*

the distribution of age classes was as follows: 35 percent 2 to 9 months old, 38 percent 7 to 12 months old, and 27 percent older than one year. This structure indicates a population turnover within about 5 years (Lechleitner 1959).

Coyotes are closely tied to jackrabbit populations over much of the western United States, and there is evidence that this interaction impacts numbers of both species (T. Clark 1972, Wagner and Stoddart 1972). Predation by coyotes on livestock and rodents increases with a decrease in jackrabbit density. Most medium-sized and large avian and mammalian predators — including coyotes, foxes, badgers, and eagles — take jackrabbits. Diseases include tularemia which, although it can infect jackrabbits, does not appear to cause cyclical epizootics. Dunn et al. (1982) reviewed the literature.

DISTRIBUTION IN COLORADO — In North America, the black-tailed jackrabbit is a species of more southerly distribution than the white-tailed jackrabbit. Black-tailed jackrabbits are restricted to areas below 2,150 m (7,000 ft) in Colorado, where they are associated with semidesert shrublands and grasslands. They are often found on the margins of cultivated lands. The density of black-

tailed jackrabbits is directly proportional to shrub density in northeastern Colorado, but white-tailed jackrabbit density is inversely proportional to shrub density (Donoho 1972). With permanent settlement of the plains and the introduction of irrigated agriculture, black-tailed jackrabbits have vastly increased and replaced white-tailed jackrabbits (Burnett 1925) and range extensions have occurred in the eastern portion of the state (Flinders and Hansen 1972). Prior to 1972, there was no documented evidence of black-tailed jackrabbits north of the Colorado River. A record from Moffat County (Meaney 1991) suggests that they may be spreading northward into what was formerly white-tailed jackrabbit habitat in extreme northwestern Colorado. *Lepus californicus melanotis* occurs on the grasslands of the eastern third of the state; *L. c. texianus* occurs in the western portion of the state.

Photograph 8-7 White-tailed jackrabbit (Lepus townsendii).

Lepus townsendii
WHITE-TAILED JACKRABBIT

DESCRIPTION — The white-tailed jackrabbit is a large hare with a white rump and tail. In summer the upper parts are pale grayish brown except for the rump and tail, which are white. There may be tical to that of the black-tailed jackrabbit; dental details mentioned in the key are not absolutely reliable.

NATURAL HISTORY — This is mostly a species of open country: prairie, open parkland, and alpine tundra. In western Colorado the species is found in semidesert shrublands and may migrate to such areas in winter. On the Pawnee National Grassland in northeastern Colorado, white-tailed jackrabbits predominated on blue grama–buffalo-grass prairie, whereas black-tails predominated in stands of four-wing saltbush. They were equally prevalent on a saltbush and grass mixture (Donoho 1972). In general, white-tailed jackrabbits cannot tolerate losses of native vegetation as well as black-tailed jackrabbits.

The diet has been studied on both prairie sites (Flinders and Hansen 1972) and in mountain parks in Colorado (Bear and Hansen 1966). In spring, summer, and early fall, grasses and sedges are favored, but in colder months forbs and shrubs become more important. In cultivated areas on the plains, winter wheat is consumed in spring and early summer. Specialized, soft fecal pellets are reingested for additional nutrition, as in other lagomorphs.

White-tailed jackrabbits are mostly crepuscular or nocturnal but can occasionally be observed moving about on cloudy days or in late afternoon. During the day they seek shelter in forms scraped out at the base of large plants. They also frequent burrows and may even have their young in underground nests, an unusual occurrence for true hares. They rely mostly on great speed for escape.

The breeding season is March through late August in south-central Colorado (Bear and Hansen 1966). Females in estrus are often followed by several males. Breeding is promiscuous. A single litter is typical in the mountains of southern Colorado, although a postpartum estrus occurs and more than one litter is possible. Litter size ranges from 1 to 11 with a mean of about 5. In North Dakota, breeding occurs from February to

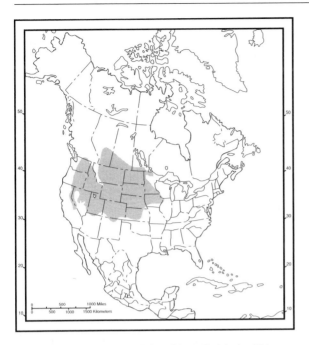

Map 8-13 Distribution of the white-tailed jackrabbit (Lepus townsendii) in North America.

a pale grayish to blackish band of hairs on the dorsal side of the tail but this stripe does not extend onto the rump. In the northern portions of the range and at higher elevations, the fall molt results in winter pelage that is almost totally white. In southern Colorado the winter pelage tends to be somewhat brownish dorsally and only slightly paler than the summer pelage (Hansen and Bear 1963). The ears are tipped with black as in the snowshoe hare, but the species in winter is readily recognizable by its much longer ears. Measurements are: total length 560–660 mm; length of tail 66–112 mm; length of hindfoot 145–175 mm; length of ear 100–115 mm; adult weight is 2.5–5 kg.

The skull has a well-developed supraorbital process (sometimes referred to as a shield) with bony anterior and posterior projections. These processes are slightly bulged dorsally and give the skull a convex appearance; the margins of the shield are often denticulate. The interparietal is indistinct. The skull of this species is virtually iden-

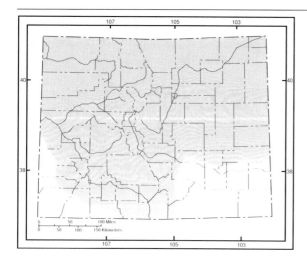

Map 8-14 Distribution of the white-tailed jackrabbit (Lepus townsendii) *in Colorado.*

mid-July with 1 to 9 young per litter (average 4.5) and 3 or 4 litters per year (T. James and Seabloom 1969). Populations on the eastern plains of Colorado may also show a higher reproductive potential than the mountain populations. At birth the young weigh 85 to 115 g, and are fully furred, with eyes open. They move about soon after birth and grow rapidly, but do not reach adult weight until about December.

Home range size and behavior are poorly known. Flinders and Hansen (1972) estimated densities of 2.2 animals per km in winter, generally a lower density than has been observed for black-tailed jackrabbits.

A large number of predators including foxes, coyotes, eagles, and humans harvest these animals, and natural population cycles recur at 8- to 10-year intervals. Like the black-tailed jackrabbit, this species is not looked on favorably by agricultural interests in Colorado, reflected in a year-round hunting season. The literature was reviewed by Dunn et al. (1982) and Lim (1987).

DISTRIBUTION IN COLORADO — The white-tailed jackrabbit is widely distributed throughout the state except in the extreme southeastern and southwestern corners. It ranges from elevations of about 1,200 m (4,000 ft) to over 4,240 m (14,000 ft) (Hoeman 1964, C. Braun and Streeter 1968). Intrusion of the black-tailed jackrabbit into white-tailed jackrabbit habitat on the eastern plains probably started around the turn of the century (H. Brown 1947, Burnett 1925) and has led to a decline in populations of the latter. *Lepus townsendii campanius* occurs in the eastern two-fifths of the state; *L. t. townsendii* occurs west of the Continental Divide.

Chapter 9

Order: Rodentia

Rodents

Rodents are the most numerous mammals in Colorado and worldwide — both as species and as individuals. Over 40 percent of Coloradan mammalian species are rodents, and there doubtless are more individual rodents in Colorado than there are individuals of all other mammals combined, humans included. Because of their great abundance and diversity, rodents are significant components of the structure and function of ecosystems, and they have been the subject of much research.

Rodents are important to people. On the negative side of the ledger, many rodents are regarded as pests because of their burrowing habits, their frequently destructive occupation of human habitations, and their competition for crops and rangeland. Several species carry diseases that are communicable to humans. On the positive side, some rodents are beneficial as sources of food or fur, and many are eminently "watchable wildlife," enriching our lives by providing nonconsumptive recreational opportunities. Further, some rodents are especially important to science, as laboratory animals and as indicators of environmental quality.

Rodents date from the late Paleocene, 65 million years ago. About 40 percent of living mammalian species are rodents; some 1,750 kinds are known. These species are classified in over 400 genera in about 50 families (Carleton 1984). Rodents are native to all major land masses except Antarctica.

Rodents range in size from the capybara (*Hydrochaeris hydrochaeris*) of South America, up to a meter long and weighing over 45 kg, to minute mice like *Baiomys* and *Micromys*, which weigh only 5 to 6 grams, the mass of a U. S. quarter. There has been an extraordinary diversification in locomotion, from primitive walking to the extreme bipedalism of kangaroo rats, the fossoriality of pocket gophers, the specialized swimming of beavers and muskrats, and through the arboreal scampering of squirrels to the remarkable gliding of "flying" squirrels. With habitats that range from wetlands to desert, from subterranean burrows to treetops, from open prairie to dense forest to open tundra, no Coloradan environment is without them. In Colorado, there are at least 59 species of rodents representing 28 genera in 7 families.

Rodents are gnawing mammals, and many are strict vegetarians (although insectivory has evolved in a number of lines). They have a pair of chisel-shaped incisors in both the upper and lower jaw. Enamel covers the anterior face of the tooth, with softer dentine making up the rest of the exposed incisor. Differential hardness of enamel and dentine allows the evergrowing incisors to be sharpened by continual nipping action, which hones the upper teeth against the lower teeth. Injury to the incisors that precludes proper opposition of upper and lower teeth may lead to formation of anomalous tusk-like structures that prevent normal feeding. A wide diastema is present, the consequence of the absence of canines and loss of a variable number of premolars. The maximal dental formula for rodents is 1/1, 0/0, 2/1, 3/3 = 22; the minimum is 1/1, 0/0, 0/0, 2/2 = 12. Cheekteeth are either ever growing or rooted. The diverse patterning of enamel on the occlusal surface of the teeth, presence or absence of strong cusps, and the arrangement of cusps are useful clues to relationships among rodents. The lower jaw articulates loosely with the skull, allowing both lateral and anterior-posterior chewing motions. The clavicle is usually well developed. Radius and ulna are separate and the elbow joint permits free rotation of the forearm. Tibia and fibula are usually separate as well, and the fibula does not articulate with the calcaneum. A baculum is typically present in males, and a homologous structure, the os clitoridis, may be present in females. Females have a duplex uterus.

For many years (until the early twentieth century), because of similarities of their gnawing dentition, rodents and lagomorphs were often grouped together in the order Glires, but distinguished as suborders Simplicidentata (the rodents proper) and Duplicidentata (for the rabbits and their kin, with their two upper incisors). There followed several decades when rodents and lagomorphs were thought to have no especially strong evolutionary connections. In recent years, however, a close relationship has been reasserted, and Stucky and McKenna (1993) included rodents, lagomorphs, and also elephant shrews (order Macroscelidea) in a single grandorder Anagalida.

There is no consensus on a proper classification of rodents at any taxonomic level. At highest levels, rodents were subdivided in the midnineteenth century into three suborders — sciuromorphs, myomorphs, and hystricomorphs — based on whether the structure and function of the infraorbital foramen and associated jaw musculature is squirrel-, mouse-, or porcupine-like, respectively. Although widely used as informal descriptions, these groups have generally been conceded to be artificial (although there

has been no agreement on an alternative arrangement that better reflects evolutionary relationships). Stucky and McKenna (1993) have actually revived formal use of the three suborders of rodents. Carleton (1984) provided a thorough and cogent review of the complex history of rodent taxonomy.

Key to the Families of the Order Rodentia Found in Colorado

1. Body covered with stiff quills intermixed with softer hairs; infraorbital foramen as large as foramen magnum . . . Family Erethizontidae, p. 295

1' Body not covered with stiff quills; infraorbital foramen smaller than foramen magnum 2

2. Infraorbital foramen small to minute, not providing passage for masseter muscle; mandibular cheekteeth four on a side 3

2' Infraorbital foramen medium sized, v-shaped, oval, or round, providing some passage for masseter muscle; mandibular cheekteeth three on a side 6

3. Postorbital processes of frontal bone prominent and sharply pointed . . . . Family Sciuridae, p. 155

3' Postorbital processes of frontal bone absent to small and blunt 4

4. External, fur-lined cheek pouches present; tail variable but not flat or scaly 5

4' External, fur-lined external cheek pouches absent; tail dorsoventrally flat and scaly . . . . Family Castoridae, p. 225

5. Forelimbs as large or larger than hindlimbs; tail short, covered with short tactile hairs; infraorbital foramen small, never completely perforating nasal septum; skull heavy and angular, auditory bullae not strongly inflated . . . . Family Geomyidae, p. 200

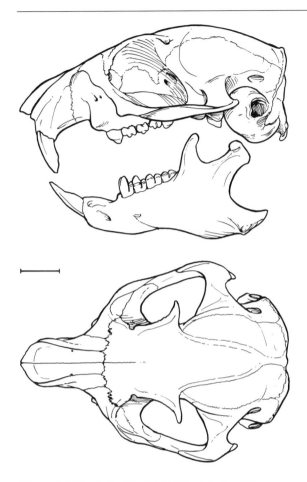

Figure 9-1 Skull of a black-tailed prairie dog (Cynomys ludovicianus) *showing prominent postorbital processes. Scale = 1 cm.*

5′ Forelimbs usually smaller than hindlimbs; tail long, usually well haired; infraorbital foramen large, completely perforating nasal septum; skull light, not angular, auditory bullae strongly inflated . . . . Family Heteromyidae, p. 211

6. Infraorbital foramen somewhat oval; total teeth 18; hindfoot and tail remarkably elongate . . . . Family Zapodidae, p. 290

6′ Infraorbital foramen not oval; total teeth 16; hindfoot and tail not notably elongate . . . . Family Muridae, p. 229

FAMILY SCIURIDAE —
Squirrels: Chipmunks, Ground Squirrels, Prairie Dogs, Marmots, and Tree Squirrels

The squirrels are a diverse group of rodents ranging from fossorial species through scansorial and arboreal forms. Colorful and mostly diurnal, they are among our most watchable smaller wildlife. They inhabit practically all habitats, from rainforest to tundra. Most are diurnal. The cheekteeth are cusped, rooted, and complex. The dental formula is 1/1, 0/0, 1–2/1, 3/3 = 20 or 22, depending on the presence or absence of a small upper premolar shed in some species as they become adults. The postorbital process is well developed and sharply pointed. The infraorbital foramen is small to minute and does not provide passage for any of the masseter muscle. The zygomatic arch is typically stout and well developed. There are four well-developed digits on the front foot (prairie dogs have five clawed front digits) and five on the rear, and usually all are clawed. The tail is well haired but varies greatly in length. Sciurid rodents date from the Oligocene, 40 million years ago. There are about 50 genera and 260 species worldwide except in parts of the Neotropics, on Madagascar, Australia, Antarctica, and in the northern Arctic. In Colorado there are 7 genera and 18 species, and 2 additional species (and an eighth genus) may occur here.

Some squirrels are not easy to identify. Chipmunks are notoriously difficult, and some people even confuse the golden-mantled ground squirrel with the chipmunks. The following key may be inadequate to separate the various chipmunks (genus *Tamias*) in some localities of sympatry. Sutton (1953), Armstrong (1972), Telleen (1976), and Bergstrom and Hoffmann (1991) have presented more detailed descriptions of Coloradan species.

Key to the Species of the Family Sciuridae Known or Expected to Occur in Colorado

1. Tail generally less than one-third total length; condylobasal length 60 mm or greater. 2

1' Tail usually greater than one-third total length; condylobasal length less than 60 mm. 5

2. Maxillary tooth rows parallel; forefoot with four clawed digits, pollex (thumb) with flat nail; total length greater than 450 mm . . . . Yellow-bellied Marmot — *Marmota flaviventris*, p. 166

2' Maxillary tooth rows converging posteriorly; forefoot with all five digits clawed; total length less than 400 mm . . . . Cynomys 3

3. Tail tipped with black . . . . Black-tailed Prairie Dog — *Cynomys ludovicianus*, p. 188

3' Tail tipped with gray or white 4

4. Tip of tail whitish, without gray center . . . . White-tailed Prairie Dog — *Cynomys leucurus*, p. 185

4' Tip of tail whitish, with gray center . . . . Gunnison's Prairie Dog — *Cynomys gunnisoni*, p. 183

5. Loose fold of skin between forelimbs and hindlimbs; infraorbital region narrow, deeply notched . . . . Northern Flying Squirrel — Glaucomys sabrinus*, p. 199

5' No loose fold of skin between forelimbs and hindlimbs; infraorbital region broad, not deeply notched 6

6. Zygomatic arches nearly parallel; jugal oriented vertically 7

6' Zygomatic arches convergent anteriorly; jugal portion of zygoma twisted toward horizontal plane 9

7. Size small, less than 350 mm; greatest length of skull less than 50 mm; anterior-ventral border of

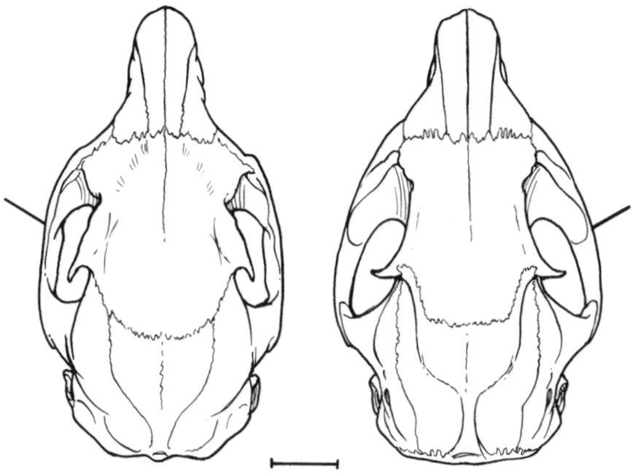

Figure 9-2 Dorsal view of skull of the fox squirrel (Sciurus niger — left) with relatively parallel and vertically oriented zygomatic arches, compared to the rock squirrel (Spermophilus variegatus — right) with anteriorly convergent and more horizontally oriented zygomatic arches. Scale = 1 cm.

orbit opposite last premolar; P^3 vestigial or absent . . . . Pine Squirrel, or Chickaree — *Tamiasciurus hudsonicus*, p. 197

7' Size large, more than 350 mm; greatest length of skull more than 50 mm; anterior-ventral border of orbit opposite first molar; P^3 usually well developed . . . . Sciurus 8

8. Ears markedly tufted; belly fur never rust-colored . . . . Abert's Squirrel — *Sciurus aberti*, p. 192

8' Ears not markedly tufted; belly fur rust-colored . . . . Fox Squirrel — *Sciurus niger*, p. 194

9. Sides of head with stripes; posterior border of zygomatic process of maxillary opposite P^3 . . . . Tamias 10

* Species of possible occurence in Colorado.

9' Sides of head without stripes; posterior border of zygomatic process of maxillary opposite M^1 14

10. Dorsal stripes (especially lateral ones) obscure; upper parts generally grayish; edges of tail often whitish . . . . Cliff Chipmunk — *Tamias dorsalis,* p. 158

10' Dorsal stripes distinct; general color of upper parts generally brownish; edges of tail buffy . . . 11

11. Size smaller; greatest length of skull less than 34 mm; length of hindfoot less than 33 mm . . . . Least Chipmunk — *Tamias minimus,* p. 159

11' Size larger; greatest length of skull more than 34 mm; length of hindfoot more than 33 mm . . . 12

12. Dorsal stripes dark brownish, usually three in number; ground color of pelage brownish to grayish; zygomatic arch weak . . . . Uinta Chipmunk — *Tamias umbrinus,* p. 164

12' Dorsal stripes black or tawny, usually five in number; ground color brighter, yellowish to reddish; zygomatic arch strong 13

13. Dorsal stripes black, ground color yellowish to brown . . . . Colorado Chipmunk — *Tamias quadrivittatus,* p. 161

13' Dorsal stripes tawny, ground color orange to reddish orange; . . . . Hopi Chipmunk — *Tamias rufus,* p. 163

14. Infraorbital foramen a narrow oval; small masseteric tubercle directly ventral to infraorbital foramen; underside of tail with white median area . . . . White-tailed Antelope Squirrel — *Ammospermophilus leucurus,* p. 168

14' Infraorbital foramen oval or subtriangular; medium to large masseteric tubercle ventral and

slightly lateral to infraorbital foramen; underside of tail without white median area . . . . *Spermophilus* 15

15. Upper parts rather uniformly grayish or brownish gray; not predominantly dappled with black or buff . . . . Wyoming Ground Squirrel — *Spermophilus elegans,* p. 170

15' Upper parts notably dappled or striped. . . . 16

16. Upper parts striped 17

16' Upper parts dappled 18

17. Upper parts with two broad white stripes bordered by darker areas; stripes not alternating with rows of spots . . . . Golden-mantled Ground Squirrel — *Spermophilus lateralis,* p. 173

17' Upper parts with alternating rows of narrow white or buffy stripes and rows of spots . . . . Thirteen-lined Ground Squirrel — *Spermophilus tridecemlineatus,* p. 177

18. Total length less than 350 mm; tail not especially bushy, shorter than 135; greatest length of skull less than 50 mm . . . . Spotted Ground Squirrel — *Spermophilus spilosoma,* p. 175

18' Total length greater than 350 mm; tail bushy, longer than 135 mm; greatest length of skull more than 50 mm 19

19. P^3 simple, less than one-fourth size of P^4; dappling of dorsal surface usually most pronounced in shoulder area; habitat in rocky areas or brushy habitats, not in tallgrass prairie . . . . . Rock Squirrel — *Spermophilus variegatus,* p. 180

19' P^3 bicuspid, with functional cutting edge, greater than one-fourth size of P^4; dappling on dorsal surface usually conspicuous to rump;

habitat in mid- to tallgrass prairie, not in rocky areas . . . . Franklin's Ground Squirrel — *Spermophilus franklinii**, p. 172

Photograph 9-1 Cliff chipmunk (Tamias dorsalis).

Tamias dorsalis
CLIFF CHIPMUNK

DESCRIPTION — The cliff chipmunk is fairly large, with obscure dorsal stripes and grayish dorsal color. The venter is whitish and the feet are brownish gray. Measurements are: total length 200–225 mm; length of tail 80–100 mm; length of hindfoot 32–35 mm; length of ear 23–26 mm; weight 50–70 g. Condylobasal length is 32–33 mm. The baculum has a thin shaft and is slightly compressed laterally. The keel of the baculum is about one-fifth the length of the tip.

NATURAL HISTORY — The cliff chipmunk is appropriately named, being largely restricted to rocky outcrops and cliff areas in piñon-juniper and ponderosa pine woodlands in extreme northwestern Colorado. No detailed studies have been made on this species in Colorado, although Cary (1911)

and Warren (1908) described habitats and observed general behavior.

Cliff chipmunks are retiring, and their drab color allows them to blend with their surroundings. They seldom venture far from dens located under rocks or in fissures and crevices of cliff faces (Hart 1971, 1976). Most foraging takes place early to midmorning and late afternoon. The cliff chipmunk is opportunistic, eating a wide variety of seeds, stems, and flower heads depending on the phenology of the plants and their proximity to dens. In Utah, mountain maple, serviceberry, balsamroot, bitterbrush, blue-grass, salsify, thistle, and wild carrot are important foods, and animal matter is not consumed (Hart 1971). Food caching occurred from June to October. Cliff chipmunks are excellent climbers and often forage in

Map 9-1 Distribution of the cliff chipmunk (Tamias dorsalis) *in North America.*

* Species of possible occurrence in Colorado.

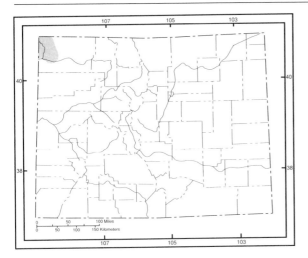

Map 9-2 Distribution of the cliff chipmunk (Tamias dorsalis) *in Colorado.*

the tops of junipers, whose "berries" (actually cones) are a favored food (Cary 1911).

Cliff chipmunks enter dormancy during the colder months in Utah (Hart 1976) and Arizona (Dunford 1974, Hoffmeister 1986), and probably also in Colorado. They are not known to make significant weight gains before entering dormancy and probably arouse periodically to feed from caches in the den.

The animals become reproductive on emergence in spring, and mating probably occurs in late April and May. Gestation period is not known but is probably one month, with only a single litter produced. About 30 percent of females studied in Arizona did not breed (Dunford 1974). The young are thought to remain below ground 35 to 45 days. J. Fitzgerald (unpublished) has observed young cliff chipmunks playing in rocks in mid-June in the Gates of Ladore area of Dinosaur National Monument, and in Utah, young have been seen as early as mid-April (Hart 1976). Dunford and Davis (1975) described vocalizations.

DISTRIBUTION IN COLORADO — Cliff chipmunks are restricted to the O-wi-yu-kuts Plateau and adjacent areas in northwestern Moffat County, north of the Yampa River and mostly west of the Little

Snake. Despite this restricted range they are not uncommon in suitable habitat. Clark and Stromberg (1987) considered them rare in adjacent Wyoming because of habitat destruction. One subspecies, *Tamias dorsalis utahensis,* occurs in Colorado. This and other Coloradan chipmunks frequently are placed in a genus *Eutamias,* with use of *Tamias* restricted to the eastern chipmunk, *Tamias striatus.* There is no consensus on generic definitions and diagnoses in the chipmunks (Levenson 1985, Patterson and Heaney 1987).

Photograph by William E. Ervin.

Photograph 9-2 Least chipmunk (Tamias minimus).

Tamias minimus
LEAST CHIPMUNK

DESCRIPTION — The least chipmunk is the smallest chipmunk in Colorado. Considerable geographic variation occurs in color and pattern. The least chipmunk usually has five dark dorsal stripes, alternating with four paler stripes. Typically the lateral blackish stripes are darker than those of other Coloradan chipmunks. The dark center stripe extends from head to tail. Two pale stripes are present on the face. Measurements are: total length 185–218 mm; length of tail 75–100 mm; length of hindfoot 28–31 mm; weight 25–60 g. Condylobasal length is less than 31 mm, and the greatest length of the skull is less than 33 mm. The baculum has a relatively long shaft and

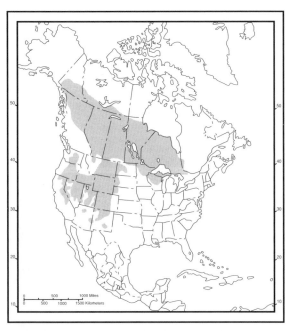

Map 9-3 Distribution of the least chipmunk (Tamias minimus) *in North America.*

a tip that is less than 29 percent of the shaft. J. A. White (1953*b*) and Lechleitner (1969) provided drawings of the bacula of Coloradan chipmunks. Because these chipmunks frequently are difficult to identify, caution is advised unless a series of specimens is available.

NATURAL HISTORY — Least chipmunks range over a wider area and in more different habitat types than any other chipmunk in the state. They occur from low-elevation semidesert shrublands, through montane shrublands and woodlands, to forest edge, to alpine tundra. Within these diverse ecosystems, they typically occupy relatively open, sunny areas on the edge of escape cover.

Least chipmunks eat a variety of fruits, berries, flowers, seeds, leaves, and stems, and also insects and carrion (Carleton 1966, Tomberlin 1969). Plant material constitutes 77 to 94 percent of the diet, and seeds 50 percent of the total. The diet changes from flowering plants in spring, to seeds and arthropods in early summer, to seeds and ber-ries in late summer and fall. Flowers of alpine parsley, dandelion, and paintbrush, and berries of *Vaccinium* and strawberry are favored (T. Vaughan 1974). Sedges, bitterroot, gilia, evening-primrose, common wild geranium, and violet are other important sources of seeds. Grass seed, currants, fungi, Douglas-fir seeds, and insects were important in Rio Grande County (Tomberlin 1969). In more xeric conditions in northwestern Colorado, a higher use of arthropods (over 70 percent of the diet), especially lepidopteran larvae, was seen (Haufler and Nagy 1984). Use of prickly-pear, thistle, and fleabane was also noted. Large aggregations of least chipmunks may occur at sites where humans feed them.

Least chipmunks are diurnal, active during the warmer months of the year, and dormant during winter. Winter dormancy is broken periodically when the animals arouse to use food stored in the den. When above ground, least chipmunks dash about searching for food with short, rapid bursts of speed. In fact, its small size and notably nervous actions help to distinguish it from Colorado's other chipmunks. Large amounts of time are spent searching for, consuming, collecting, or transporting food in the capacious internal cheek pouches.

Least chipmunks excavate burrows beneath tree roots, fallen logs, or rocks and bushes, and also use these features for feeding platforms and observation posts (T. Vaughan 1974, Telleen 1978). The tunnel system includes a nest lined with grasses, leaves, and other materials. Home ranges were 1.5 to 1.8 ha in Montana (Martinsen 1968), although Friedrichsen (1977) calculated minimum home range of 0.2 ha and densities of 54.3 animals per ha in a provisioned population in Rocky Mountain National Park. In Alberta, maximum distances between captures ranged from 143 to 413 m (Meredith 1974).

Least chipmunks are monestrous. The breeding season varies with elevation and snow conditions. Vigorous mating chases occur soon after the animals emerge from hibernation. Most individuals

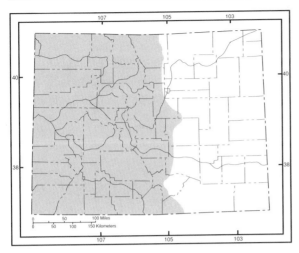

Map 9-4 Distribution of the least chipmunk (Tamias minimus) in Colorado.

extreme northwestern Colorado, north of the Yampa River and east of the Green River in Moffat County; *T. m. operarius* has the broadest distribution, occupying the Front Range and all of mountainous central and southwestern Colorado.

Photograph 9-3 Colorado chipmunk (Tamias quadrivittatus).

probably breed from late March to early July in Colorado (T. Vaughan 1969, Skryja 1974). Females enter estrus within one week of emergence. A significant number of females do not breed, possibly because of insufficient weight when entering hibernation the previous fall. Gestation probably takes four weeks (Criddle 1943). Litter size ranges from about four to six. The young are blind and naked at birth. They are furred and the eyes open at about two weeks of age. Least chipmunks are weaned and emerge from the natal den at one month of age. Weasels, martens, hawks, foxes, coyotes, and bobcats are predators. Despite its abundance, the biology of this species is poorly known in Colorado, in part because it is difficult to distinguish from other chipmunks.

DISTRIBUTION IN COLORADO — The least chipmunk is found throughout the western two-thirds of Colorado to elevations above treeline. It is a common mammal over most of its range in Colorado and is highly variable geographically, both in external appearance (Armstrong 1972) and physiology (Willems and Armitage 1975*a, b, c*). *Tamias minimus caryi* is restricted to the San Luis Valley; *T. m. consobrinus* occurs over most of northwestern Colorado; *T. m. minimus* is restricted to

Tamias quadrivittatus
COLORADO CHIPMUNK

DESCRIPTION — The Colorado chipmunk is large, similar in size to the Uinta chipmunk. The central dorsal stripe is black and very distinct; the dark lateral stripes are more reddish brown. White lateral stripes are also usually well defined. In animals with recently molted pelage the dorsal background color is bright reddish brown paling to orange-buff on the sides. The ventral color is pale gray. Measurements are: total length 200–245 mm; length of tail 90–110 mm; length of hindfoot 31-37 mm; length of ear 20–23 mm; weight 45–90 g. Condylobasal length is 31–35 mm. The width of the base of the baculum is less than one-fourth the length of the shaft and the keel height is one-fourth the length of the tip. For comparisons with similar species, see descriptions of the Uinta, Hopi, and least chipmunks.

Map 9-5 *Distribution of the Colorado chipmunk* (Tamias quadrivittatus) *in North America.*

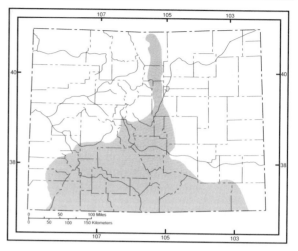

Map 9-6 *Distribution of the Colorado chipmunk* (Tamias quadrivittatus) *in Colorado.*

NATURAL HISTORY — The Colorado chipmunk has not been studied extensively despite its relatively large range and local abundance. Colorado chipmunks occupy rocky, broken terrain in open woodlands and shrublands, mostly in foothills and canyons. At lower elevations they occur in piñon-juniper woodlands and montane shrublands and at higher elevations they are found in montane forests.

Colorado chipmunks feed on seeds, berries, flowers, and herbage of a variety of plants. Common foods include mountain mahogany, prickly-pear, juniper "berries," currants, wild cherry, and snowberry (Cary 1911). The diet is undoubtedly supplemented by insects and carrion as available. All chipmunks are agile climbers, and it is not surprising to see the animals foraging high in trees and shrubs or on cliff faces. Some food materials are stored in the burrow for consumption during periods of below-ground activity. In Arizona the animals depend on free water although they also

obtain water from plant material (Hoffmeister 1986).

Radio-tracking studies found home ranges in Colorado to be 3 to 7 ha, but trapping indicated home ranges of less than 1 ha (Bergstrom 1986, 1988). As with the other chipmunks the species is not active above ground during winter but probably does arouse periodically to eat. Activity peaks during early morning and late afternoon (Cary 1911).

Colorado chipmunks are monestrous with a 30- to 33-day gestation period. Most breeding occurs in April or May. A single litter of about five young is born, furless except for vibrissae. Young are weaned at six to seven weeks of age (Armstrong 1987).

DISTRIBUTION IN COLORADO — A common species over most of its range, the Colorado chipmunk occurs in southern Colorado, where it reaches elevations of 3,200 m (10,500 ft). Its northern and eastern limits are in the Front Range, where it is restricted to the foothills along with the rock squirrel, Mexican woodrat, and rock mouse (Armstrong 1987). Along the Front Range, the Colorado chipmunk seems to occur mostly below the 2,130 m (7,000 ft) contour, and the Uinta chipmunk occurs above it (Bergstrom and Hoffmann 1991). One subspecies, *Tamias quadrivittatus quadrivittatus,* occurs in Colorado. Previously, the Hopi chipmunk (now known as *T. rufus*) in Colorado was considered a subspecies of the Colorado chipmunk (*T. q. hopiensis*), but this population is now recognized as a distinct species (Patterson 1984). Older accounts of studies at lower elevations in western Colorado and eastern Utah attributed to this species probably apply to the Hopi chipmunk (*T. rufus*).

Photograph by Rick Wicker,
Denver Museum of Natural

Photograph 9-4 Hopi chipmunk (Tamias rufus).

Tamias rufus
HOPI CHIPMUNK

DESCRIPTION — From the Colorado chipmunk this species is distinguished by somewhat smaller size and a dorsal pelage that generally lacks significant amounts of black in the stripes, resulting in a more orange red to buff pelage. Measurements are: total length 190–221 mm; length of tail 83–95 mm; length of hindfoot 31–35 mm; length of ear 15–22 mm. Condylobasal length is 31–34 mm. The auditory bullae are generally larger (especially in length) whereas the nasals are shorter and the interorbital region more narrowed than in the Colorado chipmunk. The baculum is also typically smaller than that of the Colorado chipmunk, with a shorter tip (Patterson 1984).

NATURAL HISTORY — This is the common chipmunk of much of the canyon and slickrock piñon-juniper country in western Colorado. Population densities appear to be highest in areas with an abundance of broken rock or rubble at the base of cliff faces or in rock formations with deep fissures and crevices suitable for den sites. Hopi chipmunks typically do not stray very far from

Map 9-7 Distribution of the Hopi chipmunk (Tamias rufus) *in North America.*

these rocky areas, although Cary (1911) thought them equally represented in extensive piñon-juniper stands on mesa tops. Some habitat manipulation, including removal by chaining and burning of piñon-juniper woodland, benefit this species in some areas because the downed wood increases edge and cover.

The diet of Hopi chipmunks in Utah was about 60 percent seeds, 32 percent flowers, and 7 percent insects (Armstrong 1982). Seeds of Indian ricegrass and penstemon are eagerly sought as are seeds of junipers, piñon, oak, skunkbrush, and other shrubs. As with other chipmunks, food is gathered rapidly and stored in cheek pouches for transport to feeding sites (usually atop a rock or log from which visibility is good) or food caches. Individuals probably drink free water from depressions when available.

Home ranges have been estimated at about 0.5 to 1 ha based on dye-marked animals in Utah (Wadsworth 1969, 1972). Chipmunks, including

163

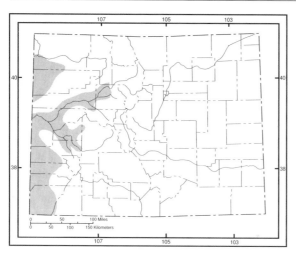

Map 9-8 Distribution of the Hopi chipmunk (Tamias rufus) in Colorado.

this species, are diurnal; activity cycles start shortly after sunrise and often do not end until nearly dark. During the heat of summer they typically are inactive at midday. Winter dormancy is shorter than for other Coloradan chipmunks, with most animals not below ground until early December and arousing in late February or early March (Wadsworth 1972).

In Colorado most breeding probably occurs in March or early April, with a gestation period of about one month. Individuals in southeastern Utah breed in late February and early March (Wadsworth 1969). Litter size ranges from two to six, with only one litter per year. The young are blind and naked at birth. The eyes open at about one month of age, and the young leave the nest when about 5 weeks old. Weaning occurs when the young are 6 to 7 weeks old. Males and females reach sexual maturity at about 11 months of age.

DISTRIBUTION IN COLORADO — The Hopi chipmunk occurs in western Colorado from the Yampa River south. It ranges eastward along the Colorado River to Eagle County and along the Gunnison to the western end of the Black Canyon. Patterson (1984) presented convincing evidence that the Hopi chipmunk is a distinct, monotypic species, as recognized here. Col-

oradan populations have been called *E. quadrivittatus hopiensis* (see Armstrong 1972 for synonymy) and *E. q. rufus* (see Hoffmeister and Ellis 1979).

Photograph by Joseph G. Hall.

Photograph 9-5 Uinta chipmunk (Tamias umbrinus).

Tamias umbrinus
UINTA CHIPMUNK

DESCRIPTION — The Uinta chipmunk is larger than the least chipmunk, and similar in size to the Colorado chipmunk. This chipmunk is often mistaken for the Colorado chipmunk; older museum specimens are often mislabeled. Uinta, Colorado, and least chipmunks all occur in north-central Colorado. Most specimens of the Uinta chipmunk are not as brightly colored as the least and Colorado chipmunks. The lateral stripes are somewhat indistinct and the flanks are grayish in color. Overall dorsal coloration tends toward brownish, but in the other two species it is more reddish yellow. The dorsal stripes are generally more distinct than those of the cliff chipmunk. Measurements are: total length 215–235 mm; length of tail 88–110 mm; length of hindfoot 33–35 mm; length of ear 16–19 mm; weight 60–70 g. Condylobasal length is 31–34 mm. The Uinta chipmunk has a longer, narrower skull, and a narrower jugal bone than does the Colorado chipmunk (Armstrong 1972). The baculum of the Uinta chipmunk has the distal half of the shaft laterally compressed with the width of the base

Map 9-9 *Distribution of the Uinta chipmunk* (Tamias umbrinus) *in North America.*

more than one-fourth the length of the tip. It has a distinctive bend lacking in the straighter baculum of the Colorado chipmunk (J. White 1953*a, b*). Behavioral and elevational differences discussed below assist in separation of these very similar species.

NATURAL HISTORY — Because of the difficulty with identification, little information is available on the natural history of the Uinta chipmunk, although it occupies a variety of habitats in Colorado. In northwestern Colorado it occupies piñon-juniper woodlands and montane shrublands, where it was considered uncommon (Finley et al. 1976). Along the Taylor River in Gunnison County they were reported from cottonwood-willow riverbottoms (Long and Cronkite 1970). More commonly, it occurs in higher elevation forest-edge situations in montane and subalpine forests (especially lodgepole pine on rubbly moraines), and it sometimes ranges into the alpine. Like the Colorado chipmunk, the Uinta

chipmunk favors rocky areas when available and is frequently common on talus slopes.

The diet is similar to that of other chipmunks, consisting of a variety of berries, fruits, and seeds as well as new terminal growth, supplemented with insects and other animal matter including carrion. As other species of chipmunks and ground squirrels, they often congregate in campgrounds where they take practically any food offered them.

Telemetry studies in the Front Range found home ranges of 2 to 5 ha (Bergstrom 1988). The animals appear to make greater use of closed understory habitats than does the least chipmunk. Good climbers, they forage on branches of conifers and shrubs. Uinta chipmunks excavate burrows under logs, rocks, shrubs, and similar surface features. On the basis of habitat, behavioral observations by Gordon (1943) probably pertain to this species.

Most individuals enter winter dens by early November. The animals are assumed to be dormant during much of the winter but probably arouse periodically to feed on stored food. Breeding occurs shortly after arousal in the spring. Gestation

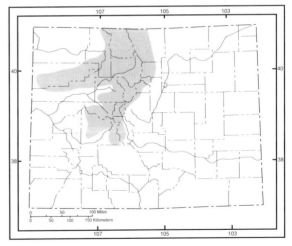

Map 9-10 *Distribution of the Uinta chipmunk* (Tamias umbrinus) *in Colorado.*

probably takes about 30 days, and one litter of three to five young is produced per season.

DISTRIBUTION IN COLORADO — The Uinta chipmunk has a complicated distribution across the the western United States, probably reflecting expansion of forest during glacial periods and contraction during interglacial intervals. At the present (perhaps interglacial) time, Coloradan populations are isolated from populations to the north and west. In Colorado they occur along the Front Range, west to Routt and Rio Blanco counties, and south to Gunnison County. Ranges of the Colorado and Uinta chipmunks are mostly parapatric in Colorado (Armstrong 1972; Bergstrom and Hoffmann 1991, Long and Cronkite 1970, J. White 1953a), although this situation needs clarification in some areas on the Western Slope. Uinta chipmunks are often sympatric with least chipmunks and golden-mantled ground squirrels (Bergstrom and Hoffmann 1991, Stinson 1978). The Uinta chipmunk ranges from as low as 1,980 m (6,500 ft) to about 3,660 m (12,000 ft). One subspecies, *Tamias umbrinus montanus,* occurs in Colorado.

Marmota flaviventris
YELLOW-BELLIED MARMOT

DESCRIPTION — Marmots, also known locally as "rockchucks" and "whistle-pigs," and sometimes mistakenly called woodchucks, are large, stout-bodied ground squirrels. Their tails are short (generally less than one-third the total length) and normally bushy. The pelage consists of long, coarse outer hairs, and shorter, woolly underfur. Individuals vary widely in color, from yellow-brown to tawny, frequently with a heavily frosted appearance due to pale tips and darker bands on some of the guard hairs. There usually is a whitish band across the nose, and the sides of the neck are typically buffy. Ventrally the fur is somewhat sparse and pale brown to yellowish. Some Colorado marmots tend toward melanism (Armitage 1961, Warren 1942). Measurements are: total length 470–680 mm; length of tail 130–210 mm; length of hindfoot 70–90 mm; and length of ear

Photograph 9-6 Yellow-bellied marmot (Marmota flaviventris).

18–22 mm; weight 1.6–5.2 kg, with males generally larger than females. The skull is broad and flat with a narrow interorbital region and well-developed postorbital processes that project posteriorly. The suture between the frontal, premaxillary, and nasal bones forms a distinct arch across the rostrum. Females have 10 mammae: 2 pectoral, 2 abdominal, and one inguinal pair. A baculum is present in males.

NATURAL HISTORY — The biology of Coloradan marmots is well known, especially near Gothic, at 2,900 (9,500 ft) in Gunnison County, where Kenneth B. Armitage, of the University of Kansas, and his coworkers at Rocky Mountain Biological Laboratory have studied them since 1962 (D. Andersen et al. 1976; Armitage 1961, 1962, 1973, 1974, 1975, 1976, 1979, 1991; Armitage and Downhower 1974; Armitage and Johns 1982; Armitage et al. 1976, 1979; Svendsen 1974, 1976). However, few studies exist on populations at lower elevations, and such studies should be encouraged.

Marmots occupy various habitats, being commonest at elevations above 2,440 m (8,000 ft) in alpine tundra, and subalpine and montane meadows. They also range down into the foothills and canyon country on either side of the mountains where rock outcrops or boulders exist along with suitably productive and succulent vegetation.

Marmots eat a variety of forbs. Less than 6.5 percent of available net primary production was consumed in one Colorado study, at least partially due to selective foraging (Kilgore and Armitage 1978). Preferred food species include dandelions, cow parsnip, chiming bells, cinquefoil, and brome. Although marmots will eat flowers of potentially toxic species such as columbine, lupine, and larkspur, they tend to avoid plant parts where such chemicals concentrate. When foraging in lush vegetation, marmots often crawl on their bellies, forming conspicuous beaten-down paths (Armitage 1962). Seeds are consumed in late summer. Marmots are not thought to be food limited over their range, although duration of snow cover affects food availability which, in turn, affects reproductive success of females (Van Vuren and Armitage 1991). Some evidence suggests that moderate grazing by livestock favors marmots by enhancing forb production (Frase and Hoffmann 1980). Cannibalism has been reported (Armitage et al. 1979).

Marmots are semifossorial, digging burrows under rocks, buildings, or other protective features. An estimated 80 percent of a marmot's life is spent in its burrow, with about 60 percent of that time in hibernation. Most home burrows are built on slopes oriented toward the northeast or southwest. Rock outcrops or boulders are usually close to the burrow entrance and serve as sites for sunning and observation (Svendsen 1976b). Trails develop between burrows.

Marmots are diurnal, with peaks of activity early morning and late afternoon. Although some individuals are solitary and transient, most are social, living in relatively stable colonies that consist of a dominant male, several females, and their offspring. Within a colony, social organization is maintained through a variety of behaviors including play, grooming, sniffing of cheek glands, and agonistic behaviors such as threat postures, chases, and fights. Males defend territories that are usually less than 1 ha in area. Territorial behaviors include tail flagging and patrolling of boundaries (Armitage 1962).

Communication is auditory, visual, and olfactory. A variety of whistles function as alert, alarm, or threat signals. Pikas and golden-mantled ground squirrels also respond to these whistles. An undulating scream is a response to fear or excitement, and a tooth chatter signals aggression (Waring 1966). Marmots scent mark with cheek glands, a behavior seen in conflict situations that probably expresses dominance (Armitage 1974, 1976).

Territories increase or decrease in size in relation to the numbers of adult males in the population (Armitage 1974). Territorial behavior and aggressive conflicts lead to development of relatively stable central colonies and peripheral "satellite" populations. Both males and females are recruited into colonies by immigration. Satellite populations tend to be less stable and have lower reproductive success compared to central colonies. Lack of suitable burrowing sites may limit distribution. Home range size has been estimated at 0.13 to 1.98 ha (Armitage 1975).

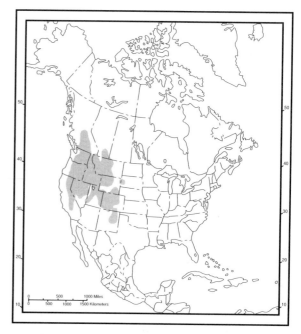

Map 9-11 Distribution of the yellow-bellied marmot (Marmota flaviventris) in North America.

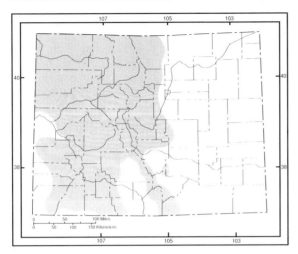

Map 9-12 Distribution of the yellow-bellied marmot (Marmota flaviventris) *in Colorado.*

Mating systems of marmots range from monogamous pairs to harems of one male with many females (Armitage and Johns 1982, Downhower and Armitage 1971). Mating probably occurs within the first two weeks following emergence from hibernation. Yearling females do not reproduce in Colorado, and as many as 75 percent of two-year-olds may not breed (Armitage and Downhower 1974). Gestation and lactation probably total about seven to eight weeks, and litter size ranges from three to eight. A single litter is produced per year (Howell 1915). The average litter size in Colorado is about four. Little is known about the development of the neonates. In mountainous regions of Colorado, young emerge from the natal den in late June and July with weaning occurring by mid-July (Armitage et al. 1976), but these stages probably vary greatly with elevation.

Marmots hibernate for up to eight months depending on local conditions. Some mortality is thought to be associated with hibernation. Marmots are regular and frequent prey of coyotes (Van Vuren 1990). Other mortality is caused by badgers, eagles, and human hunters, and diseases including plague. A little over 10 percent of a marmot's time is spent in vigilance for predators. This percentage increases when alarm calls are heard and decreases when marmots are in

groups, have good visibility, and have burrows nearby and plentiful (H. Carey and Moore 1986). Frase and Hoffmann (1980) summarized the general literature on the yellow-bellied marmot, and Armitage (1991) provided a thorough synthesis of three decades of research at Gothic, north of Crested Butte.

DISTRIBUTION —Yellow-bellied marmots occur mostly at higher elevations over the western two-thirds of the state, from as low as 1,650 m (5,400 ft) to over 4,270 m (14,000 ft). *Marmota flaviventris luteola* occurs throughout most of the occupied range in Colorado; *M. f. notioros is* found only in the Wet Mountains; *M. f. obscura* occurs in the Sangre de Cristo Range. The marmot is classified as a small game species in Colorado (Table 3-1) with no closed season.

Ammospermophilus leucurus
WHITE-TAILED ANTELOPE SQUIRREL

DESCRIPTION — White-tailed antelope squirrels are characterized by having single white lateral stripes that run from behind the shoulder to the hip. Striping is absent from the head. The dorsum is reddish brown to ash gray, and the venter is somewhat paler. The slightly bushy tail is whitish below and black to dark gray dorsally. While running, the animals carry the tail curved over the rump, revealing the flashy white undersurface, and leading to the common name antelope squirrel. Measurements are: total length 190–240 mm; length of tail 55–90 mm; length of hindfoot 35–45 mm; length of ear 9–11 mm; weight 80–110 g. A small masseteric tubercle lies directly below the oval, infraorbital foramen. Males have a baculum. Although chipmunks and golden-mantled ground squirrels may resemble this species superficially, they are readily separated by having more dorsal stripes, the pale stripes bordered by black.

NATURAL HISTORY — The biology of white-tailed antelope squirrels is poorly known in Colorado, the northeastern limit of their range. They in-

Photograph 9-7 White-tailed antelope squirrel (Ammospermophilus leucurus).

Map 9-13 Distribution of the white-tailed antelope squirrel (Ammospermophilus leucurus) *in North America.*

habit semidesert shrublands, piñon-juniper woodlands, montane shrublands, and occasionally are found in lowland riparian communities. They occupy burrows dug by other species such as kangaroo rats or small ground squirrels, and also dig their own burrows under bushes, clumps of grasses, or at the base of trees, often in sandy soils near rock outcrops. White-tailed antelope squirrels appear "nervous," seldom remaining still, but rather racing furtively to gather food or nest material and then retreating to the burrow. The tail is invariably held erect, curving over the body when the animals are moving.

No studies of the food habits of this species have been made in Colorado. Farther west they are omnivorous, with flowers, fruits, and seeds making up about one-half to three-quarters of the diet (Armstrong 1982, W. Bradley 1968). These foods are supplemented with green matter, insects, small lizards, rodents, and carrion. These ground squirrels may capture and feed on pocket mice (Morgart 1985). Remains of insects may be conspicuous at the entrance of burrows (W. Bradley 1967). Some food is transported in the internal cheekpouches to be stored in the burrow. They do not need free water for drinking.

White-tailed antelope squirrels are diurnal, with peaks of activity in morning and late afternoon;

in extremely hot weather they may virtually disappear below ground, a behavioral strategy for avoiding heat stress (W. Bradley 1967, Kavanau and Rischer 1972). Physiologically they show increased tolerance of dehydration, salivate (to increase evaporative cooling), and tolerate hyperthermia for short periods of time (Bartholomew and Hudson 1959, J. Hudson 1962). Antelope squirrels avoid cold weather by retreating to burrows but are not reported to hibernate.

Home ranges cover as much as 6 ha with daily movements often encompassing 1.6 ha (Bradley 1967). Little is known about social behavior. In Utah, the species dominated Hopi chipmunks in areas of range overlap (Armstrong 1982). They seem to be uncommon in Colorado, with only one or a few individuals observed in any particular area.

Breeding probably occurs from February to April; most litters are born in March and April (Arm-

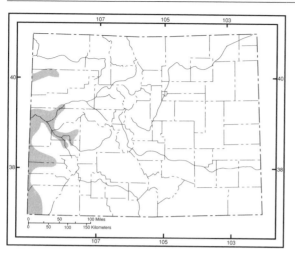

Map 9-14 Distribution of the white-tailed antelope squirrel (Ammospermophilus leucurus) in Colorado.

Photograph 9-8 Wyoming ground squirrel (Spermophilus elegans).

strong 1982). Antelope squirrels are monestrous. In Nevada, gestation takes 30 to 35 days, and litter sizes ranged from 5 to 11 (average 7.8) (Hoffmeister 1986). Mortality may be as much as 80 percent during the first year of life (Bradley 1967). Belk and Smith (1991) reviewed the literature.

DISTRIBUTION IN COLORADO — The white-tailed antelope squirrel occurs in the western third of the state to about 2,100 m (7,000 ft) in elevation. Cary (1911) reported it as common at a number of sites. Finley et al. (1976) attempted to secure specimens from some of the same sites in northwestern Colorado sampled by Cary 70 years previously and concluded that the species is becoming uncommon, perhaps as a result of human encroachment or unknown environmental changes. *Ammospermophilus leucurus cinnamomeus* occurs south of the Colorado River drainage in the southwestern corner of the state; *A. l. pennipes* occurs in the Colorado and Gunnison drainages and along the White River in Rio Blanco County. McCoy and Miller (1964) discussed the ecological distribution of the subspecies.

Spermophilus elegans
WYOMING GROUND SQUIRREL

DESCRIPTION — This medium-sized ground squirrel has a fairly long tail. The upper parts are drab buffy gray. A few individuals may show a slight dappling of blackish hairs. The underparts are buff to grayish. The tail is grayish to light brown beneath and has a border of white or buff. Measurements are: total length 250–335 mm; length of tail 65–100 mm; length of hindfoot 39–49 mm; weight 300–500 g. The skull is similar to other ground squirrels in this genus with a somewhat narrow braincase and interorbital region. The wide zygomatic arches are not parallel, and the upper surface of the jugal lacks an angular process. The infraorbital foramen is oval or subtriangular, with a large masseteric tubercle ventral to the foramen. Males have a baculum, and the testes are scrotal during the breeding season. At times individuals of this species are confused with prairie dogs, especially the Gunnison's prairie dog, from which it can be told by its smaller size, longer tail, relatively uniform color, and lack of facial markings.

NATURAL HISTORY — Wyoming ground squirrels occupy grasslands and semidesert shrublands.

Photograph by J. Perley Fitzgerald.

The diet consists mostly of grasses and forbs, with the latter most often consumed (House 1964, T. Clark 1968), although a study in Larimer County found no preferred food plants (Hansen and Johnson 1976).

Wyoming ground squirrels live in groups, but these colonies appear to be little more than aggregations of individuals in favorable habitats. However, males may defend territories during the breeding season, and females may maintain territories around natal burrows (Fagerstone 1982). In suitable habitat on the plains, densities may reach up to 44 animals per ha (House 1964). In mountainous meadows in Colorado numbers ranged from 14 (May) to 48 animals per ha (June) (Zegers 1977, Zegers and Williams 1979). Because their burrowing undermines pastures and their foraging may compete with livestock, Wyoming ground squirrels have been considered pests and control measures have been imposed for decades (Burnett 1931).

Wyoming ground squirrels mate soon after emergence from hibernation. Females typically show behavioral estrus and mate within five days of emergence. Gestation probably averages 22 to 23 days. Females have only one estrous cycle and one litter of from 3 to 11 young annually, with an average of 4 to 5. Males and females can both breed following their first hibernation cycle but apparently breeding success of yearling females is influenced by environmental conditions. Neonates are blind and naked, with hair first appearing at 10 days of age, tooth eruption at 13 days, and eyes opening at 21 to 24 days. Young remain below ground for about a month after birth. The animals are weaned by the fifth or sixth week. Within 100 days of birth the young reach adult size (T. Clark 1970; R. M. Denniston 1957; Fagerstone 1982, 1988; Zegers 1977).

As is true of most sciurids, Wyoming ground squirrels are strictly diurnal, emerging from burrows soon after sunrise and retreating before sunset. Peak activity is generally in early morning with a lesser peak in late afternoon. Behaviors include

fighting, running, chasing, feeding, alert postures, digging, hay gathering, and tail flicking. The animals frequently spend time above ground in alert upright positions (T. Clark and Denniston 1970). This has led to one of their common names, "picket pins," for their resemblance to a stake driven into the ground to tether a horse. When alarmed the animals have a high-pitched alarm call, a twittering trill given as they dive into the burrow (Fagerstone 1987a). Up to 40 percent of above-ground activity is spent feeding, 36 percent in alert postures, and less than 5 percent in chasing and fighting (Zegers 1981).

Animals begin to hibernate as early as late July; most animals are below ground by mid-September. On the Laramie Plains of Wyoming they first appeared from hibernation in early April (T. Clark 1970) but in Middle Park, Colorado, they emerged in mid-March (Fagerstone 1988). Males typically emerge one to two weeks before females. Average weight losses during hibernation range from 0.7 to 0.8 g per day, with juveniles showing

Map 9-15 Distribution of the Wyoming ground squirrel (Spermophilus elegans) *in North America.*

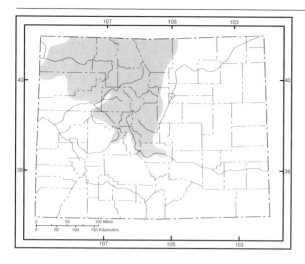

Map 9-16 Distribution of the Wyoming ground squirrel (Spermophilus elegans) *in Colorado.*

slightly lower daily losses than adults (Hansen and Reed 1969). Hibernation is believed to be triggered mostly by reduced food consumption but arousal and emergence are under exogenous controls such as snow cover and air temperature. Harlow and Menkens (1986) found that Wyoming ground squirrels and white-tailed prairie dogs in the laboratory entered torpor at 7°C.

Generally survival rates are quite high during the winter, but a considerable population loss to predation occurs during summer (T. Clark 1970; Fagerstone 1982, 1988; Zegers and Williams 1979). A large number of predators feed on Wyoming ground squirrels, including raptors, badgers, coyotes, bobcats, weasels, and rattlesnakes. Red-tailed hawks and goshawks had a 17 percent kill efficiency when hunting these squirrels (Pfeifer 1980). Sylvatic plague may be a factor influencing densities of Wyoming ground squirrels in some areas (J. Fitzgerald 1970, J. Fitzgerald and Lechleitner 1969). Humans have used a variety of control practices including the poison 1080 (sodium monofluoroacetate) to eliminate the species on pasture and agricultural lands. Zegers (1984) reviewed the literature on *S. elegans*.

DISTRIBUTION IN COLORADO — Wyoming ground squirrels are found in northwestern and central

Colorado between 1,830 and 3,660 m (6,000–12,000 ft) in elevation. Hansen (1962) reported on the dispersal of the species southward into Colorado and suggested that the rate of movement approached 2.4 km per year since 1930. At that time he speculated that their dispersal "is a natural consequence of past geologic events and not caused by modern man." This conclusion may not sufficiently weigh the impacts of livestock grazing and reduction of prairie dogs through intensive poisoning campaigns, however. These human impacts, and differences between prairie dogs and Wyoming ground squirrels in resistance to plague, may, in fact, account for some of the rapid spread of this species in Colorado.

Previously, this species in Colorado was known as Richardson's ground squirrel (*Spermophilus richardsoni*). J. Robinson and Hoffmann (1975), Nadler et al. (1971), and Fagerstone (1982) presented data on a number of criteria that justified separation of *S. elegans* from *S. richardsoni*, the latter being a species of the northern Great Plains. One subspecies, *Spermophilus elegans elegans*, occurs in Colorado. The Wyoming ground squirrel is categorized as a small game species in Colorado (Table 3-1).

Spermophilus franklinii
FRANKLIN'S GROUND SQUIRREL

DESCRIPTION — Franklin's ground squirrel is a long, slender ground squirrel, larger than the thirteen-lined ground squirrel, which may occupy similar habitat. Hall (1955) was reminded of a long-tailed weasel when he watched the squirrel moving about. Others (J. K. Jones et al. 1983) have described its long gray bushy tail as suggestive of the eastern gray squirrel (*Sciurus carolinensis*). Color of the dorsum is olive-gray to buff-gray, becoming paler on the sides with the underparts yellowish white to olive-gray. Faint dappling is noticeable along the back and sides. The head tends to be grayer than the body. The tail is blackish mixed with paler buff and bordered in white. To-

Map 9-17 Distribution of Franklin's ground squirrel
(Spermophilus franklinii) *in North America.*

tal length ranges from 360 to 412 mm; tail, 123–160 mm; hindfoot, 42–56 mm; ear, 13–18 mm; and weight 375–540 g. The skull is long and narrow with little apparent inflation of the cranium.

NATURAL HISTORY — Franklin's ground squirrel is an animal of tall- and mixed-grass prairie, tending to favor heavy, dense cover of grasses and associated forbs. It also invades openings in forest edge including margins of riparian woodland. Biology of the species has not been well studied in plains states bordering Colorado. The species is more solitary than most other ground squirrels, usually occurring in colonies of no more than a dozen individuals (J. K. Jones et al. 1983). Burrows are generally constructed on sloping ground with one or two entrances bordered by conspicuous dirt mounds. The diet is omnivorous, with up to 30 percent animal matter when insects and nestling mammals are available. Breeding occurs in April or May with females giving birth in May or June to about 6 to 9 young. Above-ground activity

may not begin until as late as May and most animals have entered hibernation by late August.

DISTRIBUTION IN COLORADO — Franklin's ground squirrel is not known from Colorado, but specimens have been taken from two nearby sites in Nebraska: along the North Platte River near Lisco, Garden County, about 50 km north of the Colorado border, and near Curtis, Frontier County, in the South Platte drainage about 130 km east of the boundary (Hall 1981). In Kansas the species has been taken in Trego County (Hall 1955) about 160 miles east of the Colorado border. J. K. Jones (1964) suggested that the range of Franklin's ground squirrel has been expanding westward and it is possible that it will eventually appear in northeastern Colorado.

Photograph by J. Perley Fitzgerald.

Photograph 9-9 Golden-mantled ground squirrel
(Spermophilus lateralis).

Spermophilus lateralis
GOLDEN-MANTLED GROUND SQUIRREL

DESCRIPTION — Medium sized, the golden-mantled ground squirrel has a distinctive reddish brown "mantle" on the head and shoulders. Two white stripes bordered by black extend from the shoulder onto the back. The eye is surrounded by a whitish eye ring. The belly is a light buffy brown to creamy white. The tail is reddish brown to yel-

173

lowish brown and not particularly bushy. Measurements are: total length 240–300 mm; length of tail 70–120 mm; length of hindfoot 38–45 mm; length of ear 16–23 mm; weight 170–290 g. The skull has a condylobasal length of about 40 mm.

NATURAL HISTORY — This is one of the more ubiquitous and easily observed small mammals in Colorado, in close company with the deer mouse and least chipmunk in its adaptability. Although the golden-mantled ground squirrel has a very broad distribution in the West and is abundant in suitable habitat, surprisingly little work has been done on its life history.

Golden-mantled ground squirrels are animals of open woodlands, shrublands, mountain meadows, and forest-edge habitat. They are not usually present in heavily wooded areas, favoring sites with good sunlight rather than shaded areas (Armstrong 1972, Cary 1911). In Colorado the species occurs in alpine tundra, montane and subalpine forests, semidesert shrublands, montane shrublands, and riparian woodlands. It is frequently found in association with different species of chipmunks, other ground squirrels, and woodrats. Although the Wyoming ground squirrel (*S. elegans*) is reported to displace this species (Carey et al. 1980, Hansen 1962), it, in turn, appears to dominate most *Tamias* species for both den sites and food in areas of sympatry.

Golden-mantled ground squirrels feed on a variety of foods; green vegetation, fungi, and seeds are consumed in quantity (Carleton 1966, McKeever 1964, Tevis 1952). Near Gothic, Gunnison County, these squirrels preferred dandelion stems but also were observed to feed on aster, sunflower, larkspur, clover, vetch, monkshood, and groundsel as well as sagebrush leaves and grass seed. Animal matter eaten includes insects, carrion, eggs, and nestling birds. Golden-mantled ground squirrels burrow beneath rocks, trees, and buildings. Burrow systems may be extensive, up to 8 m in length with side tunnels and chambers and usually several entrances. Depth is

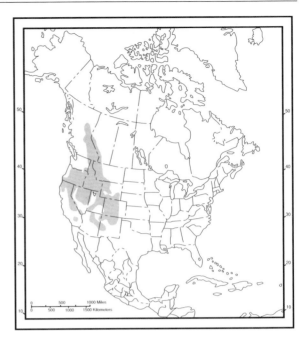

Map 9-18 Distribution of the golden-mantled ground squirrel (Spermophilus lateralis) *in North America.*

usually not more than 20 to 30 cm. A nest is constructed from grasses and leaves.

Golden-mantled squirrels are monestrous. Mating occurs within a few weeks following emergence in the spring. Gestation is probably 28 to 30 days. A single litter of altricial young is produced annually. Litter size ranges from two to eight with an average of five. As with most other ground squirrels, animals first breed at one year of age. Young are about 90 percent of adult size at two-and-one-half months of age (McKeever 1964, Skryja and Clark 1970, Tevis 1955).

Golden-mantled ground squirrels are mostly solitary and demonstrate territorial behavior near their dens. However, they may congregate in large numbers at artificial feeding sites in campgrounds and heavily used tourist areas. In such areas, dominance hierarchies form, determining access to provisioned resources. Diurnal activities begin soon after sunrise and give way to midday inactivity on hot days. Home ranges vary from 1

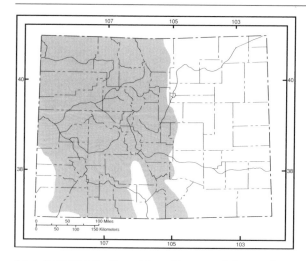

Map 9-19 Distribution of the golden-mantled ground squirrel (Spermophilus lateralis) *in Colorado.*

to 12 ha depending on season and habitat; a density of five animals per ha was found in a meadow along the Cache la Poudre River, Larimer County (Gordon 1938), and Friedrichsen (1977) found 8.8 per ha in a provisioned population in Rocky Mountain National Park.

In Colorado most golden-mantled ground squirrels are in hibernation by mid-October, several weeks ahead of chipmunks at the same elevation. They emerge in March, April, or May depending on elevation. Females typically emerge several weeks later than males. Hibernating squirrels aroused about every 5 days when entering and coming out of hibernation but periods of inactivity lasted as long as 14 days during the peak of dormancy (Jameson 1964). Males stored more fat than females prior to hibernation, and animals from 2,900 m (9,500 ft) had larger body sizes and fat stores than animals from lower elevations (Blake 1972). At room temperatures, animals from higher elevations also entered torpor more frequently than those from lower elevations. In California, emergence of females was related to snow cover of less than 50 percent (Bronson 1980).

Most individuals probably do not survive more than two or three years in the wild. A variety of

mortality factors contributes to population turnover, including predation by small and medium-sized carnivores, death during hibernation, and disease, including sylvatic plague (A. Carey et al. 1980). Bartels and Thompson (1993) provided a thorough review of the literature.

DISTRIBUTION IN COLORADO — Golden-mantled ground squirrels are common over much of the western two-thirds of the state at elevations from 1,600 m to 3,800 m (5,200–12,500 ft). *Spermophilus lateralis lateralis* occurs over most of that area; *S. l. wortmani* is known only from along the Little Snake River in Moffat County, being mostly an animal of adjacent southwestern Wyoming. In some older references, this species is treated in a genus *Callospermophilus;* that name is usually used today at the subgeneric level.

Photograph 9-10 Spotted ground squirrel (Spermophilus spilosoma).

Spermophilus spilosoma
SPOTTED GROUND SQUIRREL

DESCRIPTION — This is a small, grayish brown squirrel dappled with indistinct buffy spots on the dorsal surface. The ventral color is paler. The tail is brown and usually tipped with black. Measurements are: total length 200–245 mm; length of tail 50–80 mm; length of hindfoot 28–35 mm; length of ear 6–8 mm; weight 100–200 g. The

175

skull is similar to that of the thirteen-lined
ground squirrel but tends to be broader at the
postorbital constriction (13–15 mm) with larger
auditory bullae. Condylobasal length: 34–40 mm.

NATURAL HISTORY — Although several studies
have been conducted in Colorado, spotted
ground squirrels have not been researched intensively. A species of semiarid grasslands, it is not as
common on the eastern plains as thirteen-lined
ground squirrels; rather, spotted ground squirrels
occur more locally in suitable habitat. They prefer deep sandy soils with sparse vegetation, including areas of overgrazed sandhills vegetation and
lightly grazed mixed-grass prairie with bunchgrasses and silvery wormwood (Armstrong 1972,
N. Green 1969, Maxwell and Brown 1968, Mohamed 1989, Streubel 1975, Tubbs 1977).

The diet of the spotted ground squirrel seems to
be somewhat less omnivorous than that of the
thirteen-lined ground squirrel. A variety of
grasses and forbs were consumed in northeastern
Colorado, most notably needle-and-thread, six-
weeks fescue, annual sunflower, *Mentzelia,* and croton (Streubel 1975). Plants were also the most
important dietary item in a New Mexico study
(Sumrell 1949). Spotted ground squirrels also
feed on kangaroo rats, insects, and lizards.

Population densities of 3.8 animals per ha in Morgan County (Streubel 1975) and 5.3 to 7.1 animals per ha in Weld County (Tubbs 1977) have
been reported, with highest populations in May
and June. In the latter population yearling adults
constituted the largest cohort with survivorship
highest in males. Adults older than two years of
age were not present. Tubbs (1977) reported
more females than males whereas Streubel
(1975) had more males than females. Home
ranges in Colorado range from 0.50 to 4.8 ha.
Males have larger home ranges than females.

Burrows of spotted ground squirrels typically have
two or three entrances at the bases of shrubs,
often silvery wormwood. These squirrels build several separate burrow systems and establish defini-

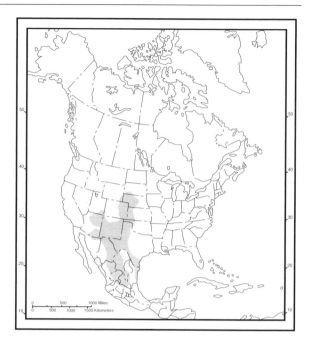

Map 9-20 *Distribution of the spotted ground squirrel*
(Spermophilus spilosoma) *in North America.*

tive surface runways between them (Streubel
1975, Tubbs 1977).

Seasonal activity patterns are similar to those of
thirteen-lined ground squirrels. Spotted ground
squirrels emerge from hibernation in early to mid-
April in northeastern Colorado. Yearlings emerge
first, followed by adult males, which precede
adult females by one to two weeks. Annual above-
ground activity averaged 115 to 135 days for
males and 95 to 125 days for females in Morgan
County (Streubel 1975). Adult males usually enter hibernation by late July or early August, and females stay active slightly longer. By late
September and early October only a few juveniles
remain above ground. Although this broad seasonal activity pattern is similar to that of the sympatric thirteen-lined ground squirrel, competition
probably is minimal because of temporal differences with annual cycles (Streubel 1975). Various
events such as emergence from hibernation,
breeding, and emergence of young occurred two

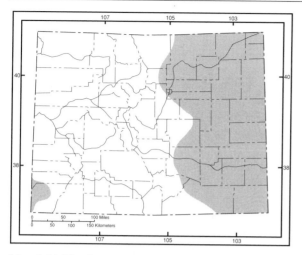

Map 9-21 Distribution of the spotted ground squirrel
(Spermophilus spilosoma) *in Colorado.*

to four weeks earlier in *S. tridecmlineatus* than in
S. spilosoma.

In Colorado, spotted ground squirrels were most
active between 1100 and 1600 hours, even on the
hottest days (Tubbs 1977). In New Mexico they
have a bimodal activity pattern with little activity
during the heat of the day (Sumrell 1949). Above-
ground activities are typically spent in feeding
and foraging behavior (66 percent), alert behavior (15 percent), investigative behavior (6 percent), and other maintenance behaviors such as
sandbathing, grooming, and sunning (8 percent).
Sexual and agonistic behaviors occupied less than
2 percent of above-ground activity, increasing to
only 7 percent during the breeding season
(Streubel 1975).

Reproductive patterns are similar to those of thirteen-lined ground squirrels. Breeding occurs in
April or May soon after emergence from hibernation. Pregnant females may be found in Colorado
from early May to late July (Streubel 1975, Tubbs
1977). Litter size varies from 5 to 12 with an average of about 7. Juveniles weigh 40 to 50 g at first
emergence from the natal burrow. Gestation is
probably the same as in thirteen-lined ground
squirrels, 27 to 28 days.

Scant information is available on predation. Bull
snakes and possibly red-tailed hawks have been reported as predators. Streubel and Fitzgerald
(1978*a*) reviewed the literature.

DISTRIBUTION IN COLORADO — Spotted ground
squirrels are widely distributed over the eastern
plains, mostly in areas of sandy soils. In suitable
habitat the species can be quite abundant but
overall it is sparsely distributed. It is most abundant in the sandhills of the northeastern part of
the state and along the Arkansas River. A considerable portion of this range has been lost to irrigated agriculture. It also occurs in the extreme
southwestern portion of the state, in Montezuma
County, where its status is uncertain. The spotted
ground squirrel in Colorado is listed as a nongame species (Table 3-1).

Spermophilus spilosoma cryptospilotus occurs in extreme southwestern Colorado; *S. s. obsoletus* occurs in northeastern Colorado, generally in the
South Platte River drainage; *S. s. marginatus* occurs over the remainder of the eastern plains.

Spermophilus tridecemlineatus
THIRTEEN-LINED GROUND SQUIRREL

DESCRIPTION — Thirteen-lined ground squirrels
are small and have a conspicuous series of alternating dark and light stripes on the back and
head. The dark stripes are each marked by a series of nearly square white spots, and the general
background color is buffy yellow, although variation is apparent (Armstrong 1971). The venter is
buffy to yellowish. Measurements are: total length
170–297 mm; length of tail 60–132 mm; length of
hindfoot 27–41 mm; weight 100–250 g. The skull
is 23 to 38 mm in condylobasal length, with postorbital breadth averaging 10.5 to 11.5 mm.

NATURAL HISTORY — Thirteen-lined ground squirrels are typical of grasslands of short and
midlength grasses and are capable of utilizing
other habitats that are heavily grazed, mowed, or

Photograph 9-11 Thirteen-lined ground squirrel (Spermophilus tridecemlineatus).

otherwise modified (Grant 1972, Moulton et al. 1981*a,b*, Lovell et al. 1985), including prairie dog towns. The species is frequently associated with heavier soils including clays, loams, or sandy-loams and is less common on sandier soils in Colorado and southeastern Wyoming (Flake 1974, Maxwell and Brown 1968, Mitchell 1972, Streubel 1975), which are usually occupied by *S. spilosoma* (Armstrong 1972, Tubbs 1977).

The diet includes both plant and animal matter. Various grasses, forbs, shrubs, fungi, lichens, and mosses are consumed; seeds are relatively unimportant relative to other plant parts (Flake 1973). The diet contains nearly 50 percent animal matter (L. Johnson 1917); insect remains constitute 30 to 70 percent of stomach contents (Flake 1973, Streubel and Fitzgerald 1978*b*). Heavy consumption of lepidopteran larvae was observed in Morgan County (Streubel 1975), as were flowers and seeds of six-weeks fescue and salt-grass in May and June. On Pawnee National Grassland, adult and larval beetles, lepidopteran larvae, and grasshoppers were most important (Flake 1973). This species is not averse to eating other vertebrates including young cottontails, lizards, snakes, and birds. Prior to hibernation, thirteen-lined ground squirrels gain weight at a rate of about 4 g per day

and may show a 30 to 40 percent increase in weight as they prepare for hibernation (Hohn 1966).

Thirteen-lined ground squirrels dig burrow systems that include relatively few deep "frost-free" nesting burrows as well as a larger number (75 to 80 percent) of shallower "retreat" burrows (Desha 1966). Burrows generally have only one entrance. Little soil is deposited around the burrow entrance, making them difficult to locate.

Thirteen-lined ground squirrels are active throughout the warmer months of the year but spend the winter in hibernation. Percentages of time spent during spring/summer and fall, respectively, in captivity were as follows: burrowing (19 and 5 percent), above-ground activity (36 and 19 percent), and resting or eating in the burrow (45 and 76 percent) (Scheck and Fleharty 1980). Of above-ground time, foraging and feeding occupied 70 percent, alert behaviors 12 percent, and maintenance behaviors 8 percent (Streubel

Map 9-22 Distribution of the thirteen-lined ground squirrel (Spermophilus tridecemlineatus) *in North America.*

178

1975). General investigative and nesting behaviors occupied most of the remaining time above ground. Depending on season and temperature the animals may show either a bimodal or unimodal diurnal cycle. In hot weather, activity ceases during the hottest part of the day. When alarmed the animals typically race to their burrows and often give a trilling alarm call as they dive underground.

The animals generally are solitary and nonterritorial although parts of the home range may be defended from intruders. Home ranges vary from 1.4 to 12 ha, with males having larger home ranges than females, especially during the breeding season. Population estimates on shortgrass prairie in Colorado ranged from 18 animals per ha on grazed prairie (Mitchell 1972) to 4.5 per ha on ungrazed prairie (Grant 1972). As would be expected, highest numbers are associated with emergence of the young of the year.

The species enters hibernation between July and October with young of the year staying above ground the longest. Lechleitner (1969) reported the species as commonly seen into late October or early November near Fort Collins, but such late activity is unusual. Prior to hibernation, animals become aggressive and intolerant of each other, reduce their home range, and become relatively inactive. Fat animals typically enter hibernation before thinner ones (McCarley 1966, Streubel 1975). Hibernating animals plug their burrow entrances and reduce heart rate from about 200 to 4 beats per minute. Body temperature during hibernation approaches one to three degrees Celsius of the ambient air temperature in the burrow. Brief periods of arousal occur about every 10 to 26 days during hibernation (Fitzpatrick 1925, G. Johnson 1928). Emergence dates in Colorado are early April or May. The seasonal activity period for adult males is only 100 to 120 days a year.

Mating occurs soon after emergence from hibernation in mid-April or early May. Females are induced ovulators, and copulation may last several minutes (G. Johnson et al. 1933). Litters number 6 to 9 (and occasionally as many as 12). Mean litter sizes of 8.1 and 6.2 are reported for Weld and Morgan counties (Flake 1974, Streubel 1975). The gestation period is 27 to 28 days; the young are born in an altricial state (Bridgewater 1966). Eyes open at about 28 days. Weaning typically coincides with the emergence of the young from their natal burrows. In some parts of their range thirteen-lined squirrels are reported to have two litters, but there is no evidence of this in Colorado.

Annual mortality has been estimated at close to 80 percent in Wisconsin (Rongstad 1965) and Texas (McCarley 1966), with juvenile males generally showing the highest losses. Most mortality occurs prior to hibernation, although a few direct observations of predation are reported in the literature. Among predators reported are bull snakes, roadrunners, swift fox, and several raptors. The first author has observed a rattlesnake eating a thirteen-lined squirrel and found the squirrels in food caches made by swift fox on the Pawnee National Grassland. Streubel and Fitzgerald (1978*b*) reviewed the literature on the species.

DISTRIBUTION IN COLORADO — Thirteen-lined ground squirrels are found across much of the eastern third of Colorado. They also occupy some of the high mountain valleys including the San Luis Valley, South Park, the Little Snake drainage in Moffat County, and the White River Plateau in Garfield County. Populations seem to have decreased in some of these mountain parklands including South Park. During 14 years of small mammal trapping in that area in the 1960s and 1970s, J. Fitzgerald (unpublished) never captured any specimens, although Ecke and Johnson (1952) commonly captured them during plague surveys. Several authors have commented on the apparent competitiveness of *S. elegans*, including its seeming ability to outcompete *S. lateralis* under sympatric conditions (Hansen 1962, Zegers 1984), and thirteen-lined ground squirrels may also be adversely affected by Wyoming ground squirrels. *Spermophilus tridecemlineatus arenicola* oc-

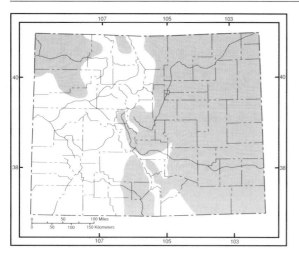

Map 9-23 Distribution of the thirteen-lined ground squirrel (Spermophilus tridecemlineatus) in Colorado.

Photograph by Joseph G. Hall.

Photograph 9-12 Rock squirrel (Spermophilus variegatus).

curs in the southeastern part of the state from the Wet Mountains east and south of the Palmer Divide; *S. t. pallidus* occurs in South Park, North Park, and throughout the northeastern Colorado; *S. t. parvus* is the subspecies of the northwestern corner of the state north of the Roan Plateau and Colorado River. *S. t. blanca* probably is restricted to the San Luis Valley; Hall (1981) mapped a puzzling extension of the range of the subspecies to western New Mexico, apparently based on a misreading of comments by Armstrong (1971). The thirteen-lined ground squirrel is classified as a small game mammal in Colorado (Table 3-1).

Spermophilus variegatus
ROCK SQUIRREL

DESCRIPTION — This species is the largest of Coloradan ground squirrels. It can even be confused with the fox squirrel unless due attention is paid to the variegated markings, less bushy tail, and grayer color. The color is grayish to blackish gray with the dorsal surface showing pale dappling. The shoulder is darker than the rump, and the flanks are brownish. Some animals are quite pale in overall color. The venter is a pale grayish brown. The bushy tail is about the same length as the head and body. Measurements are: total length 440–530 mm; length of tail 160–230 mm; length of hindfoot 53–63 mm; length of ear 17–27 mm; weight 650–1,000 g. The skull is large and robust, averaging 55 to 60 mm in condylobasal length. The masseteric tubercle lies ventral to the oval infraorbital foramen.

NATURAL HISTORY — This is probably our least known ground squirrel; no detailed studies have been done on its ecology in the state. The rock squirrel is a mammal of rocky hillsides, rimrock, and canyons, requiring boulders, talus, or tangles of dense vegetation under which to burrow (Armstrong 1972, Cary 1911, Steiner 1975). Piñon-juniper woodlands and montane shrublands are the ecosystems in which they are most likely to be found, but they also occur in montane forest, riparian woodlands, orchards, and increasingly in rock outcrops in cultivated and urban areas. Such extensions are possible because of the plasticity of the species in adapting to novel denning sites including tire piles, dumps, auto junkyards, riprap, construction debris, and woodpiles (Quinones 1988). In Utah they readily colonize abandoned woodrat dens (Juelson 1970).

Rock squirrels are opportunistic feeders, especially during times of low food availability. They are expert climbers and often feed in trees and bushes, and they also bury food — traits that may cause the casual observer to mistake them for fox squirrels. During the growing season, diet tends toward green material and flowering parts. In New Mexico flowers of skunkbrush, gooseberry, and oak were especially important (Stalheim 1965). Later in the season, seeds, fruits, and acorns are often eaten. Piñon nuts, acorns, and juniper "berries" are important foods in Colorado (Cary 1911). Damage to orchards and other crops has been reported in some areas. As with most other sciurids, carrion and insects are eaten. Cannibalism occurs as well as predation on cottontails and nestling birds and eggs. Large internal cheek pouches aid in transport of seeds and other food items. Rock squirrels do not seem to store food regularly in the den, relying instead on fat accumulation for winter survival (Oaks et al. 1987).

Rock squirrels are usually colonial, with dominant males defending colony boundaries during the breeding season. Mature dominant females apparently control prime burrow sites as subordinate males are forced to peripheral habitats. Home ranges of about 0.09 to 0.45 ha frequently overlap between adult males and one or more females. Densities probably average about 5 or 6 individuals per ha but can vary from about 2 to 13 depending on habitat quality and season. During the nonbreeding season, adults occupy individual home ranges separate from members of the opposite sex (K. Johnson 1979, 1981; Juelson 1970). In a New Mexico population, density of adults was low (fewer than 2 animals per ha), and individual home ranges were large (3.8 and 7.9 ha for females and males, respectively), overlapping for all sex and age classes (Shriner and Stacey 1991). The animals were only moderately social, and adults did not interact outside the breeding season.

Rock squirrels are diurnal, with one or two activity peaks, depending on temperature. They seek refuge at extreme temperatures. Communication is by postures, vocalizations, and scentmarking. Familiar squirrels approach each other head on and make nasal contact. Unfamiliar animals approach one another at an angle and use threat displays to

Map 9-24 Distribution of the rock squirrel (Spermophilus variegatus) *in North America.*

assert dominance. Vocalizations are mostly warning calls given by colonial females (Krenz 1977). Rock squirrels have dorsal skin glands, which males rub against rocks during the breeding season (Juelson 1970), and cheek glands, which both sexes rub against rocks and sniff during intraspecific encounters (K. Johnson 1979). They also use specific sites for urination and defecation, suggesting scent mounds. The function of these behaviors is not known.

Rock squirrels dig extensive burrow systems beneath objects. These systems usually are shallow but may reach close to 6 m in length. Side tunnels often are associated with the main tunnel, and as with most ground-dwelling sciurids, feces are typically deposited in tunnels outside the nest (Juelson 1970, Stalheim 1965). Tree bark frequently is stripped for nesting material, and leaves and grass are used also (R. Bradley 1929, Steiner 1975).

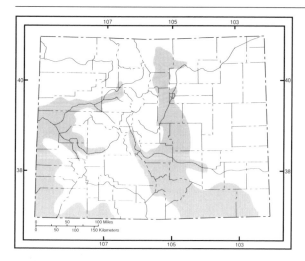

Map 9-25 Distribution of the rock squirrel (Spermophilus variegatus) *in Colorado.*

Males reportedly take several weeks to reach reproductive condition following emergence in the spring. (In most other ground squirrels, males are already in breeding condition at emergence.) Breeding occurs within one to two weeks after males come into season. Based on studies in Utah (Juelson 1970) and Texas (K. Johnson 1979) most breeding in our area probably occurs between late March and early June depending on elevation. In Arizona, mating occurred from mid-April to early July, lasting nine weeks in any one year, and this timing was closely associated with heavy summer rains (Ortega 1990). The gestation period is unknown but is presumably about a month. Contrary to some earlier reports, Ortega (1990) found rock squirrels to be monestrous, having a single litter per year. Embryo counts range from 3 to 9 with an average of 5. Average above-ground litter size is 4.8 in Arizona. In Utah mean embryo counts were 6.1. Four weaned pups are the average. Studies in Utah and elsewhere suggest that young stay in the burrow until 8 to 10 weeks of age, an unusually prolonged time below ground for a ground squirrel (Juelson 1970, Stalheim 1965). By two months postemergence, young approximate 90 percent of adult length but they may take two years to reach full weight. Juvenile animals may disperse in late summer,

fall, or the following spring. In New Mexico, apparently only yearling males dispersed; yearling females remaining near their natal site (Shriner and Stacey 1991).

In colder parts of the range, rock squirrels hibernate. Little time was spent in dormancy at Colorado National Monument (P. Miller 1964). As with other ground squirrels the species shows diurnal activity patterns, with most activity occurring in the middle of the day during the colder months but taking on a bimodal pattern during the warm season. During extremely hot weather the animals aestivate (Juelson 1970, K. Johnson 1979).

Rock squirrels are important in plague epizootics over much of their range, with mortality reaching 40 to 60 percent (Barnes 1982, Quinones 1988). During 1974 and 1985, slightly over 40 percent of human plague cases were associated with rock squirrels. Life span may exceed three years in wild populations. Most larger raptors and ground predators prey on this species. The literature was reviewed by Oaks et al. (1987).

DISTRIBUTION IN COLORADO — Rock squirrels are found in foothills and valleys below 2,530 m (8,300 ft). They occur in a band along the Front Range north nearly to the Wyoming border, up the Arkansas Valley, and eastward in southeastern Colorado to Baca County. They also occur in roughlands at lower elevations in western Colorado south of the Roan Plateau. Small colonies have been making significant range extensions along riparian woodland corridors on the northeastern plains of Colorado. Populations are now well entrenched in Fort Collins (Quinones 1988), and they are spreading eastward along the Cache la Poudre River. In Greeley several animals established a small colony in 1989 in riprap along the Poudre. Similar populations have existed near Windsor for about a decade. These pioneering populations are almost exclusively associated with rock, concrete, abandoned autos, and similar materials used to stabilize river banks (J. Fitzgerald, unpublished). These populations represent an eastward extension of the range of some 50 km. One subspecies, *Spermophilus variegatus grammurus,* occurs in Colorado. The rock squirrel is considered a small game mammal in Colorado (Table 3-1).

Cynomys gunnisoni
GUNNISON'S PRAIRIE DOG

DESCRIPTION —This species is the smallest of Colorado's prairie dogs. Dorsal color is yellowish buff to cinnamon with numerous interspersed black hairs. The ventral color is slightly paler. The top of the head, cheeks, and superciliary line above the eyes are darker than the rest of the body but do not show the striking pattern exhibited by the white-tailed prairie dog. The terminal one-third of the tail is gray to dirty white in color. Measurements are: total length 300–390 mm; length of tail 40–64 mm; length of hindfoot 53–61 mm; weight 450–1,350 g. Males are heavier than females. Overall, the species is darker and less strikingly patterned than the white-tailed prairie dog. Because of its dark color and relatively small size, Gunnison's prairie dog is often mistaken for the Wyoming ground squirrel, from which it is distinguished by its relatively shorter tail, stockier build, and distinctive vocalizations. The skull of Gunnison's prairie dog differs from that of the white-tailed prairie dog in having a more broadly spreading zygomatic process of the maxillary, smaller and more oblique mastoids, and smaller auditory bullae. Females have 10 mammae.

NATURAL HISTORY — Gunnison's prairie dogs inhabit grasslands and semidesert and montane shrublands. The diet consists mostly of grasses and sedges. In Costilla County, grasses constituted 81 percent of the diet (Longhurst 1944); other plants included borages, goosefoot, pigweed, lupine, dandelions, and mustards. In South Park, fescues, June-grass, muhly, sedges, rushes, paintbrush, senecio, chiming bells, prairie sage, big sage, and rabbitbrush were commonly used (J. Fitzgerald and Lechleitner 1974). Flowers and other succulent parts of forbs and shrubs are also consumed but the animals do little digging for

Photograph by J. Perley Fitzgerald.

Photograph 9-13 Gunnison's prairie dog (Cynomys gunnisoni).

roots and tubers. About 60 percent of the time above ground is spent foraging and feeding (J. Fitzgerald and Lechleitner 1969). Clipping of standing vegetation has not been documented. As with all species of prairie dogs and most ground squirrels, they gather grasses and forbs for nesting materials, especially in late summer. Free water is not required.

Reproduction occurs shortly after emergence from hibernation. Mating was observed in South Park in late April and May. Gestation is unknown but is estimated at about 30 days. Pups are

183

thought to remain below ground for four to five weeks after birth. Lactating females were noted in South Park in May and June with first appearance of pups in the first week of July. Females have one litter per year with an average of three to four young (range three to eight) (Pizzimenti and Hoffmann 1973). The southwestern subspecies may have slightly smaller litters (Longhurst 1944). Sex ratios favor males at birth; adult populations slightly favor females. Such unequal sex ratios have been reported in black-tailed prairie dogs and are attributed to increased chance for mortality in young males.

Gunnison's prairie dogs hibernate. In central Colorado around 3,500 m (10,000 ft) individuals entered burrows by October and emerged in mid-April. Hibernation periods at lower elevations are shorter and some individuals may even appear above ground in the winter months (Raynor et al. 1987).

The animals are diurnal, with bimodal peaks of activity typical during warmer times of the year. Although brief showers do not interrupt activity, periods of prolonged rain or snow cause the animals to retreat to their burrows. Prairie dogs are considerably more cautious in their behaviors on cloudy, overcast days than on days with bright sunshine. Alarm calls are used in response to predators, and all individuals within hearing range probably benefit. Interestingly, their alarm calls appear to have semantic properties; in an experimental situation, Gunnison's prairie dogs appeared to distinguish between (and announce information about) individual "predators" (in this case, researchers clothed in different ways) (Slobodchikoff et al. 1991).

Populations of Gunnison's prairie dogs consist of loose aggregations similar to the clans described for white-tailed prairie dogs. They are considerably less social than black-tailed prairie dogs; colony organization is more similar to the less social ground squirrels (Scheffer 1947). However, organized subgroups do exist in the colony. Females and young are more closely linked to specific loca-

tions within a colony than are males. Most agonistic behavior is related to disputes over feeding areas or specific burrow clusters rather than to discrete territorial boundaries such as the coteries observed in black-tailed prairie dogs.

Densities of Gunnison's prairie dogs range from 5 or 6 to over 57 animals per ha in especially favorable habitat (Burnett and McCampbell 1926, J. Fitzgerald and Lechleitner 1974, Lechleitner et al. 1962, Raynor 1985b). Burrow systems and mound construction are less well developed than in black-tailed prairie dogs. In South Park only 13 percent of burrows had well-developed mounds, and 77 percent had little or no excavated dirt.

Predators include badgers, golden eagles, coyotes, bobcats, and red-tailed hawks. Plague and poisoning have had major impacts on the distribution of this species in Colorado (Ecke and Johnson 1952; Lechleitner et al. 1962, 1968; J. Fitzgerald 1970, 1993; Pizzimenti 1981; Raynor 1985a). Pizzimenti and Hoffmann (1973) reviewed general literature on the species.

Map 9-26 Distribution of Gunnison's prairie dog (Cynomys gunnisoni) *in North America.*

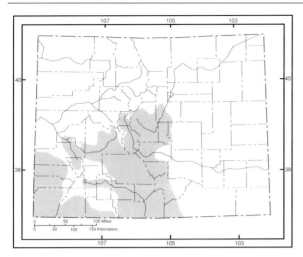

Map 9-27 Distribution of Gunnison's prairie dog (Cynomys gunnisoni) *in Colorado.*

DISTRIBUTION IN COLORADO — Gunnison's prairie dogs are restricted to southwestern and south-central Colorado. They range in elevation from 1,830 to 3,660 m (6,000–12,000 ft). Plague and poisoning have caused considerable retraction of the species (particularly *C. g. gunnisoni*) in parts of Colorado and New Mexico. An epizootic in the 1940s greatly reduced numbers of this prairie dog in South Park (Ecke and Johnson 1952). J. Fitzgerald (1978) reported most colonies gone from the park. Recently, however, an active colony has been documented near Hartsel (Robert B. Finley, pers. comm.). *Cynomys gunnisoni gunnisoni* occurs in the Gunnison River drainage, the upper Arkansas and South Platte drainages, and in the San Luis Valley. This subspecies is extinct over much of its former range, although in 1991 R. B. Finley (unpublished) found small colonies in many areas of south-central Colorado. *C. g. zuniensis* occurs at lower elevations in southwestern Colorado in Montezuma, La Plata, Dolores, San Miguel, and Montrose counties. All Coloradan prairie dogs are considered small game species (Table 3-1) and are provided no protection from harvest.

Cynomys leucurus
WHITE-TAILED PRAIRIE DOG

DESCRIPTION — White-tailed prairie dogs can be distinguished from other prairie dogs in Colorado by the presence of a short, white to grayish white tip on the tail, whitish gray to yellowish buff body color, and distinctive dark facial markings, consisting of black to dark brown cheek patches that extend to above the eye (most prominent in summer pelage). The ventral color is slightly paler than the dorsum. Measurements are: total length 315–400 mm; length of tail length 40–65 mm; length of hindfoot 60–65 mm, length of ear 8–14 mm; weight 650–1,700 g. Males are typically larger than females. White-tailed and black-tailed prairie dogs are similar in total length, but the latter has a tail 30 percent longer. Male white-tailed prairie dogs average heavier than adult black-tailed prairie dogs. The skull of the white-tailed prairie dog is not as heavy as that of the black-tail. Females usually have 10 mammae.

NATURAL HISTORY — White-tailed prairie dogs are animals of open shrublands, semidesert grasslands, and mountain valleys. In Colorado, the species is most often encountered in semidesert shrublands. Occasionally they invade pastures and agricultural lands at lower elevations. Their colonies, like those of black-tailed prairie dogs, are important to over 60 vertebrate associates (Campbell and Clark 1981).

White-tailed prairie dogs feed on a wide range of grasses, forbs, and woody plants. They may prefer grasses and sedges when available (Tileston and Lechleitner 1966). Sage, saltbush, winterfat, rabbitbrush, goosefoot, and dandelions are consumed. Unlike black-tailed prairie dogs, they do not intentionally clip taller vegetation. Animal matter is not important in the diet.

White-tailed prairie dogs frequently occur in loosely organized colonies, termed "clans" by Tileston and Lechleitner (1966) but considered by Hoogland (1981) to be equivalent to wards in black-tailed prairie dogs. Colonies may occupy

185

Photograph by J. Perley Fitzgerald.

Photograph 9-14 White-tailed prairie dog (Cynomys leucurus).

Population densities vary between years and sites, ranging from 0.8 to 12.6 animals per ha in a four-year study of six sites in Wyoming (Menkens and Anderson 1989). A density of 1.5 animals per ha was estimated for North Park, Colorado, after emergence of young of the year (Tileston and Lechleitner 1966). Density in most colonies increases by 1.5 to 4 times with emergence of young of the year. Home ranges have been estimated at 5.9 to 6.9 ha, although typical movements are much more restricted and home ranges seldom exceed 1 ha in dense populations. Overgrazing by livestock may favor increases in density on favorable sites. Emigration is believed important in new colony establishment (T. Clark 1977, Tileston and Lechleitner 1966).

White-tailed prairie dogs are diurnal, with a bimodal activity period during the warmer months of spring and summer and unimodal patterns in cooler weather. In Wyoming the animals have been shown to hibernate (Bakko and Nahorniak 1986), as long suspected. Harlow and Menkens (1986) contrasted hibernation of white-tailed prairie dogs with torpor in black-tailed prairie dogs. The period of hibernation varies from about three to six months, and many adults are dormant by mid-August. However, that period may be shorter at lower elevations, as J. Fitzgerald (unpublished) has observed white-tailed prairie dogs near Rangely and Grand Junction active in December and early January. Hibernating animals probably emerge in late February or early March in most areas in Colorado.

White-tailed prairie dogs spend almost two-thirds of their lives in their burrows. These intensively used structures are laboriously constructed. A burrow re-excavated in Montana comprised 29 m of passages and contained a turning bay, sleeping quarters, two hibernacula, and a maternity area (J. Burns et al. 1989).

White-tailed prairie dogs are monestrous, breeding in late March and April soon after they emerge from hibernation (Tileston and Lechleitner 1966). Gestation takes about 30 days (Bakko

hundreds of hectares on favorable sites, for example, along Interstate 70 from west of Grand Junction to Cisco, Utah. Sociality is not as pronounced as in black-tailed prairie dogs, sociality being restricted mostly to female-young and young-young interactions. Colony members benefit from group response to alarm calls, and their burrowing activities collectively favor development of broad-leafed herbaceous vegetation (T. Clark 1977, Hoogland 1981, Tileston and Lechleitner 1966).

Map 9-28 *Distribution of the white-tailed prairie dog* (Cynomys leucurus) *in North America.*

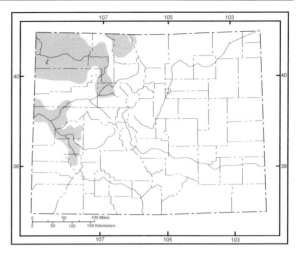

Map 9-29 *Distribution of the white-tailed prairie dog* (Cynomys leucurus) *in Colorado.*

and Brown 1967); the young are born in late April or early May. Litter sizes average 5.6 young. Pups do not appear above ground until late May or June when they are close to one month old.

Mortality is caused by a variety of predators including eagles, hawks, badgers, coyotes, black-footed ferrets, and rattlesnakes. Tileston and Lechleitner (1966) reported only 25 percent of marked animals present the following summer. Plague is an important disease over much of the species' range (T. Clark 1977, Ubico et al. 1988). Poisoning and habitat losses due to agriculture and urbanization also contribute to population declines. However, their tendency to inhabit shrublands, have dispersed burrows, and maintain relatively low densities aids in their ability to survive plague epizootics and poisoning campaigns. In Wyoming, epizootics of plague were short lived, with density and survival increasing within one to two years (Menkens and Anderson 1991). Literature was reviewed by T. Clark et al. (1971) and T. Clark (1977, 1986). Clark and others working on

black-footed ferret recovery have conducted intensive and extensive studies of the white-tailed prairie dog in Wyoming and adjacent areas (Campbell and Clark 1981, Clark et al. 1982, 1984, 1989).

DISTRIBUTION IN COLORADO — White-tailed prairie dogs inhabit northwestern and west-central Colorado, to elevations over 3,050 m (10,000 ft) although most records are from below 2,600 m (8,500 ft). According to recent black-footed ferret surveys in northwestern Colorado (Grode and Renner 1986), populations in Colorado appear to be stable or increasing. The increase probably is due largely to termination of active poisoning campaigns in the late 1960s and early 1970s. The last known population of black-footed ferrets was associated with a white-tailed prairie dog colony near Meeteetse, Wyoming (T. Clark et al. 1988). With continued success of the black-footed ferret recovery program, western Colorado and eastern Utah may some day see that fascinating species restored to selected white-tailed prairie dog colonies. *Cynomys leucurus* is monotypic; geographic variation across its range does not suggest the existence of subspecies.

Cynomys ludovicianus
BLACK-TAILED PRAIRIE DOG

DESCRIPTION — Black-tailed prairie dogs are reddish cinnamon in summer to more reddish in winter. The venter is a paler buffy brown, yellow, or white. Albino individuals are not uncommon. The tail is long compared to that of other prairie dogs and is conspicuously tipped with black to brownish black hairs. As with many mammals in Colorado, the summer pelage is short and rather coarse. Winter pelage is longer and more lax. Measurements are: total length 336–410 mm; length of tail 60–93 mm; length of hindfoot 48–68 mm; length of ear 8–14 mm; weight 525–1,350 g. Females typically are slightly smaller than males. The skull is robust, and the occipital region has an oval shape when viewed from behind. The jugal bone is thick and heavy, especially where it joins the rather stout zygomatic process of the maxillary. The cheekteeth are large, stout, and expanded laterally. Females have eight functional mammae. Hoogland (1987) described the use of molar attrition to determine the age of live animals.

NATURAL HISTORY — Black-tailed prairie dogs are among the most intensively studied of rodents, mostly because of their supposed negative impact on agriculture, but also because of their complex and fascinating social structure and behavior. They create an environment that is inviting to other animals; 64 species of vertebrates have been found on prairie dog colonies (Campbell and Clark 1981).

Black-tailed prairie dogs form large colonies or "towns" in shortgrass or mixed prairie. Among North American mammals, prairie dogs, along with pocket gophers (Huntley and Inouye 1988) and beavers (Naiman et al. 1988), have had profound environmental and historical impact (Whicker and Detling 1988). Historical estimates suggest that 20 percent of the shortgrass and mixed prairie may once have been inhabited by prairie dogs (Lauenroth 1979). Over much of

© 1993 Wendy Shattil/Bob Rozinski.

Photograph 9-15 Black-tailed prairie dog (Cynomys ludovicianus).

that area they have been extirpated or severely controlled.

Black-tailed prairie dogs consume large quantities of annual forbs and native grasses (Bonham and Lerwick 1976, Gold 1976, Hansen and Gold 1977, Klatt 1971, Klatt and Hein 1978, Uresk 1984). Grasses and sedges are preferred. Western wheatgrass, buffalo-grass, grama, Russian-thistle, pigweed, and ragweed are common food items. During late fall, winter, and spring, these prairie dogs frequently dig and eat roots of forbs and grasses. While foraging for these foods they sometimes select a small area, perhaps 1.5 to 4.5 m in diameter, and dig many circular pits 7.5 to 13 cm deep to access these roots (Tileston and Lechleitner 1966). They also commonly cut vegetation that they do not eat, perhaps to keep cover down and thus allow ready detection of aerial predators. Their habits of clipping vegetation, consuming roots, and moving dirt for crater mounds leads over time to markedly different vegetation composition than on areas surrounding the prairie dog town.

Black-tailed prairie dogs dig complex burrow systems, the entrances marked by conspicuous mounds. Mounds may be shaped like domes or craters. Dome mounds are gently rounded hummocks of subsoil brought up from the burrows. Crater mounds are conical, volcano-like, constructed of a mixture of subsoils and surface soils. The prairie dogs mix about 220 kg of soil per burrow system (Whicker and Detling 1988). Burrow systems may number from 50 to 300 per ha, so the total soil movement and mixing by a major colony can be tremendous (Archer et al. 1987, J. King 1955, O'Meilia et al. 1982, E. White and Carlson 1984).

Prairie dog towns and social systems are organized spatially around the burrow system. Black-tailed prairie dogs spend hours working on these burrows and construction and repair of their associated mounds (Cincotta 1989, J. King 1955, Sheets et al. 1971). Collection of surface soils for construction of crater mounds requires moving soil over a 1-m radius from the mound itself. This movement may be accomplished by digging trough- or trench-like furrows and pushing soil toward the mound with the front feet, or throwing the dirt toward the mound using the rear feet. Crater mounds are carefully formed when soils are moist; the animals push soil with their head, shoulders, and forelimbs and tamp the soil around the entrance with their noses. When the soils have dried the impressions left by their noses are clearly visible in the adobe-like material. The density of the burrow entrances varies greatly among towns. An average density of 104 en-

trances per ha was reported for one town north of Fort Collins (Tileston and Lechleitner 1966). However, only about 12 percent of entrances were used at any one time.

Towns vary greatly in size, ranging from a few animals to thousands of individuals. Present-day colonies generally range from less than 10 ha to several hundred ha (Dahlsted et al. 1981, C. Knowles 1986), with populations of hundreds of animals. The larger towns are divided into smaller assemblages by topographic features or by social units and territorial defense. Topographic subdivisions are called wards, smaller social units within wards are coteries. The number of wards and coteries within a town varies considerably from one town to another. Tileston and Lechleitner (1966) estimated one ward in their study to encompass 3 ha, the eight included coteries averaging 0.21 ha each. Estimated density was about six animals per ha when the population was at its peak following emergence of young of the year. In early spring the population was about one-third that size. Average densities ranging from 10 to 55 animals per ha have been reported (Archer et al. 1987, C. Knowles 1986, O'Meilia et al. 1982).

Territory size for one coterie is usually a quarter ha or less, and is defended against members of other coteries. The activities of coterie members are usually confined to this territory. Each coterie is a well-knit social unit with a dominant male and a weakly developed dominance hierarchy. In general, the majority of interactions between members of a coterie are cohesive, although infanticide by females of close kin has been observed (Hoogland 1985). Increased size and complexity of colonies allow individuals to decrease time spent on alert and thus increases time available for other activities (Devenport 1989, Hoogland 1979a, b).

Communication between prairie dogs involves tactile, visual, olfactory, and auditory stimuli. All species of prairie dogs have a variety of calls used for passing information from individual to individual or to the group as a whole. The commonly heard

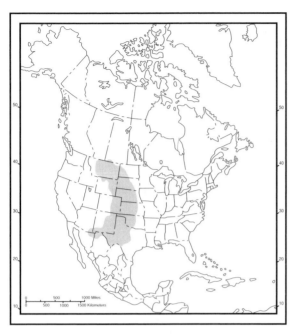

Map 9-30 Distribution of the black-tailed prairie dog (Cynomys ludovicianus) *in North America.*

"bark" or "alarm call" of black-tailed prairie dogs is familiar to anyone who has visited one of their towns. Several calls function for different situations, including alert, threat, "pleasure," and warning (Hoogland 1983, Waring 1970).

Black-tailed prairie dogs are diurnal and active above ground all year. However, during periods of inclement cold weather they may stay below ground for several days (A. Davis 1966). Their eyes have only cones, and they are almost blind in dim light. The animals appear above ground in the morning soon after sunrise and disappear in the late afternoon before sunset. Above-ground activity periods are bimodal in the warmer months, with peaks in early to midmorning and again in mid- or late afternoon. Above-ground activity diminishes in winter by as much as 45 percent. Most winter activity above ground occurs during midday when temperatures are highest. Most time above ground, especially during the growing season, is spent foraging and feeding.

Black-tailed prairie dogs have only one estrous cycle and one litter of young per year. In Colorado, they breed in February and early March. The proportion of yearling females that contributes to breeding seems to vary widely with location, probably reflecting differences in nutrition, population structure, and social stress. In Colorado 33 percent of yearlings reproduced. The young, numbering about four to five per litter with a range of one to eight, are born in late March and April. Gestation is estimated at 30 to 35 days. Young are blind, naked, and helpless at birth and remain in the burrow for four to seven weeks. By three weeks of age, hair covers the body and they begin to crawl. Eyes do not open until the animals are about five weeks old. The young are weaned when they come above ground, in late May or early June, weighing 100 to 125 g. They gain weight readily, spending much of the summer and fall foraging, so that by late fall weight approaches that of adults (Anthony and Foreman 1951, G. Johnson 1927, Koford 1958, Stockrahm and Seabloom 1988, Tileston and Lechleitner 1966).

At first emergence, pups are wary and do not venture far from the burrow entrance. However, they gradually expand their travels and in a few weeks scurry about their own coteries, mixing and playing with other litters. Activities include chasing, mock fighting, and wrestling. Adults rarely show play behavior in the wild. Pups also spend considerable amounts of time soliciting attention from their mothers (R. E. Smith 1958). Adults show frequent contact behaviors including mutual grooming, naso-nasal contact (wrongly interpreted as a "kiss"), anal sniffing, chasing, agonistic behavior, and use of vocalizations.

Many studies clearly indicate the integral role of prairie dog towns in contributing to species diversity of prairie ecosystems (T. Clark et al. 1982). For example, species like black-footed ferrets, prairie rattlesnakes, and burrowing owls are closely linked to prairie dog burrow systems for food and cover. In turn, prairie dog populations were probably influenced by heavy grazing by bison, which "disturbed" the prairie, facilitating colonization, although not all authors agree on this (see Slobodchikoff et al. 1988).

Prairie dogs of all species are subject to high mortality from a variety of terrestrial and avian predators including golden eagles, red-tailed and ferruginous hawks, coyotes, badgers, bobcats, foxes, black-footed ferrets, and rattlesnakes. Tileston and Lechleitner (1966) reported only 45 percent of marked black-tailed prairie dogs recaptured the following year. In other studies mortality has ranged from 14 to 55 percent. Diseases include plague, which can eliminate entire populations. Humans are by far the most effective control agent, with millions of hectares of prairie dog towns eliminated by intensive and extensive poison campaigns waged since agriculture invaded the range of the species. Prairie dogs may be as much a symptom of poor range management as they are a cause of degradation. Irrigation and careful range rotation can be effective controls on their populations in many situations (Fagerstone 1979). Much as they have been persecuted by agricultural interests, it is clear that land use managers have a responsibility for trying to maintain as many viable populations as possible in order to sustain diversity of our vanishing prairie lands in Colorado.

Despite persecution, in local areas prairie dogs have made a successful comeback and are abundant. In urban areas they become accustomed to humans (R. Adams et al. 1987). These urban colonies can precipitate conflicts, because some people are concerned about public health and nuisance problems, but others enjoy these interesting mammals as part of their shrinking natural world and want to retain them. T. Clark (1971b, 1986) reviewed the extensive literature on the black-tailed prairie dog.

DISTRIBUTION IN COLORADO — Black-tailed prairie dogs are not uncommon in most of the counties of the eastern plains, especially those immediately along the Front Range. The greatest difference in distribution from the early 1900s is a decrease in

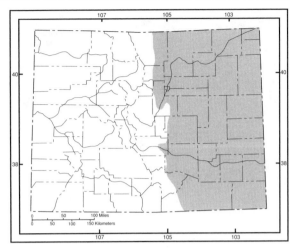

Map 9-31 Distribution of the black-tailed prairie dog (Cynomys ludovicianus) *in Colorado.*

size of colonies, with few now exceeding 40 ha and most being smaller than 20 ha (Lechleitner 1969). Because most of the eastern plains is in private ownership it is likely that total numbers of the species will decline over time as development pressures grow. On public lands such as the Pawnee National Grassland in Weld County and the Comanche National Grassland in Baca and Las Animas counties, pressure from livestock interests keeps populations at low numbers. Pawnee National Grassland has over 78,000 ha of public lands, but prairie dogs occupy less than one-half of 1 percent of the area. Such low numbers and the dispersion of colonies have reduced the distribution and affected the ecology of other species dependent on prairie dogs or their burrows. Although prairie dogs have been eliminated from millions of hectares of their former range, they are still abundant in many localities. Some of the highest densities presently found in Colorado are on lands held by developers adjacent to or within urban areas such as Denver, Boulder, and Aurora. These holdings usually were farmed but no longer are used for agriculture, being left "idle" until economic conditions permit profitable development. Black-tailed prairie dogs are able to colonize such disturbed areas with high success. One subspecies, *Cynomys ludovicianus ludovicianus,* occurs in Colorado.

Photograph by J. Perley Fitzgerald.

Photograph 9-16 Abert's squirrel (Sciurus aberti).

Sciurus aberti
ABERT'S SQUIRREL

DESCRIPTION — Also called tassel-eared squirrel, Abert's squirrel in its rich winter pelage has to rank as one of Colorado's most beautiful mammals. A large tree squirrel, the species is polymorphic in coat color along the Front Range (Nash and Ramey 1970). The gray phase has a white belly and dark lateral stripes; other color phases are solid colored: jet black, dark brown, or pale brown. Proportional prevalence of various color phases varies with location, although all three color phases may occur in a single litter. The predominant color along the Front Range is black. Coat-color polymorphism and geographic variation have been studied, and the former found to be stable in populations since the turn of the century (Hancock and Nash 1982; Hoffmeister and Diersing 1978; Ramey and Nash 1976*a, b*). The ears have conspicuous tufts of hair, most noticeable in fresh winter pelage. In southwestern Colorado, almost all Abert's squirrels are salt-and-pepper gray, often marked with a broad, dorsal patch of rust-red hairs. Measurements are: total length 450–580 mm; length of tail 200–300 mm; length of hindfoot 65–75 mm; length of ear 35–45 mm; weight 550–750 g. The skull resembles that of the fox squirrel but lacks the typical reddish tinge common in the latter species. The ventral anterior border of the orbit is opposite the first molar, and the third upper premolar is large and well developed.

NATURAL HISTORY — Abert's squirrels have been fairly well studied in Colorado. They are ecologically dependent on ponderosa pines for both nesting sites and food and thus are restricted to open montane forests (J. Keith 1965, D. Patton 1977, M. Snyder 1992). They feed on inner bark, seed, twigs, buds, and cones of ponderosa pines. Only about 10 percent of the weight of twigs cut is actually consumed. Abert's squirrels appear to select trees with low levels of certain monoterpenes and can reduce ponderosa pine cone production by up to 74 percent, depending on numbers of squirrels and the rate of cone production (Capretta et al. 1980). During winter, Abert's squirrels feed almost exclusively upon the phloem (inner bark) of particular individual trees. These target trees represent less than 10 percent of the trees in stands populated by Abert's squirrels along the Front Range and are chemically and physiologically different from trees not selected (M. Snyder 1992, 1993; Snyder and Linhart 1993). The squirrels are probably important agents of natural selection in southwestern ponderosa pine woodlands. Fungi and carrion are eaten, and bones and antlers are often gnawed for their mineral content. Food caches are not established.

Abert's squirrels are diurnal and active year round. Winter foraging focuses on terminal twigs in the tree crown. They gnaw through the base of a twig, strip the needle clusters, remove the outer bark, eat the inner bark, and drop the remaining part of the twig. These feeding sites are recognizable by the severed needle clusters and bare, discarded twigs at the base of trees (Snyder 1992).

At night and when inactive during the day, the squirrels retreat to tree nests. Occasionally animals of different ages and sexes share the same nest, especially in winter and spring. Nests are typically in ponderosa pine, with most nest trees having a diameter of more than 0.3 m. Nests are either constructed from pine twigs up to 60 cm in length and 2 cm in diameter or "excavated" in the mass of twigs that proliferates from dwarf mistletoe infestations. Nest chambers are lined with grass and other soft materials. Nests are 5 to 18 m above ground. The nest is frequently located on the south side of the tree and near the trunk; such areas would receive early sun and be somewhat protected from wind. Abert's squirrels appear to do best in ponderosa pine stands with close to 60 percent canopy closure and over 220 stems per ha (Farentinos 1972*c*; D. Patton 1977, 1984).

Although not territorial, Abert's squirrels are mostly solitary except during the breeding season. Home ranges in Colorado ranged from about 5 to 20 ha depending on season and sex of the animal. Mean home range size for both sexes is about 8 ha. Males typically have larger home ranges, especially when breeding, although adult females may cover large distances in summer (Farentinos 1979).

Abert's squirrels show a variety of visual displays and have several vocalizations. Displays include tail flaring, tail flicking, and foot stomping, all of which are associated with varying degrees of alarm or investigative behavior when examining inanimate objects. Calls include alarm barks, tooth chattering, screams, and clucks. Changes in position of the tail and ears and general body posture are used during agonistic displays in the mating season, communicating degrees of dominance or subordinance (Farentinos 1974).

As in other tree squirrels, courtship is marked by frantic chases, with males following estrous females up and down trees and over the forest floor. Such chases may continue for several hours and result in multiple copulations by the same or different males. Dominant males mate first but in prolonged chases completely subordinate males may also have a chance to mate. Aggressive behaviors are typical during these chases with the female attacking her male admirers or giving vocalizations and threat displays. Males also engage in male-male aggressive behaviors during the chase (Farentinos 1972*b*, 1980; Rice 1957).

Map 9-32 Distribution of Abert's Squirrel (Sciurus aberti) *in North America.*

Most mating occurs in April or May in Colorado with only one litter per year. Gestation takes about 46 days. Litters average three (range, two to four — Farentinos 1972*b*). Young squirrels are naked at birth. The eyes are open and the pelage is well developed by about six weeks of age. Young animals may leave the nest at about nine weeks of age but still rely on the female until about two and one-half months old.

Population dynamics of the species are poorly known. Sex ratios strongly favor males, 1.4:1 (Farentinos 1972*b*, J. Keith 1965). Population estimates range from 12 to 30 animals per km^2 in the Black Forest of El Paso County, and from 82 to 114 animals per km^2 near Boulder (Farentinos 1972*a*). Spring populations are lowest. Adults made up between 53 and 65 percent of populations near Boulder. Annual mortality ranged from 22 to 66 percent in Arizona, with the speculation that severe snow conditions can lead to high mortality (R. Stephenson and Brown 1980).

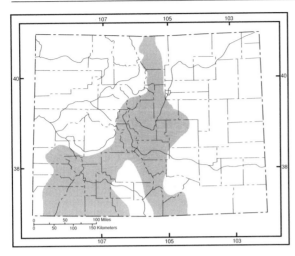

Map 9-33 Distribution of Abert's Squirrel (Sciurus aberti) *in Colorado.*

Information on predation is sparse. Hawks (especially goshawks) may be the most capable predators, as most terrestrial carnivores are not very successful at catching this arboreal species. Martens generally occur at higher elevations than do these squirrels. Food availability is probably important, as ponderosa pine seed crops are variable. Nash and Seaman (1977) reviewed the literature on the species.

DISTRIBUTION IN COLORADO — Abert's squirrels are common in ponderosa pine forests in southern and central Colorado, and their distribution has generated interest (Ramey and Nash 1971). During the late Pleistocene, Abert's squirrels occurred only as far north as central Arizona and New Mexico. Their occurrence in Colorado is thus a result of post-Pleistocene dispersal (R. Davis and Brown 1989). Extensions of their known range have occurred in recent years in southeastern (Mellott and Choate 1984) and western Colorado (R. Davis and Bissell 1989). Earlier this century, the species was not common in Colorado but subsequently increased after closure of the hunting season (Wade 1935). Abert's squirrel is classified as a small game mammal in Colorado (Table 3-1). *Sciurus aberti mimus* occurs in southwestern Colorado; *S. a. ferreus* occurs in the Front Range, Sangre de Cristos, and Wet Mountains.

Sciurus niger
FOX SQUIRREL

DESCRIPTION — The fox squirrel is a large tree squirrel, gray brown above, shading to reddish brown laterally. The belly is rufous, yellowish brown, or whitish. The tail is bushy, grayish red dorsally and red below. Measurements are: total length 450–600 mm; length of tail 170–300 mm; length of hindfoot 50–75 mm; length of ear 19–33 mm; weight 400–1,100 g. The skull is very similar to that of Abert's squirrel although it often has a reddish tinge. The skull of the fox squirrel will fluoresce red under ultraviolet light, a character unique to this mammal and caused by normal erythropoietic porphyria (Flyger and Levin 1977).

NATURAL HISTORY — Despite the fox squirrel's abundance and ubiquity along river bottoms and in urban areas of the eastern plains, few studies have been done on the species in Colorado. It is mostly an inhabitant of open deciduous forest. In Colorado, the western margin of its range, it is associated with lowland shelterbelts and urban areas as well as riparian woodlands (Hoover and Yeager 1953). The creation of urban landscapes with mixed coniferous and deciduous trees has allowed the species to do well in many cities in the state, including extralimital populations at such unlikely places as Steamboat Springs (Armstrong, unpublished).

The diet has been well studied in the eastern United States (Nixon et al. 1968, Korschgen 1981). Fox squirrels eat a variety of foods including nuts such as acorns and walnuts, twigs, buds, and tender leaves of many tree species including cottonwood and elm, various berries, apples, Russian-olives, and other fleshy fruits, small grains, and corn (Yeager 1959). Fox squirrels also readily take food placed out for songbirds and feed on eggs of birds, nestlings, and other animal protein. Bones and antlers are also consumed, especially by pregnant and lactating females.

The animals are diurnal and active year around. Individuals become active at or shortly after sun-

Photograph 9-17 Fox squirrel (Sciurus niger).

Home ranges of fox squirrels are between 0.4 and 16.4 ha, depending on habitat and population density (Flyger and Gates 1982). In Nebraska, home ranges averaged 7.5 ha for males and 3.5 ha for females, with yearlings having the largest home ranges (C. Adams 1976). In cottonwood river bottoms near Greeley, squirrels ranged over 1 to 2 ha (Graham 1977). In late summer and early fall young animals tend to disperse from their natal areas. Movements may exceed 3 km in some instances.

Fox squirrels live in nests that they construct, or they utilize available tree cavities, bird houses, and similar spaces. Cavities must have an opening of about 7 by 9 cm. The edges of such openings are gnawed and smoothed by the squirrels in their daily activity and movement (Baumgartner 1943). Nests are constructed from leaves, twigs, and bark of deciduous trees; layers of these materials are built up into a compact, durable structure. The nest chamber is hollowed out as construction occurs and is lined with finer and softer materials including shredded bark, grasses, and shredded leaves. Artificial materials are readily used. Nests are typically located close to the crotch of main limbs or near the top of the main trunk usually at least 6 m above the ground (Baumgartner 1940, J. Stoddard 1920, R. Packard 1956). Although tree cavities are reported to provide more protection to fox squirrels in the winter months, in urban areas in Colorado the animals usually are forced to rely on leaf nests for their cover because of urban forestry practices that prune out dead materials.

The fox squirrel has two breeding seasons per year. In Greeley, fox squirrels have their first season from mid-January to late March. The second season runs from late June through July. Breeding is characterized by mating chases similar to those described for Abert's squirrels (McCloskey and Shaw 1977). During the breeding season males lose considerable weight and tend to eat little. Females remain in estrus for about 10 days. Gestation takes 44 to 45 days, and the young are born naked and blind (Baumgartner 1940, L. G.

rise and exhibit morning and late afternoon activity peaks during the warmer months. In the winter the animals are most active during midday (Hicks 1949, Bakken 1959). Fox squirrels have well-developed behaviors to reduce predation and defend resources. These behaviors include habits of freezing in position, running around to the opposite side of a tree trunk when approached, or vocalizing with warning and alarm barks when danger appears (Bakken 1959, Zelley 1971). Access to resources is determined by chases, with adult males being most aggressive.

Map 9-34 Distribution of the fox squirrel (Sciurus niger) *in North America.*

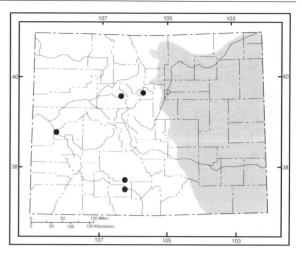

Map 9-35 Distribution of the fox squirrel (Sciurus niger) *in Colorado. Solid circles represent extralimital introductions.*

Brown and Yeager 1945). Litter size probably averages a little below three in Colorado, although a mean of 3.7 has been reported (R. Hoover and Yeager 1953). In Greeley two is the average based on observations of females with young newly emerged from the nest. Pelage development and eruption of the incisors occurs at about 4 weeks. Ears open at 3 weeks and eyes at 5 weeks of age. Young are weaned by 10 weeks of age and are self-sustaining at 3 to 4 months (D. Allen 1942, Baumgartner 1940).

Both sexes can breed at 10 or 12 months of age. Yearling females have only one litter in their first breeding year. In subsequent breeding years two litters are expected up until the death of the female. Males with scrotal testes can be observed during most months except late summer and fall.

Population biology is poorly understood. Adult fox squirrels can live over 12 years in the wild (Koprowski et al. 1988). However, few survive more than 5 or 6 years. An urban, adult female watched

by the first author and his wife in Greeley lived over 6.5 years. That female raised two litters of offspring each year of her adult life. Mortality in Colorado is mostly caused by hunting, traffic accidents, and predation by great horned owls, red-tailed hawks, domestic cats and dogs, foxes, and coyotes. Plague has been associated with urban populations in Denver and Greeley (B. Hudson et al. 1971).

DISTRIBUTION IN COLORADO — Fox squirrels are common in riparian woodlands along the South Platte and Republican rivers. They have extended their range along most tributaries of these rivers and are penetrating the foothills along riparian corridors as high as Evergreen (2,285 m [7,500 ft]) for example. Many populations are the result of deliberate introductions made in the early 1900s and more recently, but a natural invasion has also occurred as plains riparian habitats have been stabilized by control of floods and prairie fires, and as humans have created more favorable environments for fox squirrels by planting deciduous trees (Armstrong 1972, R. Hoover and Yeager 1953). Because they are more tolerant of human disturbance and tend to dominate Abert's squirrels in direct competitive interactions, fox squirrels may have a long-term negative impact on populations of Abert's squirrels in some areas, including the Black Forest between Denver and Colorado Springs. One subspecies, *Sciurus niger rufiventer,* occurs in Colorado. Fox squirrels are designated as small game mammals (Table 3-1).

Tamiasciurus hudsonicus
PINE SQUIRREL, CHICKAREE, OR "RED SQUIRREL"

DESCRIPTION — The pine squirrel is our smallest and noisiest tree squirrel, its chattering vocalizations as diagnostic as its appearance. There is considerable color variation throughout its wide range. In northern and central Colorado, little or no red is seen in the dorsal pelage. Squirrels from farther south may have somewhat brighter dorsal colors, but nowhere in Colorado does this species deserve the common name —"red squirrrel"— it bears elsewhere over its broad range. The summer pelage is usually more reddish than the grayer winter pelage. The eyes have a conspicuous white eye ring, and the venter is white. The tail is dark, ranging from blackish gray to reddish brown, often fringed with white. The ears may show tufts, longer in winter pelage. Measurements are: total length 300–350 mm; length of tail 115–135 mm; length of hindfoot 45–55 mm; length of ear 19–30 mm; weight 190–260 g. The skull is more delicate than that of the other two tree squirrels, and the premolar is either reduced in size or absent. The anterior ventral border of the orbit is opposite the premolar. The male pine squirrel has an extremely small baculum compared to members of the genus *Sciurus,* and females have a unique coiled vagina.

NATURAL HISTORY — Pine squirrels are common throughout subalpine and montane forests in Colorado, except in stands of ponderosa pine occupied by Abert's squirrels. Where Abert's squirrels are absent from ponderosa pine, pine squirrels can be expected, at least in low numbers. They also occasionally use riparian cottonwood stands (Armstrong 1972, Ferner 1974, Finley 1969, Hatt 1943).

Photograph 9-18 Pine squirrel or chickaree (Tamiasciurus hudsonicus).

Chickarees eat a variety of foods including buds, berries, and leaves of plants, although seeds of conifers and fleshy fungi are the staples (Obbard 1987). These squirrels have coevolved with the conifers upon which they feed (C. Smith 1970). Because most conifers, except the serotinous lodgepole pines, have cones that mature in the fall and release their seeds, squirrels have to harvest "green" cones and store them in caches before they release their seeds. This necessity results in tremendous energy expense and activity on the part of the squirrels. On a quiet late summer or early fall day one can hear the animals at work

197

clipping and dropping cones to the ground. Squirrels in productive trees can cut a cone every two or three seconds (Armstrong 1987). An Alaskan study indicated that one squirrel may cache up to 16,000 cones per year (C. Smith 1968). Cones are typically cached in large middens at the base of selected feeding trees. Middens may be as much as 9 m across and over 0.5 m in depth, consisting of cone scales, cores of eaten cones, and stored uneaten cones. Large middens are the result of years of accumulated materials by generations of squirrels. As middens accumulate debris and increase in size, their function in holding moisture and maintaining cool temperatures for cone storage increases, resulting in added value in keeping cones viable or available for food for several years. Nursery workers and foresters collect cones from such middens as a source of seed for commercial or reforestation purposes (Finley 1969).

In Colorado, nests in lodgepole pines are constructed of twigs, leaves, and grasses. Nests are from 3 to 20 m above the ground (average 5.3 m), typically in trees within the interior of closed canopy stands (Hatt 1943, Rothwell 1979). In other areas, use of tunnels in surface litter and hollow logs is noted, but this is not common in the Southern Rockies (Obbard 1987). In Alaska and Canada the animals may burrow under the winter snow in search of food caches made during more hospitable times. In our area, pine squirrels typically locate caches under dense tree canopy, thereby shielding their stores from significant snow accumulation.

Pine squirrels are active year-round, starting at dawn in warmer weather. Activity usually wanes during the middle of the day but picks up in late afternoon until dusk. During cold weather most activity occurs during midday. Thermoregulation is a problem for the species, and activity outside the nest generally ceases when air temperatures fall below −32°C. Temperatures in the nest during the winter may keep metabolic demand close to basal levels, whereas activity outside the nest may result in two to four times the basal energy

Map 9-36 Distribution of the pine squirrel, or chickaree, (Tamiasciurus hudsonicus) in North America.

needs. Food caches are usually located close to the nest tree, reducing time spent out of the nest in cold weather (Pauls 1978).

Chickarees are strongly territorial, linked to defense of food supplies and caches (Gurnell 1984, Hatt 1943, Kemp and Keith 1970, C. Smith 1968). Territories vary in size from about 0.4 to 2 ha per individual, depending on adequacy of cone crops and season. The degree of aggressive territorial behavior is related to the amount of available food in a given area (Rusch and Reeder 1978, C. Smith 1968). In Colorado, lodgepole pine has a relatively consistent cone crop, but cone production in spruces and firs is much more variable. This variation in productivity influences sizes of territories. Territorial defense is reduced during years of abundant cone crops. Density estimates range from 50 to 250 animals per km^2 in coniferous forests similar to those found in Colorado (Obbard 1987).

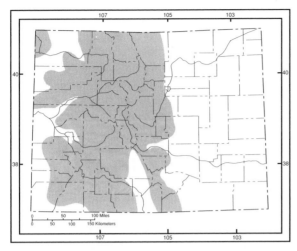

Map 9-37 Distribution of the pine squirrel, or chickaree, (Tamiasciurus hudsonicus) *in Colorado.*

In Colorado, pine squirrels breed from mid-April through mid-June; only one litter is produced a year. Average litter size is just over three, with a range of two to five (Dolbeer 1973). Females are sexually receptive for only one day and are spontaneous ovulators (Lair 1985a). Gestation is estimated to take 33 to 35 days (Lair 1985b), and most squirrels in Colorado are born in mid-May to mid-July. Young squirrels are able to leave the nest at about 40 days of age and start foraging and collecting food when about one and one-half months of age. The squirrels breed first as yearlings. Numbers of adult females breeding varied from 59 to 89 percent in Colorado.

Chickarees have lived up to nine years in captivity, but in the wild less than 5 percent live beyond their fifth year. Average annual mortality is estimated to be 67 percent in juveniles, 34 percent in yearlings, and 61 percent in adults (Obbard 1987). Most mortality is probably the result of weather and related fluctuations in cone production. Predators include martens, red fox, lynx, red-tailed hawks, goshawks, great horned owls, and eagles. The pine squirrel is recognized as a small game mammal in Colorado and may be harvested during the fall. Colorado is one of the few states that allow its harvest, but in Canada the species is an important furbearer with up to three

million animals taken per year for their pelage. Although some individuals argue that pine squirrels damage coniferous trees by cutting cones and clipping shoots, Maser et al. (1978) suggested that these damages may be more than offset by their dispersal of mycorrhizal-forming fungi, which are also important to conifer success. The literature on this squirrel is reviewed by Obbard (1987) and Flyger and Gates (1982).

DISTRIBUTION IN COLORADO — The pine squirrel is common in suitable forested habitat in Colorado at elevations from 1,830 to 3,660 m (6,000–12,000 ft). One subspecies, *Tamiasciurus hudsonicus fremonti,* occurs in the state.

Glaucomys sabrinus
NORTHERN FLYING SQUIRREL

DESCRIPTION — The northern flying squirrel is a strikingly handsome animal, with long, velvet-soft, smoky gray-brown fur (paling to white below) and a broad, flattened tail. A broad flap of well-furred skin stretches from wrists to ankles and forms the gliding membrane (patagium). Measurements are: total length, 310–340 mm; length of tail, 145–160 mm; length of hindfoot, 40–45 mm; length of ear, 25–30 mm; weights range to 190 g. Females have four mammae, and males have a well-developed baculum.

NATURAL HISTORY — Flying squirrels do not fly, of course, but they are capable of magnificent glides, launching themselves from high in one tree and gliding gracefully or acrobatically to an adjacent tree 40 m or more away. The broad tail serves as a rudder and allows dramatic turns in midair. Further, a quick flick of the tail just before landing positions the squirrel to alight head up, ready to scamper to the far side of the tree.

Habitat in the Uinta Mountains of Utah is dense spruce-fir or aspen forest. These squirrels are mostly cavity nesters, building nests of grass and lichens in holes abandoned by woodpeckers or sapsuckers, but occasionally remodeling a nest of a chickaree or a large bird.

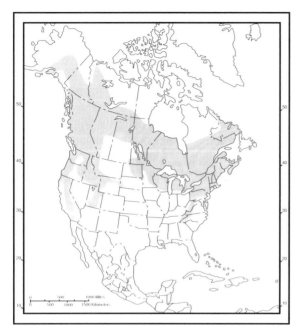

Map 9-38 Distribution of the northern flying squirrel (Glaucomys sabrinus) *in North America.*

Much of the diet is fungi and lichens, and the animals are much less dependent on seeds than most other tree squirrels. They do eat buds and staminate cones of conifers and a considerable amount of animal matter in season, including insects and nestling birds.

Females probably produce one litter of three to six (mode, four) altricial young per year after a gestation period of 37 to 42 days (Wells-Gosling and Heaney 1984). Development is fairly rapid, and the young take their "maiden flight" at about the time of weaning, roughly 10 weeks of age. Wells-Gosling and Heaney (1984) reviewed the literature.

DISTRIBUTION IN COLORADO — The northern flying squirrel is a species of boreal forest, ranging from coast to coast across southern Canada and the Upper Midwest, and extending southward through the Sierra Nevada, the Northern and Middle Rockies, and the Appalachians. The animals are not known to occur in Colorado, al-

though Durrant (1952) reported flying squirrels from extreme northeastern Utah, and T. Clark and Stromberg (1987) noted a specimen from Sweetwater County, Wyoming, just north of the Colorado boundary. There is a small possibility that *G. s. lucifugus* will be found in extreme western Moffat County, west of the Green River, at highest elevations on Hoy Mountain and adjacent uplands (where a number of mammalogists have searched for them over the years without success).

FAMILY GEOMYIDAE — Pocket Gophers

Pocket gophers are fossorial, herbivorous rodents restricted to North and Middle America. Fossils are known from the Oligocene and Miocene. Periods of climatic change and glaciation have played major roles in the distribution pattern of the living species. Because of their relatively sedentary behavior and underground habits, pocket gophers have undergone much genetic isolation and microevolution; close to 300 named subspecies for the 18 living species in the 3 genera are found in the United States. For the student of microevolution and systematics, gophers offer much opportunity for study, because populations inhabiting mountain valleys only a few kilometers apart may be distinct.

The common name "gopher" is applied colloquially to a wide range of burrowing rodents, but the term is properly restricted to pocket gophers. Pocket gophers are named for the conspicuous, external, fur-lined cheek pouches that open on either side of the mouth. The family Heteromyidae (pocket mice and kangaroo rats) also has such external cheek pouches, but the cheek pouches of other rodents are internal, opening inside the mouth cavity. Pocket gophers are heavy-bodied, short-tailed mammals with powerful forelimbs equipped with stout claws for digging. They are specialized for a fossorial existence with sturdy skulls, small eyes, small ears, and relatively short fur that does not collect dirt and debris loosened during their tunneling activities. All members of the group dig complex burrow systems, periodically marked by piles of soil pushed to the

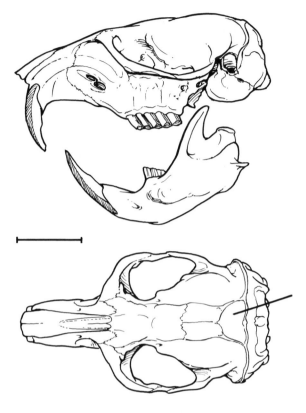

Figure 9-3 Skull of the northern pocket gopher (Thomomys talpoides) *showing the interparietal broader than long. Scale = 1 cm.*

surface. Pocket gophers are not gregarious but are strongly territorial in defense of burrow systems. They are active the year round even under the severest of winter conditions.

The dental formula is 1/1, 0/0, 1/1, 3/3 = 20. The skull has a pronounced interorbital constriction and small auditory bullae. The cheekteeth are ever growing, and enamel is reduced. The incisors are large with broad cutting surfaces. The presence or absence of grooves and the number of grooves on the upper incisors are of taxonomic importance. Males of all species have a baculum. Sexual dimorphism is pronounced—males are typically much larger than females, often by close to 40 percent of body weight. Literature on the

family was reviewed by Chase et al. (1982) and Teipner et al. (1983). A great deal of important research on pocket gophers was conducted in the 1960s and 1970s by the Colorado Cooperative Pocket Gopher Project, so much is known about these intriguing animals (but many fascinating questions remain unanswered). G. Turner et al. (1973) reviewed earlier literature and discussed pocket gophers of Colorado in detail. All pocket gophers in Colorado are classified as small game mammals (Table 3-1).

Key to the Species of the Family Geomyidae Found in Colorado

1. Upper incisors without a longitudinal groove . . . . *Thomomys* 2

1′ Upper incisors with one or two longitudinal grooves 3

2. Sphenoidal fissure absent; incisive foramen opening anterior to infraorbital foramen; ear typically less than 6.9 mm. Interparietal is broader than long . . . . Northern Pocket Gopher — *Thomomys talpoides*, p. 204

2′ Sphenoidal fissure present; incisive foramen opens posterior to anterior opening of infraorbital foramen; ear more than 6.9 mm. Interparietal longer than broad . . . . Botta's Pocket Gopher — *Thomomys bottae*, p. 202

3. Upper incisor with one longitudinal groove; color dark with orange-yellow cheeks . . . . Yellow-faced Pocket Gopher — *Cratogeomys castanops*, p. 209

3′ Upper incisor with two longitudinal grooves; color pale without conspicuous difference in cheek color . . . . Plains Pocket Gopher — *Geomys bursarius*, p. 207

Photograph by R. B. Forbes.

Photograph 9-19 Botta's pocket gopher (Thomomys bottae).

Thomomys bottae
BOTTA'S POCKET GOPHER

DESCRIPTION — Botta's pocket gophers, also called valley pocket gophers, are small and vary widely in color and size; to describe this variation, six distinct subspecies are recognized in Colorado. They vary from yellowish in western Colorado to reddish brown in the southeast. The venter is slightly paler than the dorsum. Measurements are: total length 200–260 mm; length of tail 60–85 mm, length of hindfoot 28–33 mm; length of ear 5–7 mm; weight 110–215 g. Males are consistently larger than females.

NATURAL HISTORY — Botta's pocket gophers prefer sandy soils of valley bottom riparian areas but will use many other areas except soils high in clay or extremely coarse substrates (R. Miller 1964). On Mesa de Maya, Las Animas County, they are found in less favorable soils (Moulton et al. 1979, 1983). They can be found in a variety of vegetation types, including agricultural land, grasslands, roadsides, open parklands, piñon-juniper woodlands, open montane forest, montane shrublands, and semidesert shrublands (Youngman 1958; C. L. Douglas 1969a; Moulton et al. 1979, 1983). Their distribution has been linked to soil preferences (Best 1973) and to limiting com-

petition with northern pocket gophers, plains pocket gophers, and yellow-faced pocket gophers, all of which appear capable of displacing the species on favored sites. T. Vaughan and Hansen (1964) located an area about 6 mi north of Cotopaxi, Fremont County, where the two Coloradan species of *Thomomys* occurred within a half mile of each other. Reciprocal transplants were made, and both species were introduced into experimental sympatry in an unoccupied area. The northern pocket gopher was the better disperser and tolerated a wider range of environmental conditions and therefore reproduced more successfully in the experimental zone. Either species might be dominant in agonistic encounters. A. Baker (1974) found the northern pocket gopher to be behaviorally dominant in the laboratory.

The diet of Botta's pocket gopher is similar to that of the northern pocket gopher. Seeds, tubers, roots, and green vegetation of a variety of forbs and grasses are eaten. Most food consists of above-ground plant parts. Succulent grasses, especially bromes, may constitute 40 to more than 80 percent of the diet. Forbs such as thistle, fleabane, and common sunflower generally make up the remainder. Insects make up less than 20 percent of stomach contents (Gottfried and Patton 1984). In Mesa Verde, piñon nuts, underground cactus parts, Indian ricegrass, rabbitbrush, and loco-weeds were eaten (C. L. Douglas 1969a). Food is stored in side tunnels of the burrow system. Coprophagy is practiced as a mechanism for maximizing nutrient uptake from ingested material.

Botta's pocket gophers, as other species of gophers, are thought to be polygynous because adult sex ratios sometimes favor females by almost three to one. However, Daly and Patton (1986) have raised questions regarding how effective male gophers can be in keeping other males from access to females because both sexes maintain exclusive territories. Breeding in Colorado probably occurs from March through July, according to work by Bandoli (1987) in New Mexico,

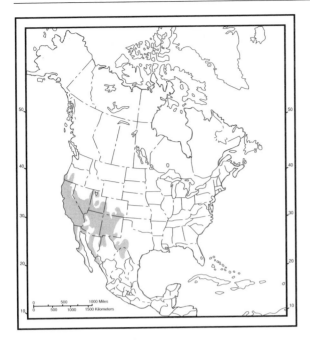

Map 9-39 *Distribution of Botta's pocket gopher* (Thomomys bottae) *in North America.*

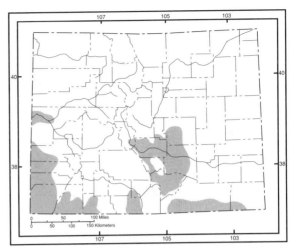

Map 9-40 *Distribution of Botta's pocket gopher* (Thomomys bottae) *in Colorado.*

where litter size ranged from 2 to 5 with an average of 2.6. Reproductively active females were found from February through April. Gestation takes about 19 days with a single litter produced each year (Schramm 1961).

Botta's pocket gophers dig complex burrow systems in well-formed soils that include both shallow and deep tunnels. In California, nests were found in burrows about 38 cm below the surface, and shallower foraging burrows were about 10 cm below ground (Gettinger 1984), but where the animals live in relatively shallow soils, such as on Mesa de Maya in southern Colorado, burrow depths averaged 15 cm (Moulton et al. 1979).

Botta's pocket gophers do not hibernate and are active at any time of the day or night. Radio-tracking studies in California found that animals spent 40 percent of their time away from the nest and tended to have bursts of activity in late afternoon (Gettinger 1984). A similar study in New Mexico found that only 19 percent of the time was spent away from the nest during the reproductive season (Bandoli 1987).

The animals are territorial, solitary, and aggressive toward other members of the species except when mating or when females are with young. Territories of males average 470 m^2 and contacted the territories of several females, whose territories average 290 m^2. The size of burrow systems of males increases in winter and spring, apparently as they search for mates (Bandoli 1981). In California, burrow systems averaged 107 m^2, with 90 percent of activity occurring within 50 m of the nest (Gettinger 1984).

Densities of 10 animals per ha are not unusual, and up to 153 per ha were reported on a favorable site during a population peak in California (Howard 1961). Young pocket gophers disperse from the natal burrow in late summer or early fall. At this time they are especially vulnerable to a variety of predators including coyotes, foxes, badgers, owls, and hawks. Significant mortality of young males is probably associated with male-male aggression and forced immigration. G. Turner et al. (1973) reviewed much of the earlier literature.

203

DISTRIBUTION IN COLORADO — Botta's pocket gophers occur in southern Colorado, where several local races have evolved. *Thomomys bottae aureus* occurs at lower elevations in southwestern Colorado, south of the Uncompahgre Plateau and southwest of the San Juan Mountains; *T. b. cultellus* occurs in the vicinity of Raton Pass; *T. b. howelli* occurs in the Grand Valley of the Colorado; *T. b. internatus* occupies the Arkansas Valley from Salida eastward to Pueblo, except for a small area around Cañon City, Fremont County, where the local race *T. b. rubidus* occurs; *T. b. pervagus* occupies the floor of the San Luis Valley west of the Rio Grande. *T. bottae* was treated by Hall (1981) as inseparable from *T. umbrinus*, the southern pocket gopher. Most mammalogists recognize Botta's pocket gopher as a distinct species, however.

Photograph by J. Perley Fitzgerald.

Photograph 9-20 Northern pocket gopher (Thomomys talpoides).

Thomomys talpoides
NORTHERN POCKET GOPHER

DESCRIPTION — The color of this small gopher varies geographically from dark brown or yellow-brown to pale, grayish yellow. Measurements are: total length 165–250 mm; length of tail 45–75; length of hindfoot 25–31; length of ear 5–7 mm; weight 100–150 g. The skull is robust, and the upper incisors lack a longitudinal groove. No sphe-

noidal fissure is present, and the incisive foramina are anterior to the infraorbital foramen. La-Voie et al. (1971) noted albinism in the species.

NATURAL HISTORY —Northern pocket gophers have been studied extensively in Colorado and elsewhere. They are the most ecologically tolerant of the gophers in the state and are found in many different habitat types including agricultural and pasture lands, semidesert shrublands, and grasslands at lower elevations upwards into alpine tundra (Armstrong 1972, Hansen and Reid 1973, P. Miller 1964). Soil development, drainage, and forage availability are factors that define their ecological limits. Grass-forb rangelands from 2,750 m to 3,350 m (9,000–11,000 ft) in elevation and with at least 50 cm of precipitation are the most productive native habitats in the state for this species (V. Reid 1973). Its broader environmental tolerance and higher vagility compared to Botta's pocket gopher, as well as possible behavioral dominance, give it a competitive and distributional advantage; however, the two species are also capable of coexistence under experimental conditions (A. Baker 1974, T. Vaughan and Hansen 1964).

Food habits of northern pocket gophers have been studied at several different localities in Colorado (J. Keith et al. 1959; Ward 1960; Ward and Keith 1962; Hansen and Ward 1966; T. Vaughan 1967, 1974). Gophers use all parts of plants, and diets vary on a seasonal basis partly in response to availability and partly because of quality and succulence. Not surprisingly, roots and tubers provide most of the winter diet, whereas spring and summer diets are usually 60 to nearly 100 percent leaves and stems. Forbs, especially composites and legumes, are the most important foods. In some locations prickly-pear, mallows, saltbush, cinquefoils, and knotweeds are also important. Grasses are seasonally and locally significant and may constitute 8 to 50 percent of the diet, with highest consumption on shortgrass prairie (T. Vaughan 1967). Locally, and especially during the winter months, northern pocket gophers can do considerable damage to conifer seedlings including lodgepole pine and Engelmann spruce (see Teipner et al. 1983). Food caches are stored in lateral tunnels usually plugged off from the main tunnel. Roots are often part of these stores, which may exceed 2 kg in weight. It appears that many caches are never used by the animals that stored them.

As other gophers, northern pocket gophers dig extensive burrow systems with both deep and shallow tunnels (Hansen and Reid 1973). Deep burrows may be more than 40 cm below the surface; burrows used in foraging are typically 10 to 30 cm deep. Northern pocket gophers also form conspicuous earthen ridges (casts or "eskers") on the surface. These ridges are composed of subsurface soils that were pushed into tunnels in the snow. As high country snow melts in spring and early summer, these garlands of soil are lowered intact to the surface, patterning High Plains grasslands as well as montane, subalpine, and alpine meadows, and influencing plant succession strongly. In northern Weld County, surface covered with gopher mounds ranged from 2.5 percent on lightly grazed sites to 8 percent on heavily grazed lands (Grant et al. 1980). Density of above-ground vegetation on such sites is highest at the margins of mounds, where infiltration of rainfall is increased.

As ecological knowledge has increased it has become apparent that burrowing by gophers over thousands of years has had a profound effect on soil development (Huntley and Inouye 1988). A high population (74 animals per ha) was estimated to move up to 400 tonnes of soil per hectare per year (Richens 1966). That kind of earth movement results in mixing and vertical cycling of soil components as organic material is incorporated into deeper layers and freshly developed parent material is exposed at the surface. Although such mounds and casts may be vulnerable to erosion, the consensus is that pocket gopher activity enhances soil formation and soil depth at lower elevations. On alpine tundra, gophers are also significant geomorphic agents. Well-vegetated sites occupied by northern pocket gophers experience soil disturbance much greater than

that on the general tundra surface, with average surface lowering of 0.0037 cm/yr, compared with 0.009 cm/yr for freeze-thaw processes, and 0.0001 cm/yr for wind and water erosion (S. Burns 1979). Burrowing has also been correlated with the presence of alpine terracettes (C. Thorne 1978).

Substantial activity by gophers in localized areas can result in predictable successional change (G. Turner 1973). Common invaders are cheatgrass, other bromes, knotweeds, gilias, and fleabane. Interestingly, common dandelion, an aggressive invader, is suppressed in areas of high gopher activity, probably because it is consumed by them. Lupines and peavines are also typically suppressed in active gopher areas. By reducing surface litter, gopher activity may impact populations of other small rodents such as *Microtus*, which are favored by a layer of thatch. The gopher often reaches very high population levels in irrigated alfalfa fields where considerable crop damage can occur (T. Vaughan 1967).

Northern pocket gophers in Colorado reproduce from mid-March through early summer; most breeding occurs in May and June right after snow melt and varies with elevation. Forage availability and quality as well as factors such as irrigation may influence the length of the breeding season. Gestation takes about 18 or 19 days. Only one litter of four to six young is produced per year. Herbicide use in western Colorado decreased litter size in one study. Older females produce the earliest litters; yearling females do not have their litters until late spring or early summer (Hansen 1960, Hansen and Bear 1964, T. Vaughan 1969). The altricial young weigh about 3 g at birth. They grow rapidly and by six months of age have almost attained adult weight (D. Anderson 1978). Although differential sex ratios are reported for several other species of gophers, it approximates 1:1 for the northern pocket gopher.

Northern pocket gophers reach highest population levels in late summer and early fall with recruitment of young of the year. Populations then

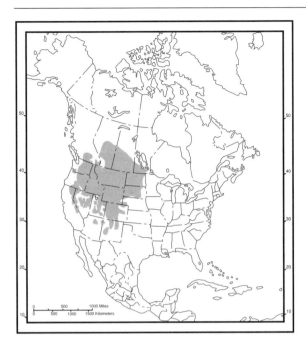

Map 9-41 Distribution of the northern pocket gopher (Thomomys talpoides) in North America.

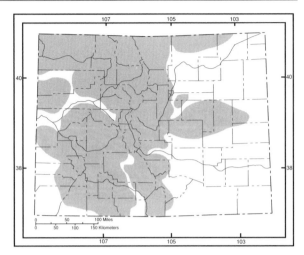

Map 9-42 Distribution of the northern pocket gopher (Thomomys talpoides) in Colorado.

decline until the next breeding season. Juveniles constitute less than 40 percent of spring populations, but in the fall they make up more than 43 percent of the population. Densities range from as low as 15 animals per ha to more than 74 animals per ha. Longevity is 1.5 to 2.5 years, with some individuals living over 5 years in the wild. Complete population turnover thus occurs every 4 to 6 years. Populations typically show fluctuations when followed over a number of years (T. Vaughan 1969, V. Reid 1973). Although pocket gophers are territorial and generally seem to make exclusive use of burrow systems, all possible combinations of adults and young were taken from the same burrow systems in spring and summer months, suggesting that intraspecific tolerance may vary, especially during the reproductive season (Hansen and Miller 1959).

Terrestrial predators of northern pocket gophers include coyotes, red and gray foxes, bobcats, badgers, spotted and striped skunks, weasels, bullsnakes, and rattlesnakes. Red-tailed and Swain-

son's hawks, goshawks, great horned, long-eared, and barn owls are effective aerial predators. Ectoparasites were studied by R. Miller and Ward (1960). G. Turner et al. (1973) reviewed much of the vast literature on the biology of the northern pocket in Colorado.

DISTRIBUTION IN COLORADO — Northern pocket gophers are common in a variety of habitats above about 1,525 m (5,000 ft) in elevation. Northern pocket gophers show wide geographic variation in color and size; nine subspecies are recognized in Colorado. *Thomomys talpoides agrestis* occurs in the San Luis Valley north and east of the Rio Grande; *T. t. attenuatus* occurs along the High Plains escarpment in northern Larimer, Weld, and Logan counties; *T. t. durranti* occurs in the vicinity of the Roan Plateau in Rio Blanco, Garfield, and Mesa counties; *T. t. fossor* occurs in the mountains of southwestern Colorado; *T. t. macrotis* is known only from Douglas County; *T. t. meritus* occurs in the mountains and parks of north-central Colorado, generally east of Moffat County and west of the Front Range; *T. t. ocius* occupies most of Moffat County; *T. t. retrorsus* occurs eastward on the eastern plains along the Platte-Arkansas Divide; *T. t. rostralis* occurs mostly in the Front Range.

© 1993 Wendy Shattil/Bob Rozinski.

Photograph 9-21 Plains pocket gopher (Geomys bursarius).

Geomys bursarius
PLAINS POCKET GOPHER

DESCRIPTION — Plains pocket gophers are pale brown to yellowish brown with a slightly paler ventral surface. By comparison the similar-sized yellow-faced pocket gopher is much darker, a rich mahogany brown. Measurements are: total length 180–300 mm; length of tail 50–90 mm; length of hindfoot 30–36 mm; length of ear 3–5 mm; weight 170–330 g. The upper incisors have two longitudinal grooves, although the inner ones may be difficult to see on some specimens. Cranial asymmetry has been noted (T. Vaughan 1961b). Plains pocket gophers are the most strongly fossorial of pocket gophers in the state. Their limbs and claws are so modified for digging that they seem to have difficulty walking, moving on the sides of their feet in an awkward manner.

NATURAL HISTORY — Plains pocket gophers occupy grasslands over the Great Plains as well as the margins of agricultural lands. They are adapted to a narrow range of conditions, requiring deep sandy to loamy soils that are well drained but moist. In Colorado they typically favor light soils of considerable depth especially in sandhills and other wind-blown soils. They appear, in part because of their larger size, to be less tolerant of harder and shallower soils than *Thomomys* (Cary 1911, P. Miller 1964, Best 1973, Moulton et al. 1983) and to be preadapted to colonize disturbed areas. Habitats include borrow pits, roadside edges, agrisystems, and lands with plant communities influenced by drought and the dust-bowl conditions of the 1930s.

Plains pocket gophers show preferences for certain plant species at certain times of the year, not necessarily in proportion to species abundance. About 64 percent of the annual diet in Washington County consisted of grasses, especially stipa, wheat-grass, and blue grama, which together composed 48 percent of the forage (G. Myers and Vaughan 1964). Significant amounts of cactus were eaten, and forbs were especially favored in spring and summer, important among them loco-weeds and globemallow. Leaves and stems accounted for only 26 percent of the diet; most food was underground parts. Studies in western Nebraska (Luce et al. 1980) showed generally similar diets, with grasses contributing the greatest fraction. Underground and above-ground plant parts were 31 and 39 percent of the diet, respectively. Four species — needle-and-thread, scouring-rush, June-grass, and Kentucky blue-grass — contributed 50 percent of the diet. Several studies indicate that plains pocket gophers can reduce production of alfalfa and forage production for livestock on native grasslands, in some cases by as much as 30 to 46 percent (Foster and Stubbendieck 1980, Luce and Stubbendieck 1981). Because of such impact, much effort has been spent on development of "control" methods for gopher populations, including toxicants and repellents. Much of that work has been conducted by researchers at the Denver Wildlife Research Center (Ward et al. 1967). However the value of the species in soil formation and in altering plant succession must be considered. In the natural ecosystem, pocket gophers are neither "good" nor "bad"; only we humans can make such subjective judgments.

In suitable habitat, conspicuous mounds of earth indicate locations of underground tunnel systems. Surface mounds consist of fresh castings from tunnels, often added to older material from other tunnel systems adjacent to the one being dug. The burrow entrance is plugged with soil except when the animals are discharging soil or emerging briefly to forage. Shallow burrows (15–30 cm deep) interconnect with deeper tunnels that reach below the frostline. Side tunnels are constructed as food caches or latrines. As with other species of gophers, soil is loosened with the strong front feet and claws or by chewing with the incisors, which angle forward. Soil is pushed to the surface with the forelimbs, chest, and neck (Downhower and Hall 1966). In Texas, burrow temperatures ranged between 23 and 33°C. Burrows typically had high humidity and elevated carbon dioxide concentrations compared to outside air. Oxygen concentration may be 20 percent lower than surface air. As in other burrow-dwelling mammals, elevated carbon dioxide and lower oxygen levels did not appear to impact the animals' physiology negatively (Kennerly 1958, 1964).

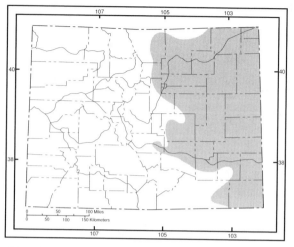

Map 9-44 Distribution of the plains pocket gopher (Geomys bursarius) in Colorado.

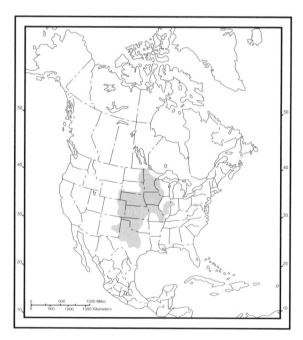

Map 9-43 Distribution of the plains pocket gopher (Geomys bursarius) in North America.

Individuals are solitary, aggressive, and territorial. Once established, burrow systems are used throughout the life of an individual. There are equally spaced periods of activity day and night (T. Vaughan and Hansen 1961). Animals were active about 34 percent of the time, with bouts of activity averaging one-half hour and resting periods averaging one hour. Density estimates for the species are few. Schmidly (1983) reported estimates of from one to 17 animals per ha in Texas. R. Beck and Hansen (1966) measured relative abundance of the species in dune sand and sandy loam habitats in Washington County, noting considerably higher activity in areas of sandy loam.

Males are polygamous and their territories may overlap those of females. Most reproduction in Colorado probably occurs during late winter and early spring. Most pregnant females were taken in April and May. The gestation period is not precisely known, but is estimated at 30 days or more. A single litter of one to six young (average, 3.5) is produced per year (T. Vaughan 1962).

A variety of terrestrial and avian predators prey on the species, particularly owls and burrowing predators such as badgers. Probably few plains pocket gophers live longer than five years. Literature on the species was reviewed by Chase et al.

(1982), Teipner et al. (1983), and G. Turner et al. (1973).

DISTRIBUTION IN COLORADO — Plains pocket gophers are a common species over most of eastern Colorado. *Geomys bursarius jugossicularis* occurs in southeastern Colorado south of the Platte-Arkansas Divide; *G. b. lutescens* is the subspecies north of that divide.

Photograph by R. B. Forbes.

Photograph 9-22 Yellow-faced pocket gopher (Cratogeomys castanops).

Cratogeomys castanops
YELLOW-FACED POCKET GOPHER

DESCRIPTION — The yellow-faced pocket gopher is slightly larger in total length than other Coloradan gophers. Most specimens are reddish brown with a yellowish orange tinge on the cheeks and neck region. The underparts are buffy. Measurements are: total length 245–300 mm; length of tail 68–80 mm; length of hindfoot 34–40 mm; length of ear less than 7 mm; weight 160–350 g. The skull is heavy and the upper incisors have a single longitudinal groove.

NATURAL HISTORY — Yellow-faced pocket gophers usually inhabit deep sandy or silty soils, relatively free of rocks. However, they also occur in shal-

lower, denser soils in some areas. In southeastern Colorado they are most often associated with grasslands but are also found in agricultural lands, roadside ditches, and montane shrublands and parklands (Cary 1911, P. Miller 1964, Moulton et al. 1983). In parts of southeastern Colorado and northeastern New Mexico, the species is apparently being displaced by *Geomys*, perhaps because of increased disturbance of native habitats (Best 1973, Moulton et al. 1983). In southwestern Texas, however, it is seemingly displacing *Geomys* in areas of increased aridity (Schmidly 1977).

Yellow-faced pocket gophers make earthen mounds at the entrance of their underground tunnels, but more frequently their surface activities result in formation of sunken plugs of soil not readily visible from a distance. Areas around such plugs are often disturbed, resulting in patches of annual or perennial forbs and grasses. Burrow depths range from 13 to 31 cm (Best 1973, Moulton et al. 1983). In the same habitats *Thomomys* burrows were somewhat shallower. Moulton et al. (1983) reported *T. bottae* and *Cratogeomys* in a zone of sympatry on Mesa de Maya, Las Animas County, with burrow systems closely overlapping but at different depths, and *Thomomys* occupying the shallower burrows. Burrow systems in Texas were from 40 to over 100 m in length with numerous side tunnels up to 3 m long (Hickman 1977). Usually burrow systems have a shallow foraging network of tunnels and a deeper system that contains the nest chamber and food stores.

Yellow-faced pocket gophers probably feed on a variety of green vegetation and root materials. Stomach contents favoring legumes and a large proportion of root materials have been described (V. Bailey 1932). Damage to crops is reported in some states. The animals harvest materials either from within the tunnel system by pulling plant roots and shoots down through the soil or by venturing out above ground to forage. When foraging above ground, plant materials are quickly clipped off close to ground level and dragged into the burrow. Once food is in the burrow system it is clipped into small pieces and carried in the cheek pouches to storage caches. Rhizomes are favored, and unused parts may be used to line the nest (Hickman 1975).

Breeding probably occurs from late March to August, with one, two, or possibly even three litters produced in a bimodal pattern, according to studies in Texas (Smolen et al. 1980), New Mexico (Hegdal et al. 1965), and Kansas (Birney et al. 1971). Most reproduction probably occurs from March to June in our area. Litter size ranges from one to five with an average of two or three. Young are born blind and naked. Cheek pouches develop after birth and are apparent only as creases in neonates (Hickman 1975). Females carry their young by the loose skin of the belly. Adult sex ratios favored females by 4:1 in southeastern New Mexico (Hegdal et al. 1965), although other studies found ratios closer to 1:1 (Smolen et al. 1980).

Yellow-faced pocket gophers usually occupy exclusive burrow systems. Occasionally more than one individual will occur together, usually during the

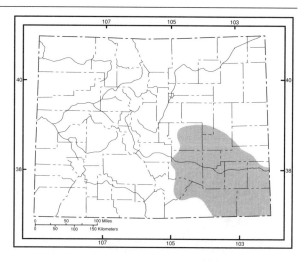

Map 9-46 Distribution of the yellow-faced pocket gopher (Cratogeomys castanops) in Colorado.

breeding season. Hegdal et al. (1965) reported multiple occupancy of burrows as common in southeastern New Mexico. These animals have relatively large home ranges and move around more than other species of gophers, probably also over land (S. Williams and Baker 1976). They do not swim very well and may be limited by water barriers more than are other gophers.

Individuals are short lived. In Texas, males survived seven months and most females survived one year, although a few survived almost two years (Smolen et al. 1980). Most small to medium-sized carnivores prey on the species; owls are especially successful. The literature was reviewed by Davidow-Henry et al. (1989).

DISTRIBUTION IN COLORADO — Yellow-faced pocket gophers occur widely in southeastern Colorado, ranging up the Arkansas Valley nearly to Florence. It is not uncommon in suitable habitat. One subspecies, *Cratogeomys castanops castanops*, occurs in Colorado. The taxonomy of the species has been unstable; at times this species has been known as *Pappogeomys castanops*, but Honeycutt and Williams (1982) have elevated *Cratogeomys* back to generic status. Common names have included chestnut-faced pocket gopher and Mexican pocket gopher.

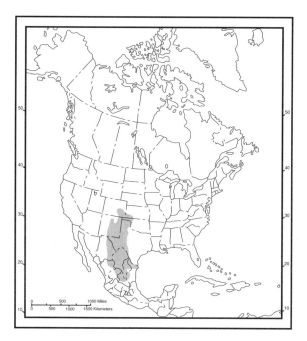

Map 9-45 Distribution of the yellow-faced pocket gopher (Cratogeomys castanops) in North America.

FAMILY HETEROMYIDAE — Kangaroo Rats and Pocket Mice

Heteromyids are small to medium-sized rodents, many of them adapted to arid and semiarid regions of western North America, Central America, and northwestern South America. The family exhibits a considerable range of locomotor morphology, and living kinds exemplify evolutionary grades in the history of the Heteromyidae. The spiny pocket mice (*Liomys* and *Heteromys*) are not at all specialized for jumping. The genera *Perognathus* and *Chaetodipus* (pocket mice) show moderate modification of limbs; when pursued they move by quadrupedal jumping (saltatory locomotion). The kangaroo rats (*Dipodomys*) and kangaroo mice (*Microdipodops*) are bipedal, strongly modified for richochetal locomotion with reduced forelimbs, greatly enlarged hindlimbs and feet, and a long, well-haired tail for balance.

All members of the family have external fur-lined cheek pouches that open alongside the mouth, similar to the geomyids. Food materials, typically seeds, are carried in these pouches to the burrow where they are stored. Pouches can be turned inside out for cleaning and tucked back into place using the forepaws. Most heteromyids are competent burrowers, digging in loose, sandy soils despite the weak forelimbs of some species. The pelage ranges from coarse and harsh to soft and silky. The skull is thin and delicately built, with inflated auditory bullae. The zygomatic arch is very thin (and easily damaged during specimen preparation or handling). The nasal bones project well beyond the upper incisors. The dental formula is 1/1, 0/0, 1/1, 3/3, for a total of 20 teeth. The incisors are thin and ever growing, and the uppers frequently show a longitudinal groove. All genera except *Dipodomys* have rooted cheekteeth. A baculum is present in males.

The evolution of this family is associated with the development of a drought-adapted flora that expanded over much of interior western North America in response to increasing aridity following uplift of the Sierra Nevada and the Rockies.

Except for the forest-dwelling *Heteromys* of northern South America and Central America, heteromyids are mostly inhabitants of desert shrublands and semiarid grasslands of the West. Fossils are known from the Oligocene, some 40 million years ago. Most species live in sandy soils, digging burrows under shrubs, trees, or herbaceous cover. They are typically nocturnal, leaving the burrow only for short periods to forage. Burrow entrances are often located in concealed areas and frequently are plugged with soil during the day. The diet is largely seeds with high protein content, but green vegetation, insects, and other invertebrates may be eaten. Many species are capable of meeting their water needs solely from the water that is produced as a by-product of the metabolism of fats. In colder areas, heteromyids undergo winter torpor. Even during favorable times of the year, above-ground activity appears to be minimized, probably to reduce predation and evaporative loss of water.

Genoways and Brown (1993) edited a comprehensive summary of the biology of the family Heteromyidae. There are 5 genera and 63 species of heteromyids, about half of which occur in the western United States. Colorado has 3 genera and 6 species, with a seventh species possible in southwestern Colorado. All Coloradan species are classified as nongame mammals (Table 3-1). Detailed studies of several species are lacking.

Key to the Species of the Family Heteromyidae Known or Expected to Occur in Colorado

1. Hindfeet greatly elongated, with soles of feet densely haired; face contrastingly marked; auditory bullae greatly inflated; cheekteeth ever growing, with simple crowns . . . . *Dipodomys* 2

1' Hindfeet not greatly enlarged, with soles of feet naked or sparsely haired; face not contrastingly marked; bullae only moderately inflated; cheekteeth rooted, with more complex crown pattern . . 3

2. Four toes on hindfoot, total length greater than 300 mm; white tip of tail longer than 25 mm

and preceded by black band . . . . Banner-tailed Kangaroo Rat — *Dipodomys spectabilis**, p. 224

2′ Five toes on hindfoot, total length less than 290 mm; white tip of tail less than 25 mm and preceded by bicolored band . . . .
. . . . Ord's Kangaroo Rat — *Dipodomys ordii*, p. 221

3. Pelage harsh; soles of feet naked; total length greater than 190 mm; hindfoot longer than 24 mm; occipitonasal length 30 mm or more . . . .
Hispid Pocket Mouse — *Chaetodipus hispidus*, p. 220

3′ Pelage not harsh; soles of feet sparsely haired; total length less than 150 mm; hindfoot less than 24 mm; occipitonasal length less than 25 mm . . . .
. . . . *Perognathus* 4

4. Tail more than one-half total length; hindfoot longer than 20 mm; antitragus lobed . . . . . Great Basin Pocket Mouse — *Perognathus parvus*, p. 218

4′ Tail less than one-half total length; hindfoot shorter than 20 mm; antitragus not lobed 5

5. Fur markedly soft and silky; total length less than 120 mm; pale postauricular patch larger than ear . . . .
. . Silky Pocket Mouse — *Perognathus flavus*, p. 216

5′ Fur not markedly soft or silky; total length greater than 120 mm; postauricular patch smaller than ear or lacking 6

6. Upper parts olive-brown, usually heavily washed with black; auditory bullae generally do not meet at anterior ventral borders . . . . . . Olive-backed Pocket Mouse — *Perognathus fasciatus*, p. 212

6′ Upper parts yellowish or reddish buff to pale brown, usually not heavily washed with black; auditory bullae usually meet at anterior borders . . . .
Plains Pocket Mouse — *Perognathus flavescens*, p. 214

Photograph 9-23 Olive-backed pocket mouse (Perognathus fasciatus).

Perognathus fasciatus
OLIVE-BACKED POCKET MOUSE

DESCRIPTION — The olive-backed pocket mouse has a dorsal pelage of olivaceous to buff, washed with black hairs. The darker hairs often form a distinct mid-dorsal band. This is the darkest of our small pocket mice, although specimens from western Colorado are much paler. A conspicuous yellowish buff lateral line typically separates the distinct dorsal color from the usually white to pale buff belly. Measurements are: total length 125–145 mm; length of tail 55–75 mm; length of hindfoot 14–19 mm; length of ear 7–12 mm; weight 10–13 g. Greatest length of the skull is 21.5–23.6 mm. The auditory bullae of the skull do not meet along their anterior margins. The interparietal bone is usually pentagonal and about equal in width to the interorbital breadth of the skull. The lower premolar is about the same length as the first lower molar. Females have three pairs of mammae.

* Species of possible occurrence in Colorado.

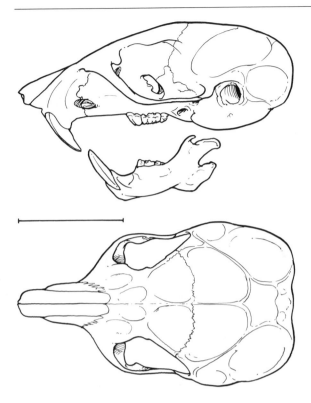

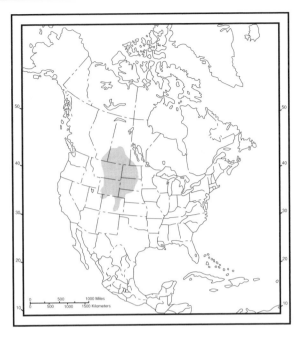

Map 9-47 Distribution of the olive-backed pocket mouse (Perognathus fasciatus) *in North America.*

Figure 9-4 Skull of the olive-backed pocket mouse (Perognathus fasciatus) *with distinct interparietal. Scale = 1 cm.*

NATURAL HISTORY — Little information exists on this species in Colorado. The olive-backed pocket mouse is an animal of mixed prairie and shrub-grassland steppe on the northern Great Plains and Wyoming Basin. In Colorado they are restricted to grasslands along the western margin of the plains and to shrub-grasslands of the northwestern part of the state (Armstrong 1972). They have also been captured in ponderosa pine with an understory of yucca (J. K. Jones 1953). Low numbers were captured in blue grama–needle-grass communities in southeastern Wyoming (Maxwell and Brown 1968). In northeastern Utah and northwestern Colorado, olive-backed pocket mice occur in sandy to gravel soils in semidesert shrublands (Hayward and Killpack 1956). They seem to prefer sites with loamy sand to clay soils and low vegetative cover, often with substantial amounts of bare ground. Typical plant associa-

tions include blue grama, needle-grass, and wheat-grass.

As with other heteromyids, olive-backed pocket mice feed selectively on a variety of seeds of grasses and forbs. Seeds of weedy species including croton, Russian-thistle, goosefoot, gaura, stipa, buckwheat, puccoon, and pigweed are frequently eaten. A captive animal ate mealworms, and it is likely that some insect matter is consumed in the wild (V. Bailey 1926, R. Turner and Bowles 1967).

Reproduction is poorly known. The species probably has one or two litters during the spring and early summer with a cessation of reproduction during hot weather. From two to nine embryos have been reported, with litters probably averaging four to six. Gestation is about one month; altricial young are produced (Pefaur and Hoffmann 1974, R. Turner and Bowles 1967).

213

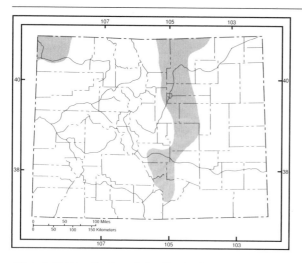

Map 9-48 Distribution of the olive-backed pocket mouse (Perognathus fasciatus) *in Colorado.*

Olive-backed pocket mice dig burrow systems, usually at the base of grass, yucca, or shrub cover. Entrances are inconspicuous and may be plugged during the daytime. Tunnels may exceed 1.8 m in depth with side tunnels used for food storage (V. Bailey 1926). Individuals probably do not move much more than 100 m from their burrows when foraging. They are inactive above ground in cold weather and probably exhibit periods of torpor. In Montana and North Dakota, densities have been estimated at 0.62 animals per ha to 4.0 animals per ha (Pefaur and Hoffmann 1975). In southeastern Wyoming, capture rates of 0.9 animals per 1,000 trap nights indicate similar low densities (Maxwell and Brown 1968). Most small to medium-sized predators probably prey on the animals, although low densities probably preclude their being common fare for any predator. Literature on the species was summarized by Manning and Jones (1988).

DISTRIBUTION IN COLORADO —Olive-backed pocket mice are restricted to extreme northwestern Moffat County and to a narrow band along the foot of the Front Range, southward to northern Las Animas, Fremont, and Custer counties. The status of the species in Colorado is poorly known, but extensive urban and agricultural de-

velopment along the Front Range corridor probably has led to local extirpation of some populations and may threaten others. Elevations of record in Colorado range from 1,525 m to 2,135 m (5,000–7,000 ft). *Perognathus fasciatus infraluteus* is found along the foot of the Front Range in north-central Colorado; *P. f. callistus* is restricted to the area north of the Yampa River in Moffat County. Systematics and geographic variation were reviewed by D. Williams and Genoways (1979).

Photograph 9-24 Plains pocket mouse (Perognathus flavescens).

Perognathus flavescens
PLAINS POCKET MOUSE

DESCRIPTION — The plains pocket mouse is pale buff to yellowish or reddish, with a variable dorsal wash of black hairs. The lateral line of buffy orange is generally less striking and the dorsal color is not as dark as that of the olive-backed pocket mouse. A buffy postauricular patch is often present. This patch is never as large as in the silky pocket mouse, and the hair is coarser. Measurements are: total length 123–145 mm; length of tail 52–71 mm; length of hindfoot 16–19 mm; length of ear 6–8 mm; weight 7–12 g. The auditory bullae typically meet at their anterior midline. As with the olive-backed pocket mouse,

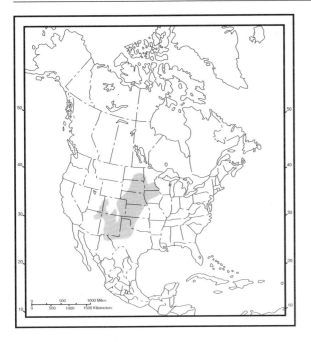

Map 9-49 Distribution of the plains pocket mouse (Perognathus flavescens) *in North America.*

the interparietal is about the same width as the interorbital breadth of the skull.

NATURAL HISTORY —The plains pocket mouse is the commonest species of *Perognathus* in grasslands on sandy to loamy sand soils in Colorado. On the eastern plains it favors sandy areas with moderate to good plant cover, although it can also tolerate a significant amount of bare ground (Maxwell and Brown 1968, Mohamed 1989). Plant communities are usually mixes of midgrass species including stipa, little bluestem, ricegrass, three-awn, and blue grama. Silvery wormwood and yucca are common associates. Highest reported capture rates are from sand sagebrush, where seven animals per 1,000 trap nights have been found (Moulton et al. 1981a). Margins of agricultural lands, including weedy fence rows, ditch banks, and grain fields, are also used (Lovell et al. 1985). In Kansas, the plains pocket mouse is one of the most abundant mammals in agriculturally disturbed sand sagebrush (K. Reed and Choate 1986). In northwestern Colorado,

highest numbers were captured in piñon-juniper stands 8 to 15 years after destruction with chains (O'Meara et al. 1981). Low numbers were captured in unchained piñon-juniper stands, where herbaceous vegetation was less well developed.

Diet of the plains pocket mouse is mostly seeds of grasses and forbs. Animals captured by Mohamed (1989) had seeds of spiderwort, ricegrass, needlegrass, lupine, scurfpea, three-awn, puccoon, bindweed, milkvetch, and *Cryptantha* in the cheek pouches. These genera include relatively common flora of the sand prairie in eastern Colorado and suggest that the mouse is a generalist in its foraging for seeds. In Utah, seeds made up 81 percent of stomach contents, including several of the species listed above (Armstrong 1982). Large seeds are stored for consumption in winter (K. Reed and Choate 1986). Arthropods made up 59 percent of the diet in the Piceance Basin of Colorado (Haufler and Nagy 1984).

The plains pocket mouse is active above ground during the warmer months. During three years of year-round trapping in Weld County, animals were captured from early March to early October (Mohamed 1989). In Kansas, they are active from March through October (K. Reed and Choate 1986). The species, like others in the genus, probably enters periods of winter torpor with arousal from time to time to eat seeds stored in the burrow system (Beer 1961).

Burrows are typically constructed at the base of clumps of vegetation, and the entrances usually are plugged during the day. Of three burrows excavated, two were shallow, less than 30 cm long and 5 cm deep, and dug into the sides of old pocket gopher mounds (K. Reed and Choate 1986). A third, whose entrance was beneath litter among sunflowers, was 2.4 m long and 0.5 m deep, the diameter of an index finger, and contained a food cache. Home ranges vary with sex and average 0.04 ha to 0.10 ha; average maximum distance moved between live captures was 22 m for males and 13 m for females (Mohamed 1989).

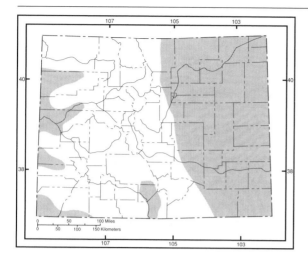

Map 9-50 Distribution of the plains pocket mouse (Perognathus flavescens) *in Colorado.*

In Kansas, average nightly movements of 20 to 30 m were documented (K. Reed and Choate 1986).

Reproduction is poorly known. In our area the species breeds from May through July. One or two litters may be born; litter size averages three to four. In Weld County, females were variously lactating, pregnant, or had uterine scars from mid-May through July. In September, only uterine scars were seen. Males with scrotal testes were captured from late April to late June (Mohamed 1989). It may be that breeding ceases with the hot summer temperatures of late July and August.

Population dynamics are poorly understood, and relative abundances are known only in terms of trapping success. Although not typically an abundant species, plains pocket mice were the fourth most common rodent in a study in Weld County (Mohamed 1989), averaging 1.2 animals per 1,000 trap nights on both snaptrap and livetrap sites (after grasshopper mice, plains harvest mice, and deer mice). In eastern Colorado, they averaged 1.01 animals per 1,000 trap nights (Moulton et al. 1981*a*). Of 13 species captured in that study, plains pocket mice were the sixth most common. In Wyoming, captures ranged from 2.7 to 7.1 animals per 1,000 trap nights (Maxwell and Brown 1968).

Information on predation is lacking. Probably snakes, grasshopper mice, and owls prey on the animals. Their small size and low population density would suggest that predation levels may be low.

DISTRIBUTION IN COLORADO —Plains pocket mice are widespread across the eastern plains with disjunct populations in the San Luis Valley and the western margin of the state to Garfield and Mesa counties. In parts of the eastern plains they are abundant, especially in sandy prairie soils. Status of the species in western Colorado is less clear. Finley et al. (1976) did not find any specimens along the Colorado River near Rifle, an area where they were reported as common by Warren (1942), and in the late 1970s Armstrong (unpublished) tried but failed to capture *P. f. caryi* at its type locality, 8 mi west of Rifle. However, they have been captured in the Piceance Basin (O'Meara et al. 1981). *P. f. flavescens* is the subspecies of the eastern plains; *P. f. relictus* is restricted to the San Luis Valley; *P. f. apache* occurs at lowest elevations in southwestern Colorado; and *P. f. caryi* occurs in the west-central valleys. The latter three subspecies were formerly known as *P. apache*, a taxon that D. Williams (1978) recognized as a synonym of *P. flavescens*. Most of the older literature refers to animals from the San Luis Valley and western Colorado as the Apache pocket mouse. In Colorado, populations on the eastern plains are not in genetic contact with those from either the San Luis Valley or the Western Slope.

Perognathus flavus
SILKY POCKET MOUSE

DESCRIPTION — The silky pocket mouse is our smallest heteromyid. The hair is fine and silky, the pale buff to pinkish brown of the dorsum interspersed with black hairs. The overall darkness of the back varies geographically. A conspicuous postauricular patch of buffy fur is present, gener-

Photograph 9-25 Silky pocket mouse (Perognathus flavus).

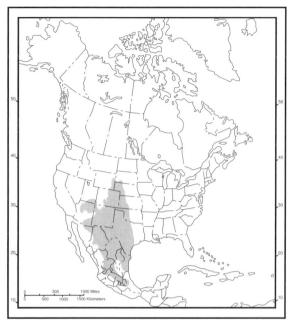

Map 9-51 Distribution of the silky pocket mouse (Perognathus flavus) *in North America.*

ally almost twice as large as the ear. Measurements are: total length 95–118 mm; length of tail 41–58 mm; length of hindfoot 12–18 mm; length of ear 4–7 mm; weight 6–9 g. The small size, relatively large ear patch, and remarkably soft fur should differentiate most specimens from adults of other small pocket mice. The interparietal bone is narrower than the interorbital breadth of the skull.

NATURAL HISTORY—Relatively little research has been conducted on silky pocket mice. The animals seem to require generally continuous short to midgrass prairie or herbaceous cover on loamy soils with small amounts of bare ground. They have been captured in low numbers on sand, loamy sand, and sandy loam soils. In southern Colorado their habitat is more varied, and included piñon-juniper woodlands in Las Animas County (Ribble and Samson 1987). The apparent scarcity of the species over much of its range may be due to competition with the plains pocket mouse which appears to be more adaptable, but the silky pocket mouse may simply be less trappable.

Food habits are similar to the other small pocket mice. Examination of 309 cheek pouches in New Mexico revealed pigweed, goosefoot, Russian-thistle, prickly-pear, globemallow, and several grasses

(Forbes 1964*a*). In Texas, several of the same plants were used as well as sand-bur, phlox, gaura, and mustards (Chapman and Packard 1974). Silky pocket mice may feed on stored seeds during midday to prepare energetically for foraging in early evening (J. Wolff and Bateman 1978).

Burrows are constructed at the base of plants such as yucca, cactus, or shrubs. Two to three burrow entrances are typical, and the openings are plugged during the day. Individual animals may maintain more than one series of burrow systems. Burrow systems have blind side tunnels used for food storage and as defecation sites. Nests are constructed from weedy or grass materials (Chapman and Packard 1974). In Colorado the animals probably live underground during the winter and have periods of torpor. The species is generally sedentary; individuals usually do not move more than 40 to 60 m from the burrow.

Pregnant females have been found from March through October. The gestation period is about

217

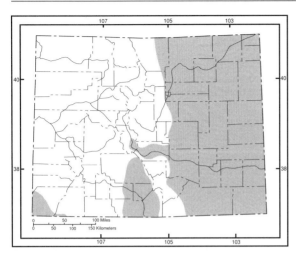

Map 9-52 *Distribution of the silky pocket mouse* (Perognathus flavus) *in Colorado.*

28 days. One litter per year of two to six young is typical, with an occasional second litter in late summer. Juveniles become sexually active after their postjuvenile molt (Eisenberg and Isaac 1963, Forbes 1964*b*).

In Texas, densities of 0.5 to 0.6 animals per ha were found, and home ranges were 0.77 to 2.4 ha (York 1949). Elsewhere, densities as high as 10 animals per ha were found (Chapman and Packard 1974). Highest numbers were reported in southwestern New Mexico, where they reached 60 animals per ha (Whitford 1976). Densities are typically low and distribution seems patchy in northern Colorado and southern Wyoming. Capture rates of 0.9 to 5.7 per 1,000 trap nights have been reported (Maxwell and Brown 1968; Moulton et al. 1981*a, b;* Ribble and Samson 1987). Mohamed (1989) did not capture the animals in a study on loamy sand to sandy loam soils in Weld County.

DISTRIBUTION IN COLORADO —*Perognathus flavus bunkeri* is the subspecies of most of the eastern plains, with populations extending up the Arkansas Valley to Salida; *P. f. hopiensis* occurs in extreme southwestern Colorado in Montezuma County; *P. f. sanluisi* is restricted to the San Luis Valley. Silky pocket mice appear to be relatively uncommon over most of their range in northern Colorado but are apparently commoner in southern parts of the state (Banta and Norris 1968; Moulton et al. 1981*a, b;* Ribble and Samson 1987). However, the status of the species is not clear, it is not known to be abundant in any location, and is in need of further study. D. Wilson (1973) argued that *P. merriami* of the Southern Great Plains is a synonym of *P. flavus,* so literature on Merriam's pocket mouse from Texas and New Mexico may be pertinent to Coloradan silky pocket mice.

Photograph by John Harris, Mammal Slide Library.

Photograph 9-26 *Great Basin pocket mouse* (Perognathus parvus)*.*

Perognathus parvus
GREAT BASIN POCKET MOUSE

DESCRIPTION — This is a long-tailed, medium-sized pocket mouse with a sandy or grayish dorsal color. The underparts are white to buff and lateral stripes are indistinct or lacking. There are patches of pale fur behind the ears. The long tail is tufted and bicolored, dark above and paler below. Measurements are: total length 148–200 mm; length of tail 77–107 mm; length of hindfoot 19–27 mm; length of ear 7–10 mm; weight 16–30 g. The antitragus is lobed. The occipitonasal length of the skull is more than 24 mm.

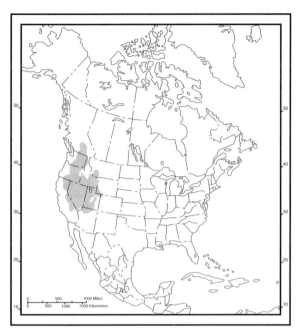

Map 9-53 Distribution of the Great Basin pocket mouse (Perognathus parvus) *in North America.*

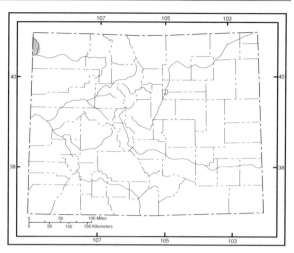

Map 9-54 Distribution of the Great Basin pocket mouse (Perognathus parvus) *in Colorado.*

NATURAL HISTORY —Great Basin pocket mice are commonest in semidesert shrublands on sandy soils dominated by sagebrush, saltbush, and greasewood with an abundant understory of annual plants (T. O'Farrell et al. 1975) and are also found in grasslands and piñon-juniper woodlands. In grasslands they are associated with stands of Indian ricegrass, bromes, needle-grass, and legumes. They prefer areas of more than 40 percent ground cover (Feldhamer 1979). Little is known of this species in Colorado.

In Utah, seeds eaten included lupine, brome, milkvetch, scurfpea, ricegrass, and needle-grass (Armstrong 1982). In eastern Washington, Great Basin pocket mice used seasonal foods including green plant material and insects, although seeds of annual grasses such as cheat-grass were also important in the diet (Kritzman 1974, T. O'Farrell et al. 1975).

Breeding begins soon after spring emergence from dormancy. Males typically are the first to ap-

pear above ground, a trait common to many mammals that enter hibernation or undergo winter torpor. Females in southern Washington bred from April to September and probably a similar breeding season occurs in northwestern Colorado. One litter per year is typical, with two litters possible in good years. Breeding success is tied to winter and spring precipitation, which affects production of annual plants. In years of poor food availability, two out of three females may not breed at all. Litter size is three to four (Dunigan et al. 1980, Kritzman 1974, T. O'Farrell et al. 1975).

Great Basin pocket mice can be common mammals in suitable habitat. In the western Great Basin, they are often the predominant small mammal, with densities ranging from 28 to 82 animals per ha (Verts and Kirkland 1988). Home ranges vary from 300 to 4,000 m^2; males have larger ranges than females (Feldhamer 1979).

Burrows are similar to those of other small pocket mice in having entrances carefully plugged during the day. Great Basin pocket mice are inactive above ground from late November to March, doubtless surviving on stored foods and undergoing periods of dormancy. Winter survival may be as high as 80 percent; close to 20 percent of populations live for two years (T. O'Farrell et al. 1975). Verts and Kirkland (1988) reviewed the literature.

DISTRIBUTION IN COLORADO —The Great Basin pocket mouse is known from only a few specimens collected in Browns Park in northern Moffat County (Bogan et al. 1988). T. Clark and Stromberg (1987) considered the species rare in Wyoming, attributing low numbers to overgrazing by livestock. One subspecies, *Perognathus parvus clarus*, occurs in Colorado.

Photograph 9-27 Hispid pocket mouse (Chaetodipus hispidus).

Chaetodipus hispidus
HISPID POCKET MOUSE

DESCRIPTION — The hispid pocket mouse is the largest pocket mouse in Colorado. Adult fur is harsh to the touch and somewhat coarse in appearance relative to that of other pocket mice. Juveniles have much softer hair. Dorsal color is yellowish to reddish buff intermixed with black hairs. The sides are paler, shading to white on the venter. The scantily haired tail is dark above and pale below and lacks the conspicuous terminal tuft of kangaroo rats. Measurements are: total length 200–260 mm; length of tail 95–126 mm; length of hindfoot 25–29 mm; length of ear 11–13 mm; weight 40–70 g. The skull, although larger (condylobasal length usually over 29 mm),

is similar to that of other pocket mice with relatively small auditory bullae and grooved incisors.

NATURAL HISTORY—The hispid pocket mouse is an inhabitant of the central and southern Great Plains. In Wyoming and Colorado the species inhabits a variety of shortgrass and midgrass communities including silvery wormwood, yucca and grass, and blue grama–needle-grass prairie, and also rather disturbed sites like weedy ditch banks, hedge rows, and dry riparian areas. Sandy loam and loamy sand soils with 8 to 40 percent bare ground are favored. In general, the species is most numerous in sites also occupied by *P. flavescens* (the plains pocket mouse) although its numbers are usually lower (Archibald 1963, J. Fitzgerald 1978, Maxwell and Brown 1968, Mohamed 1989, Moulton et al. 1981a, b).

Diet is similar to that of other heteromyids and consists of a variety of seeds, including sagebrush, prickly-pear, bluestems, annual sunflower, primrose, mallow, legumes, and witchgrass. Carabid beetles were an important food in Texas, especially during spring (Alcoze and Zimmerman 1973).

Hispid pocket mice reproduce during the spring and summer months in Colorado. Females have been captured with embryos in July and with uterine scars in mid-June, indicating spring litters. Males with scrotal testes were captured from mid-May to late September (Mohamed 1989). Other authors report similar breeding patterns with litter size ranging from two to nine and an average of five or six. Two or more litters are produced (Asdell 1964, Bee et al. 1981). Young leave the nest at one month of age.

Abundance has been reported in terms of animals captured per trap night in Colorado and southeastern Wyoming. The index ranged from 0.21 per 1,000 trap nights in shortgrass prairie and grazed riparian habitats (Moulton et al. 1981a) to 4.1 per 1,000 trap nights in a yucca and grass area on sandy loam (Maxwell and Brown 1968).

Map 9-55 *Distribution of the hispid pocket mouse* (Chaetodipus hispidus) *in North America.*

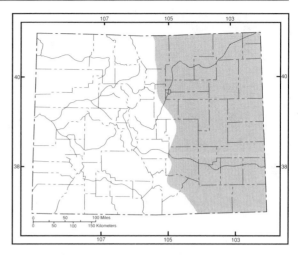

Map 9-56 *Distribution of the hispid pocket mouse* (Chaetodipus hispidus) *in Colorado.*

Hispid pocket mice are mostly solitary, each individual constructing its own burrow complex, although in captivity several individuals may tolerate one another (Williams 1968). Burrow systems are usually at the base of a shrub, yucca, or bunchgrass. The number of entrances to such systems ranges from one to several, typically plugged during the day. Soil plugs resemble those of small pocket gopher mounds. Depths of burrows may be as much as 38 cm. Nests are globular, constructed from grasses, and relatively large, measuring 4 by 3 cm (Blair 1937, Thompson and Barrett 1969). In areas with high populations of kangaroo rats, hispid pocket mice may be subject to severe competition.

In northeastern Colorado, the earliest captures of hispid pocket mice were in mid-April and the latest were in late September. The animals moved 10 to 23 m between livetrap captures. Home ranges were 0.24 to 0.34 ha. The mice retreated to burrow systems during winter. In such burrows they probably undergo intermittent periods of torpor, arousing from time to time to feed on stored seeds. Above-ground activity occurred when temperatures were as low as –10°C (Mohamed 1989). Predators include rattlesnakes and mammalian and avian carnivores, especially owls. Poulson (1988) provided a review of the literature.

DISTRIBUTION IN COLORADO —The hispid pocket mouse occurs on the eastern plains. In suitable habitat the animals are common. One subspecies, *Chaetodipus hispidus paradoxus*, occurs in Colorado. This species was formerly known as *Perognathus hispidus*. We follow J. Hafner and Hafner (1983) in according the hispid pocket mice generic rank as *Chaetodipus*.

Dipodomys ordii
ORD'S KANGAROO RAT

DESCRIPTION — Ord's kangaroo rat is a large heteromyid with a long, tufted tail, short forelimbs, and elongate hindfeet with five toes and densely haired soles. The upper parts are brownish yellow washed with black. The ventrum, legs, flanks, upper lips, and facial patterns are bright white. Black facial lines are present on the sides of the nose. The fur is sleek and silky. The tail is dark on its dorsal and ventral surfaces and white laterally. Measurements are: total length 240–280 mm;

221

Photograph 9-28 Ord's kangaroo rat (Dipodomys ordii).

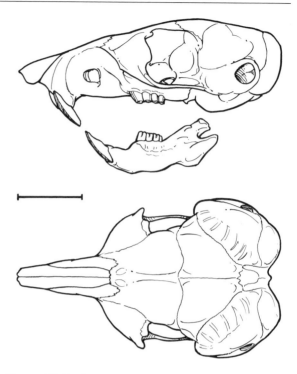

Figure 9-5 Skull of Ord's kangaroo rat (Dipodomys ordii) showing inflated auditory bullae and weak zygomatic arch. Scale = 1 cm.

length of tail 133–163 mm; length of hindfoot 39–43 mm; length of ear 12–15 mm; weight 55–85 g. Males are larger than females. The skull has greatly inflated auditory bullae, and the zygomatic arches are fragile and easily broken. The upper incisors are grooved. Geographic variation in color and size was described by Armstrong (1972). In extreme southwestern Colorado, the much larger banner-tailed kangaroo rat is undocumented but may be present at lowest elevations in La Plata and Montezuma counties. It differs from Ord's kangaroo rat in having four toes on the hindfeet and a striking white-tipped tail with a solid black band proximal to the white tip.

NATURAL HISTORY—This species is the widest-ranging kangaroo rat, capable of occupying a variety of habitats from semidesert shrublands and piñon-juniper woodlands to shortgrass or mixed prairie and silvery wormwood in Colorado, Utah, and Wyoming. It also invades dry, grazed, riparian areas if vegetation is sparse (Moulton et al. 1981a, b). Ord's kangaroo rats are commonest on sandy soils that allow for easy digging and construction of burrow systems. However, Ribble and Samson (1987) reported them in open areas with decreased canopy cover, increased shrub cover, and increased soil compaction. In suitable habitat they often are abundant and conspicuous.

Ord's kangaroo rats feed on a variety of seeds throughout the year, supplementing the diet with insects and flower parts. Up to 10 percent of the winter diet on Pawnee National Grassland is insects, especially larval beetles and moths; seeds typically represent 85 to 95 percent of the diet (Flake 1973). Important plant species included milkvetch, Kochia, Russian-thistle, spiderwort, grama, and sagebrush. In southeastern Utah cheekpouch contents included seeds of mustards, Russian-thistle, brome, fescue, primrose, dock, lupine, and Indian ricegrass (Armstrong 1982). Seeds gleaned from the ground or harvested directly from plants are manipulated with the dainty forepaws and tucked into the cheek pouches for transport to the burrow system, where the pockets are turned inside out and the materials disgorged.

Ord's kangaroo rats, as with other heteromyids, do not require free water but rather produce metabolic water from the oxidation of their foods. Many studies have been conducted on the physiological adaptations of kangaroo rats to life in stressful climatic conditions (Gettinger et al. 1986). When free water is available the animals use the forepaws to scoop water into the mouth (Allan 1946), and captives consume large amounts.

Well named, kangaroo rats typically move using bipedal locomotion, unlike pocket mice. The tail is used to maintain balance and facilitate direction of movement. When chased the animals are capable of making quick, erratic escape movements (Bartholemew and Caswell 1951). They are nocturnal, and most activity occurs during the first few hours of night. Males are more active than females. Activity is reduced under full moon conditions, at which time they are more secretive in their movements. Although active year-round, capture rates have been low in November, December, and January in Colorado (Flake 1973, Mohamed 1989). In Utah, animals were active on the surface about one hour per night, with 95 percent of that time spent foraging (Langford 1983). Other above-ground activity includes digging, sandbathing, and scent marking around the burrow entrance. During activity, body temperature is raised 1.6 to 3 degrees above resting temperatures of 37°C (B. Wunder 1974).

The breeding season and its length are variable, being regulated by the female's cycle, which is strongly affected by rainfall and appearance of green vegetation (Hoditschek and Best 1983). In Colorado, Ord's kangaroo rats breed from February through August, although testes start to show regression in July (Flake 1974). In southeastern Utah, and probably western Colorado, breeding occurs from late March through July with litters perhaps slightly larger than for eastern Colorado (Armstrong 1982). Mean embryo counts average 2.9 with a range of two to four. Gestation is about 30 days (Duke 1944). Young are altricial. Hair develops in about one week; the eyes open at two weeks of age. By five to six weeks of age the young approach the size of adults. The young remain with the female for several months. Male siblings eventually become aggressive, which leads to a breakup of the family group (Eisenberg 1962). Sexual maturity is reached at about 83 days of age (W. Jones 1985), and individuals can reproduce as yearlings (Garner 1974).

Burrows of Ord's kangaroo rat are constructed under shrubs, yucca, or grass clumps, or along exposed cut banks and arroyos. The burrow systems have several entrances and a complex of tunnels (Warren 1942). A nest is constructed of convenient plant materials including bark, yucca fibers, and dried grasses. Burrow entrances are typically plugged during the daytime. Burrows are dug primarily using the hind limbs although the animals may gnaw through roots or use the teeth to loosen materials. Laundre (1989) and Reynolds and Wakkinen (1987) provided measurements of burrows in Idaho.

Capture rates in Colorado are variable. Moulton et al. (1981a, b) found them most abundant (4.49 captures/1,000 trapnights) in grazed silvery wormwood and lowest in riparian woodland in Yuma County. In eastern Wyoming, Maxwell and Brown (1968) found highest numbers in sand dunes (59.4), yucca-grasslands (15.5), and sage-grasslands (9.9). In Texas, average densities of 15.6 animals per ha (range 9.9–26.9) were calculated. Individual movement usually was less than 0.22 ha (Garner 1974). Lusby et al. (1971) captured kangaroo rats in Mesa County in only 5 of 10 years, with densities when present of only 0.04 animals per ha. Kangaroo rats may be effective behavioral competitors with other species (Langford 1983); it is possible that densities of hispid pocket mice are kept low in areas with high densities of kangaroo rats.

Although kangaroo rats may occur in high densities on suitable sites, they are agonistic toward each other in captivity (Eisenberg 1962). Intrusion results in chases and fighting bouts marked by kicking, biting, and wrestling. They also drum

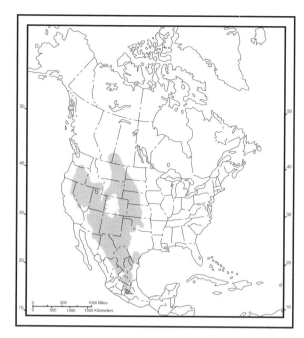

Map 9-57 Distribution of Ord's kangaroo rat (Dipodomys ordii) in North America.

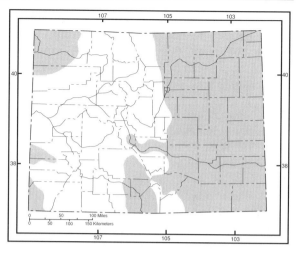

Map 9-58 Distribution of Ord's kangaroo rat (Dipodomys ordii) in Colorado.

their feet and tooth-chatter during agonistic encounters. Maintenance behaviors include prolonged periods of washing and grooming, and considerable time spent in sandbathing. Sandbathing consists of loosening sandy soils and rolling and submerging in them. When kangaroo rats are deprived of the opportunity to sandbathe, their pelage becomes greasy. Sandbathing sites are conspicuous in areas occupied by kangaroo rats, but other species such as spotted ground squirrels also make and use such depressions.

Many predators take kangaroo rats. Coyotes, swift foxes, and owls are proficient predators. Captives may live up to five years but in the wild most animals survive no longer than two or three years. Garrison and Best (1990) reviewed the extensive literature on Ord's kangaroo rat.

DISTRIBUTION IN COLORADO —Ord's kangaroo rats are common small mammals in suitable habitat over their entire range. The animals are highly variable geographically, and eight subspecies oc-

cur in Colorado. Two subspecies are rather widespread: D. o. luteolus occurs on the northeastern plains and D. o. richardsoni is known from the southeastern part of the state. Other subspecies are restricted to particular river valleys, separated by inhospitable uplands from adjacent populations. D. o. evexus occurs in the Arkansas Valley of Chaffee and Fremont counties, from Salida to Cañon City; D. o. longipes occurs in the San Juan watershed of extreme southwestern Montezuma County; D. o. montanus occurs in the San Luis Valley; D. o. nexilis occurs in the San Miguel and Dolores river valleys in southwestern Colorado; D. o. priscus inhabits the Yampa Valley in northwestern Colorado; D. o. sanrafaeli occurs in the Colorado River drainage in western Colorado.

Dipodomys spectabilis
BANNER-TAILED KANGAROO RAT

DESCRIPTION — The banner-tailed kangaroo rat is a large rodent, similar in color to the much smaller Ord's kangaroo rat except that the tail, with its large white tip and proximal black band, is even more striking. Measurements are: total length 310–350 mm; length of tail 180–210 mm;

Map 9-59 Distribution of the banner-tailed kangaroo rat (Dipodomys spectabilis) *in North America.*

length of hindfoot 47–51 mm; weight 90–135 g. Only four toes are present on the hindfoot. The lateral tail stripes only extend about half the length of the tail.

NATURAL HISTORY —Banner-tailed kangaroo rats favor well-developed desert or semidesert grasslands with some exposed soil. Large mounds are excavated to form extensive burrow systems at the base of shrubs, yucca, or cactus. Over time such burrowing mounds can reach heights over 1 m and diameters in excess of 4.5 m. Multiple entrances with well-developed trails radiate from the mound (Hoffmeister 1986, Holdenried 1957). The animals are mostly nocturnal. Behaviors are similar to those of Ord's kangaroo rat, with food cached in the burrow system. Breeding probably occurs from late winter to August. Near Santa Fe, New Mexico, breeding started in December and ended in August with up to three litters per year (Holdenried 1957). Gestation is estimated to be about 22 days. Best (1988) provided a thorough review of the literature.

DISTRIBUTION IN COLORADO —The banner-tailed kangaroo rat is a species of semiarid grasslands in New Mexico, West Texas, Mexico, and northern Arizona. Overgrazing by livestock may prevent occupancy of much of this region by banner-tails, which seem to prefer well-developed grassland on clay soils (Findley et al. 1975, Hoffmeister 1986). *Dipodomys spectabilis clarencei* is known from northern San Juan County, New Mexico, including the areas around Fruitland and Blanco less than 30 km from the Colorado border. Occurrence in Colorado has not been documented, but banner-tailed kangaroo rats may eventually be found in southern La Plata or Montezuma counties, especially on the Southern Ute Indian Reservation.

FAMILY CASTORIDAE — Beavers

The family Castoridae includes a single extant genus with two species, the European beaver (*Castor fiber*) and the American beaver (*C. canadensis*). These are among the largest of living rodents, with some adults weighing over 40 kg. Specializations for an aquatic existence include nictitating membranes, which cover the eyes while underwater, valvular ears and nostrils, and webbed hindfeet. The tail is broad and paddle-like, flattened dorsoventrally. Beavers are widely distributed across the Holarctic Region. Both species are valued furbearers. Populations in parts of Europe and North America have rebounded from overharvesting during the 1700s and 1800s, when felt hats made of beaver fur were a necessity of fashion (see Chapter 3). The geologic range of the family dates from the Oligocene; some fossil forms reached the size of modern black bears.

Castor canadensis
AMERICAN BEAVER

DESCRIPTION — This is the largest rodent in North America. Coloradan specimens not infrequently reach over 24 kg (Denny 1952). Measurements are: total length 850–1,200 mm; length of tail 200–350 mm; length of hindfoot 180–200 mm; length of ear 27–30 mm; weight 16–32 kg. Males are usually slightly larger than females. The

© 1993 Wendy Shattil/Bob Rozinski

Photograph 9-29 Beaver (Castor canadensis).

pelage has long, shiny guard hairs and dense, softer underfur. Pelage color varies from blackish to dark brown and chestnut. Kits have a darker pelage than adults. The long guard hairs may create a coarse appearance. The ears are short and rounded. The tail is flat, scaly, and sparsely haired. The legs are short and the hindfeet are webbed. The small forepaws are surprisingly dexterous. The toes of the hindfeet have split nails used to comb the fur. Other aquatic adaptations include valvular ears and nostrils, a nictitating membrane over the eyes, and lips that close behind the incisors. The skull is strongly built with a small infraorbital foramen. The incisors are large and their enamel faces are orange-red. The anterior surface of each incisor usually is greater than 5 mm wide. A baculum is present in males but the sexes are difficult to distinguish externally because the digestive and urogenital openings are enclosed in a common cloaca. Denny (1952) described palpation for the baculum as a method for sex determination. Both sexes have well-developed castor glands anterior to the cloacal opening, illustrated in Svendsen (1978).

NATURAL HISTORY: Beavers are semiaquatic mammals, constructing complex dams, lodges, and canal systems in order to minimize time spent on land foraging for food. Beavers are widespread over North America in a variety of habitat types adjacent to water. In Colorado they are commonest in areas with abundant aspen, cottonwood, or willow especially in broad glacial valleys with low stream gradients (Retzer et al. 1956, Rutherford 1964). Beavers are capable of invading anthropogenic water systems including reservoirs, canals, and irrigation ditches as long as food resources are available. Even in urban areas, such as Denver, beavers are fairly common, often causing localized destruction of tree plantings. Beavers fascinated Colorado's pioneer naturalists just as they do us today, and early accounts (such as Mills 1913 and Warren 1927) deserve rereading not only as sources of information but as sources of enjoyment and inspiration as well. Earliest European exploration and exploitation of the area now known as Colorado focused on the beaver, whose dense fur makes a superlative hatter's felt. Indeed, one could argue that the beaver was saved from extinction in the mid-nineteenth century by the fickle winds of fashion, as Chinese silk replaced beaver felt as the material of choice for gentlemen's hats.

Beavers are "choosy generalists" in their food selection (S. Jenkins and Busher 1980). They eat a wide variety of plant parts and species, but locally can be quite selective. The staple foods of beavers in Colorado are bark, buds, leaves, and twigs of quaking aspen, willows, and cottonwoods (Rutherford 1964, Yeager and Rutherford 1957). Such species are especially important as winter food. Alder, river birch, oakbrush, and conifers are used much less frequently. The more varied spring and summer diet includes a variety of aquatic and terrestrial herbaceous plant material, and in North Park nonwoody plants were the main summer food (D. MacDonald 1956).

Beavers usually do not range more than a few hundred meters from water while foraging, and most food is taken within a hundred meters of water. A cardiogastric gland in the stomach and a lobed caecum containing microflora aid in digestion of woody material. The animals also are coprophagous, reingesting their feces generally during midday in the lodge (Buech 1984). About

33 percent of the cellulose from the woody plant materials consumed is actually digested, a level roughly equal to other nonruminant mammals (A. Currier et al. 1960). Beaver intake of woody food ranges from 0.05 to 2.5 kg/day (Novak 1987). Beavers may "waste" 10 to 64 percent of trees cut for food, with greatest losses in large-diameter trees, which are felled for access to their smaller, upper branches. The beaver's tail serves as an important fat-storage center (Aleksiuk 1970).

Food supply and degree of siltation regulate time of abandonment of lodges and ponds. Beavers are excellent "engineers," building dams, lodges, bank burrows, and canals to regulate water levels and to provide shelter and waterways for floating food and construction materials to the main pond (Warren 1927). The pond provides safe passage beneath winter ice. Sticks, rocks, mud, and similar objects are used in construction. Many materials are moved by holding them tucked to the chest with the forelimbs or carried in the mouth. Dams are constructed with materials embedded in the streambed and anchored by piling and interlacing other materials. Some dams may be as much as 2 to 2.5 m high and several hundred meters in length. In many cases water management by beavers is beneficial for fish and recovery of overgrazed, eroded streambanks (Call 1970, Hill 1982).

In areas where waterways freeze in winter, beavers typically store food in underwater caches where it is available for use throughout the colder months. Food caches are started by constructing floating rafts of cuttings and placing other materials under the structure. Over time, waterlogging sinks the structure. Unpalatable or already utilized foods such as alder and peeled aspen logs may be deliberately added to the cache, possibly to add weight for submergence (Slough 1978). Such stored food consists of twigs, branches, and small trees. Caches may exceed 6 m in diameter and 3.6 m in height.

Beavers are crepuscular to nocturnal under most situations and do their tree cutting after dark (Tevis 1950), although those who fish quiet trout streams know that it is not unusual to find animals out during the daytime. Most construction of dams occurs in spring after flood runoff and in the fall in preparation for the winter. Beavers can cut through a 12-cm–diameter willow in about three minutes. The record felled tree had a diameter of 1.67 m and a height of over 30 m (Belovsky 1984, Rue 1964). When constructing the winter food cache in the fall, a colony usually can harvest a mature aspen tree every other night.

Lodges may be constructed as conical units totally surrounded by water or built partially on land. On larger riverways they are generally of the latter type because of spring flooding and difficulty of building dams. Effects of flooding on a colony in northeastern Colorado were documented by Rutherford (1952). In some instances burrows are constructed in stream banks with little or no evidence of associated lodge construction. Studies of beaver in low elevation riparian habitats in South Dakota suggest that lodge site selection is based in part on degree of cattle grazing and slope of the bank. They seemingly favor areas with lower grazing and with deep water close to steep banks (Dieter and McCabe 1989). The typical beaver lodge has an underwater entrance one meter or less below the water surface, which leads into a feeding chamber and an elevated, drier sleeping chamber. The internal chambers usually are about 1.3 m by 1.7 m and up to 1 m high. The largest lodge ever recorded was over 2 m high (above the water) and over 12 m in diameter. Temperatures in beaver lodges in December are relatively stable, averaging about 1°C, and fluctuating by less than one degree (Stephenson 1969).

Beavers are highly social animals, living in family or extended family units called colonies. A colony typically consists of adults and their yearling and juvenile offspring. The size of colonies in Colorado ranges from 4.5 to 7.8 animals (Hay 1958, D. MacDonald 1956, Rutherford 1964), and the rule of thumb in crude field surveys is that an active lodge or bank den represents five animals. The entire family unit defends the colony area from

Map 9-60 Distribution of the beaver (Castor canadensis) *in North America.*

the colony and seeking their own territories. Entire colonies of beavers may make much shorter movements up or downstream as food supplies are exhausted (Neff 1959). Rutherford (1956) noted disproportionate sex ratios in trapped beavers favoring females by 1.25:1, but he concluded that there was no reason to believe that ratios were other than 1:1.

Monogamous, beavers mate in January, February, or early March. Gestation takes 104 to 111 days (Hediger 1970). In Colorado the average litter size was 2.7 for animals above 1,525 m (5,000 ft) and 4.4 for females at lower elevations. These differences may be a response to lower nutritional levels at higher elevations because of the prolonged length of winter ice conditions (Rutherford 1955, 1956). One beaver from Weld County weighed 31 kg (69 lbs) and contained eight fetuses, the largest number reported in the state (Hay 1957). Kits are born furred with their eyes partly open (Guenther 1948). They grow rapidly and are weaned by about six weeks of age. Most females have their first litter at three years of age, although in good habitat or in areas with low population density yearlings may reproduce (Hill 1982). In suitable habitats, most females three years or older can be expected to breed. A survey in Colorado found a pregnancy rate of 75 percent for mature females and 33 percent for females of all ages (Rutherford 1956).

Home range size is difficult to assess. Summaries of studies suggest that on streams beavers may cover 0.8 to 0.9 km (Novak 1987), and others have found nearest-neighbor distances of 0.7 to 1.5 km. Territories of colonies range from 0.4 to 8 ha; 1.6 to 3.2 ha is about average in Colorado, depending on such things as valley and stream width, food availability, and stream gradient (Rutherford 1964). A number of studies, concentrating on management, regulation, population estimation, and long-term effects on the landscape, have been conducted in Colorado (Harper 1968; Neff 1957, 1959; Packard 1947; Yeager and Rutherford 1957; and others cited in this account). Although beavers are associated with

other beavers. However, the adult female is the dominant family member in many activities including constructing and maintaining the lodge, building the food cache, and maintaining dams (Hodgdon and Larson 1973). Adult females tail-slap a warning twice as frequently as adult males, and their tail slaps are more effective in causing others to move to deep water. Adult males tend to inspect dams more closely and more regularly than females once the dam is built. Mounds made of mud and castor gland secretions are constructed at strategic locations around the colony to mark its boundaries (Aleksiuk 1968).

Young animals typically disperse from the colony at two years of age with birth of the new litter. Most movements of young are less than 16 km, with an average of about 7 km in Idaho (Leege 1968). Rutherford (1956) concluded that two-year-old animals are considerably more susceptible to trapping than one-year olds because of emigration. Serious fights may occur in late winter and spring when young animals are leaving

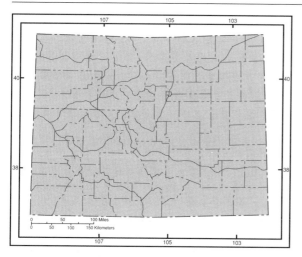

Map 9-61 Distribution of the beaver (Castor canadensis) *in Colorado.*

streams in mountainous areas, lowland reaches of all major drainages in the state also support large populations. Recent estimates of the beaver population in Denver range from 60 to 90 individuals based on winter counts of lodges, bank dens, and food caches (J. Brinker, pers. comm.).

Predators include wolves, coyotes, bear, river otter, lynx, bobcat, and mountain lions. A young kit in the collection at the University of Northern Colorado was taken from a coyote in South Park. The kit was severely wounded and died several hours later. Tularemia is an important epizootic disease, locally decimating beavers. Other causes of mortality include starvation and drowning in spring floods (Rutherford 1952). Estimation of mortality in juvenile, yearling, and adult populations is problematic because of difficulty in accurate aging and possible trap bias. That caveat aside, approximately 30 percent mortality is estimated for all age classes combined (Bergerud and Miller 1977). Humans are by far the most important limiting factor; most states, including Colorado, have regular trapping seasons for their harvest. Beaver have a considerable economic impact, both positive and negative. Harvest for fur in North America averages over a half million pelts per year, with a value of $10 to $20 per pelt.

Beavers are managed as furbearers in Colorado, and 5 to 10 thousand animals are harvested annually (Table 3-2). Beavers respond to exploitation with changes in life-history patterns. In heavily harvested populations in Alaska, females breed first at younger ages and smaller sizes and suffer higher mortality. Further, as survivorship of adults decreases, colony sites are freed for dispersing young (Boyce 1981).

Beavers manage watersheds, slowing spring run-off (hence reducing floods) and raising the water table, often with net benefits in forage available for livestock. On the debit side of the ledger, they harvest landscape plantings and interfere with human engineers, for example, by plugging culverts and tunneling into canal banks. Few would argue that beaver are not among our most fascinating and watchable wildlife species. The extensive literature on the American beaver was reviewed by Yeager and Hay (1955), S. Jenkins and Busher (1979), Hogdon and Larson (1980), Hill (1982), and Novak (1987).

DISTRIBUTION IN COLORADO —Beavers occur statewide in suitable habitat, marked by adequate supplies of water and food, whether in the alpine zone or on the eastern plains. One subspecies, *Castor canadensis concisor*, occurs in Colorado; the type locality of the subspecies is Monument Creek, southwest of Monument, El Paso County.

FAMILY MURIDAE — Rats, Mice, and Voles

The family Muridae is by far the largest group of rodents and probably the most significant ecologically as well. Other than Antarctic cap ice, virtually no terrestrial habitat on Earth is without one or more species. Because most are primary consumers and many have high rates of reproduction, murids tend to be the most abundant mammals in many of the world's ecosystems, thus figuring prominently in energy flow.

The taxonomic treatment of New World rats and mice has been a matter for considerable heated debate. A number of authorities have argued from a variety of data that all rats, mice, gerbils, hamsters, voles, and lemmings properly belong in a single family, Muridae (Ellerman 1940, Hershkovitz 1962, Hooper and Musser 1964, Carleton and Musser 1984). Other authors (for example, Honacki et al. 1982 and numerous earlier authorities) have regarded American forms as separate, classifying them in the family Cricetidae — a group with representatives in the Old World as well. That approach was followed by most North American mammalogists until rather recently. In this traditional view, two families were recognized for rats and mice in North America. These were the Muridae, composed of Old World rats and mice (represented in North America by the introduced Norway rat and house mouse), and the Cricetidae, containing all of the native rats, mice, and voles.

For present purposes, we follow Carleton and Musser (1984) and recognize a single family, Muridae, of which three subfamilies occur in Colorado. The subfamily Sigmodontinae includes all of the New World rats and mice. These animals formerly were included in a subfamily Cricetinae within the family Cricetidae; at present, however, the name Cricetinae is reserved for Old World mice, including the hamster. As presently understood, the Holarctic subfamily Arvicolinae contains the voles and lemmings. These animals previously were classified in a subfamily Microtinae in the family Cricetidae. The Old World subfamily Murinae is represented in Colorado by the introduced Norway rat and house mouse.

Although most people readily recognize murid rats and mice as a coherent group, the family is extraordinarily difficult to define and diagnose. For nearly all characters there are exceptions and many common features of the group appear to have evolved repeatedly, either as convergent or parallel traits. A trait that does unite all murids, however, is a relatively high, narrow infraorbital foramen that passes the anterior portion of the masseteric muscle. The dental formula is simple, usually 1/1, 0/0, 0/0, 3/3 = 16 teeth.

Murid rodents occur essentially worldwide. One or another group is native to all continents except Antarctica. The few oceanic islands (including Iceland and New Zealand) without native murids have been populated by species introduced by humans.

The Muridae are remarkably diverse, with over 1,100 species in some 260 genera arranged in 15 subfamilies (Carleton and Musser 1984). This is by far the largest family of rodents and of mammals, including over half of all rodents and about a quarter of all extant mammals. The family encompasses a range of diets, dental adaptations, habits, habitats, locomotor modes, and reproductive patterns nearly as broad as the Rodentia as a whole. The family appears in the fossil record in the Late Eocene of China and in the early Oligocene in North America. In Colorado there are 2 native subfamilies, with 10 genera, and at least 25 species; an additional 2 species in 2 genera in a third subfamily are introduced.

Key to the Subfamilies of the Family Muridae Found in Colorado

1. Cheekteeth all cusped, upper molars with cusps arranged in three longitudinal rows; tail scaly, round in cross-section, and sparsely haired .... Murinae, p. 265

1′ Cheekteeth either cusped or prismatic; if upper molars with cusps, then cusps not in three rows; tail variable 2

2. Ears well haired but relatively inconspicuous; skull with braincase strongly constricted at level of the rostrum; stout body with tail not as long as head and body .... Arvicolinae, p. 269

2′ Ears sparsely haired, usually conspicuous; skull not strongly constricted at level of rostrum; body not usually stout, tail often as long or longer than head and body .... Sigmodontinae, p. 231

SUBFAMILY SIGMODONTINAE — NEW WORLD RATS AND MICE

The subfamily Sigmodontinae consists of a large number of attractive rats and mice, previously referred to as cricetines. They come in various shades of gray and brown, usually have prominent ears and eyes, and well-furred tails. They typically make a living on the surface of the ground, not underneath the litter, and mostly are nocturnal. Colorado supports a fairly high diversity of sigmodontines, and their ecological and geographical relationships are of considerable interest. All Coloradan species are listed as nongame mammals (Table 3-1).

These comments aside, sigmodontines are difficult to generalize. Many genera have prismatic cheekteeth with enamel ridges surrounding lakes of dentine. In genera with cusped teeth, the cusps of the upper molars are aligned in two parallel, longitudinal rows. The infraorbital foramen is medium-sized, and its dorsal border has a posteriorly directed notch. The incisive foramina are longer than the molar toothrow. The tail, unlike that of the many Old World rats and mice (Murinae), is usually well haired and not scaly.

In the context of the following key, we note that hybridization has been reported among eastern, white-throated, and Southern Plains woodrats in southeastern Colorado and adjacent Oklahoma (Birney 1973, Finley 1958, Huheey 1972, D. Spencer 1968). Readers should be aware that firm identifications are not always possible without the aid of comparative specimens.

Key to the Species in the Subfamily Sigmodontinae Known or Expected to Occur in Colorado

1. Occlusal surface of molars flat; complicated pattern of exposed dentine lakes surrounded by enamel borders 2

1′ Occlusal surface of molars not flat; with enameled cusps. In older animals cusps may be worn

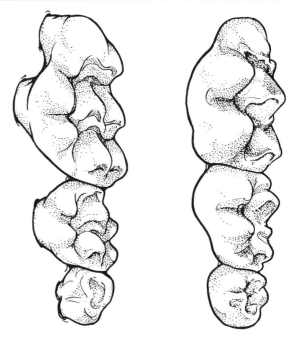

Figure 9-6 Comparative patterns of upper molars: house mouse (Mus musculus — left) *with the cusps in three rows, deer mouse* (Peromyscus maniculatus — right) *with cusps in two rows.*

away exposing dentine but patterns of dentine not as above 9

2. Ears hidden in pelage, well haired; pelage harsh; skull with strongly developed supraorbital ridges on parietal bones; molars without V-shaped re-entrant angles, cusps forming sigmoidal lophs; dorsal and ventral colors similar . . . .
. . . Hispid Cotton Rat — *Sigmodon hispidus,* p. 249

2′ Ears conspicuous, sparsely haired; pelage not especially harsh; skull without strongly developed supraorbital (temporal) ridges on parietal bones; molars with V-shaped re-entrant angles, cusps not forming sigmoidal lophs; dorsal color conspicuously darker than ventral color . . . . *Neotoma* 3

3. Tail conspicuously bushy; soles of hindfeet well haired from heel to proximal tubercle . . . .
. . . Bushy-tailed Woodrat — *Neotoma cinerea,* p. 254

3′ Tail not conspicuously bushy; soles of hindfoot naked or sparsely haired to heel. 4

4. Nasal septum intact (when viewed through incisive foramina, vomer forms solid plate separating right and left nasal cavities) 5

4′ Nasal septum with conspicuous notch on posterior margin (when viewed through incisive foramina vomer separated posteriorly from maxillaries creating a notch) 6

5. Dorsal color of adults steel gray; anterior palatine spine not forked (when viewed through incisive foramina, anterior palatine spine arises from anterior margin of palatine and projects forward between foramina usually one-half to one-third length of foramina) . . . . Southern Plains Woodrat — *Neotoma micropus,* p. 262

5′ Dorsal color buff washed with black; anterior palatine spine forked . . . . Eastern Woodrat — *Neotoma floridana,* p. 256

6. Anterior palatine spine blunt and stout . . . . Desert Woodrat — *Neotoma lepida,* p. 258

6′ Anterior palatine spine sharply pointed 7

7. Antero-internal re-entrant angle of first upper molar deep (extends more than halfway across crown) . . . . Mexican Woodrat — *Neotoma mexicana,* p. 260

7′ Antero-internal re-entrant angle of first upper molar shallow or not apparent 8

8. Hairs of throat lead gray at base; tail with moderately long hair, not sharply bicolored . . . . Stephens' Woodrat — *Neotoma stephensi*,* p. 264

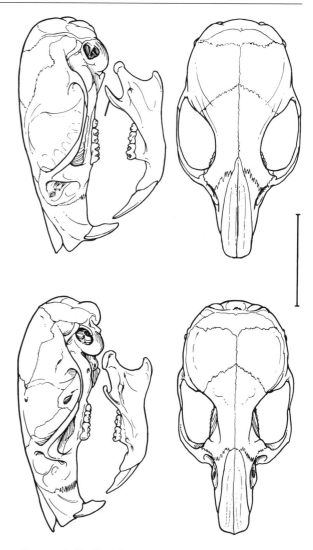

Figure 9-7 Skull of the deer mouse (Peromyscus maniculatus — bottom) *and the northern grasshopper mouse* (Onychomys leucogaster — top) *showing the high coronoid process of the mandible on the latter. Scale = 1 cm.*

8′ Hairs of throat white at base; tail with very short hair, sharply bicolored . . . . White-throated Woodrat — *Neotoma albigula,* p. 252

* Species of possible occurrence in Colorado.

9. Upper incisors with anterior longitudinal groove . . . . Reithrodontomys 10

9′ Upper incisors without longitudinal groove . . . 11

10. Narrow, distinct dorsal stripe on tail; well-developed, blackish mid-dorsal stripe; braincase breadth less than 9.7 mm . . . . Plains Harvest Mouse — *Reithrodontomys montanus*, p. 235

10′ Wide, distinct dorsal stripe on tail; mid-dorsal stripe not well defined; braincase breadth more than 9.7 mm . . . . Western Harvest Mouse — *Reithrodontomys megalotis*, p. 233

11. Tail short, less than half length of head and body; coronoid process of dentary higher than condyloid process . . . . Northern Grasshopper Mouse — *Onychomys leucogaster*, p. 247

11′ Tail long, more than half length of head and body; coronoid process no higher than condyloid process . . . . *Peromyscus* 12

12. Tail obviously shorter than head and body . . . 13

12′ Tail about as long or longer than head and body 14

13. Tail sharply bicolored; hindfoot 21 mm or less; greatest length of skull less than 27 mm . . . . Deer Mouse — *Peromyscus maniculatus*, p. 242

13′ Tail not sharply bicolored; hindfoot more than 21 mm; greatest length of skull more than 27 mm . . . . White-footed Mouse — *Peromyscus leucopus*, p. 240

14. Ear usually less than 20 mm . . . . Brush Mouse — *Peromyscus boylii*, p. 237

14′ Ear 20 mm or longer 15

15. Ear usually more than 22 mm, longer than hindfoot; rostrum short; dorsal color dull buff . . . . Piñon Mouse — *Peromyscus truei*, p. 246

15′ Ear less than 22 mm, shorter or as long as hindfoot; rostrum relatively long; dorsal color more gray or brighter buff 16

16. Dorsal color bright buffy to orangish; tail well haired, almost bushy; first and second upper molars without well-developed accessory tubercle between primary outer cusps . . . . Canyon Mouse — *Peromyscus crinitus*, p. 238

16′ Dorsal color grayish; tail not notably well haired; first and second upper molars with accessory tubercle between primary outer cusps . . . . . . Northern Rock Mouse — *Peromyscus nasutus*, p. 244

Reithrodontomys megalotis
WESTERN HARVEST MOUSE

DESCRIPTION — The western harvest mouse is similar to the plains harvest mouse but larger. Color ranges from buffy to grayish brown. A poorly defined mid-dorsal blackish wash is typical. The tail is bicolored, the dorsal stripe being half the width of the tail. Measurements are: total length 113–160 mm; length of tail 48–74 mm; length of hindfoot 15–18 mm; length of ear 12–17 mm; weight 9–21 g. The skull usually is more than 21 mm in greatest length. For more detailed comparisons between Colorado's two harvest mice, see Photo 9-31 and the account of the plains harvest mouse.

NATURAL HISTORY —No detailed investigations have been made on the western harvest mouse in Colorado. On the eastern plains, it occurs in riparian communities, weedy disturbed areas, margins of wetlands, and relatively dense, tall stands of grasses. In western Colorado it may occupy drier habitats, including semidesert shrublands in washes and relatively dry riparian sites as well as the margins of irrigated agricultural lands.

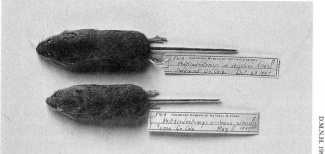

Photograph 9-31 Museum study skins of Reithrodontomys megalotis (above) *and* Reithrodontomys montanus (below). *Note wider dorsal tail stripe on* R. megalotis.

Photograph 9-30 Western harvest mouse (Reithrodontomys megalotis).

Western harvest mice are largely granivorous, feeding on seeds of grasses or forbs. Insects are frequently eaten, and green vegetation is consumed to some extent, probably in part for its moisture content. Harvest mice may use runways made by other species such as voles. They are gregarious and huddle together in the winter for mutual warmth. In Nevada they are reported to hibernate (J. O'Farrell 1974), and short periods of winter torpor probably occur in our area.

Home range estimates vary from 3,500 m² to a radius of about 70 to 100 m from the burrow (Meserve 1977). Densities have been estimated to range from 4 to 11 animals per ha to as high as 60 animals per ha in New Mexico (Whitford 1976). Most activity occurs at night.

The western harvest mouse is polyestrous, and in Colorado breeding probably occurs from March through late fall. Males are polygamous with a dominance hierarchy. Baseball-sized nests are woven from grasses or other long-fibered plant materials. The nest chamber is lined with soft, fluffy plant material including milkweed and thistle down as well as cottonwood "cotton." Nests are located in depressions on the ground or above ground level in clumps of grass, low shrubs, or weeds. A postpartum estrus allows females to have from 2 to 5 litters per season in our area, although captive individuals have had up to 14 litters per year (Richins et al. 1974). Gestation takes about 18 days, and the weight of an average litter at birth is about half the weight of the mother. Litter size ranges from three to seven with an average of four. Sex ratios slightly favor males at birth. The young are altricial but grow rapidly and are weaned at about three weeks. Females reach breeding age in about three or four months.

Most long-lived individuals are females, but, in general, populations turn over annually. The status of the species varies with location. In some areas populations can be relatively high. However, feral populations of the house mouse (*Mus*

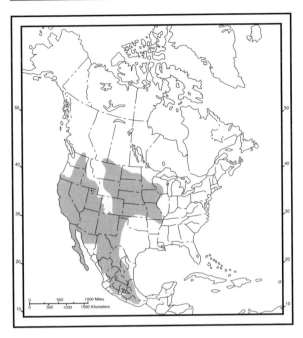

Map 9-62 *Distribution of the western harvest mouse* (Reithrodontomys megalotis) *in North America.*

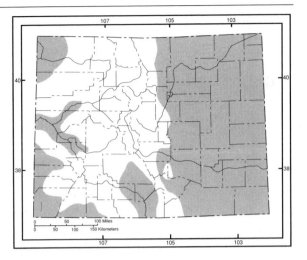

Map 9-63 *Distribution of the western harvest mouse* (Reithrodontomys megalotis) *in Colorado.*

musculus) may displace and outcompete the western harvest mouse. Most small to medium-sized predators feed on the species when the opportunity presents itself. Webster and Jones (1982) reviewed the literature on the species.

DISTRIBUTION IN COLORADO —The western harvest mouse occurs widely on the eastern plains as well as in the San Luis Valley, and at lower elevations in valleys of the Western Slope. It appears to be commoner on the eastern plains than the plains harvest mouse, using riparian areas as well as drier upland sites. *Reithrodontomys megalotis aztecus* occurs in southwestern Colorado from the Colorado drainage southward, in the San Luis Valley, and in southeastern Colorado, south of the Arkansas-Platte Divide; *R. m. dychei* occurs across the northeastern and east-central plains; *R. m. megalotis* is the subspecies of extreme western Moffat and Rio Blanco counties.

Reithrodontomys montanus
PLAINS HARVEST MOUSE

DESCRIPTION — The plains harvest mouse is the smallest of Coloradan sigmodontines, a slender mouse that superficially resembles the deer mouse (*Peromyscus maniculatus*). Gray-brown in color, it has a distinctive darker, mid-dorsal stripe. The venter and hindfeet are white. The tail is bicolored with a thin black dorsal stripe, only one-fourth the width of the tail. Measurements are: total length 111–146 mm; length of tail 48–62 mm; length of hindfoot 15–17 mm; length of ear 12–16 mm; weight 10–14 g. Rather difficult to distinguish from the western harvest mouse, plains harvest mice are slightly smaller externally and cranially (greatest length of the skull is less than 21 mm although the braincase is relatively broader), have a more pronounced mid-dorsal dark patch, and a narrower tail stripe than the western harvest mouse. Generally the tail is equal to or shorter than the head and body in the plains harvest mouse and longer than the head and body in the western harvest mouse. From the deer mouse, both harvest mice are readily distinguished by their grooved upper incisors. The molars are rooted and cusped. Females have three pairs of mammae.

235

Photograph 9-32 Plains harvest mouse
(Reithrodontomys montanus).

NATURAL HISTORY — The plains harvest mouse is
a species of semiarid grasslands in the central and
southern Great Plains. It favors well-developed
grass and forb cover of low or moderate height or
pastures where scattered rock provide cover. In
eastern Colorado, Moulton et al. (1981*a, b*) found
the species in ungrazed and grazed grassland, in
silvery wormwood prairie, and in grazed riparian
areas. Mohamed (1989) found it in moderately
grazed yucca-grassland communities on sandy
soils in Weld County. In southeastern Wyoming,
it was commoner on sites with less than 40 percent bare ground (Maxwell and Brown 1968).
This mouse is also found in margins of croplands
along fence rows and in similar disturbed but productive weedy habitats, but it is not as common in
such areas as the western harvest mouse.

The diet is similar to that of the western harvest
mouse, consisting mostly of seeds supplemented
by some green material, berries, fruits, and insects. Grasshoppers are important food items during the warmer months. Plains harvest mice may
store foods underground for winter use.

Plains harvest mice are active year-round. Most
foraging occurs at night. Home range estimates
vary from 0.04 to 0.84 ha (Wilkins 1986). Mean
home ranges in Oklahoma approximated 0.17 ha
for males and 0.21 for females (Goertz 1963). Harvest mice are excellent climbers and locate their
nests either in low shrubs and weeds, suspended
above the ground in taller grasses, inside objects
such as tin cans, or under objects on the surface

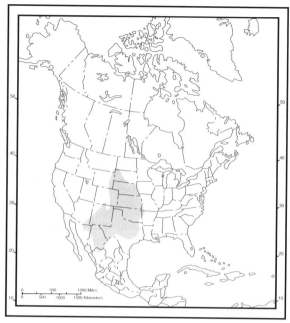

Map 9-64 Distribution of the plains harvest mouse
(Reithrodontomys montanus) *in North America.*

of the ground. The nest is similar to that of the
western harvest mouse, consisting of grasses
shaped into a small sphere (H. Brown 1946),
roughly 6 by 10 cm.

Plains harvest mice probably reproduce in Colorado during all but the coldest winter months. Females are polyestrous, having several litters per year
of one to nine young with an average litter size of
four. Gestation takes about three weeks. The altricial young develop more rapidly than those of the
western harvest mouse, are weaned at about two
weeks of age, and leave the nest at about three-and-
a-half weeks of age (Lerass 1938). At five weeks of
age the young are the size of adults, and at two
months of age they are capable of breeding.

Populations do not appear to be as dense as those
of the western harvest mouse. In Texas, density estimates were below 2 animals per ha (Schmidly
1983), and in Kansas densities of up to 6.8 animals per ha were reported (H. Brown 1946).
Most individuals live less than one year. They are

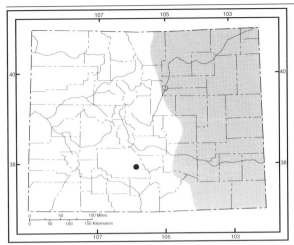

Map 9-65 Distribution of the plains harvest mouse (Reithrodontomys montanus) *in Colorado. Solid circle represents a record of occurrence.*

Photograph 9-33 Brush mouse (Peromyscus boylii).

Photograph by R. B. Forbes.

preyed on by a variety of small and medium-sized predators. Literature on the species was reviewed by Wilkins (1986).

DISTRIBUTION IN COLORADO —The species is widely distributed across the eastern plains of Colorado. It does not appear to be particularly abundant, however, and populations may be affected by prolonged grazing of upland prairie. *Reithrodontomys montanus albescens* is the subspecies of the eastern plains; *R. m. montanus* may occur in the San Luis Valley, based on a single problematic specimen captured by the Gunnison Expedition in 1853. For a synopsis of the history of this population, see Armstrong (1972).

Peromyscus boylii
BRUSH MOUSE

DESCRIPTION — Brush mice are large, long tailed, and short eared, gray-brown to buff-brown with a whitish gray venter. The sides are often brighter orange-brown. The feet are white but the ankles are gray or dusky. The indistinctly bicolored tail is longer than the length of the head and body. Hair on the tail is rather sparse so that scales are apparent. Measurements are: total length 180–220 mm; length of tail 80–115 mm; length of

hindfoot 20–24 mm; length of ear 15–22 mm (usually less than 20 mm); weight 20–30 g. The hindfoot is usually longer than the ear.

NATURAL HISTORY — Brush mice have been poorly studied over most of their range. In Colorado they typically occur in montane shrublands — especially oakbrush and mountain-mahogany — and piñon-juniper woodlands. They usually favor areas of rough, broken terrain with boulders and heavy brush. They also occur in riparian cottonwood stands, willow thickets, or brushy salt-cedar (tamarisk) bottoms.

Brush mice are good climbers and frequently forage in trees and shrubs. Over most of their range, acorns are a staple of the diet. Juniper "berries," mistletoe, and prickly-pear are also important foods. Insects are eaten whenever possible, accounting for 30 to 50 percent of the diet in California and New Mexico (Jameson 1952, Smartt 1978). In Utah and Arizona, stomachs of brush mice contained over 80 percent seeds (Duran 1973, Armstrong 1982).

The brush mouse probably breeds from late winter through early fall in Colorado, with a peak during the warmer spring months. Several litters are produced per year. Most breeding success probably occurs during the warmer spring

Map 9-66 Distribution of the brush mouse (Peromyscus boylii) in North America.

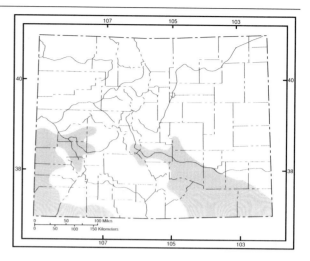

Map 9-67 Distribution of the brush mouse (Peromyscus boylii) in Colorado.

months. Litter size ranges from one to six with an average of three. Some animals may live over 18 months in the wild but most die before one year of age. Nests, open on top and similar to those of goldfinches, are built in sheltered areas under rocks and debris or in crevices in cliff faces. Woodrat dens (even occupied dens) are used as cover by brush mice and other rock-dwelling species of Peromyscus. Geluso (1970) found brush mice associated with white-throated woodrats in the canyon country in the Oklahoma Panhandle, and Armstrong (1979, 1982, 1984) documented their occurrence with several species of Neotoma in southeastern Utah.

Home ranges of brush mice are 0.09 ha to 0.35 ha. Densities varied from 0.7 to about 6 animals per ha in Missouri (L. N. Brown 1964), and 0.48 to 0.56 animals per ha in Texas (Garner 1967).

DISTRIBUTION IN COLORADO —The brush mouse occurs in the rough, broken country of southeastern Colorado from Salida in Chaffee County east to Colorado Springs in El Paso County and south onto the Mesa de Maya and the canyons of Baca County. In western Colorado the species occurs south and west of the San Juan Mountains northward to western Gunnison and Delta counties. Svoboda et al. (1988) captured specimens in the San Luis Valley. One subspecies, Peromyscus boylii rowleyi, occurs in Colorado.

Peromyscus crinitus
CANYON MOUSE

DESCRIPTION — The canyon mouse is small to medium-sized with ears as long as the hindfoot. The tail is generally longer than the head and body. The fur is long and silky with the dorsal color a bright ochraceous buff. The bases of hairs are lead gray. The sides are even more brightly colored than the back. A yellow-orange to buff pectoral spot is generally present in Coloradan populations. The belly is white to gray and the feet are white. The bicolored tail, typically longer than the head and body, has a pronounced terminal tuft, and the scales are usually visible through the thin covering of hair. Measurements are: total length 160–190 mm; length of tail 82–110 mm, length of hindfoot 18–25 mm; length of ear 17–23 mm; weight 12–30 g. The maxillary tooth row

Photograph by Claude Steelman/Wildshots.

Photograph 9-34 Canyon mouse (Peromyscus crinitus).

is typically less than 4 mm long. The skull is fragile with a long slender rostrum. Zygomatic breadth is only slightly greater than cranial breadth. The nasals are long, narrowing posteriorly. The premaxillary ends at about the level of the posterior margin of the nasals. Females are typically somewhat larger than males and have four inguinal mammae.

NATURAL HISTORY — Canyon mice, as the name implies, are mostly animals of dry, rocky canyon country. Their distribution is somewhat patchy and often what appears to be suitable habitat may not be occupied. They often inhabit talus and outwash rubble, or eroded, exposed sandstone "slickrock" (Armstrong 1979). Habitat includes piñon-juniper woodlands and montane and semidesert shrublands. They seem to favor exposed sunny slopes in northwestern Colorado (Finley et al. 1976).

Canyon mice are omnivorous and feed on seeds, berries, fruits, fungi, and insects (Armstrong 1982). Seeds are more important in winter, and insects may dominate the diet during the warmer months. Free water is not needed and efficiency of the kidneys is equal to or greater than that of the kangaroo rats (MacMillen 1983). When deprived of food and water in the laboratory, individuals enter a daily torpor. This may be a mechanism for coping with the dry environments in which the mice live.

Egoscue (1964*b*) studied reproduction in this species under laboratory conditions in Utah. Canyon mice are seasonally polyestrous. Most breeding in Colorado probably occurs in spring, early summer, and fall; reproductive activity ceases during extremely hot or cold weather. An estrous cycle is completed in about 6 days. Gestation takes from 24 to 31 days with an average of three young (range one to five) per litter. A postpartum estrus occurs, and lactating females have a longer gestation. The number of litters per year probably varies depending on food availability and seasonal temperatures. In the laboratory up to eight litters per year were produced, but probably two or three are more typical of wild animals. Young, although blind and naked at birth, are slightly more precocial than newborn deer mice, but have a longer period of postnatal development. Neonates are large, as seems to be typical of arid-land *Peromyscus* (Layne 1968). The young open their eyes around two weeks of age and are weaned at one month. Females can begin to breed as early as 75 days of age but most actually do not begin to reproduce until four to six months old. Females have lived to almost four years of age in the laboratory.

In laboratory studies canyon mice were most active at night under conditions approximating close to full-moon intensities. In nature they tend to forage primarily at night during the hours when light conditions are fairly dim and they are less conspicuous to predators. Individuals are tolerant of one another and sites suitable for occupancy usually have good populations. Densities in southeastern Utah range from about one to six animals per ha up to 43 animals per ha on the tops of isolated buttes inaccessible to other species. Home ranges averaged 0.36 ha in southeastern Utah (D. W. Johnson 1981). As with other *Peromyscus*, the species is vulnerable to predation by a variety of hawks, owls, snakes, and small to medium-sized mammals including weasels, skunks, ringtails, foxes, and coyotes. D. W.

Map 9-68 Distribution of the canyon mouse (Peromyscus crinitus) in North America.

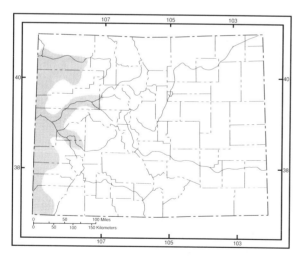

Map 9-69 Distribution of the canyon mouse (Peromyscus crinitus) in Colorado.

Johnson and Armstrong (1987) reviewed the literature on the species.

DISTRIBUTION IN COLORADO —The canyon mouse inhabits the canyonlands along the western border from the southern half of Moffat County to Montezuma County. Little is known about its status in the state. One subspecies, *Peromyscus crinitus auripectus*, is known to occur in Colorado, but *P. c. doutti* may be present west of the Green River in extreme western Moffat County.

Peromyscus leucopus
WHITE-FOOTED MOUSE

DESCRIPTION — The white-footed mouse closely resembles the deer mouse but is larger and has a less distinctly bicolored tail. The tail is usually longer than that of the deer mouse, generally exceeding 65 mm in length. The color is pale gray-brown to buffy with white underparts and feet. Most individuals are grayer in overall color than deer mice of similar size. The white hairs of the belly are gray at their bases. Measurements are: total length 150–200 mm; length of tail 60–100 mm; length of hindfoot 19–24 mm, length of ear 13–16 mm; weight 20–36 g. Greatest length of the skull is usually more than 27 mm, and the hindfoot is usually longer than 21 mm. For additional comparisons with the deer mouse see the account of that species. Females have three pairs of mammae.

NATURAL HISTORY — Although studied extensively in the eastern United States, a detailed study of this species from our part of the range would be useful. White-footed mice range widely in eastern North America in habitats ranging from deciduous forest to brushy fields. In Colorado white-footed mice are associated with rank, weedy vegetation, especially cottonwood riparian habitat, or even stands of the exotic phreatophyte, tamarisk. They also occur in rocky canyon country in the Raton Section of southeastern Colorado along the boundary with New Mexico and Oklahoma. The density of shrub cover appears to influence positively the presence of the animal in our part of the range. Studies by D. Wilson (1968) and Holbrook (1978) in New Mexico, Geluso (1971) in the Oklahoma Panhandle, and

Photograph by Roger W. Barbour.

Photograph 9-35 White-footed mouse (Peromyscus leucopus).

Kaufman and Fleharty (1974) in Kansas pertain to ecology and habitat preferences in Colorado.

White-footed mice feed on a variety of plant and animal foods. Insects are often the most common item in stomach samples, followed by seeds of a variety of plants, and together these constitute over 60 percent of the diet. Caches of food probably are made, as food-caching behavior is seen in the laboratory.

White-footed mice are semiarboreal, scampering easily among tree and shrub branches and climbing relatively smooth-barked trunks. The shorter-tailed deer mice, by comparison, are much more terrestrial animals. In areas with competition from even better climbers (rock mice, canyon mice, or piñon mice), white-footed mice tend to be mostly terrestrial foragers (Thompson and Conley 1983).

White-footed mice are polyestrous. In our area they probably breed during all but the coldest months. Ovulation is spontaneous, and females typically exhibit postpartum estrus. Gestation ranges from 22 to over 30 days depending on whether females are nursing a previous litter (Svihla 1932). Lactating females require about 25 percent more energy intake than nonlactating females or males. The average number of young per litter is four, with a range of one to seven.

The young develop relatively rapidly: eyes and ears open by two weeks of age. The young are weaned at about one month of age and attain adult size by about six weeks. Females are sexually mature at that time. Sexual maturity can be delayed by the presence of feces or urine of other white-footed mice (Rogers and Beauchamp 1976).

Nests are built from a variety of locally available plant materials including shredded bark, leaves, grass stems, and down of milkweed as well as feathers and hair if available. Nests are used for resting, warmth, and protection of young; nest building increases during cold weather or when young are about to be born. Despite their climbing ability, white-footed mice frequently nest on the ground under sheltering objects including rocks and fallen trees.

These animals are mostly nocturnal with higher trappability under conditions of high humidity, high temperature, and cloud cover (Drickamer and Capone 1977). Some diurnal activity is re-

Map 9-70 Distribution of the white-footed mouse (Peromyscus leucopus) *in North America.*

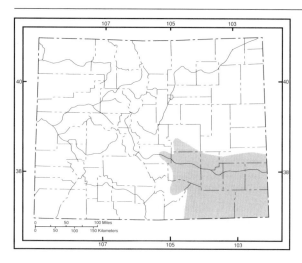

Map 9-71 Distribution of the white-footed mouse (Peromyscus leucopus) in Colorado.

Photograph 9-36 Deer mouse (Peromyscus maniculatus).

ported during the winter months. Animals exhibit torpor, especially under conditions of food deprivation or low temperature. Such torpor may last three or more hours and does not necessarily occur every day. The frequency of torpor increases with colder temperatures (D. Snyder 1956).

Home ranges typically have been estimated at less than 0.10 ha, larger in the breeding season and smaller during winter (Stickel 1968); males have slightly larger home ranges than females. Few animals are thought to survive more than one year, suffering predation by nocturnal avian and mammalian carnivores as well as harsh environmental conditions. Literature on the white-footed mouse was reviewed by Lackey et al. (1985).

DISTRIBUTION IN COLORADO —The white-footed mouse is known to occur only in the southeastern part of the state, throughout the lower Arkansas drainage, where it is common in suitable habitat. One subspecies, *Peromyscus leucopus tornillo*, is found in the state. A second subspecies, *P. l. aridulus*, is of possible occurrence in northeastern or east-central Colorado.

Peromyscus maniculatus
DEER MOUSE

DESCRIPTION — This is a highly variable mouse, both externally (Armstrong 1972) and physiologically (Wasserman and Nash 1979). Dorsal color ranges from grayish brown, to rufous orange, to pale buff. The underparts and feet are white. Juveniles are medium gray, darker than most adults. The ears are conspicuous but usually shorter than the hindfoot. The tail is distinctly bicolored and obviously shorter than the head and body. Measurements are: total length 135–180 mm; length of tail 57–78 mm; length of hindfoot 17–21 mm; length of ear 14–21 mm; weight 14–27 g. Accessory labial tubercles are present on the first two upper molars. The maxillary toothrow is usually less than 4 mm long (that of the white-footed mouse is often more than 4 mm). Females have six mammae, four inguinal and two pectoral. The species is sometimes difficult to tell from the white-footed mouse but usually the deer mouse has a shorter skull (greatest length less than 27 mm), a shorter hindfoot (less than 21 mm), and the tail is more distinctly bicolored. The zygomatic arches of the white-footed mouse show a slight but distinct bowing compared to the straighter arches in the deer mouse.

NATURAL HISTORY — The deer mouse is the widest ranging and commonest small mammal in North America, and it has been the subject of extensive research. In Colorado, deer mice are found from the tops of the highest peaks to lowest elevations, surviving practically anyplace where cover occurs, including burrows of other animals, cracks and crevices in rocks, surface debris and litter, human structures, and virtually every native habitat except well-developed wetlands (Finney 1962, J. Fitzgerald 1978, Mohamed 1989, Moulton 1978, Ribble and Samson 1987, Samson et al. 1988, Stinson 1978, O. Williams 1955a). Deer mice may be thought of as mammalian "weeds," not in a pejorative sense, but because they are adapted to exploit disturbed habitats. The disturbance may be due to heavy grazing (Lusby et al. 1971, Moulton et al. 1981a, b), land-clearing (T. O'Meara et al. 1981), mining, construction, avalanches, fire, or landslides. Anything that disturbs the habitat of specialists creates habitat for this quintessential generalist (Armstrong 1977a). For example, deer mice were the first small mammals to colonize the barren alluvial fan produced by the Lawn Lake flood in Rocky Mountain National Park in 1982 (Armstrong, 1993). Where specialized kinds of *Peromyscus* are present, deer mice may be scarce or absent locally (C. L. Douglas 1969b, Armstrong 1979).

Deer mice eat practically anything from insects and other small invertebrates to carrion, fungi (O. Williams and Finney 1964), bone, and various plant parts, particularly seeds (Jameson 1952). Leaves and bark are eaten when other materials are in short supply. Seeds accounted for 69 to 76 percent of the stomach contents of mice from Colorado and Wyoming, and insects accounted for 14 to 25 percent (O. Williams 1955c, 1959).

Pregnant females have been captured from February through November in northeastern Colorado (Beidleman 1954, Flake 1974) and in January in north-central Colorado (E. Reed 1955), supporting the notion that deer mice breed almost year around in the state. Variability is introduced by elevation and food availability. Differences in re-productive strategies are seen in comparisons between populations at high and low elevation sites (Halfpenny 1980, A. Spencer and Steinhoff 1968). Generally speaking, litter size and age at weaning were greater at higher elevation; number of litters per year and birth weights were greater at lower elevation. In northeastern Colorado litter size averaged 4.7 and ranged from two to eight (Flake 1974). The gestation period is 24 to 28 days. Females have several litters per year. Pups are weaned at about 25 days of age (Jameson 1953). Breeding begins at seven to eight weeks of age, allowing many young of the year to enter the pool of reproductive animals before the onset of winter. The gray juvenile pelage takes almost a month to replace, starting at 30 to 45 days of age, with a brown subadult pelage. The rich, brown adult pelage comes in at about four months of age and is then replaced in a pattern of spring (vernal) and fall (autumnal) molts.

Deer mice use the same trails repeatedly, and trails can get as wide as 30 cm as variations are added.

Map 9-72 Distribution of the deer mouse (Peromyscus maniculatus) *in North America.*

243

Map 9-73 Distribution of the deer mouse (Peromyscus maniculatus) *in Colorado.*

There are a number of different home or nest sites within a given home range, and the animals move among them (Stickel 1968). Although active throughout the year, the colder months cause a number of changes. During winter, deer mice use runways beneath the insulating blanket of snow.

Merritt and Merritt (1978*b*, 1980) compared home ranges during summer and winter at a subalpine forest site in the Front Range. They found that subnivean home ranges averaged 0.015 and summer home ranges averaged 0.026 ha; in both situations, males had larger home ranges than females, as was found by O. Williams (1955*b*). The reduction in size of winter home ranges, short-term torpor, and aggregate nesting are the combined strategies used by deer mice to mitigate energetic losses during cold temperatures and seasons of reduced food availability. Densities of deer mice are variable, depending on season, habitat, food availability, predators, and presence of other small rodents (Armstrong, 1993; Catlett and Brown 1961; C. L. Douglas 1969*b;* Merritt and Merritt 1980).

Deer mice that survive to adulthood probably do not live much past one year of age. Numerous

predators feed on mice, including snakes, owls, hawks, coyotes, foxes, badgers, weasels, and grasshopper mice. Papers edited by J. King (1968) provided a thorough synopsis of the earlier literature on this and other species of *Peromyscus,* and Kirkland and Layne (1989) edited an essential update.

DISTRIBUTION IN COLORADO —The deer mouse is surely the commonest mammal in Colorado, occupying most habitats at all elevations. *Peromyscus maniculatus nebrascensis* is the subspecies of northwestern Colorado and most of the eastern plains; *P. m. rufinus* occurs in southwestern and south-central Colorado and throughout the central and northern mountains; *P. m. luteus* occurs along the eastern margin of the state, mostly in the Republican and Arikaree drainages.

Photograph 9-37 Northern rock mouse (Peromyscus nasutus).

Peromyscus nasutus
NORTHERN ROCK MOUSE

DESCRIPTION — The northern rock mouse has long ears and is rather similar in appearance to the piñon mouse. However, the pelage is grayish brown, less buffy than that of the piñon mouse, with whitish to silver-gray underparts. Furthermore, the bicolored tail is usually slightly longer than the head and body, and the ears usually are

Map 9-74 *Distribution of the northern rock mouse* (Peromyscus nasutus) *in North America.*

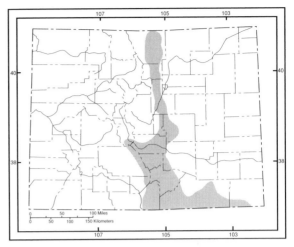

Map 9-75 *Distribution of the northern rock mouse* (Peromyscus nasutus) *in Colorado.*

less than 22 mm long, equal to or shorter than the hindfoot. Measurements are: total length 170–200 mm; length of tail 80–100 mm; length of hindfoot 22–25 mm; length of ear 21–24 mm; weight 25–30 g. No definitive cranial characteristics readily distinguish the rock mouse from the piñon mouse or the brush mouse, although the rostrum usually is distinctively slender and long.

NATURAL HISTORY — As the name suggests, the northern rock mouse lives in rocky canyons, cliffs, cuestas, and exposed hogbacks that provide numerous cracks, fissures, and overhanging ledges. The animals occupy colluvial debris at the bases of such outcrops. The rock mouse is almost always captured under ledges or rocks and not in areas devoid of rock cover, where deer mice are commoner.

Rock mice are associated with montane shrubland and piñon-juniper woodlands along the Eastern Slope. Oakbrush, piñon, juniper, skunkbrush, mountain-mahogany, choke cherry, and bitterbrush are common woody species that provide cover and seeds for food. Other plant materials and insects are also consumed.

In northern Colorado female rock mice breed from April through August with a peak of activity in June; males enter breeding condition earlier, in March. October breeding has been noted (Cinq-Mars and Brown 1969, Kisiel 1971). (Late breeding in *Peromyscus* is often associated with low precipitation or warmer than usual temperatures.) Litter size ranges from two to six with an average of four. As with other *Peromyscus*, the species is polyestrous.

DISTRIBUTION IN COLORADO —The northern rock mouse has a restricted geographic range in Colorado, occurring northward along the foothills of the Sangre de Cristos and the Front Range to terminate abruptly near the Wyoming border. It extends eastward in the roughlands of the Raton Section of southeastern Colorado to southwestern Baca County and westward to the eastern part of the San Luis Valley. The rock mouse in Colorado was previously known as *Peromyscus difficilis*. A number of authors (reviewed by Carleton 1989) have argued that northern populations warrant recognition as a full species. One subspecies, *Peromyscus nasutus nasutus* (named on the basis of specimens from Estes Park), occurs in Colorado.

Peromyscus truei
PIÑON MOUSE

DESCRIPTION — This mouse is large, buff-colored, and long-eared, with a tail slightly shorter than the head and body (based on specimens from our area). The distinctive ears are the longest of any species of *Peromyscus* in Colorado, usually exceeding 22 mm. The dorsal color is pale buff to rich grayish brown with the tail distinctly bicolored. The venter is white but the hairs have gray bases. The hindfeet are either white or pale grayish. The fur is long and soft. The tail is covered with short hairs, generally concealing the scales. Hairs at the tip of the tail are longer. Measurements are: total length 187–198 mm; length of tail 90–103 mm; length of hindfoot 23–25 mm; length of ear 23–30 mm; weight 20–28 g. The piñon mouse differs from the rock mouse and the brush mouse, the other two long-eared species of *Peromyscus* in Colorado, in having ears longer than the hindfoot and a tail usually no longer than the head and body. The skull is large, with large, inflated auditory bullae. Greatest length of skull is 28–29 mm, similar to that of the rock mouse, but relatively broader and with a less elongate rostrum.

NATURAL HISTORY — The piñon mouse is the most characteristic mouse of piñon-juniper woodlands. Indeed, the animals seldom are taken from areas lacking junipers, which are used for cover and food, although on occasion the animals do occur in sagebrush stands, and Hoffmeister (1986) reported them from cottonwood river bottoms in Arizona. Although frequently associated with rocky canyon country, in Mesa Verde the species does not require rocky terrain but thrive in piñon-juniper stands on flat areas, although highest numbers are in rocky areas (C. L. Douglas 1969b). Destruction by chaining and overgrazing of piñon-juniper woodlands is detrimental to the species (O'Meara et al. 1981).

Piñon mice are opportunistic omnivores, but seeds and cones ("berries") of junipers are the staple of the diet. Feeding sites in the crotch of a tree are marked with food debris and feces. In-

Photograph by Claude Steelman/Wildshots.

Photograph 9-38 Piñon mouse (Peromyscus truei).

sects are eaten when available as are fungi, staminate cones of pines and junipers, some flowers, and some carrion. Smartt (1978) reported common usage of juniper staminate cones, prickly-pear, mistletoe, and arthropods in addition to pistillate cones of juniper in New Mexico. Under severe water deprivation the animals may become torpid.

Home ranges of piñon mice in southwestern Colorado were 0.8 to 1.4 ha (C. L. Douglas 1969b); home ranges of males were larger than those of females. The animals are tolerant of crowding and show little

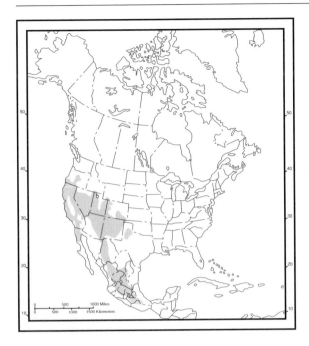

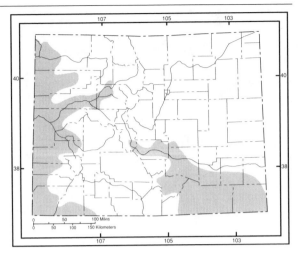

Map 9-77 Distribution of the piñon mouse (Peromyscus truei) in Colorado.

Map 9-76 Distribution of the piñon mouse (Peromyscus truei) in North America.

evidence of territorial behavior. Piñon mice are active year around; most foraging is nocturnal.

The animals are seasonally polyestrous, and females exhibit postpartum estrus. Breeding occurred on Mesa Verde from April through September (C. L. Douglas 1969b). An average of four young (range three to six) are born following a gestation period of 25 to 27 days. Eyes open at three weeks of age. Young mice are weaned at about five weeks and females may start breeding when two months old. Population turnover is high, and probably only 2 to 3 percent of animals that breed as juveniles live to breed again the following spring (Svihla 1932, Douglas 1969b). Hoffmeister (1981) reviewed the literature on the species.

DISTRIBUTION IN COLORADO —Piñon mice occupy semiarid roughlands on both sides of the Continental Divide, a general range similar to that of the brush mouse, but unlike the brush mouse they are found north of the Colorado River Valley to southwestern Moffat County. Piñon mice often

are abundant in suitable habitat. One subspecies, Peromyscus truei truei, occurs in Colorado.

Onychomys leucogaster
NORTHERN GRASSHOPPER MOUSE

DESCRIPTION — The northern grasshopper mouse is a stout-bodied, short-tailed mouse that superficially resembles a deer mouse. The dorsal color is gray in juveniles, molting to cinnamon-buff or reddish brown, and becoming gray again in very old animals. The underparts and distal part of the tail are white. Measurements are: total length 128–158 mm; length of tail 34–52 mm; length of hindfoot 20–23 mm; length of ear 14–19 mm; weight 23–45 g. The skull is distinctly heavier than that of the deer mouse, but otherwise similar, although the third upper molar is reduced in size and the coronoid process of the mandible is as high or higher than the condyloid process. Indeed, the latter character distinguishes the species from any other mouse in Colorado.

NATURAL HISTORY — Grasshopper mice occur in semiarid grasslands, sand hills, and open semidesert shrublands. They seem to reach highest densi-

247

© 1993 Wendy Shattil/Bob Rozinski.

Photograph 9-39 Northern grasshopper mouse (Onychomys leucogaster).

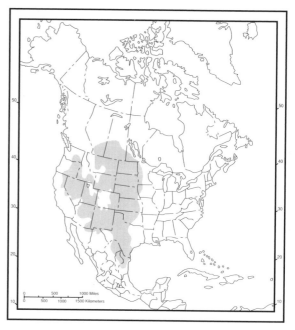

Map 9-78 Distribution of the northern grasshopper mouse (Onychomys leucogaster) *in North America.*

ties on overgrazed rangelands, which typically have high populations of insects and numerous blowouts (patches of windblown soil) that are loose enough for burrowing by mice and for their seemingly obligatory dustbathing. However, Mohamed (1989) found them to be the most abundant rodents on moderately grazed sand prairie, and Flake (1973) captured large numbers on shortgrass prairie in northeastern Colorado.

This is the most thoroughly carnivorous of North American mice, the bulk of the diet being composed of grasshoppers, crickets, and ground-dwelling beetles. Seeds are also eaten, especially in winter. Green vegetation seems not to be used. Hansen (1975) reported a diet of 87 percent arthropods, 7 percent grasses and forbs, 4 percent seeds, and 1 percent mammal and reptile remains. Flake (1973) reported 74 percent of the stomach volume to be animal matter, mostly insect larvae, beetles, grasshoppers, and small vertebrates. Plant matter averaged 25 percent by volume. Although grasshopper mice readily kill small mice and other vertebrates, the importance of such animals in the diet is not well understood. In interspecific bouts in the laboratory small mammals up to the size of hispid cotton rats and hispid pocket mice are readily killed by grasshopper mice (Ruffer 1968). Because of the animal protein in their diet, grasshopper mice have a

strong acrid odor, probably in the urine, and can be identified by smell.

Carnivory and insectivory have led to adaptive changes in behavior relative to other small sigmodontines. Similar to some carnivores, they are monogamous and both adults care for the young. Burrow openings are small and go almost straight down for several inches before angling off (Ruffer 1965a). They mark territories and have a well-developed repertoire of vocalizations (Hildebrand 1961, M. Hafner and Hafner 1979). In confined laboratory situations, dominant animals chase subordinates and usually kill them within 24 hours. Because they are active hunters, home ranges and territories are rather large, averaging 2.3 ha (Blair 1953), and population densities often are relatively low, although on suitable sites they can be one of the commoner small mammals (Flake 1973, Mohamed 1989, Moulton et al. 1981a, b). They are mostly nocturnal and are active year around.

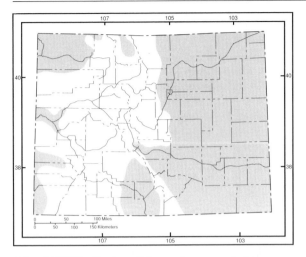

Map 9-79 Distribution of the northern grasshopper mouse (Onychomys leucogaster) in Colorado.

Grasshopper mice have young from March through September (Flake 1974) with a short postpartum estrous. Gestation is 26 to 37 days for nonlactating females (Egoscue 1960), up to 47 days for lactating females (Svihla 1936). Litter size ranges from one to six with an average of four. In Colorado probably three to four litters per year are produced. Young females can reproduce at six months of age. Newborn young are blind and hairless. Hair develops and incisors begin to erupt at a little over one week of age. Eyes are open by 20 days and young are weaned by about 25 days (Svihla 1936, Ruffer 1965b).

Mortality from predation is relatively low, and local populations probably are not regulated by predators (Egoscue 1960, McCarty 1978). Plague ecologists have suggested that the species may be an important reservoir for the disease in the western United States because of their carnivory and wide distribution (R. Thomas 1988, R. Thomas et al. 1989). Wild mice probably do not survive more than one or two years, but in captivity they have lived more than four years (Egoscue 1960). Riddle and Choate (1986) provided a thorough review of systematics, and McCarty (1978) reviewed the literature on the species.

DISTRIBUTION IN COLORADO —The northern grasshopper mouse is common over much of semiarid Colorado at lower elevations. *Onychomys leucogaster arcticeps* is the subspecies of northwestern Colorado, North Park, and the eastern plains; *O. l. pallescens* occurs in the San Luis Valley and in the valleys of the southwestern and west-central parts of the state, from the Grand Valley southward.

Photograph by Roger W. Barbour.

Photograph 9-40 Hispid cotton rat (Sigmodon hispidus).

Sigmodon hispidus
HISPID COTTON RAT

DESCRIPTION — Hispid cotton rats have harsh, dark-colored pelage. Dorsal color is blackish brown interspersed with yellowish to buffy hairs. The underparts are paler in color, tending toward gray. The tail is sparsely haired revealing the scales underneath. The length of the tail is less than that of the head and body. The ears are small but well haired. Measurements are: total length 224–265 mm; length of tail 81–166 mm; length of hindfoot 28–35 mm; length of ear 16–24 mm; weight 100–225 g. Males are typically slightly larger than females. Molars are rooted and high-crowned. Their occlusal surface has large, flattened cusps (sometimes described as lozenge-shaped), arranged in a sigma-shaped pattern (hence the generic name). The skull is

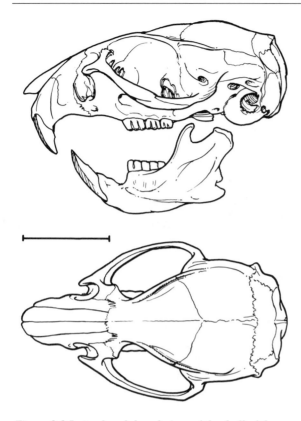

Figure 9-8 Lateral and dorsal views of the skull of the hispid cotton rat (Sigmodon hispidus). *Note the prominent supraorbital ridges. Scale = 1 cm.*

long, narrow, and stout with well-developed su-praorbital (temporal) ridges. The infraorbital foramen is prominent, and the infraorbital plate of the zygomatic arch has a pronounced, blunt, spine-like, anterior projection unlike that of any other rodent in Colorado. Females typically have five pairs of mammae.

NATURAL HISTORY — Little is known about the species in Colorado other than general observations on the rapid range expansion of the animal in southeastern Colorado. The hispid cotton rat is an animal of grasslands, especially where forbs and shrubs are well developed (Fleharty and Mares 1973). In Colorado it is associated usually with midgrass and tallgrass prairie or weedy areas in riparian zones that provide good canopy cover.

It is not found in wooded areas and appears to favor moist sites when available.

The diet is primarily grasses, with forbs and insects also consumed as available (Fleharty and Olson 1969). Cotton rats will clip and leave some vegetation during their foraging activities. In northern parts of their range, probably including Colorado, individuals gain significant weight during the fall to store as fat and metabolize during cold weather (Fleharty et al. 1972).

Cotton rats may be active any time of the day or night but are mostly nocturnal or crepuscular. They use burrow systems especially during cold weather in northern parts of their range. Globular or cup-shaped nests of grasses may be located either under surface objects or in burrows (Shump 1978, Shump and Christian 1978).

Polyestrous, cotton rats are induced ovulators with a postpartum estrus. Gestation averages 27 days (Meyer and Meyer 1944). Litter size ranges from one to 15 with an average of 6 to 7 in northern parts of their range in Kansas (Kilgore 1970). Older females typically have the largest litters. Studies on cotton rats in adjacent Kansas (Fleharty and Choate 1973, Kilgore 1970) suggest the probability that those in southwestern Colorado breed during the warmer months.

Newborn young are relatively precocial, weighing close to 7 g and having a coat of fine hair. They are capable of coordinated movements within hours after birth. The eyes open usually within 36 hours and growth is rapid for the first 40 days of life, averaging close to 2 g per day. Weaning occurs at about two weeks of age. The animals are essentially full grown in 100 days (Meyer and Meyer 1944, Svihla 1929). Females have shown signs of estrus as early as 10 days of age, with pregnancy being recorded in females about 40 days old. Males typically have sperm in the epididymis by three months of age (Fleharty and Choate 1973, Meyer and Meyer 1944).

Map 9-80 *Distribution of the hispid cotton rat* (Sigmodon hispidus) *in North America.*

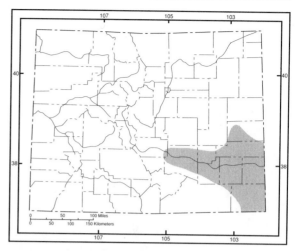

Map 9-81 *Distribution of the hispid cotton rat* (Sigmodon hispidus) *in Colorado.*

Cotton rats are extremely prolific and populations can grow rapidly; in southern parts of their range cyclic peaks and crashes are common. In northern areas population cycles are not well documented, but population crashes do occur. In Kansas low population numbers (0.02 animals per ha) occur in the spring with peaks (20 animals per ha) in the fall (Fleharty et al. 1972). Mean life expectancy is about two months with few individuals living more than 10 months. Studies of population dynamics suggest that dominant animals are more susceptible to trapping than juveniles, making it difficult to make accurate density estimates. This phenomenon appears to be the result of social structure and avoidance by subordinates of traps visited by dominant individuals (Summerlin and Wolfe 1973).

Home ranges average 0.20 to 0.40 ha. Males have larger home ranges than females, and adult home ranges are larger than those of subadults and juveniles. Females maintain exclusive home ranges and dominance systems develop in some

populations (Fleharty and Mares 1973). Individuals of all ages and both sexes may disperse, the net effect of which is to reduce population pressures and local densities. A number of studies (summarized by G. Cameron and Spencer 1981) have suggested that high population densities of cotton rats may have a negative effect on populations of species of *Microtus* and *Reithrodontomys*, some of which may be due to a predilection of cotton rats to feed on the young of these species. Hawks and owls prey heavily on cotton rats, as do mammalian carnivores such as foxes, coyotes, skunks, weasels, and domestic pets. Cameron and Spencer (1981) reviewed the rich literature on the species.

DISTRIBUTION IN COLORADO —First collected in Colorado in Baca County in 1946 (Goldman and Gardner 1947), the hispid cotton rat has been extending its range up the Arkansas River and its tributaries (Armstrong 1972, Hansen 1963). More recently, hispid cotton rats have been collected from Otero and Pueblo counties (A. Carey 1978, Mellott and Fleharty 1986) and Fremont County. They are now a common species in suitable habitat. When first discovered, Coloradan cotton rats were named by Goldman and Gardner (1947) as a new subspecies, *Sigmodon hispidus alfredi*, but

251

Armstrong (1972) suggested that Coloradan cotton rats probably were not a peripheral isolate and predicted that this name eventually will be judged a junior synonym of *S. h. texianus*.

Photograph by Claude Steedman/Wildshots.

Photograph 9-41 White-throated woodrat (Neotoma albigula).

Neotoma albigula
WHITE-THROATED WOODRAT

DESCRIPTION — The white-throated woodrat is medium-sized and brown with short, dense, soft fur. The dorsal pelage is washed with black whereas the throat and chest are white, the individual hairs white to their bases. The tail is distinctly bicolored, dark brown above and whitish below. Measurements: total length 300–354 mm; length of tail 126–147 mm; length of hindfoot 33–37 mm; length of ear 26–30 mm; weight 150–280 g. The skull has a pointed anterior palatal spine. The posterior margin of the palate is concave, as is the dorsal margin of the foramen magnum. The interorbital region is only slightly arched. The anterointernal re-entrant angle of M^1 is generally shallow. As in other woodrats, males have a pronounced midventral scent gland.

NATURAL HISTORY — The white-throated woodrat is an animal of varied habitats. Although often associated with rocky canyon country, it also does well in shrublands or areas with prickly-pear and candelabra cactus (cholla) well away from rocks. In the southwestern part of its range in Colorado it is typically associated with piñon-juniper woodlands or juniper and shrub communities with prickly-pear. In southeastern Colorado the species occupies a broader range of habitats from riparian lands and grasslands to rocky hillsides with cover of junipers. Occurrence, habitat use, and location of den sites of the white-throated woodrat are influenced by sympatry of other species of woodrats (Finley 1958).

Cactus is the main food of this woodrat. Woodrats can metabolize the oxalic acid in cacti without ill effect whereas it is normally toxic to other mammals. The cactus diet is supplemented with juniper needles, yucca blades, and leaves, buds, and reproductive structures of other plants, including piñon, cottonwood, sagebrush, serviceberry, saltbush, mountain-mahogany, winterfat, blackbrush, oakbrush, skunkbrush, pigweed, ragweed, blue grama, cheat-grass, goosefoot, and milkweed (Finley 1958). Food caches are made in dens. The high water content in cacti satisfies water needs.

In Colorado, the house or den of this species away from rocky areas is typically constructed from cactus joints or juniper sticks with other materials such as sticks of sage, cow dung, bones, snakeskin, feathers, hardware, and trash when available. The houses are often built at the base of cholla, juniper, or shrubs, with the nest chamber itself usually located down in the ground at the base of the pile. Houses may be as much as 2 m in diameter and a meter high, but most are much smaller. In rocky country, houses are typically constructed under overhanging rock or in piles of fallen rocks at ground level, not usually on cliff faces. Dens in rocky areas typically conform to the space available at the construction site. Houses and dens usually have a central chamber at or above ground level, with several entrances. The domed nest is constructed of fine-fibered plant materials, especially shredded bark of juniper and yucca or, less commonly, grasses. Nests range from about 15 to 25 cm in diameter.

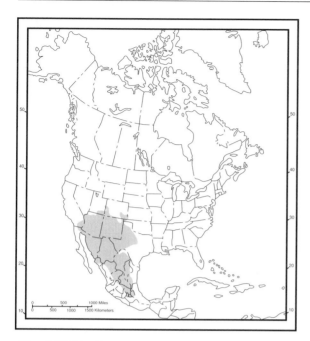

Map 9-82 *Distribution of the white-throated woodrat* (Neotoma albigula) *in North America.*

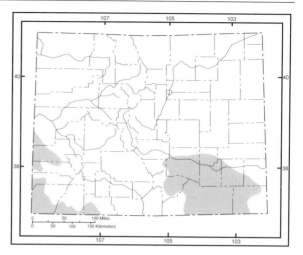

Map 9-83 *Distribution of the white-throated woodrat* (Neotoma albigula) *in Colorado.*

White-throated woodrats typically have two, but occasionally three, young per litter. Most breeding in our area probably occurs during the late winter and spring until about mid-June. Females apparently have a postpartum estrus and may have two litters sharing the same nest at the same time (Finley 1958). Newborn are large, weighing about 11 g. The eyes open at about 15 to 19 days and the young grow rapidly. Attempts are made to eat cactus as early as the seventeenth day; nest building is attempted at a little over one month of age. Young females may reach sexual maturity in as little as 3 months although most probably do not breed until closer to 10 months of age.

White-throated woodrats are solitary animals, with little social interaction between adults except for mating. However, individual home ranges often overlap significantly and animals may share foraging areas, although the den area is defended exclusively. Minimum home ranges have been estimated as being generally less than 500 m^2 (Boggs 1974). Density estimates, based on active den sites or trapping, range from as low as one to as high as 12 animals per ha. With their dependence on prickly-pear and cholla for both food and shelter, highest densities are often on heavily grazed rangeland (Vorhies and Taylor 1940).

Activity is mostly nocturnal, and the animals are active year-round (Macêdo and Mares 1988). Males scent mark with a midventral scent gland at a high rate during the breeding season. This marking is often associated with agonistic behavior. It is performed mostly by the dominant animal during paired encounters in captivity, and it may serve to delineate territories in the wild, especially during the breeding season (Howe 1977). Ventral rubbing is performed by males, as the gland is not well developed in females. Individuals of both sexes perform perineal drags, however, in which the animal deposits scent by lowering its hind end and slowly moving forward. Some scent may also be deposited while sandbathing. The odor of woodrats is quite distinctive and once one has smelled it one quickly learns to recognize when these animals have been about.

Males have a higher rate of survival than do females, but few probably survive much beyond a year or so in the wild. Maximum longevity in captivity is about five years (Landstrom 1971). Macêdo and Mares (1988) reviewed the literature on the species.

DISTRIBUTION IN COLORADO —The white-throated woodrat is found in southeastern Colorado, south of the Arkansas River, and in the southwestern part of the state, on escarpments, mesas, and valley floors in the San Juan and Dolores watersheds. It reaches its elevational limit at about 2,140 m (7,000 ft). *Neotoma albigula warreni* is the subspecies of southeastern Colorado where it has hybridized with *N. micropus* in localized areas (Finley 1958, Huheey 1972); *N. a. laplataensis* occurs in the San Juan drainage; *N. a. brevicauda* occurs in the Dolores–San Miguel watershed.

Photograph 9-42 *Bushy-tailed woodrat* (Neotoma cinerea).

Photograph by J. Perley Fitzgerald.

Neotoma cinerea
BUSHY-TAILED WOODRAT

DESCRIPTION — The bushy-tailed woodrat is large and has a bushy tail (especially pronounced in mature males); its ears are larger than those of other woodrats in our state. Although variable, color is typically ochraceous buff to gray, often washed with black. The sides are buffy. The venter is white with the hairs gray at their bases. White hairs on the chest and throat are usually white to their base. The tail is dark gray above and whitish below. The feet are white. The soles

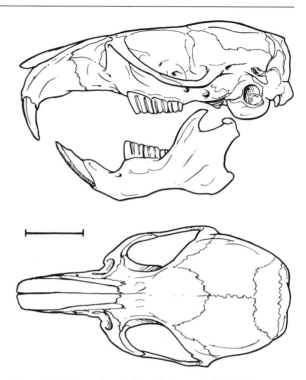

Figure 9-9 *Lateral and dorsal views of the skull of the bushy-tailed wood rat* (Neotoma cinera). *Scale = 1 cm.*

of the hindfeet are fully furred from the proximal tubercle to the heel. Measurements are: total length 340–420 mm; length of tail 142–176 mm; length of hindfoot 40–46 mm; length of ear 30–33 mm; weight 270–299 g. The skull has a narrow, channeled, interorbital region. The temporal ridges are separated by a narrow interparietal usually not much wider than its length. The nasal septum has a maxillovomerine notch, and the anterior palatine spine is slender and pointed.

NATURAL HISTORY — This is a species of mountains and roughlands of western North America, the northernmost of woodrats. In Colorado this is the woodrat of montane and subalpine forests — especially Douglas-fir, ponderosa pine, and aspen communities — and alpine talus. The animals often are quite common around old mining camps and diggings at higher elevations. It also occurs in lower elevation canyon country in semidesert shrublands, and piñon-juniper wood-

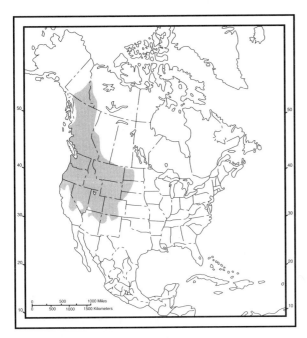

Map 9-84 *Distribution of the bushy-tailed woodrat* (Neotoma cinerea) *in North America.*

lands, typically in rimrock, rock outcrops, and similar geologic features.

The bushy-tailed woodrat is an excellent climber and favors vertical crevices high on cliff walls rather than sites at ground level or in horizontal crevices. However, in the absence of other kinds of woodrats, bushy-tailed woodrats use practically any available opening, including caves. They also construct houses at the base of trees, on or under partly fallen trees, in tree cavities close to the ground, and in abandoned or occupied buildings and mineshafts. In wooded areas the den is usually built from sticks, branches, bones, and similar debris. As with other woodrat species a cup-shaped nest is constructed and lined with fine plant fibers. Although the nest is often within the den, in well-protected areas such as rafters or walls in an abandoned cabin or a shallow cave or mine, the nest may be completely exposed.

Bushy-tailed woodrats feed on a wide variety of plant materials. Leaves of forbs and shrubs are fre-

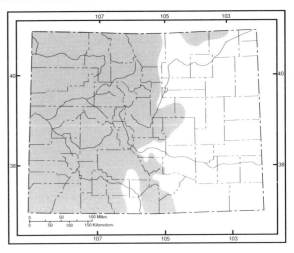

Map 9-85 *Distribution of the bushy-tailed woodrat* (Neotoma cinerea) *in Colorado.*

quently used as are needles of coniferous trees. Food considered by Finley (1958) to be particularly important when available included juniper "berries," fungi, chokecherry, aspen, rose, snowberry, currant, goldenrod, mountain mahogany, saltbush, piñon pine, rabbitbrush, prickly-pear, skunkbrush, Russian-thistle, and hackberry. Additional foods include bristlecone pine needles and bark, goosefoot, mustards, and a wide variety of composites.

Bushy-tailed woodrats are the characteristic "pack rats" of the high mountains. They frequently collect bones, dung, and old rags as well as bright objects including bottle caps, pieces of aluminum, metal, buttons, cans, and silverware, and place them in their dens. Practically every old abandoned cabin and mine building in the mountains of Colorado has dens of this species and characteristic black, tar-like varnish formed by years of urination and fecal deposition in established "toilets." Once one is familiar with the odor of the species it is easy to detect its presence in such areas.

Bushy-tailed woodrats probably breed in Colorado from April through August depending on elevation, with a potential of two litters per year.

Litter size ranges from one to six with an average of three to four.

DISTRIBUTION IN COLORADO —The bushy-tailed woodrat has the broadest range of any of the woodrats, generally occurring throughout the mountains and foothills and along the High Plains escarpment on the Wyoming-Nebraska-Colorado border. *Neotoma cinerea arizonae* is the subspecies of the canyons and plateaus at lower elevations on the Western Slope; *N. c. orolestes* occurs throughout the central mountains; *N. c. rupicola* occurs on the High Plains escarpment of northern Weld and Logan counties.

Photograph by Roger W. Barbour.

Photograph 9-43 Eastern woodrat (Neotoma floridana).

Neotoma floridana
EASTERN WOODRAT

DESCRIPTION — The eastern woodrat is a large sigmodontine with a relatively short, sparsely haired tail that is not scaly. The fur is relatively long, soft, and fine. The color is brownish gray washed lightly with black, paler on the sides. The ventral color is whitish with the bases of the hairs lead gray. The throat and chest are white and the hairs white to their bases. The tail is bicolored, white below and blackish brown above. Measurements are: total length 340–380 mm; length of tail 139–159 mm; length of hindfoot 38–43 mm; length of ear 18–28 mm; weight 275–400 g. The skull is relatively long with a condylobasal length greater than 43 mm. The nasals are also long, usually more than 19 mm. The interorbital region is not strongly arched. The nasal septum is intact, lacking a maxillovomerine notch. The posterior margin of the palate is notched or concave. This is the only woodrat in Colorado with a forked anterior palatal spine. As with all woodrats the cheekteeth are prismatic. Females have four mammae.

Some woodrats in Colorado can be difficult to identify. The eastern woodrat is sympatric in many areas with the Southern Plains, Mexican, white-throated, or bushy-tailed woodrats. The eastern woodrat differs from the Southern Plains woodrat by having brownish rather than slate gray pelage (at least in adults), having a forked anterior palatine spine, and nasals that usually exceed 19 mm. From the Mexican woodrat, the eastern woodrat differs in having a paler dorsal pelage, throat hairs white (not gray) at their bases, an intact nasal septum, and a forked anterior palatine spine. From the white-throated woodrat, the eastern woodrat differs in its slightly larger size, more robust and arched skull, and intact nasal septum (no maxillovomerine notch).

NATURAL HISTORY — Although over most of its range the eastern woodrat inhabits deciduous forest, in Colorado it occurs on the eastern plains, where it occupies rocky draws or riparian woodland and well-developed shrublands with yucca and cactus. Eastern woodrats in Colorado are marginal populations of the species. Its environment here is much drier — with greater extremes of temperature — than habitat farther east in its extensive range.

In Colorado eastern woodrats eat a variety of fruits, twigs, bark, and leaves from locally available plants including cottonwood, several species of *Atriplex*, rabbitbrush, snakeweed, choke cherry, poison ivy, skunkbrush, currant, rose, greasewood, snowberry, cholla, prickly-pear, yucca, various grasses, pigweed, ragweed, gumweed,

Map 9-86 Distribution of the eastern woodrat (Neotoma floridana) *in North America.*

sunflower, evening-star, Russian-thistle, and scurfpea (Finley 1958). Bones are also consumed, probably as a source of calcium. Cactus joints and leaves of shrubs appear to be the most important food items. Food is stored in the house, with increased storage activity in fall and winter. Free water is not necessary.

The eastern woodrat is polyestrous, with a gestation period of 32 to 38 days. Litter size averages three with a range of one to six (Birney 1973, Rainey 1956). The animals probably breed in our area from early spring through late summer. Each estrous cycle lasts from four to six days. Two to three litters are possible because females typically have a postpartum estrus (Rainey 1956).

Young are blind and naked at birth and capable of only weak movements. However, even at this early stage of development the incisors have broken through the gumline. The young weigh about 12 g at birth. Their ears open by 10 days of age and the eyes are open by 15 days of age. Full

adult weight is not reached until about eight months of age (W. Hamilton 1953, P. Pearson 1952, Rainey 1956, D. Spencer 1968). Although females can breed at five or six months of age, in our area they probably do not have young until after their first winter.

Eastern woodrats are mostly nocturnal, solitary animals, active all year round. Greatest activity occurs from nightfall to about midnight, and especially between 2030 and 2230. They are most active on dark nights with little or no moonlight, although juveniles may be active in late afternoon (Finley 1959, Wiley 1971).

As other woodrats, eastern woodrats construct complex houses that provide cover and protection from predators and the physical environment. Houses are constructed from practically any movable materials including sticks, stalks of herbaceous plants, cactus joints and other vegetation, stones, dried fecal materials, bones, feathers, hides of dead animals, and human trash. Houses generally take on a conical shape, especially if constructed at the base of a tree or cactus. However, in rocky areas they conform to the shape of the overhangs, crevices, and rock outfall under which they are built. These homes may exceed a meter in height and diameter but are typically smaller than those of other species occupying the same general area. Eastern woodrats use less cactus in house construction than do white-throated or Southern Plains woodrats. Houses are augmented throughout the lifetime of the occupant. A path may surround the house, with the debris pushed to one side of the path forming a conspicuous ridge. Side paths radiate into surrounding vegetation. Inside the house is a series of tunnels, passages, and chambers above or sometimes below ground. Two or three cup-shaped nests, made of yucca fibers, soft grasses, fur, feathers, and shredded bark are found in some of the chamber areas in the house (Finley 1958, Fitch and Rainey 1956, Rainey 1956).

The house is typically defended against other eastern woodrats. Such territorial defense is especially

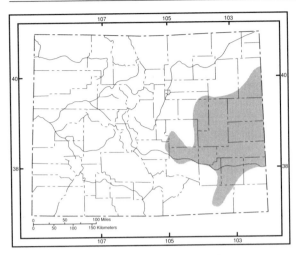

Map 9-87 Distribution of the eastern woodrat (Neotoma floridana) *in Colorado.*

marked in females during the reproductive season. Severe fights occur, with the front paws held like boxing gloves while the animals jab with their front feet and slash with their incisors. Individuals grind their teeth and thump their feet during aggressive interactions. Foot thumping also occurs when the animals are nervous or excited, as when detained in a livetrap.

Because woodrats tend to occupy linear habitats along rock outcrops or streamcourses, densities are difficult to estimate, so some authors have used counts of active houses to project numbers. In habitats with favorable sites for houses, densities have approximated about one animal per hectare. Home ranges are associated with the area immediately around the house and are usually less than 0.25 ha (Goertz 1970). Home ranges overlap in favorable habitat.

Individuals can live up to three years but most probably survive less than one year in the wild. Great horned owls, skunks, and long-tailed weasels are effective predators. Wiley (1980) reviewed literature on the species.

DISTRIBUTION IN COLORADO —The eastern woodrat is a species of the deciduous forests of the eastern United States. Eastern Colorado represents the western limit of its distribution. In this state the species occurs north of the Arkansas River to western El Paso County and north and east to Yuma County. Populations are localized in suitable habitat. In Oklahoma, *N. floridana* has hybridized with *N. micropus* (D. Spencer 1968). One subspecies, *Neotoma floridana campestris,* occurs in Colorado.

Photograph 9-44 Desert woodrat (Neotoma lepida).

Neotoma lepida
DESERT WOODRAT

DESCRIPTION — The desert woodrat is small and yellow-buff to buffy gray. The tail is sharply bicolored and short haired. The underparts are whitish to buff. White hairs on the chest are usually gray at their bases except for a small patch or midventral strip with white bases. Measurements are: total length 266–295 mm; length of tail 110–126 mm; length of hindfoot 31–33 mm; length of ear 28–30 mm; weight 100–140 g. The skull is not strongly arched in the interorbital region. A maxillovomerine notch is present in the nasal septum. The anterior palatal spine is stout and blunt. Small size, pale color, and generally naked soles of the hindfeet separate this species from *N. cinerea*. From *N. mexicana* it differs in having a much less arched skull, some hairs on the chest white to their bases, and a blunt anterior palatal spine.

NATURAL HISTORY — The desert woodrat has not been as intensively studied as some other species of *Neotoma*. It is mainly a species of canyonlands and semiarid shrublands of the Great Basin (Llewellyn 1981), reaching eastern limits in northwestern and west-central Colorado. Desert woodrats tend to locate dens among fallen rock slabs and boulders, in ledges and crevices along rock faces, or occasionally in trees (especially juniper).

Desert woodrats apparently feed on a wider variety of food items than Colorado's other woodrats. The animals are not as closely associated with cactus as other species, and much less of the diet is cactus, although it is readily eaten if available. Other dietary items include stems, twigs, bark, berries, and seeds of locally common xerophytic shrubs and forbs. Saltbush, juniper, and Russian-thistle are frequently used as well as greasewood, snakeweed, sagebrush, and yucca. In Utah, 88 percent of the diet was shrub and forb material. Juniper branches and leaves are important foods, especially in the winter months. The animals also eat Mormon tea (*Ephedra*) and piñon nuts. Food stored in the den consisted mainly of juniper leaves and "berries" in Utah (Stones and Hayward 1968).

Desert woodrats in Colorado do not appear to construct houses away from rocky areas to any significant extent (Finley 1958). All animals studied by Finley were taken at rock dens, but Cary (1911) discussed and illustrated a house made of cow dung and prickly-pear pads near Rangely. On his collection site he reported houses numerous enough to resemble "muskrat houses on a marsh." It may be that heavy livestock grazing over much of northwestern Colorado since the time of Cary's work has reduced the amount of habitat away from rocky areas suitable for the species. In Utah, houses were most abundant in dense stands of juniper, and nests were located in juniper trees (Stones and Hayward 1968).

Map 9-88 *Distribution of the desert woodrat* (Neotoma lepida) *in North America.*

Dens in rock shelters are typically constructed of small sticks, plant stalks, and cacti, with reportedly fewer bones than found in bushy-tailed woodrat dens. Dens are rarely constructed in vertical crevices but typically are found in horizontal crevices and under boulders. Size of dens varies widely, with some being built in crevices that would not be used by larger woodrats; at other times the size of the den may equal that of one constructed by a bushy-tailed woodrat. This similarity may stem from the fact that, in areas of sympatry, dens are occupied serially by different species of woodrats (Armstrong 1982). An average den is constructed in seven to ten nights of activity (Bonaccorso and Brown 1972). As with other species of woodrat, dens have more than one entrance. The nest is usually a ball-shaped mass of finely shredded bark, grass, or similar material. In Utah, oval, circular, or gourd-shaped nests were made with shredded juniper bark (Stones and Hayward 1968).

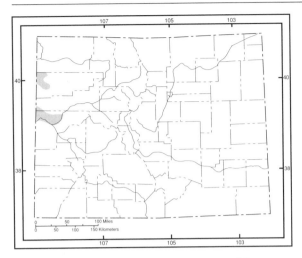

Map 9-89 Distribution of the desert woodrat (Neotoma lepida) *in Colorado.*

The species is polyestrous, reproducing throughout the warmer months. Two litters are probably typical in Colorado, although up to four litters per year have been reported from farther southwest. The gestation period is 30 to 36 days; litters range from one to five, with an average of slightly more than two (G. Cameron 1973; Egoscue 1957, 1962b; Egoscue et al. 1970). The young are relatively precocial, with incisors present at birth (which grip the nipples of the mother so tightly that suckling young are dragged as the mother scurries to deeper cover to escape perceived danger). The young grow rapidly and their eyes open at about 12 days. They are weaned at about four weeks of age. Females can reproduce at about three months of age.

The desert woodrat is mainly nocturnal although there are several reports of its moving about in the daytime. The animals forage or collect materials for the nest within about 100 m of the den. Males are more active outside the den than are females.

In juniper and sage-juniper woodland in Utah densities varied from 4.5 to 7.7 animals per ha; these same sites contained 12 and 21 houses per ha, respectively. Only about 37 percent of houses were occupied, usually by a single adult. Animals

moved between houses readily, and young animals usually took up occupancy of existing but previously unoccupied houses (Stones and Hayward 1968).

DISTRIBUTION IN COLORADO —The desert woodrat is restricted to northwestern and west-central Colorado, along the Colorado and White rivers, north and south of the Roan Plateau. One subspecies, *Neotoma lepida sanrafaeli*, occurs in Colorado.

Photograph 9-45 Mexican woodrat (Neotoma mexicana).

Neotoma mexicana
MEXICAN WOODRAT

DESCRIPTION — This species is a medium-sized woodrat. Dorsal color of animals from along the Front Range is usually dark gray, often washed with black. Specimens from southwestern Colorado are more grayish buff on the dorsum whereas those from the San Luis Valley and southeastern Colorado are grayish yellow to gray-buff. The sides are a paler grayish buff. The underparts are whitish with all hairs gray at their bases. There is typically a dusky line or ring around the mouth. The short-haired tail is distinctly bicolored, blackish above and whitish gray below. The feet are white. Measurements are: total length 297–380 mm; length of tail 124–178 mm; length of hind-

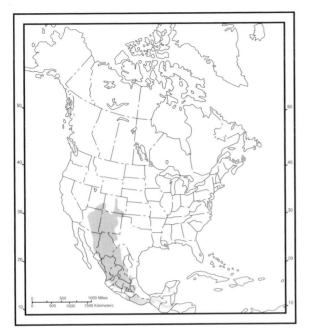

Map 9-90 Distribution of the Mexican woodrat (Neotoma mexicana) *in North America.*

foot 29–38 mm; length of ear 26–28 mm; weight 149–255 g. The skull is large and often arched in the interorbital region. A maxillovomerine notch divides the nasal septum. The anterior palatal spine has a sharp tip. In most specimens the anterointernal fold of M^1 is deep, extending more than halfway across the crown.

NATURAL HISTORY — The Mexican woodrat is a species of semiarid canyonlands and foothills below about 2,600 m (8,500 ft) in Colorado. It is invariably associated with rocky slopes and cliffs in montane shrublands, piñon-juniper woodlands, or montane forests. Like all woodrats, the species is herbivorous; leaves compose up to 90 percent of stomach contents (Armstrong 1982). Buds, flowers, and cones of a variety of species are also eaten. Finley (1958) reported the species to be a food generalist, eating practically any kind of plant available and especially oak, sagebrush, juniper, ponderosa pine, skunkbrush, mountain-mahogany, choke cherry, winterfat, snowberry, currant, rabbitbrush, and yucca. Cactus does not

appear to be used much in Colorado. Acorns, piñon nuts, and juniper "berries" are important foods. The species cuts and caches large amounts of foliage. Greatest collecting activity occurs in the fall. The ability to concentrate urine is not as well developed as that of the white-throated woodrat, and the animals will take free water if available (Brownfield and Wunder 1976).

Mexican woodrats are active year around, mostly at night. Unlike some other woodrats in Colorado they do not build houses away from rocky areas; rock shelter apparently is essential (Finley 1958). Dens and nests typically are beneath ledges or in fissures of cliffs. Both horizontal and vertical crevices are used. They also use abandoned or seasonally occupied buildings or mine tunnels and will adopt houses constructed by other species of woodrats. Their dens are typically built of small and medium-sized sticks, twigs, and leaf cuttings. Much of the material probably also is used for food. Nests are either cup-shaped or ball-shaped masses of shredded bark from juniper or sage, or yucca fibers. Woodrats are popularly "packrats," and other materials, including bones, feathers, and dung, are gathered to add to the house. Fecal material accumulates rapidly around active den sites and this, along with fresh clippings of vegetation, makes it easy to determine their presence.

The tendency of the Mexican woodrat to occur at lower elevations reduces possible interaction with the bushy-tailed woodrat. In areas of sympatry the latter species often constructs its dens higher up on cliff faces, but the Mexican woodrat uses crevices closer to ground level. Where the species do not coexist, Mexican woodrats use the entire cliff face. In areas of sympatry with white-throated woodrats, such as in southeastern and southwestern Colorado, Mexican woodrats tend to make more use of the rocky, steep sides of canyons whereas white-throated woodrats use the valley floor. In certain locations, dens of both species are found in the same rocky habitat. Populations of eastern and desert woodrats in Colorado are largely allopatric to the Mexican woodrat.

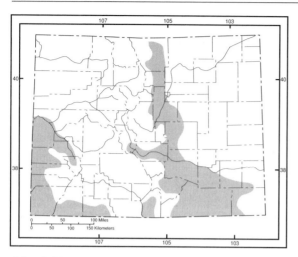

Map 9-91 *Distribution of the Mexican woodrat* (Neotoma mexicana) *in Colorado.*

Mexican woodrats are seasonally polyestrous and breed from late March to mid-June in Colorado. A postpartum estrus occurs, and typically two litters are produced per year. Gestation takes from 31 to 34 days; a litter averages three young, with a range of two to five. Females born early, in April and May, can breed late in their first year and usually produce two young per litter (L. N. Brown 1969). Males typically do not breed until after their first winter. Maximum size of testes occurs in April. Howe (1978) reported considerable agonistic behavior associated with mating in the Mexican woodrat in the laboratory. During mating encounters males made wheezy, gasping sounds when approaching estrous females. Cornely and Baker (1986) reviewed literature on the species.

DISTRIBUTION IN COLORADO —The Mexican woodrat is found in a narrow band along the Front Range and in southeastern Colorado, south of the Arkansas River. It also occurs in the volcanic San Luis Hills and in the canyon country of southwestern Colorado. *Neotoma mexicana fallax* is the subspecies of the Front Range, from the Arkansas River northward nearly to the Wyoming border, and extending westward up the Arkansas Valley to about Salida.; *N. m. inopinata* occurs in southwestern Colorado south of the Gunnison and

Colorado rivers; *N. m. scopulorum* occurs in southeastern Colorado south of the Arkansas River and also in the San Luis Valley.

Photograph 9-46 *Southern plains woodrat* (Neotoma micropus).

Neotoma micropus
SOUTHERN PLAINS WOODRAT

DESCRIPTION — Formerly called the gray woodrat, the southern plains woodrat is of medium size with a dense, soft, slate to ash gray pelage. The tail is relatively short and sparsely haired, dusky gray above and paler whitish gray below. The venter is gray and the throat and chest are white. The feet are white. As with other woodrats the vibrissae are long and conspicuous. Measurements are: total length 310–411 mm; length of tail 130–175 mm; length of hindfoot 30–45 mm; length of ear 25–30 mm; weight 180–320 g. The skull has a strongly arched interorbital region, no maxillovomerine notch, and a short palatal bridge usually with a posterior median spine. Females have two pair of mammae.

NATURAL HISTORY — The southern plains woodrat is associated with a variety of semiarid and desert grassland environments including shrub- and cactus-grasslands of the Southern Great Plains. In Colorado the species is largely restricted to grasslands with prickly-pear and candelabra cactus (cholla). A few individuals have also been captured in yucca-grass communities and on rocky outcrops in mixed shrub stands. Houses are built at the bases of cholla or yucca, and sometimes under rockfalls and rocky overhangs (Finley 1958). The animals are not as typically associated with rocky areas as are Mexican and white-throated woodrats.

In Colorado the diet appears to be mostly joints of cholla. A wide variety of other plants is also consumed, including yucca, prickly-pear, juniper, currant, blue grama, milkweed, Russian-thistle, and copper mallow (Finley 1958). Although captive animals drink readily, free water is not needed, as cactus in the diet provides ample water in the wild.

A typical house is constructed at the base of a tree cactus and is constituted largely from the joints of the cactus, supplemented with other materials including cow dung, small stones and sticks, prickly-pear pads, stalks of herbaceous plants, feathers, and bones. Houses are usually less than a meter in height and usually have a well-worn path around the outside. The house has several entrances usually bordered by cactus joints. Passages lead to a central chamber or to smaller side chambers. The ball-like nest is located in a side chamber and is constructed from softer, finer plant materials such as grass or yucca fibers. This species shows some preference for underground nest locations (Finley 1958).

A territory around the house is defended, and individuals usually stay in the same den throughout their lives. As with other woodrats, a variety of small mammals (including desert shrews), lizards, and insects are commensals in houses of southern plains woodrats. The animals are largely nocturnal and solitary. Most activity occurs before midnight. Unlike the situation reported in other species, there does not seem to be any correlation between trapping success and intensity of moonlight or cloud cover (Braun and Mares 1989). Movement is usually limited to roughly 15 m or so from the den. Home ranges are estimated at 258 m² to over 1,300 m²

Map 9-92 Distribution of the southern plains woodrat (Neotoma micropus) *in North America.*

with those of males being larger than those of females (Braun and Mares 1989).

Southern plains woodrats in our area are probably capable of having two or three litters a year. Females may have a postpartum estrus although this is not necessarily typical. For most females gestation takes 33 to 35 days although much variation is reported (Birney 1973). Pregnant females show abdominal hair loss and enlargement and swelling of the mammae. Litter size averages two to three. Growth of young animals is similar to that of the eastern woodrat, the eyes opening and juvenal pelage complete at about two weeks of age. By three months of age they have attained about 85 percent of adult weight (Wiley 1984).

Woodrats are seemingly nervous animals while active outside the den, ears in constant motion and whiskers twitching. They have excellent hearing and use it as a primary sensory mechanism to avoid predators. Braun and Mares (1989) reviewed the literature on the species.

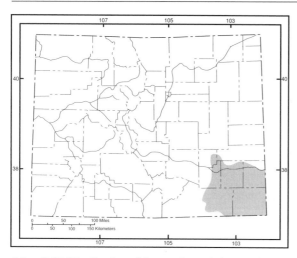

Map 9-93 Distribution of the southern plains woodrat (Neotoma micropus) in Colorado.

Map 9-94 Distribution of Stephen's woodrat (Neotoma stephensi) in North America.

DISTRIBUTION IN COLORADO —The species is largely restricted to the eastern plains south of the Arkansas River, with only a few specimens from Crowley and Bent counties north of the river. In localized areas in Colorado it has hybridized with N. albigula (Finley 1958, Huheey 1972), and in Oklahoma with N. floridana (D. Spencer 1968). One subspecies, Neotoma micropus canescens, occurs in Colorado.

Neotoma stephensi
STEPHENS' WOODRAT

DESCRIPTION — Stephens' woodrat is small and pale yellow to buff gray in color. The belly and throat are white, the hairs of the throat gray at their bases. The tail is indistinctly bicolored with the hairs relatively long and slightly bushy at the tip. Measurements are: total length 280–333 mm; length of tail 112–144 mm; length of hindfoot 30–33 mm; length of ear 27–30 mm. Any small, pale-colored woodrat from lower elevations in extreme southwestern Colorado should be examined by an expert for identification.

NATURAL HISTORY — In northern Arizona the species is typically associated with piñon-juniper woodlands, rock debris at the base of cliffs, or rocky outcrops. T. Vaughan (1980) reported that most nests near Flagstaff were located at the base of junipers. The diet is almost exclusively "berries" and leaves of juniper (Vaughan 1982). Mormon tea is also eaten. The animals probably breed from March to August with one or two young per litter (range one to three). Probably two litters are produced per year. C. Jones and Hildreth (1989) reviewed the literature.

DISTRIBUTION IN COLORADO — Stephens' woodrat is a species of probable occurrence in Colorado. It ranges over much of northern and central Arizona and western New Mexico, barely extending into southern Utah. It occurs within a few kilometers of Colorado's southern border, near Navajo Reservoir, and may be expected on the Southern Ute Reservation in the vicinity of Arboles. Neotoma stephensi relicta is the subspecies to be expected in Colorado.

SUBFAMILY MURINAE — OLD WORLD RATS AND MICE

Murine rodents typically have sparsely haired, scaly tails and cusped teeth. Cusps of the upper molars are arranged in three longitudinal rows. The palate terminates beyond the plane of the last molars. The dental formula is 1/1, 0/0, 0/0, 3/3 = 16. Members of the group are highly adaptable and often commensal or competitive with humans. In Colorado two genera and two species are present, house mice and Norway rats. Introduced Eurasian species, they both first reached North America with early European colonists but undoubtedly other individuals entered the United States later at major ports along both coasts. House mice have traveled with humans on ships, trains, and trucks to become established practically everywhere except polar areas. Similarly, Norway rats have been introduced to many parts of North America and reside in practically every major city on the continent. In Colorado they are more restricted to urban areas or feed lots than are house mice. Murine rodents in Colorado are not listed as wildlife (Table 3-1) and receive no protection under the law; hence they can be trapped or otherwise destroyed without license or limit.

Key to the Species of the Subfamily Murinae Known or Expected to Occur in Colorado

1. Length of skull less than 20 mm; total length less than 200 mm; first upper molar longer than combined length of second and third molars . . . . House Mouse — *Mus musculus*, p. 265

1′ Length of skull more than 20 mm; total length more than 200 mm; first upper molar shorter than combined length of second and third molars 2

2. Tail shorter than head and body; M^1 without distinct outer notches on first row of cusps . . . . Norway Rat — *Rattus norvegicus*, p. 267

2′ Tail longer than head and body; M^1 with distinct outer notches on first row of cusps . . . . Black Rat — *Rattus rattus*[*]

Photograph 9-47 House mouse (Mus musculus).

Mus musculus
HOUSE MOUSE

DESCRIPTION — This small, slender, brown to blackish brown mouse has a sparsely haired, scaly tail. The underparts are slightly paler in color than the dorsum without any clear line of demarcation. The ears are relatively large and sparsely haired. Measurements are: total length 130–200 mm; length of tail 60–105 mm; length of hindfoot 14–21 mm; length of ear 11–18 mm; weight 18–23 g. The skull is flattened and has a short rostrum. Cusps of the molars are aligned in three longitudinal rows. The first upper molar is longer than the combined length of the second and third molars. Superficially this species could be confused with the harvest mouse (*Reithrodontomys*). However,

[*] Couplet after Hall (1981); feral populations not reported from Colorado.

265

harvest mice have grooves on the upper incisors, which are lacking in the house mouse. House mice also have a characteristic, strong, musky odor produced by anal glands. Once acquainted with that odor a human can recognize the presence of a house mouse in a closed trap simply by the scent. Females have five pairs of mammae.

NATURAL HISTORY — As the common name implies, house mice frequently live alongside humans, in dwellings, grain bins, barns, warehouses, or other structures. House mice also survive as feral populations at lower elevations over much of Colorado, living along fence rows, ditch banks, rights-of-way, abandoned fields, or croplands. House mice frequently are termed "commensals" of people, but that is largely inaccurate. Commensalism is a symbiotic relationship in which one species benefits and a second is affected neither positively nor negatively. By that definition, house mice are not commensals, but often are competitors of humans for growing and stored food and other resources.

House mice are active year-round although in cold weather they may spend considerable amounts of time huddled together in communal nests. They are mostly nocturnal and secretive, traveling along or under objects at ground level or along baseboards and in crawlspaces beneath buildings. In the wild they use established runways, making rapid, furtive movements and pausing only briefly to gather or consume food. Nests are constructed from whatever materials are handy including cloth and paper scraps, corn husks, grass, leaves, and feathers. Nests are hidden under or in objects such as furniture and old mattresses. In our region it is not unusual for house mice to invade houses in the fall and early winter and then to disperse to outdoor environments during the warmer months.

Opportunistic in their diet, house mice eat everything from grains and vegetable crops to insects, carrion, glue, and leather. Feeding, defecation, and urination by house mice on stored grains can cause tremendous annual losses of such crops. If food is plentiful the animals make food caches near the nest site. Water is consumed if available but is not required.

House mice are polyestrous, with females coming into heat about every five days. Gestation takes about 19 days, and 2 to 13 young are produced. Average litter size is four to seven. In Colorado probably five to seven litters are produced annually; most breeding occurs from late spring through early fall. The young are blind and naked at birth, but, by two weeks of age, they are well furred and the eyes are open. The young are weaned at about three weeks. Juvenile house mice are ready to breed by six weeks of age (Breakey 1963).

House mice communicate by scent, vocalizations, and postures. They have a variety of chirps, squeaks, and "songs." Scent marking involves urination and use of a preputial gland.

The prolific reproductive ability and social nature of house mice allow populations to increase rapidly. Phenomenal densities can be attained when resources are effectively unlimited, at least for certain periods. Under natural conditions, stable family groups form with one male and one or more females (Crowcroft and Rowe 1963). They maintain territories and expel other mice from the occupied area. Adult males are more aggressive than females and are most active in territorial maintenance. Levels of aggression in males increase with increases in population density. The family group shares a nest until one of the females becomes aggressive as a result of pregnancy. If both females become pregnant at the same time, they may make a communal nest that they eventually will share with their offspring of a couple of generations. As young males mature their aggression increases and eventually causes them to leave this communal nest.

Individuals disperse into suitable adjacent habitats including abandoned fields, ditch banks, and croplands where they may displace small native rodents, such as harvest mice. Most house mice probably do not survive more than six or seven months in the wild but have lived up to six years in captivity.

A diversity of wild carnivores preys on house mice including foxes, coyotes, weasels, hawks, owls, and snakes. Domestic pets also kill house mice but may not eat them, perhaps because of their odor. W. Jackson (1982) provided a general review of the literature on this species and on the Norway rat.

DISTRIBUTION IN COLORADO — The house mouse thrives in occupied homes, urban and rural, and around agricultural areas where cereal grains are grown, stored, or fed. The species probably lives in all major cities and towns in Colorado as well as in adjacent farmlands, ranchlands, and "waste" areas. It can be locally abundant, even in native habitats. Probably at least two subspecies, *Mus musculus brevirostris* and *M. m. domesticus*, have been introduced to North America. The status and distribution of these taxa in Colorado have not been studied, however.

Rattus norvegicus
NORWAY RAT

DESCRIPTION — The Norway rat is large and heavy bodied with a long, sparsely haired, scaly tail. The upperparts are usually brown to brownish black and the underparts are paler. Occasionally some individuals show a high degree of spotting or splotching with white. The pelage is somewhat coarse. The ears are conspicuous and covered with short hairs. Measurements are: total length 300–480 mm; length of tail 150–255 mm; length of hindfoot 30–44; length of ear 18–21 mm; weight 150–540 g. Anal scent glands produce a musky odor. Males have a baculum. Females have six pairs of mammae. The skull is long and narrow with conspicuous temporal ridges. The length of the first upper molar is less than the combined length of molars two and three. Although superficially similar in size and appearance, Norway rats can be distinguished from woodrats (*Neotoma*) by their naked tail, poorly

Photograph 9-48 *Norway rat* (Rattus norvegicus).

haired ears, and relatively coarser hair. The cheek teeth of woodrats are prismatic but those of Norway rats have well-defined cusps arranged in three rows.

NATURAL HISTORY — Norway rats typically live in close commensal or competitive associations with humans, occupying buildings, sewer systems, outbuildings around farms, rubble, and land fills. They can be found in tunnel systems on vacant lots and weedy agricultural lands, usually not far from urbanized areas. One of us (JPF) live trapped rodents for the U.S. Fish and Wildlife Service Wildlife Research Center while attending graduate school at Colorado State University in the middle and late 1960s. Norway rats in many different color patterns — from nearly all white to spotted to the more typical brown — were found along ditch banks and railroad rights-of-way several kilometers from Fort Collins and nearby towns.

Similar to house mice, Norway rats are omnivorous, eating practically any organic matter. When available, cereal grains and native seeds are heavily used. Rats will also kill birds, including domestic poultry; small mammals and young of larger mammals, including baby pigs and lambs; snakes; and similar prey. Cannibalism is not uncommon, especially by large males and under crowded conditions. Individuals typically require at least 20 to 30 g of food per day, and can consume up to one-third of their body weight daily.

267

Nests of grasses, cloth, paper, and leaves are concealed under or in various objects on the surface of the ground. Well-developed colonies dig complex tunnel systems, which may be as much as half a meter below the ground level. Such tunnels usually have a main entrance and several escape holes. Digging is done with the forefeet, and loosened soil is pushed to the surface using the head, chest, and forefeet.

Norway rats are agile climbers and good swimmers. It is not unusual to see them swimming along the margins of irrigation ditches that pass through towns and cities on the plains, where they may be confused with muskrats. During spring and summer rat populations expand into agricultural lands and weedy areas but during the colder months the animals congregate again around farms and urban areas.

Norway rats are mostly nocturnal in areas where they are subject to disturbance by humans. However, in areas with little disturbance or in areas with plentiful food supplies such as poorly managed landfills, they may be active at any time. Most foraging occurs shortly after dark and again just before daylight. Rats live in colonies usually numbering about 12 to 15 individuals dominated by an older, adult male. At extremely high population levels social pressures result in increased fighting, physiological stress, reduced breeding, and increased mortality. Male Norway rats can breed year around but females are seasonally polyestrous, producing about five litters a year, primarily in spring and summer. The gestation period is 21 to 26 days. Litter size ranges from 2 to 22, with an average of 7 to 11 young. Pups are blind, naked, and helpless at birth. Eyes open at two weeks of age, with weaning completed at three weeks. Juveniles are sexually mature at about three months of age.

Most medium to large carnivores prey on Norway rats. Weasels, foxes, skunks, large snakes, hawks, and owls are probably most important in such predation. Humans constantly wage extermination campaigns against the animals, using burrow fu-

migants, toxicants, or poisoned foods. Most Norway rats probably die in their first year of life and a rare individual survives to two or three years of age.

Norway rats are vectors for a variety of diseases dangerous to humans including typhus, plague, tularemia, and occasionally rabies. Contamination of crops by urination and defecation as well as direct consumption of human food result in millions of dollars in losses annually in the United States alone. Their gnawing activity can also destroy underground utility cables and water pipes. From a positive standpoint domesticated laboratory rats have contributed to much beneficial research in the areas of medicine and pharmacology. Calhoun (1962) provided the most detailed study of this species in the United States, and W. Jackson (1982) reviewed the general biology.

DISTRIBUTION COLORADO — Norway rats are relatively common in most cities on the eastern plains. One subspecies, *Rattus norvegicus norvegicus*, occurs in Colorado.

SUBFAMILY ARVICOLINAE — VOLES, MEADOW MICE, MUSKRAT

Arvicolines are stocky, blunt-nosed, usually dark-colored rodents, mostly of small to medium size. Previously, they were known as the Microtinae, or microtine rodents, treated as a subfamily of the Cricetidae (for further comment, see the general account of the family Muridae); many of the references cited herein will refer to them as such, and the informal name "microtine" doubtless will continue to be used for the group. Arvicolines are an important part of the vertebrate prey base and as such are an essential component in many ecosystems. Many of the species experience pronounced population fluctuations and can reach high numbers in certain years (Lidicker 1988, Taitt and Krebs 1985). Arvicolines generally make a living at the interface of soil and vegetation, spending most of their time in runways and burrows. This habit may have led to an evolutionary

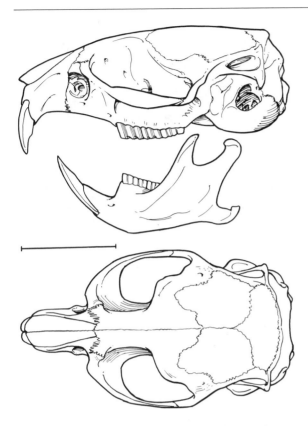

Figure 9-10 Skull of a representative arvicoline rodent, the meadow vole (Microtus pennsylvanicus) *showing the blocky appearance of the braincase. Scale = 1 cm.*

reduction in the size of their ears and eyes. Unlike sigmodontines, arvicolines are almost strictly herbivorous (except for the muskrat), feeding on green vegetation as long as it is available.

Arvicolines all have prismatic cheekteeth with deep infoldings of enamel and complex patterns of dentine. The skull is heavy and sharply angular with a stouter zygomatic arch than most sigmodontines. The braincase typically is constricted at the level of the rostrum, giving it a blocky appearance. The tail is not as well haired as that of many sigmodontines and is often shorter than the length of the head and body. The pinnae are typically small, well haired but difficult to see because of the length of the general pelage. Five genera and nine species of arvicolines live in Colorado. A

sixth genus, *Synaptomys*, may eventually be discovered in the state. Coloradan arvicolines other than the muskrat are categorized as nongame mammals (Table 3-1). General biology of many of the species in Colorado was reviewed by M. L. Johnson and Johnson (1982) and in volumes edited by Merritt (1984) and Tamarin (1985). The latter two works include chapters on energetics and thermoregulation by Bruce A. Wunder (1984, 1985), a distinguished zoologist at Colorado State University who has spent many years working with various species of arvicoline rodents, often on Coloradan populations. Gaines (1985) summarized much of the work on the genetics of New World arvicolines.

Key to the Species of the Subfamily Arvicolinae Known or Expected to Occur in Colorado

1. Tail sparsely haired, scaly, laterally compressed; condylobasal length of skull more than 55 mm . . . . Muskrat — *Ondatra zibethicus*, p. 287

1′ Tail haired, not scaly, round; condylobasal length of skull less than 35 mm 2

2. Cheekteeth rooted, height of crown decreases with wear. 3

2′ Cheekteeth evergrowing, height of crown maintained despite wear 4

3. Mid-dorsal fur reddish; palate terminates posteriorly as transverse shelf; inner re-entrant angles of lower molars about equal in depth to outer re-entrant angles . . . . Southern Red-backed Vole — *Clethrionomys gapperi*, p. 270

3′ Mid-dorsal fur grayish brown; palate with median spinous process, not terminating as transverse shelf; inner re-entrant angles of lower molars deeper than outer re-entrant angles . . . . Heather Vole — *Phenacomys intermedius*, p. 272

4. Tail short, as long as or slightly longer than hindfoot 5

4′ Tail longer, obviously longer than hindfoot . . .
. . . . *Microtus* 6

5. Tail slightly longer than hindfoot, sole of hindfoot densely haired; auditory bullae conspicuous dorsally; no obvious groove on face of upper incisor . . Sagebrush Vole — *Lemmiscus curtatus*, p. 285

5′ Tail no longer than hindfoot, sole of hindfoot not densely haired; auditory bullae not conspicuous dorsally; well-developed groove on face of upper incisor . . . . Southern Bog Lemming — *Synaptomys cooperi**, p. 289

6. Tail one-third or more total length . . . .
. . . Long-tailed Vole — *Microtus longicaudus*, p. 274

6′ Tail less than one-third total length 7

7. Belly buff; third upper molar with four dentine lakes . . . Prairie Vole — *Microtus ochrogaster*, p. 280

7′ Belly gray or whitish; third upper molar with five dentine lakes 8

8. Second upper molar with four dentine lakes and a rounded posterior loop . . . .
. . . Meadow Vole — *Microtus pennsylvanicus*, p. 283

8′ Second upper molar with four dentine lakes but lacking a rounded posterior loop 9

9. Incisive foramina narrow and constricted posteriorly; mammae eight; tail usually more than 36 mm . . Montane Vole — *Microtus montanus*, p. 278

9′ Incisive foramina broad, short, truncated posteriorly; mammae four; tail usually less than 35 mm . . . . . . Mexican Vole — *Microtus mexicanus*, p. 276

Photograph by Roger W. Barbour.

Photograph 9-49 Southern red-backed vole (Clethrionomys gapperi).

Clethrionomys gapperi
SOUTHERN RED-BACKED VOLE

DESCRIPTION — One of Colorado's most beautiful small mammals, the red-backed vole has a broad, reddish mid-dorsal stripe extending from forehead to tail. The background color is grayish brown. The ventral color is grayish with the bases of the hairs black. The bicolored tail is relatively long for an arvicoline rodent but does not approach that of the long-tailed vole. The ears are short and partly hidden by the body fur. Measurements are: total length 125–152 mm; length of tail 33–44 mm; length of hindfoot 17–19 mm; length of ear 12–16 mm; weight 20–38 g. The skull resembles that of *Microtus*, with a blocky shape and prismatic cheekteeth although the cheekteeth are different in that they are rooted (thus showing distinct patterns of wear), not rootless (and hence ever growing) as in *Microtus*. The lower molars have inner and outer re-entrant angles of about the same depth. The angles are generally opposite one another so that they almost meet in the middle of the tooth. In *Microtus* and

* Species of possible occurrence in Colorado.

Map 9-95 Distribution of the southern red-backed vole (Clethrionomys gapperi) *in North America.*

Phenacomys, by contrast, inner and outer re-entrant angles of the lower molars are notably offset from each other. The palate ends at the level of M³ in a simple, transverse shelf with no posterior projection. Females have four pair of mammae.

NATURAL HISTORY — Red-backed voles are mostly associated with mesic coniferous forests at middle elevations in Colorado, occurring in both upper montane and subalpine forests (Armstrong 1977*a*; Merritt and Merritt 1978*a, b*; G. Williams 1955*a*). They are often common in mature lodge-pole pine stands or in mixed spruce-fir forests with good cone production and an abundance of surface litter including stumps, logs, and exposed roots of fallen trees. In such habitats chickarees are often abundant and red-backed voles frequently use the middens of the squirrels for cover and as a food source. Red-backed voles also use aspen woodlands although usually such habitats are more favorable for long-tailed and montane voles (Armstrong 1972, 1977*a*). Other habitats include

grassy meadows, willow riparian areas, talus, and krummholz.

Globular nests of grasses, mosses, and similar soft materials are constructed under suitable surface objects. Runways are not as well developed as in some other voles. Microhabitat studies (Armstrong 1977*a*, Belk et al. 1988, Wywialowski and Smith 1988) indicate strong affinity for situations with substantial ground cover or surface litter.

Red-backed voles are opportunistic feeders, eating a variety of fungi, roots, bark, berries, other fruit, seeds, and leaves (Merritt and Merritt 1978*a*, O. Williams 1955*c*). Seed consumption increases in winter, and fungi are often favored in summer (O. Williams and Finney 1964). Red-backed voles drink more water than some other small rodents, and this may relate to their selection of mesic sites. Daily metabolism was calculated at 6.45 kcal/day for voles averaging 19.1 g in body weight. Metabolic demand increases at a rate of 0.02 kcal/gram/day for each degree below the thermoneutral point of 26°C (Merritt and Merritt 1978*a*).

Red-backed voles are seasonally polyestrous with a postpartum estrus. The mating system is promiscuous. Gestation lasts about 18 days with the length of the breeding season estimated to be about seven months on Rabbit Ears Pass in Routt County (T. Vaughan 1969). On the Front Range the breeding season is at least seven-and-a-half months. Animals begin to breed in late winter and continue to produce litters into late fall. Litter size ranges from four to eight; the average is about six (Merritt and Merritt 1978*a*, T. Vaughan 1969). Females are reproductively mature at 3 to 4 months but most males do not breed until about 11 months of age. Young are naked, blind, and toothless at birth, weighing about 2 g. By day 4, skin pigmentation is developing rapidly, the animals have developed some sense of equilibrium, and they are able to crawl by day 5. Body hair is developed by the end of the first week as the incisors erupt. Eyes open by two weeks of age, about the same time that the young begin to eat

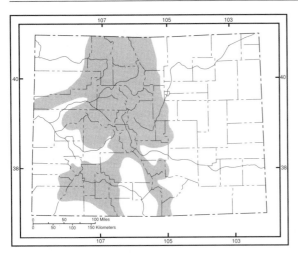

Map 9-96 Distribution of the southern red-backed vole (Clethrionomys gapperi) *in Colorado.*

solid food. The young usually are weaned by three weeks of age (Merritt 1981).

Red-backed voles are active year around, occupying home ranges of 0.01 to 0.5 ha. Density in Boulder County ranged from 2 to 48 animals per ha with highest numbers in late summer and early fall (Merritt 1985, Merritt and Merritt 1978*a,b*). Fall freezes and spring thaws were times of greatest vulnerability of voles. T. Vaughan (1969) estimated populations at fewer than 2.4 animals per hectare on Rabbit Ears Pass. Multiyear population cycles do not seem to occur in this species as they commonly do in other arvicolines.

Red-backed voles are most active at dusk and at night during the warmer months. During winter the animals become more diurnal as they are active under the snowpack (Merritt 1984). The animals reportedly are "shy," "nervous," and not especially social. Some aggression is shown during male-male and female-female encounters, but males and females get along well together and may share a nest. Females are sensitive when young are in the nest, and disturbance may result in cannibalism, abandonment, or movement of young. Longevity is usually one year or less, with

some animals surviving for up to 20 months (Merritt and Merritt 1978*a*).

Most mortality probably results from predation, fall freezes and spring thaws, and starvation during winter (Merritt 1984). A number of inconclusive and contradictory studies have been conducted on possible interspecific competition between this species and other small mammals including the meadow vole and deer mouse (Merritt 1981). During the breeding season the red-backed vole may be able to locally displace other species from woodland habitats but in turn may be displaced from grassy areas. Merritt (1981) reviewed the literature on the species.

DISTRIBUTION IN COLORADO — Red-backed voles are found throughout the mountains of the state. *Clethrionomys gapperi galei* is the subspecies of the central and northern mountains generally north of the upper Gunnison and Arkansas rivers; *C. g. gauti* is the subspecies in the mountains of the southern third of the state.

Phenacomys intermedius
HEATHER VOLE

DESCRIPTION — The heather vole is small and has a tail only slightly longer than the hindfoot. The pelage is long and soft, and dorsal color ranges from brown to grayish. The venter is silver gray. The tail is bicolored, dark above and pale below, often with a sprinkling of white hairs over the dorsal surface. The feet are white to pale gray. Usually there are stiff, orange hairs in the ears. Measurements are: total length 130–140 mm; length of tail 31–34 mm; length of hindfoot 16–19 mm; length of ear 13–17 mm; weight 30–50 g. The skull of adults is blocky with a square braincase and prominent supraorbital and lateral ridges. The palate does not end in a sharply transverse shelf as in *Clethrionomys*. The cheekteeth are rooted and without cusps, similar in general occlusal appearance to the teeth of other voles. However, the molars of the lower jaw have inner (lingual) re-entrant angles that are much deeper than the outer (buccal) re-entrant angles, extend-

Photograph by C. W. Schwartz/Animals Animals.

Photograph 9-50 Heather vole (Phenacomys intermedius).

Map 9-97 Distribution of the heather vole (Phenacomys intermedius) *in North America.*

ing more than halfway across the tooth surface. The first lower molar shows a high variability in number of closed occlusal triangles (three to seven) (McAllister and Hoffmann 1988). Females have four pairs of mammae. Superficially the heather vole may closely resemble some smaller specimens of the montane vole from which it can be separated by the rooted cheekteeth with their deep inner re-entrant angles.

NATURAL HISTORY — Heather voles occupy stands of spruce, fir, lodgepole, aspen, and ponderosa pine, and grassy meadows in montane forests, subalpine forests, and alpine tundra. Although never particularly abundant, they are generally adaptable to a number of different habitats (Negus 1950). In Colorado they are most often associated with moist to seasonally dry areas close to water. Armstrong (1977a) found them most common in spruce and lodgepole forests with ground cover of *Vaccinium*, such as frequently occur on glacial moraines.

Heather voles appear to be most active at night, foraging for green vegetation, bark of trees and shrubs, seeds, berries and fungi (Foster 1961, O. Williams and Finney 1964). The diet includes foliage and fruits of willows, myrtle blueberry, snowberry, and bog birch; kinnikinnnik may constitute the bulk of the diet locally. Bark of willow, birch,

laurel, and blueberry as well as seeds and lichens are important during fall, winter, and spring. The diet is broader than that of most *Microtus* and seems to include less abrasive plant materials. The animals store food (including fruits) in caches close to burrow entrances, which are used both summer and winter.

Heather voles are seasonally polyestrous. Most breeding occurs between May and September, with populations at higher elevations having a shorter season. Gestation is 19 to 24 days, and litter size is two to nine with an average of five or six. Overwintering females produce larger litters than do females having litters in their first summer. Studies in Colorado (Halfpenny and Ingraham 1983) suggest that litters from our area are slightly larger than those of northern populations. Individual females probably do not have more than three litters per year. Young females are of breeding age in four to six weeks, but males do not breed until the following year. As with other mice, young are blind, naked, and

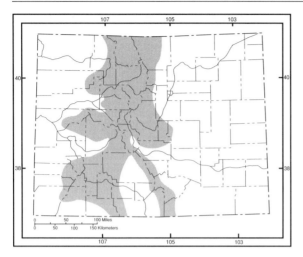

Map 9-98 Distribution of the heather vole (Phenacomys intermedius) *in Colorado.*

helpless at birth. In Colorado, newborn animals gained on average 0.82 g per day. Incisors erupted at one week, eyes opened at about 15 days, and young walked at about 16 days of age (Halfpenny and Ingraham 1983).

Population biology of the species is poorly known. A number of authors have reported it difficult to trap (S. Anderson 1959, Pruitt 1954, T. Vaughan 1969, O. Williams 1952), and livetrap mortality is high. Females show higher ratios of capture in traps than do males although sex ratios at birth approximate one to one. Density estimates from the Northern Rockies range from 0.5 to 10 animals per ha, but such estimates may be affected by low trapability (McAllister and Hoffmann 1988).

Heather voles are active year around. In summer they live in shallow burrow systems, usually less than 20 cm deep in the Northern Rockies (I. Cowan and Guiget 1956). Entrances usually are hidden by surface litter or overhanging vegetation. Nests are made of grasses and other dried vegetation with a diameter of 10 to 15 cm. Winter nests reportedly have thicker walls and are better insulated. Winter nests under snow cover may be located on the surface of the ground in protected

areas under shrubs, dead timber, or rock overhangs. Although most activity appears to be solitary, winter huddling by family groups is reported in Canada (Banfield 1974). Predators include marten, occasionally long-tailed weasels (Quick 1951), and several species of owls and hawks. The literature on the species was reviewed by McAllister and Hoffmann (1988).

DISTRIBUTION IN COLORADO — The heather vole is known from scattered records throughout the high mountains and plateaus of the state, but local distribution of the species is poorly known. Elevations of captured animals range from 2,130 m (7,000 ft) to above timberline (Armstrong 1972). One subspecies, *Phenacomys intermedius intermedius*, occurs in Colorado.

Photograph by Roger W. Barbour.

Photograph 9-51 Long-tailed vole (Microtus longicaudus).

Microtus longicaudus
LONG-TAILED VOLE

DESCRIPTION — This vole is fairly small bodied and long-tailed (the tail is greater than one-third the length of the head and body). Dorsal color is reddish brown to brownish gray interspersed with numerous black-tipped hairs. The ventral surface is gray to buff-gray. Measurements are: total length 174–196 mm; length of tail 53–68 mm; length of hindfoot 20–22 mm; length of ear 13–

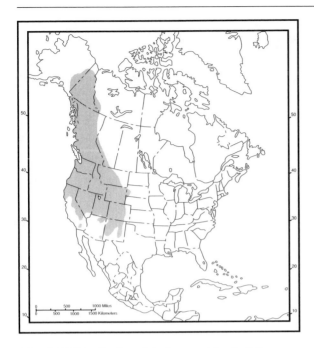

Map 9-99 *Distribution of the long-tailed vole* (Microtus longicaudus) *in North America.*

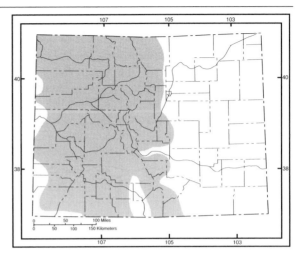

Map 9-100 *Distribution of the long-tailed vole* (Microtus longicaudus) *in Colorado.*

17 mm; weight 36–59 g. The skull is long and flattened with large, rounded auditory bullae. The first lower molar has a large anterior lake of dentine followed by five triangles and a crescent-shaped posterior prism. The second upper molar has four triangular prisms. By contrast, the meadow vole, which can approximate the size and even the tail length of the long-tailed vole, has five triangles on the second molar. Females have four pair of mammae.

NATURAL HISTORY — Long-tailed voles are most often associated with marshy to dry grassy areas adjacent to water in the mountainous parts of the state. They may be especially abundant in aspen woodlands. They have a wide ecological tolerance (perhaps because they are poor competitors with other arvicolines such as montane and meadow voles or because they are not obligatory runway builders) and can be found in sedge-forb meadows on alpine tundra, subalpine meadows and forests, riparian willow and alder thickets, and even in grassy, halophytic, semidesert shrublands or be-

neath sagebrush in western Colorado. Fires or clear cutting may favor this species, especially several years into succession (Van Horne 1982).

Long-tailed voles feed mostly on green vegetation, especially from dicots, as well as on fruits and seeds. During the winter, bark, buds, and twigs of most locally common trees and shrubs, including spruce, aspen, oak, and snowberry are also consumed. Fescues, sedges, yarrow, and Oregon-grape are also commonly used. O. Williams and Finney (1964) reported the fungus *Endogone* in the diet in populations west of Boulder. Free water is probably consumed if available but does not appear to be required.

This vole breeds from mid-April or early May to October (Conley 1976). Most litters are born during late spring and summer. In the laboratory, mean litter size is about five and ranges from one to seven (Colvin and Colvin 1970). Studies in Alaska suggest that few females have more than two litters in their lifetime and that most adults die in their first year of life (Van Horne 1982).

Long-tailed voles may be active both day and night and do not make well-defined runways. Nests of grass and stems of forbs are located underground or under surface litter. Greatest distance between captures (a rough index of home range) averaged 53 m in California. In Alaska, animals were mostly nocturnal, and home ranges of males were larger than home ranges of females (Van Horne 1982). Long-tailed voles are less aggressive than either montane or Mexican voles. Finley et al. (1986), Randall and Johnson (1979), and others suggest that long-tailed voles are displaced in the presence of more dominant species.

Densities of 5 to 120 animals per hectare have been reported in California (Jenkins 1948) and New Mexico (Conley 1976), respectively. Ten to 20 animals per ha is probably average for populations in good habitat when not undergoing major population cycles. Population dynamics have not been studied in detail although workers in Washington speculate that three-year cycles occur, whereas both annual and possibly longer population cycles seem to occur in New Mexico (Conley 1976). Documentation of predation is poor; however, several species of owls, prairie falcons (Marti and Braun 1975), weasels (Hayward 1949), and martens are known predators. Literature on the long-tailed vole was reviewed by Smolen and Keller (1987).

DISTRIBUTION IN COLORADO — The long-tailed vole is a common mammal over the mountain and plateau country of the western two-thirds of Colorado. According to Armstrong (1972), one subspecies, *Microtus longicaudus longicaudus*, occurs in Colorado. However, Hoffmeister (1986) considered *M. l. mordax* to be a valid name for some populations from the Four Corners region (although Long 1965 considered *M. l. mordax* to be a synonym of *M. l. longicaudus*).

Microtus mexicanus
MEXICAN VOLE

DESCRIPTION — This short-tailed vole has a tail less than 30 percent of the length of the head and body, and usually less than 35 mm. The dorsal pelage is typically dark brown with the venter buffy to ochraceous gray. The length of the hind-

Photograph 9-52 Mexican vole (Microtus mexicanus).

foot is usually less than 20 mm. Measurements are: total length 122–154 mm; length of tail 20–34 mm; length of hindfoot 16–21 mm; length of ear 13–16 mm; weight 28–32 g. The skull is short and broad with the zygomatic breadth usually greater than 60 percent of the condylobasal length. The

Map 9-101 Distribution of the Mexican vole (Microtus mexicanus) *in North America.*

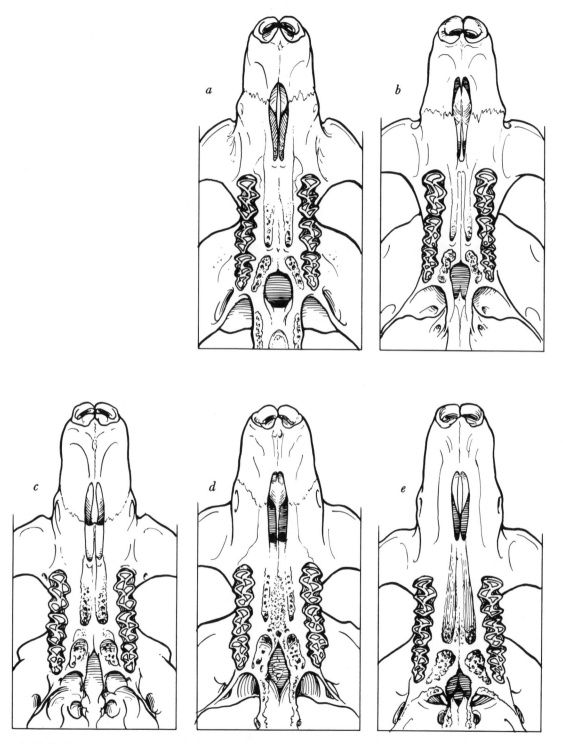

Figure 9-11 Occlusal views of upper cheek teeth and incisive foramina of: A. montane vole (Microtus montanus): B. meadow vole (Microtus pennsylvanicus); C. prairie vole (Microtus ochrogaster); D. Mexican vole (Microtus mexicanus); E. long-tailed vole (Microtus longicaudus).

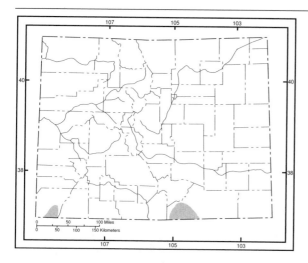

Map 9-102 Distribution of the Mexican vole (Microtus mexicanus) *in Colorado.*

last upper molar has five dentine lakes, similar to *M. pennsylvanicus* and *M. montanus*. Unlike *M. pennsylvanicus*, the second upper molar has only four dentine lakes with no posterior accessory loop. *M. mexicanus* differs from *M. montanus* in having incisive foramina broad and rounded posteriorly rather than narrow or abruptly constricted posteriorly. The jugal of the zygomatic is expanded, and the posterior margin of the palate is notched or grooved. Females have only two pair of mammae whereas other arvicolines in Colorado typically have three or more pairs. Animals can easily be confused with *Phenacomys intermedius* and *M. montanus* unless the skull is carefully checked.

NATURAL HISTORY — Little is known about the biology of this arvicoline in Colorado. The Mexican vole appears to favor drier sites with abundant grass. It usually occurs in grassy areas in ponderosa pine woodland or savannah, piñon-juniper woodlands, or montane shrublands. However, observations in Colorado, New Mexico (Finley et al. 1986), and Arizona (Hoffmeister 1986) suggest that it can survive in a wide variety of habitats, including dense midgrasses, riparian areas, sagebrush, the lower margins of spruce-fir forests, and forest-meadow ecotones. It apparently is not un-

common to have Mexican, long-tailed, and meadow voles in the same general areas at higher elevations in southeastern Colorado, with the long-tailed vole perhaps being displaced by the Mexican vole (Finley et al. 1986).

Little is known about reproduction in the species. Keller (1985) listed it as a seasonally restricted breeder. In New Mexico, Conley (1976) reported breeding from May through November. Data from Arizona suggest that females breed from April through August with lower litter size than typical for most arvicolines (L. N. Brown 1968). Litter size ranges from one to four (mean, 2.2–2.5), in keeping with the small number of mammae.

Annual fluctuations ranged from 15 to 50 animals per hectare in New Mexico, but the animals are thought not to exhibit cyclical populations. Mexican voles in Arizona maintain two peaks of activity, one during the middle of the day and the other in early evening. Predators are probably similar to those of other voles, including snakes and most avian and mammalian carnivores.

DISTRIBUTION IN COLORADO — Mexican voles were first documented in Colorado at Mesa Verde (Rodeck and Anderson 1956). Recent interpretations of former collections (see discussion in the account of the montane vole) and new collections indicate that specimens of Mexican voles have previously been misidentified and that they may occur fairly regularly in southeastern Colorado (Finley et al. 1986). Studies in New Mexico (Findley et al. 1975) suggest that the species has made significant range expansions in recent times. One subspecies, *Microtus mexicanus mogollonensis*, is currently recognized in Colorado.

Microtus montanus
MONTANE VOLE

DESCRIPTION — The montane vole is a medium-sized vole with a tail less than 40 percent of the length of the head and body. The dorsal color is grayish brown to brownish yellow. The venter is

Photograph by Roger W. Barbour.

Photograph 9-53 Montane vole (Microtus montanus).

silver gray with white-tipped, black hairs. The tail is indistinctly bicolored. Measurements are: total length 140–182 mm; length of tail 34–62 mm; length of hindfoot 17–22 mm; length of ear 11–18 mm; weight 35–60 g. The skull is stout with a square brain case. The last upper molar has five dentine lakes and the second molar has four. The incisive foramina are narrow and constricted posteriorly. The posterior edge of the premaxillaries does not extend beyond the posterior margins of the nasals. Females have four pairs of mammae.

NATURAL HISTORY — Montane voles generally occupy moist to wet habitats with thick grass or forb cover, including aspen stands. They also occur in drier grasslands with forbs and sagebrush, but usually in lower numbers (Armstrong 1977a). Typically they are found close to water although in winter they may move farther away by using tunnels under the snow.

Montane voles are highly selective feeders; five plant species constituted nearly 70 percent of the diet. Summer food consists mostly of leaves of forbs (80 percent), and includes grasses and sedges (9 percent) and fungi (3 percent) (T. Vaughan 1969). Grasses, bark, and twigs may become more important in winter after forbs have become less palatable. Seeds are not utilized to any extent (T. Vaughan 1974).

Montane voles construct well-developed runways and may be active at any time of day or night. They build a globular underground or surface nest of grass, about 13 cm in diameter with two entrances, in a shallow burrow system (Jannett 1982).

Montane voles are polygynous, except at low densities, when they may be monogamous by default. They do not form pair bonds. Adult, breeding montane voles are territorial, although male and female territories exhibit some overlap (Jannett 1980).

They probably reproduce from April to October in Colorado. Litter size averages 6 with a range of 2 to 10. Females are polyestrous with a postpartum estrus. Ovulation is induced; gestation takes about 21 days (Keller 1985, T. Vaughan 1969). At low population densities, females abandon the brood nest when the young are about 15 days old. At high densities, females remain at the nest and are tolerant of the young, allowing offspring from at least two litters to nest with her. During certain population densities and demographic conditions, breeding occurs in winter under the snow (Jannett 1980). Adults maintain separate nests and paternal care of young is nonexistent under natural conditions (McGuire and Novak 1986). Males, in fact, are less active than females during this period and spend much time resting in the nest or in a runway.

Young voles breed first in the year of their birth. Survival rates of early summer litters, and their young produced at the end of the breeding season, are important in determining the size of populations in the fall (T. Vaughan 1969). Large litter size and relatively few litters per year are adaptations to the constraints of a short growing season. As with other arvicolines, populations can show large fluctuations, often in three- to four-year cycles. On Rabbit Ears Pass, variation in densities from less than one to over 30 animals per ha were found during a three-year study (T. Vaughan 1974). However, studies in marshland adjacent to the Great Salt Lake in Utah over a

Map 9-103 Distribution of the montane vole (Microtus montanus) *in North America.*

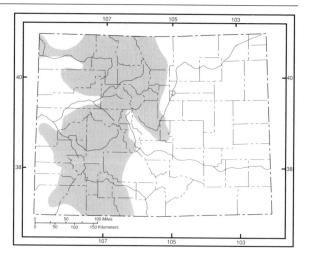

Map 9-104 Distribution of the montane vole (Microtus montanus) *in Colorado.*

nine-year period showed no dramatic crashes (Negus et al. 1986).

Predators include coyotes, weasels, kestrels, Swainson's and red-tailed hawks, and great horned owls (Jannett 1984). In optimal habitats for meadow voles, montane voles were excluded, but the latter species has broader ecological tolerances and agonistically dominated meadow voles (Stoecker 1970). More research is needed on factors regulating the distributional patterns and interactions of Coloradan voles.

DISTRIBUTION IN COLORADO — The montane vole is found throughout the mountains of Colorado and locally is quite common, from about 1,830 m (6,000 ft) in elevation to well above treeline. Dalquest (1975) reported the species from Raton Pass, Las Animas County; Mellott and Choate (1984) published new records from 32 km northwest of Trinidad. However, a review by Finley et al. (1986) corrected the identification of the specimens, recognizing them as *M. mexicanus*. Thus, to date no records of this species are known from Colorado south of the Arkansas River and east of the Sangre de Cristo Range. *Microtus montanus fusus* occurs in the southern and south-central mountains generally south of the Colorado River; *M. m. nanus* occurs in the mountainous northern portion of the state, generally north of a line from about Glenwood Springs to Pikes Peak (S. Anderson 1954).

Microtus ochrogaster
PRAIRIE VOLE

DESCRIPTION — This species is medium sized with a gray-brown to reddish brown dorsum and a pale buffy to grayish buff belly. Ventral color separates it readily from other voles in Colorado, all of which are silver gray beneath. Measurements are: total length 150–190 mm; length of tail 33–45 mm; length of hindfoot 20–23 mm; length of ear 11–15 mm; weight 50–75 g. The bicolored tail is short relative to other voles of eastern Colorado, typically less than 30 percent of the length of head and body. The skull is similar to others of the genus; however, the third lower molar has three loops of dentine but no triangles. The last upper molar has four dentine lakes somewhat similar to the pattern of the sagebrush vole de-

Photograph 9-54 Prairie vole (Microtus ochrogaster).

scribed below. The posterior margins of the premaxillary extend beyond the margins of the nasals. Females have six mammae.

NATURAL HISTORY — As the name implies, the prairie vole is adapted to the grasslands of interior North America. In northeastern Colorado it inhabits upland swales, grassy areas, edges of irrigation ditches and fence rows, and even the fringes of wooded riparian habitat consisting of open stands of willow and cottonwood (Archibald 1963, Cruzan 1968, R. Mitchell 1972, J. Fitzgerald 1978, Moulton et al. 1981*a, b*). Along the northern Front Range, the animals occupy the grassy understory of shrublands in many foothills canyons. In southeastern Colorado it has been reported from sage-grassland, grass-forb, and shrub woodland communities (A. Carey 1978, M. Reed and Choate 1988). In areas of sympatry with *Microtus pennsylvanicus* in northeastern Colorado, the prairie vole invariably occupies drier sites and usually occurs at lower densities than does the meadow vole.

In dense vegetation, well-developed, extensive runway systems are formed, but such trails are not always conspicuous on drier sites. The number of runways is positively correlated with vole density (D. Carroll and Getz 1976). The species can construct shallow (usually less than 10 cm) burrow sys-

tems in friable soils using such burrows as shelters from which to make periodic foraging expeditions. Nests, constructed to 30 cm deep in the burrow system, are of grasses, shredded bark, and similar materials and may contain large amounts of stored food including seeds and roots. If vegetation is dense the species uses surface grass nests located in depressions or sheltered by surface objects. Prairie voles are active at all times of the year and at any time of day although most activity in the warm summer months occurs at dusk or at night.

Prairie voles feed on stems, leaves, and underground parts of a wide variety of plants. Grasses are common food items but laboratory studies indicate that prairie voles cannot survive on a strict grass diet (Batzli and Cole 1979). They also feed on the bark of trees and shrubs. Arthropods can be important food items, especially in late summer. Food caches of seeds, cuttings, and roots are often stored in burrow systems.

Prairie voles have a high degree of sociality compared to many other species of *Microtus*. They are monogamous (J. A. Thomas and Birney 1979), unusual in mammals — only about 12 percent of mammalian species are monogamous (Eisenberg 1981). Groups are formed by the addition of the offspring and other nonrelated adults (Getz and Carter 1980, Getz et al. 1990). Mates form strong pair bonds and both parents assist in rearing young and in maintaining trails and burrows. Home ranges average about 0.1–0.25 ha, decreasing in size with increased population size and/or herb production. Home ranges of family units overlap and aggression associated with territoriality may be shown around the nesting burrows (Getz 1962).

The species is polyestrous with breeding occurring throughout the year although the prevalence of pregnant females declines in the colder winter months. In the extremely hot, dry weather of midsummer, breeding may also taper off. Peaks of breeding activity seem to coincide with increased precipitation during the growing season. Females must be near males to come into estrus. They exhibit postpartum estrus and show induced ovula-

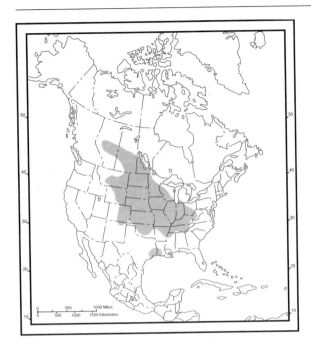

Map 9-105 Distribution of the prairie vole (Microtus ochrogaster) *in North America.*

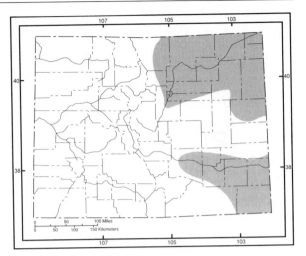

Map 9-106 Distribution of the prairie vole (Microtus ochrogaster) *in Colorado.*

tion about 10 hours after copulation. Gestation takes about 21 days, and the young are born naked and blind. Litters probably average three to four young with a range of one to seven. The young grow rapidly, gaining 0.6 to 0.8 g per day, and are weaned by about four weeks of age. Suppression of growth and reproductive maturity occurs as long as the young remain in the family group; dispersal is necessary for full maturation. Young female prairie voles can breed at about five weeks of age when two-thirds grown. Males reach sexual maturity one or two weeks later.

Populations fluctuate widely in sites of known occurrence. Long-term research in some areas suggests that the species is not characterized by years of cyclical peaks and declines, but rather annual peaks of population highs and lows (Abramsky and Tracy 1979). In other studies cycle intervals of two to four years have been noted. The reasons for population cycles are poorly understood but may be associated with disease, quality of foods, or physiological responses to subtle environ-

mental changes. Survival of early juveniles and females were the best predictors of population growth in Kansas, where a two-year cycle occurred during a four-year study (Gaines and Rose 1976).

Prairie voles are short lived, with mortality of adults during the breeding season ranging from 20 to 70 percent per month. Mortality in winter decreases to less than 50 percent. Captive voles have lived 16 months; in the wild, few live more than one year. All of the small to medium-sized carnivores prey on these voles, with birds of prey being particularly effective. Stalling (1990) reviewed the literature on the species.

DISTRIBUTION IN COLORADO — The prairie vole is locally common in suitable habitat along the lower South Platte and Republican rivers. It has recently been reported also from several sites in southeastern Colorado (A. Carey 1978, M. Reed and Choate 1988). *Microtus ochrogaster haydenii* may be the only subspecies in Colorado. *M. o. taylori* is a subspecies named from southwestern Kansas and known from within a few miles of the Colorado border near Holly. That subspecies has been reported as extirpated at the type locality (Choate and Williams 1978). Whether it exists in Colorado is not known.

Photograph 9-55 Meadow vole (Microtus pennsylvanicus).

Microtus pennsylvanicus
MEADOW VOLE

DESCRIPTION — This species is fairly large and dark with a gray belly. Dorsal color is usually dark gray-brown to chestnut. The tail is bicolored and scantily haired. The tail is longer than in most prairie voles but relatively shorter than in the long-tailed vole. The ears are rounded and inconspicuous beneath the long fur of the head. Younger animals are typically darker than older individuals. Measurements are: total length 155–192 mm; length of tail 35–67 mm; length of hindfoot 20–24 mm; length of ear 11–18 mm; weight 35–75 g. Females have four pairs of mammae. The skull is similar to that of other members of the genus, and identification is based on characters of the occlusal surface of the rootless cheek-teeth. The second upper molar has four dentine lakes plus a rounded posterior loop. The last upper molar has five rounded dentine lakes. The premaxillaries do not extend past the posterior margins of the nasals, and the nasals are rounded posteriorly. The incisive foramina are long and relatively narrow, showing only slight expansion anteriorly.

NATURAL HISTORY — The meadow vole has the widest distribution of any species of *Microtus*, and its biology has been studied extensively in eastern North America. The meadow vole is invariably associated with moist habitats. In mountainous areas it requires moist to wet meadows or bog habitats with lush cover of grasses, forbs, rushes, or sedges. On the eastern plains and along the foothills it is most common in marshy wetlands along riparian corridors. Ecology and competitive interactions between this and other *Microtus* species have been studied locally (Cruzan 1968) and more generally (Koplin and Hoffmann 1968). When found in association with other voles the meadow vole typically occupies the wetter areas. The prairie vole displaces it in drier habitats of the eastern plains; long-tailed and montane voles may displace it in drier montane habitats (Douglass 1976).

As with other voles, the food is largely green plant material during the warmer months. Clover, alfalfa, and dandelions are readily consumed. During winter, dried grass and herbaceous matter, bark, twigs and buds are eaten. The animals build winter food caches. Meadow voles tend to eat more grasses and sedges than do other voles, in keeping with the moist environments they occupy.

Meadow voles are active year around at any time of the day or night, with diurnal activity increasing under dense cover and during the winter when snow covers and protects the runway. Runways littered with grass clippings lead between nests and foraging areas. Nests are globular, built of grass and similar materials. The nest may be located on the surface in protected areas or housed within the burrow. Meadow voles swim readily and in very wet areas they tend to build their nests on high points of ground or in well-drained clumps of grass.

Meadow voles are capable of breeding year around but probably most success in Colorado occurs during the spring, summer, and early fall. Breeding males are attracted to estrous females and compete for mating opportunities. Females are polyestrous with a postpartum estrus. Ovulation is induced by copulation, and gestation takes

Map 9-107 Distribution of the meadow vole (Microtus pennsylvanicus) *in North America.*

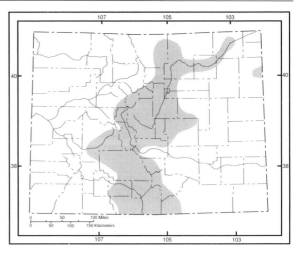

Map 9-108 Distribution of the meadow vole (Microtus pennsylvanicus) *in Colorado.*

21 days. As with other arvicolines, the young are born naked, blind, and helpless. Litter size ranges from one to 11 with an average of four to six (Keller 1985). Females of large body size have the largest litters. Size of litters has not been statistically correlated with latitude or elevation, but summer litters are 10 to 14 percent larger than those at other seasons. Young meadow voles grow rapidly, reaching weaning age by two weeks and breeding age by about six weeks.

Individuals are solitary and intolerant of conspecifics. Males are particularly aggressive when in reproductive condition or when populations are high (Getz 1960, 1962). Vocalizations often accompany aggressive threats (Krebs 1970). Home range size ranges from about 160 to 3,500 m² and those of males are larger than those of females (Van Vleck 1969). Home ranges decrease in size when populations are high and during the winter. Individuals, especially males, often shift home ranges. Defended areas, or territories, are small — roughly 7 m in diameter (Getz 1961).

Populations cycle in numbers both seasonally and also every two to five years. Densities during population peaks sometimes reach hundreds of individuals per hectare. At low points in the cycle, densities may be only a few animals per hectare. Cycles have been associated with a variety of causes including food quality, predation, local climate, physiological stress, and genetically linked behaviors (Krebs and Myers 1974). Some individuals in populations readily disperse, perhaps an adaptation for survival in environments where suitable habitat is limited and often not contiguous. The dispersing individuals apparently differ in genetic and behavioral makeup from sedentary ones (Krebs 1970).

Mortality is high — few animals live to one year of age and juvenile mortality is often close to 90 percent. Mean survival time of adults averages about eight to ten weeks, with adult females surviving slightly longer than males. Most aerial or terrestrial predators — including owls, hawks, bitterns, snakes, coyotes, foxes, weasels, and larger shrews — prey on meadow voles, especially when populations of the rodents are high. Reich (1981) reviewed the literature on the species. Tamarin (1985) edited a comprehensive review of the biology of North American members of the genus.

DISTRIBUTION IN COLORADO — Meadow voles are locally common in favorable habitat. Their distribution in Colorado is in discontinuous pieces, probably a remnant of a more nearly continuous range in glacial times recently past. *Microtus pennsylvanicus finitis* is restricted to the Republican watershed in Yuma County; *M. p. modestus* occurs in the mountains and parklands of south-central Colorado, including the wetlands of the San Luis Valley; *M. p. uligocola* occurs in the South Platte River to its headwaters in the mountains of the Front Range (S. Anderson 1956).

Photograph by Andrew Langford.

Photograph 9-56 Sagebrush vole (Lemmiscus curtatus).

Lemmiscus curtatus
SAGEBRUSH VOLE

DESCRIPTION — The sagebrush vole is small and short tailed with dense, long, soft pelage. The dorsal pelage is buff-gray to gray with paler sides. The venter is buff to silver gray, and the tail is indistinctly bicolored. Hairs are dark gray at their bases. The tail is well haired but short, only about as long as the hindfoot. The ears are small, averaging slightly more than half the length of the hindfoot. The posterior soles of the feet are well haired. Measurements are: total length 100–142 mm; length of tail 16–30 mm; length of hindfoot 14–18 mm; length of ear 9–16 mm; weight 17–38

g. The skull is generally similar to that of other arvicolines but has well-developed auditory bullae that extend back beyond the occipital condyles and hence are readily visible from above. The last upper and lower molars typically have only four dentine lakes compared to the five present in other arvicolines in Colorado. The pattern of the lakes consists of anterior and posterior loops separated by two more-or-less triangular prisms. The inner and outer re-entrant angles are about equal in depth. The molars are ever growing. Females have four pair of mammae.

NATURAL HISTORY — The species is aptly named; it is strongly tied with sagebrush and may be locally abundant on well-managed sagebrush–wheatgrass rangeland. It is also found in brushy canyon and hill country where sage, rabbitbrush, and wheat-grasses are common plant associates.

Sagebrush voles are strict herbivores feeding on a variety of green vegetation, mostly grasses. Leaves and other softer tissues are consumed, but seeds (except for those of wheat-grass) are not typically eaten. Forbs and woody plants reported in the diet include greasewood, rabbitbrush, sage, winterfat, several species of mustard, lupine and other legumes, and several composites (Maser et al. 1974, F. Miller 1930). Legumes made up much of the stomach contents in a South Dakota study. Inflorescences, bark, and twigs of sagebrush are important in the winter months. Occasionally, sagebrush voles steal clippings accumulated by deer mice (Maser et al. 1974). Cut vegetation may be stored in loose piles near burrow entrances or along runways.

Sagebrush voles are active year around at practically any time of the day. Most activity occurs during late afternoon and early night. Activity also picks up around dawn. Runway systems are wider than those of *Microtus*, although typically not as distinct because they are in areas with a sparser understory. The voles dig clusters of burrows with multiple entrances (range 8 to 30), usually located at the base of shrubs, especially sagebrush. Abandoned pocket gopher systems are also utilized (F. Miller 1930, Warren 1942). Burrows, aver-

Map 9-109 *Distribution of the sagebrush vole* (Lemmiscus curtatus) *in North America.*

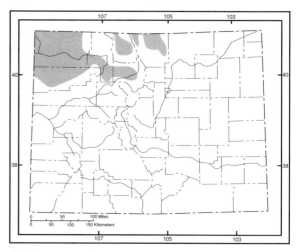

Map 9-110 *Distribution of the sagebrush vole* (Lemmiscus curtatus) *in Colorado.*

aging about 45 mm in diameter, can go as deep as 46 cm and are littered with clippings of vegetation. Nest chambers are lined with leaves and stems of grasses and have multiple entrances (Dearden 1969). Snow tunnels are used in winter and also have cuttings of vegetation at scattered intervals. Fecal material is often deposited in scat piles along runway systems but not in the underground burrow system.

Sagebrush voles occur singly or in pairs. During the breeding season a mated pair shares a nest and continues to do so after young are born. The male, although present, does not actively participate in the care of the young as is seen in the prairie vole (Hofmann et al. 1989, Mullican and Keller 1986).

Sagebrush voles are polyestrous and capable of breeding year around, but most breeding occurs in the warmer spring and early summer months (W. James and Booth 1952, Maser et al. 1974). Breeding activity may be significantly reduced dur-

ing extremely hot weather or periods of low precipitation. Probably three to four litters are produced annually in Colorado. The estrous cycle lasts about 20 days. Gestation takes about 25 days followed by a postpartum estrus. Four to six altricial young are born. The young are weaned at about three weeks and capable of breeding at about two months of age. Embryo counts and trapping ratios tend to favor males slightly, but data may be skewed by trapping techniques or the behavior of males, especially during peaks in population cycles.

Numbers show extreme local variation. They may increase dramatically in years with mild winters or with increased summer and fall precipitation. In sagebrush habitat in Idaho, densities ranged from 4 to 16 animals per ha (Mullican and Keller 1986).

A variety of predators probably feed on the sagebrush vole — owls are particularly successful. Bobcats, foxes, coyotes, weasels, rattlesnakes, and bullsnakes undoubtedly take their toll. The species is considered by public health experts to be one of the primary reservoirs of sylvatic plague in Washington. Literature on the sagebrush vole was reviewed by L. Carroll and Genoways (1980).

DISTRIBUTION IN COLORADO — Sagebrush voles are associated with shrublands in northwestern and north-central Colorado. They do not seem to be common in any locality but this may be due in part to lack of information. One subspecies, *Lemmiscus curtatus levidensis*, occurs in Colorado. For a number of years this animal was considered to represent the Holarctic genus *Lagurus*, and *Lemmiscus* was considered a subgenus. We follow Carleton and Musser (1984) in use of the generic name *Lemmiscus* for the sagebrush vole.

Photograph 9-57 Muskrat (Ondatra zibethicus).

Ondatra zibethicus
COMMON MUSKRAT

DESCRIPTION — The muskrat is by far the largest and most specialized of the arvicoline rodents in Colorado. The body is stocky with a large, rounded head. The laterally flattened, scaly tail is about as long as the head and body. The hindfeet are enlarged and partially webbed, with stiff hairs fringing the toes. The forefeet are small and dexterous. The mouth can be closed behind the incisors, and the ears are valvular, both adaptations for their semiaquatic life. The eyes are relatively small and the ears are short, rounded, and barely visible above the surrounding fur. Most muskrats in Colorado have rich reddish brown to blackish brown pelage with slightly paler underparts. The gray-brown underfur is very soft, overlain by longer, coarser guard hairs. The dense underfur is nearly impervious to water. The winter pelage has a lustrous sheen. Measurements are: total length 450–550 mm; length of tail 200–250 mm; length of hindfoot 65–78; length of ear 19–21 mm; weight 650–1800 g. Females have three pair of mammae, and males have a well-developed baculum.

The skull is typical of that of the arvicolines, stoutly built and angular with an abrupt constriction at the anterior margin of the braincase. The incisive foramina are narrow and long. The ever-growing incisors are long and yellowish. The molars are rooted; the crown pattern consists of lakes of dentine and ridges of enamel.

Small muskrats might be confused with Norway rats, from which they differ by having a laterally compressed tail and webbed hindfeet. The cheek-teeth of the Norway rat show rows of cusps and not lakes of dentine. From beavers, muskrats differ in much smaller size and a relatively longer, laterally compressed tail (in contrast to the dorsoventrally flattened tail of the beaver).

NATURAL HISTORY — Because of its wide distribution and economic importance as a furbearer, the muskrat has been studied extensively, although detailed studies of muskrat populations in Colorado have not been made. Muskrats are semiaquatic animals occupying practically all aquatic habitats, from cat-tail marshes and ponds to lakes and rivers. In Colorado they range from the edges of the alpine tundra through all other ecosystems in the riparian zone. At highest elevations they are largely restricted to beaver ponds. In agricultural areas they frequently use irrigation ditches for movement to more permanent water sources. They live in burrows in banks along the water source or in conical houses constructed of leafy vegetation. Colorado has restricted areas of marshland, so most muskrats live in bank burrows. Burrowing can damage earthen dams and unlined irrigation ditches and canals.

Map 9-111 Distribution of the muskrat (Ondatra zibethicus) *in North America.*

Muskrats are primarily herbivorous but they will eat carrion, fish, crayfish, and molluscs, especially when plant materials are scarce or animal matter readily available. Obvious signs of muskrat activity are cut, floating strands of vegetation, and feeding platforms located on floating, matted vegetation or on flattened areas on banks adjacent to water. Large numbers of muskrats in an area may decimate emergent vegetation creating a situation termed "eat-out." This condition can affect nesting success of waterfowl, so populations of muskrats are frequently controlled in waterfowl production areas.

Muskrat houses are built from the most common emergent vegetation including sedges, rushes, and cat-tails. Bank dens also are excavated. One to several nest chambers are hollowed out in the house or burrow and lined with plant material. The nest chambers are above the waterline and the den is accessible only through underwater tunnels. The size and development of houses varies with season, being larger and better insulated in

winter. Small "feeding houses" may be constructed away from the main den. Most house-building activity occurs in spring, following ice breakup, or during late summer and early fall. Houses have a usable life span of five to six months. During the winter several individuals may huddle in the nest for warmth. Abandoned dens frequently are used by waterfowl as nesting platforms.

Both sexes are territorial, and dominance hierarchies establish individual territories. Competition for breeding territories is intense. Females may be more aggressive than males and have been known to kill intruders (Errington 1963). Typically, juveniles and low-ranking animals are forced to occupy marginal habitat or migrate to new locations.

The mating structure is promiscuous or loosely monogamous (Errington 1963). Scent marking with the perianal musk glands is frequent prior to breeding. Mating occurs while the animals are partially submerged. Muskrats are polyestrous, with a cycle of about 30 days (Beer 1950). Muskrats in north-temperate areas (including Colorado) are seasonal breeders, the first litters typically being born in late April or May. Probably two litters are typical for our area, and three are relatively uncommon. In the southeastern United States, up to five litters are produced. Gestation takes 25 to 30 days, with litter size ranging from four to eight. Newborn muskrats are naked and blind, with round tails. By about two weeks of age, they are furred with the eyes open. They are weaned by four weeks. The tail becomes conspicuously compressed laterally during the second month of development. Muskrats generally first reproduce following their first winter although some precocial breeding is reported by individuals from early litters (Errington 1963).

Muskrats are mostly crepuscular to nocturnal. Major activity peaks occur in late afternoon and near midnight, but in quiet, undisturbed areas they may be active during the daytime. Home ranges of individuals or family groups composed of females and young are typically small, and most activity occurs within 15 m of the nest (MacArthur

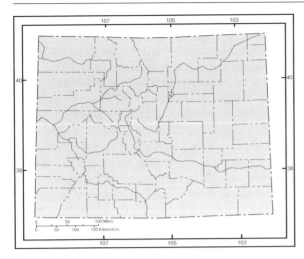

Map 9-112 *Distribution of the muskrat* (Ondatra zibethicus) *in Colorado.*

1978). Males may participate in parental care and are very tolerant of the young (Errington 1940).

Populations of muskrats are prone to 5- to 10-year cyclical fluctuations related to disease and other density-dependent control mechanisms. In good habitat, populations can exceed 55 animals per ha, although such numbers rapidly deplete food reserves (Willner et al. 1980). Dispersal occurs in spring due to thawing and the increase in hormonal levels associated with breeding.

Muskrats, especially kits, are preyed on by a variety of species, especially mink and raccoon. Other terrestrial predators include foxes, coyotes, and dogs. Avian predators take relatively few muskrats. Zoonotic diseases include tularemia, hemorrhagic disease, and leptospirosis. Although prices and harvest fluctuate widely, muskrats are the most valuable semiaquatic furbearer in North America (Perry 1982, Willner et al. 1980). Over 5 million animals are harvested most years and they are valued at $10 to $20 million. Populations in some parts of the United States are highly managed. Humans are the major population control, and up to 80 percent harvest can occur without depleting managed populations. Colorado has a liberal trapping season for the species. Willner et

al.(1980), Perry (1982), and Boutin and Birkenholz (1986) reviewed the literature.

DISTRIBUTION IN COLORADO — Muskrats occur statewide, wherever there is sufficient permanent water and a food supply, from the edges of alpine tarns to riparian wetlands on the plains and in semidesert valleys. They are often abundant locally. *Ondatra zibethicus cinnamominus* is the subspecies of the eastern plains; *O. z. osoyoosensis* is the subspecies of the western two-thirds of the state.

Synaptomys cooperi
SOUTHERN BOG LEMMING

DESCRIPTION — The southern bog lemming is heavyset with a large head and a very short tail. The tail is about the same length as the hindfoot. The pelage is longer and coarser than that of other prairie-dwelling voles. Dorsal color varies from golden brown to brownish gray with a somewhat grizzled appearance. The flanks may show white hairs in the vicinity of glands, most pronounced in adult males. The venter is slate to silvery gray in color. Measurements are: total length 125–155 mm; tail length 17–25 mm; hindfoot 17–26 mm; ear 10–14 mm; weight 35–55 g. The skull is robust and the upper incisors have a shallow but conspicuous lateral groove on the anterior surface. That character along with the robust build and short tail distinguish it from other voles of northeastern Colorado.

NATURAL HISTORY — The southern bog lemming has yet to be documented in Colorado but may be expected. These voles tolerate a variety of habitat types ranging from upland grasslands to mesic grassland and sedge areas and riparian gallery forest with adequate ground cover. The animal could occur in Colorado in ungrazed riparian habitats along the Republican River. Habitats favorable for meadow voles and short-tailed shrews could support bog lemmings (Armstrong 1972).

Bog lemmings are active year around, building runway systems and grass nests similar to those of other microtines. Studies summarized by J. K.

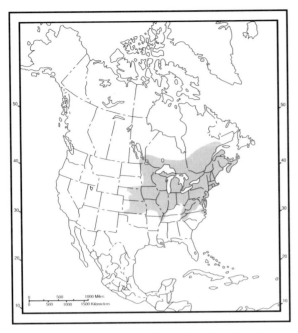

Map 9-113 Distribution of the southern bog lemming (Synaptomys cooperi) in North America.

Jones et al. (1983) for the northern Great Plains suggest that bog lemmings are often active during daylight hours. Grasses and sedges are preferred foods, and fecal material is reported to be large and bright green as opposed to the darker feces of other voles. Bog lemmings probably breed during the spring and summer on the western edge of their range, litter size averaging about three. Linzey (1983) reviewed the literature on the species.

DISTRIBUTION IN COLORADO — The southern bog lemming is mostly a species of the southern part of the boreal forest and the mixed deciduous forests of the northeastern United States and southern Canada, extending westward onto the edge of the Great Plains. It is not uncommon in eastern Nebraska and eastern Kansas, but J. K. Jones (1958) considered the species to be relictual in western Nebraska. No specimens of the southern bog lemming are known from Colorado, but the species has been collected in Dundy County, Nebraska, about 25 km east of the Colorado border (J. K. Jones 1958).

FAMILY ZAPODIDAE — Jumping Mice

This is a family of small to medium-sized mice with long tails, long hindlegs, and hindfeet adapted for saltatory, or jumping, movement. The skull has a large infraorbital foramen and the upper incisors are grooved on the anterior surface. The dental formula for Coloradan species is 1/1, 0/0, 1/0, 3/3 = 18, a tooth count unique among mammals in the state. Premolars are reduced in size. Molars are rooted and cusped. The enamel shows much infolding, with one lingual fold and four labial folds (Whitaker 1972).

Zapodids typically inhabit areas of lush herbaceous vegetation. The family is an old one dating back to the Oligocene, some 40 million years ago. There are 4 genera and 11 species of zapodids in northern Eurasia and North America. Some authorities (including Klingener 1984) have treated the Holarctic zapodids as a subfamily of the Dipodidae, the family of the jerboas, Old World analogues of North American kangaroo rats. We use the family name Zapodidae because of convention, to preclude confusion. One genus with two species occurs in Colorado. Krutzsch (1954) discussed the taxonomy and distribution of these mice in North America. The Coloradan species are somewhat difficult to distinguish, and specimens from along the foot of the Front Range should be examined by a mammalogist with access to comparative reference material.

Key to the Species of the Family Zapodidae Found in Colorado

1. Skull relatively small and light with narrow braincase and small molars; palatal breadth at last molar usually less than 4.2 mm; incisive foramina usually less than 4.6 mm; maxillary toothrow 3.7 mm or less. Tail distinctly bicolored, dark above and yellow to whitish below, ochraceous lateral line usually indistinct to lacking; mid-dorsal blackish patch poorly defined . . . . Meadow Jumping Mouse — *Zapus hudsonius*, p. 291

1' Skull relatively large and heavy with wider braincase and larger molars; palatal breadth at last molar usually greater than 4.4 mm; incisive foramina usually more than 4.6 mm; maxillary toothrow usually more than 3.7 mm. Tail less distinctly bicolored, ochraceous lateral line usually distinct; blackish mid-dorsal patch prominent . . . .
. . Western Jumping Mouse — *Zapus princeps*, p. 293

Photograph by Roger W. Barbour.

Photograph 9-58 Meadow jumping mouse (Zapus hudsonius).

Zapus hudsonius
MEADOW JUMPING MOUSE

DESCRIPTION — The meadow jumping mouse is small with large hindlegs and hindfeet and a long, sparsely haired tail that usually makes up at least 60 percent of the total length. The dorsal color is grayish to yellowish brown and the sides are paler. The venter is white. The pelage is rather harsh in texture relative to that of most other small mice. Intermixed dark hairs in the dorsal area form an indistinct mid-dorsal band or stripe, usually less pronounced than in the larger western jumping mouse. Measurements are: total length 187–255 mm; length of tail 108–155 mm; length of hindfoot 28–35 mm. The skull is small and light with a narrower braincase and smaller molars than in *Z. princeps*. The upper incisors have a distinct anterior groove and are orange.

The baculum, usually less than 4.9 mm in length, is relatively simple with a thin shaft curving slightly upward and tapering gradually from the base to near the tip. Females have eight mammae.

NATURAL HISTORY — Beyond habitats of capture, virtually no details are known of the biology of the meadow jumping mouse in Colorado. This account draws on work from the Upper Midwest and Northeast and may not be applicable to our area.

The meadow jumping mouse is a prairie species, occupying a variety of habitats but is most common in rank, lush vegetation along watercourses or in herbaceous understories in wooded areas. Most specimens from Colorado appear to be from tallgrass habitats near water; G. Jones and Jones (1985) reported the species from wetlands surrounded by sagebrush habitat in El Paso County.

Diet of the meadow jumping mouse is mostly seeds and fruits, fungi, and insects. Animal matter is thought to be most important in the early part of the season, and seeds become important as particular plants mature in summer and early fall. The animals are not reported to cache food, but they do store body fat in preparation for hibernation.

Home ranges have been estimated at 0.08 to 0.35 ha with males having slightly larger average home ranges (Quimby 1951). The species is reported to shift home ranges and wander, perhaps in response to loss of moist habitat in hot weather. In suitable habitat, densities can approach 50 mice per ha but seasonally numbers from 7 to 15 per ha are probably more typical.

A burrow and nest are used for shelter with nests typically several centimeters below ground, but well above the water table. The nest is constructed of grasses, leaves, or woody material. Nests are typically located in protected areas under logs, at the base of bushes, or in similar places. Because meadow jumping mice live in rather tall, dense vegetation, when undisturbed they move by "crawling" or by short hops along the ground. When pressed, however, they can make prodigious leaps, changing

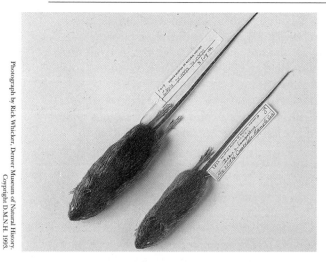

Photograph 9-59 Museum study skins of Zapus princeps *(above — left) and* Zapus hudsonius *(below — right). Note larger size and more distinct lateral line on* Z. princeps.

Map 9-114 Distribution of the meadow jumping mouse (Zapus hudsonius) *in North America.*

course in midair by using the tail as a rudder. After a few such leaps they remain motionless in the shadows. They are good climbers, swimmers, and diggers; the latter behavior probably is used in the search for fungi. Although they often live in habitat occupied by voles and other runway-using rodents, jumping mice do not use such runs with any regularity. Instead, they move along natural features of the terrain. Although generally nocturnal or crepuscular, it is not unusual for the animals to be active during daylight.

Meadow jumping mice are capable of breeding virtually throughout their period of above-ground activity, with most reproduction probably occurring between early June and mid-August. Most females seem to have two litters per year and some have three. Litter size varies from two to eight with an average of four to five. The young are born after a gestation period of 17 to over 21 days (Quimby 1951). The length of gestation is increased in lactating females. The young are naked at birth. The incisors erupt at about 13 days and the eyes open during the fourth week. The young reach minimum adult weight by about two months of age.

The animals are mostly solitary, but aggression between individuals does not occur when captives are housed together (Whitaker 1963). A number of sounds are reported, including chirping and clucking noises and, when excited, drumming with the tail (Whitaker 1963).

Jumping mice hibernate during the colder months; shorter day length seems to stimulate fat deposition. Individuals studied in the laboratory were capable of weight gains of up to 2.0 g per day for brief periods. Individuals may gain over 100 percent of their original body weight, with average daily gains of about 1.0 g per day. Body temperatures and breathing are variable and unstable during hibernation. The animals enter hibernation in October and emerge in late April and early May (Whitaker 1963). Mortality approaching 70 percent occurs during hibernation, possibly related to the rapid weight loss that occurs when first entering dormancy. During their above-ground cycle meadow jumping mice are preyed on by a wide variety of ground and aerial preda-

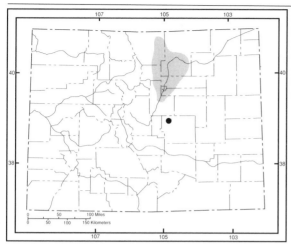

Map 9-115 Distribution of the meadow jumping mouse (Zapus hudsonius) *in Colorado. Solid circle represents a record of occurrence.*

tors including weasels, skunks, badgers, foxes, owls, and hawks. Whitaker (1972) reviewed the literature on the species.

DISTRIBUTION IN COLORADO — The meadow jumping mouse is known in Colorado on the basis of fewer than 50 specimens from Larimer, Weld, Boulder, Jefferson, Denver, Adams, and Arapahoe counties (Armstrong 1972). An intriguing recent report from El Paso County (G. Jones and Jones 1985) was the first from south of the Platte-Arkansas Divide. Individuals also have been captured in recent years near Platteville and at various localities along the mountain front south of Boulder (Bernardo Garza, U. S. Fish and Wildlife Service, pers. comm.). Judging from its limited ecological and geographic distribution in Colorado, the meadow jumping mouse probably is an Ice Age relict, perhaps once widespread in a tallgrass prairie across the eastern plains but now restricted to scattered localities on the Colorado Piedmont. Similarly relict populations are known from the White Mountains of Arizona and the Sacramento Mountains and Rio Grande Valley of New Mexico (Hafner et al. 1981). Doubtless the practice of expanding natural wetlands into irrigation reservoirs over the past century has had a negative impact on populations. Because of the apparent rarity

of this species and the difficulty of distinguishing the two species of *Zapus,* caution in identification is encouraged. Much work remains to understand the status and biology of the meadow jumping mouse in Colorado, at the western limits of its range. One subspecies, *Zapus hudsonius preblei,* is known in Colorado. Krutzsch (1954) described the subspecies on the basis of a specimen from Loveland.

Photograph 9-60 Western jumping mouse (Zapus princeps).

Zapus princeps
WESTERN JUMPING MOUSE

DESCRIPTION — The western jumping mouse strongly resembles the meadow jumping mouse. The dorsal surface is yellowish gray, and adults have a distinct blackish mid-dorsal patch. The venter is white, limited by a yellowish to buffy lateral line. This species is somewhat larger than the meadow jumping mouse; measurements are: total length 204–260 mm; length of tail 112–148 mm; length of hindfoot 27–33 mm; length of ear 13–17 mm; weight 19–37 g. The skull is larger and heavier and the molars are larger than those in Z. hudsonius. The baculum resembles that of the meadow jumping mouse but is usually longer than 5.1 mm.

NATURAL HISTORY — The western jumping mouse is an inhabitant of riparian communities at moderate to high elevations in Colorado, usually between 1,830 m and 3,500 m (6,000–11,500 ft). The species

293

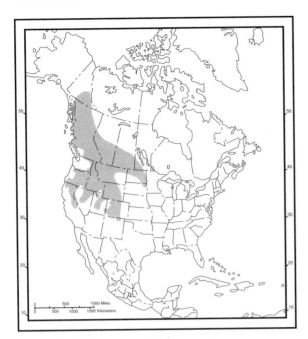

Map 9-116 Distribution of the western jumping mouse (Zapus princeps) in North America.

is most abundant in streamside alder, willow, and aspen stands with a well-developed understory of forbs and grasses. Individuals also occur in bogs and marshes, and even occasionally on the fringes of dry meadows or sagebrush stands.

Because of their rather brief period of summer activity, these animals feed mostly on high-energy food sources that allow rapid deposition of fat in preparation for the next period of hibernation. Seeds and arthropods formed the bulk of the diet (40 and 33 percent, respectively) of animals on Rabbit Ears Pass, Colorado (T. Vaughan and Weil 1980), whereas 82 percent of the diet was seeds in Grand Teton National Park, Wyoming (T. Clark 1971*a*). Insects have sometimes been thought to be incidental food items. However, habitat conditions and competition with other vertebrates for seeds may affect optimal foraging, and, at least locally, cause shifts to increased consumption of insects (T. Vaughan and Weil 1980).

Western jumping mice breed during summer. Pregnant females have been captured in June and July, and lactating animals have been found into late August in southern Wyoming (L. N. Brown 1967*a*). The gestation period is estimated to be 18 days, and only one litter is produced each year. Litter size ranges from three to eight with an average of five. A substantial proportion of females may not breed; L. N. Brown (1967*a*) reported that only 40 of 75 females examined showed signs of having bred in his study population in the Medicine Bow Mountains. Low fecundity may be a correlate of potentially great longevity. Perhaps because they are deep hibernators, western jumping mice are remarkably long lived for small mammals, sometimes surviving four years or longer. Marked longevity is often associated with deep hibernation. A mammal that hibernates 8 or 9 months each year only "lives hard" about a quarter of its life.

Western jumping mice are most active at night but are occasionally seen in the daytime by anglers and others wandering along streambanks. Their season of above-ground activity is extremely short at high elevations — estimated at 100 days on Rabbit Ears Pass (T. Vaughan and Weil 1980) and 87 days in Utah (Cranford 1978). At lower elevations the animals may be above ground an additional 30 or 40 days. Hibernacula used by the western jumping mouse in the Wasatch Mountains of Utah were typically 50 to 60 cm below ground where mean soil temperature was 4 to 5°C. Nest chambers averaged 14 cm in diameter and were lined with dried plant materials including bark, soft stems, leaves, and pine needles. The burrow entrance to such hibernacula was plugged with 15 to 30 cm of soil (Cranford 1978).

L. Myers (1969) reported an average home range of 3,075 m^2 for males and 2,350 m^2 for females at an elevation of 2,900 m (8,850 ft) near Gothic, Gunnison County. Stinson (1977*b*), working in an aspen forest at 2,900 m (9,650 ft) in Boulder County, reported similar home ranges. On his study site, home ranges of males varied from about 300 to 3,300 m^2 and those of females were from 680 to 1,275 m^2. Females tended to show

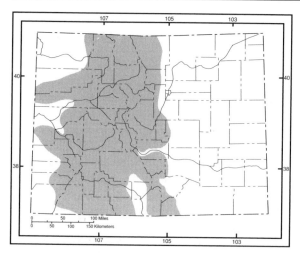

Map 9-117 Distribution of the western jumping mouse (Zapus princeps) *in Colorado.*

moderate territoriality and more uniform spacing than males. Population density estimates range from 28 to 35 per ha in Boulder County (Stinson 1977a) to 3.2 animals per ha in southeastern Wyoming (L. N. Brown 1970).

Contrary to studies of the meadow jumping mouse, Cranford (1978) found no correlation in Utah between increased fat deposition and either temperature or photoperiod; rather, fat deposition depended on availability of seeds. The onset of weight gain begins about one month before the animals enter hibernation, and western jumping mice gain weight at an average rate of 0.65 g per day with a maximum of 2.1 g per day. Up to two-thirds of the dry body weight can be in fat reserves, compared to one-half of the body weight for meadow jumping mice. Weight loss of hibernating western jumping mice averaged 0.07 g per day (Cranford 1978).

Annual mortality is probably very high as a result of the rigor of hibernation as well as predation and disease. Data on predation are lacking but probably all terrestrial carnivores and most aerial ones are potential enemies.

DISTRIBUTION IN COLORADO — The western jumping mouse occurs throughout the mountainous

western two-thirds of the state, mostly along streams and in moist meadows from about 1,830 m to 3,500 m (6,000–11,500 ft). One subspecies, *Zapus princeps princeps*, occurs widely in Colorado. The type locality is Florida, La Plata Co., Colorado. Probably *Z. p. utahensis* is the subspecies west of the Green River in extreme northwestern Colorado.

FAMILY ERETHIZONTIDAE — New World Porcupines

This family of New World rodents is characterized by a robust build and modification of some of the guard hairs into sharp, barbed quills. The feet are plantigrade and modified for an arboreal life — broad, scaly soles assist in climbing and clinging to branches. The skull has a large infraorbital foramen, typically larger than the foramen magnum. The cheekteeth are rooted and have complex occlusal surfaces characterized by many infoldings of the enamel. The dental formula is 1/1, 0/0, 1/1, 3/3 = 20. The family evolved in South America, and fossils date from the Oligocene. Two genera (*Erethizon* and *Coendou*) invaded North America by the late Pliocene; the former reached the United States and Canada. Five genera and 12 species are presently recognized in the family. *Erethizon dorsatum* is the only porcupine north of Mexico.

Erethizon dorsatum COMMON PORCUPINE

DESCRIPTION — The porcupine is the second largest rodent in Colorado, outweighed only by the beaver. Porcupines have stout bodies, relatively short legs, and short, thick, heavy tails used as a brace while climbing or perching. Many of the guard hairs on the back and tail are modified into sharp, barbed quills. Measurements are: total length 640–930 mm; length of tail 150–300 mm; length of hindfoot 85–125 mm; length of ear 20–40 mm; weight 4–18 kg. The skull is stout and broad with heavy ridges forming in older animals. The infraorbital foramina are slightly larger than the foramen magnum. Incisors are stout and ever

Photograph 9-61 Common porcupine (Erethizon dorsatum).

growing. Cheekteeth are rooted and have deeply folded enamel on the outer edges. The occlusal surface of each cheektooth shows both dentine and enamel folds. Earle and Kramm (1980) provided techniques for determining age.

Younger animals are generally dark, and older animals are more yellowish. Color variation is mostly due to the color of the coarse, long, stiff, guard hairs, which can exceed 10 cm in length. The underfur is long, soft, and dark. The quills are whitish yellow with dark tips. The venter lacks quills but has underfur and short guard hairs. There are four digits on the front feet and five on the hind. The soles of the feet are oval and covered with black, scaly plates, which assist the animal in gaining traction while climbing. Females have four mammae, and males have a distinctive baculum that is flattened dorsoventrally with a bulbous base.

NATURAL HISTORY — Porcupines are mostly associated with conifers in montane and subalpine forests and piñon-juniper woodlands. In addition, they occupy cottonwood-willow forests in river bottoms, aspen groves, and semidesert shrublands. Individuals are often observed above timberline and occasionally even on the open grasslands of eastern Colorado. Despite their abundance, there is a dearth of studies on porcupines from the Rocky Mountain Region.

The cambium, phloem, buds, and foliage of shrubs, saplings, and trees are a mainstay of the porcupine's diet. They eat leaves, buds, and young shoots of grasses and forbs during the warmer months, and concentrate on inner bark in winter. Cambium, buds, and needles of conifers, especially ponderosa pine, lodgepole pine, and Douglas-fir, are important foods in Colorado. There is considerable variation in the amount of damage done to individual trees by their foraging, with some trees in a stand showing extensive use while others may be virtually untouched. Such foraging patterns are poorly understood. In an investigation of this phenomenon in the Front Range, trees fed upon by porcupines were closer to steep, rocky outcrops (where dens might be located) and had more tannins in their phloem than trees not selected by porcupines (Habeck 1990). In some parts of Colorado (including the Piceance Basin) porcupines may invade alfalfa fields during the summer, causing considerable damage.

Porcupines are active year around and may be observed moving at any time of the day or night although they are usually considered nocturnal. During the day they typically seek refuge under rocks, in hollows, or in the crotch of a tree. These sites may be accompanied by fecal piles. Linear daily movements during summer ranged from 111 to 129 m, and home ranges averaged 14 ha (Marshall et al. 1962). Although not considered territorial, porcupines do defend particularly good feeding sites.

Porcupines are generally solitary, except for females with their young. During winter, however, individuals may concentrate in den sites such as caves, abandoned buildings, hollow trees, and brush piles. These denning sites are not defended. Densities are extremely variable between winter and summer and as a consequence of food availability. Densities of 0.77 and 9.5 animals per km^2 were reported for Arizona and Wisconsin, respectively (Taylor 1935, Kelker 1943). In Idaho shrub desert, home ranges were 0.07 ha in winter and 23.1 ha in spring and summer (Craig and Keller 1986). One male had a home range of 61.7 ha. These home ranges are smaller than those reported

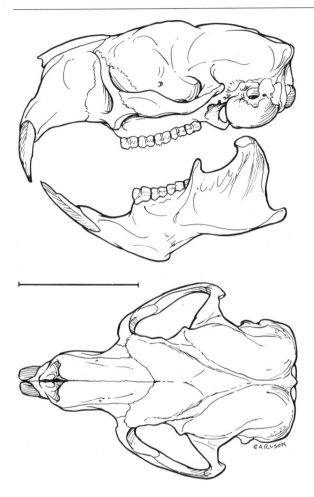

Figure 9-12 Lateral and dorsal views of the skull of the common porcupine (Erethizon dorsatum). *Scale = 1 cm.*

from forested habitats of the western United States.

Vocalizations include subdued grunts and whines used by females with their young, and grunts, whines, and shrill screeches used by males during the breeding season. The latter cries may be confused with sounds made by wild felids (Dodge 1982). One of us (JPF) kept a young male porcupine, which had lost one of its hindlegs in a coyote trap, for almost a year. When approached he would make a number of grunts and whines interpreted as greeting and care-soliciting sounds. Vision is poor,

but hearing and olfaction are good. They stand on their hindlegs to assess a passing scent.

Porcupines are monestrous or seasonally polyestrous; most breeding takes place in fall or early winter. Sex ratios tend to favor females up to as much as 100:30, but more typically 100:80 or 90 is to be expected in this polygamous species. Adults form only brief associations to breed and usually separate within six hours following copulation (Shadle 1951, Shadle et al. 1946). The gestation period is about 210 days (remarkably long for a rodent or for any mammal of its size) and the young are born in the spring. A single young is typical although twins have been reported. Young porcupines are precocial, born well furred with soft quills that harden quickly after delivery. The young begin to take solid food when only a few days old and forage with the mother at one to two weeks of age. They are weaned at about four months of age. Males are sexually mature at about 16 months and it is assumed that females reach sexual maturity at approximately the same age (Shadle 1952, Tyron 1947).

A porcupine's first alarm reaction is to remain still. When threatened, it typically assumes a hunched posture with quills erected. The animal moves in a circle, keeping its armament "pointed" toward the enemy, and thrashes or waves the well-muscled tail at the source of danger. Unfortunately for thousands of Coloradan porcupines annually, this technique is not an effective defense against motor vehicles.

Quills have microscopic, imbricate (overlapping, shingle-like) barbs. They are not ejected, but they are only loosely attached at their bases and so are readily shed and become imbedded upon contact. Porcupines are very adept at removing quills with their teeth and forefeet from their own bodies, as is neccessary after an aggressive interspecific encounter. Longevity may exceed ten years in captivity, but in the wild they only survive five to seven years. Toothwear and malocclusion often become problems as individuals age (Dodge 1982).

Map 9-118 *Distribution of the common porcupine* (Erethizon dorsatum) *in North America.*

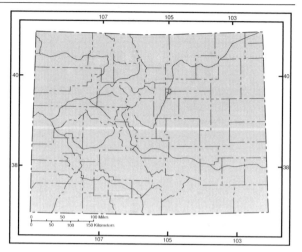

Map 9-119 *Distribution of the common porcupine* (Erethizon dorsatum) *in Colorado.*

To be quilled by a porcupine is a painful and educational experience. Every attempt should be made to remove all quills from the victim. If a quill breaks off in the wound it may start an infection or continue to penetrate tissue, doing further damage. Quills should be pulled with pliers with a straight, even motion, gripping each quill as close to the skin as possible. Porcupines in Colorado have few effective natural enemies. Animals that become proficient in killing them attempt to get at the underbelly, which is devoid of quills. In midsummer of 1975 Fitzgerald (unpublished) found the skin of an adult porcupine in an open meadow in South Park, 150 m from the nearest trees. The meat had been thoroughly eaten from the skin, and the skin was opened from tail to throat along the belly. The predator could not be determined. Fishers are reported to kill and devour porcupines in the manner described above but fishers are not known to occur in Colorado. Native predators in the state include coyotes, lynx, bobcats, mountain lions, and black bears. Humans are by far the most important enemy of porcupines, due both to control programs

and road kills. The porcupine is classified as a small game mammal in Colorado (Table 3-1). Timber producers often seek control of porcupines because their tree-girdling activity causes damage to commercial forests, although such damage is generally not excessive (Curtis 1941, 1944; Van Deusen and Myers 1962). At times porcupines may cause crop damage and most ranchers and pet owners are also typically "antiporcupine" because of the injury inflicted on careless pets and livestock unwary enough to nudge a porcupine. Woods (1973), Costello (1966), and Dodge (1982) reviewed the literature.

DISTRIBUTION IN COLORADO — Porcupines occur throughout the state but are commonest in the forested, mountainous portions, especially in areas with coniferous trees. It is not unusual, however, to find individuals in sagebrush flats or even on open prairie on the eastern plains. No modern taxonomic revision exists, but three subspecies have been ascribed ranges in Colorado: *Erethizon dorsatum bruneri* along the break of the High Plains in extreme northern Weld and northwestern Logan county; *E. d. couesi* in the extreme southwestern part of the state; and *E. d. epizanthum* over most of the western two-thirds of Colorado.

Chapter 10

Order: Carnivora

Carnivores

The order Carnivora is a diverse group of mammals, including both terrestrial and marine species. Terrestrial forms range in size from the huge brown and polar bears, weighing over 700 kg, to the diminutive least weasel, which weighs only 50 g. Marine carnivores include the true seals, the fur seals (or sea lions), and the walrus. Elephant seals are larger than any of the land carnivores; bulls weigh up to 3,600 kg.

Marine carnivores frequently have have been treated as a separate order, the Pinnipedia (Ewer 1973, Lawlor 1979, Nowak 1991, Simpson 1945). That arrangement makes the pinnipeds by far the most recently evolved mammalian order, dating only to the Miocene. Today pinnipeds usually are considered to be carnivores, but there is no firm agreement on whether the group is a natural (monophyletic) one. Fossil evidence suggests a diphyletic origin for the pinnipeds: fur seals and walruses took to the Pacific Ocean and true seals entered the Atlantic Ocean in two separate evolutionary origins from different ancestors around 25 million years ago (Tedford 1976). Other recent evidence, combining morphology and biochemistry, suggests that the group is in fact monophyletic (Arnason and Widegren 1986; Wyss 1987, 1988, 1989). In any event, however, the pinnipeds belong in the Carnivora (Stucky and McKenna, 1993).

Within the terrestrial carnivores (the fissipeds), there are 7 families, some 92 genera, and about

240 species (Nowak 1991). Carnivores evolved in the early Paleocene, probably from insectivore ancestors. The oldest fossils are from North America. Although there were numerous carnivorous marsupials, terrestrial members of the Carnivora were absent from the Australian region until the dingo was introduced by humans. Many canivores are valued as furbearers; Deems and Pursley (1983) summarized the legal status of furbearers in North America. In part because of their commercial value, introductions have led to the establishment of populations of carnivores worldwide except in Antarctica.

The carnivores represent a broad adaptive radiation in size, locomotion, dentition and diet, behavior, and reproductive patterns. Terrestrial carnivores are either plantigrade or digitigrade with four or five toes. All digits are clawed, and neither hallux nor pollex is opposable. As is typical of many cursorial mammals, the clavicle is reduced or absent. The radius is separate from the ulna, and the tibia is not fused to the fibula. The atlas has large wing-like processes. The sacrum is well developed, usually consisting of three fused vertebrae. Dentition is variably modified for true carnivory, insectivory, or omnivory. The dental formula (3/3, 1/1, 2–4/2–4, 1–4/1–5) ranges from 26 teeth in the aardwolf to 50 teeth in the bat-eared fox, both insectivorous mammals. Two species, the insectivorous sloth bear and the sea otter (which feeds mostly on marine invertebrates), have lost two upper or two lower incisors,

299

respectively. In many carnivores the last upper premolar and the first lower molar form powerful shearing teeth, the carnassial pair. Among Coloradan carnivores, the carnassials are best developed in the felids and canids, poorly developed in the procyonids and mustelids, and least developed in the bears, which have bunodont, crushing teeth well suited to their generally omnivorous diet. The canines are typically enlarged, pointed, and curved, serving as piercing and stabbing weapons. The orbits communicate with the temporal fossae, and the zygomatic arch is strongly developed. The braincase is large and the brain has well-developed cerebral hemispheres.

Most land carnivores are solitary except during the breeding season, although some species pair (foxes) and others live in packs (wolves, dholes, Cape hunting dogs). The uterus is bicornuate or bipartite. The placenta is usually endotheliochorial in structure and zonary in shape. Males have a baculum. Females of most species have a single litter each year, although some species (bears, for example) have young only every second or third year and a few species of viverrids (mongooses and allies) have more than two litters per year. Gestation periods range from about 50 to 250 days, variation being due to delayed implantation of the early embryo in a number of mustelids and ursids. Litter size ranges from one in some ursids to 13 in some mustelids. Neonates are typically altricial but usually are haired. One or both parents are involved in rearing the young and learned behaviors are important in the development of hunting skills.

Key to the Families of the Order Carnivora Found in Colorado

1. Muzzle short and broad, total teeth 30 or less; claws retractile . . . . Family Felidae, p. 364

1' Muzzle usually not short and broad, total teeth more then 32; claws not retractile 2

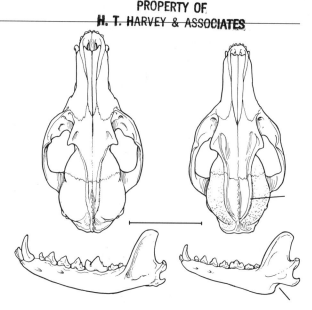

Figure 10-1 Dorsal views of the skulls and lateral views of rami of red fox (Vulpes vulpes — left) and gray fox (Urocyon cinereoargenteus — right) to show presence of prominent lyre-shaped temporal ridges and the notch in ramus of the latter. Scale = 1 cm.

2. Cheekteeth bunodont, lacking conspicuous cutting edges; tail either shorter than hindfoot or banded with hairs of contrasting color 3

2' Cheekteeth not totally bunodont, secondont teeth present; tail not as above 4

3. Tail shorter than hindfoot, not banded . . . . Family Ursidae, p. 317

3' Tail longer than hindfoot and conspicuously banded with hairs of contrasting color. . . . . Family Procyonidae, p. 324

4. Hindfoot with four toes; total teeth 42 . . . . Family Canidae, p. 301

4' Hindfoot with five toes; total teeth less than 42 . . . . Family Mustelidae, p. 330

FAMILY CANIDAE — Dogs, Foxes, and Allies

Members of this family are typically dog-like in appearance, with long legs; a long, usually bushy tail; long ears; and a pointed, sharp muzzle. Feet are digitigrade with four toes on the hindfoot and four or five toes on the forefoot. Claws are nonretractile. The rostrum is long, and the auditory bullae are well developed. The dental formula for all Coloradan canids is 3/3, 1/1, 4/4, 2/3 = 42 teeth. The carnassial teeth are well developed, and the canines are long and conical. Most canids are excellent thermoregulators, and several species live in extremely cold climates. Other species are adapted for semiarid to arid conditions where salivation and panting are used as cooling mechanisms. Sweat glands are restricted to the pads of the feet. Canids are monestrous, and Coloradan species generally breed in January, February, and March. Burrows or other dens are typically used as whelping sites, and litters usually range from three to six young. The baculum is well developed, and males are generally larger than females. The family contains 16 genera and 36 species and is native to all land areas of the world except Antarctica, the Australian region, and some oceanic islands. The domestic dog, *Canis familiaris*, has been introduced to ecosystems worldwide. The family dates from the late Eocene. In Colorado there are three genera and six species, of which one, the gray wolf, was extirpated about 50 years ago.

Key to the Species of the Family Canidae Found in Colorado

1. Postorbital processes thin and concave 2

1′ Postorbital processes thick and convex. . . . . *Canis*[*] 5

2. Backs of ears red and cheeks reddish; tail with black dorsal mane and black tip; skull with conspicuous lyre-shaped temporal ridges; mandible notched on posterior end of horizontal ramus . . . . Gray Fox — *Urocyon cinereoargenteus*, p. 315

2′ Backs of ears not red; tail without dorsal mane; skull without conspicuous lyre-shaped temporal ridges; mandible not notched on posterior end of horizontal ramus . . . . Vulpes 3

3. Tip of tail white, ears with black tips, upper body reddish; length of maxillary toothrow greater than 55; condylobasal length greater than 125 . . . . Red Fox — *Vulpes vulpes*, p. 312

3′ Tip of tail black, ears without black tips, upper body buffy gray to reddish gray; length of maxillary tooth row less than 55 mm; condylobasal length less than 125 mm 4

4. Ears longer, greater than 75 mm from notch; auditory bullae larger . . . . Kit Fox — *Vulpes macrotis*, p. 308

4′ Ears shorter, 75 mm or less from notch; auditory bullae smaller . . . . Swift Fox — *Vulpes velox*, p. 310

5. Total length greater than 1.4 m; greatest length of skull greater than 230 mm; condylobasal length greater than 200 mm; tips of upper canine teeth usually not extending below a line connecting mental foramina of mandible when jaws are closed; tail held high while runnin . . . . Gray Wolf — *Canis lupus*, p. 305

---

* Skulls of domestic dogs, depending on breed, are often difficult to distinguish from either wolf or coyote. The ratio of palatal width (distance between inner margins of alveoli of first upper molars) to length of upper cheektooth row (from anterior alveolar margin of first premolar to posterior alveolar margin of the last molar) is about 95 percent accurate for distinguishing dogs and coyotes. If the tooth row is three times the palatal width or greater it is a coyote. If the ratio is less than 2.8 the animal is a dog.

5′ Total length less than 1.4 m; greatest length of skull less than 230 mm; condylobasal length less than 200 mm; tips of upper canines extending below a line connecting anterior mental foramina of mandible; tail held low while running . . . . Coyote — *Canis latrans*, p. 302

Photograph by William E. Ervin.

Photograph 10-1 Coyote (Canis latrans).

Canis latrans
COYOTE

DESCRIPTION — The coyote is a slender, furry canid about the size of a small German shepherd dog. The tail is bushy and usually held low. The ears are pointed and held erect. Color varies considerably depending on season and location. Dorsal color is tawny gray, and animals from desert areas or low elevations are usually paler than those from other habitats. The face, forelegs, and ears tend to be reddish to brownish buff. The tail sports a black tip, and often the neck and shoulder areas have black-tipped hairs forming a "saddle." The throat and belly are paler than the rest of the body. Measurements are: total length 1,050–1,400 mm; length of tail 300–400 mm; length of hindfoot 175–220 mm; length of ear 80–130 mm; weight 9–16 kg, with a range for adult males of 8–20 kg and slightly smaller for adult females (7–18 kg). The largest reported coyote weighed almost 34 kg and was over 1,600 mm in

length. The skull is usually less than 220 mm long. Females have eight mammae.

Coyotes can generally be differentiated from wolves on the basis of longer and more pointed ears, more pointed rostrum, smaller size (usually less than 20 kg), a smaller nose pad (about 25 mm in diameter), and a hindfoot pad with a diameter of 32 mm or less (compared to 38 mm or greater in the wolf). See the key for differentiation of coyote and dog skulls. Coyotes are adaptable and hybridize with domestic dogs, rendering positive identification of some specimens almost impossible. Tooth sections and tooth-wear patterns can be used for determining age. (W. Bowen 1982).

NATURAL HISTORY — Coyotes are probably the best studied of all wild carnivores, mostly because of long-term efforts by the livestock industry to reduce populations. Coyotes are one of the most widespread and adaptable carnivores in North America. Elimination of the gray wolf, human modification of the environment, and possible human translocation of coyotes have enabled the species to colonize the entire United States (Bekoff 1982, Gier 1975, Voight and Berg 1987). Coyotes occur at all elevations and in all ecosystems in Colorado; they are least abundant in dense coniferous forest. In areas where they are subject to human control efforts they are restricted to broken, rough country with abundant shrub cover and a good supply of lagomorphs or rodents. Prior to efforts to eliminate them, they probably reached their greatest numbers on the plains of North America (Gier 1975).

Coyotes are truly opportunistic in their diet (Murie 1935), although they prefer animal matter, which composes roughly 90 percent of the diet (Bekoff 1977). In much of the West and Midwest, jackrabbits, cottontail rabbits, and rodents make up the bulk of the diet (Andrews and Bogess 1978, T. Clark 1972, Hilton 1978, Van Vuren 1990), with rodents most important as summer prey and lagomorphs important as winter prey. Fawns and carrion of livestock and big game are also eaten (Andelt 1987, Andrews and Bogess 1978, R. Cook et al. 1971, A. Todd and Keith 1983). Plant material consumed generally consists of fruit, berries, and cultivated crops including melons and carrots. In southeastern Colorado, juniper "berries" were a major component of the winter diet; rodents were important in spring, ungulate fawns in June, and grasshoppers were eaten when available in summer (Gese et al. 1988*b*). An adult coyote requires 600 g of meat per day (250 kg/yr) and a lactating female requires half again as much (Gier 1975).

Most literature suggests that the bulk of coyote predation on game and livestock is targeted at young animals, and it is not clear whether they also seek malnourished or weaker individuals (Andelt 1987). Coyotes readily prey on fawns (G. White et al. 1987). They have greater difficulty taking adult wild ungulates, but, in Colorado, coyotes do kill healthy adult deer (Compton 1980, Dorrance 1965). Social hunting and the accumulation of deep snow both enhance the ability of coyotes to prey on healthy adult ungulates (Gese et al. 1988*b*).

Coyote social structure is centered around mated pairs and their pups and is based on a dominance system. In some situations, especially where winter-kill ungulates provide an important food resource, larger groups may form that include nonbreeding adults. These additional group members are from previous years' litters and assist in the care of the young of the year. Extended family groups serve to defend better the concentrated resources provided by ungulate carcasses (Andelt 1985; Andelt et al. 1980; Bekoff and Wells 1980; Camenzind 1974, 1978). In other areas, group size decreases in fall when pups disperse, and groups form in winter as pairs come together for breeding (Gese et al. 1988*b*). Transient or lone individuals also occur and tend to be either young dispersing animals or older nonbreeding individuals that may have been displaced by younger animals. In Colorado, 78 percent of individuals in a population were resi-

Map 10-1 Distribution of the coyote (Canis latrans) *in North America.*

dents and 22 percent were transients (Gese et al. 1988*a*).

Visual communication, including a variety of facial and postural expressions (Bekoff 1974), and vocal communication (Lehner 1978*a, b*) are frequent and ongoing between members of the group and are also used in intergroup communication. Vocalizations include yips, howls, and short dog-like barks. Olfactory communication is also significant; scent marking with both urine and feces may have a territorial function, and urine is especially important during courtship (Wells and Bekoff 1981). Packs of coyotes defend territories but pairs or solitary animals do not (Bekoff and Wells 1980).

Courtship activities start two to three months before actual mating (Bekoff and Diamond 1976, Bekoff and Wells 1982). Pairing for several years may occur between adults but the social bond need not be permanent. Coyotes are monestrous with females in breeding condition for about five days, usually between January and March (Kennelly and Johns 1976). Gestation takes about 63 days and litters average five or six young (Bekoff and Diamond 1976). Litter sizes may fluctuate by one or two young depending on the abundance of rodents and the density of the coyote population (Gier 1968, Knowlton 1972). Sex ratios approximate 1:1. Compensatory reproduction is thought to occur in areas where coyotes are subjected to prolonged control (Andelt 1987, Voigt and Berg 1987).

Natal dens are generally excavated in areas with heavy cover including shrub thickets, downed timber, steep banks, or rocky areas. Young may emerge from the den as early as the second or third week and are weaned at about six weeks of age. During this time, important developmental interactions occur during play with littermates. These play fights, with aggression, submission, and posturing, establish the groundwork for future dominance relationships. Dispersal, if it occurs, is usually at six to nine months of age, but it may be slowed or halted when population densities are high (Voigt and Berg 1987).

Both sexes can breed as yearlings, but the percentage of yearling females actually breeding fluctuates widely from year to year, from 0 to 75 percent. Estimates of percentage of total breeding females in populations range from 33 to 90 percent (Gier 1968, Gipson et al. 1975, Knowlton 1972). Variations in breeding success are attributed to differences in food resources, severity of the winter, population density, and an individual's status in the population (Voigt and Berg 1987).

Population density is variable and may be closely related to the density of jackrabbits and snowshoe hares (T. Clark 1972, Gross et al. 1974, A. Todd and Keith 1983). In Wyoming, densities were 0.5 animals per km^2 before pups emerged from the den. Following whelping, densities increased almost threefold (Camenzind 1978). In sagebrush areas in Utah and Idaho, densities were 0.1 to 0.3 animals per km^2 (T. Clark 1972). One denning pair per km^2 was estimated as maximum for the rolling plains of eastern Colorado and Kansas, with up to three denning pairs per km^2 in more eroded "badlands" environments (Gier 1975). Densities of from 0.2 to 0.4 animals per km^2 are probably representative over much of coyote range (Knowlton 1972).

Coyotes may be active at any time although most activity occurs in the evening. Home ranges vary widely, from about 4 to 5 km^2 in Texas to as large as 143 km^2 in central Washington (Voigt and Berg 1987). In southeastern Colorado, the mean annual home range was 11.3 km^2 (range 2.8–32 km^2) for residents and 106 km^2 (range 61–185 km^2) for transients (Gese et al. 1988a). Male and female home ranges are about equal in size in a given area, probably because many of the studies on home range have involved pairs on territories.

Depredation by coyotes on livestock, especially sheep, has been a concern of ranchers for over a century. For much of this period, active control efforts have been pursued with governmental funding. Controversy and emotions run high on the issue of coyote control. Research efforts have led to the development of more effective and humane methods, but much work is still needed (Andelt 1987). Five percent losses of domestic sheep to coyotes in Colorado have been reported based on questionnaires (Sterner and Shumake 1978). Locally, aspects of coyote behavior relating to the potential for various "repellents" to reduce coyote predation on livestock have been pursued (Lehner 1976, Lehner et al. 1976, Olsen and Lehner 1978). The extirpation of the gray wolf appears to have removed competition and predation pressure on coyotes, allowing them to expand in abundance and distribution (Carbyn 1987), despite vigorous eradication efforts on behalf of the livestock industry.

Coyotes may live 13 to 15 years (Gese 1990, Knowlton 1972) but such longevity is very rare. Annual mortality is estimated as high as 40 to 70 percent in juveniles and about 35 to 40 percent in animals

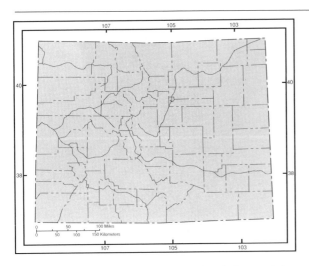

Map 10-2 Distribution of the coyote (Canis latrans) in Colorado.

Photograph 10-2 Gray wolf (Canis lupus).

Canis lupus
GRAY WOLF

over one year of age. Depending on location, human-caused mortality has been estimated to range from 38 to 90 percent (Voigt and Berg 1987). Coyotes are also susceptible to distemper and canine hepatitis but rarely show evidence of rabies (Pence and Custer 1981).

Coyotes may partially restrict populations of other small carnivores, including foxes, bobcats, and possibly badgers, by direct predation or competition for food (Gier 1975, Linhart and Robinson 1972, Rathbun et al. 1980, Sargeant 1982). On the other hand, cooperative hunting with badgers may occur (Dobie 1961). Literature on the species was reviewed by Bekoff (1977, 1978, 1982) and Voight and Berg (1987). Works by Young and Jackson (1951) and Murie (1940) are classics on the species.

DISTRIBUTION IN COLORADO — In Colorado, coyotes are common statewide in all habitats and at all elevations. They are managed and harvested as furbearers (Tables 3-1, 3-2). *Canis latrans latrans* occurs on the eastern plains; *C. l. lestes* occurs in western Colorado except the extreme southwest, where *C. l. mearnsi* occurs.

DESCRIPTION — The gray wolf is a large, powerful canid with a long bushy tail and erect ears, more rounded than those of the coyote. The legs are longer, the feet larger, and the chest narrower than on a comparable-sized dog. When the animal is running, the tail is held high, but it does not curl up onto the back. The fur is thick, long, and coarse. There is much individual variation in color and not much geographic pattern. Most gray wolves are not actually pure gray in color. Dorsal color is more often a pale tan to cream, mixed with darker and paler hairs. Darker hairs often are concentrated on the dorsum; the extremities, lower body, and facial areas are paler. Adults almost invariably have white around the mouth. Cary (1911) noted that in Colorado, mountain-dwelling animals were darker than those from the plains. However, Young and Goldman (1944) indicated that pelage was relatively pale for both subspecies in Colorado and that there was wide variation in color even in littermates, citing a litter of six from near Pueblo in which two pups were almost white, two were intermediate, and two were gray-black to brownish black. Measurements are: total length 1.3–1.6 m (although a few males may measure close to 1.8 m); length of tail 360–500 mm; length of hindfoot 70–90 mm; weight 18–80 kg. Adults are about 700 mm tall at the shoulder. Males are usually slightly larger than females. The skull is 230–290 mm in greatest length with a zygomatic breadth of 120–150 mm. The sagittal crest is typically prominent. Females have 10 mammae. As with most canids, a well-developed precaudal or tail gland is located on the dorsal side of the tail near its base. Anal glands are also present. Hybrids between gray wolves, red wolves (*C. rufus*), coyotes, and domestic dogs are not uncommon, and in the disturbed habitats of the present ranges of gray and red wolves, hybrids with coyotes or dogs are obscuring the original gene pools.

NATURAL HISTORY — Gray wolves once ranged over much of North America. Populations were apparently highest in habitats with plentiful large prey, principally ungulates (Young and Goldman 1944). Wolves spend almost their entire active life hunting or eating. Most time is spent traveling in search of food, with an average of 36 km between kills in Michigan (Mech 1970). Wolves locate prey by direct scent, tracking, and chance. Wolves may survive up to two weeks without a kill, although such an interval would be atypical. An adult wolf can consume about 9 kg of food at one meal. A maintenance diet for an adult is 1.7 kg of food per day (Mech 1970), and they can consume up to 0.21 kg prey/kg of wolf per day (Carbyn 1983). Wolves are specialized for a meat diet, and there are no accounts of them feeding on vegetation. Large mammals (beavers and ungulates) account for 56 to 96 percent of the diet of the wolf, with deer, moose, bighorn sheep, and similar-sized species among the most frequent prey (Paradiso and Nowak 1982). During their long tenure in Colorado, wolves undoubtedly dined on elk, mule deer, bison, and mountain sheep. Unfortunately, their tendency to harvest domestic livestock led to their demise.

Wolves are social animals that typically live in packs. A pack is composed of 2 to 8 animals, although packs of up to 36 animals have been reported in Alaska (R. L. Rausch 1967). Although variable, most packs consist of at least one pair of

Map 10-3 *Historic and present distribution of the gray wolf* (Canis lupus) *in North America. After Paradiso and Nowak (1982).*

breeding adults, pups, and extra adults that may or may not breed (Carbyn 1987). Lack of breeding in subordinates is often the result of lack of copulation attempts rather than gonadal repression (Packard et al. 1983). Packs typically show linear dominance hierarchies that are separate for males and females. The alpha male is the leader of the pack. The alpha female, although dominant over other females, may be submissive to other males for purposes of mating (Mech 1970). Alpha males may become less important in breeding once they take over pack leadership. The dominant animals typically have first choice of food, bedding sites, and mates, and often show leadership in hunting or moving from one hunting area to another. Wolves may exhibit territoriality, especially when high populations curtail the size of available hunting area (Peters and Mech 1975, Harrington and Mech 1983).

There is considerable variation in the size of home ranges. Minimum home ranges are upward

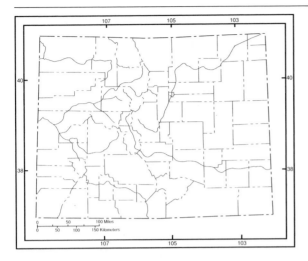

Map 10-4 Historic distribution of the gray wolf (Canis lupus) *in Colorado.*

from 94 km^2 for a pack of 2 animals to more than 13,000 km^2 for a pack of 10 animals. It appears that, at a minimum, a single wolf requires 50 to 1,300 km^2 (Paradiso and Nowak 1982). Daily movements range from one to 19 km depending on season and prey availability (Carbyn 1987). With these space requirements it is difficult to imagine the animals ever again roaming free in Colorado, although areas such as Rocky Mountain National Park (area about 1,500 km^2) are mentioned from time to time as possible restoration sites.

Mated pairs may remain together for life but supportive data other than zoo observations are lacking. Breeding occurs between January and April. In Colorado, wolves probably mated in late January and February. Copulation is typical of canids — the pair form a tie achieved by the vaginal sphincter muscle of the female locking around the bulbous base of the penis. A typical copulation lasts up to 30 minutes. The blind, helpless young are born in March, April, or May following a 63-day gestation. A den is usually used for the birthing site and may consist of a hole dug by the wolves, an enlarged burrow dug originally by another mammal, a shelter under rock overhangs, the interior of a beaver lodge, or the area under a

stump or in a hollow log. Litter size ranges from one to 11 with an average of six (Mech 1974). Eyes open at about 12 to 13 days, and pups are weaned at about five weeks. They emerge from the den at about three weeks of age (Young and Goldman 1944). Within a few weeks of emergence pups are typically moved to one of several other home sites used while they mature. Pups normally do not travel and hunt with the pack until fall. The female is usually provisioned by the male or other pack members for four to six weeks following the birth of the pups. Wolves are most sedentary when females have pups in the den. The young are sexually mature at two years of age but often do not breed until three years (R. L. Rausch 1967, Mech 1970).

Other than humans, wolves have no predators. Disease including parasites, malnutrition, and injuries and accidents take their toll. The literature was reviewed by Mech (1974), Paradiso and Nowak (1982), and Carbyn (1987).

DISTRIBUTION IN COLORADO — Historically, wolves occupied every county in Colorado, but the advent of the livestock industry and inherent fear of the animals by the general public led to their extirpation. No authentic records of wolves in Colorado exist past 1935 although occasionally hunters, trappers, and others report seeing them. Periodically, interest develops in the release of wolves into Rocky Mountain National Park. The high degree of human development in the valleys bordering the Park, the limited size of the Park, opposition by the livestock industry, and lack of support from the Colorado Division of Wildlife are formidable obstacles. The present ecosystem in and surrounding Rocky Mountain National Park seems inadequate to sustain a viable wolf population. *Canis lupus nubilus* occurred in Colorado westward to the Continental Divide; *C. l. youngi* occurred west of the Divide.

Gray wolves formerly occupied most of North America except for the southeastern states (the range of the red wolf) and the dry desert of Baja California. Today the species is gone from the

307

contiguous United States except for remnant populations in Minnesota, Wisconsin, Michigan, Idaho, Montana, and Washington.

Photograph 10-3 Kit fox (Vulpes macrotis).

Vulpes macrotis
KIT FOX

DESCRIPTION — This species is a dainty fox of the desert Southwest. It closely resembles the swift fox, *Vulpes velox*, in appearance but has larger ears and a generally more angular appearance. See the account of the swift fox for distinction between the two aridland foxes. The dorsal color of the kit fox varies from yellowish gray to grizzled. The underfur is thick and harsh in texture. The underparts are usually paler yellow to white. The sides of the muzzle are dark, and the tail is black tipped. Measurements are: total length 730–840 mm; length of tail 260–323 mm; length of hind-foot 113–137 mm; length of ear 78–94 mm; weight 1.5–2.5 kg. Females average 15 percent lighter in weight than males. Kit foxes are known to hybridize with swift foxes and red foxes, *Vulpes vulpes* (Rohwer and Kilgore 1973, Thornton et al. 1971). A number of authors (most recently Dragoo et al. 1990) have suggested that kit and swift foxes are conspecific. However, in Colorado the animals are strongly separated by the Southern Rocky Mountains. Even if the genetic situ-

ation were unequivocal in the narrow zone of intergradation or hybridization in southern New Mexico, arid land foxes in Colorado are reproductively isolated from one another and have distinctive ecological (and hence management) requirements.

NATURAL HISTORY — The kit fox occupies semidesert shrubland and margins of piñon-juniper woodlands over much of the Southwest. Saltbush, shadscale, sagebrush, and greasewood are common woody plants of typical kit fox habitat. In Utah, the species preferred areas with less than 20 percent ground cover and pale, loamy soils (McGrew 1977). In Colorado National Monument, they were observed most frequently in mixed juniper-sagebrush communities and in rimrock (P. Miller 1964). A small population in semidesert shrubland in Delta and Montrose counties is being investigated at the present time.

The kit fox appears to rely heavily on lagomorphs as the staple diet, at least in the cold desert regions of Utah where 94 percent of the diet of a family of kit foxes consisted of black-tailed jackrabbits (Egoscue 1962a). O'Neal et al. (1986), working in the same area, also reported high use of jackrabbits. Similar to the swift fox, their numbers appear to be regulated in part by the size of lagomorph populations. Kangaroo rats are also important prey in both California (McGrew 1979) and Utah (O'Neal et al. 1986). If preferred prey is unavailable, the kit fox is opportunistic and will feed on ground-nesting birds, especially horned larks (O'Neal et al. 1986), reptiles, and insects.

The species is semifossorial and digs its own dens, which normally have multiple entrances (Egoscue 1962a). Dens are clustered and not randomly distributed. The animals move from one den to another, especially during summer when pups are present. Kit foxes are active year round. Most foraging is done at night, and the animals normally do not move more than 3 km from their dens. Home range estimates vary from 252 to 1,120 ha (T. O'Farrell 1987, O'Neal et al. 1986). Home ranges overlap and evidence of territoriality is

Map 10-5 Distribution of the kit fox (Vulpes macrotis) in North America.

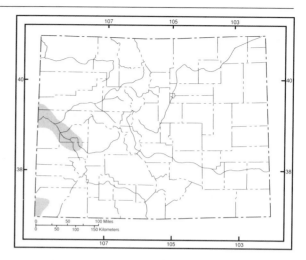

Map 10-6 Distribution of the kit fox (Vulpes macrotis) in Colorado.

lacking. Densities have been estimated to range from one individual per 43 ha to 1/1,036 ha (Egoscue 1965, Morrell 1972).

Kit foxes pair in late fall, when females select and clean out dens. Females are monestrous, and breeding occurs in December, January, and February. Some females may breed as young as 10 months of age (O'Farrell 1987). The gestation period is unknown but probably is similar to the 51 days reported for *V. velox.* Litters of four or five pups are born in February or March with a sex ratio of 1:1. Pups first emerge from the den at about four to five weeks of age and begin foraging with the parents when three to four months old. In Utah, dispersal occurs in October with young of the year showing the longest movements (Egoscue 1956, 1962a).

The extent of monogamy in kit foxes is not clear. Some pairs appear to be monogamous and to mate for life whereas others do not. Pair bonds

last at least through one breeding season, and males will sometimes father two litters. Males provision the female for the first few weeks that she is nursing the young, as she stays with the pups. At weaning, both adults bring food back to the den for the first few months; they do not regurgitate food (Egoscue 1962a, Morrell 1972).

Few data exist on mortality in kit foxes, but coyotes are thought to be major predators, causing almost half the observed mortality in radio-collared animals in California (T. O'Farrell 1987) and Utah (O'Neal et al. 1986). Mortality from motor vehicles was also significant (14 percent) in the latter study. Agricultural conversion of native habitat, trapping, shooting, and predator poisoning are all factors that have negative impacts on kit fox populations. Literature on the species was reviewed by McGrew (1979), Morrell (1975), and T. O'Farrell (1987).

DISTRIBUTION IN COLORADO — Although categorized as a furbearer (Table 3-1), geographic distribution and status of the kit fox in Colorado are poorly known but presently are under study by personnel of the Colorado Division of Wildlife and the University of Northern Colorado. To date only one small population has been located, near Delta. Although the status of the kit fox is largely unknown, Colorado has had a liberal hunting and trapping season on the species for many years. Colorado represents the eastern edge of the range, which encompasses semidesert and canyon country of the southwestern and west-central portions of the state. No verified specimens have been taken from north of the Grand Valley, although the Division of Wildlife receives periodic reports from northwestern Colorado. Present published records are limited to those of Egoscue (1964*a*), P. Miller (1964), and P. Miller and McCoy (1965). A specimen from McElmo Canyon, Montezuma Co., was reported as *Vulpes macrotis neomexicana*; those from Colorado National Monument were reported by P. Miller and McCoy 1965) as *V. m. arsipus*.

Photograph 10-4 Swift fox (Vulpes velox).

Vulpes velox
SWIFT FOX

DESCRIPTION — The swift fox is small and slender. The dorsal pelage ranges from yellowish to buffy gray, with the underfur tan and interspersed with multicolored guard hairs so that the overall dorsal color is fairly dark. The ventral pelage ranges from white to yellow. Conspicuous black marks are present on either side of the snout, and the tail is always tipped with black.

The black facial marks clearly separate the species from young coyotes. Measurements are: total length 700–880 mm; length of tail 240–350 mm; length of hindfoot 113–135 mm; length of ear 56–75 mm; weight 1.8–3.0 kg. Males average 8 percent heavier than females. Adults stand about 300 mm at the shoulder. The ears are typically shorter than those of the closely related kit fox, *Vulpes macrotis*. Other differences between the two species include more open, rounded eyes in the swift fox compared to slit-like eyes of the kit fox, and a shorter, broader muzzle in the former species. Females have eight mammae. In zones of contact, swift and kit foxes hybridize in western Texas and eastern New Mexico (Thornton et al. 1971, Rohwer and Kilgore 1973). In Colorado, the two species are strongly separated by the Southern Rocky Mountains.

NATURAL HISTORY — The swift fox, along with the black-tailed prairie dog and the white-tailed jackrabbit, is an animal of grasslands. It occupies shortgrass and midgrass prairies over most of the Great Plains, including eastern Colorado. In northeastern Colorado, the swift fox appears to be most numerous in areas with relatively flat to gently rolling topography (M. Cameron 1984, Loy 1981) and rare in terrain that is highly eroded with gullies, washes, and canyons. However, habitat occupied on the Pinon Canyon Maneuver Site in southeastern Colorado is more diverse (Rongstad et al. 1989).

Swift foxes are excellent diggers and excavate their own dens, which are typically located on flat areas or along slopes or ridges that afford good visual fields. In northern Colorado, dens are typically on sites dominated by blue grama or buffalo grass. The soil accumulated at the burrow entrance may be visible for several hundred meters, although typically not forming as large a mound as that from badger excavations (M. Cameron 1984, Loy 1981). More than one den is used at a time. Dens used for whelping typically have three to six entrances; dens used by solitary foxes usually have only one or two entrances. Dens excavated in Colorado were simple structures with

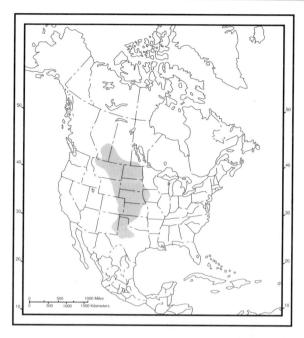

Map 10-7 Distribution of the swift fox (Vulpes velox) *in North America.*

most tunnels located about 40 cm below the surface (Loy 1981). More complex dens have been found in Oklahoma and Texas (Cutter 1958a, Kilgore 1969). Scats and prey remains litter the tunnel floors.

Swift foxes are almost entirely carnivorous, preying on a variety of small rodents, lagomorphs, birds, and similar quarry (Cutter 1958b). Studies over much of their range indicate that jackrabbits compose the bulk of the diet, supplemented by ground squirrels, prairie dogs, and many species of ground-nesting birds. In Colorado, an analysis of swift fox scats revealed that 66 percent of the biomass ingested was from lagomorphs, 11 percent from rodents, 10 percent from insects, and 4 percent from birds (M. Cameron 1984). Not unexpectedly, consumption of ground-nesting birds increased in the spring and summer months. In Kansas, mammals, especially rabbits, composed 65 percent of the diet; the remainder was mostly birds and carrion (Zumbaugh et al. 1985). No sex

or age differences in diet were seen. Use of lagomorphs, especially cottontails, also was high in southern Colorado (Rongstad et al. 1989). When food is plentiful, swift foxes kill and cache excess prey in shallow, poorly covered holes. In Colorado, lagomorphs, prairie dogs, and thirteen-lined ground squirrels have been excavated from such caches (Loy 1981; J. Fitzgerald, unpublished).

Swift foxes live in pairs, and occasionally in trios of one male and two females. The seasonal pair bond is strong, and males assist in provisioning the young. Whether monogamy is lifelong for a given pair is not clear. The animals are most active at night. However, they may forage in late evening or early morning and also spend time sunning at the den entrance on favorable days. They do not hibernate.

Swift foxes mate in late December, January, and February, at which time the animals become highly vocal (Avery 1989). Females are monestrous. Both parents assist in rearing the young, which are born in late March, April, or early May following a gestation period of 51 days. Litter size ranges from one to eight, with four to five young the average. The altricial pups develop rapidly. Their eyes and ears are opened by the end of the second week and they first come above ground at about four to five weeks of age (Kilgore 1969). The young gradually learn their surroundings and will hunt with the adults as they get older. They typically disperse in September and October. Females may breed in their first year (Kilgore 1969, Loy 1981).

A variety of predators, principally coyotes and eagles, kill swift foxes (L. N. Carbyn, pers. comm.; J. Fitzgerald, unpublished). Covell and Rongstad (1990) suggested that coyotes and eagles are major regulators of numbers of swift foxes. Humans are also important causes of mortality, due to road kill and deliberate harvest. The species is very "naive" and easy to trap. Locally, populations have been reduced or exterminated by over-zealous hunting, trapping, and poisoning

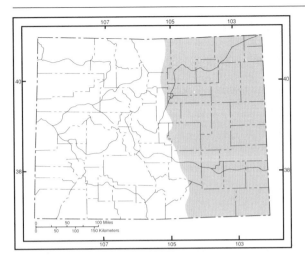

Map 10-8 Distribution of the swift fox (Vulpes velox) *in Colorado.*

campaigns. On the Pinon Canyon Site, mortality of all sex and age classes was 44 percent, with pups showing 62 percent mortality (Covell and Rongstad 1990). It appears that in times of low rabbit densities, swift fox populations decline as well. Few adults survive past their fourth year in the wild although captive females have bred successfully until six years of age and one male until his tenth year. The literature on the species was reviewed by Egoscue (1979) and Scott-Brown et al. (1987).

DISTRIBUTION IN COLORADO — The swift fox was extirpated in the late 1800s and early 1900s over much of its range in North America, probably due to its susceptibility to poisoning and trapping activities aimed at wolves and coyotes. Some states, including South Dakota, Wyoming, Nebraska, and Kansas are now experiencing local recoveries. In other areas, such as Colorado, the species never reached the extreme low numbers experienced elsewhere. Cary (1911) and Warren (1942) indicated that populations were low but present. Lechleitner (1969) remarked: "Nowhere are they presently abundant and I do not expect they will ever again become common on our plains." In fact, it appears that the density of swift foxes in certain areas on the eastern plains of

Colorado is high (Cameron 1984, Covell and Rongstad 1990, Loy 1981, Rongstad et al. 1989). Harvest records from the Colorado Division of Wildlife show annual harvests between 2,000 and 3,300 during the early 1980s when fur prices were high. The low harvest of 210 for 1990 (Table 3-2) may be more a reflection of fur prices than of abundance of foxes, although Covell and Rongstad (1990) reported difficulty in finding swift foxes on the Comanche National Grassland and in areas with high coyote density. Trap loss may be additive and not compensatory mortality in this species. The species is being reviewed at the present time for listing under the Endangered Species Act. In Colorado, the subspecies *Vulpes velox velox* can be expected from any county on the eastern plains where native prairie occurs.

Photograph by Bill Bevington.

Photograph 10-5 Red fox (Vulpes vulpes).

Vulpes vulpes
RED FOX

DESCRIPTION — The red fox is a slender, dog-like mammal with a long, sharp-pointed muzzle, and a long, bushy, white-tipped tail. Measurements are: total length 940–1045 mm; length of tail 310–380 mm; length of hindfoot 145–160 mm; length of ear 80–89 mm; weight 3–7 kg with females smaller than males (Storm et al. 1976). The tail is approximately 70 percent as long as the body.

The ears are pointed and held erect; the feet, nose, and backs of the ears are typically black. Three color phases — red, cross, and silver — exist; the red phase is the commonest in the wild. The typical red phase has a dorsal pelage of reddish yellow with the underparts yellow to white. The so-called cross-fox has a yellowish dorsum with a dark cross of hairs extending over the shoulders and on the dorsal midline. The silver fox is black with silver tips on some or all of the guard hairs, lending the pelage a frosted or silvery appearance. Melanistic foxes, lacking these silver tips, are not uncommon in the foothills of the Front Range. In all color phases, the tip of the tail is white. The skull is relatively slender with a long, narrow rostrum. The sagittal crest is well developed, especially in older animals. The postorbital processes of the frontal bones are thin and concave. Females have eight mammae. Males have a well-developed baculum with a long, broad urethral groove and a slightly expanded distal end.

NATURAL HISTORY — There are no detailed ecological studies of the red fox in the Rocky Mountain region. Across North America the red fox is commonest in open woodlands, pasturelands, riparian, and agricultural lands. It favors areas with a mixture of these vegetation types occurring in small mosaics with good development of ground cover (Ables 1975). Red foxes also do well on the margins of urbanized areas and are common in open space and other undeveloped areas adjacent to cities along the Front Range corridor. In the mountains they occur in montane and subalpine meadows as well as in alpine and forest edges, usually near water. Semidesert shrublands are not utilized to any great extent, except local riparian wetlands and areas adjoining irrigated agriculture.

Limited studies of food habits in Colorado indicate the species is adept at taking ground-nesting birds and their eggs, including sage grouse, pheasants, and waterfowl as well as jackrabbits, cottontails, and occasionally pocket gophers (Hogue 1958). Small rodents, including deer mice and voles, rabbits, birds, and insects are common dietary items (Scott 1943, Findley 1956, Korschgen 1959, Stanley 1963). Voles are often reported as the major prey (Voigt 1987). Fruits, nuts, and berries are also eaten (Samuel and Nelson 1982). In general, red foxes are opportunistic and eat whatever is available, including some carrion and domestic poultry.

Red foxes make efficient use of prey, having an average intake requirement of about 223 kcal/kg/day, with a mean assimilation efficiency of 91 percent (Vogtsberger and Barrett 1973). Foxes require 2.2 to 2.5 kg per individual per week. Fox pups in the den on a diet of jackrabbits, ducks, and duck eggs, consumed 1.3 to 1.9 kg per pup per week (Sargeant 1978). Prey biomass required for a mated pair plus five young ranges from 18.5 to 20.4 kg/km^2, assuming a territory size of 7.8 km^2.

The species is generally nocturnal or crepuscular in its hunting habits, but in winter may sun outside the den or increase daytime foraging activity, perhaps as a result of difficulty finding food (Ables 1969). Dens are the focal points for rearing pups during the spring and summer months. Natal dens are built in late winter, usually in well-drained, loose soils surrounded by good vegetative cover. In good weather foxes simply curl up on the surface and do not utilize dens for protection. Dens are usually in burrows previously excavated by other mammals, including badgers and marmots in our area, but they can dig their own dens if necessary. Most dens have at least 2 openings but some have up to 12 or more in areas of traditional use (Ables 1975).

Foxes are often together in pairs or family groups, except during fall after dispersal of the young. Social units in red fox populations are families: a mated pair and their young, or occasionally one male and several females with kinship ties, some of which have young. Nonbreeding females help rear young in such groups. Both members of the pair provision the young (Voigt 1987).

Map 10-9 Distribution of the red fox (Vulpes vulpes) *in North America.*

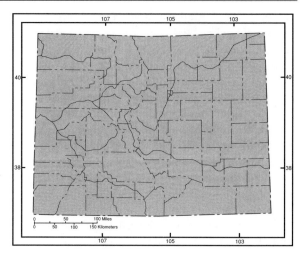

Map 10-10 Distribution of the red fox (Vulpes vulpes) *in Colorado.*

Red foxes are monestrous. Estrus lasts one to six days and the gestation period is about 52 days (Asdell 1964). Females and males may breed as juveniles, depending on population size, mortality, and food availability. Mating in the central United States occurs in the winter months from December through March. Most matings in Colorado probably occur in January and February. Young are born in March or early April on the eastern plains. Litter size is usually four to five (Lloyd 1975) but is reported to range from one to 17 (Holcomb 1965). Larger litters are usually associated with populations that have high annual mortality (Voigt 1987). The young mature rapidly and their eyes open by nine days of age. They remain in the den for the first month of their lives (Ables 1975). Sex ratios may slightly favor males over females (Storm et al. 1976). Pups are reported to be moved to different den sites one or more times.

Juveniles disperse in the fall. Considerable variation exists in distances moved, but an average of 29 to 30 km for males and 16 km for females is not unusual in the Midwest (R. Phillips et al. 1972). Actual dispersal distances may relate to the distance that places the disperser beyond home ranges established by resident foxes (D. W. Macdonald and Bacon 1982).

Home ranges are exclusive (but undefended) areas whose borders are visited every one to two weeks (Sargeant 1972). Home ranges have been estimated to be as small as 57 ha in urban areas, up to 6,000 ha in less diverse habitats (Ables 1969, Storm 1965). Males defend the territory of the mated pair during the breeding season.

Humans are the principal source of mortality, accounting for 80 to 90 percent in the central United States, with hunting, trapping, and automobiles being the major agents. Coyotes, eagles, and bobcats may also kill red foxes (Storm et al. 1976). Rabies and mange may cause some mortality but do not seem to be common in Colorado. Samuel and Nelson (1982) and Voigt (1987) reviewed the literature.

DISTRIBUTION IN COLORADO — The red fox has the widest geographic distribution of any carnivore, occurring naturally over most of North America and Eurasia as well as north Africa. It has also been introduced to other areas, including Australia, either to be hunted or to help control pest mammals, such as rabbits. In Colorado the species occurs throughout the state except for the southern half of the eastern plains. The red fox is listed as a furbearer in Colorado (Table 3-1).

For many years the North American red fox was known as *Vulpes fulva* and considered to be distinct from the Eurasian red fox, *V. vulpes*. Churcher (1959) determined that the two populations are conspecific, so the older name, *V. vulpes*, applies. One subspecies, *Vulpes vulpes macroura*, is currently recognized in Colorado. However, subspecific assignment of red foxes in Colorado has been complicated by the recent expansion of foxes in the eastern part of the state, and also by foxes escaped (or freed) from fox farms. Whether red foxes on the eastern plains dispersed from the mountains (the range of *V. v. macroura*) or from the east (the range of *V. v. regalis*) is unknown.

Urocyon cinereoargenteus
GRAY FOX

DESCRIPTION — The gray fox is a slender canid with a bushy, black-tipped tail. It is shorter and more robust than the red fox, an impression enhanced by the relatively short ears and muzzle. The dorsal color is grizzled gray. The ears, neck, and legs are reddish buff. The throat, upper chest, and belly are usually whitish. The dorsal surface of the tail is grayish with a blackish median mane that terminates in a black tip. Measurements are: total length 800–1,130 mm; length of tail 275–430 mm; length of hindfoot 100–150 mm; length of ear 65–70 mm; weight 3–7 kg, with males slightly heavier than females. The skull has distinctive, lyre-shaped temporal ridges rather than a saggital crest. The dentary has a deep notch on the posterior end of the horizontal ramus. Females have six mammae. The baculum

Photograph by Joseph G. Hall.

Photograph 10-6 Gray fox (Urocyon cinereoargenteus).

has a long urethral groove and a well-developed keel.

NATURAL HISTORY — Except for limited research in Utah, California, Arizona, and Texas, little is known of the biology of the gray fox in the West. In Colorado, gray fox habitat is usually rough broken terrain in semidesert shrublands, montane shrublands, piñon-juniper and riparian woodlands, orchards, and weedy margins of croplands. Gray foxes do not appear to occupy intensive agricultural lands or higher elevations in the mountains. Competition with red foxes, swift foxes, or kit foxes may influence their distribution in many areas of the West where they seem to occupy habitats in between those preferred by the other species. Gray foxes tolerate urbanized environments within their preferred habitats and live in suburban areas in California (T. Fuller 1978).

Gray foxes are secretive and mostly nocturnal, and they may be more common in a given area than direct observations suggest. They den in rocky outcrops, brush piles, hollow trees, or burrows. Dens are commonly close to water in the East. The animals climb trees and rock ledges with ease.

Gray foxes are more omnivorous than other Coloradan foxes. In Zion National Park, Utah, foods

Map 10-11 Distribution of the gray fox (Urocyon cinereoargenteus) *in North America.*

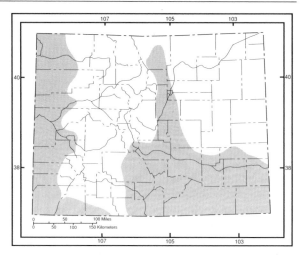

Map 10-12 Distribution of the gray fox (Urocyon cinereoargenteus) *in Colorado.*

included fruits, arthropods, small mammals, some carrion, reptiles, and a few birds (Trapp and Hallberg 1975). Their diet in that area was more herbivorous and insectivorous than in eastern studies. In the Southwest, mammals were present in about 60 percent of stomachs examined, arthropods were found in 55 percent, and plants were found in 40 percent (Turkowski 1969). Studies in the East showed cottontail rabbits to be especially important prey, but rodents may be more important than lagomorphs over much of the gray fox's western range, with *Peromyscus, Microtus, Spermophilus, Neotoma,* and *Thomomys* identified as prey. Juniper cones and prickly-pear fruits are eaten, as are acorns (Trapp and Hallberg 1975, Turkowski 1969).

Reproductive biology is poorly known. Gray foxes are monestrous with mating occurring from January to March over much of their range, but data for the Rocky Mountain region are lacking. The gestation period is about 59 days. Litter size aver-

ages 3.8 and ranges from one to seven young (Fritzell 1987). Dispersal occurs in fall or winter. Females reach sexual maturity at about 10 months and are capable of breeding their first year, but many may not breed as yearlings (Wood 1958). However, data summarized by Trapp and Hallberg (1975) suggest that populations of gray foxes appear to be composed mostly of juveniles (48 to 73 percent), suggesting that breeding by juvenile females is important to population success. Sex ratio probably is close to 1:1, although in some studies males are favored.

Home ranges averaged 30 to 200 ha for gray foxes in Utah (Trapp 1978) and California (Fuller 1978). Home ranges in the East apparently are larger, in some cases more than 500 ha (Fritzell 1987). Gray foxes may be territorial, as exclusive areas of occupancy are established and scent marking is common. Mean distances moved in foraging in Utah were 475 m for males and 600 m for females (Trapp 1978). Estimated densities ranged between one and two animals per km^2 (Fritzell 1987).

Little is known of mortality, although attrition in young is probably high. Golden eagles, coyotes, and bobcats attack gray foxes. Rabies outbreaks occur periodically in the eastern United States. The literature on the species was reviewed by Fritzell and Haroldson (1982) and Fritzell (1987).

DISTRIBUTION IN COLORADO — Gray foxes are widely distributed along the foothills of the Eastern Slope, in southeastern Colorado, and at lower elevations on the Western Slope. Little is known of its abundance or population dynamics, although it is listed as a furbearer (Table 3-1) and several hundred are harvested annually (Table 3-2). One subspecies, *Urocyon cinereoargenteus scottii*, occurs in Colorado.

FAMILY URSIDAE — Bears

The family Ursidae contains the largest of the living terrestrial carnivores, the polar bear (*Ursus maritimus*) and the brown bear (*Ursus arctos*); Alaskan brown bears weigh up to 700 kg. Bears have five nonretractile digits on each foot with well-developed claws. The front claws are longer than the hind claws. The skull is stoutly built with the auditory bullae only moderately inflated. Incisors are unspecialized, and the canines are large, conical, and somewhat curved. The dental formula is 2-3/3, 1/1, 4/4, 2/3 = 40 or 42 teeth. Premolars are typically poorly developed and may number from one to four. The fourth premolar is almost always present but lacks the third or inner root. Premolars and molars are bunodont with low, rounded cusps; sectorial carnassial teeth are absent. The stomach is simple, and there is no caecum. Males have a well-developed baculum and typically average one-fourth to one-fifth larger than females.

Closely allied with canids, the first ursids appeared relatively recently in the fossil record, during the Miocene Epoch, about 29 million years ago. Although some controversy exists over the taxonomy of the ursids, most authorities recognize three genera and eight species. Bears are found in North America, Eurasia, and the Andes of South America. One species lived in the Atlas mountains of North Africa into the nineteenth century until it was exterminated by humans.

One genus and two species are known from Colorado.

Key to the Species of the Family Ursidae Found in Colorado

1. Claws of fore- and hindfeet of about equal length; length of last upper molar less than 1 times length of first upper molar; length of maxillary toothrow less than 110 mm . . . . Black Bear — *Ursus americanus*, p. 317

1′ Claws of forefeet longer and larger than claws of hindfeet; length of last upper molar more than 1 times length of first upper molar; length of maxillary toothrow more than 110 mm . . . . Brown Bear — *Ursus arctos*, p. 321

Photograph 10-7 Black bear (Ursus americanus).

Ursus americanus
BLACK BEAR

DESCRIPTION — A medium-sized bear, this species is Colorado's largest surviving carnivore. Color varies greatly, from black to pale brown or (rarely) even blond. In a Coloradan population, 83 percent of bears of both sexes were brown (T. Beck 1991), not unusual for black bears in mountainous regions of the West. Considerable seasonal color change occurs as a result of bleaching and fading of the pelage. Subadults may change color with age, usually going from brown to black but the reverse also occurs. A white chest blaze is not uncommon for Coloradan animals. The muzzle is typically pale brownish yellow. Measurements are: total length 1.4–1.95 m; length of tail 80–125 mm; length of hindfoot 190–280 mm; length of ear 60–80 mm; weight 90 kg, although some individuals weigh as much as 225 kg. In west-central Colorado, weights of 51 adult bears ranged from 59 to 159 kg, with adult males heavier than adult females at all seasons (T. Beck 1991).

Some adult black bears closely resemble brown bears, *Ursus arctos*, in appearance and can be misidentified in the field. The black bear generally lacks the mane of hairs present on the shoulders of the brown (or grizzly) bear, and the tips of the hairs are not grizzled as they are in many individuals of *U. arctos*. When standing, the rump usually appears as high or higher than the shoulder area whereas grizzlies usually appear slightly higher in the shoulder. There is considerable overlap between the size of foot pads for Coloradan black bears and Yellowstone grizzly bears, and identification on the basis of tracks is not always possible (T. Beck 1991). In general, the claws on the front feet of black bears are not as strongly developed as on most individual grizzly bears, and are not much larger than the rear claws. The skull typically has a straight profile; most grizzly bears have a shortened, dished face and slightly shorter ears. Females have six mammae.

NATURAL HISTORY — Black bears can survive in practically any habitat that offers sufficient food and cover, from the deserts of Arizona to the coniferous forests of northern Canada. In Colorado the species is most common in montane shrublands and forests, and subalpine forests at moderate elevations, especially in areas with well-developed stands of oakbrush or berry-producing shrubs such as serviceberry and choke-cherry. However, the animals also occupy habitats ranging from the edge of the alpine tundra to the lower foothills and canyon country. Extensive work on the species has been done by T. Beck (1991) in western Colorado and McCutchen (1987, 1989) in Rocky Mountain National Park.

Detailed studies of food habits of black bears have not been conducted in Colorado. However, black bears are omnivorous and the diet depends largely on what kinds of food are seasonally available, although their mainstay is vegetation. In spring, emerging grasses and succulent forbs are favored. In summer and early fall, bears take advantage of a variety of berries and other fruits. In late fall, preferences are for berries and mast (acorns), where available. When the opportunity is present, black bears eat a diversity of insects, including beetle larvae and social insects (ants, wasps, bees, termites, etc.), and they kill a variety of mammals, including rodents, rabbits, and young or unwary ungulates (Gill and Beck 1990). Carrion may be eaten at any time, but is especially important in spring, a fact formerly exploited by spring bear hunters, who attracted the animals with bait. In some areas in Idaho, black bears were effective predators on elk calves, killing 37 percent of tagged young (Schlegal 1977). The extent and significance of similar predation on wild ungulates in Colorado is unknown. Domestic sheep and cattle may also be taken, and black bears frequently raid apiaries and orchards. Ample food supplies are critical to black bear survival in spring, when they emerge from dormancy, and in the late summer and fall when they are putting on fat for winter.

There are four physiological phases in the annual cycle of black bears, closely tied to nutritional needs: hibernation, walking hibernation, normal activity, and hyperphagia (Gill and Beck 1990). During hibernation, black bears may exist more than 200 days without eating, drinking, defecating, or urinating. A fecal plug blocks the intestinal tract until spring. During this period many individuals of both sexes shed the outer layers of their foot pads. New pads develop and harden on emergence in the spring. Black bears normally lose 20 to 27 percent of their body weight during hibernation (Folk et al. 1977, R. Nelson et al. 1973). Hibernation is marked by a drop of 50 to 60 percent in metabolic and heart rates. The body temperature remains high, however, dropping only 7 or 8°C. Thus, bears can arouse fairly quickly when disturbed in their hibernacula. Energy is supplied from fat storage, and metabolized nutrients can be resynthesized into protein (R. Nelson and Beck 1984). The walking hibernation stage lasts for at least two to three weeks following emergence from the hibernation den. At that time, black bears are not inclined to feed or drink appreciably, and apparently urination rates are low. In Montana, bears continued to lose weight from April to as long as late July (Jonkel and Cowan 1971). By late July, they start to gain weight at an average of 0.7 kg per day. The normal activity phase is characterized by an increase in metabolic demand, and bears forage selectively for plant materials with high sugar and starch content and readily digestible animal protein. The hyperphagic phase is characterized by gorging during late summer and fall, with preferences shown for foods high in fat, sugar, and starch.

Black bears are retiring and secretive animals, for the most part, typically staying close to rough topography or dense vegetation that provides escape cover. Numbers are usually low in any particular locale, making it difficult to census and study the animals.

In Colorado, winter denning may begin as early as the first week in October and extend to late December. Peaks of denning activity occur in the third and fourth weeks of October for females, and the second and third week of November for males (T. Beck 1991). In Colorado, black bears generally use rock cavities (60 percent of dens examined) or excavations under shrubs and trees for den sites. Dens dug under serviceberry bushes were favored over other shrub types. In some instances the animals simply curl up under protective cover and sleep on the ground. Of dens examined 53 percent had definitely been used in previous years, and most dens showed some degree of prior use (T. Beck 1991).

Black bears in Colorado probably breed from early June to perhaps mid-August, according to studies in Montana (Jonkel and Cowan 1971). Females remain in estrus until bred or until the follicles degenerate. Ovulation is induced by copulation. The gestation period is seven to eight months, with implantation delayed until November or December. Cubs are born in the den in late January or February, while the mother is in hibernation. Litter size is two or three (Kolenosky and Strathearn 1987). Typically, black bear populations in the western United States have lower productivity than those in the East. Bears in parts of Colorado have some of the higher success rates reported in the West (T. Beck 1991). Based on a small sample size, the average Colorado litter size is two, and occasionally three (T. Beck 1991). The age of adult females bearing their first litter averaged five years with a range of three to seven. Frequencies of litters for females ranged from one to four years, with most females having a litter every other year.

At birth the cubs weigh only 225 to 250 g and are blind, naked, and helpless. Birth weight is only about 1/200th the weight of the mother, compared to about 1/15th for a newborn human. Cubs weighed in dens in Colorado averaged 1.5 kg in late February and early March, and 2.9 kg in late March (T. Beck 1991). The cubs grow rapidly and are weaned by September. They stay with the female during their first year of life. They disperse at the age of one and a half in spring or summer when the female comes into estrus again.

Black bears are typically solitary, except for family groups (a sow and cubs), or aggregations at concentrated food resources, where bears may show a relatively high tolerance for each other. At such times the animals maintain temporal spacing through dominance behaviors such as threat displays. Bears may forage at any hour, but most activity tends to be diurnal or crepuscular. Most nocturnal behavior is observed in spring and fall.

319

Map 10-13 Distribution of the black bear (Ursus americanus) *in North America.*

Signs of bear activity in an area include large piles of scat, rotten logs ripped open, and broken, bent, or stripped branches on fruiting bushes. Black bears can climb trees, and it is not unusual to see climbing scars on large aspen trunks. Black bears as well as grizzly bears will also mark trees by biting and clawing the trunk about one to two meters off the ground. Such marking behavior is thought to increase in midsummer, possibly relating to the onset of the breeding season.

Black bear populations are difficult to estimate. In Colorado, densities were estimated at one animal per 5.6 to 7.7 km^2 during early summer, with considerable increase in numbers starting in mid-August when migrant animals moved into mast-producing areas. Compared to populations in other parts of the country, this is a very low density (T. Beck 1991). McCutchen (1987) estimated one bear per 26 to 31 km^2 in Rocky Mountain National Park, and considered that area to represent

some of the least productive bear habitat in Colorado.

Home range depends on topography, food availability, and the sex and age of the individual. In mountainous parts of Colorado, some individual bears show seasonal migrations of 13 to 36 km from summer foraging sites to areas where fall mast and berry production are high (T. Beck 1991). Adult males appear to have the largest home ranges, and nonbreeding females have the smallest home ranges. Annual home range estimates in Colorado varied from 4 to 189 km^2, and home ranges for more than one year varied from 14 to 199 km^2 for resident adult females. For adult males, annual home range varied from 31 to 145 km^2, and total home ranges were 223 to 451 km^2 (T. Beck 1991). In Idaho, home ranges of adults varied from 16.6 to 130.3 km^2, with overlap of home ranges being common (Amstrup and Beecham 1976). Males tended to show larger daily movements (average 1.7 km) than females (average 1.4 km). In Montana and Arizona, little home range overlap was observed except between adult males in Arizona (Jonkel and Cowan 1971, LeCount 1977). In Arizona, home ranges were 13 km^2 for subadult females and 42 km^2 for subadult males.

Black bears have low biotic potential, due to the advanced age at which breeding starts, small litter size, and infrequency of litters. Therefore, they are sensitive to overhunting. In many states improper management has led to significant population declines. In Colorado, annual survival rates in a population partly protected from hunting by boundary closures were 0.56 for cubs, 0.94 for yearlings, and 0.70 to 0.96 for adults and subadults combined. Survival beyond six months of age was mostly dependent on an individual's interactions with humans. On the Black Mesa 26 percent of tagged animals were killed by humans, and about 85 percent of all subadult and adult mortality was human-caused (T. Beck 1991). No evidence exists for compensatory reproductive success in hunted populations. Most black bears do not live more than 8 to 10 years in the wild, al-

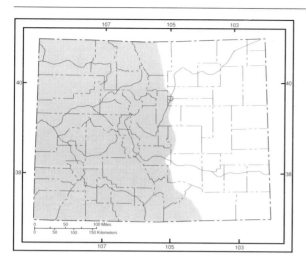

Map 10-14 Distribution of the black bear (Ursus americanus) in Colorado.

Photograph 10-8 Grizzly or brown bear (Ursus arctos).

though one captured individual was about 14 years old (T. Beck 1981). The literature was reviewed by Pelton (1982) and Kolenosky and Strathearn (1987).

DISTRIBUTION IN COLORADO — Black bears are locally common in suitable habitats in the western two-thirds of the state. Highest population densities occur in the montane shrublands from Walsenburg and Trinidad west to the San Luis Valley, in the San Juan Mountains, and in the canyon country of west-central Colorado. Black bears are big game mammals in Colorado (Table 3-1). In 1992, Colorado's voters passed a referendum halting spring bear hunting and banning the use of bait and dogs for hunting. Biologists of the Colorado Division of Wildlife and several environmental groups had been concerned that overharvest of females was leading to decline of bear populations in a number of the game management units.

Ursus americanus amblyceps, the subspecies of the Southern Rockies, once occurred statewide except in extreme northeastern Colorado, where *U. a. americanus* probably occurred.

Ursus arctos
BROWN OR GRIZZLY BEAR

DESCRIPTION — The grizzly or brown bear is a large, brownish ursid. Some individuals from western North America show a grizzled or silver-tipped appearance on their dorsal guard hairs. Other individuals are brown with a paler wash of yellowish on the shoulders and back. There is usually a pronounced mane of long hairs on the shoulders; the rest of the fur is dense, long, and coarse, at its finest in late fall and early spring. The shoulder region appears higher than the rump on most individuals because of a well-developed mass of muscle overlying the scapula. The claws on the front feet are very long and only slightly curved. The skull generally has a dished-in profile with the rostrum sloping gradually from the forehead. Females have six mammae. Few records exist on actual sizes of grizzly bears. Measurements are: total length 1.7–2.8 m; length of tail 70–80 mm; length of hindfoot 230–280 mm; length of ear 100–130 mm. An adult grizzly stands about 1,050 to 1,350 mm at the shoulder and most adults weigh 135 to 275 kg. The largest grizzly handled in the Greater Yellowstone Ecosystem weighed 509 kg (Craighead 1979). It appears that the grizzlies from Colorado were somewhat smaller than those from farther north.

NATURAL HISTORY — Grizzly bears were not limited to any particular habitat. Coloradan specimens were taken from prairie grasslands to alpine tundra. Productive grizzly bear habitat provides a variety of locally abundant foods that can be used sequentially by season (Jonkel 1987). Unlike the black bear, the grizzly does not climb trees; its activities are strictly terrestrial. The species is mostly crepuscular to nocturnal, especially in areas where it is threatened by humans.

The grizzly is largely a vegetarian, with up to 90 percent of the diet composed of plant material. Based on research in the Greater Yellowstone Ecosystem (summarized by F. Craighead 1979 and Schullery 1980, 1986), one can infer the ways in which Coloradan grizzlies once made their living. Depending on location, they probably fed on grasses, sedges, roots, and succulent forbs in alpine tundra and subalpine forests, supplemented by small mammals such as marmots, pocket gophers, and ground squirrels excavated from their dens, and the occasional large mammal or carrion. At lower elevations, the staple was probably grasses and succulent forbs supplemented with fruits such as choke cherries and currants. Colorado is not noted for the large crops of blueberries and raspberries characteristic farther north, and the availability of such foods was limited for the bears. Following severe winters, carrion (especially winter-killed deer, elk, other wildlife, and livestock) was plentiful. In Yellowstone, grizzlies have been observed killing several different ungulates, with many becoming adept at killing elk calves (Steve and Marilyn French, pers. comm.). Young adult grizzlies are the most effective hunters. The animals have also been observed to work equally hard excavating talus slopes at high elevations seeking adult miller moths (the same insects that appear in large numbers at lower elevations many springs and summers during migration). Of Colorado's native ungulates, probably only bighorn sheep and pronghorn were relatively secure

from periodic grizzly attacks because of their habitats and their speed and agility.

Good habitat for grizzly bears frequently contains food supplies that are seasonally and elevationally restricted. In such situations, the animals may have distinct and well-defined seasonal home ranges reached by long migration corridors, sometimes more than 65 km long. Home ranges have been estimated at 57 to 2,600 km^2 in the Greater Yellowstone Ecosystem, which encompasses Yellowstone National Park and the adjacent national forests. This vast ecosystem is barely large enough to contain the wanderings of some individuals and the spatial demands of a viable population (J. Craighead and Mitchell 1982). Individual animals have been reported to move up to 10 or 11 km daily in that area.

Grizzlies, as black bears, den in the winter months. They typically enter dens in late October or early November and come out between late March and early May. In the den they exhibit physiological patterns similar to those described for the black bear. Dens typically are located on steep slopes at high elevations. Dens are excavated into the soil; natural shelters are not used (F. Craighead and Craighead 1972).

Grizzly bears are polygamous and may mate as early as mid-May or as late as mid-July. Most breeding occurs in June. Estrous continues for up to two months (J. Craighead et al. 1969). Copulation may last from 10 to 60 minutes depending on individuals, and females may mate more than once, even accepting more than one male on the same day. Delayed implantation occurs, and cubs are born in the den in late January (J. Craighead et al. 1976). Average litter size is 2.24 for Yellowstone, with an average reproductive cycle of 3.4 years. Female grizzlies typically produce their first litters at 5.5 years of age and breed throughout their lifespan (J. Craighead and Mitchell 1982). Thus, grizzly bears have considerably lower biotic potential than even the black bear. The oldest breeding female in Yellowstone was approximately 25 years of age.

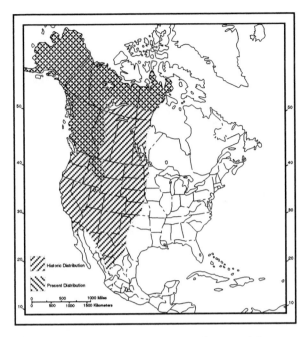

Map 10-15 *Historic and present distribution of the grizzly or brown bear* (Ursus arctos) *in North America. After Rausch (1963).*

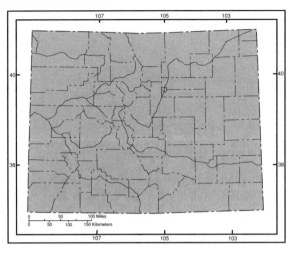

Map 10-16 *Historic distribution of the grizzly or brown bear* (Ursus arctos) *in Colorado.*

Sex ratios appear to approximate 1:1 in cubs but may slightly favor females in adults. In Yellowstone, the age structure of the population was: 19 percent cubs, 13 percent yearlings, 25 percent two- to four-year-olds, and 44 percent adults (J. Craighead and Mitchell 1982). Such age structure is probably essential for maintaining populations in other areas. Mortality is almost invariably caused by humans. Mills (1919) summarized observations of grizzly bears from the northern Front Range. Literature on the species was reviewed by J. Craighead and Mitchell (1982), Jonkel (1987), and Pasitschniak-Arts (1993).

DISTRIBUTION IN COLORADO — Although grizzly bears were once common throughout Colorado, there are presently no known populations (Armstrong 1972, Cary 1911, Warren 1942). In the contiguous United States, relatively few grizzlies remain, primarily in Yellowstone and Glacier national parks. Other remnants exist in parts of Idaho, Montana, and Wyoming. The species is

listed as "threatened" under federal law and as "endangered" by the state of Colorado.

In 1979, to the surprise of many, an adult female grizzly attacked a guide named Ed Wiseman near Platoro Reservoir on the northeastern edge of the San Juan Mountains (Barrows and Holmes 1990). Wiseman, an experienced hunter and outfitter, stated that he managed to kill the animal using a hand-held arrow. He was severely injured but recovered from the incident. The animal's skull, skeleton, and skin are housed in the collection of the Denver Museum of Natural History. This animal was the last specimen to be collected in Colorado, although periodic rumors of additional individuals still circulate. If any animals remain in the state, they probably do not constitute a viable population. This is an unfortunate but real price that is paid for "progress and development" and for maintenance of the livestock industry.

Because of extraordinary individual and geographic variation, the taxonomy of the large brown bears of North America has long been a subject of controversy. Previously, a large number of separate species were recognized (Hall 1981), of which four were named from Colorado type localities (Armstrong 1972). However, until recent decades most authors have treated Coloradan grizzly bears as *Ursus horribilis*. R. L. Rausch (1953, 1963) recognized all of the brown and grizzly bears of North America as conspecific with the Eurasian brown bear, *Ursus arctos*. One subspecies, *Ursus arctos horribilis*, occurred in Colorado.

FAMILY PROCYONIDAE — Raccoons, Ringtails, and Allies

The family Procyonidae includes small to medium-sized mammals with pointed snouts, and in many species, long tails ringed with contrasting colors and distinctive facial markings. The ears are small to medium, and the face is typically short and broad. The feet have five digits with well-developed claws, variously nonretractile or retractile. The foot posture is plantigrade or semiplantigrade. The skull is robust and lacks an alisphenoid canal except in the lesser panda, *Ailurus fulgens*. The number of teeth ranges from 36 to 40, with the loss of some premolars. The dental formula is 3/3, 1/1, 4/4, 2/2 = 40 teeth for Coloradan species. The incisors are unspecialized. Typical of carnivores, the canines are well developed. However, the carnassials are poorly developed. The molars are often broad and somewhat triangular or rounded. The stomach is simple, and a caecum is absent. Most procyonids are good climbers, typically sheltering in trees or rock crevices. They are crepuscular or nocturnal, and omnivorous in their diets. The species are social to varying degrees; some are solitary, some form pairs, and others live in family groups. Females are monestrous, having a single estrous cycle during a restricted breeding season. Males are typically about one-fifth larger than females and have a well-developed baculum.

The Procyonidae is a rather old lineage, dating from the Oligocene Epoch in North America, approximately 40 million years ago. Procyonids appear to be closely related to the ursids. There are 7 genera and 19 species. Aside from the lesser or red panda of Asia, all of the genera are restricted to the New World. In Colorado there are two genera, each represented by a single species.

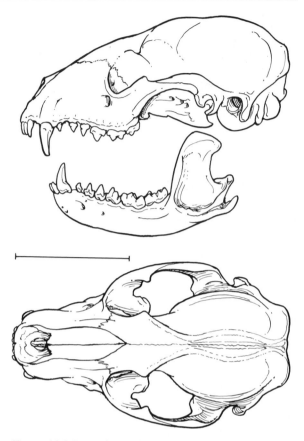

Figure 10-2 Lateral and dorsal views of the skull of the raccoon (Procyon lotor). *Scale = 1 cm.*

Key to the Species of the Family Procyonidae Found in Colorado

1. Animal slender; tail longer than head and body; rings on tail incomplete ventrally; posterior margin of bony palate not extending much beyond last molar . . . . Ringtail — *Bassariscus astutus*, p. 325

1' Animal robust; tail shorter than head and body; rings on tail complete ventrally; posterior margin of bony palate extending well beyond last molar. . . . . Raccoon — *Procyon lotor,* p. 327

Photograph 10-9 Ringtail (Bassariscus astutus).

Bassariscus astutus
RINGTAIL

DESCRIPTION — The ringtail, also called cacomistle, ringtail cat, miner's cat, rock cat, and civet cat, is a small, slender carnivore with a long tail. The dorsum is yellowish buff with black-tipped guard hairs, and the venter is whitish. The tail is white marked with a black tip and seven or eight dark bands that are incomplete ventrally. The ears are conspicuous. The muzzle is pointed, and the face is contrastingly marked with whitish areas around the eyes and below each ear. Measurements are: total length 615–850 mm; length of tail 310–440 mm; length of hindfoot 56–78 mm; length of ear 44–50 mm; weight 800–1,350 g, with males slightly larger than females. The claws are semiretractile. The skull is slightly elongated with well-developed postorbital processes. The carnassial teeth are poorly developed. The posterior margin of the palate extends to the level of the last molars. Females have four mammae.

NATURAL HISTORY — The ringtail inhabits arid and semiarid habitats throughout the Southwest. In Colorado it is typically associated with rocky canyon country and foothills areas of piñon-juniper woodlands, montane shrublands, or mixed conifer-oakbrush. In California it has been reported to be common in riparian woodlands

(Kaufmann 1987) and has usually been considered to remain close to surface water (Grinnell et al. 1937, Lechleitner 1969). However, studies of Coloradan animals suggest that the animals are good at urine concentration and probably do not require free water (Richards 1976).

Ringtail ecology is poorly known. Ringtails are omnivorous and their diet varies with food availability. They feed on various small mammals including deer mice, ground squirrels, woodrats, lagomorphs, and bats. Birds, lizards, and insects may also be taken, the latter being important seasonally. Summaries of food habit studies in other states indicate that mammals, fruits, and arthropods compose over 80 percent of the diet (Kaufmann 1987). Traces of carrion (deer) have also been reported. In Texas, plant material constituted over 70 percent of the diet locally and seasonally; juniper "berries," cactus, and hackberry may be important (Toweill and Teer 1977).

Ringtails are agile, active carnivores and excellent climbers. They can move rapidly up rock faces using such techniques as chimney stemming, ricocheting, and power leaps. The hindfoot rotates 180 degrees during vertical descents (Trapp 1972). They appear to be mostly nocturnal, shy, and retiring animals and are seldom observed even in areas where they are relatively common. Ringtails den in rock crevices, under large boulders, in hollow logs and trees, or in old buildings.

Mating occurs in the spring, generally in March in Utah. Gestation takes 51 to 54 days. The young are born in late April, May, or early June. Captive animals can produce a second litter upon the death of the first. Litters average three to four young, with a range of one to five (E. Bailey 1974, Poglayen-Neuwall and Poglayen-Neuwall 1980).

The young are altricial and weigh about 28 g at birth. The eyes open during the third and fourth weeks, and the teeth erupt during the fourth or fifth week. Both parents are reported to provision the young, although the male's role is unclear. The male may be kept away from the young until

Map 10-17 Distribution of the ringtail (Bassariscus astutus) *in North America.*

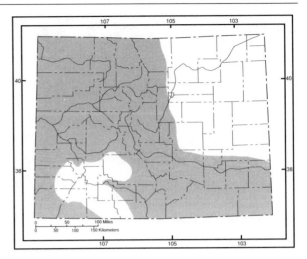

Map 10-18 Distribution of the ringtail (Bassariscus astutus) *in Colorado.*

they are four weeks of age; in fact, he may be totally excluded from the den (Kaufmann 1987). The young begin foraging with the female at about two months of age, and weaning occurs between three and five months. Both sexes are reproductively mature at about 10 months of age (E. Bailey 1974, Poglayen-Neuwall and Poglayen-Neuwall 1980, Toweill and Toweill 1978).

Reported densities range from about two animals per km^2 in juniper and oak woodlands in Texas to 20 animals per km^2 in riparian woodlands in central California (Kaufmann 1987). In Utah, densities were 1.5 to 2.9 animals per km^2 in piñon-juniper and riparian woodlands (Trapp 1978). Populations in favorable areas in Colorado are probably at densities similar to or lower than those observed in Utah. Annual population peaks coincide with birth of young in June. Home ranges in Texas were linear and averaged 20 ha for females and 43 ha for males (Toweill and Teer 1980). In Utah monthly home ranges averaged 136 ha (49 to 233 ha range) but individuals also showed indications of shifting on a seasonal basis (Trapp 1978).

The social behavior of ringtails is unknown but home ranges often overlap and some individuals may use common latrines where scat piles accumulate (Trapp 1978). Males mark their home ranges with urine. Both sexes have anal glands whose secretions are emitted when the animal is alarmed. The species has been reported to travel in pairs but few data exist to suggest that permanent bonds are formed. The vocalizations include apparent contact calls, distress and alarm calls, and threat sounds (Poglayen-Neuwall and Poglayen-Neuwall 1980, Willey and Richards 1981).

Mortality factors are not well known but great horned owls, snakes, and domestic cats and dogs have been reported to kill ringtails. Trapping and encounters with automobiles take their toll. The literature on the species was reviewed by Poglayen-Neuwall and Toweill (1988) and Kaufmann (1987).

DISTRIBUTION IN COLORADO — Our understanding of ringtail distribution in Colorado has grown in the past two decades, due largely to the

326

work of Richard E. Richards of the University of Colorado at Colorado Springs. Ringtails are far more widely distributed than was previously recognized, being present in roughlands at moderate elevations (to above 2,800 m) on either side of the Continental Divide (Gavin and Richards 1993, Willey and Richards 1974). Ringtails are categorized as furbearers in Colorado (Table 3-1). The species is probably most common in the canyon country of the southwestern part of the state. One subspecies, *Bassariscus astutus flavus*, occurs in Colorado.

Photograph 10-10 Raccoon (Procyon lotor).

Procyon lotor
RACCOON

DESCRIPTION — Raccoons are stocky carnivores with bushy tails and relatively long legs. The forepaws have elongated digits adapted for searching, grasping, and manipulating food. The dorsal color is blackish to brownish gray and the underparts are paler grayish brown. The tail has four to seven dark bands separated by lighter bands of hair. The dark bands are usually complete ventrally. A blackish mask extends across the area of the eyes. The ears are conspicuous and rounded. The feet are plantigrade. Measurements are: total length 600–950 mm; length of tail 190–405 mm; length of hindfoot 80–140 mm; weight 1.5–22 kg, with an average of 3–9 kg. Height at the shoulder is about 230–300 mm. Males are typically slightly larger than females. The skull is stout, with prominent postorbital processes. The cheek teeth are robust, and the carnassials poorly developed. The posterior margin of the palate extends well beyond the last molars. The animals lack a caecum, and the intestine is short. Females have six mammae and males have a well-developed baculum.

NATURAL HISTORY — The raccoon has been studied intensively in North America, especially in the eastern portions of its range. Detailed studies have not been made in the Rocky Mountain region, however, where the animals have increased remarkably in recent decades. The raccoon is adaptable and occupies habitats ranging from hardwood swamps, marshlands, and upland mixed or deciduous forests in the East to riparian gallery forests, montane parks, and semidesert shrublands in the West. It is typically found near water. Raccoons need suitable den sites, which may be hollow trees, logs, rock crevices, caves, culverts, burrows excavated by other mammals, brush piles, muskrat houses, or buildings (usually abandoned but sometimes even while occupied by humans). They are opportunistic, and make much use of abandoned burrows (Berner and Gysel 1967, Shirer and Fitch 1970). In south-central Wyoming, J. Fitzgerald (unpublished) recovered raccoon skulls up to 10 km from water and tree cover in white-tailed prairie dog towns, and observed their tracks around playas in such country. In Colorado the animals are commonest in lowland riparian habitats, irrigated croplands, and urbanized areas of the eastern plains and foothills, but are not uncommon along streams and reservoirs in mountain parklands.

Raccoons are most active from sunset to sunrise although at times they may forage during the daytime. Most activity occurs before midnight (Ellis 1964). During winter, they may sleep for extended periods, especially if snow cover accumulates. When warm spells occur, they may arouse and become active, depending on stored fat reserves rather than feeding (W. Hamilton 1936, Sharp and Sharp 1956, Stuewer 1943). In Colorado the length of winter inactivity varies from year to year, and in mild winters the animals are active practically year around.

Literally hundreds of different food items have been reported in the literature, varying with season and locality. Except during spring, vegetation is more important than animal foods. Raccoons are omnivorous opportunists, feeding on berries, garden and field crops, mast (acorns), and fruits including wild plums, cherries, and grapes. Animal food consists mostly of arthropods, especially crayfish, but birds, eggs, small mammals, fish, snakes, lizards, and amphibians are also eaten. Carrion from such large mammals as horses, cattle, and deer are consumed occasionally. Along the South Platte River in Colorado during fall, plant material constituted 73 percent of the diet and animal matter the remaining 27 percent (of which 13 percent was insects). Over half of the food volume was corn (Tester 1953).

Raccoons breed from December to June in Kansas (Stains 1956) and their cycle, at least in eastern Colorado, is probably similar. The peak of breeding activity in that state occurs in February, with young born in April or May. Most authors have reported a gestation period of 63 to 65 days (Kaufmann 1982). Data are conflicting on whether the females are induced ovulators, as spontaneous ovulation also occurs (Sanderson and Nalbandov 1973). Copulation may last for up to one hour, and adult males are polygynous. Expectant mothers typically move into a birthing den several days before parturition and may tear pieces of wood, bark, or similar materials to form a shallow bed. Litter size ranges from one to eight with means of two to five (Asdell 1964). Sex ratios of litters approximate 1:1, although sex ratios vary widely for adults.

The young are altricial, with eyes and ears opening at about 20 days. Teeth begin to erupt at about one month of age. Young raccoons begin

to walk at about the fifth week of age and can run and climb by seven weeks. After the eighth week the young are able to leave the den and follow the mother when she forages. Young are typically weaned by three months of age (W. Hamilton 1936; Montgomery 1964, 1968, 1969; Stuewer 1943). About 50 to 60 percent of juvenile females successfully mate, and the remainder breed as yearlings (Stuewer 1943, Wood 1955). Late litters may be the offspring of juvenile females (Sanderson and Nalbandov 1973). Males are sexually mature as juveniles but are not thought to contribute significantly to breeding until they are yearlings.

The social behavior of raccoons is poorly known. The most typical social unit consists of a mother and her young of the year. In some cases the young disperse in the fall and early winter; in other instances they stay with the female through the winter and disperse in spring or summer (Fritzell 1977, Schneider et al. 1971, Sharp and Sharp 1956). In North Dakota some yearling females were observed to stay with the female and not disperse (Fritzell 1978a). Sometimes yearlings leave in pairs and stay together until late spring.

Most adults seem to be solitary although congregations of two to two dozen may share winter dens. Whereas pairs and small groups likely represent sibling associations or family groups, larger aggregations probably do not. Temporary feeding groups also form in areas of abundant food resources. Generally, as the breeding season approaches, the incidence of fighting between adults increases and they become more solitary.

Dominance hierarchies form in certain situations. Raccoons appear to recognize their neighbors, and form dominant-subordinate relations with them more quickly than with strangers (Barash 1974). Probably, dominance relationships come into play at concentrated food resources and during the breeding season, and are facilitated by recognition of neighbors. Mutual avoidance plays a major part in their day-to-day activities.

The degree to which raccoons may be territorial is not clear (Kaufmann 1982, Lotze and Anderson 1979). Although no territories have been measured, home ranges have. Home ranges of males rarely overlap by more than 10 percent, and radio-tracked males rarely came closer to each other than 2 km (Fritzell 1978a). By contrast, home ranges of females overlap extensively, as do male-female home ranges.

In optimal urban habitat in Ohio, home ranges were 5 ha (C. Hoffmann and Gottschang 1977) whereas in prairie regions in North Dakota, home ranges averaged 2,560 ha for males and 806 ha for females (Fritzell 1978b). In Colorado most home ranges not in urban areas are probably linear because of the dependence on riparian habitat over much of the state. Densities of 0.5 to 1.0 animals per km^2 and 1.5 to 3.2 animals per km^2 have been found in North Dakota and Manitoba, respectively (W. Cowan 1973, Fritzell 1978b); similar densities can be expected for Colorado.

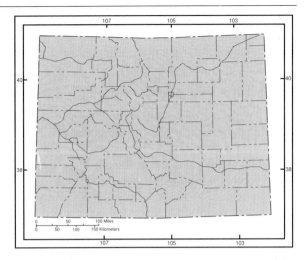

Map 10-20 Distribution of the raccoon (Procyon lotor) *in Colorado.*

Most mortality in raccoons appears to be attributable to humans or to starvation. Raccoons may live up to 16 years in the wild, but few live past their second year. In Missouri, only an estimated one raccoon in 100 lived to age seven (Sanderson 1951). Estimated population turnover time was 7.4 years, with adult mortality averaging 56 percent. Similar figures were reported from Manitoba, where yearling mortality was 60 percent and mortality for all age classes combined was over 50 percent (W. Cowan 1973). Mountain lions, bobcats, wolves, coyotes, gray and red foxes, and great horned owls are predators of raccoons. Raccoons harbor a wide variety of endo- and ectoparasites. Canine distemper is probably the most effective disease in regulating populations (Habermann et al. 1958, V. Robinson et al. 1957), including populations in Colorado. The extensive literature on raccoons was reviewed by Kaufmann (1982), Lotze and Anderson (1979), and Sanderson (1987).

DISTRIBUTION IN COLORADO — Raccoons occur throughout Colorado along riparian corridors, to elevations of about 3,050 m (10,000 ft). One of us (JPF) routinely saw raccoon tracks and had reports of tracks from the South Platte River in South Park at 2,900 m (9,500 ft) in elevation dur-

Map 10-19 Distribution of the raccoon (Procyon lotor) *in North America.*

ing the late 1960s and early 1970s. Raccoons are reported from Trappers Lake at an elevation of about 3,050 m (10,000 ft) in northeastern Garfield County (McKean and Burkhardt 1978).

Raccoons have undergone considerable range extension since the early 1940s (Sanderson 1987). This extension is surely due to their adaptability and ability to benefit from anthropogenic changes. For such a widespread and relatively common mammal, their biology is poorly known, however, especially in the West. In Colorado, studies designed to elucidate their present range, abundance, and ecological role would be beneficial. The animals are furbearers (Table 3-1) and several thousand are harvested annually (Table 3-2).

As Finley et al. (1976) and Armstrong (1972) indicated, the paucity of specimens in museum collections makes it difficult to assess taxonomic relationships of Coloradan populations. *Procyon lotor hirtus* occurs on the eastern plains; *P. l. pallidus* occurs in the western third of the state; *P. l. mexicanus* occurs in the San Luis Valley.

FAMILY MUSTELIDAE — Weasels and Allies

The family Mustelidae is a diverse adaptive radiation of terrestrial, semifossorial, arboreal, aquatic, and marine mammals. Mustelids generally rely on dens for protection when not foraging and are crepuscular or nocturnal. Most mustelids seek vertebrate prey but many are opportunistic, feeding on either plant or animal food as available. In size, mustelids range from the diminutive least weasel, measuring about 200 mm long and weighing about 50 g, to the giant otter of South America, which measures 2 m in length and weighs up to 34 kg. Mustelids are sexually dimorphic; males are typically one-quarter larger than females. The legs of most species are short, and the body of most is elongate. The tail is usually long and often bushy. The feet are plantigrade, semiplantigrade, or digitigrade. All feet have five digits with well-developed nonretractile or semiretractile

claws. The ears are short and rounded. Anal musk glands, whose secretions vary from merely pungent to memorably obnoxious, are well developed in most species. The skull is stout and lacks an alisphenoid canal. The face is typically short and broad, and the braincase is flattened. The condylar process of the dentary locks tightly into the flanged glenoid (mandibular) fossa so that the jaws close tightly and do not disarticulate when gripping prey. The dental formula for Coloradan mustelids is 3/3, 1/1, 2–4/3–4 = 32 to 38 teeth. Most commonly the dental formula is 3/3, 1/1, 3/3 = 34. The carnassial pair (fourth upper premolar and first lower molar) is well developed in most species. The single upper molar is normally large and dumbbell shaped or squarish. The upper toothrow may show an angle at the junction of the last premolar and first molar. The stomach is simple and lacks a caecum. Females are monestrous and many species show induced ovulation and delayed implantation. Males have well-developed bacula. The family is rather old, dating from the Oligocene Epoch, approximately 40 million years ago. There are 23 genera and about 65 species of mustelids, distributed worldwide except in Australia, the Antarctic, and most oceanic islands. Several species have been introduced into some of these areas. Many species are prized for their fur. In Colorado there are 8 genera and 12 species of mustelids.

Key to the Species of the Family Mustelidae Known or Expected to Occur in Colorado

1. Premolars 4/4 2

1' Premolars 4/3, 3/3, or 2/3 4

2. Dorsum dark brownish bordered dorsolaterally by two paler brown bands from shoulder to rump; length of tail about one-fourth total length; sagittal crest greatly enlarged and overhanging occiput . . . . Wolverine — *Gulo gulo*, p. 348

2' Dorsum blackish, dark brownish, or yellowish brown, not bordered by paler lateral bands; length of tail usually more than one-third total length; sagittal crest neither greatly enlarged nor overhanging the occiput. . . . . *Martes* 3

3. Dorsum brown to yellowish brown; greatest length of skull 90 mm or less . . . . American Marten — *Martes americana*, p. 332

3′ Dorsum grizzled black to dark brown; greatest length of skull greater than 90 mm . . . . Fisher — *Martes pennanti**, p. 335

4. Premolars 4/3; hindfeet webbed . . . . Northern River Otter — *Lutra canadensis*, p. 361

4′ Premolars 3/3 or 2/3; hindfeet not webbed . . . 5

5. Premolars 2/3; tail completely white . . . . Common Hog-nosed Skunk — *Conepatus mesoleucus*, p. 359

5′ Premolars 3/3; tail color variable, never completely white 6

6. Dorsal color black with white spots or stripes; posterior margin of palate not extending much beyond upper molars; auditory bullae small and flattened 7

6′ Dorsal color variable but not black with white spots or stripes; posterior margin of palate extending well beyond upper molars; auditory bullae not notably small and flattened. 9

7. Upper body generally with two continuous, longitudinal white stripes merging anteriorly in the head and neck region (rarely all black, but never with broken white stripes or spots); skull arched, highest just behind orbits; greatest length of skull more than 65 mm . . . . Striped Skunk — *Mephitis mephitis*, p. 356

7′ Upper body generally with four or more broken white stripes, breaking into spots or

blotches posteriorly; skull not highly arched, highest above posterior portion of bullae; greatest length of skull less than 65 mm . . . . *Spilogale* 8

8. Tip of tail white . . . . Western Spotted Skunk — *Spilogale gracilis*, p. 352

8′ Tip of tail with at least some black hairs . . . . Eastern Spotted Skunk — *Spilogale putorius*, p. 354

9. Front claws longer than 30 mm; white medial stripe on head and neck; greatest length of skull more than 90 mm . . . . American Badger — *Taxidea taxus*, p. 350

9′ Front claws shorter than 30 mm; no medial white stripe on head; greatest length of skull less than 90 mm . . . . *Mustela* 10

10. Hindfoot more than 55 mm; greatest length of upper tooth row more than 20 mm in males and 17.8 in females; greatest length of skull more than 60 mm 11

10′ Hindfoot less than 50 mm; greatest length of upper tooth row less than 20 mm in males and less than 17.8 in females; greatest length of skull less than 55 mm 12

11. Dorsal color buffy to yellowish white with a black facial mask; legs, feet, and tip of tail also black; distance between canines greater than distance between medial margins of auditory bullae . . . . Black-footed Ferret — *Mustela nigripes*, p. 341

11′ Dorsal color uniformly brown to dark brown, except for possible white throat or chest patch; distance between canines about equal to distance between medial margins of auditory bullae . . . . Mink — *Mustela vison*, p. 345

12. Tail with conspicuous black tip. 13

* Species of possible occurrence in Colorado.

12′ Tail without conspicuous black tip; at most a few black hairs . . . .
. . . . Least Weasel — *Mustela nivalis*,* p. 344

13. Ventral color yellowish orange in summer pelage; tail more than 44 percent of length of body; greatest length of skull usually more than 44 mm; auditory bullae relatively short; postglenoid length usually less than 46 percent of greatest length of skull . . . .
. . . . . Long-tailed Weasel — *Mustela frenata*, p. 338

13′ Ventral color white in summer pelage; tail less than 44 percent of body length; greatest length of skull usually less than 44 mm; auditory bullae relatively long; postglenoid length usually more than 46 percent of greatest length of skull . . . . . .
. . . . Ermine, or Short-tailed Weasel — *Mustela erminea*, p. 336

Martes americana
AMERICAN MARTEN

DESCRIPTION — The American marten — often called pine marten, or simply marten — is weasel-like, smaller than an average house cat, with a pointed face and conspicuous, rounded ears. The long, bushy tail accounts for about one-third of the animal's total length. The dorsal color is highly variable from dark brown to pale brownish yellow with the ventral surface sometimes slightly darker except for an orange to yellow-orange chest or throat patch. The tail and legs are usually darker than the body. The borders of the ears are often paler than the rest of the body. This prized furbearer has long, glossy, relatively stiff guard hairs and dense, silky underfur. Measurements are: total length 460–750 mm; length of tail 170–250 mm; length of hindfoot 75–98 mm; length of ear 45–55 mm; weight 0.5–1.2 kg. Females have eight mammae. Martens are digitigrade and equipped with semiretractile claws. The hind-

* Species of possible occurrence in Colorado.

Photograph 10-11 American marten (Martes americana).

limbs, like those of tree squirrels, have excellent rotational ability, enabling them to descend trees headfirst and to climb rapidly. Techniques have been developed to determine age (Strickland and Douglas 1987).

NATURAL HISTORY — The marten is an inhabitant of subalpine spruce-fir and lodgepole pine forests, alpine tundra, and occasionally montane forests (Yeager and Remington 1956). It is generally associated with older growth or mixed-age stands of spruce-fir and lodgepole pine. Over 30 percent canopy cover of coniferous trees is thought necessary for suitable marten habitat, with an optimum of 40 to 60 percent for resting and foraging (A. Allen 1982, Koehler and Hornocker 1977, W. Spencer et al. 1983). Moderate timber harvest may be favorable to martens by creating seral shrub and herb stages that enhance the prey base and berry crops. Overgrazing may reduce quality of habitat.

Martens den in tree cavities, logs, rock piles, and burrows, and frequently rest on tree limbs during the day. Large-diameter snags are important den sites in Wyoming (T. Clark and Campbell 1977) and California (S. Martin and Barrett 1983). Objects on the forest floor, including logs, rock piles, stumps, windthrown trees, and slash are thought to be important in providing not only den sites but also access in winter to subnivean rodent populations (T. Clark and Campbell 1977, Hargis and McCullough 1984).

A variety of prey is taken; however, voles and other mice may constitute over 60 to 88 percent of the diet. Pine squirrels are captured in their arboreal retreats, and chipmunks, ground squirrels, snowshoe hares, cottontails, pikas, and shrews are also eaten. In Manitoba, up to 53 percent of the diet was snowshoe hares. Winter food in Colorado is mostly voles (83 percent occurrence in samples), shrews, insects, and vegetable matter (C. Gordon 1986). Remains of snowshoe hare and beaver occurred in 7 percent of samples. Carrion is utilized as are berries when available. Birds are apparently taken only rarely. Martens pursue prey on the ground as well as in the trees (T. Clark and Campbell 1977). Martens cache food, often at a resting site (Henry et al. 1990). Adult martens require about 80 kcal/day for resting metabolism (Worthen and Kilgore 1981). This is roughly equivalent to three voles per day.

Usually crepuscular to nocturnal in habits, martens are active year around. However, diurnal activity may occur in summer where ground squirrels are important prey or in very cold winter weather. Coarse woody debris, such as is found in old-growth forests, provides access to subnivean resting sites, which are important to marten energetics in winter (Buskirk et al. 1989). In general,

the animals are more active in summer than winter. Martens seem to avoid traveling across open areas more than 100 to 250 m wide, although they have been observed in alpine boulder fields up to 3.2 km from timber (Streeter and Braun 1968). Travel routes are not used in any regular pattern.

The species does not appear to be territorial. Home ranges reported in the literature vary from less than one to almost 16 km^2, depending on season, location, and availability of food; the range is larger for eastern and northern animals than for animals farther south (Strickland and Douglas 1987). In Wyoming, average home ranges from telemetry studies were 2.0 to 3.2 km^2 for males and 0.8 km^2 for females (T. Clark et al. 1989, T. Clark and Campbell 1977). Home ranges of similar size were estimated from mark-recapture studies in Montana (V. Hawley and Newby 1957).

Populations within a given area can fluctuate widely because of variation in reproductive success and resident mortality as well as large numbers of highly mobile transient individuals. Some 65 percent of individuals in a Montana population were transients (on site no longer than one week) or temporary residents (on site less than three months) (V. Hawley and Newby 1957, Weckworth and Hawley 1962). In Wyoming also, both males and females averaged 145 days for their length of stay on the study site (T. Clark, Campbell, and Hauptman 1989). Population densities of 0.7 to 1.7 martens per km^2 have been reported (V. Hawley and Newby 1957). An apparent increase of martens occurred in the early 1950s in Colorado (Yeager and Remington 1956). Other than harvest records, detailed population information since that time is lacking. Clearly, however, perpetuation of old-growth forests is central to the maintenance of healthy marten populations.

Martens communicate by scent marking and vocalization. In addition to anal glands, both sexes have abdominal glands whose location is indicated by short hair (probably from wear) that is stained. The animals drag their bellies on logs

Map 10-21 Distribution of the American marten (Martes americana) in North America.

and branches to deposit scent, especially during the breeding season. Vocalizations include huffs, growls, screams, and something akin to a chuckle, the latter being used during the breeding season (Belan et al. 1978, Markley and Bassett 1942).

Most breeding occurs between late July and early September. Studies of captive animals suggest that polygamous matings are common and that two periods of estrus may occur if breeding is not successful the first time (Markley and Bassett 1942). In captivity, males became increasingly aggressive during the breeding season, sometimes killing their female penmates. Female-to-female aggression also increased in the breeding season, marked by vicious fighting. Summaries of field studies and scarring of pelts of males suggest that fighting, especially among males, may also be common in the wild (Strickland and Douglas 1987). Induced ovulation is suspected, based on work summarized for various mustelids (Ewer 1973). Delayed implantation occurs. Gestation

ranges from 230 to 275 days (Strickland and Douglas 1987). However, the actual developmental time from implantation to parturition is slightly less than one month (Jonkel and Weckwerth 1963). In northern populations, parturition dates range from mid-March to late April (Strickland et al. 1982). Martens have only one litter of one to five young (average slightly less than three) per year.

Both sexes are reproductively active at about 12 to 15 months (Strickland and Douglas 1987, Strickland et al. 1982). However, annual fecundity rates vary widely even within populations, making it difficult to estimate annual production. Some of this variance has been attributed to fluctuations in annual prey base. A 13-year study in Ontario reported an average of 80 percent conception in yearling females and 93 percent success in females older than one and a half years (Strickland and Douglas 1987). One of the reproductive females was estimated to be about 14 years old. Sex ratios of young are about 1:1, but males usually outnumber females in surveys of trapped animals by as much as three to one. Males may be more susceptible to trapping because of their much larger home ranges, a fact that was most noticeable in populations trapped during the fall rather than winter (Yeager 1950).

Young are altricial but partly furred. Ears open at about three weeks, and eyes open at slightly over one month of age. By about one and a half months they can leave the nest and are very active soon after that. Permanent dentition is complete by 18 weeks and the young approximate adult size at about three months. Males grow more rapidly than females (Brassard and Bernard 1939, Remington 1952).

Mortality probably is due mostly to trapping. The animals are relatively easy to capture, and unless monitored closely, populations can be overharvested (Strickland and Douglas 1987). There are scattered reports of predation by coyotes, red foxes, lynx, mountain lions, eagles, and great horned owls. The literature on the species was re-

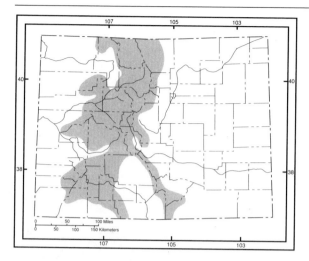

Map 10-22 Distribution of the American marten (Martes americana) *in Colorado.*

viewed by T. Clark et al. (1987), Strickland et al. (1982), and Strickland and Douglas (1987).

DISTRIBUTION IN COLORADO — Martens are harvested as furbearers (Table 3-1). They occur in most areas of coniferous forest in the higher mountains of Colorado. One subspecies, *Martes americana origenes*, occurs in the state.

Martes pennanti
FISHER

DESCRIPTION — The fisher is a large mustelid, similar in appearance to the marten. However, it lacks the orange to white chest or chin patch of the latter species. Color is typically dark brown to blackish, with the legs, tail, and rump darker than the rest of the body. Late winter and summer pelage is often paler than that of late fall and early winter. The head and shoulders are often grizzled silvery gold, and white patches may be present around the genitals or between the forelegs. Males are about 20 percent longer than females and may weigh nearly twice as much. Measurements are: total length 830–1,030 mm; length of tail 340–420 mm; length of hindfoot 90–130 mm; length of ear 40–60 mm; weights 2–5.5 kg. The skull is similar to that of the marten but usually is

more than 95 mm in length, with the outside length of the fourth upper molar more than 9.5 mm and the length of the first lower molar more than 11 mm.

NATURAL HISTORY — Fishers are most often associated with dense mixed deciduous-evergreen forest over their range in North America. The animals seem to avoid large openings in forested areas. Optimal habitats probably have more than 50 percent canopy closure, trees more than 25 cm in diameter, and at least two stories of canopy cover (Douglas and Strickland 1987). Fishers are solitary animals, rarely together except for the breeding season. Home range estimates vary from 15 to 35 km^2 with extensive overlap of males and females. Daily movements average about 2 km, with animals using temporary sleeping sites in hollow trees, beaver lodges, or burrows, or under logs, brush piles, and rock falls. Natal dens are typically in hollow trees. Powell (1981) reported that most animals mate from March to May, with delayed implantation contributing to a gestation period of about 11 months. Parturition occurs from February to May, with an average litter size of three.

Fishers are opportunistic carnivores feeding on the most available species of mammals and birds. Although fairly adept climbers, most hunting takes place on the ground. Snowshoe hare, voles, tree squirrels, mice, and carrion of ungulates commonly show up in dietary studies. Porcupines are a favored prey species in many areas. They typically are killed by repeated bites to the face (which is not protected by quills). When the prey is near death it is turned over and opened along the unprotected belly. Estimates of energy demands suggest that adult fishers need from 200 to 660 kcal/day, roughly equivalent to two squirrels or a dozen or more mice (Powell 1981). Literature on the species was reviewed by Powell (1981) and Douglas and Strickland (1987).

DISTRIBUTION IN COLORADO — Fishers are distributed across much of northern North America, although the range has contracted since

Map 10-23 Distribution of the fisher (Martes pennanti) *in North America.*

permanent European settlement (Douglas and Strickland 1987). The fisher is not firmly documented from the Southern Rockies. Specimens are known from the Yellowstone Region (Long 1965) and the Bighorn Mountains (T. Clark and Stromberg 1987) of Wyoming. Durrant (1952) listed a record of the species from the Uinta Mountains of Utah based on photographs of a single set of tracks. Armstrong (1972) discussed some early references to the fisher in Colorado, but did not find them convincing. Hoffmann et al. (1969) were of the opinion that the southern limit of the range of the fisher is in northwestern Wyoming and central Idaho. Recently the skull of an individual taken south of Aspen, Pitkin County (estimated by Elaine Anderson of the Denver Museum of Natural History to be about six years old) was submitted to Colorado Division of Wildlife personnel. The general opinion was that it represented remains of a captive animal clandestinely and unlawfully released into the wild by a nature photographer. The Wyoming Game and Fish

Commission has recently reported fisher sightings close to the Colorado-Wyoming border in the Snowy Range (Anonymous 1992), but those observations have not been verified. Based on the weight of presently available evidence, we believe it unlikely that the fisher has ever existed in the wild in Colorado.

Photograph by Bill Bevington.

Photograph 10-12 Ermine (Mustela erminea).

Mustela erminea
ERMINE, OR SHORT-TAILED WEASEL

DESCRIPTION — Also called short-tailed weasel, the ermine is a small, short-legged, slender-bodied mustelid with a short, black-tipped tail. It is the smallest carnivore known to occur in Colorado (the least weasel, *M. nivalis*, is smaller but has not been recorded in Colorado). Color varies with season. In summer, the dorsal color is chocolate to pale brown with a black tip on the tail. The venter is whitish to buff. In winter the animals are snow white except for the black tip on the tail. Measurements are: total length 190–245 mm; length of tail 42–66 mm, usually less than 44 percent of the head and body; length of hindfoot 23–31 mm; length of ear 13–16 mm; weight 30–200 g. Males are much larger than females. The soles of the feet are well-haired. Seasonal color change involves an orderly molt, and individuals are a mottled brown and white for periods in the fall and spring. The spring molt may be triggered by lengthening photoperiod, but colder temperatures may slow the rate of change (Bissonette and Bailey 1944, Rust 1962). The anal glands produce a secretion with a strong odor. Postglenoid length of the skull is usually more than 46 percent of condylobasal length. The auditory bullae are relatively long relative to those of the long-tailed weasel, about equal in length to the maxillary toothrow. Females have eight to 10 mammae.

NATURAL HISTORY — The ecological requirements of the ermine in the Southern Rocky Mountains are poorly understood. Studies in California (B. Fitzgerald 1977) and Canada (Simms 1979a) suggest that moist areas in early successional stages are favored. Coloradan records are from above 1,830 m (6,000 ft) in elevation, and observations of the animals have been made in alpine tundra (Dixon 1931) and subalpine forests (Hayward 1949). In South Park, where long-tailed weasels were relatively common, J. Fitzgerald (unpublished) captured only two ermines in 14 years of small mammal trapping. Both animals were from a moist hay meadow interspersed with willow stands in which long-tailed weasels were never captured. The latter were frequently seen and live trapped on drier upland sites adjacent to the hay meadow and along banks of the stream running through the area.

Ermines appear to be more nocturnal than long-tailed weasels and are active year round (Erlinge 1979). Bouts of foraging activity lasting about one hour are followed by rest periods. The animals can climb to prey on small semiarboreal rodents when necessary (Nams and Beare 1982). In Idaho, short-tailed weasels repeatedly followed the same hunting circuits without reliance on a home den (Musgrove 1951), although other reports indicate that weasels typically use a random search pattern when hunting.

No studies on the species' food habits have been reported for Colorado, with the exception of un-

successful attempts on pikas (Dixon 1931). In northern portions of the range, ermines prey on voles, other mice, shrews, and similar small mammals (Fagerstone 1987b, Hall 1951). Mice occurred in 59 percent of stomachs in Minnesota (Aldous and Manweiler 1942). In New York, arvicolines (microtines) accounted for about 36 percent of remains in digestive tracts, and *Peromyscus* accounted for 11 percent (W. Hamilton 1933). In California 54 percent of the winter mortality in a montane vole population was attributed to ermine predation (B. Fitzgerald 1977). Captive short-tailed weasels ate an average of 14 g of vole per day in the winter during that study. Shrews are also commonly eaten. Carrion, insects, and bird and fish remains are also part of the diet. It appears that there is some separation of feeding niches between sexes, females being more specialized (Raymond et al. 1990). The animals may be selective of prey; captive animals chose red-backed voles over deer mice (Nams 1981).

Ermines may exhibit marked population cycles, thought to correlate with fluctuations in arvicoline rodents (B. Bailey 1929, B. Fitzgerald 1977, MacLean et al. 1974). Population estimates of 4 to 11 animals per km^2 (the latter in preferred habitat) have been made in Alberta (Soper 1919) and Ontario (Simms 1979b). Estimates of home range vary widely, males typically having home ranges two to four times larger than those of females. In California, home ranges were 3 to 7 ha during winter (B. Fitzgerald 1977). In Ontario, home ranges were 10 to 25 ha, with some animals moving over 500 m per day on their hunting rounds (Simms 1979b).

Young are born in May, June, or July. Delayed implantation leads to a gestation period of about 270 days, and parturition occurs about four weeks after implantation of the blastocyst (W. Hamilton 1933, Svendsen 1982). Females become reproductively active soon after parturition, and most are bred by late summer. A single litter of six to nine young is reared by the female (W. Hamilton 1933). Females are reproductively mature at about two and a half months of age; some even

Map 10-24 *Distribution of the ermine, or short-tailed weasel* (Mustela erminea) *in North America.*

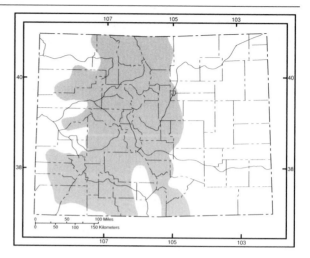

Map 10-25 *Distribution of the ermine, or short-tailed weasel* (Mustela erminea) *in Colorado.*

breed prior to weaning. Males are thought to breed at about one year of age (B. Hamilton 1933). Young are raised in nest burrows, which are often remodeled from vole burrows or located under rock piles, tree roots, or similar structures (B. Fitzgerald 1977, Hall 1951). Teeth appear at about three weeks of age, and the eyes are open by six weeks. Animals about six to seven weeks of age spend considerable time playing (W. Hamilton 1933).

Annual survival rates are about 40 percent. Life expectancy is less than two years, although animals up to seven years of age have been reported (summarized in Fagerstone 1987*b*). Most mortality is attributed to lack of food and to predation by a variety of terrestrial and avian predators. Harvest of the species usually is low in the United States, but some individuals are killed by automobiles. Svendsen (1982), C. King (1983), and Fagerstone (1987*b*) reviewed the literature on the species.

DISTRIBUTION IN COLORADO — The ermine is considered a furbearer in Colorado (Table 3-1), but only a few dozen are harvested annually. It occurs widely in mountainous areas of Colorado, where a single subspecies, *Mustela erminea muricus*, is known.

Mustela frenata
LONG-TAILED WEASEL

DESCRIPTION — This is the largest of the three North American weasels. In summer the dorsal color varies from pale to rich brown depending on the individual and the subspecies. Ventral color ranges from rusty orange to yellowish and some individuals may have white on the throat and chin. Some specimens from extreme southeastern Colorado show conspicuous white facial markings and are often referred to as "bridled" or "masked" weasels (and sometimes mistakenly identified as black-footed ferrets). In winter the color is white except for the black tip on the tail. Individuals are mottled brown and white for a period of weeks during fall and spring molts. A detailed discussion of molting patterns was provided by Hall (1951). The tail is long, typically more than 44 percent of the length of the head and body. Measurements are: total length 318–441

Photograph by Robert E. Barber.

Photograph 10-13 Long-tailed weasel (Mustela frenata).

mm; length of tail 111–160 mm; length of hind-foot 38–50 mm; length of ear 16–26 mm; weight 110–300 g. As with many mustelids, males are larger than females. Condylobasal length is greater than 40 mm. Females have eight mammae.

NATURAL HISTORY — Long-tailed weasels are common but rarely observed. They are present in all habitat types. Their distribution is probably more dependent on prey species availability in particular habitats than on vegetation or topography.

Long-tailed weasels are active year around and day and night. In a study in central Colorado, they were most active morning and late afternoon; 98 percent of captures were made in the daytime (Svendsen 1982). Activity periods are probably keyed to prey activity. When hunting, long-tailed weasels often carry the tail at a 90-degree angle above the body, especially when running or alarmed. Long-tailed weasels are seemingly curious, and when frightened into a hole will often pop their heads out for another look after a few minutes.

Voles, deer mice, other mice, chipmunks, shrews, pocket gophers, ground squirrels, prairie dogs, pikas, nestling rabbits, birds, and reptiles have been reported in the diet of long-tailed weasels. Small mammals compose between 50 and 80 percent of the annual diet (Fagerstone 1987b, Quick 1951, Svendsen 1982). Weasels also prey on eggs of grouse and waterfowl. Egg predation is reported in introduced greater prairie chicken populations in northeastern Colorado (Grant Beauprez, personal communication). A small amount of vegetable matter and berries is also eaten. In general, any prey species small enough to be subdued is potential food. Generally, weasels kill above-ground prey by hugging the animal with the four limbs and severing the spinal cord by biting at the nape of the neck. Prey captured in burrows are killed by grasping the throat and suffocating the animal (Byrne et al. 1978, Glover 1943).

The elongate body with its high surface-to-volume ratio has a high energetic cost to weasels. The estimated metabolic rate of the long-tailed weasel, which averages about 1 kcal/hour, is about 50 percent higher than that of more compact mammals of equivalent weight (J. Brown and Lasiewski 1972). Long-tailed weasels consume between 20 and 40 percent of their body weight daily, and the young have higher metabolic needs than adults (Fagerstone 1987b). The increased metabolic demands caused by the elongated shape are probably compensated for by the additional underground foraging areas that can be accessed, and by killing much prey underground with throat bites and suffocation, a procedure that may require less energy than the nape attack used above ground.

Home ranges estimated from tracking animals on snow near Gunnison were 83 to 125 ha (Quick 1951). Another study found home ranges of 12 to 16 ha (Svendsen 1982). Home ranges of females were typically included within the larger home range of adult males. In Kentucky, home ranges of males were small (10–24 ha) in areas where food was abundant, and winter home ranges were smaller than summer ranges (Fagerstone 1987b). Animals in winter tended to make more frequent but shorter hunting forays from the den, perhaps as a strategy for reducing heat loss.

Density of weasels was estimated to be 0.8 per km^2 across all habitats in Gunnison County, ranging from aspen-sagebrush to alpine tundra (Quick 1951). Studies in the East (summarized by Fagerstone 1987*b*) reported densities of 0.4 to 38 animals per km^2. In many areas where long-tailed and short-tailed weasels are sympatric, the latter are more numerous. However, that condition does not hold true for the Southern Rocky Mountains, including Colorado, based on numbers of animals in collections (Armstrong 1972) and general field observations.

Long-tailed weasels live in nests constructed inside burrows abandoned by other species, under fallen trees and rocks, in rotten logs, or in similar structures. Nests are made of grass and fur of small mammals. The animals communicate by odor and sound. Captive animals used one site for a latrine whereas in wild animals latrines are located at the entrances of burrows, in side chambers in the burrow, and in some cases in nests. Scats are deposited on rocks along trails, at times with more than one scat on the same rock, suggesting repeated visits to the site (Hall 1951, Polderboer et al. 1941, Quick 1951). Anal glands are well developed and emit a pungent odor. Their function is not known, but they probably play a role in notifying conspecifics of an individual's presence. In addition to scent marking, weasels also communicate with vocalizations, including a trill (used in various behavioral contexts), a screech (used when surprised), and a squeal (produced under duress or pain) (Svendsen 1976*a*).

The social structure of long-tailed weasels is not well studied. They are generally solitary except during the breeding season. However, pairs of long-tailed weasels have been observed together at other times. Long-tailed weasels may have a variable social structure, being more social when resources are abundant, and more solitary in less optimal habitat (Fagerstone 1987*b*). Residents of both sexes maintain territories, and they allow overlap only with individuals of the opposite sex;

Map 10-26 Distribution of the long-tailed weasel (Mustela frenata) *in North America.*

transients do not have territories (Svendsen 1982).

Most breeding occurs during July and August. A female mates with the adult male(s) whose home range encompasses hers. Males may form transitory pair bonds with females for several weeks but leave before the young are born (W. Hamilton 1933). Delayed implantation occurs, with gestation taking 220 to 237 days. Parturition occurs about 27 days postimplantation. Only one litter is reared per year, and most litters are born in April or May. Litter size averages about seven with up to nine young reported (Wright 1942, 1947, 1948*a, b*).

The young are blind and poorly haired at birth. Soft white fur develops quickly, to be replaced by pigmented hair within a few weeks. At five weeks of age the eyes open and tooth eruption is sufficient to allow eating meat. At six weeks scent glands are developed, and the young are weaned

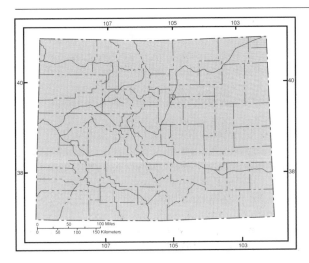

Map 10-27 Distribution of the long-tailed weasel (Mustela frenata) *in Colorado.*

and begin to forage with the mother (W. Hamilton 1933). The young stay with the female until seven weeks or so in age. Animals reach adult weight by about three months of age, at which time females are capable of breeding (Wright 1948a), which they are likely to do with the male whose home range encompasses their natal site. This male is not necessarily their father, due to high population turnover. Males reproduce at 15 months of age.

The long-tailed weasel is preyed upon by a wide variety of predators, ranging from coyotes and foxes to snakes and owls (Svendsen 1982, Fagerstone 1987b). A mathematical model suggests that raptor predation could conceivably be sufficient to limit weasel populations (Powell 1973). Terrestrial carnivores such as foxes may also act to limit weasel numbers. The literature was reviewed by Svendsen (1982) and Fagerstone (1987b). Long-tailed weasels are not infrequently killed by automobiles, and trappers harvest a few hundred each year (Table 3-2).

DISTRIBUTION IN COLORADO — The long-tailed weasel is distributed over all of Colorado although it seems to be most abundant in the mountains at moderate to high elevations.

Mustela frenata longicauda occurs on the east-central and northeastern plains; *M. f. neomexicana* occurs in the roughlands of southeastern Colorado; *M. f. nevadensis* occurs throughout the mountainous western two-thirds of the state.

Photograph by Kathleen A. Fagerstone.

Photograph 10-14 Black-footed ferret (Mustela nigripes).

Mustela nigripes
BLACK-FOOTED FERRET

DESCRIPTION — The black-footed ferret is the largest member of the genus *Mustela* in Colorado, being slightly larger than the mink. The black-footed ferret has the elongate body shape and short legs typical of the genus but is distinguished by its black facial mask, feet, and legs. The moderately long tail is tipped with black. The general pelage color is yellow buff, paler around the face, abdomen, and throat, and darker brown down the top of the head and back. The fur, including the guard hairs, is relatively short and fine textured. The ears are conspicuous and rounded. Measurements are: total length 457–572 mm; length of tail 90–150 mm; length of hindfoot 57–73 mm; length of ear 29–31 mm; weight 530–1300 g. Females are usually about 10 percent smaller than males. The skull greatly resembles that of the mink. However, in the mink the distance between the bases of the upper canines is less than the width of the basioccipital bone (measured at the level of the foramina located midway along the medial sides of the tympanic bullae); in the black-footed ferret the distance is equal to or greater than the width of the basioccipital (T. Clark et al. 1988). Females have three pairs of mammary glands. The species is similar in appearance to the European polecat, or domestic ferret, *Mustela putorius*, which sometimes is released by irresponsible pet owners. The black-footed ferret may have evolved from an ancestral stock of Siberian ferrets (*M. eversmanni*) that successfully crossed the Bering land bridge in the Pleistocene (E. Anderson et al. 1986).

NATURAL HISTORY — Prior to the discovery of a population of black-footed ferrets at Meeteetse, Wyoming, in 1981, the black-footed ferret (federally listed as endangered) was one of America's most poorly understood carnivores. Since 1981, over 115 articles have been published on the animal, and its biology is better known than that of most other mustelids. Black-footed ferrets have co-evolved with prairie dogs; their ranges and habitats closely overlap (Hall 1981; Fagerstone 1987b). Black-footed ferrets have historically occupied areas ranging from the shortgrass and midgrass prairie to semidesert shrublands. Presently they are known to exist only in a remnant restored population in the Shirley Basin of Wyoming and in captive breeding populations at various locations across the country. The success of the captive breeding program and resulting release of animals to the wild suggest that at some time in the future a number of western states, including Colorado, may once again have free-ranging populations.

Black-footed ferrets use prairie dog burrows for living quarters and as nursery dens to rear their young, and they prey on these animals as well (Hillman and Clark 1980). They will excavate dens in search of prey and in preparation of home dens. Their digging activity may result in the formation of characteristic "troughs" consisting of excavated subsoil thrown out in a relatively narrow, linear pattern with a conspicuous medial trench (T. Clark 1989, T. Clark et al. 1988).

At the Meeteetse site, most digging activity occurred between October and January. Above-ground activity of black-footed ferrets increased over the winter months, probably corresponding with the onset of the reproductive season in February (T. Clark 1989, Richardson et al. 1987). Most above-ground activity was at night, between 0100 and 0400, although bimodal peaks of nightly activity occurred in summer (Biggins et al. 1986, Fagerstone 1987b). Most daylight activity was limited to the first five hours after sunrise. Individuals, particularly juveniles, were mobile, frequently changing locations within the prairie dog town or moving between adjacent towns (T. Clark 1989, Fagerstone 1987b).

Prairie dog remains were present in over 86 percent of scats examined (Campbell et al. 1987, Sheets et al. 1972). To a much lesser degree, mice, ground squirrels, lagomorphs, birds, reptiles, and insects are eaten. No data exist to indicate that the species can survive without prairie dogs as a food base; in fact, the distribution of ferrets suggests that they are entirely dependent on prairie dogs. Adult ferrets seem to require one prairie dog every 2 to 6 days on the average (Fagerstone 1987b). This intake would require that a ferret be able to access about 100 prairie dogs per year, or 19 to 38 ha of prairie dog habitat. Further research may indicate that the animals can survive with lesser demands on the prairie dog resource if supplemented with other dietary items.

The density of black-footed ferrets at Meeteetse ranged from one animal per 49 ha to one per 74 ha (T. Clark 1989). Estimated population numbers for July based on spotlight counts were 88, 129, and 56 for 1983, 1984, and 1986, respectively. Population estimates for September, based on live-trapping mark and recapture, were 125 and 30 animals for 1984 and 1985 (Forrest et al. 1988). The smallest prairie dog colony in Meeteetse that supported a litter of black-footed ferrets was 49 ha. In South Dakota, five litters of ferrets were reported on black-tailed prairie dog towns smaller than 40 ha (Hillman et al. 1979).

Home range size for black-footed ferrets at Meeteetse averaged 40 to 60 ha (T. Clark 1989), although individual monthly ranges varied from 1.2 to 258 ha, depending on sex and season (Fagerstone 1987*b*). Juveniles typically stay close to the natal den, and even by late August their activity is contained within an area of 4 ha or less. However, during September and early October considerable dispersal of juveniles occurs, with movements of up to 7 km (Fagerstone 1987*b*).

The species is presumed to be polygynous, on the basis of home range size and the fact that home ranges of adult males usually encompass those of several females (Fagerstone 1987*b*). Animals of the same sex are thought to be intolerant of each other. Data on reproductive biology are scant. Breeding activity probably occurred from mid-February through March at Meeteetse (T. Clark et al. 1986). Copulation in captive animals occurred in March and April. Early estrus has been induced in captive females by manipulation of the light cycle. Copulation lasts for up to three hours and is believed to induce ovulation. Delayed implantation does not occur, and gestation takes about 42 to 45 days. Most litters in the wild probably are born in May. Litter size averages 3.5 with a range of one to five. Only one litter is born per year. The young first appear above ground in July when about three-quarters grown. Sexual maturity is reached at one year of age (J. Carpenter and Hillman 1978, Forrest et al. 1988, Hillman 1968, Hillman and Linder 1973, Linder et al. 1972).

A variety of predators, including great horned owls, golden eagles, coyotes, badgers, and domestic dogs, kills ferrets. Canine distemper was responsible for elimination of many of the Meeteetse ferrets (E. Thorne and Williams 1988), a factor that prompted the capture of the survivors for maintenance in captivity. Black-footed ferrets from South Dakota also were susceptible to canine distemper, resulting in loss of a captive colony (J. Carpenter et al. 1976). Loss of prey base by epizootics of plague impacts populations (Barnes 1993; J. Fitzgerald 1993; Ubico et al. 1988), as

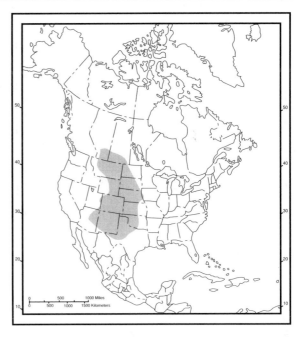

Map 10-28 Historic distribution of the black-footed ferret (Mustela nigripes) *in North America.*

do poisoning programs to control prairie dog or other rodent populations (T. Clark 1989, Fagerstone 1987*b*). Twenty-five percent (103 individuals) of all known museum specimens of black-footed ferrets were killed by predator and rodent control agents, mostly in the 1920s.

Prospects for survival of the black-footed ferret are uncertain, depending on the success of restorations. Captive ferrets have lived up to 11 years, and animals over one year of age typically breed every year (Fagerstone 1987*b*). However, the potential loss of viability of black-footed ferret populations due to small population size and inbreeding effects are of concern (T. Clark 1989). The literature on the species was reviewed by Casey et al. (1986), T. Clark (1989), Fagerstone (1987*b*), Henderson et al. (1969), Hillman and Clark (1980), and Reading and Clark (1990).

DISTRIBUTION IN COLORADO — The original range of the black-footed ferret closely approxi-

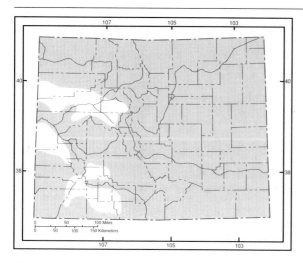

Map 10-29 *Historic distribution of the black-footed ferret* (Mustela nigripes) *in Colorado.*

Map 10-30 *Distribution of the least weasel* (Mustela nivalis) *in North America.*

mated the range of prairie dogs. Despite considerable search time in western Colorado and on the eastern plains by various personnel from state and federal agencies, no live ferrets have been found, although several skulls have been recovered. E. Anderson et al. (1986), Armstrong (1972), and Torres (1973) reviewed the status and historical records of the species in Colorado. *Mustela nigripes* is monotypic.

Mustela nivalis
LEAST WEASEL

DESCRIPTION — The least weasel is the smallest carnivore in North America. It is similar in color to the ermine, in both summer and winter pelages. However, the tail is one quarter or less the length of the head and body and it lacks a conspicuous black tip, although a few sparse black hairs may be present. Measurements are: total length 184–237 mm; length of tail 25–40 mm; hindfoot 16–31 mm; length of ear 11–14 mm (J. K. Jones 1964, Hall 1951). Greatest length of the skull is usually less than 34 mm. Skulls of *Mustela nivalis* and *M. erminea* may be difficult to separate, but for many specimens the skull of *M. nivalis* is narrower and has a relatively greater height (J. K. Jones et al. 1983). The ratio of the height at the

anterior margin of the basioccipital to mastoid breadth in *M. nivalis* is from 0.64 to 0.76 whereas for *M. erminea* the ratio is from 0.59 to 0.68.

NATURAL HISTORY — On the northern Great Plains the least weasel occupies meadows, grasslands, and woodlands and is commonest in marshy areas (J. K. Jones et al. 1983). On the margins of its range the species tends to be associated with riparian areas. The behavior and diet are similar to those of the ermine. Unlike other weasels, least weasels do not show delayed implantation and females may produce several litters in one year. Litter size ranges from one to 10, and gestation lasts about 35 days (Fagerstone 1987b).

DISTRIBUTION IN COLORADO — The least weasel has not been documented in Colorado but is known to range in Nebraska to within about 50 km of the Colorado border (Swenk 1926). Any small weasel from northeastern Colorado should be examined carefully, and any specimen obtained should be submitted to an expert with comparative material for study.

Photograph by Robert E. Barber.

Photograph 10-15 Mink (Mustela vison).

Mustela vison
MINK

DESCRIPTION — The mink is similar to the American marten in general size and appearance, although its ears are less conspicuous. Typical of many mustelids, the legs are short and the body is long and slender. The fur is soft and glossy with thick underfur and long guard hairs. Glands at the base of hairs produce water-repellent oils that prevent the hair from becoming waterlogged. Color varies from rich chestnut brown to blackish, with the venter slightly paler. Some individuals have white patches or spots on the throat, chest, or abdomen. The tail is long and well furred, about one-third to one-half of the total length. The toes of the feet are partially webbed. Measurements are: total length 491–720 mm; length of tail 158–194 mm; length of hindfoot 57–75 mm; average weights from central Idaho are 780 and 525 g for males and females, respectively. Males are about 10 percent larger than females (and may be nearly double the weight) (Whitman 1981). The skull is stout, with the palate extending beyond the last molar. The auditory bullae are conspicuous. As with other mustelids, the up-

per molars are dumbbell-shaped. Females have six to eight mammae. The testes are permanently scrotal. Anal glands are well developed in both sexes. A variety of techniques, including skull measurements, development of the baculum, size and color of nipples, and evidence of penis scars on dried pelts all have been used to determine age and sex of mink or their remains (Linscombe et al. 1982). Skulls of mink and black-footed ferret are very similar; for detailed comparison, see the account of the latter species.

NATURAL HISTORY — Despite its importance as a furbearer, relatively few intensive studies have been carried out on mink in the wild, and none has been done in the Southern Rocky Mountains. Although mink can be found in practically any habitat type, they are obligate riparian animals, never found far from permanent streams, wetlands, or other surface water. A number of specific factors affect the presence and density of mink. Den sites, such as abandoned beaver lodges and muskrat dens, are very important (Schladweiler and Storm 1969). Other factors include permanence of water and abundance of wetland habitat (A. Allen 1983), development of shoreline vegetation including willow and emergent vegetation (Marshall 1936, Mason and MacDonald 1983), crayfish abundance (Burgess and Bider 1980), availability of logjams for fall and winter hunting sites (Melquist et al. 1981), and abundance of muskrats (Errington 1943). Reaches of stream where banks have been degraded by livestock are avoided (Eberhardt and Sargeant 1977), as are ephemeral streams and streams of high gradient. Thus, mink are less abundant in Colorado than in some other parts of North America.

Food habits of mink in Colorado are unknown, but thorough studies have been possible elsewhere because mink use regular latrine sites, providing concentrated sources of scats for analysis. Considerable data are also available from examination of intestinal tracts of trapper-killed mink. The animals are generalists, eating a variety of animal prey including muskrats, cottontails, deer mice, voles, ground- and marsh-nesting birds and

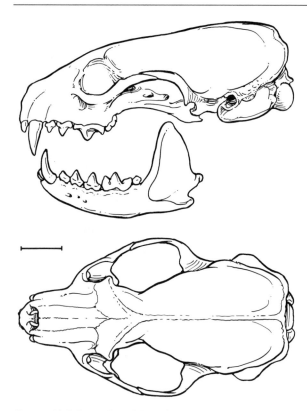

Figure 10-3 Lateral and dorsal views of the skull of the mink (Mustela vison). *Scale = 1 cm.*

Because of their importance in commercial fur farming, reproduction in mink is well known (Enders 1952, Hansson 1947, Venge 1959). Mink are polygamous. Both sexes mate with multiple partners; in fact, a given litter may have more than one father. No pair bond is formed. The breeding season is late February to early April. Females are polyestrous throughout this period until they are bred, with cycles of 7 to 10 days. Ovulation is induced by copulation. Gestation period is highly variable, 40 to 74 days (average, 51), because delayed implantation occurs in females that breed early in the season whereas it does not seem to occur in late-breeding females (Eagle and Whitman 1987). There is one litter of one to eight (average five) young per year, born in late April and May.

The young are altricial at birth, with eyes opening at about three weeks of age. By fall, they are close to adult weight. Males and females are reproductively mature at about ten months of age and are reproductive for about seven years. Young stay with the female until fall, and littermates may travel together when dispersing (Eagle and Whitman 1987, Linscombe et al. 1982).

Mink are active year around, and much of their foraging occurs along or in the water. In winter they are mainly diurnal and occasionally active at night as well. Activity may be connected to that of their prey. The animals are inactive during cold periods after heavy snows (Marshall 1936). Except for brief periods of mating, mink are solitary. Mink den in burrows close to streambanks and often use abandoned muskrat dens and beaver lodges. Mink are generally considered territorial, maintaining intrasexual territories with little or no overlap between individuals of the same sex (Powell 1979). Whitman (1981) found in Idaho that they did not defend territories against other minks of the same sex. Territories are marked with the secretions of scent glands.

Home ranges vary in size, with age and sex of the resident, social tolerance, and availability of food including seasonal foods such as spawning fishes (Marshall 1936, McCabe 1949, Melquist et al.

their eggs, frogs, snakes, fish, insects, and crayfish as well as small amounts of plant material. Mammalian prey is most important. Fish enhancement projects that improve stream habitat may also benefit mink by increasing aquatic food species. Game fishes such as trout are less regularly taken by mink than are slower moving species such as carp, minnows, and suckers. Fish appear to become increasingly important during the winter months, apparently offsetting some dependence on birds and invertebrates during the warmer seasons. In waterfowl production areas, mink can be important predators on ducks, especially if nesting habitat is concentrated (Cowardin et al. 1985, Schladweiler and Tester 1972). Males appear to feed on larger prey than females. Plant materials are thought to be taken incidentally while eating animal prey. Surplus prey is cached.

Map 10-31 Distribution of the mink (Mustela vison) *in North America.*

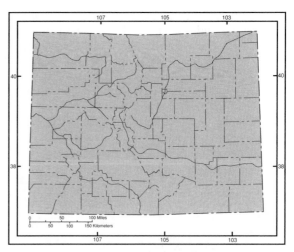

Map 10-32 Distribution of the mink (Mustela vison) *in Colorado.*

1981, J. Mitchell 1961). Also mink seldom range far from water, a characteristic that constrains their movements along narrow, linear corridors. In Sweden, males utilize 2.5 to 5.5 km of shoreline; females 0.5 to 3 km (Gerell 1970). Females have been estimated to occupy home ranges of 8 to 20 ha, whereas males may use areas up to 1,626 ha. Home ranges of females may overlap portions of the home range of adult males (Whitman 1981). Some of the increased size of home ranges of males may be attributable to breeding activities.

Densities of mink vary with habitat, season, and abundance of prey. Furthermore, methods for estimating populations vary widely and contain inaccuracies (Eagle and Whitman 1987). In Montana, riverine populations ranged from 8 to 22 mink per square mile (259 ha) (Mitchell 1961). In marsh habitat in Wisconsin, populations fluctuated between 7 and 24 mink on 445 ha over a 5-year period (McCabe 1949). Density was 0.6 females per km^2 during the winter in Michigan

(Marshall 1936). In northwestern Colorado, density was estimated at 1.7 mink per square mile (259 ha) (McKean and Burkhard 1978).

Mink are not thought to be heavily preyed upon, although they have been killed by great horned owls as well as a variety of mammalian carnivores including wolves, bobcats, and fishers (Linscombe et al. 1982). Trapping is the greatest source of mortality in most areas. In trapped populations in Montana, juvenile to adult ratios of 4:1 have been found (Lechleitner 1954). Population turnover was about three years in Montana (J. Mitchell 1961). Mink are also very sensitive to water pollution by mercury and polychlorinated biphenyls (PCBs), although the degree to which they are impacted by these contaminants in the wild is not known. Linscombe et al. (1982) and Eagle and Whitman (1987) reviewed the literature on the species.

DISTRIBUTION IN COLORADO — Although widespread across Colorado, mink seem not to be abundant, and only a few hundred are trapped annually (Table 3-2). Perhaps because of their commercial value, few museum specimens exist (Armstrong 1972). Portions of the Yampa and Eagle drainages, North Park, and the White River

Plateau were important mink habitats earlier in this century. Finley et al. (1976) cited only one report in the Piceance Basin and White River area since pioneer times. Two subspecies are ascribed ranges in Colorado, *Mustela vison energumenos* in the central and western parts of the state, and *M. v. letifera* on the eastern plains.

Photograph by Claude Steelman/Wildshots.

Photograph 10-16 Wolverine (Gulo gulo).

Gulo gulo
WOLVERINE

DESCRIPTION — The wolverine is the largest terrestrial mustelid. Blocky and bear-like in appearance, it has a broad head and short heavy neck. Unlike bears, the tail is bushy and relatively long, about one-fourth the length of the body. The ears are short and rounded. The feet are large with semiretractile claws. During the winter stiff hairs develop between the toes and on the soles of the feet. Coloration varies widely with individuals and is typically medium brown to dark brown with broad yellowish brown lateral stripes extending from the neck to the rump and joining at the base of the tail. A pale facial mask is often present. The venter is generally paler, and there may be white to yellowish tan spots on the throat and chest. Measurements of males are: total length 900–1125 mm; length of tail 190–260 mm; length of hindfoot 180–192 mm (Hall 1981). Males average 10 percent longer and 30 percent heavier than females. Weights range from 7 to 32 kg (Nowak 1991). The skull is massive, with a short muzzle, powerful jaws, and strong teeth. The auditory bullae are moderately inflated. Females have four mammae.

NATURAL HISTORY — Wolverines are animals of boreal forests and tundra. In Canada and Alaska, they prefer marshy areas such as the lowland spruce forests that support extensive wetlands (D. Wilson 1982). Large and diverse ungulate populations are also an important component of wolverine habitat (Hornocker and Hash 1981, van Zyll de Jong 1975). Wolverines have historically had one of the lowest densities of any carnivore.

Wolverines eat small rodents, rabbits, porcupines, ground squirrels, marmots, birds and eggs, fish, carrion, and plant material, especially roots and berries. They do attack large game, including moose and caribou, but most ungulate remains in their diet are probably from carrion. In winter the diet is mostly carrion and mammalian prey, with more diversity at other times of the year. Wolverines fed on kills made by mountain lions in Montana (Hornocker and Hash 1981). Wolverines cache surplus food, marking the site with urine and scent (Hash 1987, D. Wilson 1982).

Wolverines are mostly nocturnal and active year around. They are typically solitary, with pairing occurring only during the brief mating season, although adult pairs occasionally travel together for brief periods in winter (Hash 1987). Young animals travel with the female in late summer and fall. Wolverines spend considerable time in marking behaviors using their anal and ventral glands to mark objects. They also bite and claw trees in a manner similar to bears (Hornocker and Hash 1981, Koehler et al. 1980). Such behaviors may be used to mark territory or label food caches. The extent to which wolverines are territorial in North America is not clear (Hash 1987). In Europe, intrasexual territories are maintained.

Map 10-33 Historic and present distribution of the wolverine (Gulo gulo) in North America. After Wilson (1982).

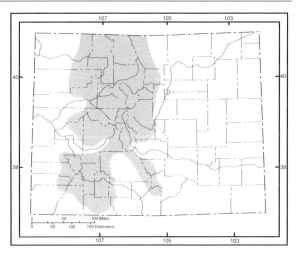

Map 10-34 Distribution of the wolverine (Gulo gulo) in Colorado.

Home ranges frequently overlapped in Montana. In Alaska and Montana they varied from 94 to 388 km^2 for females and from 422 to 666 km^2 for males (Hornocker and Hash 1981, Hash 1987). Lactating females had the smallest home ranges. The size of home ranges is probably increased by movements of ungulate prey and heightened activity by males during the breeding season. Individual wolverines may move over 30 km in one night (D. Wilson 1982). Movements of dispersing juveniles seeking suitable habitat may exaggerate the size of "home ranges" reported in the literature.

According to studies in Alaska, the Yukon, and elsewhere, wolverines can breed from late spring until early fall (Magoun and Valkenburg 1983, Rausch and Pearson 1972). Delayed implantation results in blastocysts not implanting until January or February. Variation in the delay of implantation results in a variable gestation period of 215 to 272 days (Mead 1981, Mehrer 1976). Active gestation is about 30 to 40 days postimplantation.

Two to five young (average two or three) are usually born in March or April. The young are born in simple, unlined natal dens in log jams, under rocks and boulders, or under tree roots (Hash 1987). Neonates are altricial but covered with fine white fur (Mehrer 1976). Reproductive success is low in wolverines, apparently in part due to loss of kits, lack of mating opportunity, and age at first litter (Hash 1987). Most females are not reproductively mature until two years of age (Liskop et al. 1981).

Most animals do not live more than 10 to 11 years in the wild, and average 4 to 6 years for animals harvested in Montana (Hash 1987). Other than humans, and an occasional wolf kill, natural enemies are few. The literature was reviewed by D. Wilson (1982) and Hash (1987).

DISTRIBUTION IN COLORADO — Although there were several records in the nineteenth century (reviewed by Armstrong 1972), populations apparently never were high, and the status of the wolverine in Colorado is uncertain at this time. The Colorado Division of Wildlife recently conducted surveys for both wolverine and lynx without finding any definitive wolverine populations in the state, although a specimen claimed to have been killed in eastern Utah (but probably taken in Rio

Blanco or Garfield County, Colorado) was recently brought to the attention of wildlife officials. Nowak (1973), Field and Feltner (1974), and Nead et al. (1984) summarized reports of the species in Colorado. One subspecies, *Gulo gulo luscus*, occurs in Colorado.

Photograph 10-17 American badger (Taxidea taxus).

Taxidea taxus
AMERICAN BADGER

DESCRIPTION — Badgers are short, stout mustelids, with thick necks and short legs specialized for digging. The legs are muscular with strong claws on the front feet that may exceed 50 mm in length. The tail is short but bushy. The general dorsal color is silvery gray, sometimes tinged with brown, yellow, or buff and grizzled with black. The snout, top of the head, feet, parts of the legs, and areas around the ears are black. A white midline stripe runs from the nose pad onto the head, which also sports white facial marks. The ventral surface is paler than the dorsum. Long guard hairs give the appearance of shagginess and of greater size. Measurements are: total length 660–889 mm; length of tail 98–174 mm; length of hindfoot 88–155 mm; length of ear 50–53 mm; weight 6–14 kg. On the northern Great Plains weights averaged 8.4 kg for males and 6.4 kg for females (Wright 1969). The skull is triangu-

lar and stoutly built. Females have eight mammae. Badgers are sexually dimorphic, with males larger than females.

NATURAL HISTORY — Badgers occur in practically all habitat types in Colorado. They prefer open habitats and avoid densely wooded areas, although they will enter forest margins. Badgers occur in grasslands, meadows in subalpine and montane forests, alpine tundra, and semidesert shrublands. Badgers in South Park not infrequently entered stands of aspen and open stands of conifers to hunt (Hetlet 1968, J. Fitzgerald, unpublished). They are most common in areas with abundant populations of ground squirrels, prairie dogs, and pocket gophers (T. Clark et al. 1982).

Badgers are opportunistic predators, eating practically any fossorial or terrestrial prey they can capture. They are excellent diggers and can quickly excavate burrows of rodents to obtain prey. The diet includes prairie dogs, ground squirrels, gophers, mice, cottontails, jackrabbits, snakes, lizards, ground-nesting birds and their eggs, and insects. The widest range of dietary items occurs during the warmer months (Lindzey 1982, Messick 1987). Prairie dogs as well as eggs of such birds as sage grouse were important items in the diet of Coloradan badgers (Hogue 1955, Warren 1942). In South Park, badgers preyed on Gunnison's prairie dogs, Wyoming ground squirrels, and golden-mantled ground squirrels (J. Fitzgerald and Lechleitner 1974; J. Fitzgerald, unpublished; Hetlet 1968). Badgers also preyed on marmots in Colorado (D. Anderson and Johns 1977). Carrion is eaten, and food caches may be made when extra prey is secured. Juveniles feed more heavily on insects and birds than do adults (Messick and Hornocker 1981).

The reproductive biology of the American badger has not been studied as intensively as that of some other mustelids. Mating occurs from late June to August (Campbell and Clark 1983, Messick and Hornocker 1981, Wright 1966). Four adult female badgers captured between mid-August and early September in South Park, Colorado, had conspicuously swollen vulvae, indicating breeding condition (J. Fitzgerald, unpublished; Todd 1980). Badgers are likely induced ovulators (Wright 1966). Following breeding, delayed implantation occurs, with the total gestation period lasting seven to eight months. Most females give birth in March or April (Messick 1987). Litter size ranges from one to four, with two the mode.

The young remain below ground about six weeks after birth. They stay with the female through the summer and disperse in the fall. Some females breed their first year, but males do not breed until they are at least one year old (Messick 1987). Sex ratios approximate 1:1. Percentage of females producing young varied from 52 to 72 percent in Idaho (Messick et al. 1981), and 40 to 52 percent of females 12 months of age had young.

Badgers are generally solitary except during the mating season and when females are rearing their young. They dig holes in pursuit of prey and also dig conspicuous burrows for dens. A burrow is usually characterized by a mound of dirt fanning out at the entrance. Average dimensions of 112 badger burrows in South Park, Colorado, were 19 cm high by 21 cm wide (Hetlet 1968). Lengths of dirt mounds at the burrow entrance averaged 102 cm and had a mean maximum depth of soil of about 13 cm. Of these burrows, 16 percent were being used by Wyoming ground squirrels or least chipmunks, and 5 percent were being used by badgers. With the exception of winter, 84 percent of badger dens dug by radio-tracked animals in Utah and Idaho were used only one day. Winter use of the same burrow is much more prolonged, up to 72 days. Of the burrows used by badgers, 85 percent had been previously excavated (Lindzey 1978, Messick et al. 1981).

Badgers are active at any time of day, but in areas with considerable human disturbance they are most active at night. During five years of study in South Park, 44 badgers were observed or captured, of which 28 were in daylight hours (J. Fitzgerald 1970 and unpublished, Hetlet 1968). In cold areas the animals are inactive for long pe-

Map 10-35 Distribution of the American badger (Taxidea taxus) *in North America.*

riods during the winter. Adaptations to prolonged periods without food include inactivity, torpor, and increased efficiency of food assimilation (Harlow 1981, Harlow and Seal 1981).

Badger populations are made up of two groups, resident adult animals and juveniles without permanent home ranges (Messick 1987). Home ranges of adults overlap, and males have larger areas than females. Home ranges reported from radio-tracking studies (summarized by Messick 1987) vary from about 130 to 237 ha (although one female covered over 800 ha). Home ranges of males in Idaho and Utah averaged 170 to 583 ha. These studies are from areas of high badger density. Few studies exist on badger populations where they are more dispersed. In South Park, an average of nine badgers occupied a 26 km^2 site over five years (J. Fitzgerald 1970; 1993). There is no evidence of territorial behavior. In parts of Idaho, seasonal crowding occurs because of agricultural practices, including burning, plowing,

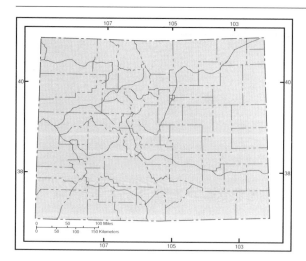

Map 10-36 Distribution of the American badger (Taxidea taxus) *in Colorado.*

and cropping of fields. Such crowding leads to increased aggression between animals (Messick et al. 1981).

A summary of data from several different studies revealed that animals less than one year of age constituted 35 to 48 percent of badger populations (Messick 1987). Sixteen to 26 percent are one year of age; 11 to 22 percent are two-year-olds, and 15 to 24 percent are between three and seven years of age. The oldest animal of known age (capture-recapture) trapped in South Park was 3.5 years old. Because of their relatively sedentary habits and longevity, badgers have proven useful in detection and assessment of levels of sylvatic plague activity in rodent populations (J. Fitzgerald 1970, 1993; Messick et al. 1983).

Badgers have few natural enemies although golden eagles, coyotes, domestic dogs, and similar predators can kill juveniles (Messick et al. 1981). Badgers tend to face danger aggressively, and most mortality is caused by vehicles or deliberate killing by humans. In Idaho, 33 percent of known mortalities were caused by automobiles and 60 percent were due directly to humans (Messick et al. 1981). Individuals up to 14 years old may occur in some populations (Crowe and Strickland

1975, Messick et al. 1981). Literature on the species was reviewed by Long (1973), Long and Killingley (1983), Lindzey (1982), and Messick (1987).

DISTRIBUTION IN COLORADO — Badgers are found throughout Colorado in all open habitats. Densities are highest in areas with abundant ground squirrels or prairie dogs. Data summarized by Messick (1987) suggest that the animal is expanding its range to the north and east in North America, but Long and Killingley (1983) presented some evidence that badgers were declining in parts of several western states. Listed as furbearers in Colorado, several hundred badgers are harvested annually (Table 3-2). Finley et al. (1976) speculated that badger populations in northwestern Colorado might be lower now than in the past because of elimination of prairie dogs. *Taxidea taxus berlandieri* is the subspecies of extreme southwestern Colorado; *T. t. taxus* occurs on the eastern plains; *T. t. montana* occurs in the western and central portions of the state.

Spilogale gracilis
WESTERN SPOTTED SKUNK

DESCRIPTION — The western spotted skunk is a small skunk, brown to black with a series of broad white stripes from the head to the base of the tail that are broken up into spots. There is also a white spot between the eyes. It is similar to the eastern spotted skunk, from which it is distinguished by being somewhat smaller, having broader white stripes that break into larger spots (see Figure 10-19), and a tail with a white tip that extends to the underside of the tail for half of its length. Armstrong (unpublished) examined a pure black individual live trapped above Boulder Canyon near Nederland. Measurements are: total length 340–482 mm; length of tail 110–160 mm; length of hindfoot 35–50 mm; length of ear 15–23 mm; weight 400–700 g. The skull is similar to that of *S. putorius*, but can be distinguished by its smaller condylobasal length, 60 mm or less.

NATURAL HISTORY — The biology of the western spotted skunk is poorly known. It is a species of

Photograph by Leonard Lee Rue III.

Photograph 10-18 Western spotted skunk (Spilogale gracilis).

Photograph by Rick Wicker, Denver Museum of Natural History. © D.M.N.H. 1993.

Photograph 10-19 Museum study skins of Spilogale gracilis *(on left) and* S. putorius *(on right). Note the white-tipped tail and larger white spots on* S. gracilis.

the semiarid West and commonest in shrub habitats in broken country. It can be found in montane forest and shrubland, semidesert shrubland, and piñon-juniper woodlands. It frequents rocky habitats and is an agile climber. Earlier this century, the species was reported as far more common than the striped skunk in a number of areas on the Western Slope (Cary 1911).

Somewhat omnivorous, western spotted skunks eat a variety of foods but seem to concentrate on arthropods, small mammals, and birds. In Texas, western spotted skunks were mostly insectivorous and carnivorous, feeding on small rodents including mice and kangaroo rats (R. Patton 1974). Bird eggs are also eaten. In Oregon, dietary items included fruit and berries, deer mice, lagomorphs, birds, and some arthropods (Maser et al. 1981). In Arizona, the skunks preyed on *Peromyscus* (Hoffmeister 1986). Food habits have not been studied in Colorado.

Male western spotted skunks become reproductive as early as June. Females enter estrus in September, and the animals mate in September or October. Delayed implantation occurs, and gestation takes 210 to 230 days. The postimplantation

period is one month. The young are born in May with an average litter size of four. Females may breed at four to five months of age. Thus most females, both adults and young of the year, breed in the fall. Some juvenile males are sexually mature in their first fall (Mead 1968b, Foresman and Mead 1973, Sinha and Mead 1976).

Little life history information has been published on the species. Adults apparently are solitary except during the mating season. The animals are strictly nocturnal and rarely seen. They den in rock crevices as well as under human habitations and outbuildings (R. Patton 1974). In Oregon, an individual den was found in a round hole in a sand dune area (Maser et al. 1981). Home range is probably not much larger than 50 ha in area, based on studies of eastern spotted skunks. Literature on the species was reviewed by Howard and Marsh (1982) and Rosatte (1987).

DISTRIBUTION IN COLORADO — The western spotted skunk is found in canyons and foothills areas at elevations generally below 2,440 m (8,000 ft) in Colorado (Armstrong 1972), on either side of the mountains. It extends northward along the foot-

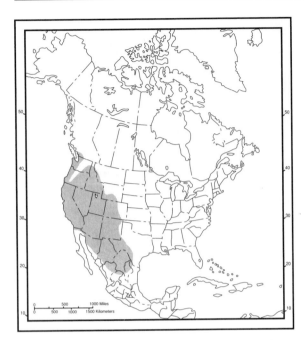

Map 10-37 Distribution of the western spotted skunk (Spilogale gracilis) *in North America.*

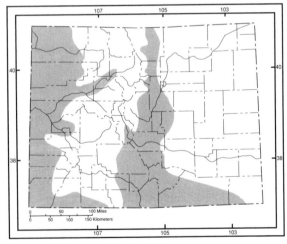

Map 10-38 Distribution of the western spotted skunk (Spilogale gracilis) *in Colorado.*

hills of the Front Range into southern Wyoming, eastward through the roughlands of southeastern Colorado, and throughout the semiarid canyon

country at lower elevations on the Western Slope. It does not appear to be common in most areas and may show fluctuations in populations, as has been noted for the eastern spotted skunk. A fur-bearer, only 88 spotted skunks were reported as harvested in 1990 (Table 3-2). One subspecies, *Spilogale gracilis gracilis*, occurs in the state.

Photograph 10-20 Eastern spotted skunk (Spilogale putorius).

Spilogale putorius
EASTERN SPOTTED SKUNK

DESCRIPTION — The eastern spotted skunk (sometimes called "civet" or even "civet cat") is a dainty black mustelid with four to six white stripes on the dorsum that are broken into spots. Spotted skunks have long, glistening, dense black fur. The ears are rounded and partially hidden in the fur. The front claws are well developed, about twice the length of the hind claws. The forehead typically has a single large white spot. The eastern spotted skunk has a black-tipped tail whereas the western spotted skunk, *Spilogale gracilis*, has a white-tipped tail (see Figure 10-18). The tail of spotted skunks is somewhat shorter than that of other genera of skunks, usually not exceeding 75 percent of the body length. Measurements are: total length 410–585 mm; length of tail 138–280 mm; length of hindfoot 38–59 mm; weight 453–885 g. Males are about 10 percent larger than females. The skull is relatively flat with little arching over the orbits, and the condylobasal length is 62 mm or less. Anal glands are well developed and produce an extremely pungent odor. Females have eight mammae. Techniques to determine age are available (Mead 1967).

NATURAL HISTORY — Relatively little is known of the ecology of spotted skunks. The species inhabits much of the Great Plains and extensions of prairie eastward into the deciduous forests. They appear to be most common in agricultural areas, in rough, broken country with abundant stands of brush, or in riparian woodlands. Their range may have expanded in some areas with agricultural expansion, including plantings of windbreaks and creation of fence rows.

Eastern spotted skunks use a variety of dens, including abandoned burrows of other mustelids, ground squirrels, pocket gophers, woodchucks (in other parts of the country), and caves, rock overhangs, and similar features as well as buildings, culverts, wood piles, and abandoned vehicles. A given den is used for three to four months and may be used sequentially by a number of individuals. Females with young protect the natal den. Underground dens typically have a nest chamber lined with grass, whereas above-ground resting sites do not contain nest materials. Dens are located close to suitable habitat or escape cover (Crabb 1948, Henderson 1976, Polder 1968).

In Iowa, insects composed the bulk of the summer diet and fruits and some cereal grains were used more in the fall. During winter, fall, and spring, small mammals (including voles, mice, and cottontails) were significant. Corn was an important component of the diet especially in the winter (Crabb 1941, Selko 1937).

Eastern spotted skunks are active year around. During cold weather their activity is restricted, and they may den communally at this time. Otherwise, they are solitary. Highly nocturnal, they rarely venture out during the daytime unless molested. They appear to be less tolerant than striped skunks of close

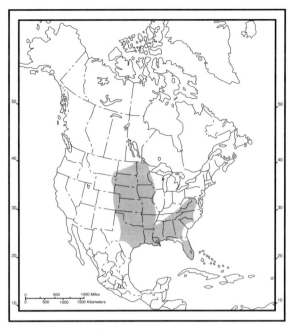

Map 10-39 Distribution of the eastern spotted skunk (Spilogale putorius) *in North America.*

contact with humans. Eastern spotted skunks are agile climbers, a characteristic that serves them well for foraging (Crabb 1948).

Spotted skunks exhibit a curious handstand posture when threatened, a prelude to spraying with the anal glands (C. Johnson 1921). The animals can sometimes be detected by the noise of their front feet patting the ground, apparently a warning behavior (Polder 1968).

Female eastern spotted skunks are polyestrous and enter estrus in late March. Spontaneous ovulators, they breed in April and give birth in June. Delayed implantation does not occur in this species, unlike the western spotted skunk. Gestation takes about 55 to 65 days. Litter size averages four to five altricial young (Constantine 1961; Mead 1968a, b).

The young are born nearly naked, blind, and deaf, yet even at birth show black and white mark-

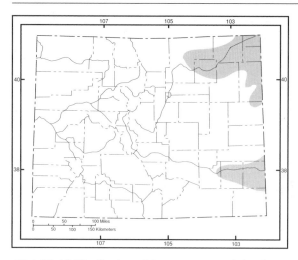

Map 10-40 Distribution of the eastern spotted skunk (Spilogale putorius) *in Colorado.*

ings. Eyes open at about 30 to 35 days of age, and scent glands are functional by 45 days. The young develop rapidly and are full grown at about three months of age (Crabb 1944).

Densities of spotted skunks averaged about 2.2 animals per km^2 in Iowa (Crabb 1948). Home ranges were 64 ha to over 530 ha, depending on habitat and sex. Males typically have larger ranges. Long-term fluctuations in abundance of the species have been documented in Kansas, probably a consequence of human activities (Choate et al. 1974).

Humans are the chief cause of mortality either directly via trapping and road kills or indirectly through habitat alteration and destruction. Diseases, including rabies, also contribute to mortality. Howard and Marsh (1982) and Rosatte (1987) reviewed the literature on the species.

DISTRIBUTION IN COLORADO — In Colorado the eastern spotted skunk is known from only a few specimens collected along the eastern border of the state. Its status in Colorado is unclear. The species has recently expanded its range on the northern Great Plains, probably as a result of human activities (J. K. Jones et al. 1983). One sub-

species, *Spilogale putorius interrupta*, occurs in Colorado.

In earlier literature, *S. putorius* and *S. gracilis* were considered to be conspecific, subspecies of *S. putorius* (Hall 1981, Van Gelder 1959). However, because *S. putorius* breeds in the spring and *S. gracilis* breeds in the fall (Mead 1968*a, b*) the two forms are reproductively isolated and thus must be recognized as separate biological species. Despite its apparent scarcity in Colorado, the eastern spotted skunk — as all skunks — is afforded no protection by the Colorado Division of Wildlife and can be trapped or hunted year round.

Mephitis mephitis
STRIPED SKUNK

DESCRIPTION — The striped skunk is a large skunk with a long bushy tail and a black background color. Most individuals have a single white dorsal stripe from the nose to the nape of the neck where it splits into two white, lateral body stripes that converge near the base of the black and white tail. The ears are small and rounded. The underfur (which may be tinged with deep reddish brown) is long, wavy, and dense, and the guard hairs are long and glossy. Measurements are: total length 580–770 mm; length of tail 190–350 mm; length of hindfoot 60–86 mm; weight 1,800–4,500 g. Considerable weight gain and loss occurs seasonally. Females are smaller than males by up to 15 percent (Hall 1981). The legs are relatively short and the soles of the feet nearly naked. Front claws are long, sometimes reaching 3 cm in length; hind claws are shorter. The skull is arched, deepest at the level of the frontals. The auditory bullae are barely inflated. The palate terminates close to the posterior border of the upper molars. Females have 10 to 14 functional mammae.

NATURAL HISTORY — No intensive research has been conducted on the striped skunk in the Rocky Mountains, and information presented below draws on studies from elsewhere. Striped

Photograph 10-21 Striped skunk (Mephitis mephitis).

skunks occur in most habitats in Colorado, except for alpine tundra. They are commonest at lower elevations, especially in and near cultivated fields and pastures (Armstrong 1972).

Striped skunks are omnivorous and opportunistic. Arthropods, especially beetles, grasshoppers, and other insects, are a mainstay of the diet. Voles, mice, ground-nesting birds and their eggs also are eaten. Plant material composes 20 percent or less of the diet and includes berries, fruit, grains, and vegetables. Insects (and to a lesser extent small mammals) are most important in the warmer months. In the fall and winter there is in-

creased use of vertebrates (including carrion) and plant foods. Both striped and spotted skunks are reported to be able to break open bird eggs by throwing them backward between the legs up against a hard surface. During the winter months 14 to 65 percent of summer and fall weight is lost (Godin 1982, Wade-Smith and Verts 1982). As with mink, striped skunks have been implicated in the destruction of nests of ground-nesting birds, including waterfowl (T. Bailey 1971) and pheasants (Kimball 1948).

Most foraging activity starts in early evening and continues through the night. Prey is located by its odor, as is apparent from watching the animals forage with their noses always to the ground. Muzzle-sized, conical pits mark places where they have foraged for ground-dwelling arthropods. Skunks pounce cat-like on prey moving on the surface of the ground.

Although skunks are mostly crepuscular and nocturnal, diurnal activity increases in the fall as the animals feed intensively to gain weight for the metabolic demands of winter. During the warmer months they often live above ground, sleeping in dense vegetation, including croplands, hay meadows, thickets, and under buildings. These bedding sites are seldom used more than one or two days. During winter, one or two alternative dens is used. Burrows abandoned by other mammals, such as marmots, badgers, foxes, and coyotes are often used as temporary shelters (Godin 1982, Houseknecht and Tester 1978, Storm 1972).

Dens usually have a single entrance and are most often built on sloping ground. Skunks are capable of digging their own burrows and will do so when no other shelter exists. Females typically use underground dens when rearing young. During the winter in colder areas (including Colorado), communal dens are used. Such groups are formed mostly of females, sometimes accompanied by one male (Houseknecht and Tester 1978, Storm 1972, Verts 1967, Wade-Smith and Verts 1982).

In cold areas striped skunks are inactive in the winter months but do not hibernate. Winter foraging activity is greatly reduced and animals spend much time in winter dens, often for several months without emerging (Mutch and Aleksiuk 1977, Storm 1972, Sunquist 1974). When in the den, periodic arousal and movement occur. These bouts of activity usually last no more than 10 minutes, two or three times a day, and do not occur every day (Sunquist 1974). In Canada, body temperatures of skunks in winter dens were about 2–3°C lower than temperatures of individuals active above ground during the same season. Males tend to be more active in cold weather than are females.

Home ranges are linear and vary with season, age, and habitat. Estimates of home ranges were from less than 1 ha to as much as 4,900 ha. Density estimates vary from 0.5 to 26 animals per km^2 with an average of about two to five animals per km^2. Length of winter, availability of winter den sites, use of communal dens, and food availability all influence density. Season of the year also affects population numbers; populations are low prior to emergence of young of the year (T. Bailey 1971, Rosatte 1987, Wade-Smith and Verts 1982).

Striped skunks are polygamous. Males increase their movements at the onset of the breeding season in search of mates. Males may form harems during the breeding season (Rosatte 1987). Skunks usually mate in February or March (W. Hamilton 1937, Seton 1929, Verts 1967). Ovulation is induced by copulation. Females are monestrous, although they will cycle again one month later if not bred during the first estrous period (Seton 1929, Verts 1967). Gestation is 59 to 77 days (Wade-Smith and Richmond 1978). Shorter gestation periods are associated with later matings, suggesting that delayed implantation occurs or is prolonged in early breeders. A litter of 5 to 8 young (range 2 to 10) is born in May or early June (Wade-Smith and Verts 1982). Striped skunks can breed at about 10 months of age. Sex ratios approximate 1:1.

Map 10-41 Distribution of the striped skunk (Mephitis mephitis) *in North America.*

Neonates weigh about 33 g, and pigmentation of the skin foreshadows the pattern of coloration. Eyes open at about three weeks of age, and ears open soon thereafter. Musk glands are developed at birth and the young can scent at a little over one week of age. Teeth begin to erupt at about one month, and weaning occurs at eight weeks. Growth continues until about breeding age. Young skunks typically stay with the female until two to four months of age (Verts 1967).

Mortality is 50 to 70 percent in juveniles, and most individuals do not live past three years of age. Great horned owls, eagles, mountain lions, bobcats, badgers, coyotes, and foxes prey on striped skunks. Rabies and distemper are important diseases, and vehicles and deliberate human persecution also account for many losses. In areas with a high incidence of rabies, skunks are often eliminated in control efforts during epizootics (Rosatte 1987). Fur trappers take several thousand striped skunks annually (Table 3-2).

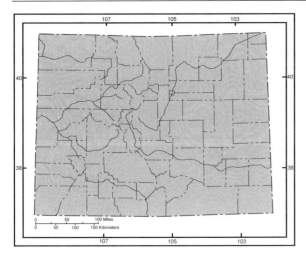

Map 10-42 Distribution of the striped skunk (Mephitis mephitis) *in Colorado.*

Photograph 10-22 Common hog-nosed skunk (Conepatus mesoleucus).

Striped skunks are well known for their potential to spray unwary aggressors. Their graphic coloration serves as a warning to would-be predators who have experience with skunks. The anal glands are equipped with sphincter muscles that allow for forceful ejection of scent up to several meters (Godin 1982). Until recently, a bath in tomato juice was the usual means of eliminating the odor. Commercial products are now available as well. The offensive odor is caused by a mercaptan, one of the class of sulfur-containing compounds familiar from its use in natural gas (which by itself is odorless) to facilitate detection of leaks. Literature on this species was reviewed by Godin (1982), Wade-Smith and Verts (1982), and Rosatte (1987).

DISTRIBUTION IN COLORADO — The striped skunk occurs throughout Colorado and is locally common up to elevations of 3,050 m (10,000 ft). *Mephitis mephitis estor* occurs in southwestern Colorado; *M. m. hudsonica* occurs in the northeastern, western, and central parts of the state; *M. m. varians* occurs on the southeastern plains and in the San Luis Valley.

Conepatus mesoleucus
COMMON HOG-NOSED SKUNK

DESCRIPTION — The hog-nosed skunk is a large skunk with a white back and black sides and venter. The muzzle and sides of the face are black and lack a white nose stripe. The nose is extended into a long, naked, flexible snout. The tail is usually completely white and proportionally shorter in length than that of the striped skunk. The fur is shorter and harsher than that of either the spotted or striped skunks. The claws on the front feet are long and stout. Measurements are: total length 450–900 mm; length of tail 190–290 mm; length of hindfoot 55–77 mm; length of ear 24–27; weight 1,500–4,500 g. The skull is highest in the parietal region with the auditory bullae moderately inflated. The palate extends posteriorly past the plane of the molars and only two premolars are present on each side of the upper jaw. Females have six mammae.

NATURAL HISTORY — This is a species of rocky canyon country in piñon-juniper woodlands and montane shrublands of the Southwest; it also has been reported from desert and grassland environments. In Colorado the few records are associated

359

Map 10-43 *Distribution of the common hog-nosed skunk* (Conepatus mesoleucus) *in North America.*

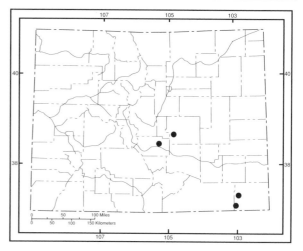

Map 10-44 *Distribution of the common hog-nosed skunk* (Conepatus mesoleucus) *in Colorado. Solid circles represent records of occurrence.*

high in old mine shafts or caves as well as occupying woodrat dens (Hoffmeister 1986).

Reproductive biology is not well known. Mating occurs in late February in Texas (Patton 1974). Gestation takes about 60 days, with litter size averaging three. Literature on this species was reviewed by Howard and Marsh (1982) and Rosatte (1987).

DISTRIBUTION IN COLORADO — Colorado represents the extreme northern edge of the range of the hog-nosed skunk. The species is known from Colorado on the basis of fewer than ten specimens collected in the 1920s in southeastern Colorado. The hog-nosed skunk in Colorado and the Oklahoma Panhandle (Caire et al. 1989) may represent a disjunct population, by several hundred kilometers from the nearest locality, in the Sandia Mountains of New Mexico (Findley et al. 1975). The present status of the species in Colorado is unknown. Two subspecies have been named from Colorado. *Conepatus mesoleucus fremonti* is reported to occur in El Paso and Fremont counties; *C. m. figginsi* was named from Baca County. In the absence of more specimens and a definitive study of geographic variation across the range of the species, these subspecific designations of Colorado

with oakbrush and piñon-juniper woodlands in southeastern Colorado.

Little information exists on the life history of the species. In Texas, they were observed to feed mostly on terrestrial insects. However, they also consumed carrion, small reptiles and mammals, and vegetable material including prickly pear fruits, berries, and nuts (V. Bailey 1932, W. B. Davis 1974, Patton 1974). They seemed to spend much of their time rooting for insects with the snout and long front claws. This rooting activity leaves large areas of disturbed litter and topsoil and is a good clue to their presence (F. Miller 1925).

Hog-nosed skunks are thought to be mostly nocturnal. They use rocky ledges, caves, abandoned mines, abandoned burrows, woodrat nests, and similar sites for denning. In Arizona they construct large, mounded grass nests up to a meter specimens should be regarded with skepticism (Armstrong 1972).

Lutra canadensis
NORTHERN RIVER OTTER

DESCRIPTION —The river otter is an elongate, robust mustelid with a thick, tapering tail. The head is relatively small and flattened with a shortened muzzle and small ears. The legs are short and the feet are large and webbed. The heels of the hindfeet have roughened pads for traction on steep, muddy streambanks. The webbed feet, powerful tail, and short fur are adaptations for an aquatic life. The short underfur is extremely dense and protected by longer glossy guard hairs. Dorsal color ranges from dark brown to chestnut with ventral coloration pale brown to silvery. The chin and throat are sometimes whitish. Measurements are: total length 880–1,300 mm; length of tail 300–510 mm; length of hindfoot 100–150 mm; weight 5–14 kg. Males are slightly larger than females. The skull has a shortened rostrum and is flattened dorsoventrally with only slightly inflated bullae. Females have four mammae.

NATURAL HISTORY — River otters inhabit riparian habitats that traverse a variety of other ecosystems ranging from semidesert shrublands to montane and subalpine forests. The species requires permanent water, of relatively high quality (although the population in the Dolores River tolerates, at least seasonally, heavy sediment loads), and with an abundant food base of fish or crustaceans. Minimum estimated water flows are 10 cubic feet (0.28 cubic meter) per second. Other habitat features that may be important include the presence of ice-free reaches of stream in winter, water depth, stream width, and suitable access to shoreline (Lytle et al. 1981, Goodman 1984). According to historical distributional records in Colorado (Armstrong 1972), relatively large rivers at low to moderate elevations were mostly used. Restored animals occupy sites in low-elevation gravel ponds and irrigation reservoirs near Fort Collins (Malville 1988), mountain lakes and

Photograph 10-23 Northern river otter (Lutra canadensis).

streams (Mack 1985), and canyon river systems at lower elevations (Malville 1990).

The diets of river otters have been studied in a number of states, but we know little about food habits in the Southern Rockies. Fishes are present in 70 to 99 percent of scat. Slow-swimming fishes, and those in greatest abundance, are principal prey. Fishes were found in 100 percent of scats examined in Grand County, Colorado (Mack 1985). Using an estimate of 1,394 kcal/animal day, Mack calculated that prey availability exceeded demand by sixfold on the restoration site, and that the area could support five reproductively active females. Crustaceans (especially crayfish) are also important food items in waters where they are abundant. Otters on the Dolores River make extensive use of crayfish (Malville 1990). Insects are also frequently reported in studies of food habits. Mammals, amphibians, and birds are utilized less than the other items. In winter, fishes may provide almost 100 percent of the diet based on studies in the Northern Rockies and the Pacific Northwest (Greer 1955, Melquist and Dronkert 1987, Melquist et al. 1981, Toweill 1974, Zackheim 1982).

Because of the river otter's aquatic life, many aspects of the species' behavior and ecology are not well studied. The animals do not hibernate and

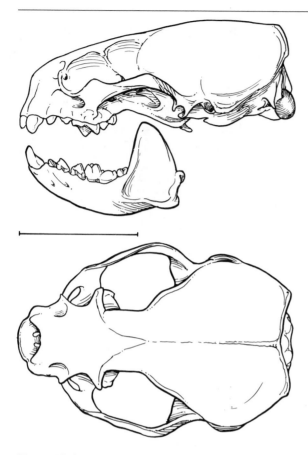

Figure 10-4 Lateral and dorsal views of the skull of a northern river otter (Lutra canadensis). *Scale = 1 cm.*

groups undoubtedly include males (Melquist and Dronkert 1987).

River otters use both terrestrial resting sites and dens when not actively moving. Beaver bank dens are particularly favored sites. They were used in 31 percent of some 1,300 observations (Melquist and Hornocker 1983). Logjams, dense riparian vegetation, and snow and ice caves were also used. Less frequent use was made of brushpiles, talus, muskrat dens, undercut banks, and beaver lodges.

A comparison of the ecology of mink and otters in Idaho revealed that the two species had differential prey selection, foraging strategy, and activity patterns (Melquist et al. 1981). In Alberta, trenching through dams by otters during the winter reduced water levels behind the dams. Otters appeared to do this to allow under-ice access to adjacent water, but it also may have improved access to air and it concentrated fish prey (D. Reid et al. 1988).

Females mate immediately after the birth of the young, probably in March and April in Colorado. Estrus may last more than 40 days, during which time males follow scent trails of females. Copulation takes 15 to 20 minutes and is accompanied by female vocalizations. Induced ovulation is thought to occur. Controversy exists (Melquist and Dronkert 1987) over whether or not delayed implantation is obligatory in the species, as some studies of southern populations suggest that it may not always occur. Total gestation period has been estimated at 290 to 375 days, with postimplantation development taking about 60 days (Liers 1951, W. Hamilton and Eadie 1964, Tabor 1974). Females retreat to secluded areas for parturition and rearing of the young, generally using abandoned dens of other aquatic mammals, especially beaver bank dens, and usually not using the same natal den more than once (Melquist and Hornocker 1983). Litter size ranges from one to six young with an average of slightly less than three (Melquist and Dronkert 1987). Sex ratios approximate 1:1.

are active year around. Otters in the Upper Colorado drainage were mostly diurnal in winter and more nocturnal in summer, with the least activity in late summer and early fall (Mack 1985). Most activity of animals in Idaho occurred near midnight and dawn (Melquist and Hornocker 1983).

River otters are social, forming family groups led by the adult female, who may exhibit territorial behavior. Yearling otters, unrelated juveniles, and occasional adult otters may join with family groups (Melquist and Hornocker 1983). Males do not stay with family units on any regular basis, except during the brief breeding period (Melquist and Hornocker 1983). Large congregations of 7 to 30 animals are sometimes observed, and these

Map 10-45 Historic and present distribution of the northern river otter (Lutra canadensis) in North America. After Toweil and Tabor (1982).

The altricial young are blind at birth but are fully furred and have open auditory canals. Young can leave the den on their own within two months, when they begin to eat solid food, and are weaned at about three months (Liers 1951).

Young otters spend some time in play, but reports of sliding on snow and mud probably appear to be exaggerated (T. Beck, personal communication, Beckel-Kratz 1977, Melquist and Hornocker 1983). Young otters remain with the female for about seven to eight months, and siblings may stay together for over a year (Melquist and Hornocker 1983). Young may disperse up to 200 km (Melquist and Hornocker 1983). Otters do not reach sexual maturity until two years of age, and males in some populations may not breed successfully until five years or older (Liers 1951, 1958). Breeding success of two-year old females ranges from 20 to 55 percent, and adult females may not breed every year (Toweill and Tabor 1982).

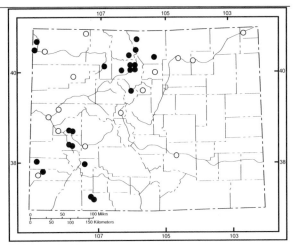

Map 10-46 Distribution of the northern river otter (Lutra canadensis) in Colorado. Open circles represent historic records of occurrence. Solid circles represent restored populations.

No long-term studies of population dynamics have been made on river otters, and turnover rates of populations are unknown. Similarly, few estimates have been made on population densities, in part because no suitable census techniques exist. Home ranges vary from 2 to 78 km long (Melquist and Hornocker 1979, 1983), with a mean length of 32 km reported for 13 telemetered animals in Colorado (Mack 1985).

Adult river otters apparently have few natural predators, although individuals have been killed by bobcats, dogs, coyotes, and foxes (Toweill and Tabor 1982). Most mortality is thought to occur from trapping and road kills. Habitat destruction and water pollution have an impact as well. Otters may live over 14 years in the wild (Melquist and Dronkert 1987). The literature on the species was reviewed by Toweill and Tabor (1982) and Melquist and Dronkert (1987).

DISTRIBUTION IN COLORADO — The river otter once occurred in most of the major river drainages of Colorado and was subsequently extirpated. Starting in 1976, Colorado initiated restoration efforts in several drainages, with an initial goal of establishing two populations (Goodman 1984). Since then, a more extensive program for restoration has been outlined (Colorado Division of Wildlife 1988). Transplants have been made in the Colorado, Gunnison, Piedra, and Dolores rivers. Reproduction apparently is low in the Colorado and Piedra release areas. Tracks and other sign of otters have also been found in the Poudre and Laramie drainages in Larimer County. These animals are thought to be stock either from the Upper Colorado River or escaped animals from Division of Wildlife facilities near Fort Collins (Malville 1988). River otters still are listed in Colorado as endangered (Table 3-1).

Historically, the subspecies *Lutra canadensis interior*, *L. c. nexa*, and *L. c. sonora* all may have occurred in Colorado. However, the paucity of specimens makes it impossible to determine historical ranges of subspecies in the state (Armstrong 1972). Otters used in recent restorations have come from at least six different states or Canadian provinces (Goodman 1984), so considerable genetic mixing has occurred.

FAMILY FELIDAE — Cats

The felids are highly specialized carnivores, adapted both behaviorally and morphologically as extremely efficient predators. Felids are more carnivorous than most other members of the order, and rarely, if ever, take vegetable matter. They kill their prey rapidly, usually with a strangulation hold on the neck or throat. This behavior, combined with their specialized dentition, renders them a formidable foe. Their dentition is specialized in the reduction of the number of teeth, and the sharpness of the canine teeth and carnassial pair (last upper premolar and first lower premolar). More than any other carnivores, the carnassials effect a scissor-like action as the jaw closes. In addition, the jaws can open to almost 90 degrees, allowing for a good hold on the throat of their prey. Felids have good visual and auditory senses, also used in hunting. Most species stalk their prey, and follow up with a short rush and pounce. The cheetah is capable of longer endurance chases than other cats.

Most felids are solitary and crepuscular or nocturnal. Most are mobile, not regularly using denning or resting areas for prolonged periods of time, except when females are rearing their altricial young. Females of most species are polyestrous but have only a single litter every one to three years. Size varies from the diminutive wildcats of Europe and Asia, weighing 3 to 8 kg, to the tiger, males of which may exceed 300 kg. The domestic cat (*Felis catus*) is thought to be descended from the wildcat, *Felis silvestris*, of the Mediterranean Region. Large felids, including tigers, lions, and leopards, sometimes attack humans. Closer to home, the number of human–mountain lion encounters in North America has increased markedly in recent years as urbanized deer populations provide an attractive food resource for lions in close proximity to humans.

Felids have a typical cat-like build, with a short muzzle, large eyes, well-developed canine and carnassial teeth, and sharp, retractile claws. Length of tail and limb proportions vary. Cats are digitigrade, walking and running on their toes rather than on the soles of their feet. The forefoot has five digits, with the pollex (thumb) reduced in size and elevated into a non–weight bearing claw. There are four digits on the hindfoot. The tooth count is 28 or 30. The eyes are frontally placed, and the pupils close vertically.

Felids evolved in the late Eocene. Modern species are found worldwide except in polar areas, on isolated oceanic islands, and Australia. Considerable controversy exists regarding the classification of the group (Nowak 1991); about 37 species are arranged in as few as four genera. Many species are categorized as threatened or endangered, often because of both overharvest for their pelage and loss of habitat. Two genera and three species occur in Colorado.

Key to the Species of the Family Felidae Found in Colorado

1. Tail more than 30 percent of length of head and body; three premolars on each side of upper jaw . . . .   Mountain Lion — *Felis concolor*, p. 365

1' Tail less than 30 percent of length of head and body; two premolars on each side of upper jaw . . . . *Lynx* 2

2. Tail more than one-half length of hindfoot; black tip on the tail incomplete ventrally; hypoglossal foramen confluent with posterior lacerate foramen* . . . Bobcat — *Lynx rufus*, p. 371

2' Tail less than one-half length of hindfoot; black tip on tail complete ventrally; hypoglossal foramen separate from posterior lacerate foramen* . . . . Lynx — *Lynx lynx*, p. 368

Felis concolor
MOUNTAIN LION

DESCRIPTION — The mountain lion is the largest cat north of Mexico, except for the jaguar, which rarely enters the United States. Other common names for this magnificent cat include puma, cougar, painter, and panther. Color is brownish to reddish brown with paler underparts. The tail is long, cylindrical, and black-tipped. The nosepad and backs of the ears are also black. Coloradan individuals are among the largest representatives of the species. Measurements are: total length 1.5–2.75 m; length of tail 600–850 mm; length of hindfoot 225–300 mm; length of ear 50–115 mm; weight 36–103 kg. Males are larger than females. The forefeet are slightly larger than the hindfeet, and their naked heelpads may measure up to 7.6 cm across on large males. Young mountain lions have spots that disappear at about one year of age. The skull is short (condylobasal length 160–

Photograph by William E. Ervin.

Photograph 10-24 Mountain lion (Felis concolor).

220 mm), broad, and heavily built. Females have eight mammae, of which only six are functional. Age can be determined by wear and appearance of teeth (M. Currier et al. 1977).

NATURAL HISTORY — Mountain lions inhabit most ecosystems in Colorado, including the eastern plains according to periodic reports. They are most common in rough, broken foothills and canyon country, often in association with montane forests, shrublands, and piñon-juniper woodlands.

Mountain lions may hunt either during the day or at night, requiring sufficient cover for stalking prey and a lack of high human activity. Most kills are reported from brushy, wooded, or rough terrain (Hornocker 1970, Young and Goldman 1946). They hunt by stealth rather than by chase, and the kill is accomplished with a final short rush and lunge.

Mountain lions prey mainly on deer in North America and also take elk and moose. In some situations they prey on mice, ground squirrels, beavers, lagomorphs, porcupines, wild hogs, raccoons, armadillos, and domestic livestock. Other

* This character trait may not always distinguish these species in the Southern Rockies; for additional distinguishing traits, see accounts of species.

carnivores, including raccoons, bobcats, and gray fox, also are eaten, especially in winter (Lindzey 1987). Some insects are eaten as well as birds, fish, and berries. Carrion apparently is eaten rarely (Russell 1978). Sheep are the most frequent livestock prey, and they sometimes are killed more than one at a time; most cattle taken are calves (Lindzey 1987). A study of lion depredation on livestock in Colorado found that transient and old lions were mostly responsible (K. Dixon and Boyd 1967).

In the West undoubtedly deer are the major prey for mountain lions (A. Anderson 1983). In Idaho deer and elk composed 70 percent of winter scats. Of the animals killed 60 to 80 percent were fawns, yearlings, or overmature individuals. It was estimated that an adult lion would have to kill a deer every two weeks to survive the winter, with annual requirements of 5 to 7 elk or 14 to 20 deer (Hornocker 1970). The importance of elk in the diet of mountain lions ranges from as low as 2 percent in Nevada to as high as 24 percent in central Idaho (K. Dixon 1982). Large prey is often moved from the site of the kill and buried with snow or surface litter. In southern Utah, increased consumption of jackrabbits and small carnivores occurred during winter (Ackerman et al. 1984).

Individual mountain lions may consume up to 4 or 5 kg of food at a meal. Free water is required, more so for females with cubs than for solitary males. In Idaho, a prey population of 200 ungulates was estimated to provide a sustainable yield of food to maintain one mountain lion (Hornocker 1970). Mountain lions on winter deer and elk ranges may be beneficial in keeping herds moving, breaking up concentrations, and reducing overbrowsing.

Mountain lions range widely and cover large distances in search of food. Distances of 30 to 40 km are easily traversed in a day, and transient individuals may move over 200 km between points of capture. Few physical barriers seem to limit their movements. Sizes of home ranges vary from about 40 to over 700 km^2 for females and from 120 to 830 km^2 for males (Lindzey 1987). Average annual home ranges of seven females on the Uncompahgre Plateau ranged from 190 to 463 km (A. Anderson et al. 1992); those of three males were 436 to 732 km^2 in the same area.

Mountain lions are solitary and do not associate with other adult lions. The exceptions are a brief period during the breeding season and when females are with cubs. Social intolerance and avoidance, rather than active defense of territory, maintain spacing (Hornocker 1969, Seidensticker et al. 1973). Females with cubs are extremely intolerant of adult males, who are likely to kill the cubs. Mountain lions, especially adult males, make scrapes (collections of leaves, dirt, and debris formed by scratching with the hindfeet), often marked with urine and feces. Such signs are often located near the margins of home ranges (Seidensticker et al. 1973).

Resident mountain lions maintain contiguous home ranges, whose size varies seasonally depending on prey density as well as a lion's sex, reproductive condition, and age. In a population, resident females typically outnumber resident males (Hemker et al. 1984). Male home ranges frequently overlap with one or more females. In western states individual mountain lions often show distinct winter-spring and summer-fall home ranges that correspond to movements of their ungulate prey and local weather conditions (Seidensticker et al. 1973). In Colorado, much of the best mountain lion habitat is at midelevations, such as the foothills of the Front Range. In these habitats resident deer herds may be relatively sedentary and lions do not make significant seasonal shifts in home range.

Densities of mountain lions under nonhunted conditions are thought to be maintained by internal population regulation rather than by their prey base. Behavioral intolerance, especially for individuals of the same sex, generally precludes high densities (Seidensticker et al. 1973). Reported densities of mountain lions vary greatly, from one animal per 333 km^2 to one animal per km^2 (A. Anderson 1983). Near Cañon City, density was estimated at one lion per 36 to 60 km^2; taking behavioral intolerance into consideration, maximum possible mountain lion density was estimated to be one animal per 25 to 50 km^2 (M. Currier 1976). Near Rifle, densities were one lion per 28 to 30 km (Brent 1983). Such estimates are usually based on population studies in fair to good habitats, and include transients; thus densities are probably much lower over all occupied habitats. The proportion of animals that are residents is 47 to 82 percent (Lindzey 1987).

Mountain lions have no set breeding season; females may come into heat at any time of the year. Due to the pattern of overlap of home ranges, males are surely polygynous, but females probably rarely breed with more than one male. Females are polyestrous and will recycle about every two weeks between estrous periods until bred (Rabb 1959, Young and Goldman 1946). Gestation lasts about 92 days. Litters are more likely to be born in spring and summer in Idaho, western Utah, and Nevada, and in late summer or fall in southern Utah and Wyoming (Lindzey 1987). Females probably average one litter every year and a half to two years. They do not prepare special natal dens for birthing. Litter size ranges from one to 6 with 2.6 the average (A. Anderson 1983).

At birth the cubs are blind and covered with fine fur with black spots. Eyes open in about 10 days, and weaning occurs at about two months. The female continues to hunt and provide food for her young during their long tutelage of 12 to 22 months. This lengthy dependence on the female keeps her reproductive potential low. Females average only four litters over a 10-year period (Russell 1978). Dispersal of young lions from the mother probably coincides with her coming back into reproductive condition. Average movements of dispersing young range from 29 to over 160 km; young females move shorter distances than males (Lindzey 1987). Two young males moved 247 and 260 km, which were among the longest reported distances moved by the species (Brent

Map 10-47 Distribution of the mountain lion (Felis concolor) *in North America.*

1983). Females are sexually mature as early as 20 months but may be prevented socially from breeding until they are older (Lindzey 1987, Seidensticker et al. 1973).

Human exploitation can have a major impact on lion populations. In a marked and radio-tagged population of 41 lions on the Uncompahgre Plateau, 50 percent had died by five and a half years of age (A. Anderson et al. 1989). The animals were studied in an area closed to hunting, but 11 of the individuals were killed illegally by humans. Twenty-two lions were captured and marked from 1981 to 1983 near Rifle and on the Uncompahgre Plateau; 14 were adults, 2 were yearlings, and 6 were kittens. Sixty percent of the animals were dead by the end of 1986. All known mortality was caused by humans, from legal and illegal harvest and accidental death in a coyote snare (Brent 1983). Prenatal mortality is estimated as high as 15 percent (Robinette et al. 1961). Mortality of

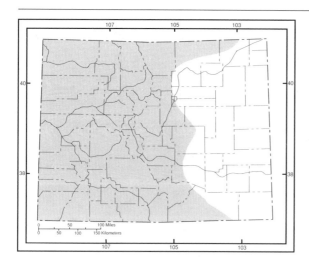

Map 10-48 Distribution of the mountain lion (Felis concolor) *in Colorado.*

cubs up to age at dispersal is 20 to 30 percent (Lindzey 1987).

Mortality factors other than humans are not well known. Disease is probably not significant, due to low densities and the solitary nature of the animals. Cubs may die from porcupine quills before they have learned the art of capturing such a difficult prey (Robinette et al. 1959). Adult males occasionally kill each other or kill and eat kittens. A few reports of adult females killing each other were also noted. Other predators, such as bears, probably kill some younger animals. Accidents occur, including lethal falls during unsuccessful predation attempts. Starvation is likewise thought to be an important agent, especially for individuals of advanced age with worn or broken teeth or for young cubs that the mother cannot maintain. Humans are the chief cause of mortality, through regulated harvest, poaching, and deliberate predator control for protection of livestock. Young animals dispersing from their mothers are especially vulnerable to harvest.

From 1929 until 1965, mountain lions were listed as predators in Colorado, and a bounty was paid. In 1965 the Wildlife Commission changed the status of mountain lions from predator to game mammal and no longer paid bounties. The present management status of the lion makes it a trophy animal, with controlled harvest of roughly 200 animals annually in Colorado. Lions evoke considerable debate. Many people view it as a species of great aesthetic value and a symbol of wilderness, and they argue against the current hunting status. On the other hand, livestock interests and wildlife managers believe that regulated harvest and management are essential. With increased development of foothills environments, providing enhanced habitat for deer, mountain lion and human conflicts are increasing. Occasionally, this situation has serious consequences, as in the case of a jogger killed in January 1991 by a mountain lion near Idaho Springs. Recently Colorado hosted a symposium dealing with conflicts between humans and mountain lions (Braun 1993). The Division of Wildlife is presently developing policies to address such conflicts. Literature on the species was reviewed by K. Dixon (1982), A. Anderson (1983), M. Currier (1983), and Lindzey (1987).

DISTRIBUTION IN COLORADO — Mountain lions have the widest distribution of any mammal in the New World, ranging from the Yukon to Tierra del Fuego. They once were distributed over all of the conterminous United States, but populations mostly have been extirpated in the East and over significant areas in the West as well. In Colorado the species is still common in much of the western two-thirds of the state, although largely eliminated from the eastern plains. One subspecies, *Felis concolor hippolestes,* occurs in Colorado.

Lynx lynx
LYNX

DESCRIPTION — The lynx is a medium-sized cat with long legs, large feet, and a short tail. The fur is long, dense, soft, and fine. The dorsal color is grizzled gray to reddish brown, often tinged with black. The legs, feet, and underparts are paler, buff to white. Although spotting may be present, it usually is more muted than in the bobcat. The ears have long, dark tufts and the face has a pro-

Photograph by William E. Ervin.

Photograph 10-25 Lynx (Lynx lynx).

nounced ruff of fur. The tail is short with a completely black tip. The hindlegs are slightly longer than the front legs. The paws are much larger than those of the bobcat and can support twice as much weight on snow. Measurements are: total length 670–1,067 mm; length of tail 95–125 mm; length of hindfoot 203–250 mm; weight 5–15 kg. Males are slightly larger than females. The skull is broad with a short muzzle. The skulls of lynx and bobcat are almost identical. In some lynx specimens the hypoglossal foramen and the posterior lacerate foramen, both adjacent to the auditory bullae, are separated (Banfield 1974); however, it is not clear whether this trait invariably distinguishes lynx and bobcat in southern populations such as ours. Females have only four mammae.

NATURAL HISTORY — Northern coniferous forests are the preferred habitat of the lynx. Uneven-aged stands with relatively open canopies and well-developed understories, favorable habitat for snowshoe hares, are ideal (Quinn and Parker 1987). Fire and some systems of clear-cutting may benefit lynxes by enhancing showshoe hare habitat. Studies of lynx in Colorado suggest a preference for dense spruce-fir stands in association with rock outcrops and large boulders. The species may not be entirely intolerant of humans, as tracks were observed around garbage dumps at a central Colorado ski area (J. C. Halfpenny, pers.

comm.). The natural history of the lynx in Colorado is generally unknown.

The principal food of North American lynx is the snowshoe hare, which composes 80 percent of the diet (Brand et al. 1976, More 1976, Nellis et al. 1972, Saunders 1963*b*). Other prey includes grouse, ptarmigan, pine squirrels, mice, ground squirrels, beavers, muskrats, and even deer, caribou, and moose. Ungulates are taken mostly as carrion or by killing fawns or calves. Most dietary diversity occurs in the warmer months. To remain in good condition, a lynx requires about four snowshoe hares per week. They kill and cache hares when they are plentiful (Nellis and Keith 1968, Brand et al. 1976). Dietary intake averaged 960 grams/day. The success rate for capturing prey was 36 percent. Because it is assumed that snowshoe hares are an important dietary component of the lynx in Colorado, most efforts to locate lynx have been directed at areas with abundant hare populations.

Lynxes are primarily solitary and nocturnal. However, they have also been observed traveling together (two females and their three young) and hunting cooperatively for marmots, ground squirrels, and snowshoe hares (Barash 1971, Carbyn and Patriquin 1983, Parker et al. 1983). Animals do not bury their scat, instead using it and urine for scent marking (Saunders 1963*a*). The animals hunt mostly on the ground but also can climb. Lynxes den or bed under ledges, trees, deadfalls, or occasionally in caves. In severe weather they may bed in thick evergreen cover.

Home ranges of lynxes have been estimated to range from 12 km^2 in Alberta and Alaska (Brand et al. 1976) to 243 km^2 in a new and expanding population that was colonizing northeastern Minnesota (Mech 1980). In the colonizing population, home ranges of females overlapped but those of males did not. There was little overlap of male and female home ranges, suggesting a pattern of spacing more similar to that of mountain lions than bobcats. Variability in size of home

Map 10-49 Historic and present distribution of the lynx (Lynx lynx) in North America. After McCord and Cardoza (1982).

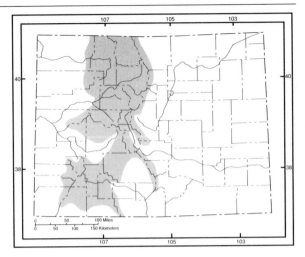

Map 10-50 Distribution of the lynx (Lynx lynx) in Colorado.

ranges is due to sex, age, reproductive status, and sometimes prey density (Brand et al. 1976).

An average density for lynxes is one animal per 20 km². Lynx population density fluctuates with cycles of showshoe hare populations. Fluctuations in the prey base involve a complex of interactions of the hares with their food supply and its quality, leading to roughly 10-year cycles of abundance and decline (Quinn and Parker 1987). Low hare populations lead to reduced lynx reproduction and loss of young due to starvation. Populations of snowshoe hares in Colorado do not appear to fluctuate cyclically (Dolbeer and Clark 1975), and it is possible that any lynx populations in the state would behave similarly.

Lynxes breed in March, April, or May in Canada and Alaska. The gestation period is about nine weeks. The single annual litter contains one to six (average, three) young. Females raise the litter, and the young disperse in the fall or the following spring. Females apparently can breed as yearlings, but breeding by such animals may be reduced or delayed if prey is scarce. Neonates are blind, and the ears are closed. They are well haired, even including some indication of the ear tufts to come (Nava 1970, Saunders 1964, Tumlison 1987).

Lynx mortality mostly appears to be due to loss of kittens during cycles of low snowshoe hare availability. Under such conditions, kitten mortality can exceed 90 percent (Brand and Keith 1979). Harvest by humans is a major mortality factor as well. Lynxes have been killed by gray wolves and wolverines, and adult male lynxes occasionally kill kittens. McCord and Cardoza (1982), Quinn and Parker (1987), and Tumlison (1987) reviewed the literature on the species.

DISTRIBUTION IN COLORADO — Historically, the lynx occurred sparsely in mountainous areas above 2,700 m (9,000 ft) in the Park, Gore, San Juan, and La Plata mountains, and the White River Plateau. They now appear to be restricted to extremely isolated areas of the mountains of the central portion of the state. Denney (1975) discussed 10 lynx reports from trappers based on a 1974–1975 survey and reported on records from

Routt, Larimer, Rio Blanco, Delta, Saguache, Archuleta, La Plata, and San Miguel counties. J. C. Halfpenny (pers. comm.) added records from Rio Blanco and Garfield counties. The Colorado Division of Wildlife is presently in the process of establishing a research protocol for study of the lynx in the state (J. Sheppard, pers. comm.). Due to a number of factors (the fragmentation of the habitat in Colorado, the fact that this state represents the southernmost distribution of the lynx in the New World, the very small number of specimens, and the difficulty of distinguishing this species from the bobcat) it is difficult to say to what extent lynxes have occupied Colorado in post-Pleistocene times. Sight reports without clear photographs or specimens must be regarded cautiously. The Nearctic lynx sometimes is treated as *Lynx canadensis*, suggesting a species distinct from the Palearctic lynx, *L. lynx*. Also, *Lynx* sometimes is considered a subgenus of *Felis*. One subspecies, *Lynx lynx canadensis*, is known from Colorado.

Lynx rufus
BOBCAT

DESCRIPTION — Bobcats are medium sized, about twice the size of a domestic cat, with a bobbed tail and long legs. The dorsal color in winter pelage is a grayish buff, whereas summer pelages are more reddish; both are marked with streaks or spots. Bobcats have one annual molt, in the fall. The summer coat is simply a worn winter pelage. A facial ruff of fur is most noticeable in winter pelage. The underside, also spotted, is white and the insides of the forelegs are marked with horizontal bands. Measurements are: total length 730–1,000 mm; length of tail 120–160 mm; length of hindfoot 143–200; length of ear 50–85 mm; weight 5–14 kg. Males are about one-third larger than females. The bobcat can be difficult to distinguish from the lynx, but differs in having shorter fur, shorter dark ear-tufts, smaller feet, a longer tail, dark bands across the front legs, and more distinct spots overall than the lynx. Both species have a black-tipped tail, but the black on the bobcat's is incomplete on the ventral surface. The

Photograph 10-26 Bobcat (Lynx rufus).

skulls are very similar, as detailed in the account of the lynx. There are 28 teeth, compared to 30 teeth in domestic cats. Females have six mammae; males have a rudimentary baculum. Methods for determining the age of bobcats have been developed (Crowe 1975).

NATURAL HISTORY — Bobcats are most common in the rocky, broken terrain of foothills and canyonlands. Preferred habitats are piñon-juniper woodlands and montane forests, although they occupy all ecosystems in Colorado, including riparian woodland on the eastern plains. They avoid unbroken grasslands, agricultural land, and densely populated areas. Favored habitats provide resting and denning sites and good cover for hunting. Females are thought to be more selective of quality habitat than males. In Montana, bobcats favored sites with at least 52 percent vertical cover (P. Knowles 1985). In Colorado, bobcats chose diurnal loafing sites in steep-sloped, rocky areas with dense vertical cover (over 70 percent) and little herbaceous ground cover (E. M. Anderson 1990). Snow cover in excess of about 15 cm restricts their movements and may cause them to follow game trails, windblown areas, roads, or similar routes.

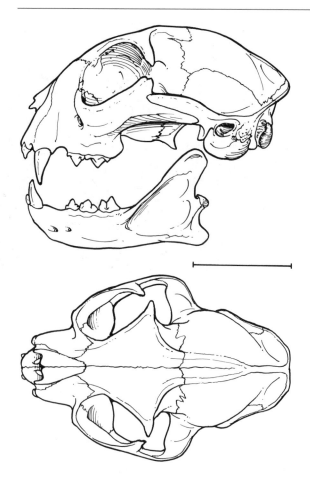

Figure 10-5 Lateral and dorsal views of the skull of a bobcat (Lynx rufus). *Scale = 1 cm.*

Bobcats hunt by stealth, relying on surprise rather than on a lengthy chase. They sit near or above a game trail and wait for prey to come by. Lagomorphs — cottontails in particular — are their specialty and compose 30 to 70 percent of the diet. In south-central and southeastern Colorado, bobcats fed on both cottontails and woodrats (E. M. Anderson 1987*b*, L. Jackson 1985). Opportunistic, bobcats will feed on practically any prey including mice, chipmunks, tree squirrels, ground squirrels, prairie dogs, snowshoe hares, porcupines, small birds, deer, amphibians, and crayfish (J. H. Jones and Smith 1979). They also kill young domestic sheep, goats, and poultry. Deer

remains were present in 34 percent of scats in Utah and Nevada (Gashwiler et al. 1960). Adult deer are killed when bedded down, by means of bites to the neck and throat, which can be made in extremely rapid succession. Juveniles and adult females are likely to feed on rodents more than do males, if rabbits are available to males. Bobcats occasionally cache food. There is little dietary overlap between coyotes and bobcats in Rocky Mountain National Park where bobcats preyed heavily on snowshoe hares and cottontails, and coyotes fed on ungulates and rodents (Makar 1980).

As with other felids, bobcats require a much higher protein diet than most other mammalian carnivores. Vegetable matter does not provide sufficient nitrogen to offset metabolic losses from liver enzyme activity. Although grass boluses are often reported in food habits studies such materials are probably used as a purgative and not as a food resource. Caged bobcats in Georgia averaged 138 kcal/kg/day in food intake although they could maintain condition on half of that intake (Golley et al 1965). Physiological studies and computer modeling in New York suggest that seasonal energetic demands are actually lowest in February and March despite cold weather because animals catabolized stored fat and reduced daily activity. Males and females both required about 374 g of food daily per kilogram of body weight in March, whereas during peak seasonal activities males needed about 760 g/kg and females about 830 g/kg (Gustafson 1984).

Bobcats are generally solitary except during the breeding season and when females are rearing young. Home ranges of males overlap with those of several females; home ranges of adult females are usually nonoverlapping (E. M. Anderson 1987*b*). However, bobcats may share refuges during inclement weather. The degree of social tolerance depends on population density, prey availability, weather, and presence and distribution of suitable dens or shelters. Subadults are tolerated on adult home ranges in most situations although there are a few reports of intense fights

Map 10-51 Distribution of the bobcat (Lynx rufus) *in North America. After McCord and Cardoza (1982).*

between adult and juvenile males; a few instances of cannibalism have been reported (McCord and Cardoza 1982, Rolley 1987).

Bobcats scent mark with feces, urine, and anal gland secretions, which are rubbed on objects or discharged on the ground. These odorous deposits may be enhanced by scrapings with the feet, which add a visual component to the signal. Marking with these secretions occurs along trails and at scent posts. Feces may be covered, or uncovered and placed on unprepared ground, or placed in a scrape made by the hindlegs. Females with kittens are responsible for most fecal marking. The use of such scent stations may serve to mark territories (T. Bailey 1974, McCord and Cardoza 1982).

Bobcats are active all year. Most hunting occurs at night or at dawn and dusk. On cloudy days in undisturbed areas, or during periods of extreme cold, they may hunt during the middle of the day.

Daily movements averaged 1.8 km for males and 1.2 km for females in Idaho, and 1 to 3 km in Colorado. Long-distance movements by young males of up to 182 km have been reported in a situation where lagomorph populations declined and local food resources became scarce. Juveniles dispersing from their natal areas may move 20 or 30 km (T. Bailey 1974, E. M. Anderson 1987*b*).

Bobcats are seasonally polyestrous and ovulate spontaneously. Previously they were thought to be induced ovulators, as are domestic cats. Females may have up to three estrous cycles over a four-month period if not bred. Although bobcats may breed at any time of the year, reproductive activity is highest in February and March in Wyoming, with most births occurring in April and May (Crowe 1975). In Utah, embryos are present in females from January to September, although mostly in March and April (Gashwiler et al. 1961). Gestation takes 60 to 70 days (E. M. Anderson 1987*a*). Females that lose a litter soon after parturition may be able to produce a second litter the same year. Average litter size was two to three (average 2.9) in the Fort Carson area (D. Jackson 1986). In that study, two females each had two litters within a nine-month period. Most adult females only have one litter per year. Kittens are nursed for about 60 days and remain with the female into the fall. In Colorado most juveniles are 9 to 11 months of age when they disperse. Some breeding occurs in yearling females, who have smaller litters and lower pregnancy rates than older females. Otherwise, females are sexually mature in their second year, as are young males (E. M. Anderson 1987*a*).

Home ranges in the West vary from 22 to over 80 km^2 for adult males, and 8 to 27 km^2 for adult females, with variation due to habitat quality (McCord and Cardoza 1982, Rolley 1987). Home ranges in southern Colorado averaged 42 to 46 km^2 for adult males and 17 to 22 km^2 for adult females (E. M. Anderson 1987*b*, D. Jackson 1986).

Although most adults in a population are residents, a small but important component are tran-

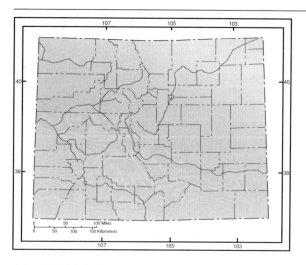

Map 10-52 Distribution of the bobcat (Lynx rufus) *in Colorado.*

sients. These individuals are quick to fill in territories left vacant by the death of the resident. Little is known about the population dynamics of bobcats in Colorado; most of the data represent harvest trends, which are subject to vagaries of trapping and inconsistency in reporting. Sex ratios of adults at Fort Carson were 0.73:1.0 males to females. Overall sex ratios were 0.79:1.0. Age ratios were 0.35 juvenile:1 adult (D. Jackson 1986). Habitat suitability, status, and management in the state for bobcats have been addressed (Alexander 1977, Donoho 1977), but additional studies on population dynamics are needed in areas of heavy trapping.

Survival rates of adult bobcats average 53 to 66 percent in populations that are trapped or hunted, and they are as high as 97 percent in protected populations (E. M. Anderson 1987a). Juvenile survival is much more variable. Mountain lions and coyotes have been implicated as predators on female bobcats, and bobcat populations may be suppressed by the latter in areas where coyote control is absent. Of animals harvested in Colorado, 61 percent were males, with adults composing about 80 percent of the take (Lipscomb et al. 1983). Limited data from the Fort Carson and Piñon Canyon studies suggest that predation and hunter harvest are the principal causes of death in bobcats, accounting for 29 and 46 percent of observed mortality, respectively (E. M. Anderson 1987b, D. Jackson 1986). Starvation and disease accounted for another 12 to 20 percent of known mortality. Annual survival rates were 0.76 for adult bobcats at Fort Carson. Literature on the species was reviewed by McCord and Cardoza (1982), E. M. Anderson (1987a), and Rolley (1987).

DISTRIBUTION IN COLORADO —Bobcats occur in the western two-thirds and southeastern sections of Colorado. We know very little about the status or ecology of the bobcat in Colorado outside of piñon-juniper woodlands and montane forests. Studies in other states suggest that populations are susceptible to overharvest when fur prices are high. Some local populations in Colorado are probably similarly overexploited. Bobcats are recognized as furbearers with a liberal season and harvest (Table 3-2). However, the U. S. Fish and Wildlife Service, under provisions of the Convention on International Trade in Endangered Species, regulates total harvest in the United States by issuing a limited number of tags to each state. All bobcats killed in Colorado must be inspected and tagged by a representative of the Colorado Division of Wildlife. *Lynx rufus baileyi* is the subspecies of southeastern and southwestern roughlands and the San Luis Valley; elsewhere in the mountains and the Western Slope, *L. r. pallescens* occurs; *L. r. rufus* is probably the subspecies in northeastern Colorado (Armstrong 1972).

Chapter 11

Order: Perissodactyla

Odd-toed Hoofed Mammals

Horses, tapirs, rhinos, asses, and zebras constitute the order Perissodactyla, the odd-toed ungulates. Perissodactyls were a dominant group during the early and mid-Tertiary, ranging across North America, Eurasia, and Africa. Of the 12 recognized families, 9 are now extinct, and the natural distribution of the remaining species is restricted to Asia, southeastern Europe, Africa, the East Indies, and parts of South and Central America. Disappearance of the perissodactyls coincided with expansion of the even-toed ungulates, the artiodactyls. Horses (*Equus caballus*) and asses (*E. asinus*) have been introduced locally in various parts of the world, including Colorado and other western states, where feral herds have become established.

The story of the evolution of the foot in the perissodactyls is well preserved in the fossil record. Perissodactyls walk on hooves, also called ungules (and hence are unguligrade), or on digits (digitigrade), and they exhibit significant loss or modification of the metacarpal and metatarsal bones, most notably an increase in their length and weight-bearing surface. There has been a reduction in the number of digits. Most members of the order have only one to three weight-bearing toes. Tapirs are the exception to this "odd-toed" formula, as their forefoot has four digits, although the outermost is reduced in size; the hindfoot has three functional digits. In all perissodactyls the main axis of the foot passes through the third and longest digit, a condition termed mesaxonic. In equids, only the third digit is functional.

The skull is elongate. The nasals are wide posteriorly. An alisphenoid canal is present. The dental formula totals 24-44, and the cheekteeth are lophodont. The general size of perissodactyls varies considerably. Some tapirs and smaller equids weigh less than 300 kg and are less than 1 m in shoulder height. At the other extreme, the white rhinoceros is one of the largest living terrestrial mammals, weighing up to 3,600 kg and standing 1.6 to 2 m high at the shoulder. Male artiodactyls lack a baculum. Females have inguinal mammae.

Modern perissodactyls are specialized to exploit grasslands and open brushy country (horses, rhinos, zebras) or dense tropical forests (tapirs). All species are grazers or browsers able to handle relatively tough, coarse foods. The stomach is simple, and breakdown of cellulose occurs largely in the small intestine and caecum. None of these animals produces a cud. Perissodactyls are slow to reach sexual maturity and are long lived, sometimes living over 30 years.

There are 3 families, 6 genera, and 17 species of living perissodactyls. In Colorado the only wild representative is the feral horse, which is in the family Equidae.

FAMILY EQUIDAE — Horses and Allies

The family Equidae evolved mostly in North America and secondarily in Asia. In North America many species arose from the early Eocene to Pleistocene times but none survived to the Recent. Speculation on the cause of extinctions of North American perissodactyls ranges from hunting by early humans to climatic change and increasing competition from artiodactyls. Equids were reestablished in North America from Spanish stock introduced as early as the mid–sixteenth century.

The family includes eight living species, all in the genus *Equus*, represented by three species of African zebras, two species of horses (domestic and Mongolian), two wild Asiatic asses, and the domestic donkey or burro. All species have a single functional, hooved digit on each foot. In the foreleg the radius and ulna are fused and weight is borne on the radius. In the hindleg the tibia is enlarged and bears weight, and the fibula is reduced. The dental formula is 3/3, 0–1/0–1, 3–4/3, 3/3 = 38 to 42. Canines are present in mature males but reduced or absent in females. Cheek teeth are homodont and lophodont, with high crowns. The skull is long with the orbit completely enclosed by bone. The nasals are long and narrow, tapering to pointed ends anteriorly. Hair is well developed; all species have coarse manes, and long, straight tail hairs.

Equids evolved on open hard ground where running speed was a selective advantage. They developed the most extreme alteration of the perissodactyl limb, which became long and slender. Only the third digit is functional. The calcaneus does not articulate with the fibula and the astragalus has a grooved, pulley-like surface for articulation with the tibia. The femur has a prominent third trochanter lacking in the artiodactyls.

Equids are highly social, forming herds of a few animals to a hundred or more during seasonal concentrations. Herds are family units, harems, or bachelor herds. Most equids are mobile and nomadic, moving in response to forage quality and availability and sources of free water. Some are territorial. Most Old World species are classified as endangered, vulnerable, or threatened because of loss of habitat and killing by humans for trophies, hides, or meat.

Large populations of feral horses ranged parts of western North America in the 1700s and 1800s but were exterminated as habitat declined and competition with domestic stock increased. Although many faunal works on mammals have tended to ignore horses and burros, or pay them token attention as "introductions," they are important inhabitants of ecosystems in several western states and their impacts on the environment cannot be ignored as state and federal agencies attempt to manage public land in the West.

Photograph 11-1 Feral horse (Equus caballus).

Equus caballus
DOMESTIC AND FERAL HORSES

DESCRIPTION — Horses are highly variable in coat color, and a wonderful vocabulary exists to define the many shades: bay, chestnut, strawberry roan, buckskin, dapple gray, and paint, to name just a few. The following measurements apply to feral horses, which are usually smaller in height and weight than domestic animals. Adults range from less than 300 kg to more than 500 kg in weight, and males are heavier than females. Shoulder height is usually 1.3 to 1.4 m. Age can be determined by tooth eruption and wear (Bone 1964). It is not always possible to distinguish feral horses from domestic herds ranging on public lands. Generally, small herds of nervous, scruffy-looking horses without apparent brands and living considerable distances from ranch dwellings can be considered feral or "wild" horses.

NATURAL HISTORY — Feral horses are associated with a variety of arid grasslands and shrublands in western North America. In Colorado the species inhabits semidesert shrublands and piñon-juniper woodlands with an understory of grasses. From 80 to more than 90 percent of the diet is grasses and sedges. During winter a variety of browse is consumed, including sagebrush, greasewood, saltbush, rabbitbrush, mountain-mahogany, juniper, Douglas-fir, and spruce (Hansen and Clark 1977). Aspen bark is also consumed when available. Microflora in the small intestine and cecum process fibrous plant material, but not as effectively as the complex gut of ruminants. Coprophagy is not uncommon. Feral horses must have free water and typically visit water holes at least daily, most frequently in late afternoon.

Feral horses have complex social behaviors, and rarely are single individuals observed. Home ranges of bands frequently overlap and are associated with the distribution of available water. Herds usually remain within 6 to 8 km from a water source. Feral horses are generally not territorial and do not defend grazing areas or watering sites (Berger 1977). Rather, social organization involves formation of harems. The mating system is polygynous and relatively few males in a population breed. Mixed bands or harems usually consist of a stallion, several mares, and their young. Mares are less aggressive than males and form complex associations with other mares in the band, establishing dominance hierarchies within the harem. Adult mares in a harem

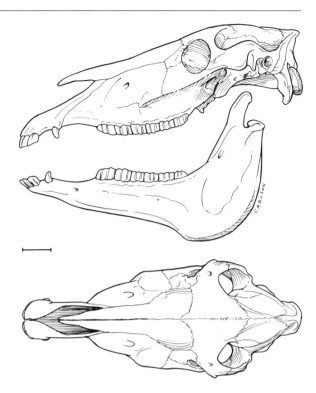

Figure 11-1 Skull of a horse (Equus caballus). *The presence of well-developed upper canines suggests that it is a male. Scale = 5 cm.*

rarely move more than 300 m from other members of the herd. At parturition females do move away from the herd, however, sometimes accompanied by nonpregnant mares. As young males reach one to three years of age, they are forced from the group by the dominant stallion and form small bachelor herds led by a young stallion dominant in the bachelor herd but not old or strong enough to usurp a harem for himself. Breeding females are reported to expel younger females from some herds. These younger females are typically taken into harems of other males.

Dominance is maintained by a variety of displays and threat postures including laying back of the ears, open-mouth displays, arching of the neck, and head-shaking. When these displays escalate, actual fighting ensues, including biting and kicking. A behavior termed *Flehmen* (which involves curling the upper lip to facilitate passage of sexual odors through the incisive foramina to the vomeronasal organ) is exhibited during precopulatory activity or during examination of urine, feces, or the fresh placenta dropped during birthing. Horses communicate through a series of vocalizations including nickers, squeals, neighs, snorts, and screams. Individual grooming, dusting, and rolling is common and mutual grooming is a daily activity used in maintaining herd integrity. Stallions do not groom or allow grooming by immature males. Use of common defecation sites may result in formation of "stud piles" of putative social value. Because males most commonly contribute to these piles they were once thought to represent territorial markers, but because territoriality has not been observed, their function is not clear.

Breeding occurs during spring and summer. The average gestation is 340 days. Foaling usually occurs in April, May, or June. A postpartum estrus

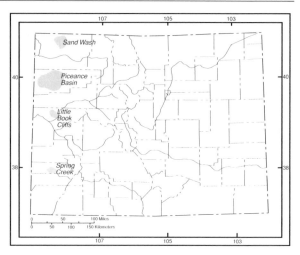

Map 11-2 *Distribution of the feral horse* (Equus caballus) *in Colorado.*

follows about one week after foaling. However, in many wild herds females only foal in alternate years. Reproductive success varies from 20 to 40 foals per 100 mares, up to 65 percent annual foaling rate for a population in Montana (Garrott and Taylor 1990). Females make up about 60 percent of the foals. Young animals are protected by the mother and by other herd members. Horses are long lived, and domestic animals often live over 30 years. This longevity is associated with a longer time to reach reproductive maturation compared to artiodactyls of similar size. Feral mares usually do not become sexually active until 3 years of age and may continue to bear young to 22 years of age. Males seldom have an opportunity to breed before they are 6 years old. Males displacing a harem stallion have been reported to cause recently conceived mares to abort through forced copulation. Reinsemination by the stallion results in the mare foaling his progeny and not that of his predecessor.

Mortality in horses is associated mostly with severe winter weather and starvation. In fact, adult survival rates of 95 and 97 percent have been documented in Nevada and Montana, respectively (Berger 1986, Garrott and Taylor 1990). Females have higher survival rates than males, and

Map 11-1 *Distribution of the feral horse* (Equus caballus) *in North America.*

most mortality occurs in animals greater than 15 years of age. Few animals prey on feral horses although mountain lions take some foals in some localities. Historically feral horses were shot for pet food or simply to reduce competition with domestic cattle, sheep, horses, or big game. Encouraged by animal rights groups, Congress enacted the Wild and Free-roaming Horse and Burro Protection Act in 1971, asserting federal ownership of feral horses on public lands. Control of populations is presently handled by periodic roundups and sales of captured animals. However, considerable research is now being conducted on the use of chemosterilants and other methods of birth control (Garrott 1991). The literature on feral horses was reviewed by Slade and Godfrey (1982).

DISTRIBUTION IN COLORADO — Feral horses occur in all of the western states except Washington. In Colorado, populations are generally small, associated with lands managed by the Bureau of Land Management in the western third of the state, especially in Moffat, Rio Blanco, Garfield, Montrose, and Mesa counties.

Chapter 12

Order:
Artiodactyla

Artiodactyls, Even-toed
Hoofed Mammals

The Artiodactyla is one of several orders of hoofed mammals, or ungulates. Generally speaking, ungulates (which include the living horses and their allies as well as a rich diversity of extinct forms) are adapted to covering large distances quickly, allowing them to exploit the abundant but often diffuse plant resources of open country. Usually the limbs are elongate, toes are reduced in number, and the collar bone (clavicle) is lost, with accompanying reduction in lateral mobility of the limbs, a trade-off for increased efficiency of fore-aft motion.

Artiodactyls represent the zenith of these ungulate trends, and the order includes most living ungulates. In all artiodactyls the first digit is missing. The second and fifth digits are reduced in more primitive forms or lost completely in more advanced forms. The main weight of the body passes equally between the third and fourth digits in most species. One genus, *Tayassu* (peccaries), has an odd number of digits, with four front toes and three hind toes. In advanced forms the metacarpal bones of the front limbs and the metatarsal bones of the hindlimbs are reduced in number and fused to form the cannon bones. The smallest of the artiodactyls is the mouse deer, *Tragulus*, which weighs about 8 kg, and the largest is *Hippopotamus*, which weighs up to 4,500 kg.

The dental formula varies although generally the upper incisors and upper canines are reduced or absent. In some species the canines are retained

and form tusks. The cheekteeth range from bunodont to selenodont and may be either high or low crowned. Molars usually are more complex than are the premolars. Many species in this order have either horns or antlers that project from the frontal bones.

More primitive artiodactyls have a simple stomach, but most living artiodactyls are ruminants, which have a complex "stomach" with three or four chambers, the anterior parts of which actually are elaborations of the esophagus. As it is harvested, forage enters the first compartment, the rumen (or paunch), a storage chamber whose bacteria help to digest some of the cellulose in the diet. In the reticulum the moistened, pulpy food is formed into cuds. From the reticulum the cud moves back to the mouth for further chewing. Then it is reswallowed and shunted to the omasum, whence finally it moves to the abomasum, the true stomach. There digestive juices subject it to further breakdown. This complex arrangement means that ruminants can gather large quantities of food rapidly and then retire to the relative safety of cover (or the herd) to ruminate, processing the food at leisure. The result is much more thorough processing of low-quality herbage than is possible for nonruminants. The caecum is small.

Artiodactyls arose in the Eocene Epoch, approximately 60 million years ago, and reached their greatest diversity in the Miocene, 25 million years ago. Today there are 9 families, 79 genera, and about 192 species distributed naturally throughout the world except in the Antarctic, the Australian region, the West Indies, and most other oceanic islands. Various species have been introduced worldwide except the Antarctic. There are three suborders of Artiodactyla: the Suina, which includes pigs, peccaries, and hippopotamuses; the Tylopoda, including camels, guanaco, vicuña, llama, and alpaca; and the Ruminantia (the largest group), including deer, giraffes, cattle, antelope, sheep, and goats. In Colorado only the suborder Ruminantia is represented in the wild by three families, seven genera, and eight species (two of which are introduced).

Key to the Families of the Order Artiodactyla Found in Colorado[*]

1. Incisors 3/3; upper and lower canines present, curving sharply outward and enlarged as tusks; slope of the braincase rising abruptly from the rostrum . . . . Family Suidae — Domestic Swine — *Sus scrofa*

1′ Incisors 0/3; canines, if present, not sharply curving or enlarged; slope of the braincase not steeply rising 2

2. Nasal and lacrimal bones joined by sutures; horns if present are permanent, not forked; horn sheath not deciduous; a single lacrimal foramina on or just within anterior rim of orbit . . . . Family Bovidae, p. 400

2′ Nasal and lacrimal bones separated by ethmoid (prelacrimal) vacuity; deciduous bony antlers or horns present at least on males; horns, if present, with a deciduous horn sheath and forked in males; two lacrimal foramina present on or just within anterior rim of orbit. 3

3. Males with deciduous antlers; dewclaws (vestigial hooves) present as reduced non–weight-bearing digits . . . . Family Cervidae, p. 381

3′ Males with forked horns; females with unforked horns or lacking horns; dewclaws absent . . . . Family Antilocapridae, p. 396

FAMILY CERVIDAE — Deer and Allies

The family Cervidae includes a variety of graceful mammals that vary in size from the diminuitive *Pudu* of the Andes to the large moose, *Alces*, which can weigh almost 1,000 kg. Male cervids are typically larger than females. In most species males have branched, deciduous antlers that function in sexual recognition, courtship displays, male-male combat, and defense. The antlers are bone and grow from pedicels on the frontal bones. New antlers are grown each year from March to September and are covered with a highly vascular, finely haired skin (velvet) that is shed after the structures mature and harden. In temperate-dwelling species the antlers are shed in late winter (mostly in February and March in Colorado, although some bucks hold their antlers until April or even early May) and mature in the fall (September and October). Two genera (*Moschus* and *Hydropotes* — the musk and water deer of Asia) lack antlers, and in the genus *Rangifer* (caribou or reindeer) both sexes have antlers.

There is a large vacuity (called rostral fenestra, prelacrimal or lacrimal vacuity, or ethmoidal vacuity) at the junction of the frontal, nasal, lacrimal, and maxillary bones. A conspicuous depression, the antorbital pit, or lacrimal fossa, is located in front of the orbits and houses the antorbital, or preorbital, glands. The upper canines may be long and pointed or short and blunt. The lower canines are reduced and incisiform, and are

[*] Because skulls of domestic sheep, goats, pigs, and cattle sometimes are found, they have been included in these keys to facilitate identification of domestic as well as wild artiodactyls.

spatulate along with the lower incisors. The cheek-teeth are brachydont and selenodont. The ulna and fibula are reduced. The stomach is four-chambered, and a cud is produced. A gall bladder is usually absent.

Breeding in temperate species typically occurs in the fall; tropical species often breed aseasonally and may have more than one estrous cycle per year. Most species have one or two young per year, but Chinese water deer may have up to four. The placenta is cotyledonary and in all but the musk deer the female has two pairs of mammae. Facial, tarsal, metatarsal, and interdigital skin glands are often well developed. The cervids are a relatively old group, dating to the Oligocene Epoch, approximately 40 million years ago. Today there are 16 genera and 38 species of cervids distributed worldwide except in sub-Saharan Africa, Australia, and Antarctica. Species have been introduced into Australia as well as New Zealand and several other oceanic islands. In Colorado there are three genera and four species of cervids (one of which is introduced).

Key to the Species of the Family Cervidae Found in Colorado

1. Antlers palmate, both sexes with elongated premaxilla and an inflated bulbous nose; pendulous skin growth on throat; nasals short, less than one-half the length from their anterior border to the anterior border of the premaxillary . . . . Moose — *Alces alces**, p. 393

1′ Antlers not palmate; premaxilla not greatly elongated; nose not particularly inflated and bulbous; no pendulous skin growth on throat; nasals long, more than one-half the length from their anterior border to the anterior border of the premaxillary. 2

2. Antlers large, directed posteriorly over shoulders; tail and rump patch yellowish; premaxillary bones reaching nasals; vomer not attached to median suture of palatine, and not separating posterior narial cavity; knob-like upper canines present . . . .
. . American Elk or Wapiti— *Cervus elaphus*, p. 382

2′ Antlers smaller, not directed posteriorly over shoulders; tail and rump patch white; premaxillary bones not reaching nasals; vomer attached to palatine suture and separating posterior narial cavity; no upper canines present
. . . . 3

3. Antlers with single main beam and simple tines; tail broad, white on undersurface, often held vertically as a flag while running; face without contrasting color between muzzle and forehead; ears about one-half length of head . . . .
. White-tailed Deer — *Odocoileus virginianus*, p. 390

3′ Antlers branching dichotomously from main beam; tail narrow, black-tipped, not held high when running; face contrastingly colored between muzzle and forehead; ears more than one-half length of head . . . .
. . . . Mule Deer — *Odocoileus hemionus*, p. 386

Cervus elaphus
AMERICAN ELK, OR WAPITI

In North America this animal is commonly called elk or wapiti, but in Europe the term elk refers to the European moose, *Alces alces*. The American *elk* is presently recognized by most authorities (McCullough 1969) as conspecific with the European red deer, *Cervus elaphus*, although formerly it was considered to be a distinct species, *Cervus canadensis*. *Cervus* and *elaphus* are Latin and Greek words, respectively, for deer.

---

* Introduced species.

Photograph 12-1 American elk, or wapiti (Cervus elaphus).

DESCRIPTION — The elk is a large cervid whose general body color is pale tan or brown. There is a contrastingly darker mane of long hairs on the neck and a paler yellowish tan rump patch. The tail is short and blends in with the rump patch. The hair is relatively long and coarse. The legs are long and the ears are large and conspicuous. Males are larger than females and may weigh over 450 kg although average weight is closer to 300 kg. There are four hooves on each foot but the two outermost are reduced to dewclaws, which are not weight bearing. Measurements are: total length 2.1–2.8 m; length of tail 100–220 mm; length of hindfoot 460–700 mm; length of ear 180–220 mm; weight 220–450 kg.

Adult males have large antlers, round in cross-section, with a main beam extending backward over the neck and shoulders. Several tines or points arise from the main beam with the tines typically not branching. Yearling males have only short "spikes," usually 30 to 45 cm in length, which are the main beams without tines. Older bulls may have up to six or seven tines off of each main beam. The skull has a large antorbital vacuity. The upper jaw has short, rounded canines and no incisors. Lower canines and incisors are spatulate and there is a diastema between them and the selenodont cheekteeth. The pattern of tooth erup-

tion and wear can be used to determine age of individuals (Quimby and Gaab 1957).

NATURAL HISTORY — Elk are among the better studied big game mammals of North America. Once the animals ranged well eastward on the Great Plains, but today they are associated with semiopen forests or forest edges adjacent to parks, meadows, and alpine tundra (R. Green 1982, Hoover and Wills 1987).

Generalist feeders, elk are both grazers and browsers. In the northern and central Rocky Mountains, grasses and shrubs compose most of the winter diet, with the former becoming of primary importance in the spring months (Kufeld 1973). Forbs become increasingly important in late spring and summer, and grasses again dominate in the fall. However, on the White River Plateau in Colorado, grasses provide from 77 to over 90 percent of the diet in summer and fall (Boyd 1970). Browse constituted over 56 percent of the winter diet. In that region forbs are little utilized except in the summer and fall. In Rocky Mountain National Park, grasses and browse are the most frequently used plant groups (Hobbs 1979; Hobbs et al. 1979, 1981, 1983). Forbs tend to be favored on drier sites, but browse is preferred in most mesic areas including aspen stands, willow communities, and moist meadows. In a study in Utah, wet meadows, dry meadows, clear-cuts, and revegetated roads were preferred grazing sites; wet meadows, revegetated roads, and mature lodgepole pine forests were preferred for resting and nongrazing activities (Collins et al. 1978).

On many elk ranges in Colorado and other western states elk have a considerable impact on aspen stands by browsing on twigs and new seedlings and feeding on the bark. Such "barking" is generally done during the fall and winter months; in heavily used stands all trees may be scarred to heights of about two meters. Scarred bark is invaded by a fungus so "barking" seriously and negatively affects the vigor and regeneration of aspen in such places as Rocky Mountain Na-

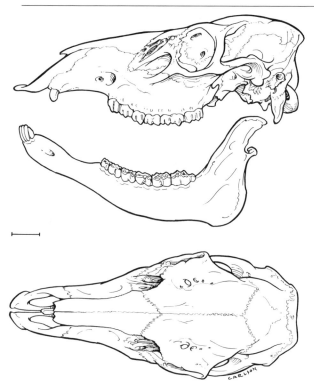

Figure 12-1 Lateral and dorsal views of skull of a cow elk (Cervus elaphus). *Scale = 5 cm.*

tional Park (Gysel 1960, Ratcliff 1941, Olmsted 1979).

Most studies of competition between elk and other species suggest that conflict and impacts are minimal, although J. Nelson (1982) suggested that competition with cattle could be high. In northeastern Colorado, considerable overlap was found in diets of elk, cattle, and wild horses (Hansen and Clark 1977). Elk appear to abandon areas being grazed by domestic sheep, and bighorn sheep seem to avoid areas being used by elk. Differences in diet tend to reduce competition between deer and elk.

Elk breed in the fall with the peak of the rut in Colorado occurring during the last week of September and first week of October (Boyd and Ryland 1971). At least some bulls have completed their antler growth and reached reproductive con-

dition by late August and early September. Breeding is typically over by late October. During the rut bulls have swollen necks and expend considerable energy in wallowing, bugling, thrashing, and digging, which serve to attract other bulls and results in sparring encounters (Struhsaker 1967). These sparring encounters are frequent, although rarely do they escalate or cause serious damage. The bugle— a loud, almost musical call— may serve as advertisement to cow elk and as a warning to potentially competing bulls. Bulls typically compete for females and attempt to gather harems consisting of adult cows and calves. Other bulls continually attempt to usurp some of these cows or copulate with estrous females, forcing the herd bull to keep a continual vigil. At this time of the year bulls lose considerable weight and many go into the winter months in poor condition. Harem size is typically between 15 and 20 cows, although some exceed 30 animals (Boyd 1978, J. Thomas and Toweill 1982).

Females are seasonally polyestrous and may undergo up to three estrous cycles at approximately 21-day intervals if successful mating does not occur. Late-breeding animals may produce calves too late in the year for the offspring to survive the winter. Most calves are born in late May or early June following a 240- to 255-day gestation period. Yearling cows can breed, but only about 29 percent of them maintain calves into the fall in Colorado, compared to 76 percent for older females (Freddy 1987). Reduced breeding in yearling females is thought to be due to weight and nutritional factors. Failure of yearling males to breed is primarily due to inability to compete with more mature bulls. Most breeding is done by males three years of age or older, and although yearling bulls can breed, pregnancy rates of cows bred by them are low. Cow:calf ratios fluctuate widely from about 18 calves per 100 cows (Cole 1969) in the Greater Yellowstone ecosystem to 71 per 100 cows on Colorado's White River Plateau (Boyd 1970). Calving grounds are carefully selected by the cows and are generally in locations where cover, forage, and water are in juxtaposition. In western Colorado most females calve within 200 m of water (Seidel 1977). A single calf is typical, and twins are rare. Calves weigh from 13 to 16 kg at birth and are precocial. They are covered with small white spots for the first few months of their lives.

Females with calves isolate themselves from the herd for the first two to three weeks. Once the calves are large enough, females with young re-join the herd. During spring and summer adult bulls usually segregate from cows, calves, and younger bulls, and form small bands of their own. Younger bulls often stay with the cow-calf herds until the rut, at which time adult bulls usually force the younger animals to leave.

Overall sex ratios are about 1:1 at birth but adult bull:cow ratios can range from as low as 10:100 to over 36:100 in relatively unhunted herds in Banff National Park (Boyd 1970, Flook 1970). Vari-ations in population structure in different herds mostly stem from hunting pressure and differen-tial winter mortality, both of which favor cows and select against bulls.

Elk tend to inhabit higher elevations during spring and summer and migrate to lower eleva-tions for winter range. However, some elk herds are relatively sedentary (Boyd 1970). Lengths of seasonal migration vary from about 6 km to over 60 km in the case of the Jackson Hole and North-ern Yellowstone herds. Migrating elk typically fol-low the melting snowpack upslope in spring; fall migrations are tied to weather and forage avail-ability. Snow depth of about 40 cm triggers elk movement to winter ranges. Although they can move through snow over a meter deep, this condi-tion forces the animals to plow through snow in single file and to change leaders as they tire.

During winter, elk form large mixed herds on fa-vored winter range. Except during the rut when dominant bulls seem to dictate most activities, old cows typically are the leaders of such herds These females may lead the herd on migrations or moves to new feeding areas. They may also be the leaders when danger threatens.

Map 12-1 Distribution of the American elk, or wapiti (Cervus elaphus) in North America.

Elk are generally nocturnal or crepuscular in their activities, although cloudy weather and free-dom from disturbance may stimulate them to for-age or move about during daylight hours. Generally elk do not move more than 1 km dur-ing their daily activities. They favor relatively steep slopes (15 to 30 percent) over flats or steeper areas although ridgetops are often used for bedding grounds. One can readily detect bed-ding sites by the distinctive odor of the animals and also by the trampled vegetation. R. Green (1982) investigated habitat selection and activity periods of elk in Rocky Mountain National Park.

Mortality is due mostly to predation on calves, hunting, and winter starvation. Black bears may become skilled at locating and feeding on young calves (Schlegal 1977), and grizzly bears regularly hunt them in Yellowstone National Park (Steve and Marilyn French, pers. comm.). Coyotes may be important predators in some areas, such as California (McCullough 1969). In Colorado, mor-

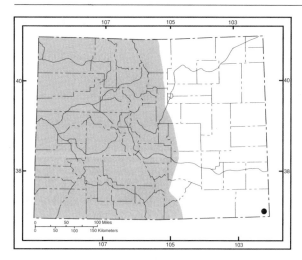

Map 12-2 Distribution of the American elk, or wapiti (Cervus elaphus) *in Colorado. Solid circle represents introduced resident population.*

tality was almost equally attributed to starvation of calves (17 percent), hunting (13 percent), and predation (13 percent) (Bear and Green 1980). Herding behavior in elk, as in other species, may have evolved as a predator defense mechanism (Geist 1982). Although elk can live up to 20 years, the rate of population turnover in hunted populations is high. Males in the population on the White River Plateau survived an average of 1.2 years and over 85 percent of females suffered mortality by their fifth year (Boyd 1970). In less heavily hunted populations, one-half of all males born in a given year probably do not survive over three years of age and one half of the females do not survive beyond age five. For reviews of the vast literature on elk biology, consult O. Murie (1951), Boyd (1978), Boyce and Hayden-Wing (1979), Peek (1982), J. W. Thomas and Toweill (1982), and Boyce (1990).

DISTRIBUTION IN COLORADO — Elk formerly occupied much of central and western North America from the southern Canadian Provinces and Alaska south to the southern United States, and eastward into the deciduous forests. This wide distribution encompassed prairie and eastern deciduous forest as well as mountainous terrain in the

West. Present populations are generally restricted to forested areas in rough country in western North America. Elk were almost extirpated from Colorado in the early 1900s when market hunting caused populations to decline to 500 to 1,000 individuals (Armstrong 1972). A very successful program of restoration (using elk from Wyoming) and careful management have led to current high elk population in Colorado. Elk are big game animals under Colorado statute, and over 50,000 were harvested in 1990 (Table 3-2).

In Colorado the species ranges throughout the western two-thirds of the state generally at elevations above 1,800 m (6,000 ft), although occasionally elk are reported in the South Platte River drainage on the eastern plains. Primeval patterns of geographic variation are not known, but *Cervus elaphus nelsoni* occurs over western Colorado whereas *C. e. canadensis* may have been the subspecies formerly inhabiting the eastern plains. *C. e. nelsoni* sometimes is called the Rocky Mountain elk to distinguish it from other subspecies, such as the Tule and Olympic elk of the West Coast.

Odocoileus hemionus
MULE DEER

DESCRIPTION — Mule deer are medium-sized cervids with conspicuously long ears and a coarse coat. The Coloradan subspecies, *O. h. hemionus*, is the largest. Males are larger than females and can weigh up to 200 kg, but the average weight is closer to 70 kg (A. Anderson et al. 1974, Hunter 1947). Does are fully grown at 2 years of age, but bucks may continue to grow until 9 or 10. The color in summer is reddish tan, and the winter pelage is brownish gray. The rump and belly are white. The face is marked: the paler muzzle contrasts with the gray forehead and brownish spots on either side of the rostrum. The tail is short and pale except for a black tip. There are four hooves on each foot, of which two are reduced to dewclaws. Metatarsal glands are well developed, usually over 100 mm in length. Measurements are: total length 1,200–1,675 mm; length of tail 100–220 mm; length of hindfoot 380–530 mm;

Photograph 12-2 Mule deer (Odocoileus hemionus).

Photograph 12-3 Hybrid of Odocoileus hemionus *and* O. virginianus. *Note small ears and long tail with black stripe.*

length of ear 180–230 mm. Mule deer stand 710–1,060 mm at the shoulder (Anderson et al. 1974). The skull has large vacuities, and there are no upper canines or incisors. The lower incisors and canines are spatulate. The dentition can be used to determine age of individuals (Robinette et al. 1957, 1977). Genetic variability in mule deer in Colorado is about average for cervids and for mammals in general (heterozygosity, 3.6 percent), but less than in white-tailed deer (M. Smith et al. 1990). This difference may reflect the management history of local populations or differences in population structure, and it clearly deserves further study.

Males have antlers that are round in cross-section and project forward and upward from the frontal bones. The antlers branch equally (dichotomously) to form four main tines although many individuals have more than that number. Young males have either simple spikes or a single fork near the tips of the antlers. The antlers are shed annually in late February or March (A. Anderson and Medin 1969, 1971; Hunter 1947). Occasional hybridization occurs between mule and white-tailed deer, the hybrid offspring showing intermediacy in appearance of such characters as tail and antlers (Photo 12-3).

NATURAL HISTORY — Mule deer occupy all ecosystems in Colorado from grasslands to alpine tundra. They reach their greatest densities in shrublands on rough, broken terrain, which provide abundant browse and cover.

A wide distribution and general adaptibility make for broad diets. In the Rocky Mountains, winter diets of mule deer consist of browse from a variety of trees and shrubs (74 percent) and forbs (15 percent). In the spring, browse contributes 49 percent of the diet, and forbs and grasses make up about 25 percent each. Summer diets are 50 percent browse, and forb consumption increases to 46 percent. Browse use increases in the fall to 60 percent while forb use declines to 30 percent (L. Carpenter et al. 1979b, Kufeld et al. 1973). Several studies in Colorado have indicated that diets containing 30 percent or more sagebrush and juniper reduce rumen microbes and are therefore deleterious (L. Carpenter 1976, Nagy and Tengerdy 1967, Nagy et al. 1964, Schwartz et al. 1980). Alldredge et al. (1974) estimated that mule deer could consume no more than about one percent of available sagebrush forage on western rangelands. When heavy snows bury grasses and forbs on such rangelands and force mule deer to consume high amounts of sage and juni-

387

per, mortality rates increase due to malnutrition. Mule deer seem to be able to survive without free water except in arid environments. However, they do drink available water and also eat snow. Additional research in Colorado on chemical composition and digestibility, shrub age structure on winter range, foraging on oak, and forage use relative to logging is reported by Dietz et al. (1962), Roughton (1972), Kufeld (1983), and Wallmo et al. (1972), respectively.

Mule deer are mostly nocturnal or crepuscular in the warmer months, becoming more diurnal in winter (Loveless 1967). Peaks of activity may occur around sunrise and sunset (L. Carpenter 1976). Activity depends on local conditions including temperature, season, weather, and forage. Over much of Colorado the species is migratory, summering at higher elevations and moving downslope to winter range. Deer on the White River Plateau make annual migrations of about 80 to 90 km (Bartmann 1968, Bartmann and Steinert 1981); on many other ranges the seasonal movements may be only a few kilometers. The routes followed are often habitual, apparently based on years of learning. Snow depth of 15 to 30 cm appears to trigger fall movements and depths over 50 cm prevent use of an area (Loveless 1967). However, Garrott et al. (1987) found that mule deer in northwestern Colorado migrated to winter range in October, before snow accumulation. They suggested that better quality forage on winter range at that time of year triggers the movements. During midwinter, deer moved to lower elevations and foraged on more protected south-facing exposures. This latter movement was timed with severity of weather.

Spring and summer ranges are most typically mosaics of meadows, aspen woodlands, alpine tundra–subalpine forest edges, or montane forest edges. Montane forests and piñon-juniper woodlands with good shrub understory are often favored winter ranges. Because of their movements the home ranges of mule deer are difficult to measure. However, seasonally the animals appear to be relatively sedentary, staying within areas of

40 to 900 ha. In areas where the animals do not migrate significant distances, annual home ranges are 7.0 to 22 km^2 (Mackie et al. 1982). Migrating individuals are philopatric, returning to the same areas year after year (Carpenter et al. 1979a, Franzen 1968).

In Colorado, mule deer breed in November and December. Females are in estrus for just a few hours but will repeat estrous cycles every three to four weeks until bred. About 70 percent of breeding occurs in a 20-day span in some populations. The gestation period averages 203 days (A. Anderson and Medin 1967). Yearling females typically produce a single fawn, and older females in good condition produce twins. Precocial at birth, fawns weigh about 4 kg. They can consume vegetation at two to three weeks of age but are not weaned until fall. Sex ratios at birth favor males slightly, but, with increasing age, females commonly exceed males by ratios of 2:1, 5:1, or higher. Nutritional factors influence fawn sex ratios, and there is some evidence that does on poorer diets have a higher proportion of male fawns. Does are solitary during fawning. They form small groups of yearlings, does, and fawns when the young are several months old. As winter approaches the size of herds increases and large numbers may congregate on wintering grounds. When not in rut, adult males often form pairs or small groups of three to five individuals. Social behavior was summarized by Geist (1981).

Mortality in mule deer varies with age class and region. In fawns annual mortality varies from 27 percent in Utah to 67 percent in one Colorado study (Anderson and Bowden 1977). Fawn mortality is due to predation and starvation. Larger fawns are more likely to survive, and smaller fawns are more likely to starve. Variability in size is great for fawns taken by predators, suggesting little selection (G. White et al. 1987). Studies in South Dakota indicated that fall populations must be at least 30 to 33 percent fawns to maintain stable numbers; up to 75 percent overwinter mortality of fawns is not unusual. Most mortality in older age classes occurs from hunting or winter starvation (L. Carpen-

Map 12-3 Distribution of the mule deer (Odocoileus hemionus) *in North America.*

About the turn of the century populations were greatly depleted in Colorado because of market hunting. The meat was used by newly arrived settlers, and it was also shipped east. The advent of a conservation ethic and a Department of Fish and Game led to recovery of this species in the state (Barrows and Holmes 1990). Mule deer populations declined again over much of the western United States in the 1950s through mid-1970s (Connolly 1981, Workman and Low 1976) due to overhunting, habitat loss, habitat alteration, and deterioration of winter ranges. Populations in many areas including Colorado are now on the increase. In fact, Colorado enjoys one of the highest mule deer populations in the United States. Indeed, in a number of urban localities herds are large enough to damage landscape plantings and to constitute a serious traffic hazard. Mule deer are hunted as big game in Colorado. In 1990, over 90,000 deer (both mule and white-tailed) were harvested (Table 3-2).

Much research on mule deer has been done in Colorado, particularly by the Colorado Division of Wildlife and Colorado State University. For management purposes, techniques for aerial surveys, ground surveys, mark and recapture, stocking rates, and modeling dynamics have been studied (Bartmann et al. 1987, Gilbert and Grieb 1957, Kufeld et al. 1980, McKean 1971, Medin and Anderson 1979).

DISTRIBUTION IN COLORADO — Mule deer are found statewide in all ecosystems. Highest densities are reached in areas like the Piceance Basin in northwestern Colorado, the Gunnison River drainage, and the foothills of the Front Range. One subspecies, *Odocoileus hemionus hemionus,* occurs in Colorado. Hall (1981) used the generic name *Dama* for the mule and white-tailed deer, but few authors have adopted this usage, instead applying the name *Dama* to the Old World fallow deer (*Dama dama,* also called *Cervus dama*), a species in a different subfamily of deer.

ter 1976). Predators include coyotes, bobcats, golden eagles, mountain lions, black bears, brown bears, and domestic dogs. Locally, coyote predation on fawns can account for significant mortality within populations; however, research summarized by Torbit et al. (1982) suggests that the costs and efforts entailed do not warrant predator control programs to reduce deer mortality. Mule deer may survive up to 20 years in the wild but such longevity is rare, and population turnover is high. In Utah only one percent of bucks examined were classed as over eight years of age (Robinette et al. 1977). Several studies suggest that annual turnovers of 28 to 43 percent of the population are not unusual in "stable" herds (Connolly 1981). In such areas about half of the mortality is fawns, and adult bucks show about one-third higher mortality than do adult does. Excellent reviews of the extensive and diffuse research literature on mule deer were provided by A. Anderson and Wallmo (1984), Mackie et al. (1982), Taylor (1956), and Wallmo (1981).

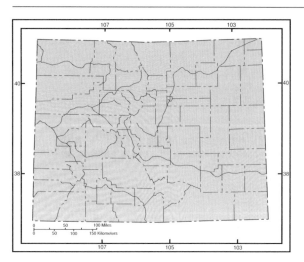

Map 12-4 Distribution of the mule deer (Odocoileus hemionus) in Colorado.

© 1993 Wendy Shattil/Bob Rozinski.

Photograph 12-4 White-tailed deer (Odocoileus virginianus). See Photograph 12-3 for O. virginanus and O. hemionus hybrid.

Odocoileus virginianus
WHITE-TAILED DEER

DESCRIPTION — White-tailed deer are medium-sized cervids with moderately long ears and wide, flat, bushy tails. The coat is coarse and not very long. Males are larger than females and may weigh over 150 kg although the average is closer to 40–180 kg. Adult white-tailed deer stand about 1 m at the shoulder. The predominant color is bright reddish in the summer and grayish in the winter. The ventral color is white. The face is not contrastingly marked but there may be a whitish spot on the throat, white eye rings, and a white ring around the muzzle. The tail is reddish brown on the dorsal surface and white ventrally. It is typically held high while running. Fawns are reddish brown with white dorsal spots, which are lost at three to four months of age. Metatarsal glands are conspicuous but usually much less than 100 mm in length. Measurements are: total length 1,340–2,060 mm; length of tail 150–330 mm; length of hindfoot 360–520 mm; length of ear 140–230 mm; weight 60 kg.

Normally only males have antlers. The antlers of older bucks have a well-defined main beam from which arises a series of nonbranching tines. Young bucks may have only simple spikes or single forks. Males typically shed their antlers in late February or March, and the new set has completed its growth by late August or early September. The skull is similar to that of the mule deer with a large antorbital vacuity and no canines or incisors on the upper jaw. The lower incisors and canines are spatulate and the cheekteeth are selenodont. Severinghaus (1949) discussed use of dental characteristics to determine age of white-tailed deer. Hybridization with mule deer occurs occasionally (see Photo 12-3).

NATURAL HISTORY — White-tailed deer are the widest-ranging cervid in North America. One of the most adaptable deer, white-tails are found from humid, tropical rainforest to the Arctic tree-limit on Hudson Bay. In our area, white-tailed deer occupy a variety of habitats, but they are typically associated with riparian woodlands and the associated irrigated agricultural lands of the eastern plains. They do not occupy dense coniferous forests or open prairie.

The species has a catholic diet, selecting the most nutritious plant matter available at any particular time. In agricultural areas, white-tailed deer often favor crops such as corn and wheat to native browse, forbs, or grasses. No detailed studies have been made on the diet of these deer in Colorado, but studies in the East (Hesselton and Hesselton 1982) have shown that browse provides only 3 to 17 percent of the diet and that grasses and forbs are much more important than in the diet of the mule deer. Mushrooms have been reported as important foods, as have a variety of fruits, acorns (mast), and other nuts. In Colorado, mast is lacking in most white-tailed deer habitat.

White-tailed deer are secretive and often difficult to observe even when they occur in large numbers. The animals are mostly crepuscular although they also move and feed at night or during daylight. Unlike mule deer, white-tailed deer do not typically make significant seasonal migrations. However, Kufeld (1992) found that 25 percent of radio-collared white-tails along the South Platte and Arkansas rivers in eastern Colorado made seasonal movements, usually from the river bottom to plains sites (often farmland) in late spring and summer, and returning to the bottomlands in the fall. Home ranges (measured as minimal convex polygons) of white-tails in that study averaged 7.7 km^2, compared with 3.9 km for mule deer in the same habitats. Home ranges tend to be elongate, and adult bucks have larger home ranges than do does (Marchinton and Hirth 1984). White-tails are good swimmers and do not hesitate to cross bodies of water, even several miles. During the winter on some northern ranges they may form relatively large herds in "yards" where they congregate for shelter from snow and cold in an area of good food reserves. In Colorado, white-tailed deer typically herd in groups of up to 20 animals in riparian woodlands during the winter months. Most groups of white-tailed deer appear to be composed of females and up to two generations of offspring. Such groups may commingle with other families and with small groups of bucks to form the winter herds.

White-tailed deer exhibit two conspicuous alarm signals, snorting and tail flagging. Snorting is more frequent in family groups of females than in groups of males and is seen when the cause for alarm is both very close or at some distance. Tail flagging occurs in both buck and doe groups but is not used when the cause for alarm is very close (Bildstein 1983, Hirth and McCullough 1977). Its function is disputed, but it seems both to signal to predators that they have been detected (so no longer have the advantage of surprise) and to alert group members and to facilitate group cohesion when the predator is at a safe distance.

White-tailed deer breed in fall with a season similar to that of the mule deer. The peak of the rut is probably early November in Colorado. During the rut adult bucks become very active and spend much of their time searching for estrous females. Bucks typically make characteristic "scrapes" at this time by pawing patches of ground upon which they urinate and leave metatarsal gland scent. Trees near such scrapes often show signs of antler rubbing. Such marked areas are believed to represent breeding-season territories, defended against other males. Females during the rut typically become more solitary, often chasing yearling fawns away and increasing their own range of movements. White-tailed deer can breed as fawns; ovulation first occurs at about six or seven months. In some studies up to 60 to 70 percent of the female fawn crop has been shown to breed successfully. Although male fawns are probably capable of breeding their first year there is no evidence that they do so.

Does are polyestrous. Estrus lasts about one day, and females who do not breed will recycle every 21 to 28 days. Females urinate more frequently during the onset of estrus (Verme and Ullrey 1984). The urine's chemistry alerts adult males, possibly during Flehmen (lip-curling) behavior whereby fluid is suctioned into the vomeronasal organ for analysis. The gestation period averages 201 days. Male:female sex ratios approximate 112:100 in utero, with younger females having a significantly greater chance of having male offspring than older females. White-tails weigh about 3 kg at birth; twins or even triplets are not

Map 12-5 Distribution of the white-tailed deer (Odocoileus virginianus) in North America.

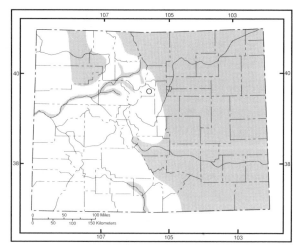

Map 12-6 Distribution of the white-tailed deer (Odocoileus virginianus) in Colorado. Open circle represents historical record of occurrence.

uncommon. Older does seem to protect their young better from predation and therefore contribute more offspring to the population than do younger deer (Mech and McRoberts 1990). Females typically become reclusive when fawning and stay away from other deer for the first month or so following parturition. Fawns begin to forage at about two to three weeks of age and are typically weaned by the fifth month. Growth is rapid and by seven to nine months fawns on good habitat may weight 50 to 55 kg. Adult bucks reach full size at four or five years of age, and females are full grown at three to four years. White-tail bucks in riparian situations on Colorado's eastern plains grow especially fine antlers and are much sought by trophy hunters.

Mortality in white-tailed deer mostly is due to hunting, winter starvation, automobile accidents, and predation. Coyotes, mountain lions, and wolves are important predators where deer populations are high; bobcats, bears, and eagles may

also kill white-tailed deer on occasion. In the eastern United States it is estimated that domestic dogs may cause mortality equal to 10 percent of the legal harvest, and automobile accidents account for 15 to 100 percent of the legal harvest in certain states. In most eastern populations the turnover rate is remarkably rapid. Rarely do bucks exceed 3.5 years of age or females 5.5 years, although in captivity white-tailed deer have lived to 20 years of age (Hesselton and Hesselton 1982).

In Colorado, where much of the hunting pressure is concentrated on mule deer in mountain environments, long-term studies of white-tail demography would be of interest. In situations of low forage availability, white-tail females delay reproduction and have a lower incidence of twinning (Verme and Ullrey 1984). Preliminary studies (such as Kufeld 1992) suggest differences in habitat requirements and demography of Coloradan populations compared to the well-studied eastern populations reviewed by Taylor (1956), Halls (1984), Hesselton and Hesselton (1982), and W. Smith (1991).

DISTRIBUTION IN COLORADO — In Colorado, white-tailed deer are rather common in river bottoms of the eastern plains, particularly in the South Platte, Arkansas, and Republican river drainages. Individuals are also known from several isolated locations in the mountains including above timberline in Rocky Mountain National Park, Middle Park, the White River drainage in Rio Blanco County, and the San Luis Valley in Rio Grande County. Almost extirpated by the 1920s, white-tails have recovered as a consequence of enforcement of game laws and restorations (Hunter 1948, Armstrong 1972). *Odocoileus virginianus dacotensis* is the subspecies ascribed a range in the South Platte drainage; *O. v. texanus* occurs in the Arkansas watershed. These subspecies may be indistinct in Colorado due to artificial introductions, movements, and spread of populations. No rigorous analysis of geographic variation exists.

Photograph 12-5 Moose (Alces alces).

Alces alces
MOOSE

DESCRIPTION — Largest of the cervids, moose are black, chocolate brown, or reddish brown with paler legs and belly. The winter pelage is grayer.

Calves are reddish or rusty and lack the white spots characteristic of other young cervids. The long hair is coarse, brittle, and longer on the neck and shoulders than elsewhere. The front legs are longer than the hindlegs, creating a sloping back. There are four hooves on each foot; two are reduced in size and elevated as dewclaws. The large head has a long, broad muzzle and a heavy, bulbous nose pad. A fold of skin, the "bell" or dewlap, dangles from the throat region. Ears are large and erect. The tail is short and inconspicuous. The skull has a greatly elongated premaxillary region. Dentition can be used to determine age of individuals (Peterson 1955, Sergeant and Pimlott 1959). Measurements are: total length 2.4–2.9 m; length of tail 75–115 mm; length of hindfoot 750–850 mm; length of ear 200–300 mm; weight 380–550 kg. The upper weight limit (550 kg) is notable and applies to *Alces a. gigas*, the Alaskan subspecies. Accurate weight and measurement data for *Alces a. shirasi*, the subspecies introduced to Colorado, are lacking. An adult moose measures around 1,900 mm at the shoulders. As with most cervids, tremendous changes in weight can occur between early spring and fall. Female moose may show a 48 percent increase in weight over this time span (Gasaway and Coady 1974).

Adult males have large palmate antlers that spread outward and backward from the skull. The total mass of the antlers can exceed 25 kg in mature bulls. Maximum antler development occurs between 8 and 13 years of age in Alaska (Gasaway 1975). Each antler has a number of points or tines that extend from the edges of the palms of the antler. The shedding and growth pattern is similar to that of other deer; in late winter bony outgrowths appear from the frontal bones. They grow through the summer and are relatively soft, covered with a finely haired, thin skin, termed *velvet*. In late summer and early fall the antlers harden and the velvet is rubbed off against bushes and trees. The hardened antlers remain on the animals through the rutting season in early winter, at which time they are shed (cast).

NATURAL HISTORY — Introduced in Colorado, moose are inhabitants of boreal forest edge and openings in forests adjacent to water. They are dependent on early successional stages in areas that have been recently burned, logged, or manipulated by beavers (Wolfe 1974). Moose require a plentiful supply of browse including stems, bark, buds, and leaves of deciduous or evergreen trees or shrubs for winter forage. Daily forage intake (dry weight) is estimated to be 5 kg in winter and about 11 kg in warmer months. Typical moose range in the Rocky Mountains includes a mixture of willow, spruce, fir, aspen, or birch. Willows are a winter staple on many western ranges (Peek 1974). During spring, summer, and fall, moose also utilize a variety of herbaceous vegetation including grasses, sedges, aquatic emergents, and forbs. In Wyoming, principal foods are willows, algae, pondweed, and occasionally sagebrush (R. H. Denniston 1956). Competition for food between moose and elk is minimal (Stevens 1974) but may increase in severe winters (K. Jenkins and Wright 1987). Habitat management plans for the introduced Colorado population recommend no more than 50 percent utilization of available annual growth of willow (Colorado Division of Wildlife, unpublished).

Moose are less social than other cervids (Altmann 1956, R. H. Denniston 1956). They are reclusive and have strong attachments to specific home ranges, although some populations make seasonal migrations and many individuals will wander considerable distances in search of suitable new habitat. Yearling animals appear to be more mobile than adults and maintain larger home ranges (Houston 1968, 1974). Philopatry, or fidelity to specific ranges, may lengthen the time for colonization of suitable adjacent habitats. Home ranges typically encompass no more than 5 to 10 km and are usually smaller in winter than in summer. Density of moose at the Colorado release site in North Park did not exceed 0.38 moose/km (Nowlin 1985).

Deep snow appears to trigger most movements in fall and winter although moose can paw through up to 40 cm of snow in search of forage. During winter, moose may "yard up," or aggregate, in riparian areas. Although high densities may be reached, moose are more typically solitary and tend to ignore each other. In North Park, cows with calves are widely dispersed throughout the year, but bulls, cows without calves, and yearlings showed a clumped pattern during winter (Nowlin 1985). The only durable social bonds are those formed between cows and their calves, and they are typically broken just before birth of the next offspring.

Moose breed in fall, from mid-September to early November (Denniston 1956), with the peak in late September and early October. At that time bulls become aggressive toward each other and may display or fight for females. Bulls rub and thrash shrubs and small trees at that time. Both males and females increase their vocalizations during the rut, using barks, croaks, and moans. At this time, bulls respond to calls that sound like the grunt of a cow moose. As with other cervids, males typically show swelling of the neck and shoulders and forage very little if at all. If not bred, females go through successive estrous cycles at 20- to 30-day intervals. Gestation lasts approximately 243 days, with most calving occurring in late May and early June (Peterson 1955). Moose do not form harems. However, small groups of bulls and cows may form in which agonistic interactions among males and among females may be exhibited (Altmann 1959). A single young is the mode, with twins occurring in only 11 to 29 percent of births. Triplets are much rarer. Nowlin (1985) reported a calf:cow ratio of 77:100, and a 12 percent twinning rate in Colorado. Moose calves weigh 12 to 13 kg at birth but may reach weights of around 175 to 180 kg by October, a gain of about 1 kg per day.

Both nutrition and population density appear to influence reproductive potential. With low populations and high forage availability yearlings breed and females have twins. In areas of high population density yearlings often do not breed and females produce a single young (Blood

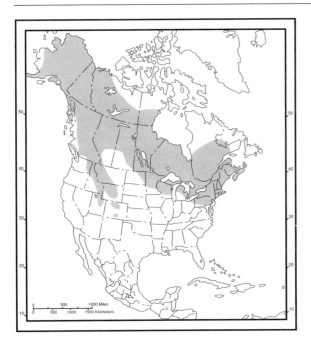

Map 12-7 Distribution of the moose (Alces alces) *in North America.*

1974). Sex ratios usually approximate 1:1 in unhunted populations, but may be as low as 40:100 bulls to cows in heavily hunted areas, although in the latter case reproductive success is apparently not significantly impaired (Bishop and Rausch 1974). An adult bull can only effectively impregnate two or three cows, indicating that a sex ratio of at least 50:100 bulls to cows is essential for good herd management (Colorado Division of Wildlife, unpublished).

The population dynamics of the introduced Coloradan animals are interesting. In 1978, four bulls and eight cows, one with a calf, were released into North Park from the Uinta Mountains of Utah. In January 1979, an additional 12 animals (one adult bull, six adult cows, three yearling cows, and two cows with calves) from Grand Teton National Park were released in the same general area along the Illinois River south and east of Walden, Jackson County (Nowlin et al. 1979). From this base, population numbers grew

to 59 in 1981 and 250 in 1990; managers project a stable population of about 500 animals. In addition, 20 animals were introduced near Spring Creek Pass northwest of Creede in 1991 and an additional 45 animals were introduced there in 1992. Illegal shooting has been the principal cause of mortality in the North Park population. Despite such mortality the growth of the population has expanded into the Laramie River drainage and has allowed controlled harvest starting in 1985, when 5 licenses for antlered animals were issued. In 1992, 63 permits were issued after a drawing; in 1993, 114 permits were granted (Colorado Division of Wildlife, unpublished).

As with other North American cervids, major mortality factors are hunting, malnutrition, and predation. In Colorado efficient moose predators are absent. Wolves are the principal predator in northern parts of the range. Black bears and brown bears also take a toll, especially on calves (Franzmann et al. 1980, Hosley 1949) but, in Colorado, moose populations do not occur in prime black bear habitat. Other predators implicated in moose kills are mountain lions, wolverines, coyotes, lynx, and domestic dogs although mortality from such carnivores is light. Snow cover in excess of 70 cm severely impairs moose movement and may result in significant winter mortality from malnutrition. As with most cervids winter mortality generally impacts calves the hardest followed by older adults and adult males. For reviews of the biology of moose, see Coady (1982), Franzmann (1978, 1981), Houston (1968), and Peterson (1955).

DISTRIBUTION IN COLORADO — Historically, moose were occasional visitors to Colorado, apparent stragglers that wandered into the northern part of the state from Utah or Wyoming (Armstrong 1972). There is no documented historical record of breeding populations of moose in Colorado prior to their introduction by the Division of Wildlife beginning in 1978 (Nowlin et al. 1979), although moose have been expanding their range southward in North America since the late 1800s (Peterson 1955).) The habitat of the origi-

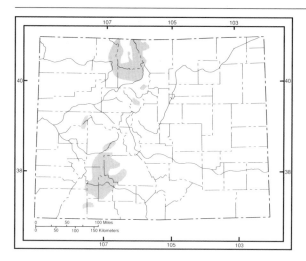

Map 12-8 Distribution of the moose (Alces alces) *in Colorado.*

nal introduced herd in North Park was willow and lodgepole pine at an elevation of 2,700 to 2,850 m (8,850–9,350 ft). Since then, animals from this population have been reported in several adjacent areas, including Middle Park, the upper reaches of the Laramie and Cache la Poudre rivers, and Rocky Mountain National Park. Other sightings have been reported in South Park, near Leadville, near Gunnison, near Yampa, and west of Denver. The nucleus of a new population is becoming established in Middle Park south of Fraser. The most recent introductions have been made in the area northwest of Creede. *Alces alces shirasi* is the subspecies of the Middle Rocky Mountains introduced in Colorado.

FAMILY ANTILOCAPRIDAE —
Pronghorn

The family Antilocapridae has an exclusively North American evolution. Only one species, the pronghorn (*Antilocapra americana*), survives today. The family is known from the middle Miocene with 13 extinct genera present during the Pliocene and Pleistocene. The pronghorn first appeared in the early Pleistocene. The pronghorn and its fossil relatives are placed in this distinct

family, although some authors (O'Gara and Matson 1975) assign the group to a subfamily Antilocaprinae within the family Bovidae. Antilocaprids and cervids have two lacrimal foramina, in contrast to bovids, which have a single lacrimal foramen inside the anterior rim of the orbit of the eye. The pronghorn frequently is called "pronghorn antelope," or simply antelope, but those are misnomers. True antelope are Old World mammals, members of the bovid subfamily Antilopinae, which includes the familiar gazelles of East Africa.

Photograph 12-6 Pronghorn (Antilocapra americana).

Antilocapra americana
PRONGHORN

DESCRIPTION — The pronghorn is a small, graceful, hoofed mammal with a decidedly large head and prominent, laterally positioned eyes. Males are larger than females. The general color is pale reddish brown to tan with two broad white bands across the throat. The ventral surface and rump are white. In males the dorsal surface of the muzzle is often dark, and black jaw patches are visible on the side of the cheeks close to the neck. The guard hairs are moderately long, hollow, brittle, and coarse with a longer, dark mane of hairs on the nape of the neck. The underfur is woolly. Hairs on the rump can be erected to form a conspicuous patch used to communicate potential

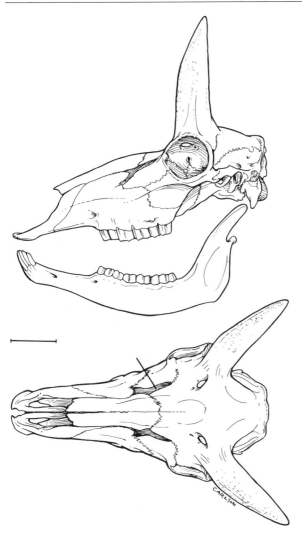

Figure 12-2 Lateral and dorsal views of the skull of a male pronghorn (Antilocapra americana). *Note the prominent ethmoid vacuity (arrow). Scale = 5 cm.*

rim of the orbit. Lower incisors and canines are spatulate and cheekteeth are hypsodont and selenodont. Dentition and incisor cementum provide useful criteria for determining age (Dow and Wright 1962, McCutchen 1969).

Males and most females have horns that are composed of laterally flattened bony cores arising from the frontal bones, covered with a keratinous mass of fused hairs that form a sheath. The sheath is shed annually following the breeding season (O'Gara et al. 1971). Horns of females usually are very short, unforked nubs. Those of males are forked about one-third of the way from the tip and may exceed 250 mm in length. Skin glands are well developed in the cheek area (the jaw patch), on the hock, between the hooves, and on the rump. Females have four mammae and a cotyledonary, epitheliochorial placenta.

NATURAL HISTORY — Pronghorns inhabit grasslands and semidesert shrublands on rolling topography that affords good visibility. They are most abundant in shortgrass or midgrass prairies and least common in xeric habitats. The average year-round diet in Colorado is approximately 43 percent forbs, 43 percent browse, 11 percent cactus, and 3 percent grass (Hoover et al. 1959). In the northern parts of the range, browse is the major food item, forming up to 64 percent of the annual diet and over 70 percent during fall and winter; forbs and grasses constitute 24 of the annual diet and 7 percent of the fall and winter diet. On more southern portions of their range pronghorns are more dependent on forbs. On Pawnee National Grassland in northeastern Colorado, grasses and forbs each represent 45 to 48 percent of the diet, and shrubs compose 5 percent or less (Schwartz and Nagy 1976).

Delicate feeders, pronghorns are more selective than sheep, cattle, and bison (Schwartz et al. 1977). However, they do consume such plants as larkspur, loco-weed, *Hymenoxys*, cocklebur, "*Haplopappus*," yucca, and needle-and-thread, which are known to be poisonous or injurious to domestic stock (Hoover et al. 1959). In northwest-

danger. Fawns are similar to adults but paler in color with indistinct markings. There are only two hooves on each foot; dewclaws are lacking. Measurements are: total length 1.0–1.5 m; length of tail 75–180 mm; length of hindfoot 400–432 mm; length of ear 140–150 mm; weight 36–70 kg. Adult pronghorns stand about 900 mm at the shoulder. The skull has an elongated antorbital vacuity and two lacrimal foramina at the anterior ern Colorado, shrubs compose over 90 percent of the fall and winter diet on sagebrush and bitterbrush range, whereas forbs account for 64 to 80 percent of the spring and summer diet (Bear 1973). In Kansas, successful populations fed largely on forbs in late spring, summer, and early autumn, on forbs supplemented with wheat in late autumn and early spring, and on wheat and alfalfa in winter (Sexson et al. 1981). The use of cultivated crops during winter, when native foods are in short supply, varies with location and degree of agricultural activity. Although pronghorn are frequently observed in wheat fields they do not appear to cause much damage to plantings (Liewer 1988).

Pronghorn may be active at any time but peaks of activity are crepuscular, especially when daytime temperatures are high. At night more time is spent bedded down than foraging. The size of home ranges occupied by pronghorns varies with season, habitat quality, population characteristics, and patterns of livestock use. Home ranges are from about 165 ha to over 2,300 ha; winter home ranges are somewhat smaller than summer ranges (Kitchen and O'Gara 1982). In certain areas adult males are territorial and maintain territories of 25 to 440 ha on good ranges. Normally, daily movements do not exceed 10 km. Pronghorns may make seasonal migrations between winter and summer ranges but, unlike most cervids, such movements appear to be tied more closely to succulence of vegetation than to weather conditions such as snow accumulation.

Pronghorn are rightly renowned for their extraordinary speed, estimates of which range beyond 100 km (60 miles) per hour. This is considerably faster, by the way, than any extant North American predator, so to understand pronghorn it is relevant to note that in the Pleistocene Epoch, cheetahs lived in the Great Basin.

Highly social, pronghorns are herd-forming mammals with numerous stereotyped behavioral patterns and several vocalizations (Kitchen 1974, Prenzlow et al. 1968, Waring 1969). In spring and summer, older, more dominant bucks are solitary whereas younger males form bachelor bands of up to a dozen or more individuals. After fawning, females form nursery bands that may include an occasional older male. During the winter large herds of mixed sex and age classes may form. Such concentrations facilitate census efforts (Bear 1969).

Pronghorns breed in the fall, from mid-September to mid-October. At this time bachelor herds tend to break up, and older males from such herds attempt to mate with does attracted to mature bucks. The dominant males attempt to retain harems or to mate with does on their territories. These sexual behaviors vary depending on a combination of range conditions and demographic factors such as population size and sex ratios. When succulent, palatable vegetation is clumped, such as in sagebrush habitats in the northern part of the range, mature bucks tend to be territorial. These territories are maintained from March through October. When sex ratios heavily favor females, when population densities are low, and in grassland areas, bucks typically form harems and territories are not maintained (Hoover et al. 1959).

Females are polyestrous, ovulation coincides with copulation, and estrus is recurrent (Pojar and Miller 1984). Females normally breed first as yearlings, and gestation lasts 252 days. Most fawns are dropped from late May to mid-June in Colorado (Hoover et al. 1959), although Pojar and Miller (1984) reported bimodal peaks of fawning in mid-June and mid-July for animals in southeastern Colorado. Twins are the rule in good habitat, and fawns weigh 3 to 4 kg at birth. Sex ratios approximate 1:1 at birth but differential mortality, including hunting of bucks, may lead to skewed ratios of one male to as many as five females. Females leave the herd to give birth, and keep the young segregated for three to six weeks. Males are sexually mature as yearlings but few breed because of competition with the more mature bucks. Although capable of breeding at five months of age, females typically do not breed until they are yearlings.

Adult pronghorn mortality is mostly due to hunting. Harvest of over 40 percent of a herd in northwestern Colorado led to significant population decline, whereas 20 percent harvest rates allowed continued population growth (Bear 1968). Accidental deaths may also be frequent in winter; pronghorn become entangled in fences obscured by drifting snow, and sometimes they are driven against fences by the wind and then suffocated during blizzards. Predation may cause localized losses to fawns of from 12 to 90 percent (Kitchen and O'Gara 1982). Great speed and keen eyes (set on the sides of the head, allowing remarkable peripheral vision but probably poor depth perception) protect pronghorn from most predators. Coyotes, bobcats, and golden eagles are among the most important predators (Hoover et al. 1959). Very few pronghorn live more than nine years in the wild but detailed studies on population turnover are lacking. Lance and Pojar (1984) reviewed diseases and parasites, and general reviews were provided by Kitchen and O'Gara

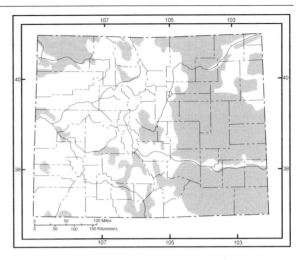

Map 12-10 Distribution of the pronghorn (Antilocapra americana) *in Colorado.*

(1982), O'Gara (1978), and Yoakum and Spalinger (1979).

DISTRIBUTION IN COLORADO — The pronghorn is an endemic North American mammal. In Colorado the species is found on the eastern plains, in the larger mountain parks and valleys, and on shrublands west of the mountains. Pronghorns were formerly very abundant throughout their range. Around 1800 more than 40 million animals were present with about two million in Colorado (Hoover et al. 1959). Subsequently, the species was seriously threatened with extinction by early market hunters. By the 1900s there were few pronghorns remaining, and many states provided them complete protection. Under this protection the animals began to increase, and limited hunting seasons have since been allowed in most states over which they once ranged. One subspecies, *Antilocapra americana americana*, occurs in Colorado.

FAMILY BOVIDAE — Bovids

The family Bovidae includes a remarkable array of browsing and grazing ungulates, from the slender, graceful antelopes of Asia and Africa to various stout, ponderous cattle. Adult dik-diks (genus *Modoqua*) of Africa may stand only about 300 mm at the shoulder and weigh 3 to 6 kg, whereas

Map 12-9 Distribution of the pronghorn (Antilocapra americana) *in North America.*

399

some breeds of domestic cattle (*Bos taurus*) and the gaur (*Bos gaurus*) of southern Asia may weigh over 1,000 kg and stand up to 2.2 m at the shoulder. Most bovids inhabit grasslands, shrublands, or desert, but some have adapted to forests, mountainous terrain, and tundra. In keeping with habitats in open country, most species are gregarious and social, and many are territorial.

Permanent, unbranched horns consisting of a bony core and a horny sheath are present on males of all species and on females of most species. Certain domestic breeds lack horns. The dental formula is 0/3, 0/1, 3/2–3, 3/3 = 30–32 teeth. The lower incisors and canines are spatulate; the cheekteeth are selenodont and typically hypsodont. There is little or no antorbital vacuity and the lacrimal and nasal bones nearly meet. The third and fourth metapodials are fused to form the cannon bone. The ulna and fibula are reduced. Only two digits, the third and fourth, bear weight. The second and fifth digits may be absent, or present as reduced dew hooves or dewclaws. The digestive system exhibits the four-chambered ruminant "stomach," and a gall bladder is typically present. There are two to four mammae usually merged into an inguinal udder. Scent glands are diverse and well developed in this group. Although 21 different glands have been reported (Gosling 1985), the most common are antorbital, interdigital, and inguinal glands. The placenta is cotyledonary.

The family Bovidae is not very old, dating from the Miocene of Europe, 30 million years ago. The rise of ruminant artiodactyls, including the bovids, may have contributed to the decline of the more primitive perissodactyls. The evolution of the bovids did create opportunities for rapid evolution of a number of large carnivores. The family has reached its greatest diversity only in the last few million years with 45 genera, and about 128 species, extant as natives or introductions in all parts of the world except the Antarc-

tic. The original distribution was limited to the Holarctic Region, Africa, and some of the larger islands of the East Indies. Cattle, sheep, and goats were domesticated very early in the Neolithic revolution, and remain important sources of meat, milk, and fiber for humans. In Colorado there are three genera and three species of wild bovids, one of which — the mountain goat — is introduced.

Key to the Species of the Family Bovidae (Including Domestic Livestock) Found in Colorado

1. Length of skull more than 350 mm; maxillary tooth row more than 120 mm; total length greater than 2 m; occipital-parietal region of skull at right angles to forehead at level of horns 2

1′ Length of skull less than 350 mm; maxillary tooth row less than 120 mm; total length less than 2 m; occipital-parietal region of skull at obtuse angle to forehead at level of horns. 3

2. Premaxillary not in contact with nasals; frontal region greatly expanded laterally, obscuring zygomatic bones in dorsal view; hair on head and front quarters conspicuously longer and shaggier than hair on hindquarters; distinct hump on shoulder; head massive; both sexes with horns . . . . Bison — *Bison bison*, p. 402

2′ Premaxillary touching nasals; frontal region narrower with zygomatic bones visible in dorsal view; hair on head and front quarters not conspicuously longer or shaggier than rest of body; no distinct hump on shoulder, or, if present, hair not elongated or shaggy on front quarters; head less massive, more slender; sexes with or without horns . . . . Domestic Cattle — *Bos taurus**

3. Color white to whitish yellow, hair long, soft, and shaggy; horns present on both sexes,

* Domestic species.

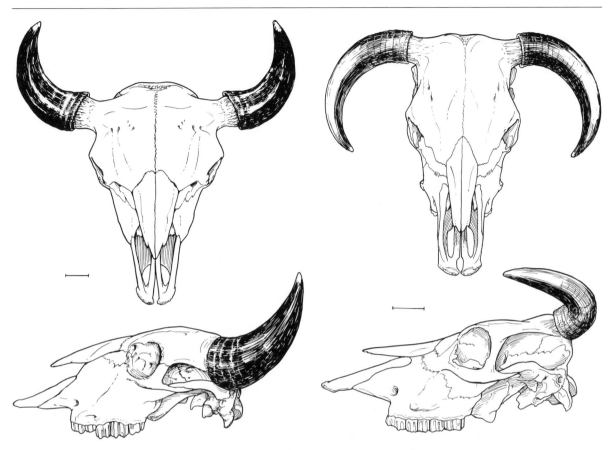

Figure 12-3 Dorsal and lateral view of bison (Bison bison — *left*) *and domestic cow* (Bos taurus — *right*) *skulls. Note that the premaxillary bones do not contact the nasals in the bison skull. Scale = 5 cm.*

relatively straight, short, slender and black; horns round in cross section . . . . Mountain Goat — Oreamnos americanus*, p. 405

3′ Color not uniformly white, or if whitish the hairs typically not long, soft, and shaggy; horns present or absent, and if present not straight, slender, and black; horns not round in cross section 4

4. Horns, if present, not highly pediceled, curling outward and downward; antorbital pits present;

premaxillae barely or not touching nasals; premolars with prominent vertical enamel ridges on labial side; beard absent. 5

4′ Horns, if present, highly pediceled, never curling outward and downward; antorbital pits absent; premaxillae broadly contacting nasals; premolars without prominent vertical enamel ridges on labial side; beard well developed . . . . Domestic Goat — *Capra hircus***

* Introduced species.
**Domestic species.

5. Horns present on both sexes, massive at base on adult males and strongly curling posteriorly, laterally, and downward; longer, straighter guard hairs mask woolly underfur; color uniform grayish brown with paler rump patch . . . . Mountain Sheep — *Ovis canadensis*, p. 408

5′ Horns variable, present or absent; if present, not massive at base on adult males and not strongly curled; pelage conspicuously woolly, color variable but usually white to pale gray, paler rump patch not typically present . . . . Domestic Sheep — *Ovis aries**

Photograph 12-7 Bison, or American buffalo (Bison bison).

Bison bison
BISON, OR AMERICAN BUFFALO

DESCRIPTION — Heavy-bodied and powerfully built, bison are the largest of North American artiodactyls and can weigh up to 1,300 kg. Bison are characterized by a massive head and neck, and a stout body that tapers from the heavy front quarters and pronounced shoulder hump to leaner flanks and hindquarters. Hair on the front quarters, neck, and most of the head is brownish black, relatively long, dense, and woolly. Hair on the hindquarters is much shorter and varies seasonally in color from chocolate brown to a paler brownish tan. A distinct beard hangs from the chin. The tail is moderately long with a tufted tip. The broad forehead has short, curved, relatively smooth horns. Males have thicker, longer horns and larger and heavier builds than females. Measurements are: total length 2.0–3.8 m; length of tail 400–600 mm; length of hindfoot 530–680 mm; weight 725–910 kg; height at the shoulder 1.5–1.8 m. The skull has a relatively narrow muzzle and an extremely broad forehead. The nasal bones are long and do not contact the premaxillary bones. Ethmoidal vacuities are lacking. Skull lengths measure 490–600 mm for the plains specimens, and the greatest width may exceed 240 mm. The cheekteeth are hypsodont and selenodont; upper incisors are lacking. Upper canines are absent although there are a few reports of vestigial canines. Tooth replacement and wear are age indicators (W. Fuller 1959).

NATURAL HISTORY — No other mammal was as important to the survival of people in western North America as the bison. Native Americans of the plains relied extensively on bison for food, shelter, blankets, and clothing. The arrival of European settlers, who saw the bison as a resource to be used and perhaps plundered, marked the beginning of the end. Slaughtered for their skins, meat, and sometimes only their tongues, decimated as a tactic in the military attempt to subdue the Plains Indians, and sometimes shot for the mere "sport" of it, bison were virtually eliminated from the entire continent in the half century between 1830 and about 1880. Perhaps the most enduring symbol of the vast grasslands that they roamed, bison have generated much inter-

---

* Domestic species.

est, and their history is both fascinating and re-markable (McHugh 1972, Roe 1970).

Historically, bison ranged over much of Colo-rado. Generally a mammal of grasslands includ-ing mountain valleys and parks, they also occupied semidesert shrublands, piñon-juniper woodlands, and even ranged onto the alpine tun-dra. Bison were the keystone species of the North American prairie. The vast herds of bison that roamed the Great Plains were a factor (along with fire and recurrent drought) in maintaining short-grass prairie (Larson 1940, Weaver and Clements 1938). Movements of these heavy-bodied, gregari-ous animals caused tremendous localized impacts including scarification of soils, elimination of much of the shallow-rooted vegetation by tram-pling and foraging, and enrichment of soils by defecation and urination. The animals' habits of dusting and mud wallowing facilitated the disper-sal of seeds of a variety of plants and produced fa-vored habitat for such species as black-tailed prairie dogs (and their specialized predator, the black-footed ferret), thirteen-lined ground squir-rels, grasshoppers (and hence grasshopper mice), horned lizards, mountain plovers, burrowing owls, and rattlesnakes. The tendency of bison to favor prairie dog colonies and burned areas also contributed to the dynamics of grassland vegeta-tion (Coppock and Detling 1986, Coppock et al. 1983*a, b*).

Adult bison require about 7.5 kg of food per day, roughly 1.5 percent of their total body weight (Hawley et al. 1981). They may range 2 to 3 km per day to meet these dietary demands. Bison are grazers, so grasses, sedges, and rushes constitute the bulk of the diet. However, in shrublands the species turns to higher percentages of browse, es-pecially in fall and winter. Studies on Pawnee Na-tional Grassland and in Colorado National Monument found bison relying most heavily on grasses and shrubs at all times of the year (Peden 1976, Wasser 1977). On Pawnee National Grass-land in northeastern Colorado bison fed on a to-tal of 36 plant species, but 11 species made up the bulk of the diet. A similar selectivity was seen in

semidesert shrublands and piñon-juniper wood-lands of western Colorado. Saltbush, needle-and-thread, sand dropseed, galleta-grass, and prickly-pear were eaten more than most other spe-cies, and some common plants, including big sagebrush and cheat-grass, were virtually ignored.

This selectivity, however, is less restrictive than that of cattle on similar ranges (Peden et al. 1974). Although reasons are not clear, bison are more effective in utilizing low protein diets dur-ing late fall, winter, and early spring than are do-mestic cattle. By contrast, studies in Utah found that bison and cattle had a 91 percent dietary overlap in an area seeded with crested wheat-grass and alfalfa. Cattle fed on shrubs more than bison did (Van Vuren and Bray 1983). Bison had more restricted diets than cattle, as was true in a shrub-steppe community where cattle fed on forbs more than bison (Van Vuren 1984).

Bison are highly gregarious mammals, with well-developed herd behaviors. They make a number of different vocalizations during the breeding sea-son; the roaring of the bulls is a common sound (Gunderson and Mahan 1980). Bison breed in Colorado from July to September. Breeding in Wind Cave National Park in South Dakota occurs from late June to mid-September, reaching its peak between July 21 and August 15. Similar time spans are reported for Yellowstone National Park herds. During the rut, herds increase in size and activity. Bulls increase the frequency of sexual in-vestigation, following females, Flehmen (lip curls and head-lifting behaviors associated with olfac-tory investigation of females), vulval exploration, vocalizations, threat postures, horning and thrash-ing of shrubs, wallowing, and fighting. As females approach estrus, bulls tend them, preventing them from engaging in normal herd routine and segregating them to the periphery of the group. Bonds that form during the rut are transitory, leading to some debate over whether females are polygamous or whether temporary monogamy oc-curs. Most females breed when two to four years old, although in some instances yearlings breed successfully (Meagher 1973). Percentages of yearlings that breed vary from 6 to 13; by contrast, the percentage of two-year-olds breeding ranges from 60 to 90. Male bison are sexually mature by their third year of age, but most breeding is done by animals several years older.

The gestation period is about 285 days, similar to that for domestic cattle. Females are at their highest reproductive peaks from three to eleven years of age. During that span they can be expected to produce two calves every three years. Some calves still nurse as yearlings. Twinning is rare. Pregnancy rates vary with different populations and herd characteristics but probably average about 60 to 70 percent of reproductively mature females. Most calving occurs from April to June. Sex ratios at birth tend to favor males, averaging about 53 to 56 percent males to females. Calf crops in extant herds average about 18 to 20 percent of the population; similar numbers were probable in historic times (H. W. Reynolds et al. 1982).

In the Henry Mountains of Utah, characterized by piñon-juniper woodlands, montane forest, and openings of sagebrush and grasses, bison social structure was very fluid. Groups of cows, calves, yearlings, and young bulls did not form stable units. Most such groups persisted for only one to four days before encountering another group and combining and separating, thus forming new groups (Van Vuren 1983). Isolated groups persisted longer. Summer home ranges averaged 52 km^2, with large amounts of overlap. This relatively closed habitat is probably the most significant factor affecting group size. Also in this area females had low calf productivity. The average number of calves per adult cow was 0.52, and suckling by yearlings occurred frequently, whereas it is an infrequent phenomenon elsewhere (Van Vuren and Bray 1986). The low forage productivity is thought to be the cause of large home ranges and low calf productivity. These conditions may be comparable to what montane populations of bison formerly experienced in Colorado.

Map 12-11 *Historic distribution of the bison, or American buffalo* (Bison bison) *in North America.*

Free-ranging bison are generally migratory, active animals. It is likely that herds occupying eastern Colorado tended to move in an east-west direction in late fall and winter so that they could seek refuge from winter storms along the eastern slopes of the Rockies. This pattern was probably reversed in spring and summer, as open, wind-swept prairies were sought as a refuge from insect pests. Bison often use well-developed trails during long-distance migrations and are not hesitant to swim rivers. In inclement weather the animals typically head into the storm, unlike domestic stock, which usually face away from the wind. This trait of bison would be valuable to breed into domestic cattle, which often are driven by prairie blizzards into fences, where they suffocate beneath snow drifts. Bison obtain forage under the snow by sweeping it away with their broad, well-haired heads. Bison are typically diurnal, with the night spent resting, or more rarely, feeding and traveling.

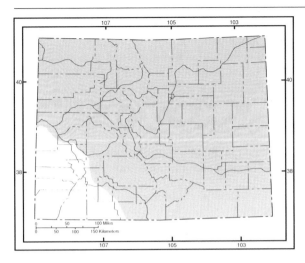

Map 12-12 Historic distribution of the bison, or American buffalo (Bison bison) *in Colorado.*

Bison mortality before the arrival of European settlers was probably limited to some losses from predators, especially wolves and to a lesser extent grizzly bears. Predation then and now probably is highest on calves or older solitary males. Other causes of death today include anthrax, and possibly brucellosis and tuberculosis, although the latter are difficult to isolate as specific mortality factors (H. W. Reynolds et al. 1982). High incidences of intestinal parasites are also thought to lead to some mortality. Drowning is a known mortality factor in Yellowstone, and it has been suggested that it was once important locally in free-ranging herds on the Great Plains. Evidence of high mortality associated with climatic factors is lacking unless snowfall is excessive or combined with crusting and ice formation. Bison are long-lived animals—some survive 20 to 40 years (Soper 1941). The literature on the biology of bison was reviewed by H. W. Reynolds et al. (1982) and Meagher (1986). McDonald (1981) discussed the complex classification and evolution of the species.

DISTRIBUTION IN COLORADO — The western limits of the historic distribution of bison appears to have been western New Mexico, Colorado, Wyoming, and Montana. In Colorado bison occupied most of the state except for the Uncompahgre Pla-

teau and the San Juan Mountains in the southwest (Meaney and Van Vuren 1993). It is generally thought that *Bison bison bison*, the plains bison, occupied eastern Colorado, and *B. b. athabascae*, the wood bison or mountain bison, occupied portions of the mountains and western Colorado. However, the distinction between the two supposed subspecies is unclear, and concrete data on original distributions of the two subspecies is lacking (Armstrong 1972). Furthermore, Meagher (1986) pointed out that convincing evidence for subspecies is lacking in studies of blood chemistry and chromosomes.

Free-ranging herds of bison can still be seen in Yellowstone National Park, and in Wood Buffalo National Park in Alberta and Northwest Territories. More closely regulated populations exist in Wind Cave and Badlands National Parks, South Dakota, and on the National Bison Range in Montana. No bison herds presently live in Colorado under anything approaching natural conditions. Certain ranches on the eastern plains and in the San Luis Valley maintain relatively large herds, but they are carefully managed and generally closely confined. The last residual herd of semi-wild bison existed in Colorado National Monument. That herd was started in 1926 from two cows and a bull provided by the Denver Mountain Parks. The source for the Denver Mountain Park herd is thought to have been Yellowstone National Park, sometime between 1914 and 1923 (P. Miller 1964). The herd of fewer than 20 animals in Colorado National Monument was studied by Capp (1964) and Wasser (1977). Because of impacts on the vegetation, the animals were removed from the monument in the late 1970s.

Oreamnos americanus
MOUNTAIN GOAT

DESCRIPTION — The mountain goat has a sturdy build with a slight shoulder hump. The pelage is white to yellowish white with long guard hairs, woolly underfur, and a prominent mane, beard, and chaps. The black horns, hooves, and nose pad contrast sharply with the white pelage. The

Photograph 12-8 Mountain goat (Oreamnos americanus).

horns, present on both sexes, are of modest length (190–300 mm), relatively thin, conical, and unbranched. Well-developed horn (postcornual) glands are present at the base of the horns. The legs are short and the hooves have a pliable, elastic, slightly convex pad that extends beyond the rim of the outer hoof wall. This pad allows for excellent traction on steep, rocky cliff faces. Dewclaws are present. Females are smaller than males. Measurements are: total length 950–1,700 mm; length of tail 80–200 mm; length of hindfoot 300–370 mm; weight 40–140 kg. The skull lacks ethmoidal vacuities and the premaxillae do not contact the nasals. The bony cores of the horns are nearly straight and round in cross-section. The posterior palate ends opposite the last upper molar. The lower incisors and canines are spatulate, the cheekteeth are selenodont and hypsodont. Techniques for determining the age of mountain goats in the laboratory have been developed (Brandborg 1955, Lentfer 1955, B. Smith 1988), mostly using dental traits and length of horns. Sex and age can be determined in the field (B. Smith 1988), albeit with difficulty, especially if herds are large (Hopkins 1992).

NATURAL HISTORY — Mountain goats are mammals of glaciated subalpine and alpine tundra in the Northern Rockies and coastal ranges of western North America. They have been introduced in various states, including Colorado. Mountain goats typically do not descend much below the level of the treeline, although they may temporarily use trees for shelter from wind and severe cold or snow. They normally also do not venture far from talus or rock faces. The best habitat appears to be a mixture of talus rock faces, alpine meadows, ridge tops, and subalpine ecotones (Saunders 1955), although in South Dakota introduced animals have thrived in montane forests on the Black Hills.

Summer forage consists of grasses and grass-like plants (50 to 95 percent of the diet) and forbs (4 to 14 percent of the diet) (Hibbs 1967, B. Johnson et al. 1978, Saunders 1955). Winter diets are also predominately grass and grass-like plants (88 to 90 percent), and browse (10 to 12 percent). Summer diets of Coloradan mountain sheep and mountain goats are similar but, in winter, goats eat fewer graminoids and more dicots than sheep (Dailey et al. 1984). Mountain goats need free water or snow and typically select ranges that have abundant supplies of salts; they are known to travel 24 km or more to visit mineral licks (Brandborg 1955, Hopkins 1992).

Depending on local topographic and climatic conditions, some populations winter at high elevations on wind-blown slopes; others migrate to treeline or even lower elevations during the winter. Migrations usually involve moves of only 4 to 6 km but some populations may move as far as 24 km. Spring migrations are slower than fall movements; older males reach the summering grounds first and nannies with kids arrive later.

The daily activity pattern consists of foraging from dawn through most of the morning, resting at midday, and foraging again during late afternoon and evening. Generally sedentary, the animals typically do not move more than 0.5 km except during seasonal migrations. However, Hopkins (1992) noted regular movements in excess of 12 km for herds using salt licks in the Gore Range. They bed on rocky shelves or vegetation, and on hot days may lie on snow patches. Caves and overhanging rocks are used for shelter if available. Considerable time is spent wallowing and dusting, especially in the warmer months. Home ranges of mountain goats are generally between 21 and 48 km^2 (Rideout and Hoffmann 1975).

Mountain goats congregate on winter ranges, especially at salt licks and during storms. In late spring and summer, males are solitary but females, yearlings, and kids disperse into herds. Although herds usually are small, in the Gore Range herds of 30 to 50 animals are not unusual. Females and kids remain separated from billies until late summer to early autumn (Hopkins 1992). The breeding season is November and early December. Male rutting behavior includes increased wandering from one band of females to another, pawing shallow pits (which results in soiled ventral parts and hind quarters), and an increase in agonistic behavior between males. Various threat postures, often involving the horns, are used. Unlike the ritualized head butting of mountain sheep, fighting is rare. However, when fighting does occur, serious injuries may result (Geist 1964).

Mountain goats are polygamous. Estrus in females lasts 48 to 72 hours, and most females first breed at about two and one-half years of age. Yearling females do not breed, although yearling males have been observed in rutting behavior. Gestation takes 178 days (Brandborg 1955), and kids are born in late May and early June. The incidence of twins ranges from 8 to 30 percent. Kids are precocious, often eating forage within a week after birth. They nurse until late August or early September. The young of the year generally constitute 20 to 56 percent of the population. In a 1981 study, ratios of kids to older animals in Colorado ranged from 18:100 to 71:100, lower reproductive success being correlated with high spring snowpack (Adams and Bailey 1982). Mountain goats generally do not show high fluctuations in populations; most studies show moderate growth or stability although introduced populations in Olympic National Park, Washington, have increased to the point that they are considered detrimental to vegetation. Status and management

Map 12-13 Distribution of the mountain goat (Oreamnos americanus) *in North America.*

in Colorado was originally studied in the context of increasing the herds (Denney 1977, Hibbs et al. 1969). More recently, concerns about habitat destruction and competition with native species predominate (Dailey et al. 1984).

Most mountain goat mortality occurs from starvation in winter and accidental deaths from avalanches and rock slides. Mountain lions are the most significant predators on mountain goats. Bobcats, coyotes, black bears, brown bears, and golden eagles also prey on them, mostly on young and infirm individuals and only occasionally on adults. Winter-killed goats are eaten by coyotes. Reviews of mountain goat biology were provided by Rideout (1978), Rideout and Hoffmann (1975), and Wigal and Coggins (1982). Colorado has a hunting season on mountain goats; 102 animals were harvested in 1990 (Table 3-2).

DISTRIBUTION IN COLORADO — Populations of mountain goats in Colorado are all the result of

407

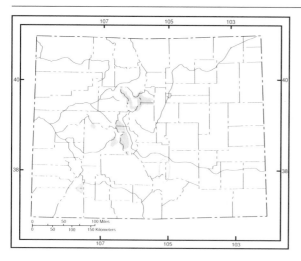

Map 12-14 Distribution of the introduced mountain goat (Oreamnos americanus) in Colorado.

Photograph 12-9 Mountain sheep, or bighorn sheep (Ovis canadensis).

introductions made in 1948, 1950, 1961, 1964, 1968, 1970, and 1971. Animals were brought from Idaho (the nearest native population), South Dakota (itself an introduced population), and British Columbia (Rutherford 1972a). Mountain goats now exist in portions of the San Juan Mountains, Gore Range, Collegiate Range (J. Bailey and Johnson 1977), and on Mount Evans. Cowan and McCrory (1970) studied geographic variation and concluded that *Oreamnos americanus* is monotypic; previously four subspecies had been recognized, with the name *O. a. missoulae* being applied to the population from the Middle Rockies introduced into Colorado.

Ovis canadensis
MOUNTAIN SHEEP, OR BIGHORN SHEEP

DESCRIPTION — Mountain sheep, also called bighorn sheep or simply bighorns, are blocky, heavily built mammals whose color varies seasonally and geographically from grayish brown to medium brown. The muzzle is grayish white and there is a paler gray rump patch, underbelly, and edging down the rear legs. Adult males have thick, massive horns that are heavily ridged, a

characteristic useful in determining the ages of individuals (Geist 1966). On adult males the horns sweep sharply outward, backward, and downward, with the tips then curving upward, eventually forming "full curls." The horns on a mature ram may measure more than 46 cm around their base and 112 cm in length. The tips of the horns are frequently worn or broken, a condition referred to as "brooming." Horns on subadults and females are shorter and more slender. Measurements are: total length 1,250–1,950 mm; length of tail 70–130 mm; length of hindfoot 310–440 mm; length of ear 90–135 mm; weight 50–125 kg. Skulls of adult males may measure up to 320 mm in length and the horns and head may weigh more than 17 kg. The skull has antorbital pits; the premaxillae either barely reach or do not touch the nasals. The premolars have prominent vertical enamel ridges on the labial side. The incisors are spatulate and the molars are long and well developed. Permanent dentition is not fully in place until four years of age (Deming 1952).

NATURAL HISTORY — Mountain sheep conjure images of pristine, wilderness conditions because of their association with the high mountains and steep canyons. In part because of impacts imposed by humans, they typically occur only on steep, precipitous terrain, although a number of herds in the state (for example, along Interstate 70 near Georgetown and in the Big Thompson Canyon west of Loveland) have become habituated to areas adjacent to busy highways. Historical evidence suggests that at one time mountain sheep were much more widely distributed, even extending onto the eastern plains in areas close to the foothills. In Colorado, mountain sheep prefer high-visibility habitat dominated by grass, low shrubs, and rock cover, areas near open escape terrain, and topographic relief. Vegetational succession, as encroachment of shrubland and forest, has led to declines in sheep in recent years on some ranges (Wakelyn 1987). The image evoked by mountain sheep and their importance as a premier game mammal in Colorado led to their designation of "state animal" in 1961. Subsequently, the Game, Fish, and Parks Department (now the Colorado Division of Wildlife) adopted the mountain sheep for its logo.

The bulk of the diet is grasses and grass-like plants, browse, and some forbs (Moser 1962, D. Smith 1954, J. Todd 1972). Specifically, grasses and sedges (46 percent), and shrubs (45 percent) constitute the bulk of the yearly diet (Todd 1975). At lower elevations browse appears to be the staple in winter. At higher elevations grasses and grass-like plants may dominate both summer and winter diets (T. Woodward 1980), although B. Johnson and Smith (1980) observed that in alpine summer ranges in New Mexico, the use of forbs and graminoids was about equal. In Colorado, winter diets of bighorns included more graminoids and fewer dicots than did the diet of mountain goats, whereas summer diets were more similar (Dailey et al. 1984). Some 80 to 90 percent of the diet of desert bighorns (*O. c. nelsoni*) was roughly equal amounts of browse and grass or grass-like materials (L. Wilson et al. 1980). Spowart and Hobbs (1985) investigated the effects of burning on competition for forage between deer and mountain sheep. They concluded that the greatest degree of competition was in the spring in situations where the two species were crowded onto limited range; otherwise, sufficient forage was available to meet the needs

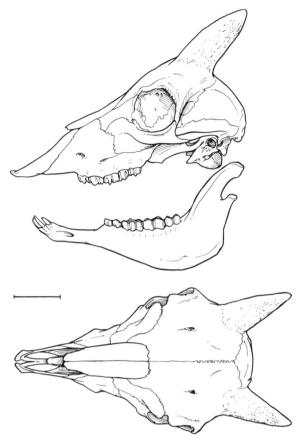

Figure 12-4 Lateral and dorsal views of the skull of a female mountain sheep, or bighorn sheep (Ovis canadensis). *Scale = 5 cm.*

of both species. Capp (1968) reported little competition among elk, deer, and mountain sheep on summer ranges in Rocky Mountain National Park, because of little range overlap. Investigations to improve bighorn ranges with fertilizer or herbicide application in Colorado were inconclusive (Bear 1978).

Mountain sheep are gregarious, social mammals. They are diurnal, with two to five foraging bouts interspersed with periods of rest, play (generally among lambs or between lamb and mother), and maintenance behaviors such as rubbing, dusting, and scratching. They have a high degree of philopatry, or site fidelity, which ties them closely to areas that are familiar and leads to slow rates of expansion. Such fidelity renders them vulnerable to increased stress levels when a disturbance to their ranges occur. During spring and summer, mountain sheep segregate by sex and age. Rams older than three or four form small bachelor herds, while females, lambs, and younger rams form larger units.

Seasonally, mountain sheep may make relatively short migrations from summer to winter ranges. Many populations effect this migration through a series of deliberate, short-distance moves using favored habitat along the way. These movements have been interpreted as seasonal drift (Moser 1962) or as short-term use of seasonal home ranges (Geist 1971) with up to four or five such areas used, depending on the herd and the terrain. Movements associated with seasonal changes can cover distances of up to 60 km although distances of 5 to 15 km are more typical. A movement of 5 to 8 km in the mountains of Colorado may lead to an elevational shift of hundreds of meters. Daily movements when on a particular seasonal range average 0.5 to 1.5 km (Oldemeyer 1966, Simmons 1961, D. Smith 1954), although Hopkins (1992) noted regular movements in excess of 12 km for herds visiting salt licks in the Gore Range. In fall, adult rams move onto the breeding/winter range several weeks before ewes, lambs, and younger rams. Barriers to movement include large expanses of timber or dense brush (which restrict the view) as well as large rivers and wide valley floors.

Mountain sheep breed in November and December in our area, although desert bighorns may initiate breeding as early as July in parts of the Southwest. Breeding attempts by mature rams decrease rapidly by January but younger rams may exhibit reproductive behaviors into April and May (Moser 1962). The species is promiscuous, with dominant males typically doing most of the breeding. Young males can breed with females in the absence of dominant rams, but unless population structure demands it, most do not contribute significantly to breeding until seven or eight years of age. Most females breed at two-and-a-half years

of age although both sexes may be mature as yearlings. Females are monestrous. Within a herd usually only one female is in estrus at any one time, leading to several rams attempting to follow and copulate with her. Gestation takes approximately 175 to 180 days. Most young are born in May or June in Colorado, with a peak in mid-June (Moser 1962), although desert bighorns may lamb as early as January in other states. Ewes segregate from the herd for about a week when lambing, and most populations have specific lambing grounds that are used year after year. A single young is the rule. Lambs at birth weigh about 3 to 5 kg. They are precocial and start to forage several weeks after birth, although they may not be weaned for five or six months.

Bighorn sheep can live up to 17 years, although individuals in the wild probably do not live much more than 10 to 12 years (Streeter 1970). The sex ratio at birth approximates 1:1, but differential mortality leads to adult ram:ewe ratios that vary widely depending on the effects of hunting and other factors. Female reproductive success also varies widely. Lamb:ewe ratios for the Pike's Peak and Georgetown herds varied from 7:100 to 95:100, based on July counts over a seven-year period; average ratios were about 59:100 (Moser 1962). Streeter (1969) reported average ratios of 59:100 for herds on Mount Evans and the Buffalo Peaks from 1966 to 1968. Woodward et al. (1974), working with a declining population in the Sangre de Cristo mountains, reported ratios of 83:100 and 72:100 in June counts.

Studies of declining populations in Colorado reported high levels of mortality in lambs (18 and 25 percent lamb survival) during late summer, fall, or winter (Streeter 1969, Woodward et al. 1974). In the Buffalo Peak study significant adult mortality (about 30 percent) also occurred. A number of researchers have suggested that most decline in Coloradan populations was due to lungworm-induced pneumonia, affecting either lambs or all age classes (Feuerstein et al. 1980, Moser 1962, Woodward et al. 1974). However, Streeter (1969) found no evidence of disease contributing

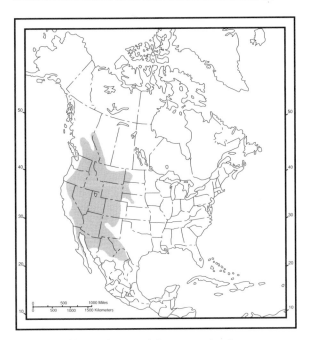

Map 12-15 *Distribution of the mountain sheep, or bighorn sheep* (Ovis canadensis) *in North America.*

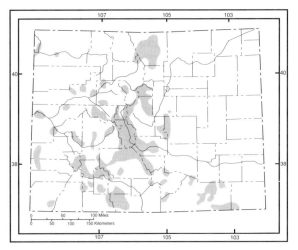

Map 12-16 *Distribution of the mountain sheep, or bighorn sheep* (Ovis canadensis) *in Colorado. Solid circles indicate extralimital introductions.*

to mortality in the Buffalo Peaks herd. In that study he attributed the decrease to an experimental either-sex hunting season conducted for three years and to a shift in behavioral patterns of the herd, leading to year-round use of their alpine range when historically they had utilized both lower elevations and alpine range.

High mortality in the first year of life is due to disease, nutrition, and weather factors. Coyotes, bobcats, mountain lion, and golden eagles are known predators on sheep, especially on young of the year. Hunting is also an important factor in shaping population structure. Colorado populations were heavily exploited by early settlers and market hunters, leading to a complete closure of hunting in 1887 (Bear and Jones 1973). In 1953, hunting was again established (Moser 1962), and limited harvest has been permitted since that time, mostly directed toward mature rams. Hunting of trophy rams and of herds of fewer than 100 animals may be deleterious because of impacts on

the gene pool and on learned behaviors (Geist 1975). However, most state wildlife agencies have continued to emphasize harvest of trophy rams and generally ignore this argument.

For many years, populations of bighorn sheep declined in Colorado, from about 7,300 animals in 1915 to around 3,000 in the late 1950s, and to about 2,200 in 1970 (Buechner 1960, Moser 1962, Bear and Jones 1973). Lungworm-pneumonia complexes have contributed to significant losses of sheep in many populations (Feuerstein et al. 1980), as have habitat changes due to plant succession (Wakelyn 1987). To offset declines in particular populations, Colorado wildlife personnel treated sheep for lungworm and pursued a vigorous program to capture and transplant excess individuals from healthy herds (Rutherford 1972b, c; Bear 1979). Population numbers have subsequently increased to 3,500 in 1979 and to 6,300 animals in 1990 (Barrows and Holmes 1990). General reviews of the abundant literature on mountain sheep were provided by Buechner (1960), Geist (1971), Lawson and Johnson (1982), Monson and Sumner (1980), Shackleton (1985), and Wishart (1978). The paper by D. Smith (1954) in Idaho is still an excellent work on the general biology and management of sheep in the Rocky Mountains, and the work of Welles and Welles (1961) is a classic on desert bighorn.

DISTRIBUTION IN COLORADO — Colorado herds are widely scattered throughout the mountains and foothills of the state. *Ovis canadensis canadensis,* the Rocky Mountain bighorn, is the native mountain sheep of Colorado; *O. c. nelsoni,* the desert bighorn, was introduced near Colorado National Monument in 1979 (Creeden 1986). In general, morphological differences between the two forms are slight, and some of the differences may be environmental rather than genetic. Horns of the desert bighorn are more slender and flare outward more than those of the Rocky Mountain subspecies, although the basal circumference of the horns is greater in the desert sheep (Buechner 1960). Generally, desert sheep are paler and typically slightly smaller than the Rocky Mountain bighorn.

Literature Cited

Ables, E. D. 1969. Activity studies of red foxes in southern Wisconsin. J. Wildl. Mgmt., 33:145–153.

———. 1975. Ecology of the red fox in North America. Pp. 216–236, *in* The wild canids: their systematics, behavioral ecology and evolution (M. W. Fox., ed.). Van Nostrand Reinhold, New York, 508 pp.

Abramsky, Z., and C. R. Tracy. 1979. Population biology of a "noncycling" population of prairie voles and a hypothesis on the role of migration in regulating microtine cycles. Ecology, 60:349–361.

Ackerman, B. B., F. G. Lindzey, and T. P. Hemker. 1984. Cougar food habits in southern Utah. J. Wildl. Mgmt., 48:147–155.

Adams, C. 1976. Measurement and characteristics of fox squirrel, *Sciurus niger rufiventer*, home ranges. Amer. Midland Nat., 95:211–215.

Adams, L. G., and J. A. Bailey. 1982. Population dynamics of mountain goats in the Sawatch Range, Colorado. J. Wildl. Mgmt., 46:1003–1009.

Adams, R. A. 1988. Trends in reproductive biology of some bats in Colorado. Bat Res. News, 29:21–25.

———. 1990. Biogeography of bats in Colorado: ecological implications of species tolerances. Bat Res. News, 31:17–21.

Adams, R. A., B. J. Lengas, and M. Bekoff. 1987. Variations in avoidance responses to humans by black-tailed prairie dogs (*Cynomys ludovicianus*). J. Mamm., 68:686–689.

Addison, E. M., I. K. Barker, and D. B. Hunter. 1987. Diseases and parasites of furbearers. Pp. 893–909, *in* Wild furbearer management and conservation in North America (M. Novak, J. A. Baker, M. E. Obbard, and B. Malloch, eds.). Ontario Trappers Association, Toronto, 1150 pp.

Alcoze, T. M., and E. G. Zimmerman. 1973. Food habits and dietary overlap of two heteromyid rodents from the mesquite plains of Texas. J. Mamm., 54:900–908.

Aldous, S. E., and J. Manweiler. 1942. The winter food habits of the short-tailed weasel in northern Minnesota. J. Mamm., 23:250–255.

Aldridge, E. R. 1976. Prey selection by *Myotis lucifugus* (Chiroptera: Vespertilionidae). Amer. Nat., 110:619–628.

Aleksiuk, M. 1968. Scent-mound communication, territoriality, and population regulation in beaver (*Castor canadensis*). J. Mamm., 49:759–762.

———. 1970. The function of the tail as a fat storage depot in the beaver (*Castor canadensis*). J. Mamm., 51:145–148.

Alexander, L. 1977. Suitability of habitat for bobcats in Colorado. Unpubl. rept., Colorado Division Wildlife, Denver, 46 pp.

Allan, P. F. 1946. Notes on *Dipodomys ordii richardsoni*. J. Mamm., 27:271–273.

Alldredge, A. W., J. F. Lipscomb, and F. W. Whicker. 1974. Forage intake rates of mule deer estimated with fallout cesium–137. J. Wildl. Mgmt., 38:508–516.

Allen, A. W. 1982. Habitat suitability index models: marten. U.S. Dept. of Interior, Fish and Wildl. Service, FWS/OBS 82/10.11:1–9.

———. 1983. Habitat suitability index models: mink. U.S. Dept. of Interior, Fish Wildl. Service, FWS/OBS 82/10.61:1–19.

Allen, D. L. 1942. Populations and habits of the fox squirrel in Allegan County, Michigan. Amer. Midland Nat., 27:338–379.

Allen, J. A. 1874. Notes on the mammals of portions of Kansas, Colorado, Wyoming, and Utah. Bull. Essex Inst., 6:43–66.

Altmann, M. 1956. Patterns of social behavior in big game. Trans. N. Amer. Wildl. Nat. Res. Conf., 21:538–545.

———. 1959. Group dynamics in Wyoming moose during the rutting season. J. Mamm., 40:420–424.

Amstrup, S. C., and J. Beecham. 1976. Activity patterns of radiocollared black bears in Idaho. J. Wildl. Mgmt., 40:340–348.

Andelt, W. F. 1985. Behavioral ecology of coyotes in south Texas. Wildl. Monogr., 94:1–45.

———. 1987. Coyote predation. Pp. 128–140, *in* Wild furbearer management and conservation in North America (M. Novak, J.A. Baker, M.E. Obbard, and B. Malloch, eds). Ontario Trappers Association, Toronto, 1150 pp.

413

Andelt, W. F., D. P. Althoff, R. M. Case, and P. S. Gipson. 1980. Surplus killing by coyotes. J. Mamm., 61:377–378.

Anderson, A. E. 1983. A critical review of literature on puma (*Felis concolor*). Spec. Rept., Colorado Div. Wildl., 54:1–91.

Anderson, A. E., and D. C. Bowden. 1977. Mule deer–coyote interactions. Pp. 15–16, *in* Colorado Game Res. Review, 1975–1976 (O. B. Cope, ed.). Colorado Div. Wildl., Fort Collins, 73 pp.

Anderson, A. E., D. C. Bowden, and D. M. Kattner. 1989. Survival in an unhunted mountain lion (*Felis concolor hippolestes*) poppulation in southwestern Colorado. P. 57 *in* Proceedings of the Third Mountain Lion Workshop, 6–8 December, Prescott, AZ (R.H. Smith, ed.). Arizona Chapter Wildlife Society and Arizona Game and Fish Department, Phoenix, 88 pp.

———. 1992. The puma on Uncompahgre Plateau, Colorado. Tech. Publ., Colorado Div. Wildl., 40:1–116.

Anderson, A. E., and D. E. Medin. 1967. The breeding season in migratory mule deer. Game Inf. Leafl., Colorado Game, Fish, and Parks Dept., 60:1–4.

———. 1969. Antler morphometry in a Colorado mule deer population. J. Wildl. Mgmt., 33:520–533.

———. 1971. Antler phenology in a Colorado mule deer population. Southwestern Nat., 15:485–494.

Anderson, A. E., D. E. Medin, and D. C. Bowden. 1974. Growth and morphometry of the carcass, selected bones, organs, and glands of mule deer. Wildl. Monogr., 39:1–122.

Anderson, A. E., and O. C. Wallmo. 1984. *Odocoileus hemionus.* Mamm. Species, 219:1–9.

Anderson, D. C. 1978. Observations on reproduction, growth, and behavior of the northern pocket gopher (*Thomomys talpoides*). J. Mamm., 59:418–422.

Anderson, D. C., K. B. Armitage, and R. S. Hoffmann. 1976. Socioecology of marmots: female reproductive strategies. Ecology, 57:552–560.

Anderson, D. C., and D. W. Johns. 1977. Predation by badger on yellow-bellied marmot in Colorado. Southwestern Nat., 22:283–284.

Anderson, E. 1968. Fauna of the Little Box Elder Cave, Converse County, Wyoming: the Carnivora. Univ. Colorado Studies, Ser. Earth Sci., 6:1–59.

Anderson, E., S. C. Forrest, T. W. Clark, and L. Richardson. 1986. Paleobiology, biogeography, and systematics of the black-footed ferret, *Mustela nigripes* (Audubon and Bachman), 1851. Great Basin Nat. Mem., 8:11–62.

Anderson, E. M. 1987*a*. A critical review and annotated bibliography of literature on the bobcat. Spec. Rept., Colorado Div. Wildl., 62:1–61.

———. 1987*b*. Bobcat behavioral ecology in relation to resource use in southeastern Colorado. Unpubl. Ph.D. dissert., Colorado State Univ., Fort Collins, 107 pp.

———. 1990. Bobcat diurnal loafing sites in southeastern Colorado. J. Wildl. Mgmt., 54:600–602.

Anderson, S. 1954. Subspeciation in the meadow mouse, *Microtus montanus,* in Wyoming and Colorado. Univ. Kansas Publ., Mus. Nat. Hist., 7:489–506.

———. 1956. Subspeciation in the meadow mouse, *Microtus pennsylvanicus,* in Wyoming, Colorado, and adjacent areas. Univ. Kansas Publ., Mus. Nat. Hist., 9:85–104.

———. 1959. Mammals of the Grand Mesa, Colorado. Univ. Kansas Publ., Mus. Nat. Hist., 9:405–414.

Anderson, S., and J. K. Jones, Jr., eds. 1984. Orders and families of mammals of the world. John Wiley and Sons, New York, 686 pp.

Andrews, R. D., and E. K. Boggess. 1978. Ecology of coyotes in Iowa. Pp. 249–265, *in* Coyotes: biology, behavior, and management (M. Bekoff, ed.). Academic Press, New York, 384 pp.

Anonymous. 1992. Fishing for fishers. Wyoming Wildl., 56:24–29.

Anthony, A., and D. Foreman. 1951. Observations on the reproductive cycle of the black-tailed prairie dog (*Cynomys ludovicianus*). Physiol. Zool., 24:242–248.

Archer, S., M. G. Garrett, and J. K. Detling. 1987. Rates of vegetation change associated with prairie dog (*Cynomys ludovicianus*) grazing in North American mixed-grass prairie. Vegetatio, 72:159–166.

Archibald, W. S. 1963. A study of small mammal–habitat association in Weld County, Colorado. Unpubl. M.S. thesis, Colorado State College, Greeley, 63 pp.

Arlton, A. V. 1936. An ecological study of the mole. J. Mamm., 17:349–371.

Armitage, K. B. 1961. Frequency of melanism in the golden-mantled marmot. J. Mamm., 42:100–101.

———. 1962. Social behavior of a colony of the yellow-bellied marmot (*Marmota flaviventris*). Anim. Behav., 10:319–331.

———. 1973. Population changes and social behavior following colonization by the yellow-bellied marmot. J. Mamm., 54:842–854.

———. 1974. Male behaviour and territoriality in the yellow-bellied marmot. J. Zool., 172:233–265.

———. 1975. Social behavior and population dynamics of marmots. Oikos, 26:341–354.

———. 1976. Scent-marking by yellow-bellied marmots. J. Mamm., 57:583–584.

———. 1979. Food selectivity by yellow-bellied marmots. J. Mamm., 60:628–629.

———. 1991. Social and population dynamics of yellow-bellied marmots: results from long-term research. Ann. Rev. Ecol. Syst., 22:379–407.

Armitage, K. B., and J. F. Downhower. 1974. Demography of yellow-bellied marmot populations. Ecology, 55:1233–1245.

Armitage, K. B., J. F. Downhower, and G. E. Svendsen. 1976. Seasonal changes in weights of marmots. Amer. Midland Nat., 96:36–51.

Armitage, K. B., and D. Johns. 1982. Kinship, reproductive strategies, and social dynamics of yellow-bellied marmots. Behav. Ecol. Sociobiol., 11:55–63.

Armitage, K. B., D. Johns, and D. C. Anderson. 1979. Cannibalism among yellow-bellied marmots. J. Mamm., 60:205–207.

Armstrong, D. M. 1971. Notes on variation in *Spermophilus tridecemlineatus* (Rodentia, Sciuridae) in Colorado and adjacent states, and description of a new subspecies. J. Mamm., 52:528–536.

——. 1972. Distribution of mammals in Colorado. Monogr., Univ. Kansas Mus. Nat. Hist., 3:1–415.

——. 1974. Second record of the Mexican big-eared bat in Utah. Southwestern Nat., 19:114–115.

——. 1977a. Ecological distribution of small mammals in the upper Williams Fork Basin, Grand County, Colorado. Southwestern Nat., 22:289–304.

——. 1977b. Distributional patterns of mammals in Utah. Great Basin Nat., 37:457–474.

——. 1979. Ecological distribution of rodents in Canyonlands National Park, Utah. Great Basin Nat., 39:199–205.

——. 1982. Mammals of the Canyon Country: a handbook of mammals of Canyonlands National Park and vicinity, Utah. Canyonlands Natural History Association, Moab, 263 pp.

——. 1984. Mammalian associates of woodrats (*Neotoma*) on the Colorado Plateau, U.S.A. Program and Abstracts, Australian Mammal Society, American Society of Mammalogists, Joint Meeting, Sydney, unpaged, microfiche.

——. 1986. Edward Royal Warren (1860–1942) and the development of Coloradan mammalogy. Amer. Zool., 26:363–370.

——. 1987. Rocky Mountain mammals, a handbook of mammals of Rocky Mountain National Park and vicinity, Colorado, revised ed. Colorado Assoc. Univ. Press, Boulder, 223 pp.

——. 1993. Effects of the Lawn Lake Flood on the local distribution of mammals. Pp. 170–191, *in* Ecological effects of the Lawn Lake flood of 1982, Rocky Mountain National Park (H. E. McCutcheon, R. Herrmann, and D. R. Stevens, eds.). Sci. Monogr., National Park Service, NPS/NRROMO/NSRM–93/21: 214 pp.

Armstrong, D. M., Banta, B. H., and E. J. Pokropus. 1973. Altitudinal distribution of small mammals along a cross-sectional transect through the Arkansas River watershed, Colorado. Southwestern Nat., 17:315–326.

Armstrong, D. M., and J. K. Jones, Jr. 1971. *Sorex merriami*. Mamm. Species, 2:1–2.

——. 1972. *Notiosorex crawfordi*. Mamm. Species, 17:1–5.

Arnason, U., and B. Widegren. 1986. Pinniped phylogeny enlightened by molecular hybridizations using highly repetitive DNA. Molec. Biol. Evol., 3:356–365.

Asdell, S. A. 1964. Patterns of mammalian reproduction, second ed. Cornell Univ. Press, Ithaca, 670 pp.

Avery, S. R. 1989. Vocalization and behavior of the swift fox (*Vulpes velox*). Unpubl. M.A. thesis, Univ. Northern Colorado, Greeley, 104 pp.

Bailey, B. 1929. The mammals of Sherburne County, Minnesota. J. Mamm., 10:153–164.

Bailey, E. P. 1974. Notes on the development, mating behavior, and vocalization of captive ringtails. Southwestern Nat., 19:117–119.

Bailey, J. A., and B. K. Johnson. 1977. Status of introduced mountain goats in the Sawatch Range of Colorado. Pp. 54–63, *in* Proc. First Internat. Mountain Goat Symp. (W. Samuel and W. G. MacGregor, eds.). Fish Wildl. Branch, British Columbia, 243 pp.

Bailey, R. G. 1978. Ecosystems of the United States. U.S. Dept. of Agriculture, Forest Service, RARE II, Map B, 1:7,500,000.

Bailey, T. N. 1971. Biology of striped skunks on a southwestern Lake Erie marsh. Amer. Midland Nat., 85:196–207.

——. 1974. Social organization in a bobcat population. J. Wildl. Mgmt., 38:435–446.

Bailey, V. 1926. A biological survey of North Dakota. N. Amer. Fauna, 49:1–226.

——. 1932. Mammals of New Mexico. N. Amer. Fauna, 53:1–412.

Baird, S. F. 1855. Characteristics of some new species of North American Mammalia, collected chiefly in connection with the U.S. surveys of a railroad route to the Pacific. Proc. Acad. Nat. Sci., Philadelphia, 7:333–336.

——. 1858. Mammals *in* Reports of explorations and surveys . . . from the Mississippi River to the Pacific Ocean. . . . , 8(1):1–757.

Baker, A. E. M. 1974. Interspecific aggressive behavior of pocket gophers *Thomomys bottae* and *T. talpoides* (Geomyidae: Rodentia). Ecology, 55:671–673.

Baker, R. J., R. J. Gress, and D. L. Spencer. 1983. Mortality and population density of cottontail rabbits at Ross Natural History Reservation, Lyons County, Kansas. Emporia State Res. Studies, 31:1–49.

Baker, R. J., and D. L. Spencer. 1965. Late fall reproduction in the desert shrew. J. Mamm., 46:330.

Bakken, A. A. 1959. Behavior of gray squirrels. Proc. Southeastern Assoc. Game Fish Comm., 13:393–406.

Bakko, E. B., and L. N. Brown. 1967. Breeding biology of the white-tailed prairie dog, *Cynomys leucurus* in Wyoming. J. Mamm., 48:100–112.

Bakko, E. B., and J. Nahorniak. 1986. Torpor patterns in captive white-tailed prairie dogs (*Cynomys leucurus*). J. Mamm., 67:576–578.

Balcombe, J. P. 1990. Vocal recognition of pups by mother Mexican free-tailed bats *Tadarida brasiliensis mexicana*. Anim. Behav., 39:960–966.

Bandoli, J. H. 1981. Factors influencing seasonal burrowing activity in the pocket gopher, *Thomomys bottae*. J. Mamm., 62:293–303.

415

———. 1987. Activity and plural occupancy of burrows in Botta's pocket gopher *Thomomys bottae.* Amer. Midland Nat., 118:10–14.

Banfield, A.W.F. 1974. The mammals of Canada. Univ. Toronto Press, Toronto, 438 pp.

Banta, B. H., and T. M. Norris. 1968. The small mammal fauna sampled along a transect of prairie in El Paso, Colorado, in 1963 and 1964. Wasmann J. Biol., 26:185–200.

Barash, D. P. 1971. Cooperative hunting in the lynx. J. Mamm., 52:480.

———. 1974. Neighbor recognition in two "solitary" carnivores: the raccoon (*Procyon lotor*) and the red fox (*Vulpes vulpes*). Science, 185:794–796.

Barbour, R. W., and W. H. Davis. 1969. Bats of America. Univ. Kentucky Press, Lexington, 286 pp.

Barnes, A. M. 1982. Surveillance and control of bubonic plague in the United States. Symp. Zool. Soc. London, 50:237–270.

Barnes, A. M. 1993. A review of plague and its relevance to prairie dog populations and the black-footed ferret. Pp. 28–37, *in* Proceedings of the Symposium on the Management of Prairie Dog Complexes for the Reintroduction of the Black-footed Ferret (J. L. Oldemeyer, D. E. Biggins, B. J. Miller, and R. Crete, eds.). Biol. Rept., U.S. Fish Wildl. Serv., 93(13):1–96.

Barrows, P., and J. Holmes. 1990. Colorado's wildlife story. Colorado Div. Wildl., Denver, 450 pp.

Bartels, M. A., and D. P. Thompson. 1993. *Spermophilus lateralis.* Mamm. Species, 440:1–8.

Bartholomew, G. A., and J. W. Hudson. 1959. Effects of sodium chloride on weight and drinking in the antelope ground squirrel. J. Mamm., 40:354–360.

Bartholemew, G. H., and H. H. Caswell. 1951. Locomotion in kangaroo rats and its adaptive significance. J. Mamm., 32:155–169.

Bartmann, R. M. 1968. Results from an 18-year deer tagging program in northwestern Colorado. Proc. West. Assoc. State Game and Fish Comm., 48:166–172.

Bartmann, R. M., and S. F. Steinert. 1981. Distribution and movements of mule deer in the White River drainage, Colorado. Spec. Rep., Colorado Div. Wildl., 51:1–12.

Bartmann, R. M., G. C. White, L. H. Carpenter, and R. A. Garrott. 1987. Aerial mark-recapture estimates of confined mule deer in piñon-juniper woodland. J. Wildl. Mgmt., 51:41–46.

Batzli, G. O., and F. O. Cole. 1979. Nutritional ecology of microtine rodents: digestibility of forage. J. Mamm., 58:583–591.

Baumgartner, L. L. 1940. The fox squirrel: its life history, habits, and management in Ohio. Wildl. Res. Sta. Release, Ohio State Univ., 138:1–257.

———. 1943. Fox squirrels in Ohio. J. Wildl. Mgmt., 7:193–202.

Bear, G. D. 1968. Hunter harvest and population trend of a small herd of antelope located in Moffat County, Colorado. Proc. Pronghorn Antelope Workshop, 3:85–91.

———. 1969. Evaluation of aerial antelope census technique. Game Inf. Leafl., Colorado Div. Wildl., 69:1–3.

———. 1973. Antelope investigations. Food habits of antelope. Game Res. Rept., Colorado Div. Wildl., Jan:37–70.

———. 1978. Evaluation of fertilizer and herbicide applications on two Colorado bighorn sheep winter ranges. Div. Rept., Colorado Div. Wildl., 10:1–75.

———. 1979. Evaluation of bighorn transplants in two Colorado localities. Spec. Rept., Colorado Div. Wildl., 45:1–12.

Bear, G. D., and R. Green. 1980. Elk investigations. Elk population and ecological studies. Wildl. Research Rept., Colorado Div. Wildl., July: 221–313.

Bear, G. D., and R. M. Hansen. 1966. Food habits, growth, and reproduction of white-tailed jackrabbits in southern Colorado. Tech. Bull., Agric. Exp. Sta., Colorado State Univ., 90:1–59.

Bear, G. D., and G. W. Jones. 1973. History and distribution of bighorn sheep in Colorado. Colorado Div. Wildl., 231 pp.

Beattie, K. H., and T. A. Pierson. 1977. What makes hunters happy? Colorado Outdoors, September–October.

Beck, R. F., and R. M. Hansen. 1966. Estimating plains pocket gopher abundance on adjacent soil types by a revised technique. J. Range Mgmt., 19:224–225.

Beck, T. D. I. 1981. Black bear investigations. Job Progress Report, Colorado Div. Wildl., P–R Proj. W–126-R–4: 305–316.

———. 1991. Black bears of west-central Colorado. Tech. Publ., Colorado Div. Wildl., 39:1–86.

Beckel-Kratz, A. 1977. Preliminary observations on the social behavior of the North American otter (*Lutra canadensis*). Otters (J. Otter Trust), 1977:28–32.

Bee, J. W., G. E. Glass, R. S. Hoffmann, and R. R. Patterson. 1981. Mammals in Kansas. Publ. Ed. Ser., Univ. Kansas Mus. Nat. Hist., 7:1–300.

Beer, J. R. 1950. The reproductive cycle of the muskrat in Wisconsin. J. Wildl. Mgmt., 14:151–156.

———. 1961. Hibernation in *Perognathus flavescens.* J. Mamm., 42:103.

Beidleman, R. G. 1950. The cinereous shrew below 6000 feet in north central Colorado. J. Mamm., 31:459.

———. 1952. Possums and points west. Colorado Conserv., 1:2–5.

———. 1954. October breeding of *Peromyscus* in north central Colorado. J. Mamm., 35:118.

Beidleman, R. G., and J. D. Remington. 1955. Another record of the least shrew from northeastern Colorado. J. Mamm., 36:123.

Beidleman, R. G., and W. A. Weber. 1958. Analysis of a pika hay pile. J. Mamm., 39:599–600.

Bekoff, M. 1974. Social play and play soliciting by infant canids. Amer. Zool., 14:323–341.

———. 1977. *Canis latrans*. Mamm. Species, 79:1–9.

———. 1982. Coyote. Pp. 447–459, *in* Wild mammals of North America: biology, management, and economics (J. A. Chapman and G. A. Feldhamer, eds.). Johns Hopkins Univ. Press, Baltimore, 1147.

———, ed. 1978. Coyotes: biology, behavior, and management. Academic Press, New York, 384 pp.

Bekoff, M., and J. Diamond. 1976. Precopulatory and copulatory behavior in coyotes. J. Mamm., 57:372–375.

Bekoff, M., and M. C. Wells. 1980. The social ecology of coyotes. Sci. Amer., 242:130–148.

———. 1982. Behavioral ecology of coyotes: social organization, rearing patterns, space use, and resource defense. Z. Tierpsychol., 60:281–305.

Belan, I., P. N. Lehner, and T. W. Clark. 1978. Vocalizations of the American pine marten, *Martes americana*. J. Mamm., 59:871–874.

Belk, M. C., C. L. Pritchett, and H. D. Smith. 1990. Patterns of microhabitat use by *Sorex monticolus* in summer. Great Basin Nat., 50:387–389.

Belk, M. C., and H. D. Smith. 1991. *Ammospermophilus leucurus*. Mamm. Species, 368:1–8.

Belk, M. C., H. D. Smith, and J. Lawson. 1988. Use and partitioning of montane habitat by small mammals. J. Mamm., 69:688–695.

Belovsky, G. E. 1984. Summer diet optimization by beaver. Amer. Midl. Nat., 111:209–222.

Benedict, A. D. 1991. A Sierra Club Naturalist's Guide to the Southern Rockies. Sierra Club Books, San Francisco, 578 pp.

Benedict, J. B. 1985. Arapaho Pass. Research Rept., Center for Mountain Archeology, Ward, Colorado, 3:1–197.

Benedict, J. B. 1992. Footprints in the snow: high-altitude cultural ecology of the Colorado Front Range, U.S.A. Arctic and Alpine Res., 24:1–16.

Benedict, J. B., and B. L. Olson. 1978. The Mount Albion complex. Research Rept., Center for Mountain Archeology, Ward, Colorado. 1:1–213.

Beneski, J. T., Jr., and D. W. Stinson. 1987. *Sorex palustris*. Mamm. Species, 296:1–6.

Berger, J. 1977. Organizational systems and dominance in feral horses in the Grand Canyon. Behav. Ecol. Sociobiol., 2:131–146.

———. 1986. Wild horses of the Great Basin: social competition and population size. Univ. Chicago Press, Chicago, 326 pp.

Bergerud, A. T., and D. R. Miller. 1977. Population dynamics of Newfoundland beaver. Canadian J. Zool., 55:1480–1492.

Bergstrom, B. J. 1986. Ecological and behavioral relationships among three species of chipmunks (*Tamias*) in the Front Range of Colorado. Unpubl. Ph.D. dissert., Univ. Kansas, Lawrence, 111 pp.

———. 1988. Home ranges of three species of chipmunks (*Tamias*) as assessed by radiotelemetry and grid trapping. J. Mamm., 69:190–193.

Bergstrom, B. J., and R. S. Hoffmann. 1991. Distribution and diagnosis of three species of chipmunks (*Tamias*) in the Front Range of Colorado. Southwestern Nat., 36:14–28.

Berner, A., and L. W. Gysel. 1967. Raccoon use of large tree cavities and ground burrows. J. Wildl. Mgmt., 31:706–714.

Best, T. L. 1973. Ecological separation of three genera of pocket gophers (Geomyidae). Ecology, 54:1311–1319.

———. 1988. *Dipodomys spectabilis*. Mamm. Species, 311:1–10.

Biggins, D. E., M. H. Schroeder, S. C. Forrest, and L. Richardson. 1986. Activity of radio-tagged black-footed ferrets. Great Basin Nat. Mem., 8:135–140.

Bildstein, K. L. 1983. Why white-tailed deer flag their tails. Amer. Nat., 121:709–715.

Birney, E. C. 1973. Systematics of three species of woodrats (genus *Neotoma*) in central North America. Misc. Publ. Mus. Nat. Hist., Univ. Kansas, 58:1–173.

Birney, E. C., J. K. Jones, Jr., and D. M. Mortimer. 1971. The yellow-faced pocket gopher, *Pappogeomys castanops*, in Kansas. Trans. Kansas Acad. Sci., 73:368–375.

Bishop, R. H., and R. A. Rausch. 1974. Moose population fluctuations in Alaska, 1950–1972. Nat. Canadienne, 101:559–593.

Bissonnette, T. H., and E. E. Bailey. 1944. Experimental modification and control of molts and changes of coat-color in weasels by controlled lighting. Annals New York Acad. Sci., 45:221–260.

Bittner, S. L., and O. J. Rongstad. 1982. Snowshoe hare and allies (*Lepus americanus* and allies). Pp. 146–163, *in* Wild mammals of North America: biology, management, and economics (J. A. Chapman and G. A. Feldhamer, eds.). Johns Hopkins Univ. Press, Baltimore, 1147 pp.

Black, H. L. 1970. Occurrence of the Mexican big-eared bat in Utah. J. Mamm., 51:190.

———. 1974. A north temperate bat community: structure and prey populations. J. Mamm., 55:138–157.

Blair, W. F. 1937. Burrows and food of the prairie pocket mouse. J. Mamm., 18:284–288.

———. 1953. Population dynamics of rodents and other small mammals. Adv. Genetics, 5:1–41.

Blake, B. H. 1972. The annual cycle and fat storage in two populations of golden-mantled ground squirrels. J. Mamm., 53:157–167.

Blake, I. H., and A. K. Blake. 1969. An ecological study of timberline and alpine areas, Mount Lincoln, Park County, Colorado. Univ. Nebraska Studies, New Ser., 40:1–59.

Blood, D. A. 1974. Variation in reproduction and productivity of an enclosed herd of moose (*Alces alces*). Proc. Internat. Congr. Game Biol., 11:59–66.

Bogan, M. A. 1972. Observation on parturition and development in the hoary bat (*Lasiurus cinereus*). J. Mamm., 53:611–614.

417

———. 1974. Identification of *Myotis californicus* and *M. leibii* in southwestern North America. Proc. Biol. Soc. Washington, 87:49–56.

Bogan, M. A., R. B. Finley, Jr., and S. J. Petersburg. 1988. The importance of biological surveys in managing public lands in the western United States. Pp. 254–261, *in* Management of amphibians, reptiles, and small mammals in North America (R. C. Szaro, K. E. Severson, and D. R. Patton, eds.). U.S. Forest Service, General Tech. Rept., RM–166, 458 pp.

Boggs, J. R. 1974. Social ecology of the white-throated woodrat (*Neotoma albigula*) in Arizona. Unpubl. Ph.D. dissertation, Arizona State Univ., Tempe, 134 pp.

Bonaccorso, F. J., and J. H. Brown. 1972. House construction of the desert woodrat, *N. lepida lepida.* J. Mamm., 53:283–288.

Bone, J. R. 1964. The age of the horse. Southwest Vet., 17:269–272.

Bonham, C. D., and A. Lerwick. 1976. Vegetation changes induced by prairie dogs on shortgrass range. J. Range Mgmt., 29:221–225.

Boutin, S. 1979. Spacing behaviour of snowshoe hares in relation to their population dynamics. Unpubl. M.S. thesis, Univ. British Columbia, Vancouver, 141 pp.

Boutin, S., and D. E. Birkenholz. 1986. Muskrat and round-tailed muskrat. Pp. 315–325, *in* Wild furbearer management and conservation in North America (M. Novak, J. A. Baker, M. E. Obbard, and B. Malloch, eds.). Ontario Trappers Assoc., Toronto, 1150 pp.

Boutin, S., B. S. Gilbert, C. J. Krebs, A. R. E. Sinclair, and J. N. M. Smith. 1985. The role of dispersal in the population dynamics of snowshoe hares. Canadian J. Zool., 63:106–115.

Bowen, G. S., et al. 1981. The ecology of Colorado tick fever in Rocky Mountain National Park in 1974. II. Infection in small mammals. Amer. J. Trop. Med. Hyg., 30:490–496.

Bowen, W. D. 1982. Determining age of coyotes, *Canis latrans,* by tooth sections and tooth-wear patterns. Canadian Field-Nat., 96:339–341.

Boyce, M. S. 1981. Beaver life-history responses to exploitation. J. Appl. Ecol., 18:749–753.

———. 1990. The Jackson Elk herd: intensive wildlife management in North America. Cambridge Univ. Press, Cambridge, 320 pp.

Boyce, M. S., and L. D. Hayden-Wing, eds. 1979. North American elk: ecology behavior and management. Univ. Wyoming, Laramie, 294 pp.

Boyd, R. J. 1970. Elk of the White River Plateau, Colorado. Tech. Bull., Colorado Div. Game, Fish, and Parks, 25:1–126.

———. 1978. American elk. Pp. 11–29, *in* Big game of North America: ecology and management (J. L. Schmidt and D. L. Gilbert, eds.). Stackpole Books, Harrisburg, Pennsylvania, 494 pp.

Boyd, R. J., and E. E. Ryland. 1971. Breeding dates of Colorado elk as estimated by fetal growth curves. Game Inf. Leafl., Colorado Div. Game, Fish, and Parks, 88:1–2.

Brach, V. 1969. Some observations on a captive desert shrew, *Notiosorex crawfordi.* Bull. Southern California Acad. Sci., 68:119–120.

Bradley, R. M. 1929. Habits and distribution of the rock squirrel in southern New Mexico. J. Mamm., 10:168–169.

Bradley, W. G. 1967. Home range, activity patterns, and ecology of the antelope ground squirrel in southern Nevada. Southwestern Nat., 12:231–252.

———. 1968. Food habits of the antelope ground squirrel in southern Nevada. J. Mamm., 49:14–21.

Brand, C. J., and L. B. Keith. 1979. Lynx demography during a snowshoe hare decline in Alberta. J. Wildl. Mgmt., 43:827–849.

Brand, C. J., L. B. Keith, and C. A. Fischer. 1976. Lynx responses to changing snowshoe hare densities in central Alberta. J. Wildl. Mgmt., 40:416–428.

Brandborg, S. M. 1955. Life history and management of the mountain goat in Idaho. Wildl. Bull., Idaho Dept. Fish and Game, 2:1–142.

Brassard, J. S., and R. Bernard. 1939. Observations on breeding and development of marten, *Martes a. americana* (Kerr). Canadian Field-Nat., 53:15–21.

Braun, C. E., ed. 1993. Mountain lion–human interaction. Colorado Div. Wildl., 114 pp.

Braun, C. E., and R. G. Streeter. 1968. Observations on the occurrence of white-tailed jackrabbits in the alpine zone. J. Mamm., 49:160–161.

Braun, J. K., and M. A. Mares. 1989. *Neotoma micropus.* Mamm. Species, 330:1–9.

Breakey, D. R. 1963. The breeding season and age structure of feral house mouse populations near San Francisco Bay, California. J. Mamm., 44:153–168.

Brent, J. A. 1983. Colorado mountain lion investigations: Northwest Region. Unpublished report, Colorado Div. Wildl., Grand Junction, 14 pp.

Brewer, W. H. 1871. Animal life in the Rocky Mountains of Colorado. Amer. Nat., 5:220–223.

Bridgewater, D. D. 1966. Laboratory breeding, early growth, development and behavior of *Citellus tridecemlineatus* (Rodentia). Southwestern Nat., 11:325–337.

Bronson, M. T. 1980. Altitudinal variation in emergence time of golden-mantled ground squirrels (*Spermophilus lateralis*). J. Mamm., 61:124–126.

Brown, H. L. 1946. Rodent activity in a mixed prairie near Hays, Kansas. Trans. Kansas Acad. Sci., 48:448–456.

———. 1947. Why has the white-tailed jack rabbit (*Lepus townsendii campanius* Hollister) become scarce in Kansas? Trans. Kansas Acad. Sci., 49:455–456.

Brown, J. H., and R. C. Lasiewski. 1972. Metabolism of weasels: the cost of being long and thin. Ecology, 53:939–943.

Brown, L. G., and L. E. Yeager. 1945. Fox squirrels and gray squirrels in Illinois. Illinois Nat. Hist. Surv. Bull., 23:449–536.

Brown, L. N. 1964. Dynamics in an ecologically isolated population of the brush mouse. J. Mamm., 45:436–442.

———. 1966. First record of the pygmy shrew in Wyoming and description of a new subspecies. Proc. Biol. Soc. Washington, 79:49–52.

———. 1967a. Seasonal activity patterns and breeding of the western jumping mouse (*Zapus princeps*) in Wyoming. Amer. Midland Nat., 78:460–470.

———. 1967b. Ecological distribution of six species of shrews and comparison of sampling methods in the central Rocky Mountains. J. Mamm., 48:617–623.

———. 1968. Smallness of mean litter size in the Mexican vole. J. Mamm., 53:185–187.

———. 1969. Reproductive characteristics of the Mexican woodrat at the northern limit of its range in Colorado. J. Mamm., 50:536–541.

———. 1970. Population dynamics of the western jumping mouse (*Zapus princeps*) during a four-year study. J. Mamm., 51:651–658.

Brown, R. N., C. H. Southwick, and S. C. Golian. 1989. Male-female spacing, territorial replacement, and the mating system of pikas (*Ochotona princeps*). J. Mamm., 70:622–627.

Brownfield, M. S., and B. A. Wunder. 1976. Relative medullary area: a new structural index for estimating urinary concentrating capacity of mammals. Comp. Biochem. Physiol., 55A:69–75.

Buchanan, E. R. 1987. Timing of ovulation and early embryonic development in *Myotis lucifugus* (Chiroptera: Vespertilionidae) from northern central Ontario. Amer. J. Anat., 178:335–340.

Buech, R. R. 1984. Ontogeny and diurnal cycle of fecal reingestion in the North American beaver (*Castor canadensis*). J. Mamm., 65:347–350.

Buechner, H. K. 1960. The bighorn sheep in the United States, its past, present, and future. Wildl. Monogr., 4:1–174.

Burgess, S. A., and J. R. Bider. 1980. Effects of stream habitat improvements on invertebrates, trout populations and mink activity. J. Wildl. Mgmt., 44:871–880.

Burnett, W. L. 1925. Jack rabbits of Colorado with suggestions for their control. Circ. Colorado State Entomol., 48:1–11.

———. 1931. Life history studies of the Wyoming ground squirrel (*Citellus elegans elegans*) in Colorado. Bull. Colorado Agric. Exp. Sta., 373:1–23.

Burnett, W. L., and S. C. McCampbell. 1926. The Zuni prairie dog in Montezuma County, Colorado. Circ. 49, Office of State Entomologist, Colorado Agric. College, Fort Collins, 15 pp.

Burns, J. A., D. L. Flath, and T. W. Clark. 1989. On the structure and function of white-tailed prairie dog burrows. Great Basin Nat., 49:517–524.

Burns, S. F. 1979. The northern pocket gopher (*Thomomys talpoides*) — a major geomorphic agent on the alpine tundra. J. Colorado-Wyoming Acad. Sci., 11:86.

Buskirk, S. W., S. C. Forrest, M. G. Raphael, and H. J. Harlow. 1989. Winter resting site ecology of marten in the central Rocky Mountains. J. Wildl. Mgmt., 53:191–196.

Byrne, A., L. L. Stebbins, and L. Delude. 1978. A new killing technique of the long-tailed weasel. Acta Theriol., 23:127–143.

Caire, W., and R. B. Finley. 1977. The desert shrew *Notiosorex crawfordi* (Coues) from northwestern Colorado. Southwestern Nat., 22:284–285.

Caire, W., J. D. Tyler, B. P. Glass, and M. A. Mares. 1989. Mammals of Oklahoma. Univ. Oklahoma Press, Norman, 567 pp.

Calhoun, J. B. 1962. The ecology and sociology of the Norway rat. U.S. Dept. Health, Education, Welfare, Public Health Serv., Bethesda, 288 pp.

Call, M. W. 1970. Beaver pond ecology and beaver-trout relationships in southeastern Wyoming. Unpubl. Ph.D. dissertation, Univ. Wyoming, Laramie, 204 pp.

Camenzind, F. J. 1974. Territorial and social behavior of coyotes (*Canis latrans*) on the National Elk Refuge, northwestern Wyoming. J. Colorado–Wyoming Acad. Sci., 7(5):56.

———. 1978. Behavioral ecology of coyotes on the National Elk Refuge, Jackson, Wyoming. Pp. 267–294, *in* Coyotes: biology, behavior, and management (M. Bekoff, ed.). Academic Press, New York, 384.

Cameron, G. N. 1973. Effect of litter size on postnatal growth and survival in the desert woodrat. J. Mamm., 54:489–493.

Cameron, G. N., and S. R. Spencer. 1981. *Sigmodon hispidus*. Mamm. Species, 158:1–9.

Cameron, M. W. 1984. The swift fox (*Vulpes velox*) on the Pawnee National Grassland: its food habits, population dynamics and ecology. Unpubl. M.A. thesis, Univ. of Northern Colorado, Greeley, 117 pp.

Campbell, T. M., III, and T. W. Clark. 1981. Colony characteristics and vertebrate associates of white-tailed and black-tailed prairie dogs in Wyoming. Amer. Midland Nat., 105:269–275.

———. 1983. Observation of badger copulatory and agonistic behavior. Southwestern Nat., 28:107–108.

Campbell, T. M., III, T. W. Clark, L. Richardson, S. C. Forrest, and B. R. Houston. 1987. Food habits of Wyoming black-footed ferrets. Amer. Midland Nat., 117:208–210.

Capp, J. C. 1964. Ecology of the bison of Colorado National Monument. U.S. Dept. of Interior, Natl. Park Serv., Washington, 30 pp.

———. 1968. Bighorn sheep, elk, mule deer range relationships. Rocky Mountain Nature Assoc., Estes Park, 75 pp.

Capretta, P. J., R. C. Farentinos, V. M. Littlefield, and R. M. Potter. 1980. Feeding preferences of captive tassel-eared squirrels (*Sciurus aberti*) for ponderosa pine twigs. J. Mamm., 61:734–737.

Carbyn, L. N. 1983. Wolf predation on elk in Riding Mountain National Park, Manitoba. J. Wildl. Mgmt., 47:963–976.

———. 1987. Gray wolf and red wolf. Pp. 358–376, *in* Wild furbearer management and conservation in North America

(M. Novak, J. A. Baker, M. E. Obbard, and B. Malloch, eds.). Ontario Trappers Association, Toronto, 1150 pp.

Carbyn, L. N., and D. Patriquin. 1983. Observations on home range sizes, movements and social organization of lynx, *Lynx canadensis*, in Riding Mountain National Park, Manitoba. Canadian Field-Nat., 97:262–267.

Carey, A. B. 1978. Distributional records for the prairie vole and hispid cotton rat in Colorado. J. Mamm., 59:624.

Carey, A. B., R. G. McLean, and G. O. Maupin. 1980. The structure of a Colorado tick fever ecosystem. Ecol. Monogr., 50:131–151.

Carey, H. V., and P. Moore. 1986. Foraging and predation risk in yellow-bellied marmots. Amer. Midland Nat., 116:267–275.

Carleton, M. D. 1966. Food habits of two sympatric Colorado sciurids. J. Mamm., 47:91–103.

———. 1984. Introduction to rodents. Pp. 255–265 *in* Orders and families of Recent mammals of the world (S. Anderson and J. K. Jones, Jr., eds.). John Wiley and Sons, New York, 686 pp.

———. 1989. Systematics and evolution. Pp. 7–141, *in* Advances in the study of *Peromyscus* (Rodentia). (G. L. Kirkland, Jr., and J. N. Layne, eds.), Texas Tech Univ. Press, Lubbock, 367 pp.

Carleton, M. D., and G. G. Musser. 1984. Muroid rodents. Pp. 289–379 *in* Orders and families of Recent mammals of the world (S. Anderson and J. K. Jones, Jr., eds.). John Wiley and Sons, New York, 686 pp.

Carpenter, J. W., M. J. G. Appel, R. C. Erickson, and M. N. Novilla. 1976. Fatal vaccine-induced canine distemper virus infection in black-footed ferrets. J. Amer. Vet. Med. Assoc., 169:961–964.

Carpenter, J. W., and C. N. Hillman. 1978. Husbandry, reproduction, and veterinary care of captive ferrets. Ann. Proc. Amer. Assoc. Zoo Vet., 1978:36–47.

Carpenter, L. H. 1976. Nitrogen-herbicide effects on sagebrush deer range. Unpubl. Ph.D. dissert., Colorado State Univ., Fort Collins, 159 pp.

Carpenter, L. H., R. B. Gill, D. J. Freddy, and L. E. Sanders. 1979*a*. Distribution and movements of mule deer in Middle Park, Colorado. Spec. Rept., Wildl. Res. Sec., Colorado Div. Wildl., 46:1–32.

Carpenter, L. H., O. C. Wallmo, and R.B. Gill. 1979*b*. Forage diversity and dietary selection by wintering mule deer. J. Range Mgmt., 32:226–229.

Carroll, D., and L. L. Getz. 1976. Runway use and population density of *Microtus ochrogaster*. J. Mamm., 57:772–776.

Carroll, L. E., and H. H. Genoways. 1980. *Lagurus curtatus*. Mamm. Species, 124:1–6.

Cary, M. 1911. A biological survey of Colorado. N. Amer. Fauna, 33:1–256.

Casey, D. E., J. DuWaldt, and T. W. Clark. 1986. Annotated bibliography of the black-footed ferret. Great Basin Nat. Mem., 8:185–208.

Cassells, E. C. 1983. The archaeology of Colorado. Johnson Books, Boulder, 325 pp.

Catlett, R. H., and R. Z. Brown. 1961. Unusual abundance of *Peromyscus* at Gothic, Colorado. J. Mamm., 42:415.

Centers for Disease Control. 1993. Hantavirus infection — southwestern United States: interim recommendations for risk reduction. Morbidity and Mortality Weekly Rept., U.S. Dept. Health and Human Services, Public Health Service, 42 (RR–11):1–12.

Chapman, B. R., and R. L. Packard. 1974. An ecological study of Merriam's pocket mouse in southeastern Texas. Southwestern Nat., 19:281–291.

Chapman, J. A. 1975. *Sylvilagus nuttallii*. Mamm. Species, 56:1–3.

Chapman, J. A., A. L. Harman, and D. E. Samuel. 1977. Reproductive and physiological cycles in the cottontail complex in western Maryland and nearby West Virginia. Wildl. Monogr., 56:1–73.

Chapman, J. A., J. G. Hockman, and M. M. Ojeda. 1980. *Sylvilagus floridanus*. Mamm. Species, 136:1–8.

Chapman, J. A., J. G. Hockman, and W. R. Edwards. 1982. Cottontails. Pp. 83–123, *in* Wild mammals of North America: biology, management, and economics (J. A. Chapman and G. A. Feldhamer, eds.). Johns Hopkins Univ. Press, Baltimore, 1147 pp.

Chapman, J. A., and G. R. Willner. 1978. *Sylvilagus audubonii*. Mamm. Species, 106:1–4.

Chase, J. D., W. E. Howard, and J. T. Roseberry. 1982. Pocket gophers (Geomyidae). Pp. 239–255, *in* Wild mammals of North America: biology, management, and economics (J. A. Chapman, and G. A. Feldhammer, eds.). Johns Hopkins Univ. Press, Baltimore, 1147 pp.

Choate, J. R. 1970. Systematics and zoogeography of Middle American shrews of the genus *Cryptotis*. Univ. Kansas Publ., Mus. Nat. Hist., 19:195–317.

Choate, J. R., and E. D. Fleharty. 1973. Habitat preference and spatial relations of shrews in a mixed grassland in Kansas. Southwestern Nat., 18:110–112.

Choate, J. R., E. D. Fleharty, and R. J. Little. 1974. Status of the spotted skunk, *Spilogale putorius*, in Kansas. Trans. Kansas Acad. Sci., 76:226–233.

Choate, J. R., and J. B. Pinkham. 1988. Armadillos in northeastern Colorado. Prairie Nat., 20:174.

Choate, J. R., and M. P. Reed. 1988. Least shrew, *Cryptotis parva*, in southwestern Kansas and southeastern Colorado. Southwestern Nat., 33:361–362.

Choate, J. R., and S. L. Williams. 1978. Biogeographic interpretation of variation within and among populations of the prairie vole, *Microtus ochrogaster*. Occas. Papers Mus., Texas Tech. Univ., 49:1–25.

Christian, J. J. 1956. The natural history of a summer aggregation of the big brown bat, *Eptesicus fuscus fuscus*. Amer. Midland Nat., 55:66–95.

Chronic, J., and H. Chronic. 1972. Prairie, peak, and plateau: a guide to the geology of Colorado. Colorado Geological Survey Bull., 32:1–126.

Churcher, C. S. 1959. The specific status of the New World red fox. J. Mamm., 40:513–520.

Cincotta, R. P. 1989. Note on mound architecture of the black-tailed prairie dog. Great Basin Nat., 49:621–623.

Cinq-Mars, R. J., and L. N. Brown. 1969. Reproduction and ecological distribution of the rockmouse, *Peromyscus difficilis*, in northern Colorado. Amer. Midland Nat., 81:205–217.

Cinq-Mars, R. J., R. S. Hoffmann, and J. K. Jones, Jr. 1979. New records of the dwarf shrew (*Sorex nanus*) in South Dakota. Prairie Nat., 11:7–9.

Clark, T. W. 1968. Food uses of the Richardson ground squirrel (*Spermophilus richardsoni elegans*) in the Laramie Basin in Wyoming. Southwestern Nat., 13:248–249.

———. 1970. Richardson's ground squirrel (*Spermophilus richardsonii*) in the Laramie Basin, Wyoming. Great Basin Nat., 30:55–70.

———. 1971*a*. Ecology of the western jumping mouse in Grand Teton National Park. Northwest Sci., 45:229–238.

———. 1971*b*. Towards a literature review of prairie dogs. J. Range Mgmt., 236:29–44.

———. 1972. Influence of jackrabbit density on coyote population change. J. Wildl. Mgmt., 36:343–356.

———. 1973. Distribution and reproduction of shrews in Grand Teton National Park, Wyoming. Northwest Sci., 47:128–131.

———. 1977. Ecology and ethology of the white-tailed prairie dog (*Cynomys leucurus*). Milwaukee Public Mus. Publ. Biol. Geology, 3:1–97.

———. 1986. Annotated prairie dog bibliography 1973–1985. Montana Bur. Land Mgmt., Wildl. Tech. Bull., 1:1–32.

———. 1989. Conservation biology of the black-footed ferret *Mustela nigripes*. Spec. Sci. Rept., Wildl. Pres. Trust, 3:1–175.

Clark, T. W., E. Anderson, C. Douglas, and M. Strickland. 1987. Martes americana. Mamm. Species, 289:1–8.

Clark, T. W., M. Bekoff, T. M. Campbell, III, T. Hauptman, and B. D. Roberts. 1989. American marten, *Martes americana*, home ranges in Grand Teton National Park, Wyoming. Canadian Field–Nat., 103:423–425.

Clark, T. W., and T. M. Campbell, III. 1977. Short-term effects of timber harvest on pine marten behavior and ecology. Idaho State Univ., Pocatello, 60 pp.

Clark, T. W., T. M. Campbell, III, and T. N. Hauptman. 1989. Demographic characteristics of American marten populations in Jackson Hole, Wyoming. Great Basin Nat., 49:587–596.

Clark, T. W., T. M. Campbell, III, M. H. Schroeder, and L. Richardson. 1988. Handbook of methods for locating black-footed ferrets. Wildl. Tech. Bull., Wyoming, Bureau of Land Management. 1:1–61.

Clark, T. W., T. M. Campbell, III, D. G. Socha, and D. E. Casey. 1982. Prairie dog colony attributes and associated vertebrate species. Great Basin Nat., 42:572–582.

Clark, T. W., and R. H. Denniston. 1970. On the descriptive ethology of Richardson's ground squirrel. Southwestern Nat., 15:193–200.

Clark, T. W., S. C. Forrest, L. Richardson, D. Casey, and T. M. Campbell, III. 1986. Descriptive ethology and activity patterns of black–footed ferrets. Great Basin Nat. Mem., 8:72–84.

Clark, T. W., D. Hinckley, and T. Rich. 1989. The prairie dog ecosystem: managing for biological diversity. Montana Bur. Land Mgmt., Wildl. Tech. Bull., 2:1–55.

Clark, T. W., R. S. Hoffmann, and C. F. Nadler. 1971. *Cynomys leucurus*. Mamm. Species, 7:1–4.

Clark, T. W., and M. R. Stromberg. 1987. Mammals in Wyoming. Publ. Ed. Ser., Univ. Kansas Mus. Nat. Hist., 10:1–314.

Clark, W. K. 1951. Ecological life history of the armadillo in the eastern plateau region. Amer. Midland Nat., 46:337–358.

Clark, W. R. 1973. Reproduction, survival, and density of snowshoe hares in northeastern Utah. Unpubl. M.S. thesis, Utah State Univ., Logan, 80 pp.

Clothier, R. R. 1955. Contribution to the life history of *Sorex vagrans* in Montana. J. Mamm., 36:214–221.

Coady, J. W. 1982. Moose. Pp. 902–922, *in* Wild mammals of North America, biology, management, and economics (J. A. Chapman and G. A. Feldhamer, eds.). Johns Hopkins Univ. Press, Baltimore, 1147 pp.

Cockrum, E. L. 1952. Mammals of Kansas. Univ. Kansas Publ., Mus. Nat. Hist., 7:1–303.

———. 1955. Reproduction in North American bats. Trans. Kansas Acad. Sci., 58:487–511.

———. 1960. The Recent mammals of Arizona: their taxonomy and distribution. Univ. Arizona Press, Tucson, 276 pp.

Cole, G. 1969. The elk of Grand Teton and southern Yellowstone National Parks. Res. Rept., Natl. Park Serv., U.S. Dept. of Interior, GRTE–N–1:1–192.

Collins, W. B., P. J. Urness, and D. D. Austin. 1978. Elk diets and activities on different lodgepole pine habitat segments. J. Wildl. Mgmt., 42:799–810.

Colorado Department of Agriculture. 1990. Vertebrate rodent infestation survey. Spec. Publ., Colorado Department of Agriculture, 70 pp.

Colorado Division of Wildlife. 1988. Draft river otter recovery plan.

———. 1990. A comparison of resident hunting participation and population trends 1960–1990. Unpublished internal report, Colorado Division of Wildlife, Denver, 21 pp.

Colvin, M. A., and D. V. Colvin. 1970. Breeding and fecundity of size species of voles (*Microtus*). J. Mamm., 51:417–419.

Compton, T. L. 1980. Coyote predation on an adult deer in southwestern Colorado. Southwestern Nat., 25:113–114.

Conaway, C. H. 1952. Life history of the water shrew *Sorex palustris navigator*. Amer. Midland Nat., 48:219–248.

——. 1958. Maintenance, reproduction, and growth of the least shrew in captivity. J. Mamm., 39:507–512.

——. 1959. The reproductive cycle of the eastern mole. J. Mamm., 40:180–194.

Conley, W. 1976. Competition between *Microtus*: a behavioral hypothesis. Ecology, 57:224–237.

Conner, D. A. 1982. Geographic variation in short calls of pikas (*Ochotona princeps*). J. Mamm., 63:48–52.

——. 1983. Seasonal changes in activity patterns and the adaptive value of haying in pikas (*Ochotona princeps*). Canadian J. Zool., 61:411–416.

——. 1984. The role of an acoustic display in territorial maintenance in the pika. Canadian J. Zool., 62:1906–1909.

——. 1985a. Analysis of the vocal repertoire of adult pikas: ecological and evolutionary perspectives. Anim. Behav., 33:124–134.

——. 1985b. The function of the pika short call in individual recognition. Z. Tierpsychol., 67:131–143.

Connolly, G. E. 1981. Trends in populations and harvests. Pp. 225–243, *in* Mule and black-tailed deer of North America (O. C. Wallmo, ed.). Univ. Nebraska Press, Lincoln, 605 pp.

Constantine, D. G. 1961. Gestation period in the spotted skunk. J. Mamm., 42:421–422.

——. 1966. Ecological observations on lasiurine bats in Iowa. J. Mamm., 47:34–41.

Cook, C. W. 1972. Energy budget for rabbits compared to cattle and sheep. Range Sci. Dept. Ser., Colorado State Univ., 13:1–17.

Cook, R. S., M. White, D. O. Trainer, and W. C. Glazener. 1971. Mortality of young white-tailed deer fawns in South Texas. J. Wildl. Mgmt., 35:47–56.

Coppock, D. L., and J. K. Detling. 1986. Alteration of bison and black-tailed prairie dog grazing interaction by prescribed burning. J. Wildl. Mgmt., 50:452–455.

Coppock, D. L., J. K. Detling, J. E. Ellis, and M. I. Dyer. 1983a. Plant herbivore interactions in a North American mixed-grass prairie. I. Effects of black-tailed prairie dogs on interseasonal above ground plant biomass and nutrient dynamics and plant species diversity. Oecologia, 56:1–9.

——. 1983b. Plant herbivore interactions in a North American mixed-grass prairie. II. Responses of bison to modification of vegetation by prairie dogs. Oecologia, 56:10–15.

Cornely, J. E., and R. J. Baker. 1986. *Neotoma mexicana*. Mamm. Species, 262:1–7.

Cornely, J. E., L. N. Carraway, and B. J. Verts. 1992. *Sorex preblei*. Mamm. Species, 416:1–3.

Costello, D. F. 1954. Vegetation zones in Colorado. Pp. iii–x, *in* Manual of the plants of Colorado (by H. D. Harrington). Sage Books, Denver, 666 pp.

——. 1966. The world of the porcupine. J. B. Lippincott Co., Philadelphia, 157 pp.

Coues, E., and J. A. Allen. 1877. Monographs of North American Rodentia. United States Geol. Surv. Terr., 11:1–1099.

Coues, E., and H. C. Yarrow. 1875. Report on the collections of mammals made in portions of Nevada, Utah, California, Colorado, New Mexico, and Arizona, during the years 1871, 1872, 1873, and 1874. . . . Explorations and surveys west of the one hundredth meridian. . . . Wheeler, 5:35–129, 96–979.

Covell, D. F., and O. J. Rongstad. 1990. 1989 annual report, ecology of swift fox on Pinon Canyon Maneuver Site. Environmental, Energy, and Natural Resources Division, Fort Carson, Colorado, 7 pp.

Cowan, I. McT., and G. J. Guiget. 1956. The mammals of British Columbia. Handbook, British Columbia Prov. Mus., 11:1–413.

Cowan, I. McT., and W. McCrory. 1970. Variation in the mountain goat, *Oreamnos americanus* (Blainville). J. Mamm., 51:60–73.

Cowan, W. F. 1973. Ecology and life history of the raccoon (*Procyon lotor hirtus* Nelson and Goldman) in the northern part of its range. Unpubl. Ph.D. dissert., Univ. North Dakota, Grand Forks, 161 pp.

Cowardin, L. M., D. S. Gilmer, and C. W. Shaiffer. 1985. Mallard recruitment in the agricultural environment of North Dakota. Wildl. Monogr., 92:1–37.

Crabb, W. D. 1941. Food habits of the prairie spotted skunk in southeastern Iowa. J. Mamm., 22:349–364.

——. 1944. Growth, development, and seasonal weights of spotted skunks. J. Mamm., 25:213–221.

——. 1948. The ecology and management of the prairie spotted skunk in Iowa. Ecol. Monogr., 18:201–232.

Craig, E. H., and B. L. Keller. 1986. Movements and home range of porcupines, *Erethizon dorsatum*, in Idaho shrub desert. Canadian Field-Nat., 100:168–173.

Craighead, F. C., Jr. 1979. Track of the grizzly. Sierra Club Books, San Francisco, 261 pp.

Craighead, F. C., Jr., and J. J. Craighead. 1972. Grizzly bear prehibernation and denning activities as determined by radiotracking. Wildl. Monogr., 32:1–35.

Craighead, J. J., F. C. Craighead, Jr., and J. Sumner. 1976. Reproductive cycles and rates in the grizzly bear, *Ursus horribilis*, of the Yellowstone ecosystem. Internat. Conf. Bear Research and Mgmt., 3:337–356.

Craighead, J. J., M. G. Hornocker, and F. C. Craighead, Jr. 1969. Reproductive biology of young female grizzly bears. J. Reprod. Fertil. Suppl., 6:447–475.

Craighead, J. J., and J. A. Mitchell. 1982. Grizzly bear. Pp. 515–556, *in* Wild mammals of North America: biology, management, and economics (J. A. Chapman and G. A. Feldhamer, eds.). Johns Hopkins Univ. Press, Baltimore, 1147 pp.

Cranford, J. A. 1978. Hibernation in the western jumping mouse (*Zapus princeps*). J. Mamm., 59:496–509.

Creeden, P. J. 1986. The ecology of desert bighorn sheep in Colorado. Unpubl. M.S. thesis, Colorado State Univ., Fort Collins, 72 pp.

Criddle, S. 1943. The little northern chipmunk in southern Manitoba. Canadian Field-Nat., 57:81–86.

Crowcroft, P., and F. P. Rowe. 1963. Social organization and territorial behavior in the wild house mouse (*Mus musculatus L.*). Proc. Zool. Soc. London, 140:517–531.

Crowe, D. M. 1975. Aspects of aging, growth, and reproduction of bobcats from Wyoming. J. Mamm., 56:177–198.

Crowe, D. M., and D. Strickland. 1975. Population structures of some mammalian predators in southeastern Wyoming. J. Wildl. Mgmt., 39:449–450.

Cruzan, J. 1968. Ecological distributions and interactions of four species of *Microtus* in Colorado. Unpubl. Ph.D. dissert., Univ. Colorado, Boulder, 129 pp.

Currie, P. O., and D. L. Goodwin. 1966. Consumption of forage by black-tailed jackrabbits on salt-desert ranges of Utah. J. Wildl. Mgmt., 30:304–311.

Currier, A., W. D. Kitts, and I. McT. Cowan. 1960. Cellulose digestion in the beaver (*Castor canadensis*). Canadian J. Zool., 38:1109–1116.

Currier, M. J. P. 1976. Characteristics of the mountain lion population near Canon City, Colorado. Unpubl. M.S. thesis, Colorado State Univ., Fort Collins, 81 pp.

———. 1983. *Felis concolor*. Mamm. Species, 200:1–7.

Currier, M. J. P., S. L. Sheriff, and K. R. Russell. 1977. Mountain lion population and harvest near Canon City, Colorado, 1974–1977. Spec. Rept., Colorado Div. Wildl. and Coop. Wildl. Research Unit, 42:1–12.

Curtis, J. D. 1941. The silvicultural significance of the porcupine. J. Forestry, 39:583–594.

———. 1944. Appraisal of porcupine damage. J. Wildl. Mgmt., 8:88–91.

Cutter, W. L. 1958a. Denning of the swift fox in northern Texas. J. Mamm., 39:70–74.

———. 1958b. Food habits of the swift fox in northern Texas. J. Mamm., 39:527–532.

Czaplewski, N. J. 1983. *Idionycteris phyllotis*. Mamm. Species, 208:1–4.

Czelusniak, J., et al. 1990. Perspectives from amino acid and nucleotide sequences on cladistic relationships among higher taxa of Eutheria. Current Mammalogy, 2:545–572.

Dahlsted, K. J., S. Sather-Blair, B. K. Worcester, and R. Klukas. 1981. Application of remote sensing to prairie dog management. J. Range Mgmt., 34:218–223.

Dailey, T. V., N. T. Hobbs, and T. N. Woodward. 1984. Experimental comparisons of diet selection by mountain goats and mountain sheep in Colorado. J. Wildl. Mgmt., 48:799–806.

Dalquest, W. W. 1947. Notes on the natural history of the bat, *Myotis yumanensis*, in California, with a description of a new race. Amer. Midland Nat., 38:224–247.

———. 1975. The montane vole in northeastern New Mexico and adjacent Colorado. Southwestern Nat., 20:138–139.

Daly, J. C., and J. L. Patton. 1986. Growth, reproduction, and sexual dimorphism in *Thomomys bottae* pocket gophers. J. Mamm., 67:256–265.

Dartt, M. 1879. On the plains and among the peaks, or how Mrs. Maxwell made her natural history collection. Claxton, Remsen and Haffelfinger, Philadelphia, 225 pp.

Dasmann, R. F. 1966. Wildlife and the new conservation. Wildl. Soc. News, 105:48–49.

Davidow-Henry, B. R., J. K. Jones, Jr., and R. R. Hollander. 1989. *Cratogeomys castanops*. Mamm. Species, 338:1–6.

Davis, A. H., Jr. 1966. Winter activity of the black-tailed prairie dog in north-central Colorado. Unpubl. M.S. thesis, Colorado State Univ., Fort Collins, 46 pp.

Davis, R., and S. J. Bissell. 1989. Distribution of Abert's squirrel (*Sciurus aberti*) in Colorado: evidence for a recent expansion of range. Southwest Nat., 34:306–309.

Davis, R., and D. E. Brown. 1989. Role of post-Pleistocene dispersal in determining the modern distribution of Abert's squirrel. Great Basin Nat., 49:425–434.

Davis, W. B. 1942. The moles of Texas. Amer. Midland Nat., 27:380–386.

———. 1974. The mammals of Texas. Bull., Texas Parks and Wildl. Dept., 41:1–294.

Davis, W. H., and R. W. Barbour. 1970. Life history data on some southwestern *Myotis*. Southwestern Nat., 15:261–263.

Deardon, L. C. 1969. Burrows of the pallid vole, *Lagurus curtatus*, in Alberta, Canada. Canadian Field-Nat., 83:282.

DeBlase, A. F., and R. E. Martin. 1981. A manual of mammalogy with keys to families of the world. Wm. C. Brown, Dubuque, 436 pp.

DeCalesta, D. S. 1971. Colorado cottontail foods. Unpubl. M.S. thesis, Colorado State Univ., Fort Collins, 71 pp.

Decker, D. J. 1989. Why manage for wildlife: an overview of wildlife values. Pp. 1–13, *in* Timber management and its effects on wildlife (J. C. Finley and M. C. Brittingham, eds.). Proc. 1989 Pennsylvania State Forest Resources Issues Conf., School of Forestry Resources, and Pennsylvania State Coop. Extension, Pennsylvania State Univ., College Park, 269 pp.

Decker, D. J., and G. R. Goff, eds. 1987. Valuing wildlife: economic and social perspectives. Westview Press, Boulder, 424 pp.

Decker, D. J., and K. G. Purdy. 1988. Toward a concept of wildlife acceptance capacity in wildlife management. Wildl. Soc. Bull., 16:53–57.

Deems, E. F., Jr., and D. Pursley. 1983. North American furbearers, a contemporary reference. International Assoc. Fish Wildl. Agencies, 223 pp.

Deming, O. V. 1952. Tooth development of the Nelson bighorn sheep. California Fish and Game, 38:523–529.

DeMott, S. L., and G. P. Lindsey. 1975. Pygmy shrew, *Microsorex hoyi*, in Gunnison County, Colorado. Southwestern Nat., 20:417–418.

Denney, R. N. 1952. A summary of North American beaver management, 1946–1948. Current Rept., Colorado Game and Fish Dept., 28:1–58.

———. 1975. The status of lynx in Colorado. Colorado Division of Wildlife, Denver, mimeo, 2 pp.

———. 1977. The status and management of mountain goats in Colorado. Pp. 29–36, *in* Proc. First Internat. Mountain Goat Symp. (W. Samuel and W. G. MacGregor, eds.). Fish and Wildl. Branch, British Columbia, 243 pp.

Denniston, R. H. 1956. Ecology, behavior and population dynamics of the Wyoming or Rocky Mountain moose, *Alces alces shirasi*. Zoologica, 41:105–118.

Denniston, R. M., II. 1957. Notes on breeding and size of young in the Richardson's ground squirrel. J. Mamm., 38:414–416.

Desha, P. G. 1966. Observations on the burrow utilization of thirteen-lined ground squirrels. Southwestern Nat., 11:408–410.

Devenport, J. A. 1989. Social influences on foraging in black-tailed prairie dogs. J. Mamm., 70:166–168.

Dice, L. R. 1943. The biotic provinces of North America. Univ. Michigan Press, Ann Arbor, 78 pp.

Diersing, V. E. 1980. Systematics and evolution of the pygmy shrews (Subgenus *Microsorex*) of North America. J. Mamm., 61:76–101.

Diersing, V. E., and D. F. Hoffmeister. 1977. Revision of the shrew *Sorex merriami* and a description of a new species of the subgenus *Sorex*. J. Mamm., 58:321–333.

Dieter, C. D., and T. R. McCabe. 1989. Factors influencing beaver lodge-site selection on a prairie river. Amer. Midland Nat., 122:408–411.

Dietz, D. R., R. H. Udall, and L. E. Yeager. 1962. Chemical composition and digestibility by mule deer of selected forage species, Cache la Poudre range, Colorado. Tech. Publ., Colorado Game and Fish Dept., 14:1–89.

Dixon, J. 1931. Pikas versus weasel. J. Mamm., 12:72.

Dixon, K. R. 1982. Mountain lion. Pp. 711–727, *in* Wild mammals of North America: biology, management, and economics (J. A. Chapman and G. A. Feldhamer, eds.). Johns Hopkins Univ. Press, Baltimore, 1147 pp.

Dixon, K. R., and R. J. Boyd. 1967. Evaluation of the effects of mountain lion predation. Job Completion Rept., Proj. W–38–R–21. Colorado Game, Fish and Parks Dept., Fort Collins, 23 pp.

Dobie, J. F. 1961. The voice of the coyote. Univ. Nebraska Press, Lincoln, 386 pp.

Dodge, W. E. 1982. Porcupine. Pp. 355–366, *in* Wild mammals of North America: biology, management, and economics (J. A. Chapman and G. A. Feldhamer, eds.). John Hopkins Univ. Press, Baltimore, 1147 pp.

Dolbeer, R. A. 1973. Reproduction in the red squirrel (*Tamiasciurus hudsonicus*) in Colorado. J. Mamm., 54:536–540.

Dolbeer, R. A., and W. R. Clark. 1975. Population ecology of snowshoe hares in the central Rocky Mountains. J. Wildl. Mgmt., 39:535–549.

Donoho, H. S. 1972. Dispersion and dispersal of white-tailed and black-tailed jackrabbits, Pawnee National Grasslands. Unpubl. M.S. thesis, Colorado State Univ., Fort Collins, 83 pp.

———. 1977. The status and management of the bobcat in Colorado. Unpubl. rept., Colorado Div. Wildl., Denver, 6 pp.

Dorrance, M. J. 1965. Behavior of mule deer in the Cache La Poudre drainage. Unpubl. M.S. thesis, Colorado State Univ., Fort Collins, 76 pp.

Douglas, C. L. 1967. New records of mammals from Mesa Verde National Park, Colorado. J. Mamm., 48:322–323.

———. 1969*a*. Ecology of pocket gophers in Mesa Verde, Colorado. Pp. 147–175, *in* Contrib. in Mammalogy (J. K. Jones, Jr., ed.). Misc. Publ. Mus. Nat. Hist., Univ. Kansas, 51:428.

———. 1969*b*. Comparative ecology of piñon mice and deer mice in Mesa Verde National Park, Colorado. Misc. Publ. Mus. Nat. Hist., Univ. Kansas, 18:421–504.

Douglas, C. W., and M. A. Strickland. 1987. Fisher. Pp. 510–529, *in* Wild furbearer management and conservation in North America. (M. Novak, J. A. Baker, M. E. Obbard, and B. Malloch, eds.). Ontario Trappers Association, Toronto, 1150 pp.

Douglass, R. J. 1976. Spatial interactions and microhabitat selections of two locally sympatric voles, *Microtus montanus* and *Microtus pennsylvanicus*. Ecology, 57:346–352.

Dow, S. A., Jr., and P.L. Wright. 1962. Changes in mandibular dentition associated with age in pronghorn antelope. J. Wildl. Mgmt., 26:1–18.

Downhower, J. F., and K. B. Armitage. 1971. The yellow-bellied marmot and the evolution of polygamy. Amer. Nat., 105:355–370.

Downhower, J. F., and E. R. Hall. 1966. The pocket gopher in Kansas. Misc. Publ. Univ. Kansas Mus. Nat. Hist., 44:1–32.

Dragoo, J. W., J. R. Choate, T. L. Yates, and T. P. O'Farrell. 1990. Evolutionary and taxonomic relationships among North American arid-land foxes. J. Mamm., 71:318–332.

Drickamer, L. C., and M. R. Capone. 1977. Weather parameters, trappability and niche separation in two sympatric species of *Peromyscus*. Amer. Midland Nat., 98:376–381.

Druecker, J. D. 1972. Aspects of reproduction in *Myotis volans*, *Lasionycteris noctivagans*, and *Lasiurus cinereus*. Unpubl. Ph.D. dissert., Univ. New Mexico, Albuquerque, 68 pp.

Duke, K. L. 1944. The breeding season of two species of *Dipodomys*. J. Mamm., 25:155–160.

———. 1951. The external genitalia of the pika, *Ochotona princeps*. J. Mamm., 32:169–173.

Dunford, C. 1974. Annual cycle of cliff chipmunks in the Santa Catalina Mountains, Arizona. J. Mamm., 55:401–415.

Dunford, C., and R. Davis. 1975. Cliff chipmunk vocalizations and their relevance to the taxonomy of coastal sonoran chipmunks. J. Mamm., 56:207–212.

Dunigan, P. F. X., Jr., W. Lei, and W. H. Rickard. 1980. Pocket mouse population response to winter precipitation and drought. Northwest Sci., 54:289–295.

Dunn, J. P., J. A. Chapman, and R. E. Marsh. 1982. Jackrabbits. Pp. 124–145, *in* Wild mammals of North America: biology, management, and economics (J. A. Chapman and G. A.

Feldhamer, eds.). Johns Hopkins Univ. Press, Baltimore, 1147 pp.

Duran, J. C. 1973. Field investigations and energy determination of stomach contents of *Peromyscus boylii* in the Granite Basin Area, Yavapai County, Arizona. Unpubl. Ph.D. dissert., Univ. Northern Colorado, Greeley, 62 pp.

Durrant, S. D. 1952. Mammals of Utah: taxonomy and distribution. Univ. Kansas Publ., Mus. Nat. Hist., 6:1–549.

Eagle, T. C., and J. S. Whitman. 1987. Mink. Pp. 613–624, *in* Wild furbearer management and conservation in North America (M. Novak, J.A. Baker, M.E. Obbard, and B. Malloch, eds.). Ontario Trappers Association, Toronto, 1150 pp.

Earle, R. D., and K. R. Kramm. 1980. Techniques for age determination in the Canadian porcupine. J. Wildl. Mgmt., 44:413–419.

Easterla, D. A. 1973. Ecology of the 18 species of Chiroptera at Big Bend National Park, Texas. Northwest Missouri State Univ. Studies, 34:1–165.

Easterla, D. A., and J. O. Whitaker, Jr. 1972. Food habits of some bats from Big Bend National Park, Texas. J. Mamm., 53:887–890.

Eberhardt, L. E., and A. B. Sargeant. 1977. Mink predation on prairie marshes during the waterfowl breeding season. Pp. 33–43, *in* Proceedings 1975 Predator Symposium (R. L. Phillips and C. Jonkel, eds.). Montana Forest Conservation Exp. Sta., Univ. Montana, Missoula, 103 pp.

Ecke, D. H., and C. W. Johnson. 1952. Plague in Colorado. Part I. Plague in Colorado and Texas. U.S. Public Health Serv., Publ. Health Monogr., 6:1–54.

Egoscue, H. J. 1956. Preliminary studies of the kit fox in Utah. J. Mamm., 37:351–357.

———. 1957. The desert wood rat: a laboratory colony. J. Mamm., 38:472–481.

———. 1960. Laboratory and field studies of the northern grasshopper mouse. J. Mamm., 41:99–110.

———. 1962*a*. Ecology and life history of the kit fox in Tooele County, Utah. Ecology, 43:481–497.

———. 1962*b*. The bushy-tailed wood rat: a laboratory colony. J. Mamm., 43:328–337.

———. 1964*a*. The kit fox in southwestern Colorado. Southwestern Nat., 9:40.

———. 1964*b*. Ecological notes and laboratory life history of the canyon mouse. J. Mamm., 45:387–396.

———. 1965. Population dynamics of the kit fox in western Utah. Bull. So. California Acad. Sci., 74:122–127.

———. 1979. *Vulpes velox*. Mamm. Species, 122:1–5.

Egoscue, H. J., J. G. Bittmenn, and J. A. Petrovich. 1970. Some fecundity and longevity records for captive small mammals. J. Mamm., 51:622–623.

Ehrenfeld, D. W. 1974. The conservation of non-resources. Amer. Sci., 64:648–656.

Eisenberg, J. F. 1962. Studies on the social behavior of heteromyid rodents. Unpubl. Ph.D. dissert., Univ. California, Berkeley, 225 pp.

———. 1964. Studies on the behavior of *Sorex vagrans*. Amer. Midland Nat., 72:417–425.

———. 1981. The mammalian radiations. Univ. Chicago Press, Chicago, 610 pp.

Eisenberg, J. F., and D. E. Isaac. 1963. The reproduction of heteromyid rodents in captivity. J. Mamm., 44:61–67.

Ellerman, J. R. 1940. The families and genera of living rodents, Vol. I. British Museum (Natural History), London, 689 pp.

Ellinwood, S. R. 1978. A survey of bats of southeast Colorado. Unpubl. M.S. thesis, Univ. Northern Colorado, Greeley, 77 pp.

Ellis, R. J. 1964. Tracking raccoons by radio. J. Wildl. Mgmt., 28:363–368.

Enders, A. C. 1966. The reproductive cycle of the nine-banded armadillo (*Dasypus novemcinctus*). Pp. 295–310, *in* Comparative biology of reproduction in mammals (I. W. Rowlands, ed.). Academic Press, London, 559 pp.

Enders, R. K. 1952. Reproduction in the mink (*Mustela vison*). Proc. Amer. Phil. Soc., 96:691–755.

Erickson, K. A., and A. W. Smith. 1985. Atlas of Colorado. Colorado Assoc. Univ. Press, Boulder, 73 pp.

Erlinge, S. 1979. Adaptive significance of sexual dimorphism in weasels. Oikos, 33:233–245.

Errington, P.L. 1940. Natural restocking of muskrat-vacant habitat. J. Wildl. Mgmt., 4:173–185.

———. 1943. An analysis of mink predation upon muskrats in north-central United States. Research Bull., Agric. Exp. Sta., Iowa State Coll., 320:798–924.

———. 1963. Muskrat populations. Iowa State Univ. Press, Ames, 665 pp.

Esch, G. W., R. G. Beidleman, and L. E. Long. 1959. Early breeding of the black-tailed jack rabbit in southeastern Colorado. J. Mamm., 40:442–443.

Ewer, R. F. 1973. The carnivores. Cornell Univ. Press, Ithaca, 494 pp.

Fagerstone, K. A. 1979. Food habits of the black-tailed prairie dog (*Cynomys ludovicianus*). Unpubl. MA thesis, Univ. Colorado, Boulder, 160 pp.

———. 1982. Ethology and taxonomy of Richardson's ground squirrel (*Spermophilus richardsonii*). Unpubl. Ph.D. dissert., Univ. Colorado, Boulder, 298 pp.

———. 1987*a*. Comparison of vocalizations between and within *Spermophilus elegans elegans* and *S. richardsoni*. J. Mamm., 68:853–857.

———. 1987*b*. Black-footed ferret, long-tailed weasel, short-tailed weasel, and least weasel. Pp. 548–573, *in* Wild furbearer management and conservation in North America (M. Novak, J. A. Baker, M. E. Obbard, and B. Malloch, eds.). Ontario Trappers Association, Toronto, 1150 pp.

———. 1988. The annual cycle of Wyoming ground squirrels in Colorado. J. Mamm., 69:678–687.

Fagerstone, K. A., G. K. Lavoie, and R. E. Griffith, Jr. 1980. Black-tailed jackrabbit diet and density on rangeland and near agricultural crops. J. Range Mgmt., 33:229–233.

Farentinos, R. C. 1972a. Observations on the ecology of the tassel-eared squirrel. J. Wildl. Mgmt., 36:1234–1239.

———. 1972b. Social dominance and mating activity in the tassel-eared squirrel (Sciurus aberti ferreus). Anim. Behav., 20:316–326.

———. 1972c. Nests of the tassel-eared squirrel. J. Mamm., 53:900–903.

———. 1974. Social communication of the tassel-eared squirrel (Sciurus aberti): a descriptive analysis. Z. Tierpsychol., 34:441–458.

———. 1979. Seasonal changes in home range size of tassel-eared squirrels (Sciurus aberti). Southwestern Nat., 24:49–62.

———. 1980. Sexual solicitation of subordinate males by female tassel-eared squirrels (Sciurus aberti). J. Mamm., 61:337–341.

Feldhamer, G. A. 1979. Vegetative and edaphic factors influencing abundance and distribution of small mammals in southeast Oregon. Great Basin Nat., 39:207–218.

Fenneman, N. M. 1931. Physiography of western United States. McGraw-Hill, New York, 534 pp.

Fenton, M. B. 1983. Just bats. Univ. Toronto Press, Toronto, 165 pp.

———. 1985. Communication in the Chiroptera. Indiana Univ. Press, Bloomington, 161 pp.

Fenton, M. B., and R. M. R. Barclay. 1980. Myotis lucifugus. Mamm. Species, 142:1–8.

Fenton, M. B., and G. P. Bell. 1979. Echolocation and feeding in four species of Myotis (Chiroptera). Canadian J. Zool., 57:1271–1277.

———. 1981. Recognition of species of insectivorous bats by their echolocation calls. J. Mamm., 62:233–243.

Fenton, M. B., P. Racey, and J. M. V. Rayner, eds. 1987. Recent advances in the study of bats. Cambridge Univ. Press, Cambridge, 470 pp.

Fenton, M. B., C. G. van Zyll de Jong, G. P. Bell, D. B. Campbell, and M. Laplante. 1980. Distribution, parturition dates, and feeding of bats in south-central British Columbia. Canadian Field-Nat., 94:416–420.

Ferguson, M. A. D., and H. G. Merriam. 1978. A winter feeding relationship between snowshoe hares and porcupines. J. Mamm., 59:878–880.

Ferner, J. W. 1974. Habitat relationships of Tamiasciurus hudsonicus and Sciurus aberti in the Rocky Mountains. Southwestern Nat., 18:470–472.

Feuerstein, V., R. L. Schmidt, C. P. Hibler, and W. H. Rutherford. 1980. Bighorn sheep mortality in the Taylor River–Almont Triangle area, 1978–1979: a case study. Spec. Rept., Colorado Div. Wildl., 48:1–19.

Field, R. J., and G. Feltner. 1974. Wolverine. Colorado Outdoors, 23:1–6.

Findley, J. S. 1955. Speciation of the wandering shrew. Univ. Kansas Publ., Mus. Nat. Hist., 9:1–68.

———. 1956. Comments on the winter food of red foxes in eastern South Dakota. J. Wildl. Mgmt., 20:216–217.

———. 1967. Insectivores and dermopterans. Pp. 87–103, in Recent mammals of the world (S. Anderson and J. K. Jones, Jr., eds.). Ronald Press Co., New York, 453 pp.

———. 1987. The natural history of New Mexican mammals. Univ. New Mexico Press, Albuquerque, 164 pp.

Findley, J. S., and S. Anderson. 1956. Zoogeography of montane mammals of Colorado. J. Mamm., 37:80–82.

Findley, J. S., A. H. Harris, D. E. Wilson, and C. Jones. 1975. Mammals of New Mexico. Univ. New Mexico Press, Albuquerque, 360 pp.

Findley, J. S., and C. Jones. 1964. Seasonal distribution of the hoary bat. J. Mamm., 45:461–470.

Finley, R. B., Jr. 1954. Notiosorex crawfordi and Antrozous pallidus from southeastern Colorado. J. Mamm., 35:110–111.

———. 1958. The woodrats of Colorado: distribution and ecology. Univ. Kansas Publ., Mus. Nat. Hist., 10:213–552.

———. 1959. Observation of nocturnal animals by red light. J. Mamm., 40:591–594.

———. 1969. Cone caches and middens of Tamiasciurus in the Rocky Mountain region. Misc. Publ. Mus. Nat. Hist., Univ. Kansas, 51:233–273.

Finley, R. B., Jr., W. Caire, and D.E. Wilhelm. 1983. Bats of the Colorado oil shale region. Great Basin Nat., 43:554–560.

Finley, R. B., Jr., J. R. Choate, and D. F. Hoffmeister. 1986. Distributions and habitats of voles in southeastern Colorado and northeastern New Mexico. Southwestern Nat., 31:263–266.

Finley, R. B., Jr., and J. Creasy. 1982. First specimen of the spotted bat (Euderma maculatum) from Colorado. Great Basin Nat., 42:360.

Finley, R. B., Jr., D. E. Wilhelm, Jr., and W. Caire. 1976. Mammals of the Colorado oil shale region. Annual progress report. Natl. Fish Wildl. Lab., U.S. Fish Wildl. Serv., Fort Collins, 49 pp.

Finney, B. A. 1962. Re-examination of small mammal populations in Moon Gulch, Gilpin County, Colorado. J. Colorado-Wyoming Acad. Sci., 5(3):42.

Fitch, H. S., P. Goodrum, and C. Newman. 1952. The armadillo in the southeastern U.S. J. Mamm., 33:21–37.

Fitch, H. S., and D. G. Rainey. 1956. Ecological observations on the woodrat, Neotoma floridana. Univ. Kansas Publ., Mus. Nat. Hist., 8:499–533.

Fitch, H. S., and L. L. Sandidge. 1953. Ecology of the opossum on a natural area in northeastern Kansas. Univ. Kansas Publ., Mus. Nat. Hist., 7:305–338.

Fitch, H. S., and H. W. Shirer. 1970. A radiotelemetric study of spatial relationships in the opossum. Amer. Midland Nat., 84:170–186.

Fitzgerald, B. M. 1977. Weasel predation on a cyclic population of the montane vole (*Microtus montanus*) in California. J. Anim. Ecol., 46:367–397.

Fitzgerald, J. P. 1970. The ecology of plague in prairie dogs and associated small mammals in South Park, Colorado. Unpubl. Ph.D. dissert., Colorado State Univ., Fort Collins, 123 pp.

———. 1978. Vertebrate associations in plant communities along the South Platte River in northeastern Colorado. Pp. 73–88, *in* Lowland river and stream habitat in Colorado: a symposium (W. D. Graul and S. J. Bissell, eds.), Colorado Chapter, Wildlife Soc. and Colorado Audubon Council, 195 pp.

———. 1993. The ecology of plague in Gunnison's prairie dogs and suggestions for the recovery of black-footed ferrets. Pp. 50–59, *in* Proceedings of the Symposium on the Management of Prairie Dog Complexes for the Reintroduction of the Black-footed Ferret (J. L. Oldemeyer, D. E. Biggins, B. J. Miller, and R. Crete, eds.). Biol. Rept., U.S. Fish Wildl. Serv., 93(13):1–96.

Fitzgerald, J. P., and R. R. Lechleitner. 1969. Sylvatic plague in Gunnison's prairie dogs and associated mammals in South Park, Colorado. J. Colorado–Wyoming Acad. Sci., 7:45.

———. 1974. Observations on the biology of Gunnison's prairie dog in central Colorado. Amer. Midland Nat., 92:146–163.

Fitzgerald, J. P., D. Taylor, and M. Prendergast. 1989. New records of bats from northeastern Colorado. J. Colorado-Wyoming Acad. Sci., 21:22.

Fitzpatrick, F. L. 1925. The ecology and economic status of *Citellus tridecemlineatus*. Studies Nat. Hist., Iowa State Univ., 11:1–40.

Flake, L. D. 1973. Food habits of four species of rodents on a short-grass prairie in Colorado. J. Mamm., 54:636–647.

———. 1974. Reproduction of four rodent species in a short-grass prairie of Colorado. J. Mamm., 55:213–216.

Fleharty, E. D., and J. R. Choate. 1973. Bioenergetic strategies of the cotton rat, *Sigmodon hispidus*. J. Mamm., 54:680–692.

Fleharty, E. D., J. R. Choate, and M. A. Mares. 1972. Fluctuations in population density of the hispid cotton rat: factors influencing a "crash." Bull. Southern California Acad. Sci., 71:132–138.

Fleharty, E. D., and M. A. Mares. 1973. Habitat preference and spatial relations of *Sigmodon hispidus* on a remnant prairie in west-central Kansas. Southwestern Nat., 18:21–29.

Fleharty, E. D., and L. E. Olson. 1969. Summer food habits of *Microtus ochrogaster* and *Sigmodon hispidus*. J. Mamm., 50:475–486.

Flinders, J. T., and R. M. Hansen. 1972. Diets and habitats of jackrabbits in northeastern Colorado. Sci. Ser., Range Sci. Dept., Colorado State Univ., 12:1–29.

———. 1973. Abundance and dispersion of leporids within a shortgrass ecosystem. J. Mamm., 54:287–291.

———. 1975. Spring population responses of cottontails and jackrabbits to cattle grazing shortgrass prairie. J. Range Mgmt., 28:290–293.

Flook, P. R. 1970. Causes and implications of an observed sex differential in the survival of wapiti. Canadian Wildl. Serv. Rept., Ser., 11:1–71.

Flyger, V. F., and J. E. Gates. 1982. Pine squirrels: *Tamiasciurus hudsonicus* and *T. douglassi*. Pp. 230–238, *in* Wild mammals of North America: biology, management, and economics (J. A. Chapman, and G. A. Feldhamer, eds.). Johns Hopkins Univ. Press, Baltimore, 1147 pp.

Flyger, V. F., and E. Y. Levin. 1977. Congenital erythropoietic porphyria: normal porphyria of fox squirrels (*Sciurus niger*). Amer. J. Pathol., 87:269–272.

Folk, G. E., J. M. Hunt, and M. A. Folk. 1977. Hibernating bears: further evidence and bioenergetics. Proc. 4th Internat. Conf. Bear Res. and Mgmt., Kalispell, Montana.

Forbes, R. B. 1964*a*. Notes on food of silky pocket mice. J. Mamm., 43:278–279.

———. 1964*b*. Some aspects of the life history of the silky pocket mouse *Perognathus flavus*. Amer. Midland Nat., 72:438–443.

Foresman, K. R., and R. A. Mead. 1973. Duration of post implantation in a western subspecies of the spotted skunk (*Spilogale putorius*). J. Mamm., 54:521–523.

Formanowicz, D. R., Jr., P. J. Bradley, and E. D. Brodie, Jr. 1989. Food hoarding by the least shrew (*Cryptotis parva*): intersexual and prey type effects. Amer. Midland Nat., 122:26–33.

Forrest, S. C., et al. 1988. Black-footed ferret (*Mustela nigripes*) population attributes at Meeteetse, Wyoming, 1981–1985. J. Mamm., 69:261–273.

Forrest, S. C., T. W. Clark, L. Richardson, D. Biggins, K. Fagerstone, and T. M. Campbell, III. 1985. Life history characteristics of the genus *Mustela*, with special reference to the black-footed ferret, *Mustela nigripes*. Pp 23.1–23.14, *in* Black-footed ferret (S.H. Anderson and D.B. Inkley, eds.). Workshop Proc., Wyoming Game and Fish Dept., Laramie.

Forsyth, D. J. 1976. A field study of growth and development of nestling masked shrews (*Sorex cinereus*). J. Mamm., 57:708–721.

Foster, J. B. 1961. Life history of the *Phenacomys* vole. J. Mamm., 42:181–198.

Foster, M. A., and J. Stubbendieck. 1980. Effects of the plains pocket gopher (*Geomys bursarius*) on rangeland. J. Range Mgmt., 33:74–78.

Franzen, R. W. 1968. The abundance, migration and management of mule deer in Dinosaur National Monument. Unpubl. M.S. thesis, Utah State Univ., Logan, 138 pp.

Franzmann, A. W. 1978. Moose. Pp. 67–82, *in* Big game of North America: ecology and management (J.L. Schmidt and D. L. Gilbert, eds.). Stackpole Books, Harrisburg, Pennsylvania, 494 pp.

———. 1981. *Alces alces*. Mamm. Species, 154:1–7.

Franzmann, A. W., C. C. Schwartz, and R. O. Peterson. 1980. Moose calf mortality in summer on the Kenai Peninsula. J. Wildl. Mgmt., 44:764–768.

Frase, B. A., and R. S. Hoffmann. 1980. *Marmota flaviventris*. Mamm. Species, 135:1–8.

Freddy, D. J. 1987. The White River elk herd: a perspective, 1960–85. Tech. Publ., Colorado Div. Wildl., 37:1–64.

Freeman, G. E. 1981. Distributional records of bats of western Colorado. J. Colorado-Wyoming Acad. Sci., 13:50.

———. 1984. Ecomorphological analysis of an assemblage of bats: resource partitioning and competition. Unpubl. Ph.D. dissert., Univ. Colorado, Boulder, 131 pp.

Freeman, G. E., and L. Wunder. 1988. Observations at a colony of the Brazilian free-tailed bat (*Tadarida brasiliensis*) in southern Colorado. Southwestern Nat., 33:102–103.

Friedrichsen, T. T. 1977. Responses of rodent populations to visitors in a national park. Unpubl. M.S. thesis, Colorado State Univ., Fort Collins, 98 pp.

Fritzell, E. K. 1977. Dissolution of raccoon sibling bonds. J. Mamm., 58:427–428.

———. 1978*a*. Aspects of raccoon (*Procyon lotor*) social organization. Canadian J. Zool., 56:260–271.

———. 1978*b*. Habitat use by prairie raccoons during the waterfowl breeding season. J. Wildl. Mgmt., 42:118–127.

———. 1987. Gray fox and island gray fox. Pp. 408–420, *in* Wild furbearer management and conservation in North America (M. Novak, J. A. Baker, M. E. Obard, and B. Malloch, eds.). Ontario Trappers Association, Toronto, 1150 pp.

Fritzell, E. K., and K. J. Haroldson. 1982. *Urocyon cinereoargenteus*. Mamm. Species, 189:1–8.

Fujita, M. S., and T. H. Kunz. 1984. *Pipistrellus subflavus*. Mamm. Species, 228:1–6.

Fuller, T. K. 1978. Variable home range sizes of female gray foxes. J. Mamm., 59:446–449.

Fuller, W. A. 1959. The horns and teeth as indicators of age in bison. J. Wildl. Mgmt., 23:342–344.

Gaines, M. S. 1985. Genetics. Pp. 845–883, *in* Biology of New World *Microtus* (R. H. Tamarin, ed.). Spec. Publ., Amer. Soc. Mammalogists, 8:1–893.

Gaines, M. S., and R. K. Rose. 1976. Population dynamics of *Microtus ochrogaster* in eastern Kansas. Ecology, 57:1145–1161.

Galatowitsch, S. M. 1990. Using the original land survey notes to reconstruct presettlement landscapes in the American West. Great Basin Nat., 50:181–191.

Galbreath, G. J. 1982. Armadillo. Pp. 71–79, *in* Wild mammals of North America: biology, management, and economics (J. A. Chapman and G. A. Feldhamer, eds.). Johns Hopkins Univ. Press, Baltimore, 1,147 pp.

Gardner, A. L. 1982. Virginia opossum. Pp. 3–36, *in* Wild mammals of North America: biology, management, and economics (J. A. Chapman and G. A. Feldhamer, eds.). Johns Hopkins Univ. Press, Baltimore, 1,147 pp.

Garner, H. W. 1967. An ecological study of the brush mouse, *Peromyscus boylii*, in western Texas. Texas J. Sci., 19:285–291.

———. 1974. Population dynamics, reproduction, and activities of the kangaroo rat, *Dipodomys ordii*, in western Texas. Graduate Studies, Texas Tech Univ., 7:1–28.

Garrison, T. E., and T. L. Best. 1990. *Dipodomys ordii*. Mamm. Species, 353:1–10.

Garrott, R. A. 1991. Feral horse fertility control: potential and limitations. Wildl. Soc. Bull., 19:52–58.

Garrott, R. A., and L. Taylor. 1990. Dynamics of a feral horse population in Montana. J. Wildl. Mgmt., 54:603–612.

Garrott, R. A., G. C. White, R. M. Bartmann, L. H. Carpenter, and W. A. Alldredge. 1987. Movements of female mule deer in northwest Colorado. J. Wildl. Mgmt., 51:634–643.

Gasaway, W. C. 1975. Moose antlers: how fast do they grow? Misc. Publ., Alaska Dept. Fish and Game, 2 pp.

Gasaway, W. C., and J. W. Coady. 1974. Review of energy requirements and rumen fermentation in moose and other ruminants. Nat. canadienne, 101:227–262.

Gashwiler, J. S., W. L. Robinette, and O. W. Morris. 1960. Foods of bobcats in Utah and eastern Nevada. J. Wildl. Mgmt., 24:226–229.

———. 1961. Breeding habits of bobcats in Utah. J. Mamm., 42:76–84.

Gavin, B. R., and R. E. Richards. 1993. Distribution update for Colorado ringtails (Carnivora: *Bassariscus astutus*): 1982–1993. J. Colorado-Wyoming Acad. Sci., 25(1):30.

Geist, V. 1964. On the rutting behavior of the mountain goat. J. Mamm., 45:551–568.

———. 1966. Validity of horn segment counts in aging bighorn sheep. J. Wildl. Mgmt,. 30:634–646.

———. 1971. Mountain sheep, a study in behavior and evolution. Univ. Chicago Press, Chicago, 283 pp.

———. 1975. Mountain sheep and man in the northern wilds. Cornell Univ. Press, Ithaca, 248 pp.

———. 1981. Behavior: adaptive strategies in mule deer. Pp. 157–223, *in* Mule and black-tailed deer of North America (O. C. Wallmo, ed.). Univ. Nebraska Press, Lincoln, 605 pp.

———. 1982. Adaptive behavioral strategies. Pp. 219–278, *in* Elk of North America, ecology and management (J. W. Thomas and D. E. Toweill, eds.). Stackpole Books, Harrisburg, Pennsylvania, 698 pp.

Geluso, K. N. 1970. Ecological distribution of *Peromyscus* (Rodentia: Cricetidae) in the Black Mesa region of Oklahoma. Unpubl. M.S. thesis, Univ. Oklahoma, Norman, 35 pp.

———. 1971. Habitat distribution of *Peromyscus* in the Black Mesa region of Oklahoma. J. Mamm., 52:605–607.

Genoways, H. H., and J. H. Brown, eds. 1993. Biology of the Heteromyidae. Spec. Publ., Amer. Soc. Mammalogists, 10:1–719.

George, S. B. 1986*a*. Evolution and historical biogeography of soricine shrews. Syst. Zool., 35:153–162.

———. 1986*b*. *Blarina brevicauda*. Mamm. Species, 261:1–9.

———. 1988. Systematics, historical biogeography, and evolution of the genus *Sorex*. J. Mamm., 69:443–461.

George, S. B., J. R. Choate, and H. H. Genoways. 1981. Distribution and taxonomic status of *Blarina hylophaga* Elliot (Insectivora: Soricidae). Ann. Carnegie Mus. Nat. Hist., 50:493–513.

George, S. B., H. H. Genoways, J. R. Choate, and R. J. Baker. 1982. Karyotypic relationships within the short-tailed shrews, genus *Blarina*. J. Mamm., 63:639–645.

Gerell, R. 1970. Home ranges and movements of the mink, *Mustela vison* Schreber, in southern Sweden. Oikos, 21:160–173.

Gese, E. M. 1990. Reproductive activity in an old-age coyote in southeastern Colorado. Southwestern Nat., 35:101–102.

Gese, E. M., O. J. Rongstad, and W. R. Mytton. 1988*a*. Home range and habitat use of coyotes in southeastern Colorado. J. Wildl. Mgmt., 52:640–646.

———. 1988*b*. Relationship between coyote group size and diet in southeastern Colorado. J. Wildl. Mgmt., 52:647–653.

Gettinger, R. D. 1984. A field study of activity patterns of *Thomomys bottae*. J. Mamm., 65:76–84.

Gettinger, R. D., P. Arnold, B. A. Wunder, and C. L. Ralph. 1986. Seasonal effects of temperature and photoperiod on thermogenesis and body mass of the kangaroo rat (*Dipodomys ordii*). Pp. 505–509, *in* Living in the cold: physiological and biochemical adaptations (H. C. Heller, X. J. Musacchia, and L. C. H. Wang, eds.). Elsevier Sci. Publ., New York, 587 pp.

Getz, L. L. 1960. A population study of the vole *Microtus pennsylvanicus*. Amer. Midland Nat., 64:392–405.

———. 1961. Home ranges, territoriality, and movement of the meadow vole. J. Mamm., 42:24–36.

———. 1962. Aggressive behavior of the meadow and prairie voles. J. Mamm., 43:351–358.

Getz, L. L., and C. S. Carter. 1980. Social organization in *Microtus ochrogaster* populations. The Biologist, 62:56–69.

Getz, L. L., N. G. Solomon, and T. M. Pizzuto. 1990. The effects of predation of snakes on social organization of the prairie vole, *Microtus ochrogaster*. Amer. Midland Nat., 123:365–371.

Gier, H. T. 1968. Coyotes in Kansas. Agric. Exper. Sta., Kansas State Univ., 118 pp.

———. 1975. Ecology and behavior of the coyote (*Canis latrans*). Pp. 247–262, *in* The wild canids: their systematics, behavioral ecology and evolution (M. W. Fox., ed.). Van Nostrand Reinhold, New York, 508 pp.

Gilbert, P. F., and J. R. Grieb. 1957. Comparison of air and ground deer counts in Colorado. J. Wildl. Mgmt., 21:33–37.

Gill, R. B. 1991. Colorado furtrapping controversy: preliminary analysis. Colorado Division of Wildlife, Denver, 21 pp.

Gill, R. B., and T. D. I. Beck. 1990. Black bear management plan 1990–1995. Division Report, Colorado Div. Wildl., 15:1–44.

Gill, R. B., and L. H. Carpenter. 1985. Winter feeding — a good idea? Proc. Western Assoc. Fish and Wildl. Agencies, 65:57–66.

Gillette, L. N. 1980. Movement patterns of radio-tagged opossums in Wisconsin. Amer. Midland Nat., 104:1–12.

Gillis, J. E. 1968. The activity of the big brown bat. Unpubl. M.S. thesis, Colorado State Univ., Fort Collins, 30 pp.

Gipson, P. S., I. K. Gipson, and J. A. Sealander. 1975. Reproductive biology of wild *Canis* in Arkansas. J. Mamm., 56:605–612.

Glass, B. P. 1966. Some notes on reproduction in the red bat, *Lasiurus borealis*. Proc. Oklahoma Acad. Sci., 46:40–41.

Glover, F. A. 1943. Killing techniques of the New York weasel. Pennsylvania Game News, 13:11–23.

Godin, A. J. 1982. Striped and hooded skunks (*Mephitis mephitis* and allies). Pp. 674–687, *in* Wild mammals of North America: biology, management, and economics (J. A. Chapman and G. A. Feldhamer, eds.). Johns Hopkins Univ. Press, Baltimore, 1147 pp.

Goehring, H. H. 1972. Twenty-year study of *Eptesicus fuscus* in Minnesota. J. Mamm., 53:201–207.

Goertz, J. W. 1963. Some biological notes on the plains harvest mouse. Proc. Oklahoma Acad. Sci., 43:123–125.

———. 1970. An ecological study of *Neotoma floridana* in Oklahoma. J. Mamm., 51:94–104.

Gold, I. K. 1976. Effects of blacktail prairie dog mounds on shortgrass vegetation. Unpubl. M.S. thesis, Colorado State Univ., Fort Collins, 40 pp.

Goldman, E. A., and M. C. Gardner. 1947. Two new cotton rats. J. Mamm., 28:57–59.

Golley, F. B., G. A. Petrides, E. L. Rauber, and J. H. Jenkins. 1965. Food intake and assimilation by bobcats under laboratory conditions. J. Wildl. Mgmt., 29:442–447.

Goodman, P. 1984. River otter recovery plan for Colorado: Draft. Colorado Div. Wildl., Denver, 14 pp. + appendix.

Gordon, C. C. 1986. Winter food habits of the pine marten in Colorado. Great Basin Nat., 46:166–168.

Gordon, K. 1938. Observations on the behavior of *Callospermophilus* and *Eutamias*. J. Mamm., 19:78–84.

———. 1943. The natural history and behavior of the western chipmunk and the mantled ground squirrel. Studies Zool., Oregon State Coll., 5:1–104.

Gosling, L. M. 1985. The even-toed ungulates: order Artiodactyla. Pp. 550–618, *in* Social odours in mammals (R. E. Brown and D. W. Macdonald, eds.). Clarendon Press, Oxford, 882 pp.

Gottfried, G. J., and D. R. Patton. 1984. Pocket gopher food habits on two disturbed forest sites in central Arizona. Research Paper, U.S. Forest Serv., RM-255:1–9.

Graf, R. P. 1985. Social organization of snowshoe hares. Canadian J. Zool., 63:468–474.

Graham, S. J. 1977. The ecology and behavior of the western fox squirrel, *Sciurus niger rufiventer* (Geoffroy), on the South Platte bottomlands. Unpubl. honors thesis, Univ. Northern Colorado, Greeley, 75 pp.

Grant, W. E. 1972. Small mammal studies on the Pawnee Site during the 1971 field season. U.S. Internat. Biol. Program Grassland Biome Tech. Rept., 163:1–51.

Grant, W. E., and E. C. Birney. 1979. Small mammal community structure in North American grasslands. J. Mamm., 60:23–36.

Grant, W. E., N. R. French, and L. J. Folse, Jr. 1980. Effects of pocket gopher *Thomomys talpoides* mounds on plant production in short grass prairie ecosystems. Southwestern Nat., 25:215–224.

Green, N. E. 1969. Occurrence of small mammals on sandhill rangelands in eastern Colorado. Unpubl. M.S. thesis, Colorado State Univ., Fort Collins, 39 pp.

Green, R. A. 1982. Elk habitat selection and activity patterns in Rocky Mountain National Park. Unpubl. M.S. thesis, Colorado State Univ., Fort Collins, 165 pp.

Greer, K. R. 1955. Yearly food habits of the river otter in the Thompson Lakes region, northwestern Montana, as indicated by scat analysis. Amer. Midland Nat., 54:299–313.

Gregg, R. E. 1963. The ants of Colorado. Univ. Colorado Press, Boulder, 792 pp.

Grinnell, J. J., J. S. Dixon, and J. M. Linsdale. 1937. Fur-bearing mammals of California. Univ. California Press, Berkeley, 2 vols.

Grode, M. R., and L. Renner. 1986. Northwest Colorado black-footed ferret search: annual and interim reports, 1983–1986. Wildlife Research Center Library, Colorado Div. Wildl., Fort Collins, unpaged.

Gross, J. E., L. C. Stoddart, and F. H. Wagner. 1974. Demographic analysis of a northern Utah jackrabbit population. Wildl. Monogr., 40:1–68.

Gruchy, D. F. 1950. Status of the opossum, *Didelphis virginiana*, in Colorado. J. Colorado-Wyoming Acad. Sci., 4:76.

Guenther, S. E. 1948. Young beavers. J. Mamm., 29:419–420.

Gunderson, H. L., and B. R. Mahan. 1980. Analysis of sonograms of American bison (*Bison bison*). J. Mamm., 61:379–381.

Gurnell, J. 1984. Home range, territoriality, caching behavior and food supply of the red squirrel (*Tamiasciurus hudsonicus fremonti*) in a subalpine lodgepole pine forest. Anim. Behav., 32:1119–1131.

Gustafson, K. A. 1984. The winter metabolism and bioenergetics of the bobcat in New York. Unpubl. M.S. thesis, State Univ. New York, Syracuse, 112 pp.

Gustin, M. K., and G. F. McCracken. 1987. Scent recognition between females and pups in the bat *Tadarida brasiliensis mexicana*. Anim. Behav., 35:13–19.

Gysel, L. W. 1960. An ecological study of the winter range of elk and mule deer in the Rocky Mountain National Park. J. Forestry, 58:696–703.

Habeck, S. A. 1990. Winter feeding patterns by porcupines (*Erethizon dorsatum*) in the Colorado Front Range. Unpubl. M.A. thesis, Univ. Colorado, Boulder, 99 pp.

Habermann, R. T., C. M. Herman, and F. P. Williams. 1958. Distemper in raccoons and foxes suspected of having rabies. J. Amer. Vet. Med. Assoc., 132:31–35.

Hafner, D. J., K. E. Peterson, and T. L. Yates. 1981. Evolutionary relationships of jumping mice (genus *Zapus*) of the southwestern United States. J. Mamm., 62:501–512.

Hafner, J. C., and M. S. Hafner. 1983. Evolutionary relationships of heteromyid rodents. Great Basin Nat. Mem., 7:3–29.

Hafner, M. S., and D. J. Hafner 1979. Vocalizations of grasshopper mice (Genus *Onychomys*). J. Mamm., 60:85–94.

Hahn, D. E. 1966. The nine-banded armadillo, *Dasypus novemcinctus*, in Colorado. Southwestern Nat., 11:303.

Halfpenny, J. C. 1980. Reproductive strategies: intra- and interspecific comparison within the genus *Peromyscus*. Unpubl. Ph.D. dissert., Univ. Colorado, Boulder, 160 pp.

Halfpenny, J. C., and K. P. Ingraham. 1983. Growth and development of heather voles. Growth, 47:437–445.

Hall, E. R. 1951. American weasels. Univ. Kansas Publ., Mus. Nat. Hist., 4:1–466.

———. 1955. Handbook of mammals of Kansas. Misc. Publ., Mus. Nat. Hist., Univ. Kansas, 7:1–303.

———. 1981. The mammals of North America. Second ed. John Wiley & Sons, New York, 2 vols.

Halls, L. K., ed. 1984. White-tailed deer: ecology and management. Stackpole Books, Harrisburg, Pennsylvania, 870 pp.

Hamilton, R. B., and D. T. Stalling. 1972. *Lasiurus borealis* with five young. J. Mamm., 53:190.

Hamilton, W. J., Jr. 1929. Breeding habits of the short-tailed shrew, *Blarina brevicauda*. J. Mamm., 10:125–134.

———. 1933. The weasels of New York. Amer. Midland Nat., 14:289–337.

———. 1936. The food and breeding habits of the raccoon. Ohio J. Sci., 36:131–140.

———. 1937. Winter activity of the skunk. Ecology, 18:326–327.

———. 1953. Reproduction and young of the Florida wood rat, *Neotoma floridana* (Ord). J. Mamm., 34:180–189.

Hamilton, W. J., Jr., and W. R. Eadie. 1964. Reproduction in the otter, *Lutra canadensis*. J. Mamm., 45:242–252.

Hammitt, W. E., C. D. McDonald, and M. E. Patterson. 1990. Determinants of multiple satisfaction for deer hunting. Wildl. Soc. Bull., 18:331–337.

Hancock, D. C., Jr., and D. J. Nash. 1982. Dorsal hair length and coat color in Abert's squirrel (*Sciurus aberti*). The Great Basin Nat., 42:597–598.

Hansen, R. M. 1960. Age and reproductive characteristics of mountain pocket gophers in Colorado. J. Mamm., 41:323–335.

———. 1962. Dispersal of Richardson ground squirrel in Colorado. Amer. Midland Nat., 68:58–66.

———. 1963. Cotton rat from Kiowa County, Colorado. J. Mamm., 44:126.

———. 1972. Estimation of herbage intake from jackrabbit feces. J. Range Mgmt., 25:468–471.

———. 1975. Plant matter in the diet of *Onychomys*. J. Mamm., 56:530–531.

Hansen, R. M., and G. D. Bear. 1963. Winter coats of white-tailed jackrabbits in southwestern Colorado. J. Mamm., 44:420–422.

———. 1964. Comparison of pocket gophers from alpine, sub-alpine and shrub-grassland habitats. J. Mamm., 45:638–640.

Hansen, R. M., and R. C. Clark. 1977. Foods of elk and other ungulates at low elevation in northwestern Colorado. J. Wildl. Mgmt., 41:76–80.

Hansen, R. M., and J. T. Flinders. 1969. Food habits of North American hares. Sci. Ser., Range Sci. Dept., Colorado State Univ., 1:1–18.

Hansen, R. M., and I. K. Gold. 1977. Black-tailed prairie dogs, desert cottontails and cattle trophic relations on shortgrass range. J. Range Mgmt., 30:210–213.

Hansen, R. M., and M. K. Johnson. 1976. Stomach content weight and food selection by Richardson ground squirrels. J. Mamm., 57:749–751.

Hansen, R. M., and R. S. Miller. 1959. Observations on the plural occupancy of pocket gopher systems. J. Mamm., 40:577–584.

Hansen, R. M., and L. D. Reed. 1969. Energy assimilation in Richardson ground squirrels. Amer. Midland Nat., 82:290–292.

Hansen, R. M., and V. H. Reid. 1973. Distribution and adaptations of pocket gophers. Pp. 1–19, *in* Pocket gophers and Colorado mountain rangeland (G. T. Turner, R. M. Hansen, V. H. Reid, H. P. Tietjen, and A. L. Ward, eds.). Exper. Sta. Bull., Colorado State Univ., 2:1–554.

Hansen, R. M., and A. L. Ward. 1966. Some relations of pocket gophers to rangelands on Grand Mesa, Colorado. Colorado Agric. Exp. Sta. Tech. Bull., 88:1–22.

Hansson, A. 1947. The physiology of reproduction in mink (*Mustela vison*, Schreb.) with special reference to delayed implantation. Acta Zool., 28:1–136.

Hargis, C. D., and D. R. McCullough. 1984. Winter diet and habitat selection of marten in Yosemite National Park. J. Wildl. Mgmt., 48:140–146.

Harlow, H. J. 1981. Torpor and other physiological adaptations of the badger (*Taxidea taxus*) to cold environments. Physiol. Zool., 54:267–275.

Harlow, H. J., and G. E. Menkens, Jr. 1986. Comparison of hibernation in the black-tailed prairie dog, white-tailed prairie dog, and Wyoming ground squirrel. Canadian J. Zool., 64:793–796.

Harlow, H. J., and U.S. Seal. 1981. Changes in hematology and metabolism in the serum and urine of the badger, *Taxidea taxus*, during food deprivation. Canadian J. Zool., 59:2123–2128.

Harper, W. R. 1968. Chemosterilant assessment for beaver. Unpubl. M.S. thesis, Colorado State Univ., Fort Collins, 40 pp.

Harrington, F. H., and L. D. Mech. 1983. Wolf pack spacing: howling as a territory-independent spacing mechanism in a territorial population. Behav. Ecol. Sociobiol., 12:161–168.

Harris, A. H. 1974. *Myotis yumanensis* in interior southwestern North America, with comments on *Myotis lucifugus*. J. Mamm., 55:589–607.

Hart, E. B. 1971. Food preferences of the cliff chipmunk, *Eutamias dorsalis*, in northern Utah. Great Basin Nat., 31:182–188.

———. 1976. Life history notes on the cliff chipmunk, *Eutamias dorsalis*, in Utah. Southwestern Nat., 21:243–246.

Harvey, M. J. 1976. Home range, movements, and diel activity of the eastern mole, *Scalopus aquaticus*. Amer. Midland Nat., 95:436–445.

Hasenyager, R. N. 1980. Bats of Utah. Publ., Utah Div. Wildl. Resources, 80–15:1–109.

Hash, H. S. 1987. Wolverine. Pp. 574–585, *in* Wild furbearer management and conservation in North America (M. Novak, J.A. Baker, M.E. Obbard, and B. Malloch, eds.). Ontario Trappers Association, Toronto, 1150 pp.

Hatt, R. T. 1943. The pine squirrel in Colorado. J. Mamm., 24:311–345.

Haufler, J. B., and J. G. Nagy. 1984. Summer food habits of a small mammal community in the piñon-juniper ecosystem. Great Basin Nat., 44:145–150.

Hawes, M. L. 1977. Home range, territoriality, and ecological separation in sympatric shrews, *Sorex vagrans* and *Sorex obscurus*. J. Mamm., 58:354–367.

Hawley, A. W. L., D. G. Peden, H. W. Reynolds, and W. R. Stricklin. 1981. Bison and cattle digestion of forages from the Slave River Lowlands, Northwest Territories, Canada. J. Range Mgmt., 34:126–130.

Hawley, V. D., and F. E. Newby. 1957. Marten home ranges and population fluctuations. J. Mamm., 38:174–184.

Hay, K. G. 1957. Record beaver litter for Colorado. J. Mamm., 38:268–269.

———. 1958. Beaver census methods in the Rocky Mountain region. J. Wildl. Mgmt., 22:395–402.

Hayward, C. L. 1949. The short-tailed weasel in Utah and Colorado. J. Mamm., 30:436–437.

Hayward C. L., and M. L. Killpack. 1956. Occurrence of *Perognathus fasciatus* in Utah. J. Mamm., 37:451.

Heberlein, T. A. 1987. A profile of the American hunter. Environment, 29(7):6–33.

Hediger, H. 1970. The breeding behavior of the Canadian beaver (*Castor fiber canadensis*). Forma et Functio, 2:336–351.

Hegdal, P. L., A. L. Ward, A. M. Johnson, and H. P. Tietjen. 1965. Notes on the life history of the Mexican pocket gopher (*Cratogeomys castanops*). J. Mamm., 46:334–335.

Hemker, T. P., F. G. Lindzey, and B. B. Ackerman. 1984. Population characteristics and movement patterns of cougars in southern Utah. J. Wildl. Mgmt., 48:1275–1284.

Henderson, F. R. 1976. How to handle problem skunks. Pp. 35–38, *in* Proc. 2nd Great Plains Wildl. Damage Control Workshop, 9–11 December 1975, Manhattan, Kansas.

Henderson, F. R., P. F. Springer, and R. Adrian. 1969. The black-footed ferret in South Dakota. South Dakota Dept. Game, Fish, and Parks Rept., Pierre, 37 pp.

Hennings, D., and R. S. Hoffmann. 1977. A review of the taxonomy of the *Sorex vagrans* species complex from western North America. Occas. Papers Mus. Nat. Hist.,Univ. Kansas, 68:1–35.

Henry, S. E., M. G. Raphael, and L. F. Ruggiero. 1990. Food caching and handling by marten. Great Basin Nat., 50:381–383.

Hermanson, J. W., and T. J. O'Shea. 1983. *Antrozous pallidus*. Mamm. Species, 213:1–8.

Hershkovitz, P. 1962. Evolution of Neotropical cricetine rodents (Muridae), with special reference to the phyllotine group. Fieldiana Zool., 46:1–524.

——. 1971. Basic crown patterns and cusp homologies of mammalian teeth. Pp. 95–150, *in* Dental morphology and evolution (A. A. Dahlberg, ed.). Univ. Chicago Press, Chicago, 350 pp.

Hesselton, W. T., and R. M. Hesselton. 1982. White-tailed deer. Pp. 878–901, *in* Wild mammals of North America: biology, management, and economics (J. A. Chapman and G. A. Feldhamer, eds.). Johns Hopkins Univ. Press, Baltimore, 1147 pp.

Hetlet, L. A. 1968. Observations on a group of badgers in South Park, Colorado. Unpubl. M.S. thesis, Colorado State Univ., Fort Collins, 30 pp.

Hibbs, L. D. 1967. Food habits of the mountain goat in Colorado. J. Mamm., 48:242–248.

Hibbs, L. D., F. A. Glover, and D. L. Gilbert. 1969. The mountain goat in Colorado. Trans. N. Amer. Wildl. Nat. Res. Conf., 34:409–418.

Hickman, G. C. 1975. The maternal behavior of a Mexican pocket gopher *Pappogeomys castanops*. Southwestern Nat., 20:142–144.

——. 1977. Burrow system structure of *Pappogeomys castanops* (Geomyidae) in Lubbock County, Texas. Amer. Midland Nat., 97:50–58.

Hicks, E. A. 1949. Ecological factors affecting the activity of the western fox squirrel, *Sciurus niger rufiventer* (Geoffroy). Ecol. Monogr., 19:287–302.

Hildebrand, M. 1961. Voice of the grasshopper mouse. J. Mamm., 42:263.

Hill, E. P. 1982. Beaver. Pp. 256–281, *in* Wild Mammals of North America biology, management, and economics (J. A. Chapman and G. A. Feldhamer, eds.). Johns Hopkins Univ. Press, Baltimore, 1147 pp.

Hillman, C. N. 1968. Field observations of black-footed ferrets in South Dakota. Trans N. Amer. Wildl. Nat. Res. Conf., 33:433–443.

Hillman, C. N., and T. W. Clark. 1980. *Mustela nigripes*. Mamm. Species, 126:1–3.

Hillman, C. N., and R. L. Linder. 1973. The black-footed ferret. Pp 10–23, *in* Proc. Black-footed ferret and prairie dog workshop (R. L. Linder and C.N. Hillman, eds.). South Dakota State Univ., Brookings, 208 pp.

Hillman, C. N., R. L. Linder, and R. B. Dahlgren. 1979. Prairie dog distributions in areas inhabited by black-footed ferrets. Amer. Midland Nat., 102:185–187.

Hilton, H. 1978. Systematics and ecology of the eastern coyote. Pp. 209–228, *in* Coyotes: biology, behavior, and management (M. Bekoff, ed.). Academic Press, New York, 384 pp.

Hirth, D. H., and D. R. McCullough. 1977. Evolution of alarm signals in ungulates with special reference to white-tailed deer. Amer. Nat., 111:31–42.

Hobbs, N. T. 1979. Winter diet quality and nutritional status of elk in the upper montane zone, Colorado. Unpubl. Ph.D. dissert., Colorado State Univ., Fort Collins, 131 pp.

Hobbs, N. T., D. L. Baker, J. E. Ellis, and D. M. Swift. 1981. Composition and quality of elk winter diets in Colorado. J. Wildl. Mgmt., 45:156–171.

Hobbs, N. T., D. L. Baker, and R. B. Gill. 1983. Comparative nutritional ecology of montane ungulates during winter. J. Wildl. Mgmt., 47:1–16.

Hobbs, N. T., J. E. Ellis, and D. M. Swift. 1979. Composition and quality of elk diets during winter and summer: a preliminary analysis. Pp. 47–53, *in* North American elk: ecology, behavior, and management (M. S. Boyce and L. D. Hayden-Wing, eds.). Univ. Wyoming, Laramie, 294 pp.

Hodgdon, H. E., and J. S. Larson. 1973. Some sexual differences in behavior within a colony of marked beavers (*Castor canadensis*). Anim. Behav., 21:147–152.

Hoditschek, B., and T. L. Best. 1983. Reproductive biology of Ord's kangaroo rat (*Dipodomys ordii*) in Oklahoma. J. Mamm., 64:121–127.

Hoeman, J. V., 1964. High altitude winter records for white-tailed jackrabbits. J. Mamm., 45:495.

Hoffmann, C. O., and J. L. Gottschang. 1977. Numbers, distribution, and movements of a raccoon population in a suburban residential community. J. Mamm., 58:623–636.

Hoffmann, R. S., and R. D. Fisher. 1978. Additional distributional records of Preble's shrew (*Sorex preblei*). J. Mamm., 59:883–884.

Hoffmann, R. S., and J. K. Jones, Jr. 1970. Influence of late-glacial and post-glacial events on the distribution of Recent mammals on the northern Great Plains. Pp. 355–394, *in* Pleistocene and Recent environments of the central Great Plains (W. Dort, Jr., and J.K. Jones, Jr., eds.). Spec. Publ. Dept. Geology, Univ. Kansas, 3:1–433.

Hoffmann, R. S., and J. G. Owen. 1980. *Sorex tenellus* and *Sorex nanus*. Mamm. Species, 131:1–4.

Hoffmann, R. S., P. L. Wright, and F. E. Newby. 1969. The distribution of some mammals in Montana. I. Mammals other than bats. J. Mamm., 50:579–604.

Hoffmeister, D. F. 1967. An unusual concentration of shrews. J. Mamm., 48:462–464.

——. 1981. *Peromyscus truei*. Mamm. Species, 161:1–5.

——. 1986. Mammals of Arizona. Univ. Arizona Press, Tucson, 602 pp.

Hoffmeister, D. F., and V. E. Diersing. 1978. Review of the tassel-eared squirrels of the subgenus *Otosciurus*. J. Mamm., 59:402–413.

Hoffmeister, D. F., and L. S. Ellis. 1979. Geographic variation in *Eutamias quadrivittatus* with comments on the taxonomy of other Arizona chipmunks. Southwestern Nat., 24:655–666.

Hoffmeister, D. F., and W. W. Goodpaster. 1962. Life history of the desert shrew, *Notiosorex crawfordi*. Southwestern Nat., 7:236–252.

Hoffmeister, D. F., and M. R. Lee. 1963. Revision of the desert cottontail, *Sylvilagus audubonii*, in the Southwest. J. Mamm., 44:501–518.

Hofmann, J. E., B. McGuire, and T. M. Pizzuto. 1989. Parental care in the sagebrush vole (*Lemmiscus curtatus*). J. Mamm., 70:162–165.

Hogdon, K. W., and J. S. Larson. 1980. A bibliography of the recent literature on beaver. Res. Bull., Univ. Massachusetts Agric. Exp. Sta., 665:1–128

Hogue, J. E. 1955. *Taxidea taxus taxus*: the brawny and belligerent badger. Colorado Conservation, 4:28–29.

———. 1958. The red fox. Colorado Outdoors, 7:12–14.

Hohn, B. M. 1966. Movement and activity patterns in a population of thirteen-lined ground squirrels, Itasca State Park, Minnesota. Unpubl. M.S. thesis, Univ. Minnesota, St. Paul, 78 pp.

Holbrook, S. J. 1978. Habitat relationships and coexistence of four sympatric species of *Peromyscus* in northwestern New Mexico. J. Mamm., 59:18–26.

Holcomb, L. C. 1965. Large litter size of red fox. J. Mamm., 46:530.

Holdenried, R. 1957. Natural history of the bannertail kangaroo rat in New Mexico. J. Mamm., 38:330–350.

Holmes, A. C. V., and G. C. Sanderson. 1965. Populations and movements of opossums in east-central Illinois. J. Wildl. Mgmt., 29:287–295.

Holst, V. D. 1985. The primitive eutherians I: orders Insectivora, Macroscelidea, and Scandentia. Pp. 105–154, *in* Social odours in mammals, vol. 1 (R. E. Brown and D. W. Macdonald, eds.). Clarendon Press, Oxford, 506 pp.

Holter, J. B., G. Tyler, and T. Walski. 1974. Nutrition of the snowshoe hare (*Lepus americanus*). Canadian J. Zool., 52:1553–1558.

Honacki, J. H., J. E. Kinman, and J. W. Koeppl. 1982. Mammal species of the world. Assoc. Systematics Collections, Lawrence, 694 pp.

Honeycutt, R. L., and S. L. Williams. 1982. Genic differentiation in pocket gophers of the genus *Pappogeomys*, with comments on intergeneric relationships in the subfamily Geomyinae. J. Mamm., 63:208–217.

Hoogland, J. L. 1979*a*. Aggression, ectoparasitism, and other possible costs of prairie dog (Sciuridae, *Cynomys* spp.) coloniality. Behaviour, 69:1–35.

———. 1979*b*. The effect of colony size on individual alertness of prairie dogs (Sciuridae: *Cynomys* spp.) Anim. Behav., 27:394–407.

———. 1981. The evolution of coloniality in white-tailed and black-tailed prairie dogs (Sciuridae: *Cynomys leucurus* and *C. ludovicianus*). Ecology, 62:252–272.

———. 1983. Nepotism and alarm calling in the black-tailed prairie dog (*Cynomys ludovicianus*). Anim. Behav., 31:472–479.

———. 1985. Infanticide in prairie dogs: lactating females kill offspring of close kin. Science, 230:1037–1038.

———. 1987. Using molar attrition to age live prairie dogs. J. Wildl. Mgmt., 51:393–394.

Hooper, E. T., and G. G. Musser. 1964. The glans penis in Neotropical cricetines (Family Muridae) with comments on classification of muroid rodents. Misc. Publ. Mus. Zool. Univ. Michigan, 123:1–57.

Hoover, R. L., C. E. Till, and S. Ogilvie. 1959. The antelope of Colorado. Tech. Bull., Colorado Div. Game and Fish, 4:1–110.

Hoover, R. L., and L. E. Yeager. 1953. Status of the fox squirrel in northeastern Colorado. J. Mamm., 34:359–365.

Hoover, R. L., and D. L. Wills, eds. 1987. Managing forested lands for wildlife. Colorado Div. Wildl. and Rocky Mountain Region, U.S. Forest Service, Denver, 459 pp.

Hopkins, A. L. 1992. Behavior and population dynamics of mountain goats in the Gore Range of Colorado. Unpubl. M.A. thesis, Univ. Northern Colorado, Greeley, 168 pp.

Hornocker, M. G. 1969. Winter territoriality in mountain lions. J. Wildl. Mgmt., 33:457–464.

———. 1970. An analysis of mountain lion predation upon mule deer and elk in the Idaho Primitive Area. Wildl. Monogr., 21:1–39.

Hornocker, M. G., and H. S. Hash. 1981. Ecology of the wolverine in northwestern Montana. Canadian J. Zool., 59:1286–1301.

Hosley, N. W. 1949. The moose and its ecology. Leafl., U.S. Fish and Wildl. Serv., 317:1–51.

House, W. A. 1964. Food habits of Richardson's ground squirrel in south-central Wyoming. Unpubl. M.S. thesis, Colorado State Univ., Fort Collins, 57 pp.

Houseknecht, C. R., and J. R. Tester. 1978. Denning habits of striped skunks (*Mephitis mephitis*). Amer. Midland Nat., 100:424–430.

Houston, D. B. 1968. The Shiras moose in Jackson Hole, Wyoming. Tech. Bull., Grand Teton Nat. Hist. Assoc.,1:1–110.

———. 1974. Aspects of the social organization of moose. Pp. 690–696, *in* The behavior of ungulates and its relation to management (V. Geist and F. Walther, eds.). IUCN Publ., 24(2):1–941.

Howard, W. E. 1961. A pocket gopher population crash. J. Mamm., 42:258–260.

Howard, W. E., and R. E. Marsh. 1982. Spotted and hog-nosed skunks. Pp. 664–673, *in* Wild mammals of North America: biology, management, and economics (J. A. Chapman and

G. A. Feldhamer, eds.). Johns Hopkins Univ. Press, Baltimore, Maryland, 1147 pp.

Howe, R. J. 1977. Scent marking behavior in three species of woodrats. (*Neotoma*) in captivity. J. Mamm., 58:685–688.

———. 1978. Agonistic behavior of three sympatric species of woodrats (*Neotoma mexicana, N. albigula*, and *N. stephensi*). J. Mamm., 59:780–786.

Howell, A. H. 1915. Revision of the American marmots. N. Amer. Fauna, 37:1–80.

Hudson, B. W., et al. 1971. Serological and bacteriological investigations of an outbreak of plague in an urban tree squirrel population. Amer. J. Trop. Med. Hyg., 20:255–263.

Hudson, J. W. 1962. The role of water in the biology of the antelope ground squirrel *Citellus leucurus*. Univ. California Publ. Zool., 64:1–56.

Huheey, C. C. 1972. Sympatric hybridization of *Neotoma albigula* and *Neotoma micropus* in southeastern Colorado: a study of karyology, blood proteins, morphology, and ecology. Unpubl. Ph.D. dissert., Univ. Illinois, Urbana, 66 pp.

Humphrey, S. R. 1974. Zoogeography of the nine-banded armadillo (*Dasypus novemcinctus*) in the United States. BioScience, 24:457–462.

Humphrey, S. R., and J. B. Cope. 1976. Population ecology of the little brown bat, *Myotis lucifugus*, in Indiana and north-central Kentucky. Spec. Publ., Amer. Soc. Mammalogists, 4:1–81.

Humphrey, S. R., and T. H. Kunz. 1976. Ecology of a Pleistocene relict, the western big-eared bat (*Plecotus townsendii*), in the southern Great Plains. J. Mamm., 57:470–494.

Hunter, G. N. 1947. Physical characteristics of Colorado mule deer in relation to their age classes. Colorado Game and Fish Dept., 38 pp.

———. 1948. History of white-tailed deer in Colorado. Colorado Game and Fish Dept., mimeo., 10 pp.

Huntley, N., and R. Inouye. 1988. Pocket gophers in ecosystems: patterns and mechanisms. BioScience, 38:786–793.

Huxley, J. S. 1953. Evolution in action. Harper and Brothers, New York, 182 pp.

Indeck, J. 1987. Sediment analysis and mammalian faunal remains from Little Box Elder Cave, Wyoming. Unpubl. Ph.D. dissert., Univ. Colorado, Boulder, 197 pp.

Ingles, L. G. 1960. A quantitative study of the activity of the dusky shrew (*Sorex vagrans obscurus*). Ecology, 41:656–660.

———. 1961. Home range and habitats of the wandering shrew. J. Mamm., 42:455–462.

Jackson, D. H. 1986. Ecology of bobcats in east-central Colorado. Unpubl. Ph.D. dissert. Colorado State Univ., Fort Collins, 116 pp.

Jackson, H. H. T. 1915. A review of the American moles. N. Amer. Fauna, 38:1–100.

Jackson, L. S. 1985. Bobcat diets and small mammal populations in southcentral Colorado. Unpubl. M.S. thesis, Colorado State Univ., Fort Collins, 82 pp.

Jackson, W. B. 1982. Norway rat and allies. Pp. 1077–1088, *in* Wild mammals of North America: biology, management, and economics (J. A. Chapman and G. A. Feldhamer, eds.). Johns Hopkins Univ. Press, Baltimore, 1147 pp.

James, T. R., and R. W. Seabloom. 1969. Reproductive biology of the white-tailed jack rabbit in North Dakota. J. Wildl. Mgmt., 33:558–568.

James, W. B., and E. S. Booth. 1952. Biology and life history of the sagebrush vole. Walla Walla College Publ., Dept. Biol. Sci., 1:23–43.

Jameson, E. W., Jr. 1952. Food of deer mice, *Peromyscus maniculatus* and *P. boylei*, in the northern Sierra Nevada, California. J. Mamm., 33:50–60.

———. 1953. Reproduction of deer mice (*Peromyscus maniculatus* and *P. boylei*) in the Sierra Nevada, California. J. Mamm., 34:44–58.

———. 1964. Patterns of hibernation of captive *Citellus lateralis* and *Eutamias speciosus*. J. Mamm., 45:455–460.

Janes, D. W. 1959. Home range and movements of the eastern cottontail in Kansas. Univ. Kansas Publ., Mus. Nat. Hist., 10:553–572.

Jannett, F. J., Jr. 1980. Social dynamics of the montane vole, *Microtus montanus*, as a paradigm. The Biologist, 62:3–19.

———. 1982. Nesting patterns of adult voles, *Microtus montanus*, in field populations. J. Mamm., 63:495–498.

———. 1984. Reproduction of the montane vole, *Microtus montanus*, in subnivian populations. Spec. Publ. Carnegie Mus. Nat. Hist., 10:215–224.

Jenkins, H. O. 1948. A study of the meadow mice of three Sierra Nevada meadows. Proc. California Acad. Sci., 26:43–67

Jenkins, K. J., and R. G. Wright. 1987. Dietary niche relationships among cervids relative to winter snowpack in northwestern Montana. Can. J. Zool., 65:1397–1401.

Jenkins, S. H., and P. E. Busher. 1979. *Castor canadensis*. Mamm. Species, 120:1–8.

———. 1980. Problems, progress, and prospects in studies of food selection by beavers. Pp. 559–579, *in* Worldwide Furbearer Conf. Proc. (J. A. Chapman and D. Pursley eds.), 1:1–651.

Johnson, B. K., R. D. Schultz, and J. A. Bailey. 1978. Summer forages of mountain goats in the Sawatch Range, Colorado. J. Wildl. Mgmt., 42:636–639.

Johnson, B. K., and D. R. Smith. 1980. Food habits and forage preferences of bighorn sheep in alpine and subalpine communities. Proc. Biennial Symp. Northern Wild Sheep and Goat Council, 1980:1–17.

Johnson, C. E. 1921. The "hand-stand" habit of the spotted skunk. J. Mamm., 2:87–89.

Johnson, D. R. 1967. Diet and reproduction of Colorado pika. J. Mamm., 48: 311–315.

Johnson, D. W. 1981. Ecology of small mammals on two isolated buttes in Canyonlands National Park, Utah. Southwestern Nat., 26:395–407.

Johnson, D. W., and D. M. Armstrong. 1987. *Peromyscus crinitus*. Mamm. Species, 287:1–8.

Johnson, G. E. 1927. Observations on young prairie dogs (*Cynomys ludovicianus*) born in the laboratory. J. Mamm., 8:110–115.

———. 1928. Hibernation of the thirteen-lined ground squirrel *Citellus tridecemlineatus* (Mitchell). I. A comparison of the normal and hibernating states. J. Exp. Zool., 50:15–30.

Johnson, G. E., M. A. Foster, and R. M. Coco. 1933. The sexual cycle of the thirteen-lined ground squirrel in the laboratory. Trans. Kansas Acad. Sci., 36:250–269.

Johnson, K. 1979. Ecology, behavior, and social organization of the rock squirrel, *Spermophilus variegatus*. Unpubl. M.S. thesis, Trinity Univ., San Antonio, 107 pp.

———. 1981. Social organization in a colony of rock squirrels (*Spermophilus variegatus*, Sciuridae). Southwestern Nat., 26:237–242.

Johnson, L. E. 1917. The habits of the thirteen-lined ground squirrel (*Citellus tridecemlineatus*) with especial reference to burrows. Quart. Rev., Univ. North Dakota, 7:261–271.

Johnson, M. K., and R. M. Hansen. 1979. Foods of cottontails and woodrats in south-central Idaho. J. Mamm., 60:213–215.

Johnson, M. L., and C. W. Clanton. 1954. Natural history of *Sorex merriami* in Washington State. Murrelet, 35:1–4.

Johnson, M. L., and S. Johnson. 1982. Voles. Pp. 326–354 *in* Wild mammals of North America: biology, management, and economics (J. A. Chapman and G. A. Feldhamer, eds.). Johns Hopkins Univ. Press, Baltimore, 1147 pp.

Jones, C. 1965. Ecological distributions and activity periods of bats of the Mogollon Mountains area of New Mexico and adjacent Arizona. Tulane Studies Zool., 12:93–100.

Jones, C., and N. J. Hildreth. 1989, *Neotoma stephensi*. Mamm. Species, 328:1–3.

Jones, C., and R. D. Suttkus. 1972. Notes on netting bats for eleven years in western New Mexico. Southwestern Nat., 16:261–266.

Jones, G. S., and D. B. Jones. 1985. Observations of intraspecific behavior of meadow jumping mice, *Zapus hudsonius*, and escape behavior of a western jumping mouse, *Zapus princeps*, in the wild. Canadian Field-Nat., 99:378–380.

Jones, J. H., and N. S. Smith. 1979. Bobcat density and prey selection in central Arizona. J.Wildl. Mgmt., 43:666–672.

Jones, J. K., Jr. 1953. Geographic distribution of the pocket mouse, *Perognathus fasciatus*. Misc. Publ. Mus. Nat. Hist., Univ. Kansas, 5:515–526.

———. 1958. A new bog lemming (genus *Synaptomys*) from Nebraska. Univ. Kansas Publ., Mus. Nat. Hist., 9:385–388.

———. 1964. Distribution and taxonomy of mammals in Nebraska. Univ. Kansas Publ., Mus. Nat. Hist., 16:1–356.

Jones, J. K., Jr., D. M. Armstrong, and J. R. Choate. 1985. Guide to mammals of the Plains States. Univ. Nebraska Press, Lincoln, 371 pp.

Jones, J. K., Jr., D. M. Armstrong, R. S. Hoffmann, and C. Jones. 1983. Mammals of the Northern Great Plains. Univ. Nebraska Press, Lincoln, 379 pp.

Jones, J. K., Jr., E. D. Fleharty, and P. B. Dunnigan. 1967. The distributional status of bats in Kansas. Misc. Publ. Univ. Kansas Mus. Nat. Hist., 46:1–33.

Jones, J. K., Jr., R. S. Hoffmann, D. W. Rice, C. Jones, R. J. Baker, and M. D. Engstrom. 1992. Revised checklist of North American mammals north of Mexico, 1991. Occas. Papers Mus., Texas Tech Univ., 146:1–23.

Jones, J. K., Jr., and R. B. Loomis. 1954. Records of the short-tailed shrew and least shrew in Colorado. J. Mamm., 35:110.

Jones, W. T. 1985. Body size and life-history variables in heteromyids. J. Mamm., 66:128–132.

Jonkel, C. J. 1987. Brown bear. Pp. 456–473, *in* Wild furbearer management and conservation in North America (M. Novak, J. A. Baker, M. E. Obbard, and B. Malloch, eds.). Ontario Trappers Association, Toronto, 1150 pp.

Jonkel, C. J., and I. McT. Cowan. 1971. The black bear in the spruce-fir forest. Wildl. Monogr., 27:1–57.

Jonkel, C. J., and R. P. Weckwerth. 1963. Sexual maturity and implantation of blastocysts in the pine marten. J. Wildl. Mgmt., 27:93–98.

Juelson, T. C. 1970. A study of the ecology and ethology of the rock squirrel, *Spermophilus variegatus* (Erxleban) in northern Utah. Unpubl. Ph.D. dissert., Univ. Utah, Salt Lake City, 173 pp.

Junge, J. A., and R. S. Hoffmann. 1981. An annotated key to the long-tailed shrews (genus *Sorex*) of the United States and Canada, with notes on Middle American *Sorex*. Occas. Papers Mus. Nat. Hist., Univ. Kansas, 94:1–48.

Kalmbach, E. R. 1943. The armadillo: its relation to agriculture and game. Texas Game, Fish and Oyster Comm., Austin, Texas, 60 pp.

Kaufman, D. W., and E. D. Fleharty. 1974. Habitat selection by nine species of rodents in north-central Kansas. Southwestern Nat., 18:443–452.

Kaufmann, J. H. 1982. Raccoon and allies. Pp. 567–585, *in* Wild mammals of North America: biology, management, and economics (J. A. Chapman and G. A. Feldhamer, eds.). Johns Hopkins Univ. Press, Baltimore, 1147 pp.

———. 1987. Ringtail and coati. Pp. 500–508, *in* Wild furbearer management and conservation in North America (M. Novak, J. A. Baker, M. E. Obbard, and B. Malloch, eds.). Ontario Trappers Association, Toronto, 1150 pp.

Kavanau, J. L., and C. E. Rischer 1972. Influences of ambient temperature on ground squirrel activity. Ecology, 53:158–164.

Kawamichi, T. 1976. Hay territoriality and dominance rank of pikas (*Ochotona princeps*). J. Mamm., 57:133–148.

Keith, J. O. 1965. The Abert squirrel and its dependence on ponderosa pine. Ecology, 46:150–163.

Keith, J. O., R. M. Hansen, and A. L. Ward. 1959. Effect of 2,4-D on abundance of foods of pocket gophers. J. Wildl. Mgmt., 23:137–145.

Keith, L. B. 1974. Some features of population dynamics in mammals. Proc. Internat. Congr. Game Biol., 11:17–58.

———. 1990. Dynamics of snowshoe hare populations. Pp. 119–195, *in* Current mammalogy (H. H. Genoways, ed.). Plenum Press, New York, 2:1–577.

Keith, L. B., and L. A. Windberg. 1978. A demographic analysis of the snowshoe hare cycle. Wildl. Monogr., 58:1–70.

Kelker, G. H. 1943. A winter wildlife census in northeastern Wisconsin. J. Wildl. Mgmt., 7:133–141.

Keller, B. L. 1985. Reproductive patterns. Pp. 725–778, *in* Biology of New World *Microtus* (R. H. Tamarin, ed.). Amer. Soc. Mammalogists, 8:1–593.

Kellert, S. R. 1977. Policy implications of a national study of American attitudes and behavioral relations to animals. U.S. Fish and Wildlife Service, Washington, 124 pp.

———. 1980. American attitudes toward and knowledge of animals: an update. Internat. J. Studies Anim. Prob., 1:87–119.

———. 1987. Social and psychological dimensions of an environmental ethics. Proc. of the Internat. Conf. on Outdoor Ethics, Lake Ozark, Missouri: 18–19.

———. 1988. Human-animal interactions: a review of American attitudes to wild and domestic animals in the twentieth century. Pp. 137–175, *in* Animals and people sharing the world (A.N Rowan, ed.). Univ. Press of New England, Hanover, New Hampshire, 206 pp.

Kellert, S. R., and J. K. Berry. 1987. Attitudes, knowledge, and behaviors toward wildlife as affected by gender. Wildl. Soc. Bull., 15:363–371.

Kemp, G. A., and L. B. Keith. 1970. Dynamics and regulation of red squirrel (*Tamiasciurus hudsonicus*) populations. Ecology, 51:763–779.

Kennelly, J. J., and B. E. Johns. 1976. The estrous cycle of coyotes. J. Wildl. Mgmt., 40:272–277.

Kennerly, T. E., Jr. 1958. Comparisons of morphology and life history of two species of pocket gophers. Texas J. Sci., 10:133–146.

———. 1964. Microenvironmental conditions of the pocket gopher burrow. Texas J. Sci., 16:395–441.

Kilgore, D. L., Jr. 1969. An ecological study of the swift fox (*Vulpes velox*) in the Oklahoma Panhandle. Amer. Midland Nat., 81:512–534.

———. 1970. The effect of northward dispersal on growth rate of young, size of young at birth, and litter size in *Sigmodon hispidus*. Amer. Midland Nat., 84:510–520.

Kilgore, D. L., Jr., and K. B. Armitage. 1978. Energetics of yellow-bellied marmot populations. J. Mamm., 60:628–629.

Kimball, J. W. 1948. Pheasant population characteristics and trends in the Dakotas. Trans. N. Amer. Wildl. Conf. 13:291–311.

King, C. M. 1983. *Mustela erminea*. Mamm. Species, 195:1–8.

King, J. A. 1955. Social behavior, social organization, and population dynamics in a black-tailed prairie dog town in the Black Hills of South Dakota. Contrib. Lab. Vert. Biol., Univ. Michigan, 67:1–123.

———., ed. 1968. Biology of *Peromyscus* (Rodentia). Spec. Publ., Amer. Soc. Mammalogists, 2:1–593.

Kirkland, G. L., Jr., and J. N. Layne, eds. 1989. Advances in the study of *Peromyscus* (Rodentia). Texas Tech Univ. Press, Lubbock, 336 pp.

Kirsch, J. A. W. 1977. The classification of marsupials. Pp. 1–50, *in* The biology of marsupials (D. Hunsaker, II, ed.). Academic Press, New York, 537 pp.

Kirsch, J. A. W., and J.H. Calaby. 1977. The species of living marsupials: an annotated list. Pp. 9–26, *in* The biology of marsupials (B. Stonehouse and D. Gilmore, eds.). Macmillan, London, 486 pp.

Kisiel, D. S. 1971. October birth by *Peromyscus difficilis nasutus* in north central Colorado. Southwestern Nat., 16:213–214.

Kitchen, D. W. 1974. Social behavior and ecology of the pronghorn. Wildl. Monogr., 38:1–96.

Kitchen, D. W., and B. W. O'Gara. Pronghorn. 1982. Pp. 960–971, *in* Wild mammals of North America: biology, management, and economics (J.A. Chapman and G.A. Feldhamer, eds.). Johns Hopkins Univ. Press, Baltimore, 1147 pp.

Kivett, V. K., and O. B. Mock. 1980. Reproductive behavior in the least shrew (*Cryptotis parva*) with special reference to the aural glandular region of the female. Amer. Midland Nat., 103:339–345.

Klatt, L. E. 1971. A comparison of the ecology of active and abandoned black-tailed prairie dog towns. Unpubl. M.S. thesis, Colorado State Univ., Fort Collins, 52 pp.

Klatt, L. E., and D. Hein. 1978. Vegetative differences among active and abandoned towns of black-tailed prairie dogs (*Cynomys ludovicianus*). J. Range Mgmt., 31:315–317.

Klingener, D. 1984. Gliroid and dipodoid rodents. Pp. 381–388, *in* Orders and families of Recent mammals of the world. (S. Anderson and J. K. Jones, Jr., eds.). John Wiley and Sons, New York, 686 pp.

Knowles, C. J. 1986. Some relationships of black-tailed prairie dogs to livestock grazing. Great Basin Nat., 46:198–203.

Knowles, P. R. 1985. Home range size and habitat selection of bobcats, *Lynx rufus*, in north-central Montana. Canadian Field-Nat., 99:6–12.

Knowlton, F. F. 1972. Preliminary interpretations of coyote population mechanics with some management implications. J. Wildl. Mgmt., 36:369–382.

Koehler, G. M., and M. G. Hornocker. 1977. Fire effects on marten habitat in the Selway-Bitterroot Wilderness. J. Wild. Mgmt., 41:500–505.

Koehler, G. M., M. G. Hornocker, and H. S. Hash. 1980. Wolverine marking behavior. Canadian Field-Nat., 94:339–341.

Koford, C. B. 1958. Prairie dogs, whitefaces, and blue grama. Wildl. Monogr., 3:1–78.

Kolenosky, G. B., and S. M. Strathearn. 1987. Black bear. Pp. 442–454, *in* Wild furbearer management and conservation in North America (M. Novak, J. A. Baker, M. E. Obbard, and B. Malloch, eds.). Ontario Trappers Association, Toronto, 1150 pp.

Koplin, J. R., and R. S. Hoffmann. 1968. Habitat overlap and competitive exclusion in voles (*Microtus*). Amer. Midland Nat., 80:494–507.

Koprowski, J. L., J. L. Roseberry, and W. D. Klimstra. 1988. Longevity records for the fox squirrel. J. Mamm., 69:383–384.

Korschgen, L. J. 1959. Food habits of the red fox in Missouri. J.Wildl. Mgmt., 23:168–176.

———. 1981. Foods of fox and gray squirrels in Missouri. J. Wildl. Mgmt., 45:260–266.

Krebs, C. J. 1970. *Microtus* population biology: behavioral changes associated with the population cycle in *M. ochrogaster* and *M. pennsylvanicus*. Ecology, 51:34–52.

Krebs, C. J., and J. H. Myers. 1974. Population cycles in small mammals. Adv. Ecol. Res., 8:267–399.

Krenz, M. C. 1977. Vocalization of the rock squirrel *Spermophilus variegatus*. Unpubl. M.S. thesis, Texas Tech Univ., Lubbock, 46 pp.

Kritzman, E. B. 1974. Ecological relationships of *Peromyscus maniculatus* and *Perognathus parvus* in eastern Washington. J. Mamm., 55:172–188.

Krutzsch, P. H. 1954. North American jumping mice (genus *Zapus*), Univ. Kansas Publ., Mus. Nat. Hist., 7:349–472.

———. 1975. Reproduction of the canyon bat, *Pipistrellus hesperus*, in the southwestern United States. Amer. J. Anat., 143:163–200.

Kufeld, R. C. 1973. Foods eaten by the Rocky Mountain elk. J. Range Mgmt., 26:106–113.

———. 1983. Responses of elk, mule deer, cattle, and vegetation to burning, spraying, and chaining of Gambel oak rangeland. Tech. Publ., Colorado Div. Wildl., 34:1–47.

———. 1992. Development of census methods for deer in plains riverbottom habitats. Job Progress Report, Project W–153–R–5, Research Center, Colorado Div. of Wildl., Fort Collins, 13 pp.

Kufeld, R. C., J. H. Olterman, and D. C. Bowden. 1980. A helicopter quadrat census for mule deer on Uncompahgre Plateau, Colorado. J. Wildl. Mgmt., 44:632–639.

Kufeld, R. C., O. C. Wallmo, and C. Feddema. 1973. Foods of the Rocky Mountain mule deer. Res. Paper, U.S. Forest Service, RM–111:1–31.

Kundaeli, J. N., and H. G. Reynolds. 1972. Desert cottontail use of natural and modified piñon-juniper woodlands. J. Range Mgmt., 25:116–118.

Kunz, T. H. 1973. Resource utilization temporal and spatial components of bat activity in central Iowa. J. Mamm., 54:14–32.

———. 1974. Reproduction, growth, and mortality of the vespertilionid bat, *Eptesicus fuscus*, in Kansas. J. Mamm., 55:1–13.

———. 1982. *Lasionycteris noctivagans*. Mamm. Species, 172:1–5.

Kunz, T. H., and R. A. Martin. 1982. *Plecotus townsendii*. Mamm. Species, 175:1–6.

Kurtén, B. 1971. The age of mammals. Columbia Univ. Press, New York, 250 pp.

Lackey, J. A., D. G. Huckaby, and B. G. Ormiston. 1985. *Peromyscus leucopus*. Mamm. Species, 247:1–10.

Lair, H. 1985a. Mating seasons and fertility of red squirrels in southern Quebec. Canadian J. Zool., 63:2323–2327.

———. 1985b. Length of gestation in the red squirrel, *Tamiasciurus hudsonicus*. J. Mamm., 66:809–810.

Lance, W. R., and T. M. Pojar. 1984. Diseases and parasites of pronghorn: a review. Spec. Rept., Wildl. Res. Sec., Colorado Div. Wildl., 57:1–14.

Landstrom, R. E. 1971. Longevity of white-throated woodrat. J. Mamm., 52:623.

Langenau, E. E., Jr., R. J. Moran, J. R. Terry, and D. C. Cue. 1981. Relationship between deer kill and ratings of the hunt. J. Wildl. Mgmt., 45:959–964.

Langford, A. 1983. Pattern of nocturnal activity of male *Dipodomys ordii* (Heteromyidae). Southwestern Nat., 28:341–346.

Larson, F. 1940. The role of the bison in maintaining the short grass plains. Ecology, 21:113–121.

Lauenroth, W. K. 1979. Grassland primary production: North American grasslands in perspective. Pp. 3–24 *in* Perspectives in grassland ecology (N. R. French, ed.). Springer-Verlag, New York.

Laundre, J. W. 1989. Horizontal and vertical diameters of burrows of five small mammal species in southeastern Idaho. Great Basin Nat., 49:646–649.

LaVal, R. K., and M. L. LaVal. 1979. Notes on reproduction, behavior, and abundance of the red bat, *Lasiurus borealis*. J. Mamm., 60:209–212.

LaVoie, G. K, G. K. Tietjen, and M. W. Fall. 1971. Albinism in *Thomomys talpoides* from Colorado. Great Basin Nat., 31:181.

Lawlor, T. E. 1979. Handbook of the orders and families of living mammals, second ed. Mad River Press, Eureka, CA, 327 pp.

Lawson, B., and R. Johnson. 1982. Mountain sheep. Pp. 1036–1055, *in* Wild mammals of North America: biology, management, and economics (J.A. Chapman and G.A. Feldhamer, eds.). Johns Hopkins Univ. Press, Baltimore, 1147 pp.

Lay, D. W. 1942. Ecology of the opossum in eastern Texas. J. Mamm., 23:147–159.

Layne, J. N. 1968. Ontogeny. Pp. 148–253, *in* Biology of *Peromyscus* (Rodentia) (J. A. King, ed.) Spec. Publ., Amer. Soc. Mammalogists, 2:1–593.

Layne, J. N., and D. Glover. 1977. Home range of the armadillo in Florida. J. Mamm., 58:411–413.

Lechleitner, R. R. 1954. Age criteria in mink, *Mustela vison*. J. Mamm., 35:496–503.

———. 1957. Reingestion in the black-tailed jack rabbit. J. Mamm., 38:481–485.

———. 1958. Movements, density, and mortality in a black-tailed jack rabbit population. J. Wildl. Mgmt., 22:371–384.

———. 1959. Sex ratio, age classes, and reproduction of the black-tailed jack rabbit. J. Mamm., 40:63–81.

———. 1964. Another record of the least shrew from Colorado. J. Mamm., 45:298.

———. 1969. Wild mammals of Colorado: their appearance, habits, distribution, and abundance. Pruett Publishing Co., Boulder, 254 pp.

Lechleitner, R. R., L. Kartman, M. I. Goldenberg, and B. W. Hudson. 1968. An epizootic of plague in Gunnison's prairie dogs (*Cynomys gunnisoni*) in southcentral Colorado. Ecology, 49:734–743.

Lechleitner, R. R., J. V. Tileston, and L. Kartman. 1962. Die-off of a Gunnison's prairie dog colony in central Colorado. I. Ecological observations and description of the epizootic. Zoonoses Res., 1:185–199.

LeCount, A. 1977. Some aspects of black bear ecology in the Arizona chaparral. Proc. Internat. Conf. Bear Res. Mgmt., 4:175–180.

Leege, T. A. 1968. Natural movements of beavers in southeastern Idaho. J. Wildl. Mgmt., 31:326–332.

Lehner, P. N. 1976. Coyote behavior: implications for management. Wildl. Soc. Bull., 4:120–126.

———. 1978a. Coyote communication. Pp. 127–162, *in* Coyotes: biology, behavior, and management (M. Bekoff, ed.). Academic Press, New York, 384 pp.

———. 1978b. Coyote vocalizations: a lexicon and comparison with other canids. Anim. Behav., 26:712–722.

Lehner, P. N., R. Krumm, and A. T. Cringan. 1976. Tests for olfactory repellents for coyotes and dogs. J. Wild. Mgmt., 40:145–150.

Lentfer, J. W. 1955. A two-year study of the Rocky Mountain goat in the Crazy Mountains, Montana. J. Wildl. Mgmt., 19:417–429.

Leonard, M. L., and M. B. Fenton. 1984. Echolocation calls of *Euderma maculatum* (Chiroptera: Vespertilionidae): use in orientation and communication. J. Mamm., 65:122–126.

Leopold, A. 1949. A Sand County almanac, and sketches here and there. Oxford Univ. Press, New York, 226 pp.

Lerass, H. J. 1938. Observations on the growth and behavior of harvest mice. J. Mamm., 19:441–444.

Levenson, H. 1985. Systematics of the Holarctic chipmunks (*Tamias*). J. Mamm., 66:219–242.

Li, C.-K., and S.-Y. Ting. 1985. Possible phylogenetic relationships: eurymylid-rodent and mimotonid-lagomorph. Pp. 35–58, *in* Evolutionary relationships among rodents (W.P. Luckett and J.-L. Hartenberger, eds.). NATO ASI Series, Series A: Life Sci., 92:1–721.

Lidicker, W. Z., Jr. 1988. Solving the enigma of microtine "cycles." J. Mamm., 69:225–235.

Liers, E. E. 1951. Notes on the river otter (*Lutra canadensis*). J. Mamm., 32:1–9.

———. 1958. Early breeding in the river otter. J. Mamm., 39:438–439.

Liewer, J. A. 1988. Pronghorn grazing impacts on winter wheat. Unpubl. M.S. thesis, Colorado State Univ., Fort Collins, 32 pp.

Lim, B. K. 1987. *Lepus townsendii*. Mamm. Species, 288:1–6.

Linder, R., B. Dahlgren, and C. N. Hillman. 1972. Black-footed ferret-prairie dog interrelationships. Pp. 22–37, *in* Proc. Symp. on Rare and Endangered Wildl. of the Southwestern United States. New Mexico Dept. Game and Fish, Santa Fe.

Lindzey, F. G. 1978. Movement patterns of badgers in northwestern Utah. J. Wildl. Mgmt., 42:418–422.

———. 1982. Badger. Pp. 653–663, *in* Wild mammals of North America: biology, management, and economics (J. A. Chapman and G. A. Feldhamer, eds.). Johns Hopkins Univ. Press, Baltimore, 1147 pp.

———. 1987. Mountain lion. Pp. 656–668, *in* Wild furbearer management and conservation in North America (M. Novak, J.A. Baker, M.E. Obbard, and B. Malloch, eds.). Ontario Trappers Association, Toronto, 1150 pp.

Linhart, S. B., and W. B. Robinson. 1972. Some relative carnivore densities in areas under sustained coyote control. J. Mamm., 53:880–884.

Linscombe, G., N. Kinler, and R. J. Aulerich. 1982. Mink. Pp. 629–643, *in* Wild mammals of North America: biology, management, and economics (J. A. Chapman and G. A. Feldhamer, eds.). Johns Hopkins Univ. Press, Baltimore, 1147 pp.

Linzey, A. V. 1983. *Synaptomys cooperi*. Mamm. Species, 210:1–5.

Lipscomb, J., H. Riffel, H. Funk, and C. Gardner. 1983. Colorado small game, furbearer and varmint harvest, 1982. Federal Aid Wildl. Rest. Proj., Colorado Div. Wildl., W-121-R:1-186.

Liskop, K. S., R. M. F. S. Sadlier, and B. P. Saunders. 1981. Reproduction and harvest of wolverine (*Gulo gulo*) in British Columbia. Pp. 469–477, *in* Proc. Worldwide Furbearer Conf. (J. A. Chapman and D. Pursley, eds.). Worldwide Furbearer Conf., Inc., Frostburg, Maryland, 2059 pp.

Llewellyn, J. B. 1981. Habitat selection by the desert woodrat (*Neotoma lepida*) inhabiting a piñon-juniper woodland in western Nevada. Southwestern Nat., 26:76–78.

Lloyd, H. G. 1975. The red fox in Britain. Pp. 207–215, *in* The wild canids: their systematics, behavioral ecology and evolution (M. W. Fox, ed.). Van Nostrand Reinhold Co., New York, 508 pp.

Long, C. A. 1965. The mammals of Wyoming. Univ. Kansas Publ., Mus. Nat. Hist., 14:493–758.

———. 1972. Notes on habitat preference and reproduction in pygmy shrews, *Microsorex*. Canadian Field-Nat., 86:155–160.

———. 1973. *Taxidea taxus*. Mamm. Species, 26:1–4.

———. 1974. *Microsorex hoyi* and *Microsorex thompsoni*. Mamm. Species. 33:1–4.

Long, C. A., and D. Cronkite. 1970. Taxonomy and ecology of sibling chipmunks in central Colorado. Southwestern Nat., 14:283–291.

Long, C. A., and R. S. Hoffmann. 1992. *Sorex preblei* from the Black Canyon, first record for Colorado. Southwestern Nat., 37:318–319.

Long, C. A., and C. A. Killingley. 1983. The badgers of the world. Charles C. Thomas Publ., Springfield, Illinois, 404 pp.

Longhurst, W. 1944. Observations on the ecology of the Gunnison prairie dog in Colorado. J. Mamm., 25:24–36.

Lotze, J.-H., and S. Anderson. 1979. *Procyon lotor.* Mamm. Species, 119:1–8.

Loughry, W. J., and G. F. McCracken. 1991. Factors influencing female-pup scent recognition in Mexican free-tailed bats. J. Mamm., 72:624–626.

Loveless, C. M. 1967. Ecological characteristics of a mule deer winter range. Tech. Bull., Colorado Div. Game, Fish, and Parks, 20:1–124.

Lovell, D. C., J. R. Choate, and S. J. Bissell. 1985. Succession of mammals in a disturbed area of the Great Plains. Southwestern Nat., 30:335–342.

Loy, R. R. 1981. An ecological investigation of the swift fox, *Vulpes velox,* on the Pawnee National Grassland, Colorado. Unpubl. M.A. thesis, Univ. Northern Colorado, Greeley, 64 pp.

Luce, D. G., R. M. Case, and J. L. Stubbendieck. 1980. Food habits of the plains pocket gopher on western Nebraska rangeland. J. Range Mgmt., 33:129–131.

Luce, D. G., and J. L. Stubbendieck. 1981. Damage to alfalfa fields by plains pocket gophers. J. Wildl. Mgmt., 45:258–260.

Lusby, G. C., V. H. Reid, and O. D. Knipe. 1971. Effects of grazing on the hydrology and biology of the Badger Wash Basin in western Colorado, 1953–1966. Water Supply Papers, U.S. Geol. Surv., 1532-D:1–90.

Lytle, T., J. Caufield, and D. Hanna. 1981. River otter restoration and monitoring. Job Progress Report. Project SE–3–3, unpaged mimeo.

MacArthur, R. A. 1978. Winter movements and home range of the muskrat. Canadian Field-Nat., 92:345–349.

MacDonald, D. 1956. Beaver carrying capacity of certain mountain streams in North Park, Colorado. M.S. thesis, Colorado A and M College, Fort Collins, 136 pp.

Macdonald, D. W., and P. J. Bacon. 1982. Fox society, contact rate and rabies epizootiology. Comp. Immun. Microbiol. Infect. Dis., 5:247–256.

Macêdo, R. H., and M. A. Mares. 1988. *Neotoma albigula.* Mamm. Species, 310:1–7.

MacInnes, C. D. 1987. Rabies. Pp. 910–929, *in* Wild furbearer management and conservation in North America (M. Novak, J. A. Baker, M. E. Obbard, and B. Malloch, eds.). Ontario Trappers Association, Toronto, 1150 pp.

Mack, C. M. 1985. River otter restoration in Grand County, Colorado. Unpubl. M.S. thesis, Colorado State Univ., Fort Collins, 133 pp.

Mackie, R. J., K. L. Hamlin, and D. F. Pac. 1982. Mule deer. Pp. 862–877, *in* Wild mammals of North America: biology, management, and economics (J. A. Chapman and G. A. Feldhamer, eds.). Johns Hopkins Univ. Press, Baltimore, 1147 pp.

MacLean, S. F., Jr., B. M. Fitzgerald, and F. A. Pitelka. 1974. Population cycles in Arctic lemmings: winter reproduction and predation by weasels. Arctic and Alpine Res., 6:1–12.

MacMillen, R. E. 1983. Water regulation in *Peromyscus.* J. Mamm., 64:38–47.

Magoun, A. J., and P. Valkenburg. 1983. Breeding behavior of free-ranging wolverines (*Gulo gulo*). Acta Zool. Fenn., 174:175–177.

Makar, P. W. 1980. Bobcat and coyote food habits and habitat use in Rocky Mountain National Park. Unpubl. M.S. thesis, Colorado State Univ., Fort Collins, 32 pp.

Malville, L. E. 1988. River otter tracking in Larimer County. Report to Colorado Div. Wildl., unpaged.

———. 1990. Movements, distribution, and habitat selection of river otters reintroduced into the Dolores River, southwestern Colorado. Unpubl. M.A. thesis, Univ. Colorado, Boulder, 67 pp.

Manning, R. W., and J. K. Jones, Jr. 1988. *Perognathus fasciatus.* Mamm. Species, 303:1–4.

———. 1989. *Myotis evotis.* Mamm. Species, 329:1–5.

Manville, R. H. 1949. A study of small mammal populations in northern Michigan. Misc. Publ. Mus. Zool., Univ. Michigan 73:1–83.

Marchinton, R. L., and D. H. Hirth. 1984. Behavior. Pp. 129–168, *in* White-tailed deer: ecology and management (L. K. Halls, ed.). Stackpole Books, Harrisburg, Pennsylvania, 870 pp.

Markley, M. H., and C. F. Bassett. 1942. Habits of captive marten. Amer. Midland Nat., 28:605–616.

Marr, J. W. 1967. Ecosystems of the east slope of the Front Range in Colorado. Univ. Colorado Studies, Ser. in Biology, 8:1–134.

Marsden, H. M., and N. R. Holler. 1964. Social behavior in confined populations of the cottontail and the swamp rabbit. Wildl. Monogr., 13:5–39.

Marshall, W. H. 1936. A study of the winter activities of the mink. J. Mamm., 17:382–392.

Marshall, W. H., G. W. Gullion, and G. Schawb. 1962. Early summer activities of porcupines as determined by radio-positioning techniques. J. Wildl. Mgmt., 26:75–79.

Marti, C. D. 1972. Notes on the least shrew in Colorado. Southwestern Nat., 15:447–448.

Marti, C. D., and C. E. Braun. 1975. Use of tundra habitats by prairie falcons in Colorado. Condor, 77:213–214.

Martin, I. G. 1980. An ethogram of captive *Blarina brevicauda.* Amer. Midland Nat., 104:290–294.

———. 1981. Tolerance of conspecifics by short-tailed shrews (*Blarina brevicauda*) in simulated natural conditions. Amer. Midland Nat., 106:206–208.

———. 1983. Daily activity of short-tailed shrews (*Blarina brevicauda*) in simulated natural conditions. Amer. Midland Nat., 109:136–144.

Martin, P. S., and R. G. Klein, eds. 1984. Quaternary extinctions, a prehistoric revolution. Univ. Arizona Press, Tucson, 892 pp.

Martin, R. D. 1986. Are fruit bats primates? Nature, 320:482–483.

Martin, S. K., and R. H. Barrett. 1983. The importance of snags to pine marten habitat in the northern Sierra Nevada. Pp. 114–116, in Snag habitat management: proceedings of a symposium (J.W. Davis, G.A. Goodwin, and R.A. Ockenfils, tech. coord.). U.S. Forest Service Tech. Rept. RM–99.

Martinsen, D. L. 1968. Temporal patterns in the home ranges of chipmunks (Eutamias). J. Mamm., 49:83–91.

———. 1969. Energetics and activity patterns of short-tailed shrews (Blarina) on restricted diets. Ecology, 50:505–510.

Maser, C., B. R. Mate, J. F. Franklin, and C. T. Dyrness. 1981. Natural history of Oregon Coast mammals. Gen. Tech. Rept. U.S. Forest Service, PNW–133:1–496.

Maser, C. E., ed. 1974. The sage vole, Lagurus curtatus (Cope 1868), in the Crooked River National Grassland, Jefferson County, Oregon: a contribution to its life history and ecology. Saugetierk. Mitt., 22:193–222.

Maser, C. E., J. M. Trappe, and R. A. Nussbaum. 1978. Fungal-small mammal interrelationships with emphasis on Oregon coniferous forests. Ecology, 59:799–809.

Mason, C. F., and S. M. MacDonald. 1983. Some factors influencing the distribution of mink (Mustela vison). J. Applied Ecol., 20:281–283.

Maxwell, M. H., and L. N. Brown. 1968. Ecological distribution of rodents on the high plains of eastern Wyoming. Southwestern Nat., 13:143–158.

McAllister, J. A., and R. S. Hoffmann. 1988. Phenacomys intermedius. Mamm. Species, 305:1–8.

McBee, K., and R. J. Baker. 1982. Dasypus novemcinctus. Mamm. Species, 162:1–9.

McCabe, R. A. 1949. Notes on live-trapping mink. J. Mamm., 30:416–423.

McCarley, W. H. 1959. An unusually large nest of Cryptotis parva. J. Mamm., 40:243.

———. 1966. Annual cycle, population dynamics, and adaptive behavior of Citellus tridecemlineatus. J. Mamm., 47:294–316.

McCarty, R. 1978. Onychomys leucogaster. Mamm. Species 87:1–6.

McCloskey, R. J., and K. G. Shaw. 1977. Copulatory behavior of the fox squirrel. J. Mamm., 58:663–665.

McCord, C. M., and J. E. Cardoza. 1982. Bobcat and lynx. Pp. 728–766, in Wild mammals of North America: biology, management, and economics (J. A. Chapman and G. A. Feldhamer, eds.). Johns Hopkins Univ. Press, Baltimore, 1147 pp.

McCoy, C. J., Jr., and P. H. Miller. 1964. Ecological distribution of the subspecies of Ammospermophilus leucurus in Colorado. Southwestern Nat., 9:89–93.

McCracken, G. F. 1984. Communal nursing in Mexican free-tailed bat maternity colonies. Science, 223:1090–1091.

McCullough, D. R. 1969. The tule elk: its history, behavior, and ecology. Univ. California Publ. Zool., 88:1–290.

McCutchen, H. E. 1969. Age determination of pronghorn by the incisor cementum. J. Wildl. Mgmt., 33:172–175.

———. 1987. Black bear species/area relationships studied at Rocky Mountain National Park. Park Sci., 7:18–19.

———. 1989. Observations of American black bear cryptic behavior in a national park. Proc. Internat. Conf. Bear Res. Mgmt., 8:20–25.

McDonald, J. N. 1981. North American bison: their classification and evolution. Univ. California Press, Berkeley, 316 pp.

McGinnies, W. J., H. L. Schantz, and W. G. McGinnies. 1991. Changes in vegetation and land use in eastern Colorado: a photographic study, 1904–1986. Agric. Res. Serv., U.S. Dept. Agriculture, ARS–85:1–165.

McGrew, J. C. 1977. Distribution and habitat characteristics of the kit fox (Vulpes macrotis) in Utah. Unpubl. M.S. thesis, Utah State Univ., Logan, 92 pp.

———. 1979. Vulpes macrotis. Mamm. Species, 123:1–6.

McGuire, B., and M. Novak. 1986. Parental care and its relationship to social organization in the montane vole (Microtus montanus). J. Mamm., 67:305–311.

McHugh, T. 1972. The time of the buffalo. Alfred A. Knopf, New York, 339 pp.

McKay, D. O., and B. J. Verts. 1978. Estimates of some attributes of a population of Nuttall's cottontails. J. Wildl. Mgmt., 42:159–168.

McKean, W. T. 1971. Stocking rates for mule deer and livestock on certain piñon-juniper areas. Game Inf. Leafl., Colorado Div. Game, Fish, and Parks, 87:1–2.

McKean, W. T., and W. T. Burkhard. 1978. Fish and wildlife analysis for the Yellow Jacket Project. Colorado Div. Wildl., Denver, 119 pp.

McKeever, S. 1964. The biology of the golden-mantled ground squirrel. Ecol. Monogr., 34:383–401.

McKenna, M. C. 1975. Toward a phylogenetic classification of the Mammalia. Pp. 21–46, in Phylogeny of the primates (W. P. Luckett and F. S. Szalay, eds.). Plenum Publishing, 483 pp.

McLean, R. G., D. B. Francy, G. S. Bowen, R. E. Bailey, C. H. Calisher, and A. M. Barnes. 1981. The ecology of Colorado tick fever in Rocky Mountain National Park in 1974. I. Objectives, study design, and summary of principal findings. Amer. J. Trop. Med. Hyg., 30:483–489.

McManus, J. J. 1970. Behavior of captive opossums, Didelphis marsupialis virginiana. Amer. Midland Nat., 84:144–169.

———. 1974. Didelphis virginiana. Mamm. Species 40:1–6.

Meacham, J. W. 1971. [No title] Bat Res. News, 12:37.

———. 1974. A Colorado colony of Tadarida brasiliensis. Bat Res. News, 15:8–9.

Mead, R. A. 1967. Age determination in the spotted skunk. J. Mamm., 48:606–616.

———. 1968a. Reproduction in eastern forms of the spotted skunk (genus Spilogale). J. Zool., 156:119–136.

———. 1968b. Reproduction in western forms of the spotted skunk (genus *Spilogale*). J. Mamm., 49:373–390.

———. 1981. Delayed implantation in mustelids, with special emphasis on the spotted skunk. J. Reprod. Fert. Suppl., 29:11–24.

Meagher, M. 1973. The bison of Yellowstone National Park. Sci. Monogr., Nat. Park Service, 1:1–161.

———. 1986. *Bison bison.* Mamm. Species, 266:1–8.

Meaney, C. A. 1986. Scent-marking in pikas (*Ochotona princeps*): test of a breeding-facilitation hypothesis. Pp. 571–577, *in* Chemical signals in vertebrates (D. Duvall, D. Muller-Schwarze, and R. M. Silverstein, eds.). Plenum Press, New York, 4:1–742.

———. 1987. Cheek-gland odors in pikas (*Ochotona princeps*): discrimination of individual and sex differences. J. Mamm., 68:391–395.

———. 1990a. Distributional extensions of mammals in Colorado. J. Colorado-Wyoming Acad. Sci., 12(1):48.

———. 1990b. Spatial utilization and scent-mark location in a territorial lagomorph. Pp. 388–393, *in* Chemical signals in vertebrates (D. W. Macdonald, D. Muller-Schwarze, and S. Natyncznk, eds.). Oxford Univ. Press, Oxford, 5:1–659.

———, ed. 1991. Colorado mammal distribution latilong study. Colorado Div. Wildl., Denver, 31 pp.

Meaney, C. A., S. J. Bissell, and J. S. Slater. 1987. A nine-banded armadillo, *Dasypus novemcinctus* (Dasypodidae), in Colorado. Southwestern Nat., 32:507–508.

Mech, L. D. 1970. The wolf: the ecology and behavior of an endangered species. Nat. Hist. Press, Garden City, New York, 384 pp.

———. 1974. *Canis lupus.* Mamm. Species, 37:1–6.

———. 1980. Age, sex, reproduction, and spatial organization of lynxes colonizing northeastern Minnesota. J. Mamm., 61:261–267.

Meaney, C. A., and D. Van Vuren. 1993. Recent distribution of bison in Colorado west of the Great Plains. Proc. Denver Mus. Nat. Hist., Series 3, 4:1–10.

Mech, L. D., and R. E. McRoberts. 1990. Survival of white-tailed deer fawns in relation to maternal age. J. Mamm., 71:465–467.

Medin, D. E., and A. E. Anderson. 1979. Modeling the dynamics of a Colorado mule deer population. Wildl. Monogr., 68:1–77.

Mehrer, C. F. 1976. Gestation period in the wolverine, *Gulo gulo.* J. Mamm., 57:570.

Mellott, R. S., and J. R. Choate. 1984. *Sciurus aberti* and *Microtus montanus* on foothills of the Culebra Range in southern Colorado. Southwestern Nat., 29:135–137.

Mellott, R. S., and E. D. Fleharty. 1986. Distribution status of the hispid cotton rat (*Sigmodon hispidus*) in Colorado. Trans. Kansas Acad. Sci., 89:75–77.

Melquist, W. E., and A. E. Dronkert. 1987. River otter. Pp. 626–641, *in* Wild furbearer management and conservation in North America (M. Novak, J.A. Baker, M.E. Obbard, and B.

Malloch, eds.). Ontario Trappers Association, Toronto, 1150 pp.

Melquist, W. E., and M. G. Hornocker. 1979. Methods and techniques for studying and censusing river otter populations. Tech Rep., Univ. Idaho For., Wildl. and Range Exper. Sta. 8:1–17 pp.

———. 1983. Ecology of river otters in west central Idaho. Wildl. Monogr., 83:1–60.

Melquist, W. E., J. S. Whitman, and M. G. Hornocker. 1981. Resource partitioning and coexistence of sympatric mink and river otter populations. Pp. 187–220, *in* Proc. Worldwide Furbearer Conf. (J. A. Chapman and D. Pursley, eds.). Worldwide Furbearer Conf., Inc., Frostburg, Maryland, 2059 pp.

Menkens, G. E., Jr., and S. H. Anderson. 1989. Temporal-spatial variation in white-tailed prairie dog demography and life histories in Wyoming. Canadian J. Zool., 67:343–349.

———. 1991. Population dynamics of white-tailed prairie dogs during an epizootic of sylvatic plague. J. Mamm., 72:328–331.

Meredith, D. H. 1974. Long distance movements by two species of chipmunks (*Eutamias*) in southern Alberta. J. Mamm., 55:466–469.

Merritt, J. F. 1981. *Clethrionomys gapperi.* Mamm. Species, 146:1–9.

———. 1984. Growth patterns and seasonal thermogenesis of *Clethrionomys gapperi* inhabiting the Appalachian and Rocky Mountains of North America. Pp. 201–213, *in* Winter ecology of small mammals (J. F. Merritt, ed.). Spec. Publ., Carnegie Mus. Nat. Hist., 10:1–380.

———. 1985. Influence of snowcover on survival of *Clethrionomys gapperi* inhabiting the Appalachian and Rocky Mountains of North America. Acta Zool. Fennica, 173:73–74.

Merritt, J. F., and J. M. Merritt 1978a. Population ecology and energy relationships of *Clethrionomys gapperi* in a Colorado subalpine forest. J. Mamm., 59:576–598.

———. 1978b. Seasonal home ranges and activity of small mammals of a Colorado subalpine forest. Acta Theriol., 23:195–202.

———. 1980. Population ecology of the deer mouse (*Peromyscus maniculatus*) in the Front Range of Colorado. Spec. Publ., Carnegie Mus. Nat. Hist., 49:113–130.

Meserve, P. L. 1977. Three-dimensional home ranges of cricetid rodents. J. Mamm., 58:549–558.

Messick, J. P. 1987. North American badger. Pp. 586–597, *in* Wild furbearer management and conservation in North America (M. Novak, J.A. Baker, M.E. Obbard, and B. Malloch, eds.). Ontario Trappers Association, Toronto, 1150 pp.

Messick, J. P., and M. G. Hornocker. 1981. Ecology of the badger in southwestern Idaho. Wildl. Monogr., 76:1–53.

Messick, J. P., G. W. Smith, and A. M. Barnes. 1983. Serologic testing of badgers to monitor plague in southwestern Idaho. J. Wildl. Dis., 19:1–6.

Messick, J. P., M. C. Todd, and M. G. Hornocker. 1981. Comparative ecology of two badger populations. Pp. 1290–1304, *in* Proc. Worldwide Furbearer Conf. (J. A. Chapman and D. Pursley, eds.). Worldwide Furbearer Conf., Inc., Frostburg, Maryland, 2059 pp.

Meyer, B. J., and R. K. Meyer. 1944. Growth and reproduction of the cotton rat, *Sigmodon hispidus hispidus*, under laboratory conditions. J. Mamm., 25:107–129.

Mighetto, L. 1991. Wild animals and American environmental ethics. Univ. Arizona Press, Tucson, 177 pp.

Miller, F. W. 1925. A new hog-nosed skunk. J. Mamm., 6:50–51.

———. 1930. A note on the pygmy vole in Colorado. J. Mamm., 11:83–84.

Miller, G. S., Jr., and G. M. Allen. 1928. The American bats of the the genera *Myotis* and *Pizonyx*. Bull. U.S. Nat. Mus., 144:1–218.

Miller, P. H. 1964. The ecological distribution of mammals in Colorado National Monument, Mesa County, Colorado. Unpubl. M.S. thesis, Oklahoma State Univ., Stillwater, 133 pp.

Miller, P. H., and C. J. McCoy. 1965. Kit fox in Colorado. J. Mamm., 46:342–343.

Miller, R. S. 1964. Ecology and distribution of pocket gophers (Geomyidae) in Colorado. Ecology, 42:256–272.

Miller, R. S., and R. A. Ward. 1960. Ectoparasites of pocket gophers from Colorado. Amer. Midland Nat., 64:382–391.

Mills, E. A. 1913. In beaver world. Houghton Mifflin, Boston, 227 pp.

———. 1919. The grizzly, our greatest wild mammal. Riverside Press, Cambridge, Massachusetts, 284 pp.

Milner, J., C. Jones, and J.K. Jones, Jr. 1990. *Nyctinomops macrotis*. Mamm. Species, 351:1–4.

Mitchell, J. L. 1961. Mink movements and populations on a Montana river. J. Wildl. Mgmt., 25:48–54.

Mitchell, R. S. 1972. Small rodents of the flood plain of the South Platte River at the proposed Narrows Reservoir site. Unpubl. M.A. thesis, Univ. Northern Colorado, Greeley, 50 pp.

Mohamed, R. M. 1989. Ecology and biology of *Perognathus* species in a grassland ecosystem in northeastern Colorado. Unpubl. Ph.D. dissert., Univ. Northern Colorado, Greeley, 177 pp.

Monson, G., and L. Sumner, eds. 1980. The desert bighorn. Univ. Arizona Press, Tucson, 370 pp.

Montgomery, G. G. 1964. Tooth eruption in preweaned raccoons. J. Wildl. Mgmt., 28:582–584.

———. 1968. Pelage development of young raccoons. J. Mamm., 49:142–145.

———. 1969. Weaning of captive raccoons. J. Wildl. Mgmt., 33:154–159.

Moore, T. D., L. E. Spence, and C. E. Dugnolle. 1974. Identification of the dorsal guard hairs of some mammals of Wyoming. Wyoming Game and Fish Dept., Cheyenne, 174 pp.

More, G. 1976. Some winter food habits of lynx in the southern MacKenzie district, NWT. Canadian Field-Nat., 90:499–500.

Morgart, J. R. 1985. Carnivorous behavior by a white-tailed antelope ground squirrel, *Ammospermophilus leucurus*. Southwestern Nat. 30:304–305.

Morrell, S. H. 1972. Life history of the San Joaquin kit fox. California Fish and Game, 58:162–174.

———. 1975. San Joaquin kit fox distribution and abundance in 1975. Admin. Rept., Wildl. Mgmt. Branch, California Dept. Fish and Game, 75–3:1–27.

Moser, D. A. 1962. The bighorn sheep of Colorado. Tech. Publ., Colorado Game and Fish Dept. 10:1–49.

Moulton, M. P. 1978. Small mammal associations in grazed versus ungrazed cottonwood riparian woodlands in eastern Colorado. Pp. 133–140, *in* Lowland river and stream habitat in Colorado: a symposium (W.D. Graul and S.J. Bissell, technical coordinators). Colorado Chapter, Wildl. Soc. and Colorado Audubon Council, Greeley, 195 pp.

Moulton, M. P., J. R. Choate, and S. J. Bissell. 1979. Sympatry of pocket gophers on Mesa de Maya, Colorado. Trans. Kansas Acad. Sci., 82:194–195.

———. 1981*a*. Small mammals on revegetated agricultural land in eastern Colorado. Prairie Nat., 13:99–104.

———. 1983. Biogeographic relationships of pocket gophers in southeastern Colorado. Southwestern Nat., 28:53–60.

Moulton, M. P., J. R. Choate, S. J. Bissell, and R. A. Nicholson. 1981*b*. Associations of small mammals on the central High Plains of eastern Colorado. Southwestern Nat., 26:53–57.

Mullican, T. R., and B. L. Keller. 1986. Ecology of the sagebrush vole (*Lemmiscus curtatus*) in southeastern Idaho. Canadian J. Zool., 64:1,218–1,223.

Mumford, R. E. 1973. Natural history of the red bat (*Lasiurus borealis*) in Indiana. Period. Biol., 75:155–158.

Murie, A. 1940. Ecology of the coyote in the Yellowstone. Fauna Ser., U.S. Nat. Park Serv. 4:1–206.

Murie, O. J. 1935. Food habits of the coyote in Jackson Hole, Wyoming. Circ., U.S. Dept. Agric., 362:1–24.

———. 1951. The elk of North America. The Stackpole Co., Harrisburg, Pennsylvania, 376 pp.

Musgrove, B. F. 1951. Weasel foraging patterns in the Robinson Lake area, Idaho. Murrelet, 32:8–11.

Mutch, G. R. P., and M. Aleksiuk. 1977. Ecological aspects of winter dormancy in the striped skunk (*Mephitis mephitis*). Canadian J. Zool., 55:607–615.

Mutel, C. F., and J. C. Emerick. 1992. From grassland to glacier, the natural history of Colorado and the surrounding region, second ed. Johnson Books, Boulder, 290 pp.

Myers, G. T., and T. A. Vaughan. 1964. Food habits of the plains pocket gopher in eastern Colorado. J. Mamm., 45:588–597.

Myers, L. G. 1969. Home range and longevity in *Zapus princeps* in Colorado. Amer. Midland Nat., 82:628–629.

Nadler, C. F., R. S. Hoffmann, and K. R. Greer. 1971. Chromosomal divergence during evolution of ground squirrel populations (Rodentia: *Spermophilus*) Syst. Zool., 20:298–305.

Nagy, J. G., H. W. Steinhoff, and G. M. Ward. 1964. Effects of essential oils of sagebrush on deer rumen microbial function. J. Wildl. Mgmt., 28:785–790.

Nagy, J. G., and R. P. Tengerdy. 1967. Antibacterial action of essential oils of *Artemisia* as an ecological factor II. Antibacterial action of the volatile oils of *Artemisia tridentata* (big sagebrush) on bacteria from the rumen of mule deer. Appl. Microbiol., 16:441–444.

Naiman, R. J., C. A. Johnston, and J. C. Kelley. 1988. Alteration of North American streams by beaver. BioScience, 38:753–762.

Nams, V. 1981. Prey selection mechanisms of the ermine (*Mustela erminea*). Pp. 861–882, *in* Proc. Worldwide Furbearer Conf. (J. A. Chapman and D. Pursley, eds.). Worldwide Furbearer Conf., Inc., Frostburg, Maryland, 2059 pp.

Nams, V., and S. S. Beare. 1982. Use of trees by ermine, *Mustela erminea.* Canadian Field-Nat., 96:89–90.

Nash, D. J., and C. A. Ramey. 1970. The tassel-eared squirrel in Colorado. Occas. Publ. Dept. Zool., Colorado State Univ., 2:1–6.

Nash, D. J., and R. N. Seaman. 1977. *Sciurus aberti.* Mamm. Species, 80:1–5.

Nava, J. A. 1970. The reproductive biology of the Alaska lynx (*Lynx canadensis*). Unpubl. M.S. thesis. Univ. Alaska, Fairbanks, 141 pp.

Nead, D. M., J. C. Halfpenny, and S. Bissell. 1984. The status of wolverines in Colorado. Northwest Sci., 58:286–289.

Neff, D. J. 1957. Ecological effects of beaver habitat abandonment in the Colorado Rockies. J. Wildl. Mgmt., 21:80–84.

⸻. 1959. A seventy-year history of a Colorado beaver colony. J. Mamm., 40:381–387.

Negus, N. C. 1950. Habitat adaptability of *Phenacomys* in Wyoming. J. Mamm., 31:351.

Negus, N. C., P. J. Berger, and B. W. Brown. 1986. Microtine population dynamics in a predictable environment. Canadian J. Zool., 64:785–792.

Nellis, C. H., and L. B. Keith. 1968. Hunting activities and success of lynxes in Alberta. J. Wildl. Mgmt., 32:718–722.

Nellis, C. H., S. P. Wetmore, and L. B. Keith. 1972. Lynx-prey interactions in central Alberta. J. Wildl. Mgmt., 36:320–329.

Nelson, J. R. 1982. Relationships of elk and other large herbivores. Pp. 443–478, *in* Elk of North America, ecology and management (J. W. Thomas and D. E. Toweill, eds.). Stackpole Books, Harrisburg, PA, 698 pp.

Nelson, R. A., and T. D. I. Beck. 1984. Hibernation adaptation in the black bear: implications for management. Proc. Eastern Workshop Bear Mgmt. Res., 7:48–53.

Nelson, R. A., H. W. Wahner, J. D. Jones, R. D. Ellefson, and P. E. Zollman. 1973. Metabolism of bears before, during, and after winter sleep. Amer. J. Physiol., 224:491–496.

Nixon, C. M., D. M. Worley, and M. W. McClain. 1968. Food habits of squirrels in southeast Ohio. J. Wildl. Mgmt., 32:294–305.

Novacek, M.J. 1985. Cranial evidence for rodent affinities. Pp. 59–81, *in* Evolutionary relationships among rodents (W.P. Luckett and J.-L. Hartenberger, eds.). NATO ASI Series, Series A: Life Sci., 92:1–721.

⸻. 1990. Morphology, paleontology, and the higher clades of mammals. Current Mammal., 2:507–543.

Novak, M. 1987. Beaver. Pp. 283–312, *in* Wild furbearer management and conservation in North America (M. Novak, J. A. Baker, M. E. Obbard, and B. Malloch, eds.). Ontario Trappers Association, Toronto, 1150 pp.

Novak, M., J. A. Baker, M. E. Obbard, and B. Malloch, eds. 1987. Wild furbearer management and conservation in North America. Ontario Trappers Association, Toronto, 1150 pp.

Nowak, R. M. 1973. Return of the wolverine. Nat. Parks Conserv. Mag., 47:20–23.

⸻, ed. 1991. Walker's mammals of the world. Fifth ed. Johns Hopkins Univ. Press, Baltimore, 2 vols.

Nowlin, R. A. 1985. Distribution of moose during occupation of vacant habitat in northcentral Colorado. Unpubl. M.S. thesis, Colorado State Univ., Fort Collins, 60 pp.

Nowlin, R. A., W. K. Seitz, and R. N. Denney. 1979. Initial progress of the Colorado moose reintroduction. Proc. N. Amer. Moose Conf. and Workshop, 15:187–212.

Oaks, E. C., P. J. Young, G. L. Kirkland, Jr., and D. F. Schmidt. 1987. *Spermophilus variegatus.* Mamm. Species, 272:1–8.

Obbard, M. E. 1987. Red squirrel. Pp. 265–281, *in* Wild furbearer management and conservation in North America (M. Novak, J. A. Baker, M. E. Obbard, and B. Malloch, eds.). Ontario Trappers Association, Toronto, 1150 pp.

O'Farrell, J. J. 1974. Seasonal activity patterns of rodents in a sagebrush community. J. Mamm., 55:809–823.

O'Farrell, M. J., and W. G. Bradley. 1970. Activity patterns of bats over a desert spring. J. Mamm., 51:18–26.

O'Farrell, M. J., W. G. Bradley, and G. W. Jones. 1967. Fall and winter bat activity at a desert spring in southern Nevada. Southwestern Nat., 12:163–171.

O'Farrell, M. J., and E. H. Studier. 1973. Reproduction, growth, and development in *Myotis thysanodes* and *M. lucifugus* (Chiroptera: Vespertilionidae). Ecology, 54:18–30.

⸻. 1980. *Myotis thysanodes.* Mamm. Species, 137:1–5.

O'Farrell, T. P. 1987. Kit fox. Pp. 422–431, *in* Wild furbearer management and conservation in North America (M. Novak, J. A. Baker, M. E. Obbard, and B. Malloch, eds.). Ontario Trappers Association, Toronto, 1150 pp.

O'Farrell, T. P., R. J. Olson, R. O. Gilbert, and J. D. Hedlund. 1975. A population of Great Basin pocket mice, *Perognathus parvus,* in the shrub-steppe of south-central Washington. Ecol. Monogr., 45:1–28.

O'Gara, B. W. 1978. *Antilocapra americana.* Mamm. Species, 90:1–7.

O'Gara, B. W., and G. Matson. 1975. Growth and casting of horns by pronghorns and exfoliation of horns by bovids. J. Mamm., 56:829–846.

O'Gara, B. W., R. F. Moy, and G. D. Bear. 1971. The annual testicular cycle and horn casting in the pronghorn (*Antilocapra americana*). J. Mamm., 52:537–544.

Oldemeyer, J. L. 1966. Winter ecology of bighorn sheep in Yellowstone National Park. Unpubl. M.S. thesis, Colorado State Univ., Fort Collins, 107 pp.

Olmsted, C. E., Jr. 1979. The ecology of aspen with reference to utilization by large herbivores in Rocky Mountain National Park. Pp. 89–97, *in* North American elk: ecology, behavior, and management (M. S. Boyce and L. D. Hayden-Wing, eds.). Univ. Wyoming, Laramie, 294 pp.

Olsen, A., and P. N. Lehner. 1978. Conditioned avoidance of prey in coyotes. J. Wildl. Mgmt., 42:676–679.

Olson, T. E., and F. L. Knopf. 1988. Patterns of relative diversity within riparian small mammal communities, Platte River watershed, Colorado. Pp. 379–386, *in* Management of amphibians, reptiles, and small mammals in North America (R. C. Szaro, K. R. Severson, and D. R. Patton, technical coordinators). Gen. Tech. Rept., U.S. Forest Service, RM–166:1–458.

O'Meara, T. E., J. B. Haufler, L. H. Stetler, and J. G. Nagy. 1981. Nongame wildlife responses to chaining of pinyon-juniper woodlands. J. Wildl. Mgmt., 45:381–389.

O'Meilia, M. E., F. L. Knopf, and J. C. Lewis. 1982. Some consequences of competition between prairie dogs and beef cattle. J. Range Mgmt., 35:580–585.

O'Neal, G. T., J. T. Flinders, and W. P. Clary. 1986. Behavioral ecology of the Nevada kit fox (*Vulpes macrotis nevadensis*) on a managed desert rangeland. Current Mammal., 1:443–481.

Orr, R. T. 1940. The rabbits of California. Occas. Papers California Acad. Sci., 19:1–227.

———. 1950. Unusual behavior and occurrence of a hoary bat. J. Mamm., 31:456–457.

———. 1954. Natural history of the pallid bat, *Antrozous pallidus*. Proc. California Acad. Sci., 28:165–264.

Ortega, J. C. 1990. Reproductive biology of the rock squirrel (*Spermophilus variegatus*) in southeastern Arizona. J. Mamm., 71(3):448–457.

O'Shea, T. J., and T. A. Vaughan. 1977. Nocturnal and seasonal activities of the pallid bat, *Antrozous pallidus*. J. Mamm., 58:269–284.

Packard, F. M. 1947. A survey of the beaver population of Rocky Mountain National Park, Colorado. J. Mamm., 28:219–227.

Packard, J. M., L. D. Mech, and U.S. Seal. 1983. Social influences on reproduction in wolves. Pp. 78–85, *in* Wolves in Canada and Alaska: their status, biology, and management (L.N. Carbyn, ed.). Rep. Ser., Canadian Wildl. Serv., 45:1–135.

Packard, R. L. 1956. The tree squirrels of Kansas. Misc. Publ. Mus. Nat. Hist., Univ. Kansas, 11:1–67.

Paradiso, J. L., and R. M. Nowak. 1982. Wolves. Pp. 460–474, *in* Wild mammals of North America: biology, management, and economics (J. A. Chapman and G. A. Feldhamer, eds.). Johns Hopkins Univ. Press, Baltimore, 1147 pp.

Parker, G. R., J. W. Maxwell, L. D. Morton, and G. E. J. Smith. 1983. The ecology of the lynx (*Lynx canadensis*) on Cape Breton Island. Canadian J. Zool., 61:770–786.

Pasitschniak-Arts, M. 1993. *Ursus arctos*. Mamm. Species, 439:1–10.

Patterson, B. D. 1984. Geographic variation and taxonomy of Colorado and Hopi chipmunks (genus *Eutamias*). J. Mamm., 65:442–456.

Patterson, B. D., and L. R. Heaney. 1987. Preliminary analysis of geographic variation in red-tailed chipmunks (*Eutamias ruficaudus*). J. Mamm., 68:782–791.

Patton, D. R. 1977. Managing southwestern ponderosa pine for Abert squirrel. J. Forestry, 264–267.

———. 1984. A model to evaluate Abert squirrel habitat in uneven-aged stands of ponderosa pine. Wildl. Soc. Bull., 12:408–414.

Patton, R. F. 1974. Ecological and behavioral relationships of the skunks of Trans-Pecos Texas. Unpubl. Ph.D. dissert., Texas A & M Univ., College Station, 199 pp.

Pauls, R. W. 1978. Behavioural strategies relevant to the energy economy of the red squirrel (*Tamiasciurus hudsonicus*). Canadian J. Zool., 56:1519–1525.

Pearson, O. P. 1942. On the cause and nature of a poisonous action produced by the bite of a shrew (*Blarina brevicauda*). J. Mamm., 23:159–166.

———. 1944. Reproduction in the shrew (*Blarina brevicauda* Say). Amer. J. Anat., 75:39–93.

———. 1946. Scent glands of the short-tailed shrew. Anat. Rec., 94:615–629.

Pearson, P. G. 1952. Observations concerning the life history and ecology of the wood rat *Neotoma floridana floridana* (Ord). J. Mamm., 33:459–463.

Peden, D. G. 1976. Botanical composition of bison diets on shortgrass plains. Amer. Midland Nat., 96:225–229.

Peden, D. G., G. M. Van Dyne, R. W. Rice, and R. M. Hansen. 1974. The trophic ecology of *Bison bison* L. on shortgrass plains. J. Appl. Ecol., 11:489–498.

Peek, J. M. 1974. On the nature of winter habitats of Shiras moose. Nat. canadienne, 101:131–141.

———. 1982. Elk. Pp. 851–861, *in* Wild mammals of North America: biology, management, and economics (J. A. Chapman and G. A. Feldhamer, eds.) Johns Hopkins Univ. Press, Baltimore, 1147 pp.

Pefaur, J. E, and R. S. Hoffmann. 1974. Notes on the biology of the olive-backed pocket mouse *Perognathus fasciatus* on the northern Great Plains. Prairie Nat., 6:7–15.

———. 1975. Studies of small mammal populations at three sites on the Northern Great Plains. Occas. Papers Mus. Nat. Hist., Univ. Kansas, 37:1–27.

Pelton, M. R. 1982. Black bear. Pp. 504–514, *in* Wild mammals of North America: biology, management, and economics (J. A. Chapman and G. A. Feldhamer, eds.). Johns Hopkins Univ. Press, Baltimore, 1147 pp.

Pence, D. B., and J. W. Custer. 1981. Host-parasite relationships in the wild Canidae in North America. II. Pathology of infectious diseases in the genus *Canis*. Pp. 760–785, *in* Proc. Worldwide Furbearer Conf. (J. A. Chapman and D. Pursley, eds.). Worldwide Furbearer Conf., Inc., Frostburg, Maryland, 2059 pp.

Perry, H. R., Jr. 1982. Muskrats. Pp. 282–325, *in* Wild mammals of North America: biology, management, and economics (J. A. Chapman, and G. A. Feldhamer eds.). Johns Hopkins Press, Baltimore, 1147 pp.

Peters, R. P., and L. D. Mech. 1975. Scent-marking in wolves. Amer. Sci., 63:628–637.

Peterson, R. L. 1955. North American moose. Univ. Toronto Press, Toronto, 280 pp.

Pettigrew, J. D. 1986. Flying primates? Megabats have the advanced pathway from eye to mid-brain. Science, 231:1304–1306.

Pettus, D., and R. R. Lechleitner. 1963. *Microsorex* in Colorado. J. Mamm., 44:119.

Pfeifer, S. 1980. Aerial predation on Wyoming ground squirrels. J. Mamm., 61:368–371.

Phillips, G. L. 1966. Ecology of the big brown bat (Chiroptera: Vespertilionidae) in northeastern Kansas. Amer. Midland Nat., 75:168–198.

Phillips, R. L., R. D. Andrews, G. L. Storm, and R. A. Bishop. 1972. Dispersal and mortality of red foxes. J. Wildl. Mgmt., 36:237–248.

Pizzimenti, J. J. 1981. Increasing sexual dimorphism in prairie dogs: evidence for changes during the past century. Southwestern Nat., 26:43–47.

Pizzimenti, J. J., and R. S. Hoffmann. 1973. *Cynomys gunnisoni*. Mamm. Species. 25:1–4.

Poché, R. M., and G. L. Bailey. 1974. Notes on the spotted bat (*Euderma maculatum*) from southwest Utah. Great Basin Nat., 34:254–256.

Poglayen-Neuwall, I., and I. Poglayen-Neuwall. 1980. Gestation period and parturition of the ringtail *Bassariscus astutus* (Lichtenstein, 1830) Z. Saugetierk., 45:73–81.

Poglayen-Neuwall, I., and D. E. Toweill. 1988. *Bassariscus astutus*. Mamm. Species, 327:1–8.

Pojar, T. M., and L. W. Miller. 1984. Recurrent estrus and cycle length in pronghorn. J. Wildl. Mgmt., 48:973–979.

Pokropus, E. J., and B. H. Banta. 1966. Observations on two Colorado shrews in captivity. Wasmann Jour. Biol., 24:75–81.

Polder, E. 1968. Spotted skunk and weasel populations den and cover usage in northeast Iowa. Proc. Iowa Acad. Sci., 75:142–146.

Polderboer, E. B., L. W. Kuhn, and G. O. Hendrickson. 1941. Winter and spring habits of weasels in central Iowa. J. Wildl. Mgmt., 5:115–119.

Poulson, D. D. 1988. *Chaetodipus hispidus*. Mamm. Species, 320:1–4.

Powell, R. A. 1973. A model for raptor predation on weasels. J. Mamm., 54:259–263.

———. 1979. Mustelid spacing patterns: variations on a theme by *Mustela*. Z. Tierpsychol., 50:153–165.

———. 1981. *Martes pennanti*. Mamm. Species 156:1–6.

Powers, R. A., and B. J. Verts 1971. Reproduction in the mountain cottontail rabbit in Oregon. J. Wildl. Mgmt., 35:605–612.

Prenzlow, E. J., D. L. Gilbert, and F. A. Glover. 1968. Some behavior patterns of the pronghorn. Spec. Rept., Colorado Div. Game, Fish, and Parks, 17:1–16.

Preston, J. R., and R. E. Martin. 1963. A gray shrew population in Harmon County, Oklahoma. J. Mamm., 44:268–270.

Pruitt, W. O., Jr. 1953. An analysis of some physical factors affecting the local distribution of the shorttail shrew (*Blarina brevicauda*) in the northern part of the Lower Peninsula of Michigan. Misc. Publ. Mus. Zool., Univ. Michigan, 79:1–39.

———. 1954. Notes on Colorado *Phenacomys* and pikas. J. Mamm., 35:450–452.

Quick, H. F. 1951. Notes on the ecology of weasels in Gunnison County, Colorado. J. Mamm., 32:281–290.

Quimby, D. C. 1951. The life history and ecology of the jumping mouse, *Zapus hudsonius*. Ecol. Monogr., 21:61–95.

Quimby, D. C., and J. E. Gaab. 1957. Mandibular dentition as an age indicator in Rocky Mountain elk. J. Wildl. Mgmt., 21: 435–451.

Quinn, N.W.S., and G. Parker. 1987. Lynx. Pp. 682–694, *in* Wild furbearer management and conservation in North America (M. Novak, J. A. Baker, M. E. Obbard, and B. Malloch, eds.). Ontario Trappers Association, Toronto, 1150 pp.

Quinones, B. E. 1988. The potential for human plague acquired from rock squirrels in the Fort Collins area. Unpubl. M.S. thesis, Colorado State Univ., Fort Collins, 56 pp.

Rabb, G. B. 1959. Reproductive and vocal behavior in captive pumas. J. Mamm., 40:616–617.

Rainey, D. G. 1956. Eastern woodrat, *Neotoma floridana*: life history and ecology. Misc. Publ. Mus. Nat. Hist., Univ. Kansas, 8:535–646.

Ramey, C. A., and D. J. Nash. 1971. Abert's squirrel in Colorado. Southwestern Nat., 16:125–126.

———. 1976a. Geographic variation in Abert's squirrels (*Sciurus aberti*). Southwestern Nat., 21:135–139.

———. 1976b. Coat color polymorphism of Abert's squirrel, *Sciurus aberti*, in Colorado. Southwestern Nat., 21:209–217.

Randall, J. A., and R. E. Johnson. 1979. Population densities and habitat occupancy by *Microtus longicaudus* and *M. montanus*. J. Mamm., 60:217–219.

Randolph, J. C. 1973. Ecological energetics of a homeothermic predator, the short-tailed shrew. Ecology, 54:1166–1187.

Ratcliff, H. M. 1941. Winter range conditions in Rocky Mountain National Park. Trans. N. Amer. Wildl. Conf., 6:132–139.

Rathbun, A. P., M. C. Wells, and M. Bekoff. 1980. Cooperative predation by coyotes on badgers. J. Mamm., 61:375–376.

Rausch, R. A., and A. M. Pearson. 1972. Notes on the wolverine in Alaska and the Yukon Territory. J. Wildl. Mgmt., 36:249–268.

Rausch, R. L. 1953. On the status of some Arctic mammals. Arctic, 6:91–148.

———. 1963. Geographic variation in size in North American brown bears, *Ursus arctos* L., as indicated by condylobasal length. Canadian J. Zool., 41:33–45.

———. 1967. Some aspects of the population ecology of wolves, Alaska. Amer. Zool., 7:253–265.

Raymond, M., J.-F. Robitaille, P. Lauzon, and R. Vaudry. 1990. Prey-dependent profitability of foraging behaviour of male and female ermine, *Mustela erminea*. Oikos, 58:323–328.

Raynor, L. S. 1985a. Dynamics of a plague outbreak in Gunnison's prairie dog. J. Mamm., 66:194–196.

———. 1985b. Effects of habitat quality on growth, age of first reproduction and dispersal in Gunnison's prairie dogs (*Cynomys gunnisoni*) Canadian J. Zool., 63:2835–2840.

Raynor, L. S., A. K. Brody, and C. Gilbert. 1987. Hibernation in the Gunnison's prairie dog. J. Mamm., 68:147–150.

Reading, R. P., and T. W. Clark. 1990. Black-footed ferret annotated bibliography, 1986–1990. Tech. Bull., Montana Bur. Land Mgmt., 3:1–22.

Reed, E. B. 1955. January breeding of *Peromyscus* in north central Colorado. J. Mamm., 36:462–463.

Reed, K. M., and J. R. Choate. 1986. Geographic variation in the plains pocket mouse (*Perognathus flavescens*) on the Great Plains. Texas J. Sci., 38:227–240.

Reed, M. P., and J. R. Choate. 1988. Noteworthy southwestern records of the prairie vole. Southwestern Nat., 33:495–496.

Reeves, H. M., and R. M. Williams. 1956. Reproduction, size, and mortality in the Rocky Mountain muskrat. J. Mamm., 37:494–500.

Reich, L. M. 1981. *Microtus pennsylvanicus*. Mamm. Species, 159:1–8.

Reid, D. G., S. M. Herrero, and T. E. Code. 1988. River otters as agents of water loss from beaver ponds. J. Mamm., 69:100–107.

Reid, V. H. 1973. Population biology of the northern pocket gopher. Pp. 21–41, *in* Pocket gophers and Colorado mountain rangeland (G. T. Turner, R. M. Hansen, V. H. Reid, H. P. Tietjen, and A. L. Ward, eds.). Colorado State Univ., Exp. Sta. Bull., 2:1–554.

Reig, O. A. 1977. A proposed unified nomenclature for the enameled components of the molar teeth of the Cricetidae (Rodentia). J. Zool., 181:227–241.

Remington, J. D. 1952. Food habits, growth, and behavior of two captive pine marten. J. Mamm., 33:66–70.

Rennicke, J. 1990. Colorado wildlife. Colorado Geogr. Ser., 6:1–138.

Retzer, J. L., H. M. Swope, J. D. Remington, and W. H. Rutherford. 1956. Suitability of physical factors for beaver management in the Rocky Mountains of Colorado. Tech. Bull., Colorado Dept. Game and Fish, 2:1–32.

Reynolds, H. C. 1952. Studies on reproduction in the opossum (*Didelphis virginiana*). Univ. California Publ. Zool., 52:223–284.

Reynolds, H. W., R. D. Glaholt, and A. L. Hawley. 1982. Bison. Pp. 972–1007, *in* Wild mammals of North America: biology, management, and economics (J. A. Chapman and G. A. Feldhamer, eds.). Johns Hopkins Univ. Press, Baltimore, 1147 pp.

Reynolds, T. D., and W. L. Wakkinen. 1987. Characteristics of the burrows of four species of rodents in undisturbed soil in southeastern Idaho. Amer. Midland Nat., 118:245–250.

Ribble, D. O., and F. B. Samson. 1987. Microhabitat associations of small mammals in southeastern Colorado, with special emphasis on *Peromyscus* (Rodentia). Southwestern Nat., 32:291–303.

Rice, D. W. 1957. Sexual behavior of tassel-eared squirrels. J. Mamm., 38:129.

Richards, R. E. 1976. The distribution, water balance, and vocalization of the ringtail, *Bassariscus astutus*. Unpubl. Ph.D. dissert., Univ. Northern Colorado, Greeley, 68 pp.

Richardson, L., T. W. Clark, S. C. Forrest, and T. M. Campbell, III. 1987. Winter ecology of black-footed ferrets (*Mustela nigripes*) at Meeteetse, Wyoming. Amer. Midland Nat., 117:225–239.

Richens, V. B. 1966. Notes on the digging activity of a northern pocket gopher. J. Mamm., 47:531–533.

Richins, G. H., H. D. Smith, and C. D. Jorgensen. 1974. Growth and development of the western harvest mouse, *Reithrodontomys megalotis megalotis*. Great Basin Nat., 34:105–120.

Riddle, B. R., and J. R. Choate. 1986. Systematics and biogeography of *Onychomys leucogaster* in western North America. J. Mamm., 67:233–255.

Ride, W.E.L. 1964. A review of Australian fossil marsupials. J. Royal Soc. Western Australia, 47:97–131.

———. 1970. A guide to the native mammals of Australia. Oxford Univ. Press, Melbourne, 249 pp.

Rideout, C. B. 1978. Mountain goat. Pp. 149–159, *in* Big game of North America; ecology and management (J. L. Schmidt and D. L. Gilbert, eds.). Stackpole Books, Harrisburg, Pennsylvania, 494 pp.

Rideout, C. B., and R. S. Hoffmann. 1975. *Oreamnos americanus*. Mamm. Species, 63:1–6.

Robinette, W. L., J. S. Gashwiler, and O. W. Morris. 1959. Food habits of the cougar in Utah and Nevada. J. Wildl. Mgmt., 23:261–273.

———. 1961. Notes on cougar productivity and life history. J. Mamm., 42:204–217.

Robinette, W. L., N. V. Hancock, and D. A. Jones. 1977. The Oak Creek mule deer herd in Utah. Resource Publ., Utah Div. Wildl., 77–15:1–148.

Robinette, W. L., D. A. Jones, G. Rogers, and J. S. Gashwiler. 1957. Notes on tooth development and wear for Rocky Mountain mule deer. J. Wildl. Mgmt., 21:134–153.

Robinson, J. W., and R. S. Hoffmann. 1975. Geographical and interspecific cranial variation in big-eared ground squirrels (*Spermophilus*): a multivariate study. Syst. Zool., 24:79–88.

Robinson, V. B., J. W. Newberne, and D. M. Brooks. 1957. Distemper in the American raccoon (*Procyon lotor*). J. Amer. Vet. Med. Assoc., 131:276–278.

Rodeck, H. G., and S. Anderson. 1956. *Sorex merriami* and *Microtus mexicanus* in Colorado. J. Mamm., 37:436.

Roe, F. G. 1970. The North American buffalo. Second ed. Univ. Toronto Press, Toronto, 991 pp.

Rogers, J. G., Jr., and G. K. Beauchamp. 1976. Influence of stimuli from populations of *Peromyscus leucopus* on maturation of young. J. Mamm., 57:320–330.

Rohwer, S. A., and D. L. Kilgore, Jr. 1973. Interbreeding in the arid-land foxes, *Vulpes velox* and *V. macrotis*. Systematic Zool., 22:157–165.

Rolley, R. E. 1987. Bobcat. Pp. 670–681, *in* Wild furbearer management and conservation in North America (M. Novak, J. A. Baker, M. E. Obbard, and B. Malloch, eds.). Ontario Trappers Association, Toronto, 1150 pp.

Rolston, H., III. 1986. Philosophy gone wild: essays in environmental ethics. Prometheus Books, Buffalo, NY, 269 pp.

Rongstad, O. J. 1965. A life history study of thirteen-lined ground squirrels in southern Wisconsin. J. Mamm., 46:76–87.

Rongstad, O. J., T. R. Laurion, and D. E. Andersen. 1989. Ecology of swift fox on the Pinon Canyon Maneuver Site, Colorado. Final Rept. to Environ., Energy, and Nat. Res. Div., Fort Carson, Colorado, 52 pp.

Roppe, J. R., and D. Hein. 1978. Effects of fire on wildlife in a lodgepole pine forest. Southwestern Nat., 23:279–288.

Rosatte, R. C. 1987. Striped, spotted, hooded, and hog-nosed skunk. Pp. 598–613, *in* Wild furbearer management and conservation in North America (M. Novak, J. A. Baker, M. E. Obbard, and B. Malloch, eds.). Ontario Trappers Association, Toronto, 1150 pp.

Rose, G. B. 1977. Mortality rates of tagged adult cottontail rabbits. J. Wildl. Mgmt., 41:511–514.

Rothwell, R. 1979. Nest sites of red squirrels (*Tamiasciurus hudsonicus*) in the Laramie Range of southeastern Wyoming. J. Mamm., 60:404–405.

Roughton, R. D. 1972. Shrub age structures on a mule deer winter range in Colorado. Ecology, 53:615–625.

Rue, L. L. 1964. The world of the beaver. J. B. Lippincott, Philadelphia, 155 pp.

Ruffer, D. G. 1965*a*. Burrows and burrowing behavior of *Onychomys leucogaster*. J. Mamm., 46:241–247.

———. 1965*b*. Sexual behavior of the northern grasshopper mouse (*Onychomys leucogaster*). Anim. Behav., 13:447–452.

———. 1968. Agonistic behavior of the northern grasshopper mouse (*Onychomys leucogaster breviauritus*). J. Mamm., 49:481–487.

Ruffner, G. A., R. M. Poché, M. Meierkord, and J. A. Neal. 1979. Winter bat activity over a desert wash in southwestern Utah. Southwestern Nat., 24:447–453.

Rusch, D. A., and W. G. Reeder. 1978. Population ecology of Alberta red squirrels. Ecology, 59:400–420.

Russell, K. R. 1978. Mountain lion. Pp. 207–225, *in* Big game of North America: ecology and management (J. L. Schmidt and D. L. Gilbert, eds.). Stackpole Books, Harrisburg, Pennsylvania, 494 pp.

Rust, C. C. 1962. Temperature as a modifying factor in the spring pelage change of short-tailed weasels. J. Mamm., 43:323–328.

Rutherford, W. H. 1952. Effects of summer flash flood upon a beaver population. J. Mamm., 34:261–262.

———. 1955. Wildlife and environmental relationships of beaver in Colorado forests. J. Forestry, 53:803–806.

———. 1956. Productivity rates, age classes and sex ratios of spring-caught beavers in Colorado. Outdoor Facts, Colorado Dept. Nat. Resources, Div. Game, Fish, and Parks, 4:1.

———. 1964. The beaver in Colorado: its biology, ecology, management, and economics. Tech. Publ., Colorado Game, Fish, and Parks, 17:1–49.

———. 1972*a*. Status of mountain goats in Colorado. Game Inf. Leafl., Colorado Div. Game, Fish, and Parks, 90:1–4.

———. 1972*b*. Status of transplanted bighorn sheep in Colorado. Game Inf. Leafl., Colorado Div. Game, Fish, and Parks, 92:1–3.

———. 1972*c*. Guidelines for evaluating bighorn sheep transplanting sites in Colorado. Game Inf. Leafl., Colorado Div. Game, Fish, and Parks, 93:1–3.

Saariko, J., and I. Hanski. 1990. Timing of rest and sleep in foraging shrews. Anim. Behav., 40:861–869.

Samson, F. B., F. L. Knopf, and L. B. Hass. 1988. Small mammal response to the introduction of cattle into a cottonwood floodplain. Pp. 432–438, *in* Management of amphibians, reptiles, and small mammals in North America (R. C. Szaro, K. R. Severson, and D. R. Patton, technical coordinators). Gen. Tech. Rept., U.S. Forest Service, RM-166:1–458.

Samuel, D. E., and B. B. Nelson. 1982. Foxes. Pp. 475–490, *in* Wild mammals of North America: biology, management, and economics (J. A. Chapman and G. A. Feldhamer, eds.). Johns Hopkins Univ. Press, Baltimore, 1147 pp.

Sanderson, G. C. 1951. Breeding habits and a history of the Missouri raccoon population from 1941 to 1948. Trans. N. Amer. Wildl. Conf., 16:445–460.

———. 1987. Raccoon. Pp. 486–499, *in* Wild furbearer management and conservation in North America (M. Novak, J. A. Baker, M. E. Obbard, and B. Malloch, eds.). Ontario Trappers Association, Toronto, 1150 pp.

Sanderson, G. C., and A. V. Nalbandov. 1973. The reproductive cycles of the raccoon in Illinois. Bull., Illinois Nat. Hist. Surv., 31:25–85.

Sandidge, L. L. 1953. Food and dens of the opossum (*Didelphis virginiana*) in northeastern Kansas. Trans. Kansas Acad. Sci., 56:97–106.

Sargeant, A. B. 1972. Red fox spatial characteristics in relation to water fowl predation. J. Wildl. Mgmt., 36:225–236.

———. 1978. Red fox prey demands and implications to prairie duck production. J. Wildl. Mgmt., 42:520–527.

———. 1982. A case history of a dynamic resource — the red fox. Pp. 121–137, in Midwest furbearer management (G. C. Sanderson, ed.) Proc. Symp. 43rd Midwest Fish and Wildl. Conf., Wichita, 195 pp.

Saunders, J. K., Jr. 1955. Food habits and range use of the Rocky Mountain goat in the Crazy Mountains, Montana. J. Wildl. Mgmt., 19:429–437.

———. 1963a. Movements and activities of the lynx in Newfoundland. J. Wildl. Mgmt., 27:390–400.

———. 1963b. Food habits of the lynx in Newfoundland. J. Wild. Mgmt., 27:384–390.

———. 1964. Physical characteristics of the Newfoundland lynx. J. Mamm., 45:36–47.

Savage, R.J.G., and M. R. Long. 1986. Mammal evolution: an illustrated guide. Facts on File, New York, 259 pp.

Scheck, S. H., and E. D. Fleharty. 1980. Subterranean behavior of the adult thirteen-lined ground squirrel (Spermophilus tridecemlineatus). Amer. Midland Nat., 103:191–195.

Scheffer, T. H. 1947. Ecological comparisons of the plains prairie dog and the Zuñi species. Trans. Kansas Acad. Sci., 49:401–406.

Schladweiler, J. L., and G. L. Storm. 1969. Den use by mink. J. Wildl. Mgmt., 33:1025–1026.

Schladweiler, J. L. and J. R. Tester. 1972. Survival and behavior of hand-reared mallards released in the wild. J. Wildl. Mgmt., 36:1118–1127.

Schlegal, M. W. 1977. Factors affecting calf elk survival on Coolwater Ridge in north central Idaho. Pp. 35–39, in Proc. Western States Elk Workshop, Colorado Div. of Wildl., Denver, 64 pp.

Schmidly, D. J. 1977. The mammals of Trans-Pecos Texas. Texas A & M Univ. Press, College Station, 225 pp.

———. 1983. Texan mammals east of the Balcones fault zone. Texas A & M Univ. Press, College Station, 400 pp.

Schneider, D. G., L. D. Mech, and J. R. Tester. 1971. Movements of female raccoons and their young as determined by radiotracking. Anim. Behav. Monogr., 4:1–43.

Schramm, P. 1961. Copulation and gestation in the pocket gopher. J. Mamm., 42:167–170.

Schowalter, D.B. 1980. Swarming, reproduction, and early hibernation of Myotis lucifugus and Myotis volans in Alberta, Canada. J. Mamm., 61:350–354.

Schullery, P. 1980. The bears of Yellowstone. Citron Printing, Denver, 176 pp.

———. 1986. The bears of Yellowstone, revised ed. Roberts Rinehart, Inc., Boulder, 263 pp.

Schultz, T. T., and W. C. Leininger. 1991. Nongame wildlife communities in grazed and ungrazed montane riparian sites. Great Basin Nat., 51:286–292.

Schwartz, C. C., and J. G. Nagy. 1976. Pronghorn diets relative to forage availability in northeastern Colorado. J. Wildl. Mgmt., 40:469–478.

Schwartz, C. C., J. G. Nagy, and W. L. Regelin. 1980. Juniper oil yield, terpenoid concentration, and antimicrobial effects on deer. J. Wildl. Mgmt., 44:107–113.

Schwartz, C. C., J. G. Nagy, and R. W. Rice. 1977. Pronghorn dietary quality relative to forage availability and other ruminants in Colorado. J. Wildl. Mgmt., 41:161–168.

Scott, T. G. 1943. Some food coactions of the northern plains red fox. Ecol. Monogr., 13:427–479.

Scott-Brown, J. M., S. Herrero, and J. Reynolds. 1987. Swift fox. Pp. 432–441, in Wild furbearer management and conservation in North America (M. Novak, J. A. Baker, M. E. Obbard, and B. Malloch, eds.). Ontario Trappers Association, Toronto, 1150 pp.

Scribner, K. T., and R. J. Warren. 1986. Electrophoretic and morphologic comparisons of Sylvilagus floridanus and S. audubonii in Texas. Southwestern Nat., 31:65–71.

Seidel, J. W. 1977. Elk calving behavior in west central Colorado. Pp. 38–40, in Proc. Western States Elk Workshop, Colorado Div. Wildl., Denver, 64 pp.

Seidensticker, J. C., IV, M. G. Hornocker, W. V. Wiles, and J. P. Messick. 1973. Mountain lion social organization in the Idaho Primitive Area. Wildl. Monogr., 35:1–60.

Seidensticker, J. C., IV, M. A. O'Connell, and A.J.T. Johnsingh. 1987. Virginia opossum. Pp. 247–263, in Wild furbearer management and conservation in North America (M. Novak, J. A. Baker, M. E. Obbard, and B. Malloch, eds.). Ontario Trappers Association, Toronto, 1150 pp.

Selko, L. F. 1937. Food habits of Iowa skunks in the fall of 1936. J. Wildl Mgmt., 1:70–76.

Sergeant, D. E., and D. H. Pimlott. 1959. Age determination in moose from sectioned incisor teeth. J. Wildl. Mgmt., 23:315–321.

Seton, E. T. 1929. Lives of game animals. Doubleday, Doran and Co., Garden City, New York, 949 pp.

Severinghaus, C. W. 1949. Tooth development and wear as criteria of age in white-tailed deer. J. Wildl. Mgmt., 13:195–216.

Sexson, M. L., J. R. Choate, and R. A. Nicholson. 1981. Diet of pronghorn in western Kansas. J. Range Mgmt., 34:489–493.

Shackleton, D. M. 1985. Ovis canadensis. Mamm. Species, 230:1–9.

Shadle, A. R. 1951. Laboratory copulations and gestations of porcupine, Erethizon dorsatum. J. Mamm., 32:219–221.

———. 1952. Sexual maturity and first recorded copulation of a 16-month male porcupine, Erethizon dorsatum dorsatum. J. Mamm., 33:329–331.

Shadle, A. R., M. Smelzer, and M. Metz. 1946. The sex reactions of porcupines (Erethizon d. dorsatum) before and after copulation. J. Mamm., 27:116–121.

Sharp, W. M., and L. H. Sharp. 1956. Nocturnal movements and behavior of wild raccoons at a winter feeding station. J. Mamm., 37:170–177.

Shattil, W., and R. Rozinsky, photo eds.; F. R. Rinehart and E. A. Webb, eds. 1990. Close to home: Colorado's urban wildlife. Roberts Rinehart, Boulder, 179 pp.

Sheets, R. G., R. L. Linder, and R. B. Dahlgren. 1971. Burrow systems of prairie dogs in South Dakota. J. Mamm., 52:451–453.

———. 1972. Food habits of two litters of black-footed ferrets in South Dakota. Amer. Midland Nat., 87:249–251.

Shirer, H. W., and H. S. Fitch. 1970. Comparison from radiotracking of movements and denning habits of the raccoon, striped skunk, and opossum in northeastern Kansas. J. Mamm., 51:491–503.

Shriner, W. M., and P. B. Stacey. 1991. Spatial relationships and dispersal patterns in the rock squirrel, *Spermophilus variegatus.* J. Mamm., 72:601–606.

Shump, K. A., Jr. 1978. Ecological importance of nest construction in the hispid cotton rat (*Sigmodon hispidus*). Amer. Midland Nat., 100:103–115.

Shump, K. A., Jr., and D. P. Christian. 1978. Differential burrowing by hispid cotton rats (*Sigmodon hispidus*: Rodentia). Southwestern Nat., 23:681–709.

Shump, K. A., Jr., and A. U. Shump. 1982a. *Lasiurus cinereus.* Mamm. Species, 185:1–5.

———. 1982b. *Lasiurus borealis.* Mamm. Species, 183:1–6.

Silver, J., and A. W. Moore. 1941. Mole control. U.S. Dept. of Interior, Fish and Wildl. Bull., 16:1–17.

Simmons, N. M. 1961. Daily and seasonal movements of Poudre River bighorn sheep. Unpubl. M.S. thesis, Colorado State Univ., Fort Collins, 180 pp.

Simms, D. A. 1979a. North American weasels: resource utilization and distribution. Canadian J. Zool., 57:504–520.

———. 1979b. Studies on an ermine population in southern Ontario. Canadian J. Zool., 57:824–832.

Simpson, G. G. 1945. The principles of classification and a classification of mammals. Bull. Amer. Mus. Nat. Hist., 85:1–350.

Simpson, M. R. 1993. *Myotis californicus.* Mamm. Species, 428:1–4.

Sinha, A. A., and R. A. Mead. 1976. Morphological changes in the trophoblast, uterus and corpus luteum during delayed implantation and implantation in the western spotted skunk. Amer. J. Anat., 145:331–356.

Skryja, D. D. 1974. Reproductive biology of the least chipmunk (*Eutamias minimus operarius*) in southeastern Wyoming. J. Mamm., 55:221–224.

Skryja, D. D., and T. W. Clark. 1970. Reproduction, seasonal changes in body weight, fat deposition, spleen and adrenal gland weight of the golden-mantled ground squirrel *Spermophilus lateralis lateralis* in the Laramie Mountains, Wyoming. Southwestern Nat., 15:201–208.

Slade, L. M., and E. B. Godfrey. 1982. Wild horses. Pp. 1089–1098, *in* Wild mammals of North America: biology, management, and economics (J. A. Chapman and G. A. Feldhamer, eds.). Johns Hopkins Univ. Press, Baltimore, 1147 pp.

Slobodchikoff, C. N., J. Kiriazis, C. Fischer, and E. Creef. 1991. Semantic information distinguishing individual predators in the alarm calls of Gunnison's prairie dogs. Anim. Behav., 42:713–719.

Slobodchikoff, C. N., A. Robinson, and C. Schaack. 1988. Habitat use by Gunnison's prairie dogs. Pp. 403–408, *in* Management of amphibians, reptiles, and small mammals in North America (R. C. Szaro, K. E. Severson, and D. R. Patton, technical coordinators). Gen. Tech. Rept., U.S. Forest Service, RM–166:1–458.

Slough, B. G. 1978. Beaver food cache structure and utilization. J. Wildl. Mgmt., 42:644–646.

Smartt, R. A. 1978. A comparison of ecological and morphological overlap in a *Peromyscus* community. Ecology, 59:216–220.

Smith, A. T., and B. L. Ivins. 1983. Colonization in a pika population: dispersal versus philopatry. Behav. Ecol. Sociobiol., 13:37–47.

———. 1984. Spatial relationships and social organization in adult pikas: a facultatively monogamous mammal. Z. Tierpsychol., 66:289–308.

Smith, A. T., and M. L. Weston. 1990. *Ochotona princeps.* Mamm. Species, 352:1–8.

Smith, B. L. 1988. Criteria for determining age and sex of American mountain goats in the field. J. Mamm., 69:395–402.

Smith, C. C. 1968. The adaptive nature of social organization in the genus of tree squirrels *Tamiasciurus.* Ecol. Monogr., 38:31–63.

———. 1970. The coevolution of pine squirrels (*Tamiasciurus*) and conifers. Ecol. Monogr., 40:349–371.

Smith, D. R. 1954. The bighorn sheep in Idaho, its status, life history, and management. Wildl. Bull., Idaho Dept. Fish and Game, 1:1–154.

Smith, G. W. 1990. Home range and activity patterns of black-tailed jackrabbits. Great Basin Nat., 50:249–256.

Smith, J. D., and T. E. Lawlor. 1964. Additional records of the armadillo in Kansas. Southwestern Nat., 9:48–49.

Smith, L. 1941. An observation on the nest-building behavior of the opossum. J. Mamm., 22:201–202.

Smith, M. H., K. T. Scribner, L. H. Carpenter, and R. A. Garrott. 1990. Genetic characteristics of Colorado mule deer (*Odocoileus hemionus*) and comparisons with other cervids. Southwestern Nat., 35:1–8.

Smith, R. E. 1958. Natural history of the prairie dog in Kansas. Misc. Publ. Mus. Nat. Hist., Univ. Kansas, 16:1–36.

Smith, R. L., D. J. Hubartt, and R. L. Shoemaker. 1980. Seasonal changes in weight, cecal length, and pancreatic function in snowshoe hares. J. Wildl. Mgmt., 44:719–724.

Smith, W. P. 1991. *Odocoileus virginianus.* Mamm. Species, 388:1–13.

Smolen, M. J., H. H. Genoways, and R. J. Baker. 1980. Demographic and reproductive parameters of the yellow-cheeked pocket gopher (*Pappogeomys castanops*). J. Mamm., 61:224–226.

Smolen, M. J., and B. L. Keller. 1987. *Microtus longicaudus.* Mamm. Species, 271:1–7.

Snyder, D. P. 1956. Survival rate, longevity, and population fluctuation in the white footed mouse, *Peromyscus leucopus*, in southwestern Michigan. Misc. Publ. Mus. Zool., Univ. Michigan, 95:1–33.

Snyder, M. A. 1992. Selective herbivory by Abert's squirrel mediated by chemical variability in ponderosa pine. Ecology, 73:1730–1741.

———. 1993. Interactions between Abert's squirrel and ponderosa pine: the relationship between selective herbivory and host plant fitness. Amer. Nat., 141:866–879.

Snyder, M. A., and Y. B. Linhart. 1993. Barking up the right tree. Nat. Hist., 102(9):44–49.

Somers, P. 1973. Dialects in southern Rocky Mountain pikas, *Ochotona princeps* (Lagomorpha). Anim. Behav., 21:124–137.

Soper, J. D. 1919. Notes on Canadian weasels. Canadian Field-Nat., 33:43–47.

———. 1941. History, range, and home life of the northern bison. Ecol. Monogr., 11:349–412.

Sorenson, M. W. 1962. Some aspects of water shrew behavior. Amer. Midland Nat., 68:445–462.

Southwick, C. H., S. C. Golian, M. R. Whitworth, J. C. Halfpenny, and R. Brown. 1986. Population density and fluctuations of pikas (*Ochotona princeps*) in Colorado. J. Mamm., 67:149–153.

Sparks, D. R. 1968. Diet of black-tailed jackrabbits on sandhill rangeland in Colorado. J. Range Mgmt., 21:203–208.

Spencer, A. W. 1966. Identification of the dwarf shrew, *Sorex nanus*. J. Colorado-Wyoming Acad. Sci., 5:89.

———. 1975. Additional records of *Sorex nanus* and *Sorex merriami* in Colorado. J. Colorado-Wyoming Acad. Sci., 7:48.

Spencer, A. W., and D. Pettus. 1966. Habitat preferences of five sympatric species of long-tailed shrews. Ecology, 47:677–683.

Spencer, A. W., and H. W. Steinhoff. 1968. An explanation of geographic variation in litter size. J. Mamm., 49:281–286.

Spencer, D. L. 1968. Sympatry and hybridization of the eastern and southern plains wood rats. Unpubl. Ph.D. dissert., Oklahoma State Univ., Stillwater, 85 pp.

Spencer, W. D., R. H. Barrett, and W. J. Zielinski. 1983. Marten habitat preferences in the northern Sierra Nevada. J. Wildl. Mgmt., 47:1181–1186.

Spowart, R. A., and N. T. Hobbs. 1985. Effects of fire on diet overlap between mule deer and mountain sheep. J. Wildl. Mgmt., 49:942–946.

Stains, H. J. 1956. The raccoon in Kansas: natural history, management, and economic importance. Misc. Publ. Mus. Nat. Hist., Univ. Kansas, 10:1–76.

Stalheim, W. 1965. Some aspects of the natural history of the rock squirrel, *Citellus variegatus*. Unpubl. M.S. thesis, Univ. New Mexico, Albuquerque, 55 pp.

Stalling, D. T. 1990. *Microtus ochrogaster*. Mamm. Species, 355:1–9.

Stanford, D. 1974. Preliminary report of the excavations of the Jones-Miller Hell Gap Site, Yuma County, Colorado. Southwestern Lore 40(3–4):29–36.

———. 1975. The 1975 excavations at the Jones-Miller Site, Yuma County, Colorado. Southwestern Lore 41(4):34–38.

Stanley, W. C. 1963. Habits of the red fox in northeastern Kansas. Misc. Publ. Univ. Kansas Mus. Nat. Hist., 34:1–31.

Steiner, A. L. 1975. Bedding and nesting material gathering in rock squirrels, *Spermophilus* (*Otospermophilus*) *variegatus grammurus* (Say) (Sciuridae) in the Chiricahua Mountains of Arizona. Southwestern Nat., 20:363–370.

Stephenson, A. B. 1969. Temperatures within a beaver lodge in winter. J. Mamm., 50:134–136.

Stephenson, R. L., and D. E. Brown. 1980. Snow cover as a factor influencing mortality of Abert's squirrels. J. Wildl. Mgmt., 44:951–955.

Sterner, R. T. and S. A. Shumake. 1978. Coyote damage-control research: a review and analysis. Pp. 297–325, *in* Coyotes: biology, behavior, and management (M. Bekoff, ed.). Academic Press, New York, 384 pp.

Stevens, D. R. 1974. Rocky Mountain elk–Shiras moose range relationships. Nat. canadienne, 101:505–516.

Stickel, L. F. 1968. Home range and travels. Pp. 373–411, *in* Biology of *Peromyscus* (Rodentia) (J. H. King, ed.). Spec. Publ., Amer. Soc. Mammalogists, 2:1–593.

Stinson, N., Jr. 1977a. Species diversity, resource partitioning, and demography of small mammals in a subalpine deciduous forest. Unpubl. Ph.D. dissert., Univ. Colorado, Boulder, 238 pp.

———. 1977b. Home range of the western jumping mouse, *Zapus princeps*, in the Colorado Rocky Mountains. Great Basin Nat., 37:87–90.

———. 1978. Habitat structure and rodent species diversity on north and south-facing slopes in the Colorado lower montane zone. Southwestern Nat., 23:77–84.

Stockrahm, D.M.B., and R. W. Seabloom. 1988. Comparative reproductive performance of black-tailed prairie dog populations in North Dakota. J. Mamm., 69:160–164.

Stoddard, J. L. 1920. Nests of the western fox squirrel. J. Mamm., 1:122–123.

Stoddart, L. C. 1985. Severe weather related mortality of black-tailed jack rabbits. J. Wildl. Mgmt., 49:696–698.

Stoecker, R. E. 1970. An analysis of sympatry in two species of *Microtus*. Unpubl. Ph.D. dissert., Univ. Colorado, Boulder, 58 pp.

Stones, R. C., and C. L. Hayward. 1968. Natural history of the desert woodrat *Neotoma lepida*. Amer. Midland Nat., 80:458–476.

Storch, G., and G. Richter. 1988. Der Ameisenbär *Eurotamandua* ein "Südamerikaner" in Europa. Pp. 211–215, *in* Messel — Ein Schaufenster in die Geschichte der Erde und Lebens (S. Schaal and E. Ziegler, eds.). Waldemar Kramer, Frankfurt am Main, 315 pp.

Storm, G. L. 1965. Movements and activities of foxes as determined by radio tracking. J. Wildl. Mgmt., 29:1–12.

————. 1972. Daytime retreats and movements of skunks on farmlands in Illinois. J. Wildl. Mgmt., 36:31–45.

Storm, G. L., R. D. Andrews, R. L. Phillips, R. A. Bishop, D. B. Siniff, and J. R. Tester. 1976. Morphology, reproduction, dispersal, and mortality of midwestern red fox populations. Wildl. Monogr., 49:1–82.

Streeter, R. G. 1969. Demography of two Rocky Mountain bighorn sheep populations in Colorado. Unpubl. PhD. dissert., Colorado State Univ., Fort Collins, 96 pp.

————. 1970. A literature review on bighorn sheep population dynamics. Spec. Rept., Colorado Div. Game, Fish, and Parks, 24:8–11.

Streeter, R. G., and C. E. Braun. 1968. Occurrence of pine marten, *Martes americana* (Carnivora: Mustelidae), in Colorado alpine areas. Southwestern Nat., 13:449–451.

Streubel, D. P. 1975. Behavioral features of sympatry of *Spermophilus spilosoma* and *Spermophilus tridecemlineatus* and some life history aspects of *S. spilosoma*. Unpubl. D.A. dissert., Univ. Northern Colorado, Greeley, 130 pp.

Streubel, D. P., and J. P. Fitzgerald. 1978a. *Spermophilus spilosoma*. Mamm. Species, 101:1–4.

————. 1978b. *Spermophilus tridecemlineatus*. Mamm. Species, 103:1–5.

Strickland, M. A., and C. W. Douglas. 1987. Marten. Pp. 530–546, *in* Wild furbearer management and conservation in North America (M. Novak, J. A. Baker, M. E. Obbard, and B. Malloch, eds.). Ontario Trappers Association, Toronto, 1150 pp.

Strickland, M. A., C. W. Douglas, M. Novak, and N. P. Hunziger. 1982. Marten. Pp. 599–612, *in* Wild mammals of North America: biology, management, and economics (J. A. Chapman and G. A. Feldhamer, eds.). Johns Hopkins Univ. Press, Baltimore, 1147 pp.

Stromberg, M. R. 1982. New records of Wyoming bats. Bat Res. News, 23:42–44.

Struhsaker, T. T. 1967. Behavior of elk (*Cervus canadensis*) during the rut. Z. Tierpsychol., 24:80–114.

Stucky, R. K., and M. C. McKenna. 1993. Mammalia. Pp. 739–771, *in* The fossil record. Second ed. (M. Benton and M. Whyte, eds.). Chapman and Hall, London, 845 pp.

Studier, E. H., and M. J. O'Farrell. 1972. Biology of *Myotis thysanodes* and *M. lucifugus* (Chiroptera: Vespertilionidae): 1. Thermoregulation. Comp Biochem. Physiol., 38:567–596.

Stuewer, F. W. 1943. Reproduction of raccoons in Michigan. J. Wildl. Mgmt., 7:60–73.

Summerlin, C. T., and J. L. Wolfe. 1973. Social influences on trap response of the cotton rat *Sigmodon hispidus*. Ecology, 54:1156–1159.

Sumrell, F. 1949. A life history study of the ground squirrel *Citellus spilosoma major* (Merriam). Unpubl. M.S. thesis, Univ. New Mexico, Albuquerque, 100 pp.

Sunquist, M. E. 1974. Winter activity of striped skunks (*Mephitis mephitis*) in east-central Minnesota. Amer. Midland Nat., 92:434–446.

Sutton, D. A. 1953. A systematic review of Colorado chipmunks (genus *Eutamias*). Unpubl. Ph.D. dissert., Univ. Colorado, Boulder, 208 pp.

Svendsen, G. E. 1974. Behavioral and environmental factors in the spatial distribution and population dynamics of a yellow-bellied marmot population. Ecology, 55:760–771.

————. 1976a. Vocalizations of the long-tailed weasel (*Mustela frenata*). J. Mamm., 57:398–399.

————. 1976b. Structure and location of burrows of yellow-bellied marmot. Southwestern Nat., 20:487–494.

————. 1978. Castor and anal glands of the beaver (*Castor canadensis*). J. Mamm., 59:618–620.

————. 1979. Territoriality and behaviors in a population of pikas (*Ochotona princeps*). J. Mamm., 60:324–330.

————. 1982. Weasels. Pp. 613–628, *in* Wild mammals of North America: biology, management, and economics (J. A. Chapman and G. A. Feldhamer, eds.). Johns Hopkins Univ. Press, Baltimore, 1147 pp.

Svihla, A. 1929. Life history notes on *Sigmodon hispidus hispidus*. J. Mamm., 10:352–353.

————. 1932. A comparative life history study of the mice of the genus *Peromyscus*. Misc. Publ. Mus. Zool.,Univ. Michigan, 24:1–39.

————. 1936. Breeding and young of the grasshopper mouse. J. Mamm., 17:172–173.

Svoboda, P. L., and J. R. Choate. 1987. Natural history of the Brazilian free-tailed bat in the San Luis Valley of Colorado. J. Mamm., 68:224–234.

Svoboda, P. L., D. K. Tolliver, and J. R. Choate. 1988. *Peromyscus boylii* in the San Luis Valley, Colorado. Southwestern Nat., 33:239–240.

Swenk, M. H. 1926. Notes on *Mustela campestris* Jackson, and on the American forms of least weasels. J. Mamm., 7:313–330.

Tabor, J. E. 1974. Productivity, survival, and population status of river otter in western Oregon. Unpubl. M.S. thesis, Oregon State Univ., Corvallis, 62 pp.

Taitt, M. J., and C. J. Krebs. 1985. Population dynamics and cycles. Pp. 567–620, *in* Biology of New World *Microtus* (R. H. Tamarin, ed.). Spec. Publ., Amer. Soc. Mammalogists, 8:1–893.

Tamarin, R. H., ed. 1985. Biology of New World *Microtus*. Spec. Publ., Amer. Soc. Mammalogists, 8:1–893.

Taylor, W. P. 1935. Ecology and life history of the porcupine (*Erethizon epixanthum*) as related to the forests of Arizona and the southwestern United States. Univ. Arizona Bull., 6:1–177.

————. 1946. Armadillos abundant in Kerr County, Texas. J. Mamm., 27:273.

————., ed. 1956. The deer of North America. The Stackpole Company, Harrisburg, Pennsylvania, 668 pp.

Tedford, R. N. 1976. Relationships of pinnipeds to other carnivores (Mammalia). Syst. Zool., 25:363–374.

451

Teipner, C. L., E. O. Garton, and L. Nelson, Jr. 1983. Pocket gophers in forest ecosystems. Gen. Tech. Rept., Intermountain Forest and Range Exp. Sta., U.S. Dept. Agric., Forest Service, INT-154:1–53.

Telleen, S. L. 1976. Identification of live Colorado chipmunks. M.A. thesis, Univ. Colorado, Boulder, 56 pp.

———. 1978. Structural niches of *Eutamias minimus* and *E. umbrinus* in Rocky Mountain National Park. Unpubl. Ph.D. dissert., Univ. Colorado, Boulder, 141 pp.

Tester, J. R. 1953. Fall food habits of the raccoon in the South Platte Valley of northeastern Colorado. J. Mamm., 34:500–502.

Tevis, L., Jr. 1950. Summer behavior of a family of beavers in New York State. J. Mamm., 31:40–65.

———. 1952. Autumn foods of chipmunks and golden-mantled ground squirrels in the northern Sierra Nevada. J. Mamm., 33:198–205.

———. 1955. Observations on chipmunks and mantled squirrels in northeastern California. Amer. Midland Nat., 53:71–78.

Thomas, D. W., M. B. Fenton, and R.M.R. Barclay. 1979. Social behavior of the little brown bat, *Myotis lucifugus*. I. Mating behavior. Behav. Ecol. Sociobiol., 6:129–136.

Thomas, J. A., and E. C. Birney. 1979. Parental care and mating system of the prairie vole, *Microtus ochrogaster*. Behav. Ecol. Sociobiol., 5:171–186.

Thomas, J. W., and D. E. Toweill, eds. 1982. Elk of North America: ecology and management. Stackpole Books, Harrisburg, Pennsylvania, 698 pp.

Thomas, R. E. 1988. A review of flea collection records from *Onychomys leucogaster* with observations on the role of grasshopper mice in the epizoology of wild rodent plague. Great Basin Nat., 48:83–95.

Thomas, R. E., M. L. Beard, T. J. Quan, L. G. Carter, A. M. Barnes, and C. E. Hopla. 1989. Experimentally induced plague infection in the northern grasshopper mouse (*Onychomys leucogaster*) acquired by consumption of infected prey. J. Wildl. Dis., 25:477–480.

Thompson, J. N., Jr., and S. D. Barrett. 1969. The nest complex of *Perognathus hispidus* (Rodentia: Heteromyidae) in Oklahoma. Proc. Oklahoma Acad. Sci., 48:105–108.

Thompson, T. G., and W. Conley. 1983. Discrimination of coexisting species of *Peromyscus* in south-central New Mexico. Southwestern Nat., 28:199–209.

Thorne, C. 1978. Preliminary assessment of the geomorphic role of pocket gophers in the alpine zone. Geografiska Annaler, 60:181–187.

Thorne, E. T., N. Kingston, W. R. Jolley, and R. C. Bergstrom, eds. 1982. Diseases of wildlife in Wyoming, second ed. Wyoming Game and Fish Dept., Cheyenne, 353 pp.

Thorne, E. T., and E. Williams. 1988. Diseases and endangered species: the black-footed ferret as a recent example. Conserv. Biol., 2:66–73.

Thornton, W. A., G. C. Creel, and R. E. Trimble. 1971. Hybridization in the fox genus, *Vulpes*, in West Texas. Southwestern Nat., 15:473–484.

Tiemeier, O. W. 1965. Bionomics. Pp. 5–37, *in* The black-tailed jackrabbit in Kansas. Tech. Bull., Kansas Agric. Exp. Sta., 140:1–75.

Tileston, J. V., and R. R. Lechleitner. 1966. Some comparisons of the black-tailed and white-tailed prairie dogs in north-central Colorado. Amer. Midland Nat., 75:292–316.

Todd, A. W., and L. B. Keith. 1983. Coyote demography during snowshoe hare decline in Alberta. J. Wildl. Mgmt., 47:394–404.

Todd, J. W. 1972. A literature review on bighorn sheep food habits. Spec. Rept., Colorado Game, Fish, and Parks Dept., 27:1–21.

———. 1975. Foods of Rocky Mountain bighorn sheep in southern Colorado. J. Wildl. Mgmt., 39:108–111.

Todd, M. 1980. Ecology of badgers in southcentral Idaho, with additional notes on raptors. Unpubl. M.S. thesis, Univ. Idaho, Moscow, 164 pp.

Tolliver, K. K., M. H. Smith, P. E. Jones, and M. W. Smith. 1985. Low levels of genetic variability in pikas from Colorado. Canadian J. Zool., 63:1735–1737.

Tomasi, T. E. 1978. Function of venom in the short-tailed shrew (*Blarina brevicauda*). J. Mamm., 59:852–854.

———. 1979. Echolocation by the short-tailed shrew (*Blarina brevicauda*). J. Mamm., 60:751–759.

Tomberlin, D. R. 1969. Population ecology of two chipmunk populations in southern central Colorado. Colorado-Wyoming Acad. Sci., 6:63.

Torbit, S. C., A. W. Alldredge, and J. Nagy. 1982. Big game in northwest Colorado: a synthesis of existing knowledge. Northwest Colorado Wildlife Consortium, Colorado Div. Wildl., Denver, 234 pp.

Torres, J. R. 1973. The future of the black-footed ferret of Colorado. Pp. 27–33, *in* Proc. black-footed ferret and prairie dog workshop (R. L. Linder and C. N. Hillman, eds.). South Dakota State Univ., Brookings, 208 pp.

Toweill, D. E. 1974. Winter food habits of river otters in western Oregon. J. Wildl. Mgmt., 38:107–111.

Toweill, D. E., and J. E. Tabor. 1982. River otter. Pp. 688–703, *in* Wild mammals of North America: biology, management, and economics (J. A. Chapman and G. A. Feldhamer, eds.). Johns Hopkins Univ. Press, Baltimore, 1147 pp.

Toweill, D. E., and J. G. Teer. 1977. Food habits of ringtails in the Edwards Plateau region of Texas. J. Mamm., 58:660–663.

———. 1980. Home range and den habits of Texas ringtails (*Bassariscus astutus flavus*). Pp. 1103–1120, *in* Proc. Worldwide Furbearer Conf. (J. A. Chapman and D. Pursley, eds.). Worldwide Furbearer Conf., Inc., Frostburg, Maryland, 2059 pp.

Toweill, D. E., and D. B. Toweill. 1978. Growth and development of captive ringtails (*Bassariscus astutus flavus*). Carnivore, 1:46–53.

Trapp, G. R. 1972. Some anatomical and behavioral adaptations of ringtails, *Bassariscus astutus*. J. Mamm., 53:547–557.

———. 1978. Comparative behavioral ecology of the ringtail (*Bassariscus astutus*) and gray fox (*Urocyon cinereoargenteus*) in southwestern Utah. Carnivore, 1:3–32.

Trapp, G. R., and D. L. Hallberg. 1975. Ecology of the gray fox (*Urocyon cinereoargenteus*): a review. Pp. 164–178, *in* The wild canids: their systematics, behavioral ecology and evolution (M. W. Fox, ed.). Van Nostrand Reinhold Co., New York, 508 pp.

Trent, T. T., and O. S. Rongstad. 1974. Home range and survival of cottontail rabbits in southwestern Wisconsin. J. Wildl. Mgmt., 38:459–472.

Trethewey, D.E.C., and B. J. Verts. 1971. Reproduction in eastern cottontail rabbits in western Oregon. Amer. Midland Nat., 86:463–476.

Trippe, T. M. 1874. Appendix to Oscines, A. Pp. 223–233, *in* E. Coues, Birds of the northwest: a hand-book of the ornithology of the region drained by the Missouri River and its tributaries. Misc. Publ., U.S. Geol. Surv. Terr., 3:1–791.

Tubbs, A. A. 1977. Ecology and population biology of the spotted ground squirrel, *Spermophilus spilosoma obsoletus*. Unpubl. D. A. dissert., Univ. Northern Colorado, Greeley, 64 pp.

Tully, R. J. 1990. Big game damage summaries, 1978–79 to 1989–90. Colorado Div. of Wildl., Denver, unpaged.

Tumlison, R. 1987. *Felis lynx.* Mamm. Species, 269:1–8.

———. 1993. Geographic variation in the lappet-eared bat, *Idionycteris phyllotis*, with descriptions of subspecies. J. Mamm., 74:412–421.

Turkowski, F. J. 1969. Food habits and behavior of the gray fox (*Urocyon cinereoargenteus*) in the lower and upper sonoran life zones of southwestern United States. Unpubl. Ph.D. dissert., Arizona State Univ, 136 pp.

———. 1975. Dietary adaptability of the desert cottontail. J. Wildl. Mgmt., 39:748–756.

Turkowski, F. J., and C. K. Brown. 1969. Notes on distribution of the desert shrew. Southwestern Nat., 14:128.

Turner, G. T. 1973. Effects of pocket gophers on the range. Pp. 51–61, *in* Pocket gophers and Colorado mountain rangeland (G. T. Turner, R. M. Hansen, V. H. Reid, H. P. Tietjen, and A. L. Ward, eds.). Exp. Sta. Bull., Colorado State Univ., 554S:1–90..

Turner, G. T., R. M. Hansen, V. H. Reid, H. P. Tietjen, and A. L. Ward, eds. 1973. Pocket gophers and Colorado mountain rangeland. Exp. Sta. Bull., Colorado State Univ., 554S:1–90.

Turner, R. W., and J. B. Bowles. 1967. Comments on reproduction and food habits of the olive-backed pocket mouse in western North Dakota. Trans. Kansas Acad. Sci., 70:266–267.

Tuttle, M. D. 1988. America's neighborhood bats. Univ. Texas Press, Austin, 96 pp.

Tyron, C. A., Jr. 1947. Behavior and post-natal development of a porcupine. J. Wildl. Mgmt., 11:282–283.

Ubico, S. R., G. O. Maupin, K. A. Fagerstone, and R. G. McLean. 1988. A plague outbreak in white-tailed prairie

dogs (*Cynomys leucurus*) of Meeteetse, Wyoming. J. Wildl. Dis., 24:399–406.

Uresk, D. W. 1984. Black-tailed prairie dog food habits and forage relationships in western South Dakota. J. Range Mgmt., 37:325–329.

Van Deusen, J. L., and C. A. Myers. 1962. Porcupine damage in immature stands of ponderosa pine in the Black Hills. J. Forestry, 60, 811–813.

Van Gelder, R. G. 1959. A taxonomic revision of the spotted skunks (genus *Spilogale*). Bull. Amer. Mus. Nat. Hist., 117:229–392.

Van Horne, B. 1982. Demography of the longtail vole *Microtus longicaudus* in seral stages of coastal coniferous forest, southeast Alaska. Canadian J. Zool., 60:1690–1709.

Van Vleck, D. B. 1969. Standardization of *Microtus* home range calculations. J. Mamm., 50:69–80.

Van Vuren, D. 1983. Group dynamics and summer home range of bison in southern Utah. J. Mamm., 64:329–332.

———. 1984. Summer diets of bison and cattle in southern Utah. J. Range Mgmt., 37:260–261.

———. 1990. Yellow-bellied marmots as prey of coyotes. Amer. Midland Nat., 125:135–139.

Van Vuren, D., and K. B. Armitage. 1991. Duration of snow cover and its influence on life-history variation in yellow-bellied marmots. Can. J. Zool., 69:1755–1758.

Van Vuren, D., and M. P. Bray. 1983. Diets of bison and cattle on a seeded range in southern Utah. J. Range Mgmt., 36:499–500.

———. 1986. Population dynamics of bison in the Henry Mountains, Utah. J. Mamm., 67:503–511.

van Zyll De Jong, C. G. 1975. The distribution and abundance of the wolverine (*Gulo gulo*) in Canada. Canadian Field-Nat., 89:431–437.

———. 1984. Taxonomic relationships of Nearctic small-footed bats of the *Myotis leibii* group (Chiroptera: Vespertilionidae). Canadian J. Zool., 62:2519–2526.

Vaughan, M. R., and L. B. Keith. 1981. Demographic response of experimental snowshoe hare populations to overwinter food shortage. J. Wildl. Mgmt., 45:354–380.

Vaughan, T. A. 1959. Functional morphology of three bats: *Eumops, Myotis, Macrotus*. Univ. Kansas Publ., Mus. Nat. Hist., 12:1–153.

———. 1961*a*. Vertebrates inhabiting pocket gopher burrows in Colorado. J. Mamm., 42:171–174.

———. 1961*b*. Cranial asymmetry in the pocket gopher. J. Mamm., 42:412–413.

———. 1962. Reproduction in the plains pocket gopher in Colorado. J. Mamm., 43:1–13.

———. 1967. Food habits of the northern pocket gophers on shortgrass prairie. Amer. Midland Nat., 77:176–189.

———. 1969. Reproduction and population densities in a montane small mammal fauna. Pp. 51–74, *in* Contributions in mammalogy (J. K. Jones, Jr., ed.). Misc. Publ. Mus. Nat. Hist., Univ. Kansas, 51:1–428.

———. 1974. Resource allocation in some sympatric subalpine rodents. J. Mamm., 55:764–795.

———. 1980. Woodrats and picturesque junipers. Pp. 387–401, in Aspects of vertebrate history (L. L. Jacobs, ed.). Mus. Northern Arizona Press, Flagstaff, 407 pp.

———. 1982. Stephen's woodrat, a dietary specialist. J. Mamm., 63:53–62.

———. 1986. Mammalogy. Third ed. Saunders College Publishing, Philadelphia, 576 pp.

Vaughan, T. A., and R. M. Hansen. 1961. Activity rhythm of the plains pocket gopher. J. Mamm., 42:541–543.

———. 1964. Experiments on interspecific competition between two species of pocket gophers. Amer. Midland Nat., 72:444–452.

Vaughan, T. A., and T. J. O'Shea. 1976. Roosting ecology of the pallid bat, Antrozous pallidus. J. Mamm., 57:19–42.

Vaughan, T. A., and W. P. Weil. 1980. The importance of arthropods in the diet of Zapus princeps in a subalpine habitat. J. Mamm., 61:122–124.

Venge, O. 1959. Reproduction in the fox and mink. Anim. Breed. Abst., 27:129–145.

Verme, L. J., and D. E. Ullrey. 1984. Physiology and nutrition. Pp. 91–118, in White-tailed deer ecology and management (L. K. Halls, ed.). Stackpole Books, Harrisburg, Pennsylvania, 870 pp.

Verts, B. J. 1967. The biology of the striped skunk. Univ. Illinois Press, Urbana, 218 pp.

Verts, B. J., and G. L. Kirkland, Jr. 1988. Perognathus parvus. Mamm. Species, 318:1–8.

Vogtsberger, L. M., and G. W. Barrett. 1973. Bioenergetics of captive red foxes. J. Wildl. Mgmt., 37:495–500.

Voigt, D. R. 1987. Red fox. Pp. 378–392, in Wild furbearer management and conservation in North America (M. Novak, J. A. Baker, M. E. Obbard, and B. Malloch, eds.). Ontario Trappers Association, Toronto, 1150 pp.

Voigt, D. R., and W. E. Berg. 1987. Coyote. Pp. 344–357, in Wild furbearer management and conservation in North America (M. Novak, J. A. Baker, M. E. Obbard, and B. Malloch, eds.). Ontario Trappers Association, Toronto, 1150 pp.

Vorhies, C. T., and W. P. Taylor. 1940. Life history and ecology of the white-throated wood rat, Neotoma albigula albigula, in relation to grazing in Arizona. Tech. Bull., Coll. Agric., Univ. Arizona, 86:454–529.

Wade, O. 1935. Notes on the northern tuft-eared squirrel, Sciurus aberti ferreus True, in Colorado. Amer. Midland Nat., 16:201–202.

Wade-Smith, J., and M. E. Richmond. 1978. Induced ovulation, development of the corpus luteum, and tubal transport in the striped skunk (Mephitis mephitis). Amer. J. Anat., 153:123–142.

Wade-Smith, J., and B. J. Verts. 1982. Mephitis mephitis. Mamm. Species, 173:1–7.

Wadsworth, C. E. 1969. Reproduction and growth of Eutamias quadrivittatus in southeastern Utah. J. Mamm., 50:256–261.

———. 1972. Observations of the Colorado chipmunk in southeastern Utah. Southwestern Nat., 16:451–454.

Wagner, F. H., and L. C. Stoddart. 1972. Influence of coyote predation on black-tailed jackrabbit populations in Utah. J. Wildl. Mgmt., 36:329–342.

Wainwright, L. C. 1968. Cottontail reproduction in Colorado. Unpubl. M.S. thesis, Colorado State Univ., Fort Collins, 57 pp.

Wakelyn, L. A. 1987. Changing habitat conditions on bighorn sheep ranges in Colorado. J. Wildl. Mgmt., 51:904–912.

Wallmo, O. C., ed. 1981. Mule and black-tailed deer of North America. Univ. Nebraska Press, Lincoln, 605 pp.

Wallmo, O. C., W. L. Regelin, and D. W. Reichert. 1972. Forage use by mule deer relative to logging in Colorado. J. Wildl. Mgmt., 36:1025–1033.

Ward, A. L. 1960. Mountain pocket gopher food habits in Colorado. J. Wildl. Mgmt., 24:89–92.

Ward, A. L., P. L. Hegdal, V. B. Richens, and H. P. Tietjen. 1967. Gophacide, a new pocket gopher control agent. J. Wildl. Mgmt., 31:332–338.

Ward, A. L., and J. O. Keith. 1962. Feeding habits of pocket gophers on mountain grasslands, Black Mesa, Colorado. Ecology, 43:744–749.

Waring, G. H. 1966. Sounds and communications of the yellow-bellied marmot (Marmota flaviventris). Anim. Behav., 14:177–183.

———. 1969. The blow sound of pronghorns (Antilocapra americana). J. Mamm., 50:647–648.

———. 1970. Sound communications of black-tailed, white-tailed and Gunnison's prairie dog. Amer. Midland Nat., 83:167–185.

Warner, R. M., and N. J. Czaplewski. 1984. Myotis volans. Mamm. Species, 224:1–4.

Warren, E. R. 1908. Further notes on the mammals of Colorado. Gen. Ser., Colorado College Publ., 33:59–90.

———. 1910. The mammals of Colorado. G. P. Putnam's Sons, New York, 300 pp.

———. 1911. The history of Colorado mammalogy. Colorado College Publ., Gen. Ser., 54 (Sci. Ser., 12):312–328.

———. 1927. The beaver, its work and its ways. Monogr., Amer. Soc. Mammalogists, 2:1–177.

———. 1942. The mammals of Colorado. Second ed., Univ. Oklahoma Press, Norman, 330 pp.

Wasser, C. H. 1977. Bison-induced stresses in Colorado National Monument. Unpublished report, National Park Service, 8 pp.

Wasserman, D., and D. J. Nash. 1979. Variation in hemoglobin types in the deer mouse (Peromyscus maniculatus) along an altitudinal gradient. Great Basin Nat., 39:192–194.

Watkins, L. C. 1977. Euderma maculatum. Mamm. Species, 77:1–4.

Weaver, J. W., and F. E. Clements. 1938. Plant ecology. McGraw-Hill Book Co., New York, 601 pp.

Webb, E. A. 1990. Introduction. Pp. 1–13, *in* Close to home: Colorado's urban wildlife. (F. R. Rinehart and E. A. Webb, eds.). Denver Mus. Nat. Hist. and Colorado Urban Wildlife Partnership, Denver, 200 pp.

Webb, E. A., and S. Q. Foster, eds. 1991. Perspectives in urban ecology. Denver Mus. Nat. Hist., Denver, 89 pp.

Weber, W. A. 1976. Rocky Mountain flora. Colorado Assoc. Univ. Press, Boulder, 479 pp.

Webster, W. D., and J. Knox Jones, Jr. 1982. *Reithrodontomys megalotis*. Mamm. Species, 167:1–5.

Weckwerth, R. P., and V. D. Hawley. 1962. Marten food habits and population fluctuations in Montana. J. Wildl. Mgmt., 26:55–74.

Welles, R. E., and F. B. Welles. 1961. The bighorn of Death Valley. Fauna Ser., Nat. Park Serv., 6:1–242.

Wells, M. C., and M. Bekoff. 1981. An observational study of scent marking by wild coyotes. Anim. Behav., 26:251–258.

Wells-Gosling, N., and L. R. Heaney. 1984. *Glaucomys sabrinus*. Mamm. Species, 229:1–8.

Werner, R. M., and J. A. Vick. 1977. Resistance of the opossum (*Didelphis virginiana*) to envenomization by snakes of the family Crotalidae. Toxicon, 15:29–33.

Westoby, M., and F. H. Wagner. 1973. Use of a crested wheatgrass seeding by black-tailed jackrabbits. J. Range Mgmt., 26:349–352.

Wheat, J. B. 1967. A paleo-Indian bison kill. Sci. Amer. 216:44–52.

Whicker, A. D., and J. K. Detling. 1988. Ecological consequences of prairie dog disturbances. BioScience, 38:778–785.

Whitaker, J. O., Jr. 1963. A study of the meadow jumping mouse, *Zapus hudsonius* (Zimmermann), in central New York. Ecol. Monogr., 33:215–254.

———. 1972. *Zapus hudsonius*. Mamm. Species, 11:1–7.

———. 1974. *Cryptotis parva*. Mamm. Species, 43:1–8.

Whitaker, J. O., Jr., C. Maser, and L. E. Keller. 1977. Food habits of bats of western Oregon. Northwest Sci., 51:46–55.

White, E. M., and D. C. Carlson. 1984. Estimating soil mixing by rodents. Proc. South Dakota Acad. Sci., 63:34–37.

White, G. C., R. A. Garrott, R. M. Bartmann, L. H. Carpenter, and A. W. Alldredge. 1987. Survival of mule deer in northwest Colorado. J. Wildl. Mgmt., 51:852–859.

White, J. A. 1953a. Taxonomy of the chipmunks, *Eutamias quadrivittatus* and *Eutamias umbrinus*. Univ. Kansas Publ., Mus. Nat. Hist., 5:563–582.

———. 1953b. The baculum in the chipmunks of western North America. Univ. Kansas Publ., Mus. Nat. Hist., 5:611–631.

Whitford, W. G. 1976. Temporal fluctuations in density and diversity of desert rodent populations. J. Mamm., 57:351–369.

Whitman, J. S. 1981. Ecology of the mink (*Mustela vison*) in westcentral Idaho. Unpubl. M.S. thesis, Univ. Idaho, Moscow, 101 pp.

Whitworth, M. R., and C. H. Southwick. 1980. Growth of pika in laboratory confinement. Growth, 45:66–72.

———. 1984. Sex differences in the ontogeny of social behavior in pikas: possible relationships to dispersal and territoriality. Behav. Ecol. Sociobiol., 15:175–182.

Wiedorn, W. S. 1954. A new experimental animal for psychiatric research: the opossum *Didelphis virginiana*. Science, 119:360–361.

Wigal, R. A., and V. L. Coggins. 1982. Mountain goat. Pp. 1008–1020, *in* Wild mammals of North America: biology, management, and economics (J. A. Chapman and G. A. Feldhamer, eds.). Johns Hopkins Univ. Press, Baltimore, 1147 pp.

Wiley, R. W. 1971. Activity periods and movements of the eastern woodrat. Southwestern Nat., 16:43–54.

———. 1980. *Neotoma floridana*. Mamm. Species, 139:1–7.

———. 1984. Reproduction in the southern plains woodrat (*Neotoma micropus*) in western Texas. Spec. Publ., Mus. Texas Tech. Univ., 22:137–164.

Wilkins, K. T. 1986. *Reithrodontomys montanus*. Mamm. Species, 257:1–5.

———. 1989. *Tadarida brasiliensis*. Mamm. Species, 331:1–10.

Willems, N. J., and K. B. Armitage. 1975a. Thermoregulation and water requirements in semiarid and montane populations of the least chipmunk, *Eutamias minimus*. I. Metabolic rate and body temperature. Comp. Biochem. Physiol., 51A: 717–722.

———. 1975b. Thermoregulation and water requirements in semiarid and montane populations of the least chipmunk, *Eutamias minimus*. II. Water balance. Comp. Biochem. Physiol., 52A:109–120.

———. 1975c. Thermoregulation and water requirements in semiarid and montane populations of the least chipmunk, *Eutamias minimus*. III. Acclimatization at a high ambient temperature. Comp. Biochem. Physiol., 52A:121–128.

Willey, R. B., and R. E. Richards. 1974. The ringtail (*Bassariscus astutus*): vocal repertoire and Colorado distribution. J. Colorado-Wyoming Acad. Sci., 7(5):58.

———. 1981. Vocalizations of the ringtail (*Bassariscus astutus*). Southwestern Nat., 26:23–30.

Williams, D. F. 1978. The systematics and ecogeographic variation of the Apache pocket mouse (Rodentia: Heteromyidae). Bull. Carnegie Mus. Nat. Hist., 10:1–57.

Williams, D. F., and J. S. Findley. 1979. Sexual size dimorphism in vespertilionid bats. Amer. Midland Nat., 102:113–126.

Williams, D. F. and H. H. Genoways. 1979. A systematic review of the olive-backed pocket mouse, *Perognathus fasciatus* (Rodentia, Heteromyidae). Ann. Carnegie Mus., 48:73–102.

Williams, G. P. 1978. Historical perspective of the Platte Rivers in Nebraska and Colorado. Pp. 11–41, *in* Lowland river and stream habitat in Colorado: a symposium (W. D. Graul and S. J. Bissell, eds.) Colorado Chapter, Wildlife Soc., and Colorado Audubon Council, 195 pp.

Williams, O. 1952. New *Phenacomys* records from Colorado. J. Mamm., 33:399.

———. 1955a. The distribution of mice and shrews in a Colorado montane forest. J. Mamm., 36:221–231.

———. 1955b. Home range of *Peromyscus maniculatus rufinus* in a Colorado ponderosa pine community. J. Mamm., 36:42–45.

———. 1955c. The food of mice and shrews in a Colorado montane forest. Univ. Colorado Studies, Ser. Biol., 3:109–114.

———. 1959. Food habits of the deer mouse. J. Mamm., 40:415–419.

Williams, O., and B. A. Finney. 1964. Endogone — food for mice. J. Mamm., 45:265–271.

Williams, O., and G. S. McArthur. 1972. New information on the least shrew in northern Colorado. Southwestern Nat., 15:448–449.

Williams, P. K. 1968. Social tendencies in *Perognathus hispidus*. Texas J. Sci., 20:95–96.

Williams, S. L., and R. J. Baker. 1976. Vagility and local movements of pocket gophers (Geomyidae: Rodentia). Amer. Midland Nat., 96:303–316.

Williams, T. R. 1957. Marten and hawk harass snowshoe hare. J. Mamm., 38:517–518.

Willner, G. R., G. A. Feldhamer, E. E. Zucker, and J. A. Chapman. 1980. *Ondatra zibethicus*. Mamm. Species, 141:1–8.

Wilson, D. E. 1968. Ecological distribution of the genus *Peromyscus*. Southwestern Nat., 13:267–274.

———. 1973. The systematic status of *Perognathus merriami*. Proc. Biol. Soc. Washington, 86:175–192.

———. 1982. Wolverine. Pp. 644–652, *in* Wild mammals of North America: biology, management, and economics (J. A. Chapman and G. A. Feldhamer, eds.). Johns Hopkins Univ. Press, Baltimore, 1147 pp.

Wilson, D. E., and J. F. Eisenberg. 1990. Origin and applications of mammalogy in North America. Current Mammal., 2:1–35.

Wilson, D. E., and D. Reeder. 1993. Mammal species of the world: a taxonomic and geographic reference. Second ed. Smithsonian Institution Press, Washington, 1206 pp.

Wilson, L. O., et al. 1980. Desert bighorn habitat requirements and management recommendations. Trans. Desert Bighorn Council, 24:1–7.

Winternitz, B. L., and D. W. Crumpacker. 1985. Species of special concern — Colorado Wildlife Workshop. Colorado Div. Wildl., Denver, 92 pp.

Wishart, W. D. 1978. Bighorn sheep. Pp. 161–172, *in* Big game of North America: ecology and management (J. L. Schmidt and D. L. Gilbert, eds.). Stackpole Books, Harrisburg, Pennsylvania, 494 pp.

Wolfe, M. L. 1974. An overview of moose coactions with other animals. Nat. canadienne, 101:437–456.

Wolff, J. O., and G. C. Bateman. 1978. Effects of food availability and ambient temperature on torpor cycles of *Perognathus flavus* (Heteromyidae). J. Mamm., 59:707–716.

Wood, J. E. 1955. Notes on reproduction and rate of increase of raccoons in the Post Oak Region of Texas. J. Wildl. Mgmt., 19:409–410.

———. 1958. Age structure and productivity of a gray fox population. J. Mamm., 39:74–86.

Woods, C. A. 1973. *Erethizon dorsatum*. Mamm. Species, 29:1–6.

Woodward, T. N. 1980. Seasonal dietary preferences of bighorn sheep. Job Progress Rept., Colorado Div. Wildl., 2:330–336.

Woodward, T. N., R. J. Gutierrez, and W. H. Rutherford. 1974. Bighorn lamb production, survival, and mortality in south-central Colorado. J. Wildl. Mgmt., 38:771–774.

Workman, G. W., and J. B. Low, eds. 1976. Mule deer decline in the West: a symposium. Agric. Exp. Sta., College Nat. Resources Utah State Univ., Logan., 134 pp.

Worthen, G. L., and D. L. Kilgore, Jr. 1981. Metabolic rate of pine marten in relation to air temperature. J. Mamm., 62:624–628.

Wright, P. L. 1942. Delayed implantation in the long-tailed weasel (*Mustela frenata*), the short-tailed weasel (*Mustela cicognani*) and the marten (*Martes americana*). Anat. Rec., 83:341–353.

———. 1947. The sexual cycle of the male long-tailed weasel (*Mustela frenata*). J. Mamm., 28:343–352.

———. 1948a. Breeding habits of captive long-tailed weasels (*Mustela frenata*). Amer. Midland Nat., 39:338–344.

———. 1948b. Preimplantation stages in the long-tailed weasel (*Mustela frenata*). Anat. Rec., 100:595–607.

———. 1966. Observations on the reproductive cycles of the American badger (*Taxidea taxus*). Symp. Zool. Soc. London, 15:27–45.

———. 1969. The reproductive cycle of the male American badger, *Taxidea taxus*. J. Reprod. Fert., Suppl., 6:435–445.

Wunder, B. A. 1974. The effect of activity on body temperature of Ord's kangaroo rat (*Dipodomys ordii*). Physiol. Zool., 47:29–36.

———. 1984. Strategies for and environmental cueing mechanisms of seasonal changes in thermoregulatory parameters of small mammals. Pp. 165–172, *in* Winter ecology of small mammals (J. F. Merritt, ed.). Spec. Publ., Carnegie Mus. Nat. Hist., Pittsburgh, 10:1–380.

———. 1985. Energetics and thermoregulation. Pp. 812–844, *in* Biology of New World *Microtus* (R. H. Tamarin, ed.). Spec. Publ., Amer. Soc. Mammalogists, 8:1–893.

Wunder, L. A. 1987. Behavior and activity pattern of a maternity colony of *Myotis lucifugus*. Unpubl. Ph.D. dissert., Colorado State Univ., 127 pp.

Wunder, L. A., and D. J. Nash. 1980. *Myotis lucifugus*. J. Colorado-Wyoming Acad. Sci., 12:7.

———. 1981. Behavior of juvenile *Myotis lucifugus* in a summer nursery colony. J. Colorado-Wyoming Acad. Sci., 13:50–51.

Wyss, A. R. 1987. The walrus auditory region and the monophyly of pinnipeds. Amer. Mus. Novit., 2871:1–31.

———. 1988. Evidence from flipper structure for a single origin of pinnipeds. Nature, 334:427–428.

———. 1989. Flippers and pinniped phylogenies: has the problem of convergence been overrated? Marine Mamm. Sci., 5:343–360.

Wywialowski, A. P., and G. W. Smith. 1988. Selection of microhabitat by the red-backed vole, *Clethrionomys gapperi*. Great Basin Nat., 48:216–223.

Yates, T. L., and R. J. Pedersen. 1982. Moles. Pp. 37–51, *in* Wild mammals of North America: biology, management, and economics (J. A. Chapman and G. A. Feldhamer, eds.). Johns Hopkins Univ. Press, Baltimore, 1147 pp.

Yates, T. L., and D. J. Schmidly. 1978. *Scalopus aquaticus*. Mamm. Species, 105:1–4.

Yeager, L. E. 1950. Implications of some harvest and habitat factors on pine marten management. Trans. N. Amer. Wildl. Conf., 15:319–335.

———. 1959. Status and population trend of fox squirrels on fringe range, Colorado. J. Wildl. Mgmt., 23:102–107.

Yeager, L. E., and K. G. Hay. 1955. A contribution toward a bibliography on the beaver. Tech. Bull., Colorado Dept. Game and Fish, 1:1–103.

Yeager, L. E., and J. D. Remington. 1956. Sight observations of Colorado martens, 1950–1955. J. Mamm., 37:521–524.

Yeager, L. E., and W. H. Rutherford. 1957. An ecological basis for beaver management in the Rocky Mountain region. Trans. N. Amer. Wildl. Nat. Res. Conf., 22:269–300.

Yoakum, J. D., and D. E. Spalinger, compilers. 1979. American pronghorn antelope. Wildl. Soc., Washington, 244 pp.

York, C. L. 1949. Notes on home ranges and population density of two species of heteromyid rodents in southwestern Texas. Texas J. Sci., 1:42–46.

Young, S. P., and E. A. Goldman. 1944. The wolves of North America. American Wildl. Inst., Washington, 385 pp.

———. 1946. The puma, mysterious American cat. American Wildl. Inst., Washington, 358 pp.

Young, S. P., and H. H. T. Jackson. 1951. The clever coyote. Wildl. Mgmt. Inst., Washington, 411 pp.

Youngman, P. M. 1958. Geographic variation in the pocket gopher, *Thomomys bottae*, in Colorado. Misc. Publ. Mus. Nat. Hist., Univ. Kansas, 9:363–384.

Zackheim, H. 1982. Ecology and population status of the river otter in southwestern Montana. Unpubl. M.S. thesis, Univ. Montana, Missoula, 100 pp.

Zegers, D. A. 1977. Energy dynamics and role of Richardson's ground squirrel (*Spermophilus richardsonii elegans*) in a montane meadow ecosystem. Unpubl. Ph.D. dissert., Univ. Colorado, Boulder, 177 pp.

———. 1981. Time budgets of Wyoming ground squirrels, *Spermophilus elegans*. Great Basin Nat., 41:222–228.

———. 1984. *Spermophilus elegans*. Mamm. Species, 214:1–7.

Zegers, D. A., and O. Williams. 1979. Energy flow through a population of Richardson's ground squirrels. Acta Theriol., 24:221–235.

Zelley, R. A. 1971. The sounds of the fox squirrel, *Sciurus niger rufiventer*. J. Mamm., 52:597–604.

Zumbaugh, D. M., J. R. Choate, and L. B. Fox. 1985. Winter food habits of the swift fox on the central High Plains. Prairie Nat., 17:41–47.

Appendix A

The Metric System

Throughout this book we use the metric system of measurement. Science, international commerce, and international athletic competition use the metric system almost exclusively. The metric system is both more logical and far easier to use than is the socalled English system (which even the English have mostly abandoned). It is more logical because it is based — at least to some extent — on the physical dimensions of the Earth rather than on the length of some forgotten monarch's appendages. The meter (m) first was defined as one ten millionth the distance from the Equator to the North Pole, as measured along a line of longitude running through Paris. The gram (g) is the mass ("weight") of one cubic centimeter (cc) of water. Hence a liter (l) of water, 1,000 cc, weighs 1,000 g, or 1 kilogram (kg).

Table A-1. Conversions and equivalencies, metric-English, English-metric.

Unit (abbreviation)	Numerical Value	To Convert	To	Multiply By	To Convert	To	Multiply By
Length							
kilometer (km)	1,000 m	km	miles	0.6	miles	km	1.6
meter (m)	100 cm	m	yards	1.1	yards	m	0.9
		m	feet	3.3	feet	m	0.3
centimeter (cm)	0.01 m	cm	inches	0.4	inches	cm	2.5
millimeter (mm)	0.001 m	mm	inches	0.04	inches	mm	25
Area							
square km (km^2)	100 hectares (ha)	km^2	$mi.^2$	0.39	$mi.^2$	km^2	2.6
hectare (ha)	10,000 m^2	ha	acres	2.5	acres	ha	0.4
square meter (m^2)	10,000 cm^2	m^2	$ft.^2$	10.8	$ft.^2$	m^2	0.09
Mass ("weight")							
metric tonne (t)	1,000 kg	tonne	ton	1.1	ton	tonne	0.9
kilogram (kg)	1,000 g	kg	pound	2.2	pounds	kg	0.45
grams (g)	0.001 kg	g	ounces	0.04	ounces	g	28

The metric system is easy to use because it is a decimal system, based on multiples of ten. That makes it much easier to manipulate with our everyday counting number system, which also is based on ten. (How mammals with 10 fingers and 10 toes ever managed to invent a measuring system in which a "foot" is subdivided into 12 inches is difficult to understand.)

Because many of us belong to generations in transition from the old system to the "new" (the "new" international system is 200 years old!), we provide here a conversion table for reference. However, rather than convert, many people find it more useful simply to "think metric": a dime weighs 2.5 g, a penny 3, a nickel 5, and quarter 6. A quart of milk is almost a liter, so it weighs almost 1 kg. A mechanical pencil is about 14 cm long and 8 mm thick, and a U. S. dollar bill is 65 mm wide and 155 mm long.

Appendix B

Glossary

This glossary is not meant to be comprehensive. Rather, it lists terms that are used repeatedly in this book but are not in general English usage and therefore often do not appear in abridged dictionaries. (Frequently such technical terminology is found in keys to species.) Further, terms in general English usage that have a distinctive definition in the context of mammalogy are listed. Technical terms that are defined where used in text are not included. Adjectives formed from nouns (such as alveolar from alveolus) generally are not included if the noun is defined, and vice versa. Terms defined or illustrated in Chapter 2 mostly are absent from the glossary.

Abiotic — Nonliving; especially physical factors and processes of ecosystems: soils, climate, and so on.

Abomasum — Most posterior compartment of ruminant "stomach"; the only chamber that actually is stomach (others are modified segments of esophagus).

Accessory Tubercle — Small, cusp-like structure on occlusal surface of tooth in addition to usual larger, higher cusps.

Aestivation — Summer dormancy; regulation to minimal physiology in avoidance of hot and/or dry weather.

Agonistic — Contesting behavior, generally between members of the same species.

Alisphenoid — Paired lateral parts of composite bony structure forming base of braincase and inner wall of orbit.

Allantois — An extraembryonic membrane of higher vertebrates (amniotes); functions as waste repository in reptilian egg and furnishes blood vessels and connective tissue in mammalian umbilicus.

Alluvium — Sediment deposited by flowing water (as opposed to colluvium).

Altithermal — Time interval after recession of last major Pleistocene glaciation characterized by climate warmer and/or drier than present; also called Hypsithermal.

Altricial — Born in highly dependent state; contrasts with precocial.

Alveolus — Socket in jaw in which tooth is rooted.

Analogous — Similarity between organisms not due to common ancestry; contrasts with homologous. Wings of bats and of butterflies are analogous structures.

Androgenic — Literally, "male forming"; descriptive of hormones that control development of male sexual characteristics.

Anterointernal Fold — Fold in enamel wall of tooth, located in medial (labial), anterior portion of crown.

Anterior — Pertaining to front of organism or structure.

Anterior Palatal Spine — Slender, forward-projecting process of maxillary bones that extends anteriorly between incisive foramina.

Antitragus — Small fleshy projection on posteroventral margin of pinna of some bats.

Antler — Deciduous, usually branched, bony growth from frontal bones of (especially male) cervids.

Antorbital — Located in front of orbit or eye.

Appendicular — Pertaining to appendages (in contrast to axial).

Apposable — Capable of being brought into contact, as apposable thumb and forefinger of human hand; sometimes "opposable."

Articular — Pertaining to point of contact between two adjacent bones.

Articulare — Bone in reptilian jaw, became mammalian ear ossicle (malleus).

Auditory Bulla — Bony capsule surrounding structures of middle and inner ear; called tympanic bulla if derived wholly from tympanic bone.

Autecological — Pertaining to ecology of single species: life histories, habitat selection, and so on; contrast with synecological.

Axial — Pertaining to axis (midline) of body, such as vertebral column; contrast with appendicular.

Baculum — Bone present in penis of many male mammals (os penis).

Basal Length — Distance from anterior margin of premaxillary bone to most anterior point on lower margin of foramen magnum.

Basilar Length — Distance from posterior margins of alveoli of upper incisors to most anterior point on lower margin of foramen magnum.

Basioccipital — Bone at base of occiput, forming ventral margin of foramen magnum.

Basisphenoid — Most posterior of several bones forming base of braincase (Figure 2-1).

Baubellum — Bone in clitoris of females of certain mammalian species (also called os clitoridis); female counterpart of baculum.

Biconcave — Shape indented from both sides.

Bicornuate — Two-horned, as a bicornuate uterus.

Bicuspid — Generic term for tooth with two cusps; especially in humans, applied to premolars.

Biomass — Total mass ("weight") of living material of site; figures in measures of productivity.

Biome — Broad, major habitat types of Earth, usually described by structure (rather than taxonomy) of vegetation; need not be geographically continuous. Examples: grassland, savanna, temperate deciduous forest.

Biota — Inclusive term for living things of particular place and time (fauna and flora and microbiota).

Biotic — Pertaining to living organisms of site; contrast with abiotic.

Blastocyst — Mammalian blastula; hollow ball of embryonic cells; stage at which embryo implants in uterine lining.

Bolus — Discrete mass of food moving through anterior organs of digestive system.

Brachydont — Descriptive of low-crowned tooth; opposed to hypsodont.

Braincase — Posterior portion of skull, which houses brain; behind rostrum.

Buccal — Pertaining to cheek cavity.

Bulla — Literally, "ball"; *see* Auditory Bulla.

Bunodont — Descriptive of low-crowned, generally rectangular tooth specialized for grinding.

Calcaneum — Heel-bone; calcaneus.

Calcaneus — Heel-bone; calcaneum.

Calcar — Cartilaginous or bony spur projecting medially from ankle of many species of bats; helps support uropatagium.

Canine — Most anterior tooth on maxilla and corresponding tooth of dentary (Figures 2-1, 2-2); never numbering more than one per quadrant.

Carapace — General term for "shell" in vertebrates, as in turtles or armadillo.

Carnassials — Specialized, sectorial cheekteeth of carnivores; in members of order Carnivora, always fourth upper premolar over first lower molar (P^4/M^1).

Carpals — Bones of wrist; compare with tarsals.

Caudal — Pertaining to tail.

Cecum — Pouch off junction of small and large intestines; especially well developed in herbivores and often site of symbiotic microbial activity.

Cementum — Bony matrix that affixes tooth in alveolus.

Cenozoic — Geologic era following Mesozoic; "Age of Mammals"; past 65 million years.

Cheekpouch — Distended or expandable area in buccal region of many rodents, usually functioning in carrying food from point of harvest to point of storage; may be fur-lined (geomyids, heteromyids) or not (sciurids).

Cheekteeth — Collective term for premolars and molars; also called postcanine teeth or (where appropriate) molariform teeth.

Chemosterilants — Chemical compounds used to preclude reproduction.

Class — Taxonomic category composed of one or more orders; example, Mammalia.

Cloaca — Literally, "sewer"; common chamber for products of urinary and digestive (and sometimes reproductive) systems.

Coevolution — Process of genetic change through time by which two or more species respond reciprocally to presence of each other in biotic community; often observed in pollination systems, seed dispersal systems, and so on.

Colluvium — Sediment deposited by gravity (contrasting with alluvium).

Commensalism — Symbiotic relationship in which one species is benefited and a second is essentially unaffected.

Condylar Fossa — Depression in squamosal bone in which condyloid process of dentary articulates (Figure 2-1).

Condyle — Rounded prominence on bone, serving as point of articulation in hinged joints.

Condylobasal Length — Measurement of skull taken in midline from posterior projections of occipital condyles to anterior border of sockets of incisors.

Coronoid — Literally, "crown-like"; process at top of ascending ramus of dentary (Figure 2-2).

Corpora — Plural of corpus.

Corpus — Literally, "body"; common descriptive term in anatomy, as in corpus luteum, "yellow body."

Countershading — Pattern of coloration of pelage in which (usually darker) dorsum contrasts with venter; thought to function in crypsis.

461

Cranial — Pertaining to cranium or braincase.

Cranial Breadth — Width of cranium (enclosing brain and sense organs) taken at broadest point perpendicular to long axis of skull.

Cranium — Portion of skull containing brain and sense organs.

Crepuscular — Active at dawn and/or dusk; contrasts with diurnal and nocturnal.

Cretaceous — Final geologic period of Mesozoic Era ("Age of Reptiles"), ending about 65 million years ago, marked by demise of ruling reptiles.

Crown — Exposed (usually enamel-covered) surface of tooth.

Cursorial — Pertaining to running.

Cusp — Projection (ridge, point, hummock, and so forth) on crown of tooth.

Deciduous — That which is shed or falls away, as leaves, milk teeth, antlers, and so on.

Deciduous Dentition — Juvenal or milk teeth, shed and replaced by permanent dentition.

Delayed Fertilization — Phenomenon (especially in some bats) wherein spermatozoa are stored in the uterus and therefore fertilization does not immediately follow copulation and insemination.

Delayed Implantation — Phenomenon wherein implantation of blastocyst in uterine lining does not immediately follow its formation.

Demography — Literally, "population mapping"; general term for population dynamics.

Density — Numbers per area.

Dental — Pertaining to teeth.

Dental Formula — Numerical description of dentition of mammal (see Table 2-1).

Dentary — Single bone that makes up half of lower jaw of mammals; composite term for entire lower jaw is mandible.

Dentine — Bone-like material that constitutes bulk of typical tooth.

Derived — Descriptive of characteristic evolutionarily different from condition in ancestor; such traits formerly termed "advanced," a term to be avoided because it may connote evolution as "progress," which implies a subjective judgment.

Dermal — Pertaining specifically to the dermis, although sometimes applied to skin more generally.

Dermis — Inner layers of skin, beneath epidermis.

Dewclaws — Small, usually vestigial, hoofed or clawed digits on various (mostly cursorial) mammals with simplified feet.

Dewlap — Pendulous, often fatty, flap of skin under neck, as in moose.

Diagnostic — Descriptive of characteristic(s) that define or unequivocally distinguish species or other taxon.

Diastema — Gap or space in toothrow, usually representing teeth lost in evolutionary reduction of dental formula; length of diastema is measured from posterior margin of alveolus of last incisor to anterior margin of alveolus of first cheek tooth.

Digitigrade — Standing on digits or "tiptoes."

Digits — Generic term for toes and fingers.

Diphyletic — Artificial taxon including groups derived from two separate ancestries.

Dispersal — Movement, especially one-way movement from place of birth to place of residence and reproduction.

Dispersion — Pattern of spacing of individuals within local population; may be uniform, clumped (contagious), or random.

Distal — Away from axis of body or other specified point of reference; contrasts with proximal.

Diurnal — Active by day.

Dormancy — Extended period of inactivity; hibernation is extreme form.

Dorsal — Referring to back or upper surface (dorsum).

Dorsoventrally — From top to bottom, as "dorsoventrally flattened."

Dorsolaterally — Pertaining to back and sides.

Dorsum — Top, back.

Echolocation — Process by which mammals (especially bats) form images and orient by emitting (usually high-frequency) sounds and processing sound waves returned as echoes from objects in environment.

Ecoregions — Extensive geographic area of continent with ecological integrity and distinctiveness.

Ecosphere — More-or-less continuous global zone of interaction between Earth and life; sum of Earth's ecosystems.

Ecosystem — Volume of environment in which biotic and abiotic factors interact in cycles of materials and flows of energy.

Ecotone — Area of overlap or interaction between adjacent, distinctive ecological communities or ecosystems.

Ectoparasites — Parasite living outside body of host; often arthropods (ticks, lice, fleas, and so on).

Emigration — Permanent movement out of an area (contrast with immigration).

Enamel — Mineral substance that covers crown of teeth of many mammals; hardest substance in vertebrate body.

Endemic — Species unique to particular place.

Endoparasites — Parasite living inside body of host; often "worms" (flukes, tapeworms, nematodes, and so on) or microbes.

Endothermy — Process of maintaining body temperature by retaining heat produced by metabolic processes; "warm-bloodedness."

Enzootic — Descriptive of disease constantly present in particular wildlife population.

Eocene — The second epoch of the Cenozoic, following Paleocene and prior to Oligocene; many modern orders of mammals arose.

Epizootic — Descriptive of disease temporarily prevalent in wild-life population.

Erythropoietic — Tissue that produces red blood cells, as bone marrow.

Estrous — Adjective describing cycle of hormones regulating reproductive periodicity in (especially nonhuman) female mammals.

Estrus — Interval of maximal sexual receptiveness of female mammal; "heat."

Ethmoid Vacuity — Hollow of nasal chamber, containing olfactory membranes. In certain artiodactyls, represented by opening in rostrum anterior to orbits, at junction of nasal, frontal, and maxillary sutures.

Exoccipitals — Lateral bones of occiput, forming sides of foramen magnum.

Exogenous — Literally, "externally born"; descriptive of processes caused from outside the organism, as an "exogenous rhythm."

Exotic — Descriptive of species not native to particular place; introduced.

External Auditory Meatus — Bony entrance to auditory bulla (Figure 2-1).

Ever-growing — See Rootless.

Femur — Bone of proximal segment of tetrapod limb; articulates with pelvic girdle to form hip.

Fenestrate — Penetrated by window-like openings.

Fertilization — Process of production of zygote (fertilized egg) from fusion of gametes (sex cells — egg or sperm); "conception."

Foramen — Opening or hole through bone, passage for nerves or blood vessels.

Foramen Magnum — Large opening for passage of spinal cord at posterior end of braincase (Figure 2-1).

Foramina — Plural of foramen.

Forb — Neologism contracted from "forest herb"; broadleafed, herbaceous plants (by contrast with grass-like plants, graminoids).

Fossa — Literally, "ditch"; depression in bone into which muscles and/or other bones fit.

Fossorial — Descriptive of subterranean locomotion of moles, pocket gophers, for example.

Frontal — Paired bones forming anterior end of braincase (Figure 2-1); point of growth of antlers, horns in artiodactyls.

Fur — Rough synonym of pelage, especially when commercially valuable.

Furbearer — Management term for mammals with commercially valuable pelage.

Game — Management term for mammals pursued for meat or "sport."

Genitalia — Male or female sexual structures; usually qualified as external or internal.

Genus — Taxonomic category composed of one or more closely related species.

Gestation Period — Duration of period of internal development of placental mammals, from fertilization (or implantation) to parturition (birth).

Girdle — Generic term for points of attachment of limbs (appendages) to body: hips, shoulders.

Glenoid Fossa — Shallow depression in scapula that accommodates head of humerus in formation of shoulder joint.

Glissant — Gliding (gravity-powered "flight," as in "flying" squirrels); opposed to volancy.

Graminoids — Grasslike plants: grasses, sedges, rushes, etc.

Grazers — Herbivores specialized for feeding (grazing) on graminoids.

Greatest Length of Skull — Overall length of skull excluding any forward projection of anterior teeth.

Guard Hair — Outer, generally longer, generally coarse, often colored hairs of pelage.

Guild — Functional subdivision of biotic community defined ecologically, usually on basis of foraging habits; examples, grazers, browsers, gleaners. Meant to transcend taxonomic limits; guild of diurnal, terrestrial seedeaters includes chipmunks and sparrows.

Habitat — Place where an organism occurs.

Habituation — Process by which an organism learns to ignore a particular stimulus (such as human presence).

Hair — Complex structure of keratin extruded from epidermal follicle in mammalian skin.

Hallux — First digit of hind foot (represented by human big toe).

Halophyte — Plant adapted to salt tolerance.

Harem — Group of two or more females more or less controlled for breeding purposes by single male.

Herbivory — Process of feeding on plant material.

Heterodont — Teeth differentiated by size and/or shape in toothrow.

Hibernaculum — Particular location or structure where hibernation is passed.

Hibernation — State of minimal physiology in winter; extreme case of dormancy.

High-crowned — Descriptive of teeth generally taller than broad; extreme case is ever-growing (rootless) teeth; hypsodont.

Holarctic — Biogeographic term: occurring in Northern Hemisphere, both New and Old Worlds (Nearctic plus Palearctic regions).

Holotype — Particular museum specimen to which scientific name is attached in original published description of species or subspecies; imprecisely called "type."

Homeostasis — Sum of processes by which organism maintains dynamic equilibrium of internal environment in face of continually changing external environment.

Homodont — Teeth undifferentiated by size and/or shape in toothrow.

Homologous — Pertaining to structures (which may or may not have same function) with common evolutionary origin; human hand and wing of bat are homologous structures; contrast with analogous.

Horizontal Ramus — Ventral portion (usually long axis) of dentary in which teeth are rooted.

Hypoglossal Foramen — Hole passing hypoglossal nerve (cranial XII) from braincase to tongue.

Hypsodont — Descriptive of high-crowned tooth.

Imbricate — Overlapping arrangement, as shingles on roof.

Implantation — Process by which blastocyst becomes embedded in uterine lining, preliminary to formation of placenta and remainder of gestation.

Immigration — Permanent movement into area (as opposed to emigration).

Incisive Foramen — Holes in anterior palate, between premaxillary and maxillary bones by which nasal and oral cavities communicate (Figure 2-1).

Incisors — Teeth (often adapted for nipping) arising from premaxillary bone of upper jaw and corresponding teeth on anterior of mandible (Figures 2-1, 2-2).

Incus — "Anvil"; one of three bones of mammalian middle ear; derived from reptilian quadrate.

Infraorbital Foramen — Foramen (opening) ventral to anterior border of orbit, penetrating zygomatic portion of maxilla (Figure 2-1).

Inguinal — Pertaining to groin.

Interfemoral Membrane — Web of skin between hind legs of bat, forming part of flight surface (=uropatagium).

Interglacial — Interval of time between successive advances of glacial ice during Pleistocene Epoch.

Interorbital Breadth — Least distance across skull as measured between orbits.

Interparietal Bone — Unpaired bone situated between parietals and anterior to supraoccipital.

Jugal Bone — Central bone of zygomatic arch, bounded anteriorly by zygomatic (malar) process of maxillary and posteriorly by zygomatic process of squamosal (Figure 2-1).

Juvenal — Adjectival form of juvenile.

Juvenile — General and somewhat loosely defined term for young mammal, beyond neonate, prior to subadult.

Keel — On calcar of some bats, a conspicuous ridge, shaped like keel of boat; presence or absence is important diagnostic feature in some species.

Keratin — Protein of which hair and nails are made.

Keystone Species — Species critical to natural function and maintenance of particular biotic community, such as beaver in riparian systems of mountain parks or bison on shortgrass prairie.

Krummholz — "Crooked wood"; twisted trees of upper treeline.

Labial — Pertaining to lips (used as term of orientation, opposed to lingual or buccal).

Lacrimal — Pertaining to tears, as lacrimal glands; as term of orientation, ventromedial area of orbit; bone at that place (Figure 2-1).

Lactation — Production and delivery of milk by mammary glands.

Lambdoidal Ridge — Ridge on skull (where occipital bone joins the parietal and squamosal) shaped like Greek letter lambda (inverted V-shaped) (Figure 2-1).

Lateral — Pertaining to side; away from midline.

Lingual — Pertaining to tongue; as term of orientation, opposed to labial.

Loph — Longitudinal or transverse ridge on occlusal surface of tooth formed by fusion and elongation of cusps.

Lophodont — Tooth characterized by well-developed lophs.

Malar Process — Extension of maxillary bone that forms anterior base of zygomatic arch; articulates with jugal bone.

Malleus — "Hammer"; one of three bones of mammalian middle ear, derived from reptilian articulare.

Mammae — Milk-producing glands; mammary glands.

Mandible — Composite structure comprising two dentary bones; length of mandible is measured on the bone itself, not including any forward-projecting incisor teeth.

Mandibular Toothrow — Teeth of dentary; length measured from anterior edge of alveolus of most anterior mandibular tooth to the posterior edge of alveolus of most posterior cheektooth.

Marsupium — Pouch of marsupial mammals in which mammae are located and externally developing young are carried.

Mastication — Process of chewing.

Masseteric Tubercle — Small projection of maxillary bone that provides additional surface area for attachment of masseter muscle.

Mastoid Bone — Bone bounded by tympanic, squamosal, and exoccipital bones; often relatively massive and protuberant and marking posterolateral corner of skull.

Mastoid Breadth — Breadth of posterior end of skull, measured at most lateral extension of mastoid bones.

Maxilla — Paired bones composing upper jaw and bearing upper cheekteeth (Figure 2-1).

Maxillary Toothrow — Collective term for teeth of maxilla (upper jaw posterior to premaxilla). Length is measured as distance from anterior margin of alveolus (socket) of canine to posterior margin of alveolus of last molar.

Maxillovomerine Notch — Fenestration in nasal septum, visible through incisive foramina.

Meatus — See External Auditory Meatus.

Mental Foramen — Conspicuous hole on lateral wall of dentary (Figure 2-2).

Mesaxonic — Pertaining to foot structure in which axis of symmetry passes through middle (third) toe, as in horse.

Metacarpal — Bones of forefoot, distal to wrist, proximal to phalanges.

Metapodials — Collective term for metatarsals and metacarpals.

Metatarsal — Bones of hind foot, distal to ankle, proximal to phalanges.

Middens — Accumulation of food wastes, generally plant material, as is produced by pine squirrels and woodrats.

Mimicry — Evolutionary tendency toward adaptive similarity in species of independent ancestry.

Molar — Cheektooth with no deciduous precursor, located posterior to premolars (Figures 2-1, 2-2).

Molt — Process of replacement of hairs, typically maturational or seasonal and often precisely patterned.

Monestrous — Descriptive of female reproductive cycle with single estrus even in particular breeding season; alternative is polyestrous.

Monogamous — Breeding system characterized by mating as pairs, one female per male.

Monomorphic — Literally, "one form"; little or no external difference in size or shape between sexes.

Monophyletic — Group of species derived from single common ancestor; in modern taxonomic practice, taxon at particular level in hierarchy is supposed to be monophyletic.

Monotypic — Descriptive of species without discernible geographic variation.

Multiparous — Pertaining to reproductive pattern in which female has several litters in a lifetime.

Nares — Nasal openings.

Nasal — Pertaining to nose; paired bones forming roof of rostrum (Figure 2-1).

Nasal Septum — Bony, longitudinal plate that subdivides nasal chamber into right and left sides.

Natality — Pattern of births in population.

Natatorial — Descriptive of swimming locomotion.

Nearctic — Biogeographic term for northern part of Western Hemisphere (New World), as opposed to Palearctic.

Neonate — Newborn.

Neotropical — Pertaining to New World (Western Hemisphere) tropics, as opposed to Paleotropical.

Niche — Sum of resource requirements of species population; description of species' multidimensional "resource space."

Nocturnal — Active at night.

Nomenclature — Naming, especially technical procedures for scientific naming.

Nulliparous — Descriptive of female that has not borne offspring.

Occipital — Pertaining to occiput; the composite bone in that region.

Occipitonasal Length — Length of skull from posterior end of occipital condyles to anterior end of nasal bones.

Occiput — Posteroventral region of skull, surrounding foramen magnum and providing insertion for cervical musculature.

Occlusal Surface — Surface of tooth that contacts corresponding tooth in opposing jaw in process of mastication.

Omasum — Third compartment of ruminant "stomach"; actually modified esophagus.

Omnivory — Feeding on both animal and plant materials.

Opposable — See Apposable.

Optic — Pertaining to eye.

Oral — Pertaining to mouth.

Orbits — Bony sockets housing eyeballs (Figure 2-1).

Order — Subdivision of taxonomic class composed of one or more families; example, Rodentia.

Orogeny — Mountain building.

Os Penis — See Baculum.

Os Clitoridis — See Baubellum.

Ossicles — Literally, "little bones"; especially bones of middle ear.

Ossified — Infused with mineral bone.

Ovary — Female gonad, produces ova (eggs) and hormones.

Oviducts — Tube through which ova and then (after fertilization) zygote move from vicinity of ovary to uterus; also Fallopian tubes.

Ovulation — Process of shedding mature egg cell from ovarian follicle into oviduct; mediated by complex system of hormones.

Palatal Breadth — Width of palate taken between any specified pair of teeth; typically excludes alveoli.

Palatal Length — Measurement from most anterior point on premaxillary bone to posterior edge of palate.

Palatine — Paired medial bones at posterior end of palate (Figure 2-1).

Palearctic — Biogeographic term for northern portion of Old World (Eastern Hemisphere), as opposed to Nearctic.

Palmate — Flattened, broad structure, reminiscent of palm of hand, as antlers of moose.

Papillae — Any small, usually fleshy protuberance, as on tongue.

Parapatric — Descriptive of geographic distributions that abut but do not overlap.

Paraxonic — Describes foot structure in which axis of symmetry passes between two toes, as in deer.

Parietal — Paired bones of sides of braincase.

Parous — Pertaining to birth, bearing of offspring; parous females are pregnant or have borne offspring previously.

Partum — Parturition.

Parturition — Process of giving birth.

Patagium — Wing membrane of bats.

Patella — Kneecap.

Pectoral — Pertaining to shoulders.

Pedicels — Permanent prominences on frontal bones that serve as base and growing point of antlers.

Pelage — Collective term for hair of mammal.

Pelt — Commercial term for pelage and underlying skin.

Pelvic — Pertaining to hips.

Pendulous — Hanging.

Perianal — Surrounding or in vicinity of anus.

Perineal — Area between genitalia and anus.

Pes — Foot.

Phalanges — Plural of phalanx.

Phalanx — Individual bones of digits (fingers, toes).

Phallus — Alternative term for penis (male intromittent organ).

Philopatry — Tendency of individuals to remain in area of their birth.

Phylogeny — Pattern of historical, evolutionary relationships of species, often expressed as "phylogenetic tree."

Pinna — Literally, "feather"; flap, typically cartilaginous, of ear.

Pistillate — Pertaining to female flower or cone of seed plant.

Placenta — Composite structure formed of fetal membranes and lining of maternal uterus; mediates chemical exchange between mother and developing offspring.

Plantar Tubercle — Elevated pad of soles of hind feet, usually of rodents.

Plantigrade — Standing on soles of feet and palms of hands.

Podials — Generic term for bones of foot.

Pollex — First digit of forefoot (represented by human thumb).

Polyestrous — Descriptive of reproductive cycle with plural estrus events in particular breeding season; alternative is Monestrous.

Polygamous — Mating system in which individual has plural mates of opposite sex.

Polygynous — Polygamous mating system in which male breeds with plural females.

Polymorphic — Descriptive of local species population with several distinctive forms, as color phases of red fox or Abert's squirrel.

Population — Individuals of same species in same general area; potential reproductive unit.

Postauricular — Positioned behind ear.

Postcornual — Positioned behind horn.

Postcranial — Descriptive of structures behind head, as "postcranial skeleton."

Postglenoid Length — Measurement from posterior margin of glenoid fossa to most distant projection of skull.

Postorbital Breadth — Smallest distance across skull as measured behind postorbital processes.

Postorbital Process — Projection of frontal bone over posterior margin of orbit.

Postorbital — Positioned behind orbit.

Postpartum — Following parturition or birthing.

Precocial — Descriptive of young born in relatively well-developed and independent condition; contrasts with altricial.

Prehensile — Capable of grasping.

Premaxillary Bone — Anterolateral bone of upper jaw, bearing upper incisor teeth (Figure 2-1).

Premolar — Cheektooth with deciduous predecessor, located posterior to canines and anterior to molars (Figures 2-1. 2-2).

Preorbital — Positioned anterior to orbit.

Preputial — Pertaining to prepuce (foreskin of penis).

Presphenoid — Anteromedial bone of composite structure forming base of braincase beneath orbits (Figure 2-1).

Prismatic — Characterized by prisms; obvious crystalline structure or shapes suggestive of crystals.

Procumbent — Anteroventrally directed.

Promiscuous — Mating system characterized by lack of pair bonding.

Proximal — Nearer axis of body or specified point of reference; contrast with distal.

Pterygoid — Literally, "wing-like"; paired bones lateral to sphenoid contributing to base of braincase (Figure 2-1).

Ramus — Literally, "branch"; divergent portions of bone or other structure, as vertical and horizontal rami of dentary.

Recruitment — Additions to a population; sum of births and immigration.

Reentrant Angles — Sharply indented fold in side of hypsodont teeth; may be on lingual or labial side of tooth.

Reingestion — Process of taking specialized feces into mouth from anus to allow second pass through digestive tract; coprophagy, cecotrophy.

Richochetal — Bipedal hopping locomotion, as in kangaroos and kangaroo rats.

Riparian — Pertaining to streamside situations.

Rooted — Describes tooth in which pulp cavity closes, tooth fuses in alveolus, and growth ceases.

Rootless — Describes tooth that continues to grow throughout life.

Rostrum — Portion of skull anterior to orbits; with lower jaw composes "muzzle."

Rostral Breadth — Breadth across rostrum, normally measured at suture between premaxillae and maxillae unless otherwise specified.

Rumen — Most anterior compartment of ruminant "stomach"; actually modified esophagus.

Ruminant — Member of suborder Ruminantia, artiodactyls with advanced, four-chambered "stomach" (first three chambers of which actually are modified esophagus).

Ruminate — Process in which ruminants "chew cud," regurgitated material partially digested in rumen and reticulum.

Rut — Period of sexual activity in male mammals, especially used with respect to cervids.

Sagittal — Arrow-shaped, as sagittal ridge or crest of skull (Figure 2-1); as term of orientation, refers to longitudinal, vertical plane through midline.

Saltatory — Pertaining to hopping locomotion.

Scansorial — Pertaining to scampering locomotion.

Scapula — Shoulder bone.

Scat — Droppings, feces, especially of mammals.

Scrotum — Sack external to abdominal cavity in which mammalian testes reside, at least while actively producing spermatozoa — in many species a cyclic, seasonal occurrence.

Sebaceous Glands — Oil-secreting glands of hair follicles.

Sebum — Lubricant secreted by sebaceous glands.

Secodont — Describing cheekteeth with cusps specialized for shearing.

Sectorial — Pertains to specialization for cutting, shearing.

Selenodont — Describing cheekteeth with crescent-shaped, longitudinal lophs.

Sphenoidal Fissure — Vertical groove or elongate foramen in posteromedial area of orbit.

Sphincter — Muscles in circular array that constrict to close an opening (lips, anus).

Squamosal — Posterolateral bones of skull to which dentary articulates (Figure 2-1).

Staminate — Pertaining to male flower or cone of seed plant.

Stapes — "Stirrup"; one of three ossicles of mammalian middle ear; homolog of reptilian ear bone (columella).

Stochastic — Describing events or processes characterized by randomness (contrasts with deterministic).

Subadult — Developmental stage of mammal, usually with nearly adult-like external appearance but sexually immature.

Subnivean — Describes space beneath snowpack.

Succession — Change in structure and floristic composition of vegetation (and dependent organisms) over time as biota changes conditions of site.

Sudoriferous Glands — Sweat glands; also known as sudoriparous glands.

Superciliary — Pertaining to eyebrows.

Survivorship — Demographic construct, describing a population's pattern of age-specific mortality.

Suture — Junction between adjacent bones; immovable joint.

Sylvatic — Literally, "of the woods"; describing wild (versus domestic or human) conditions, especially diseases.

Symbioses — Ecological systems in which two or more coexisting species interact: competition, predation, mutualism, and so on.

Sympatry — Overlap of geographic ranges of species.

Symphysis — Point of attachment of symmetrical bones, as pubic symphysis, mandibular symphysis.

Synecological — Pertaining to ecology of two or more species interacting in community: predator-prey systems, competition, and so forth; contrasting with autecological.

Tarsals — Bones of ankle; compare with carpals.

Territory — Portion of home range of individual defended against other individuals of same species.

Thoracic — Pertaining to chest region.

Tibia — One of two bones of distal segment of vertebrate hind limb.

Tragus — Flap of tissue appended to inner edge of pinna; especially prominent in bats.

Tympanic Membrane — Ear drum.

Type — See Holotype.

Ungulate — Informal, inclusive term for hoofed mammals; not a formal taxonomic unit.

Ungules — Hooves.

Unguligrade — Standing on hooves.

Unicuspid — Tooth with single cusp, as most canines.

Uropatagium — See Interfemoral Membrane.

Vacuity — Space, usually in bone, typically accommodating glandular tissue.

Vagility — Capacity of species to move, especially across barriers, to expand geographic range.

Valvular — Capable of closing, as a valve.

Venter — Lower (belly) surface.

Ventral — Pertaining to venter; opposed to dorsal.

Vibrissae — Whiskers; stiff hairs, usually with tactile function.

Volancy — Muscle-powered flight, as in bats.

Vomer — Bone forming base of braincase, posterior roof of nasal passage (Figure 2-1).

Vulva — External genitalia of female mammal.

Zoonoses — General term for wildlife diseases.

Zygomatic — Pertaining to cheek bone.

Zygote — Fertilized egg; product of fusion of egg and sperm nuclei.